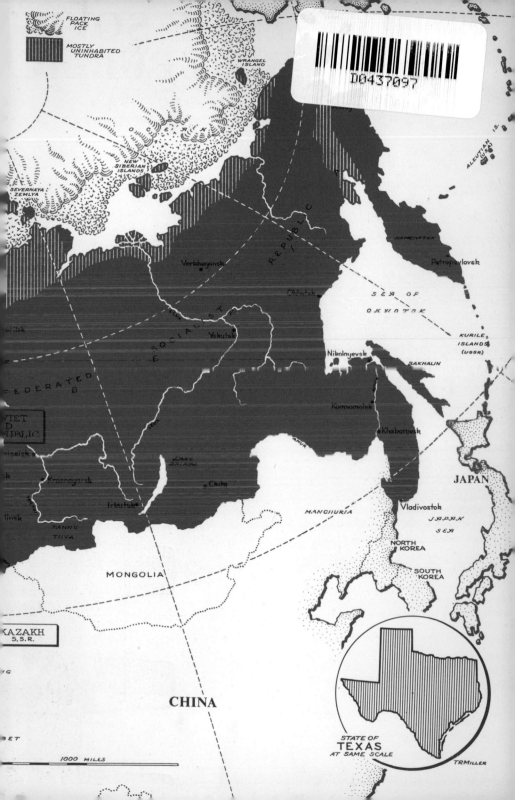

FLOATING
PACK
ICE

MOSTLY
UNINHABITED
TUNDRA

D0437097

WRANGEL
ISLAND

NEW
SIBERIAN
ISLANDS

SEVERNAYA
ZEMLYA

KAMCHATKA

Petropavlovsk

Verkhoyansk

SOCIALIST   REPUBLIC

Okhotsk

SEA   OF

OKHOTSK

Yakutsk

KURILE
ISLANDS
(USSR)

Nikolayevsk

SAKHALIN

FEDERATED

Komsomolsk

TET
D
UBLIC

Khabarovsk

niseisk

Krasnoyarsk

LAKE
BAIKAL

Chita

JAPAN

AMUR

linsk

Irkutsk

MANCHURIA

JAPAN

Vladivostok

SEA

TANNU
TUVA

NORTH
KOREA

MONGOLIA

SOUTH
KOREA

KAZAKH
S.S.R.

CHINA

STATE OF
TEXAS
AT SAME SCALE

TRMiller

1000 MILES

BET

INSIDE RUSSIA TODAY

BOOKS BY JOHN GUNTHER

INSIDE RUSSIA TODAY

INSIDE AFRICA

INSIDE U.S.A.

INSIDE LATIN AMERICA

INSIDE ASIA

INSIDE EUROPE

THE RIDDLE OF MACARTHUR

EISENHOWER

ROOSEVELT IN RETROSPECT

BEHIND THE CURTAIN

DEATH BE NOT PROUD

D DAY

THE TROUBLED MIDNIGHT

DAYS TO REMEMBER
(with Bernard Quint)

MEET NORTH AFRICA
(with Sam and Beryl Epstein)

ALEXANDER THE GREAT

INSIDE
RUSSIA
TODAY

by
JOHN GUNTHER

HARPER & BROTHERS

NEW YORK

Dedicated with Love to
G., V., and G.G.
Russian Experts

It is better to have a world united than a world divided. But it is also better to have a world divided than a world destroyed.

WINSTON CHURCHILL

Russia is sublime—a universal, ordered chaos.

DOSTOEVSKY IN 1871

What was scatter'd in many volumes, and observ'd at several times by Eye-witnesses, with no cursory pains I laid together, to save the Reader a far longer travaile. . . .

—JOHN MILTON
Brief History of Muscovia

CONTENTS

MAPS

THE UNION OF SOVIET
SOCIALIST REPUBLICS

ARCTIC

NORWEGIAN SEA

SPITZBERGEN

FRANZ JOSEF LAND

BARENTS SEA

UNITED KINGDOM

ESTONIAN S.S.R.

NORWAY

LATVIAN S.S.R.

SWEDEN

NOVAYA ZEMLYA

DENMARK

Murmansk

KARA SEA

FINLAND

(WEST) **GERMANY** (EAST)

BALTIC SEA

Tallin

Archangel

Vorkuta

LITHUANIAN S.S.R.

Riga

Leningrad

R U S S I A N

POLAND

Vilnius

BELORUSSIAN S.S.R.

Minsk

SOVIET S

HUNG.

★ Moscow

Gorky

Perm

R SOC

Kiev

Kazan

EUROPE ASIA

Tobolsk

RUMANIA

Kishinev

Kharkov

Sverdlovsk

URAL MOUNTAINS

Odessa

Saratov

Kuibyshev

Chelyabinsk

BULGARIA

Sevastopol

Magnitogorsk

Omsk

Nov

BLACK SEA

Rostov-on-Don

Stalingrad

Uralsk

Astrakhan

Karaganda

Semip

MOLDAVIAN S.S.R.

TURKEY

Batum

ARAL SEA

LAKE BALKHASH

UKRAINIAN S.S.R.

Tiflis

Yerevan

CASPIAN SEA

GEORGIAN S.S.R.

Baku

Tashkent

Alma-Ata

SYRIA

Frunze

ARMENIAN S.S.R.

Ashkhabad

Bukhara

IRAQ

AZERBAIJAN S.S.R.

Samarkand

Stalinabad

Merv

IRAN

SAUDI ARABIA

AFGHAN.

KASHMIR

PAK.

TURKMEN S.S.R.

UZBEK S.S.R.

TADZHIK S.S.R.

KIRGH S.S.R.

FLOATING
PACK ICE

MOSTLY
UNINHABITED
TUNDRA

ALASKA
(USA)

BERING
SEA

WRANGEL
ISLAND

Anadyr

O C E A N

NEW
SIBERIAN
ISLANDS

ALEUTIAN IS

SEVERNAYA
ZEMLYA

Petropavlovsk

R E P U B L I C

Verkhoyansk

Okhotsk

SEA OF
OKHOTSK

S O C I A L I S T

Yakutsk

KURILE
ISLANDS
(USSR)

Nikolayevsk

SAKHALIN

F E D E R A T E D

Komsomolsk

Khabarovsk

IET
UBLIC

JAPAN

Krasnoyarsk

Chita

JAPAN
SEA

Irkutsk

MANCHURIA

Vladivostok

insb

TANNU
TUVA

NORTH
KOREA

MONGOLIA

SOUTH
KOREA

AZAKH
S.S.R.

CHINA

STATE OF
TEXAS
AT SAME SCALE

1000 MILES

TRMiller

FOREWORD—
THE SPUTNIKS AND THE FUTURE

FOR a long time I have wanted to write an Inside book about the Soviet Union, and this is it. In general it follows the pattern of *Inside Europe*, *Inside U.S.A.*, *Inside Africa*, and so on, but the canvas is more restricted—still, big enough. After all, the Soviet Union covers close to one-sixth of the land surface of the globe, and has put its own moons into the sky. I have added "Today" to the title not in relation to any particular date but because, even if the substratum of the Soviet system has not changed, today's Russia is an altogether different thing from Russia under Stalin. This is a new Russia we are inspecting, at least to a degree, and it poses new, peculiar, and baffling problems.

What I have tried to do most of all, with what measure of success I do not know, is give a *picture* of this cumbrous, slippery giant, with its evolving strains and issues—to try, perhaps vainly, to convey to the reader something of what it is *like*, its essential quality and atmosphere since Stalin's death. Also I have included (a) some brief historical passages, because an indispensable key to what is going on in Russia is its continuity with the past; (b) an informal *Who's Who* of Russian leaders, especially those about whom information is otherwise scant; and (c) descriptive material about major Soviet sights and cities. More and more Americans and western Europeans are visiting the USSR year by year, and such material may be useful.

Then too this book is, obviously, a reporter's job, and I have sought earnestly to describe the current political situation and events. The Table of Contents spells all this out. In trying to transmit objectively my impression of some of the fascinating and quickly shifting factors at play I have used the instrument of quotation a good deal more than in any other of my books, because it seemed wise, so far as possible, to let the story come out of the Russians' own outspoken mouths. For much of this quoted material, but not all, I am indebted to the *Current Digest of the Soviet Press*, the admirable magazine published in New York under the auspices of the Joint Committee on Slavic Studies. This surveys with intent and discriminating eye the whole of the Soviet press, and quotes from it impartially, without comment, week by week.

Now as to my terms of reference. My wife and I went to Russia late in

1956, and had a vivid, stimulating, and productive visit. We traveled about twelve thousand miles in the Soviet Union, mostly by air, and visited the most important of its constituent republics. We had some weeks in Moscow and managed to see other principal cities, such as Leningrad and Kiev. We visited Odessa, Yalta in the Crimea, several other Black Sea ports, Tiflis (now known as Tbilisi) in the Caucasus, and the remote, romantic cities of Central Asia—Alma-Ata, Tashkent, Bukhara, and Samarkand. It is my duty to report that one mosque in Bukhara has been converted into a poolroom, not very handsome, and that Samarkand, the pivot of the old Silk Road to China, has traffic lights more or less like those on Fifth Avenue.

This was my fourth visit to the Soviet Union. I went there first as a correspondent of the Chicago *Daily News* in 1928, long before American recognition of the USSR. On that trip I traveled a good deal along the Volga, saw something of the Ukraine, and penetrated (it was easy enough in those days) to Armenia, Azerbaijan, and some of the shaggy valleys of the Caucasus. Altogether I stayed in Russia about five months. Then I went to Moscow again in 1935, again as a correspondent for the Chicago *Daily News*, and once more in 1939, as representative of the *Reader's Digest*, the North American Newspaper Alliance, and the National Broadcasting Company.

I applied for a Soviet visa several times after the war, but was always refused. In 1948, however, my wife and I managed to visit four Iron Curtain countries—Poland, Hungary, Czechoslovakia, and Yugoslavia. This, naturally, added to our experience of eastern Europe, and taught us something of the nature of Communist regimes. Russia itself continued to refuse to let us in —both in 1949 and again in 1951. Finally in 1956, following the general loosening up that came after Stalin's death, visas were granted and we took our trip. Having thus been in Russia in 1928, 1935, 1939, and now once more in 1956, I can at least try to see it in perspective. These years are neatly spaced out and each is, or was, a crucial year. Nineteen twenty-eight marked the beginning of the first Five-Year Plan, and 1935 saw the Stalin dictatorship in full ugly flower. We all know that World War II followed the Russo-German Pact in 1939, and 1956 was a year of surpassing interest, if only because de-Stalinization was brought out into the open, and Hungary exploded.

*

Russia is never easy to write about. It is an extremely complicated country, which moreover is not at all like what many people think it to be, and which is apt to stir up passionate partisan feelings in the observer. I have tried to let the facts fall where they may. My point of view is quite simple; that it is high time that we in America accept the facts of life, and, no matter how distasteful and repugnant we find Soviet institutions, adjust ourselves to the necessity of having to live in a world side by side with them. Also it is our duty to learn more, if only as a matter of self-preservation, and to try to understand something of the nature of the Russian people, who can be angels one minute and devils the next, and who, more than any other I know in the world, give constantly the note of striving for fulfillment, and have so much force, discipline, and faith in spite of their bleak totalitarian surroundings.

One obstacle that the writer of good will must hurdle is preconception on the part of his readers. People are shocked, I do not know why, even by such a simple fact as that the Soviet Union produced and consumed last year 27,000,000 bottles of champagne—good champagne too. In New York last week I met an educated, sophisticated lady who could not believe it when I told her that Russians make automobiles that run, who asked if Soviet citizens lived on "estates," and who did not know that it is impossible to buy a copy of the *New York Times*, or for that matter any other American newspaper, on a Moscow newsstand.

There are frightful evils, cruelties, and suppressions in the Soviet Union today. But also there are some astonishing accomplishments, mostly in such fields as education, science, and technology. Who amongst us knows that the Soviet Union graduates every year four times more doctors of medicine than does the United States? (I didn't, until I got there.) Who knows that there are 41,000 teachers of English in the USSR today? (How many teachers of Russian in the United States?) There are more than two million students in Soviet colleges today, including those taking correspondence courses—more than in all western Europe, and a Moscow university student is *paid* to go to school, instead of paying. The Russians succeeded in making a hydrogen bomb before we did.[1] An industrial atom power plant has been functioning in the USSR for more than three years, and tourists can freely see an atomic pile in operation twenty minutes from the center of Moscow.

Some questions we must ask are these. But Russia is a country where simple "yes" or "no" answers are hard to come by; dubieties are more conspicuous than certitudes. Several times in this book I shall seemingly contradict on one page what I have said on another. Anyway—

[1] The United States was the first to produce a thermonuclear "device," but the Russians came first with an actual bomb.

Who (or *what*) runs Russia?
What has the Soviet Union *got?*
What are current trends?
Is the "New Look" genuine?
Why doesn't the government do more for the people?
How much socialism remains—if any?
Is peaceful coexistence possible?

One more preliminary word. I went to Russia for *Collier's* Magazine which disappeared while we were en route, and what I wrote appeared instead in my old friend, *Look,* and in the *Sunday Times* in London. *Look* used my material in a single long article, running to fourteen thousand words. This material, which was a kind of hors d'oeuvre to the book to come, this book, comprised only a minute fraction of what is before the reader now. Perhaps I might add another point—that I give less emphasis than most writers on Russia to industry and agriculture. I know perfectly well how important these realms are but for several reasons I have not singled them out for special attention, although they are not neglected. Mostly I have wanted to stress aspects of the Soviet Union and its formidable power that are less well known, for instance convulsions among the youth, problems in education, technological advance, science, and emerging social patterns.

The Russians are a terrific, a tremendous, a magnificent people. In some respects they closely resemble Americans—in good humor, robustness, curiosity, gregariousness, capacity for analysis, capacity for organization, inventiveness, aptitude for technical skills, and so on. (There are differences, too.) During our whole trip I never saw an unfriendly face, or—with one possible exception—encountered the slightest rudeness of any kind. This is particularly remarkable considering that a Cold War is going on, with the United States as the "enemy." The one thing that is certain in Russia today is that nobody wants a war. On the other hand, the Russian government is, in most respects, an appallingly unpleasant government from our point of view. But it would be the gravest of errors to underestimate its power or to ignore or minimize the potentiality of the Soviet Union. Obviously, if it did not have *something,* it would not be the incandescent preoccupation that it is everywhere. With the future of the world, no less, at stake, we at least owe it to ourselves to be informed, and without facile optimism either.

*

About the Sputniks

On October 4, 1957, as this book was being put to press, the Russians discharged their first Sputnik into the heavens. The brief passage above referring to Soviet technological advance was, incidentally, written long before this prodigious and epochal event. Now, although I had hoped to make this Foreword as short as possible, I should perhaps write one more word. Also I have added a good many references to the Sputniks at appropriate intervals in the body of the text that follows, for instance in Chapter XIII, as well as consideration of an even more pregnant topic, ballistic missiles, in Chapter XVIII. But I did not find it necessary to change the tone or text of anything I had already written.

"Sputnik" has two meanings in the Russian language. First, in the astronomical sense, it means "moon" or "satellite"; second, it means "traveling companion" (*not*, as is sometimes said, "fellow traveler" in the political sense). The interpreter who accompanies you on a trip through Russia, or any friend or even governess or valet whom you take with you somewhere on a journey, is a "sputnik." Outside scientific circles it was commonly thought, after the first sensational release of these man-made satellites circling the earth at 18,000 miles an hour, that the Russians had two Sputniks in the sky; actually there were five: (1) the first Sputnik itself, which was let loose by a carrier rocket; (2) its rocket case, cylindrical in shape; (3) its protective nose cone, which was designed to fall off, and did; (4) Sputnik II together with its carrier rocket; (5) the nose cone of Sputnik II.

October 4, 1957, is beyond doubt a supreme date in the history of mankind, if only because it inaugurated the Space Age. Man, for the first time since his birth some millions of years ago, managed to propel something off the earth into the space beyond space, and get signals from it. The handful of embarrassed American officials who, in the first hours of Sputnik I's flight, sought to laugh it off or dismiss it as a fancy, inconsequential toy should be pitied rather than scorned for their flagrant blindness—not merely for failing to appreciate the significance of Sputnik itself, but for their stubborn unwillingness to concede the realities of Soviet scientific advance, devotion to research, and concentration of resource to a single purpose. A principal aim of this book is to show, by implication at least, *why* such accomplishments come about, and rise inevitably not merely from individual brilliance on the part of Russian theoreticians and technicians, but as a result of skillful planning, leadership, and cohesion of activity in the nation as a whole.

The plain fact of the matter is that the propulsion of the Sputniks into space was an unequivocal, electric defeat for the United States and the free world—a defeat, moreover, in a field which Americans had come to think of complacently as their very own, the application of science to technology. Americans should have faced up to this challenge with better grace and realism.

Sputnik I looked something like a ball of yarn with darning needles stuck through it. It measured 22 inches across, weighed 183.92 pounds, left the earth at a speed of approximately 26,400 feet a second, and reached a maximum height of 560 miles. It circled the earth about fifteen times a day, once every hour and thirty-five minutes. What stunned American observers was not merely the extraordinary skill and precision of instrumentation required to place such an object in orbital flight, at the exact right speed, level, and direction, but its size. The American artificial moon in process of gestation was designed to reach a weight of twenty-one and a half pounds. The first Soviet satellite was eight times heavier. This meant, in turn, either that the Russians had a new and extraordinarily efficient rocket fuel, or that their launching mechanism was of unprecedented power.

On November 3 came Sputnik II. If we had been shocked before, we were doubly shocked now. This satellite weighed more than half a ton (1,120.26 pounds) and reached a height of 960 miles or more. The mechanism used to launch it probably had something like a million pounds of thrust, and was thus roughly three times more powerful than any known in the United States. Moreover—what really challenged the imagination of the world—Sputnik II carried a passenger, Laika, the dog which for a week had what was certainly the most fantastic ride in history. In that time Laika went around the earth ninety times and traveled 3,500,000 miles.

Some consequences—

This is a book about Russia, not about the United States, and we need not mention here the reasons for the comparative failure as of the moment of American missile development, caused by indifference to research, obscurantism, rivalries between the services, faulty leadership, lack of engineering personnel, stereotyped ideas about old-fashioned air power, and fear of spending money. It is always unwise to underestimate adversaries. For a generation, it has been part of the American folklore to think that Russians are hardly capable of operating a tractor. Not since Pearl Harbor has the

United States suffered such a jolt. Perhaps it may turn out to be a salutary jolt.

Obviously, if the Russians are capable of creating a multisection rocket that could shoot anything so heavy as Sputnik II into the sky, with delicate accuracy and precision, they can perform similar wonders in the realm of missiles. In fact the Soviet ICBM, or intercontinental ballistic missile, was successfully tested a few weeks *before* the first Sputnik went up, and (we know now) used the same launching mechanism. If the rocket could carry Sputnik, it can also carry easily enough a hydrogen bomb warhead. On the other hand, there are differences between Sputniks and missiles. A missile has to hit a target, and the re-entry problem is abstruse—that is, how to get missiles down to the ground without their burning up in the earth's atmosphere. Whether the Russians have actually solved this problem, as they claim, is unknown.

Even so, Soviet work on Sputniks and missiles has changed irremediably the world strategical picture. American prestige has gone down; what is much more telling, the United States can no longer claim with reason to be the world's first scientific power, in an era when science, as well as prestige, counts for so much. At the moment the United States is, for the first time in its recent history, being forced to pursue its international affairs from a position of relative weakness and inferiority, not from one of undisputed strength. This position may, of course, be soon redressed. But, thinking strictly in terms of today, consider the fact that American policy toward the Soviet Union is largely based on two elements, containment and the deterrent power of "massive retaliation." Neither is out of the window as yet—we still seek to "contain" the USSR and the Strategic Air Command certainly still has the capacity for massive retaliation—but both concepts seem, late in 1957, to be somewhat out of date and a little sour. What good is "containment" if the Russians have reached, not merely the Middle East, but are exploring the way to the moon? What good is massive retaliation, if the Russians have a capacity for massive retaliation equivalent to ours?

American policy toward Russia and Russian policy toward America have both been based to a degree on fear; in the first case, American fear of Soviet *subversion*; in the second, Soviet fear of direct American *attack*. This equilibrium has been substantially altered by the Sputniks. It is not merely subversion or infiltration that we have to fear nowadays, at home or in the neutralist or uncommitted countries of the world, but the possibility of surprise attack by a superior instrument; and to an extent the Russians have (as of the moment) canceled out the theoretical possibility of automatically successful American military attack on the Soviet Union. The USSR has something—something important—that the USA hasn't got.

But the Sputniks, extensive as their potential military significance is, should not be thought of only in military terms. They represent a magnificent advance in the realm of pure and applied science, in the benefits of which the whole world should share, and to which the rest of the world should contribute, without any feeling of grudge or humiliation. Their challenge is, moreover, symbolic in other fields. When I think of the Sputniks I do not think merely of brisk little artificial moons parading neatly in the sky, but of children getting education in remote villages where education was unknown forty years ago, of the whole fabric of Soviet society with its multifarious political, social, and economic challenges. The Soviet Union is, most of us know, an inexpressibly dreary, crude, and repellent dictatorship, with its people brutally flattened down into absolutist conformity, but it has lessons for us that we should heed, even so. The song of the Sputniks should be listened to with attention and without fear or prejudice, not merely for themselves but for what they signify in the growth and development of contemporary world society. For us merely to build bigger and better Sputniks will not be enough.

J. G.

INSIDE RUSSIA TODAY

CHAPTER I

Getting In

The primeval tomtom still beats while the atom bomb ticks. Russia is straddling the centuries, in victory more than ever pounding backward to Peter the Great and racing to overtake Henry Ford . . . before she has caught up with Thomas Jefferson.

—ANNE O'HARE MCCORMICK

There are no experts on Russia—only varying degrees of ignorance.

—PAUL WINTERTON

THE Union of Soviet Socialist Republics is the largest political organism in the world, almost three times the size of the United States, and it dominates not merely one continent, but two. It contains fifteen different republics, and is the world's first socialist state, run in all its monolithic immensity by a single party, the Communist party. It passed its fortieth birthday last year, and is both the second industrial and second military power in the world—perhaps, since the Sputniks, the first military power.

Correctly, the name of this gigantic agglutination of territories and peoples is, in Russian, *Soyuz Sovetskikh Sotsialisticheskikh Respublik.* Some observers think that, despite its weight and girth, despite supersonic missiles and the significance of the artificial moons, it is still a house of cards, which could be spilled by one swift jab. Some do not. In any case its relations with the United States and the free world form incomparably the most important, difficult, and dangerous problem in the world today, on which peace and, no doubt, the future of mankind depend.

Geographically the Soviet Union, covering 8,602,700 square miles, is big enough to make most comparisons sound incredible. This mastodon of a

1

country is bigger than all Latin America; it is bigger by far than China and India put together; its European section alone is bigger than all the rest of Europe; it covers between a sixth and a seventh of the total land surface of the globe, and is more than twice as big as any other country in the world.

The Soviet Union spreads over not less than 160 degrees of longitude, or nearly halfway around the earth, and, as one fanciful observer put it, the sun takes eleven hours to cross it. From Moscow to Vladivostok is further than from Moscow to New York. Mr. Khrushchev, in his TV interview to the United States, nettled some listeners by mentioning mildly that his country had more "room" than the United States, but this was a quite tactful way of putting it, since the Soviet Union is nearly three times bigger. Also, something seldom realized, it is the European (and Asian) country geographically closest to the United States, with what is almost a common frontier; only fifty-six miles separate the extreme eastern edge of Siberia from the extreme western edge of Alaska, across the Bering Strait. In more senses than one, Russia is right next door.

The USSR has, moreover, increased substantially in size since World War II. Estonia, Latvia, and Lithuania, which had belonged to Czarist Russia but which became free after World War I, were annexed; so were parts of East Prussia, including towns like Tilsit (now Sovetsk) and Königsberg (now Kaliningrad) which could hardly by any stretch of the imagination be called Russian at all; so were Bessarabia, Ruthenia (giving the Soviet Union a frontier with Hungary and Czechoslovakia), parts of Finland and, in the Far East, the Kuriles and southern Sakhalin Island. In terms of politics and spheres of influence, Russian expansion was even more conspicuous. We may toll off familiar names—Czechoslovakia, Poland, Rumania, Hungary, Albania, Bulgaria, East Germany, Yugoslavia (in a manner of speaking), China, Manchuria, the Mongolias, Tibet, North Korea, North Vietnam. One commentator has calculated that the Communist "empire" between 1945 and 1950 expanded at the rate of "fifty to sixty square miles an hour."[1] There were, however, certain Soviet losses and withdrawals during the same period —for instance, in Austria, Greece, Iran, and Finland[2]—but these are in no way comparable to the gains.

To return to the Soviet Union itself. The great Eurasian plain, stretching

[1] Marguerite Higgins, "Mr. Dulles and Soviet Policy," New York *Herald Tribune*, February 27, 1956.
[2] The Porkkala naval base, seized after World War II, was given back to Finland in 1955.

from the Carpathians to the edge of China, has several distinguishing features. One is that it lies much further north than most people, who do not look at a map closely, are apt to realize. There are, for instance, no cities of consequence in Canada above Edmonton, on the 54th degree of latitude. But more than *fifty* Russian cities, including Moscow, are situated above this northerly line. Another is that the plain is largely unbroken, and is by far the most extensive such unit in the world. The flatness is unending; you can travel three thousand miles or more in the Soviet Union, and never see a protuberance higher than a few hundred feet. Several historians, like Spengler, hold that this characteristic has markedly influenced the Russian temperament. Third, the Urals are generally supposed to be a kind of frontier between European and Asian Russia, or, for that matter, between Europe and Asia, but this is not the case. Contrary to most thought, the Urals are a meager little range from the point of view of height, seldom rising to more than sixteen hundred feet; as a barrier, they have no more consequence than pimples.[3]

Eurasia is, the geographers tell us, a single indivisible continent, with no true physical line of demarcation. So far as ethnic or racial distribution is concerned, Asia begins not at the Urals but at the Volga, deep in what we think of as "European" Russia.

Much of the endlessly vast plain is heavily forested; the *taiga*, as part of the wooded area is called, is in fact the largest uninterrupted forest bloc, if such a term may be used, in the world. Other locutions with which we should be acquainted are *tundra*, which signifies the northern marshland, and *steppe*, which for some reason connotes to most non-Russians the idea of dry, sterile soil. Actually steppe means any extensive grassland, or prairie, and steppe soil can be inordinately rich. The black earth or chernozem belt, in what is called "the great agricultural triangle" in south central Russia, is of unmatched fertility and resource.

Immense and fruitful rivers cut their way across the giant plain. The rivers were the roads of ancient Russia, and, supplemented by canals, still are; more than a third of all Russian freight was carried by river or canal before the Revolution, even though many rivers were icebound for long months. Russia has 225,000 miles of river, of which perhaps 70,000 are navigable. Of the nine longest rivers in the world, four are Russian (Ob, Amur, Lena, and Yenisei); the Ob is the fourth longest river in the world, and the Volga,

[3] The Urals are a fabulously rich depository of basic mineral wealth, however, and also, a minor but interesting point, of precious stones, particularly emeralds. Much Czarist jewelry came from here.

which is two miles wide at Kuibyshev, and which ties much of European Russia together like a greenish golden rope, drains an area three times the size of France.[4]

The Soviet Union is, in short, big; but also a great deal of it, particularly on its northern rim, is waste. You can do something, if you work hard enough, with a desert, and the Russians have done much to reclaim and make useful deserts in Kazakhstan and elsewhere; the Arctic regions are more difficult to cultivate, to tame. One-third of the country lies on a line north of Newfoundland, and not less than three-quarters of its land is, for purposes of agriculture at least, marginal or useless.

*

In the Soviet immensity live 200,200,000 people, almost 10 per cent of the human race. (If you add the population of China and the satellites the figure is more than 900,000,000, or approximately one-third of the human race.) Russia, plus the European satellites, has roughly the same population as all the rest of Europe; one out of every two Europeans, in other words, lives under Communism, if all Russians are considered to be European.[5] Also, of course, there are substantial numbers of Communists in France, Italy, and other non-Communist countries, and some countries are coming closer to Communism precipitously, like Indonesia. On the other hand, a steady, if small, flow of people trickles out of the Soviet orbit into the democratic world; about twelve to fifteen thousand persons manage to cross from East Germany to West every month.

The Soviet Union is not a country, but a patchwork, and contains today citizens of no fewer than sixty different nationalities, who may be further subdivided into 169 distinct groups. Most of these are, however, so small as to be negligible. Some authorities give the total number of different ethnic groups as 180. Between 20 and 25 per cent of the total population is non-Slav, and 22 per cent is considered to be "non-white." Most of the non-whites are Mongols or Mongoloid. There are no Negroes, except a handful who come mainly from the United States. Religious statistics are difficult to ob-

---

[4] Most Russian rivers—a peculiar physical characteristic—incline to the right side of their banks; the high bank, on the right, is called colloquially the "mountain bank," the low on the left the "meadow bank." See Baedeker's *Guide to Russia*, published in 1914, and still an invaluable work of reference. Readers of Chekhov, Turgenev, and other Russian classics will have come across this characteristic of Russian rivers many times.

[5] Bertram D. Wolfe, *Three Who Made a Revolution*, p. 13.

tain, but there are probably 25,000,000 Moslems and 2,500,000 Jews. The Soviet Union is one of the most important Moslem powers in the world, and is the second Jewish power.

Of the total population of 200,200,000 Soviet statisticians classify roughly 117,000,000 as workers, including the intelligentsia, and 83,000,000 as peasants on collective farms. The peasantry, as recently as 1926, comprised a majority of the population; today it is a minority. The urban population is given as 86,000,000, three times the figure twenty years ago; dwellers in urban or semiurban communities now comprise 43 per cent of the population, as against 18 per cent in 1926, and the country has no fewer than 135 cities with a population exceeding 100,000.[6] Three of the Union republics— the Ukraine, White Russia (Belorussia) and Lithuania—have lost rather than gained population in recent years, for a variety of reasons. The forced collectivization of agriculture hit the Ukraine with particular brutality, and millions of kulaks (rich peasants) starved or were transported. Also, the Ukraine and White Russia bore the brunt of the Nazi invasion, and countless numbers of their people were taken prisoner by the Germans, or crossed the line voluntarily. Finally, the Nazis exterminated several hundred thousand Ukrainian and White Russian Jews.[7]

*

So much by way of introduction. Now let us bite into this colossal body and see what we find. First, how to get there.

The Intourist Apparatus

Visas for Russia are comparatively easy to obtain nowadays. Soviet visa policy toward Americans is more liberal than vice versa. You go to any travel agency that has an arrangement with Intourist, the official Russian agency, like the Cosmos Travel Bureau in New York City, and apply for a tourist visa. The

[6] There are 106 in the United States.

[7] Within limits, there is no reason to doubt the accuracy of the Soviet estimate that, as of April 1, 1956, the population of the Union was 200,200,000. This figure was substantially lower than foreign calculations, and the Russians, if they had wanted to juggle figures, would have been tempted to put them high, not low. But the Soviet Union has not held a census since 1939, which means that no current population statistics can be altogether accurate. The next census, for which elaborate preparations are being made, will be held in 1959. Several explanations are given for the comparatively low total of 200,200,000—huge losses during the war, a sharp decline in the birth rate in postwar years, and inaccurate estimates of the population of several annexed areas. New York Times, February 3, 1957.

formalities are simple. Formerly applicants for a Soviet visa had to fill out an involved questionnaire, and even submit an autobiography. Then in the great majority of cases nothing whatever happened. You were not accepted; you were not refused. All that *did* happen was that you never got the visa. Today applicants fill out nothing more than a brief form containing questions asked by almost every country, like date and place of birth. The only "sensitive" questions are whether you have ever been in Russia before, and for what reason, and whether you have any relatives there. The above refers only to tourist visas. If you want a visa for an extended stay, for instance as a permanently accredited journalist, the procedure is more elaborate. Tourist visas are, moreover, as a rule restricted to thirty days, and getting an extension may present heroic difficulties.[8]

The Russians boast that no Americans are refused visas these days, but this is not quite true. There are a few black-listed characters, and some visitors are not given the full thirty days but may be restricted to fifteen, eight, or even four. But some astounding examples have occurred recently of people getting in who could not conceivably have got in at all ten, five, or even three years ago. Invitations have been extended to well-known anti-Soviet refugees in the United States, and writers notorious for their hostility to the Soviet regime have been admitted, which certainly seems to indicate that the regime has confidence in itself. I even know one defector who got a visa. He was a Russian official who skipped over the wall in a Soviet consulate abroad years ago and eventually became a naturalized American citizen. Several reasons exist for the new Russian visa policy. (1) The authorities want to be able to say that *Russia* is not responsible for the Iron Curtain. (2) They hope that other countries will, in turn, be more liberal about giving visas to Russian citizens whom they want to send abroad. (3) For some time the Soviet government has been worried to an extent about being "culturally isolated" from the rest of the world. It does not want to be cut off from the main streams of technical accomplishment. (4) Tourist traffic brings in a certain amount of foreign currency, which is always useful.

The Russians realize perfectly well that to let in tourists without limit is

---

[8] In general practice you are pitched out on the thirtieth day no matter what. We were lucky and got two extensions. Intourist has no authority over extensions; this is strictly a matter for the Foreign Office. And often Intourist does not know what the Foreign Office, in its maddening way, is doing. Once, the story goes, a correspondent was refused an extension in Moscow and then, arriving at the frontier on his way out, was picked up off the train and categorically sent back to Moscow— even though he didn't want to go back—because permission for him to be extended finally came through, but only after he had boarded the train.

a risk. Tourists bring in fresh air from the world outside, which can be dangerous. We Americans, on our side, would do well to take advantage of the new Soviet visa policy, and pump as many tourists into the USSR as possible. A tourist is a valuable article of export. Every chink in the armor should be explored, and anything is to the good that serves to bring light and stimulus to people in Russia, and show them how *we* live. More on this later.

In any case some 480,000 tourists from 84 countries visited the Soviet Union in 1956, four times the number in 1955, and a surprisingly high figure. Most were from the satellites. No fewer than 1,733 delegations came, a rise of 600 per cent over the preceding year. Of the total number of visitors, about 2,500 were Americans. Intourist now has contracts with 67 companies in 40 countries, and the number of visitors next year is expected to rise substantially.[9] Thirty thousand youngsters from all over the world came to the Moscow Youth Festival alone in 1957.

Your Intourist tickets cost $30 per day per person for the de luxe class, exclusive of transportation. You buy them in New York or elsewhere before you set out. If you join a tour instead of traveling independently, rates are much lower—$20 a day or even $10. The joke is that for $30 a day you get a toilet that flushes, for $20 a toilet that doesn't flush, and for $10 no toilet at all. (Actually I only encountered one toilet in the Soviet Union that didn't flush; on the other hand, I seldom found a washbowl that drained properly. Usually they have some kind of stoppage, leak, or gurgle, no matter how de luxe your surroundings may be.)

Thirty dollars a day may seem expensive but actually it is quite cheap. For $30 you get: (a) the best available suite or room in the best hotel; (b) four meals a day; (c) a limousine and chauffeur for a certain number of hours a day, which meant, in our case, since we each had a ticket, practically unlimited service; (d) an interpreter ditto; (e) free entrance to museums and the like; and (f) a kickback of 25 rubles a day cash. This at par is only $6.25 but it is useful and in theory is supposed to pay for laundry, theater tickets, drinks and so on. Tobacco and alcohol are not included in the global $30. In our case, the $6.25 was never enough, but if you need more you can always cash an American Express check or any foreign currency at any Intourist office or the State Bank, which will be glad to take your money.

This is a good moment for bringing up an abstruse subject. As of the time

[9] *Pravda*, July 25, 1957, as translated by the *Current Digest of the Soviet Press*, September 4, 1957. The *Current Digest* is, as noted in the Foreword, published by the Joint Committee on Slavic Studies of the American Council of Learned Societies and the Social Science Research Council, and is an invaluable, in fact indispensable, guide to and record of day-to-day Soviet affairs. Its editor is Leo Gruliow.

we were in Russia, the official exchange rate was four rubles to a dollar, so that the ruble was worth twenty-five cents in foreign terms. This figure does not accurately reflect purchasing power. A truer value would be ten rubles to the dollar, with the ruble worth ten cents, or even less. Rubles can be bought abroad for as little as three cents, but it is strictly illegal to bring them in or to engage in any black market operations. Visitors may however legally purchase Finnish marks at a cheaper rate outside and convert these into rubles in Russia at six to the dollar. Early in 1957 it was announced that, to attract tourists, a special rate of ten to a dollar would apply to foreign visitors. Nevertheless, all transpositions from rubles into dollars or vice versa in this book will—for the sake of uniformity and convenience—be calculated at the official figure.[10]

A word about tourism in reverse. Normally few Russians ever get exit visas for travel abroad to countries in the free world. The reason, if not obvious, will become so before this book progresses much further. If Russians were permitted to travel indiscriminately, they would see what the rest of the world is like, realize how appallingly low their own standard of living is by comparison, and perhaps, to put it mildly, become disgruntled. Soviet officials going abroad and members of various scientific and cultural exchange groups are carefully handpicked. But, remarkable as the fact may be, the Soviet government is now permitting a good deal of external tourist traffic. About 560,000 Soviet citizens went abroad last year, mostly to the eastern European satellites, but in all to sixty-one different countries. Some five thousand were even permitted to go take cruises to ports in Italy, France, and Scandinavia—most of them trade-union members chosen for seniority or good behavior. Another limiting factor is that these cruises are expensive, and only people fairly high up can afford to go. Only 350 Russians visited the United States. The Russians say that many more would have sought American visas, but did not do so because they refused to submit to finger-printing.

[10] Perhaps we should also have a word here—at the outset—about something else that may be puzzling to the general reader, in the field of terminology. "Soviet Union" means the same as "Union of Soviet Socialist Republics" (USSR), the correct name for the country. Often I use "Russia" as a synonym for this as a matter of euphony or convenience, but strictly speaking to do so is not correct. "Russia," except when used in the historical or general sense, means technically the Russian Soviet Federated Socialist Republic, the RSFSR or Russia proper, the chief division of the Soviet Union. As to "Soviet" I use it as a blanket adjective or noun to indicate both "Communist" and "Russian" characteristics. Actually "Soviet" is an old word which means "council." Sometimes I use "Bolshevik" as a synonym for "Communist," even though this usage is not quite correct. Russians themselves have not used the term "Bolshevik" officially for some years, except in such an appellation as "Old Bolshevik." The word means "majority."

Flight to Moscow

You can reach Moscow from western Europe by train, or fly in by any of several routes. SAS, the Scandinavian airline, has good services to Moscow and Leningrad several times a week; so have the Finns. Except for the satellite lines (Polish, East German, and Czechoslovakian), these are the only foreign companies serving Russia. Of course the Soviet airline, Aeroflot, on which more later, operates many flights abroad.[11] For most visitors the easiest way to fly in is from Copenhagen. SAS and Aeroflot arrange their timetables so that one or the other is available six days a week.

Why are SAS and the Finnish Aero O/Y the only non-Communist lines allowed in? The answer could not be simpler; Sweden and Finland are not members of NATO, the North Atlantic Treaty Organization, which is one of the Soviet Union's pet hates. Also Sweden, Denmark, and Norway (which operate SAS jointly) are small countries, which Russia does not fear, and their line has no "imperialist" connotation. Recently, as a special and signal concession, a KLM (Dutch) plane was permitted to fly into Leningrad, for just one trip, in order to carry some Rembrandts being exchanged by Russian and Dutch museums. Also, as a matter of personal courtesy, the American and British ambassadors are allowed to fly in and out of Russia by American Air Force or RAF military transport planes. Otherwise foreign planes are unknown. No private flying of any kind is permitted in the Soviet Union. Another curiosity is that when SAS and the Russian authorities made their agreement the Swedes (also the Finns) were forbidden to use anything but two-motor planes. SAS, an up-to-date airline, was hard put to it to find any two-motor ships left in its stable and had to resort to using an old type of craft known as a Scandia. The reasons why the Russians will not permit DC-6s, DC-7s, Constellations or similar four-engine craft to fly inside Russia are: (a) they do not as yet have operational four-motor ships of their own to compete and they do not want to be at a disadvantage on jointly shared runs; (b) they are not particularly fond of having new types of passenger aircraft seen and admired by their own people; (c) they lack airport facilities.[12]

The Scandinavian pilots flying into Russia are subject to a good many somewhat trying regulations. On the run to Moscow they are obliged to stay within a strip twenty kilometers wide, no matter what the weather. If bad

[11] See Chapter XVIII below.
[12] On the other hand the Russians are now flying jets on their long international runs, the only full jets operated by any airline in the world.

weather develops during a flight they are forbidden to land anywhere except at Riga, a small intermediary airport at Velikiye Luki, and Moscow itself. Actually the air strip at Velikiye Luki is so inferior that no Swedish plane has ever cared to land there even in an emergency; the Swedes always carry enough gasoline to get back to Riga. The Russians have given the Swedes categorical assurance that if any SAS plane runs out of fuel in bad weather and has to be led in, it will be permitted to land anywhere, as a matter of emergency, but the Swedes say that they don't want to take a chance on landing at an unknown airport with passengers and they have never been allowed to experiment by practice runs. Every SAS plane carries a Russian-speaking crewman, so that, if it has to be talked in by ground approach at some airport where nobody speaks English, there will be no language difficulty. The Swedes have stricter operating procedures—in regard to ceiling, visibility, et cetera—than Aeroflot or the satellite lines; also the Swedes complain that the quality of Russian gasoline is not up to theirs. One curious point is that SAS has had to promise never to permit any printed matter to be taken off its planes. All copies of western newspapers and magazines must be carefully removed from the cabin while SAS craft rest on Russian airports.

We took off from Copenhagen on a disagreeably wet and smeary morning; the sky looked like a nest of mottled, twisting snakes. The plane (SAS) was full up with members of an Italian anti-Fascist delegation, all women, who furiously wrote letters as we flew. Our pilot (Norwegian) shop-talked to us; he said that Russian planes were good and Russian pilots superb.

Presently Riga rose out of an icy mist; this city, once as proud and charming as any in Europe, was before the war the capital of independent Latvia. At the end of the runway stood two or three small planes which I think were made of papier-mâché. What they could be for I do not know, unless they were dummies to mislead aerial photographers. The first physical impression I had of Russia, as we descended from the plane, was the quality of the metal ladder set against the side of the plane—flimsy, antique, short by half a step, and made of some queer light metal ornately engraved. Dozens of times later I saw similar ladders, which creak and bend under even a modest weight.

Stepping on Russian soil is always an adventure. In the old days, the Soviet customs examination was one of the toughest in the world. Every page of a book might be scrutinized, and tubes of toothpaste slit open. Today, bags are not even taken off the plane, and no examination of luggage takes place at all. We could have brought in contraband rubles, insurrectionary printed matter, dope, firearms, or what you will. Nobody would have known the dif-

ference. No bag was opened or looked at. This is standard procedure throughout the Soviet Union today for everybody.[13] Russians are a great people for
going the whole hog. It is all or nothing. Once they decided on a liberal visa
policy, they also decided that what the traveler carried was his own business
and that he would be taken on faith. The passport examination at Riga was
extremely cursory. There was no standing in line (even in Scandinavia or
England you wait before a booth or table); not a single question was asked
and, so far as I remember, I never once opened my mouth. Twice, within
Russia, we did not even have to surrender our passports when registering in
a hotel, something that would not happen in France or Italy. On arrival in
Moscow, however, your passport *is* held for a couple of days, and it must be
visaed specifically for each Russian city you plan to visit. But to return to
Riga. The waiting room was cold; no heat at all, and we froze. An MVD man
in green uniform took our passports, and we filled out a slip, of a type familiar
all over Europe, itemizing the foreign currency we carried. We went in to
lunch, a quite good lunch, and half an hour later our passports were handed
to us as we reboarded the plane. That was all. I couldn't help reflecting that
it was certainly easier for an American to get into Russia than for a Russian
—or American for that matter—to get into the United States.
     For mile after mile, en route to Moscow, we saw not a single light. I won-
dered how many brightly lit towns and villages and glowing ribbons of automobile headlights one would have seen in an analogous flight in the United
States, say from Denver to St. Louis. Here it was like flying over the dead
side of the moon. Then an immense lustrous constellation of light flung itself
quivering over the eastern sky, and we knew that we must be approaching
Moscow. The scene at the airport, Vnukovo, was like that at any eastern
European city. Slavs always seem to be confused, even when they aren't. The
porters look like anybody else. But our bags got to the Intourist lobby faster
than bags get from a plane to the waiting room at Idlewild. I had asked for
reservations at the Hotel National, and we went up to the attendant. He
said, "Ah, you are going to the Metropole." I said, "No, the National." He
said, "Yes, precisely, the National." So we went to the National, without
further argument. Before we boarded our car, which was duly waiting, something happened that I thought was moderately astonishing. We picked up
an outrider. A Russian youth came up as we stumbled through the chaotic,
friendly crowds and asked us for a lift into town. I thought, "Here we have

[13] Except, of course, for travelers overtly suspected of smuggling. An American
woman was arrested at the Moscow airport recently for trying to take out contraband silver. New York *Herald Tribune*, April 20, 1957.

been in Moscow less than five minutes, and already we have a spy." I was quite wrong. Our outrider was not a spy. He simply wanted a ride into town. He was a minor airport official who spoke good English. He told us that he earned 1,000 rubles a month ($250), and was devoted to the works of Ernest Hemingway. Within Moscow we passed a line of tanks grinding heavily along. I looked at them with some curiosity, having forgotten that November 7, the great Soviet holiday, was approaching. The tanks were, of course, coming into the city to take part in the celebrations. But the Hungarian crisis was bursting out at just this time and some reflection of my thought must have crossed my face because our outrider laughed quickly and said, "If those tanks were for anything except November 7, you wouldn't see them!"

It was surprising to hear talk so frank.

Then another small thing happened. During the flight I had asked our pilot what our altitude was. He told me, and added, "Does it bother you?" I said, "No." Halfway into Moscow, having finished his disquisition on Mr. Hemingway, our outrider suddenly exclaimed, "I understand you were troubled by the altitude today." I would have paid no attention to this except to think that it was remarkable that any such minor point should be reported at all, quite aside from being reported inaccurately, if I had not met the same observation the next day. An official of the hotel greeted us warmly, "I hope you had a nice flight, but I was sorry to learn that the altitude had bothered you!" News in Moscow certainly does get around. Perhaps I should add that no episode similar to this ever occurred again.

How to Live on Thirty Dollars a Day

The Intourist system works more or less like this. Each hotel has what is known as a Service Bureau, and this becomes your headquarters. One must exclude altogether from one's mind comparisons to a great European or American hotel. A Russian hotel may be very good, but it simply is not *like* a western hotel. No flower shops or cashier's desk behind grilles; no concierge as in Europe; no vitrines skillfully illuminated; no mail chutes or shining banks of elevators; no bulletin boards with neat white-on-black announcements. If any single thing does not exist in Moscow, it is a bellboy in uniform.[14] True, some new hotels in Moscow, like the Sovetskaya, have miles of marble halls and are decorated with unparalleled magnificence; even so, the

---

[14] The ancient wheezing men who run the ancient wheezing elevators wear a kind of shabby uniform, however.

impression they convey is bleak, and there is always a militiaman outside the door.[15]

The lesser hotels give the impression of being establishments run by doctrinaire but amiable lunatics. You can do thus and so. You cannot do thus and so. But the glint in the eye of the chambermaid who touches your cashmere sweater, enraptured, to feel its texture, is profoundly human, and almost everybody is good-humored.

Intourist has four hotels in Moscow—the National, the Metropole, the Savoy, and the Leningradskaya. Normally these are the only hotels tourists are likely to see. Another, the Moskva, is reserved mostly for Russian guests, diplomats, and delegations, as is the Sovetskaya. During the Stalin years, legend had it that a good Soviet citizen would walk around the block rather than come anywhere near the Moskva—because it was the chief hotel assigned to foreigners. In all of Moscow today, a city of 4,800,000 people, these six are the only good hotels.[16] And, in all of Moscow, outside the hotels, there are only three first-class restaurants. One is the Praga, a six-story establishment somewhat like the old Haus-Vaterland in Berlin, overwhelmingly sumptuous and at the same time crude; a good Georgian restaurant called the Aragvi; and the Ararat, which is Armenian. Oddly enough no really good Chinese restaurants exist, although the city is full of Chinese. Visitors should perhaps be warned that a good dinner for two in these restaurants, which are off the Intourist circuit and which do not accept Intourist vouchers, will cost at least fifty dollars, if you calculate your rubles at par.

As we left the Aragvi one day two Russians at the next table who had been watching us murmured, "Thank you for giving us all that good American money!"

Intourist operates directly under the Ministry of Foreign Trade. The Service Bureaus differ according to the character of the hotel and temperament of the manager. Ours was run by a friendly, alert and hard-working man, Alexander Rogov. His office—the whole Service Bureau—consisted of only one small room, and had a crowded informal atmosphere. Five or six pretty girls who speak foreign languages expertly—Larissa, Tamara, and three Ninas—do their duties with beguiling and characteristically Russian volatility, alternations of emotion, a bit of the gay old *nichevo* spirit, and efficiency. One handles theater tickets, another railway transportation,

[15] Militiamen are cops. They belong to the MVD, and wear long blue coats with red and white tabs. Most are friendly, somewhat stupid yokels who do not have much importance except as symbols of authority. They are no more menacing than a cop sauntering down the street in New York.

[16] A new thirty-story hotel, the Ukraine, with 1,026 rooms, opened in 1957.

another local visas, another automobiles, and so on. On arrival, you address yourself to the manager and he works out a kind of plan for your visit, and introduces you to your interpreter. He will say that he assumes that you will want to see such and such a factory, such and such a collective farm, visit the University, and so forth. I surprised Mr. Rogov at our first meeting by telling him, however, that the first three things I wanted to see were: (a) a really good lunatic asylum; (b) an academy where young artists were trained; (c) a musician. Within forty-eight hours all three were dutifully produced, and the musician was none other than the pianist Emil Gilels.[17]

The hotel we stayed in, the National, fronts Manezhny Place, built to commemorate the Russian victory over Napoleon, and has an enthralling view of the crimson walls and omelette-yellow palaces of the Kremlin. I liked it very much. It is shabby and antique and worn out in spots, but clean and well serviced. Local telephone calls are free, and so is mineral water, the admirable Narzan. Maybe the first thing I noticed in Moscow as against 1939 was that the Narzan bottles are now capped with a regular metal disc, as we cap bottles, instead of being plugged with a bit of cork and rusty wire. Laundry comes back in a day. Since your Intourist vouchers, in their orange-colored booklet, cover lodging and food, you never get a hotel bill, and signing chits is unknown. Telegrams, pressing, drinks, long-distance phone calls, are paid for in cash as you go along.

The chambermaids wear black dresses and white aprons and caps and look identical. As a matter of fact, almost all servants in Russia, if of the older generation, look astoundingly alike. I had noticed the guardian of the cloakroom at the Riga airport, a tottering but sturdy old man in a blue smock, with a totally shaved skull and drooping white mustachios. A survivor from a Tolstoy novel, obviously. Now in Moscow I saw him again. But this time he was the doorman outside the National. Then I saw him once more. He was now the elevator operator in the Metropole. And I saw him half a dozen times later—he was a porter in Kiev and a messenger in Leningrad. Today, as yesterday, there are universal Russian types.

[17] I must add a word about the marked friendliness as well as competence of the Intourist organization as we saw it. The organization made only three slips during our whole tour. Once a chauffeur misunderstood directions and got lost, and once a car failed to pick us up at a foreign embassy. And once when we wrote from Leningrad to Moscow asking that tickets be reserved for a special ballet we wanted to see, the message was not delivered. As against this I can remember all sorts of agreeablenesses. Day after day Intourist did things right. One night no tickets could be had for *Anna Karenina* at the Moscow Art Theater for love or money. But trust Intourist. We were whisked over to the theater with a special guide who led us into the director's box.

Our quarters were enormous. Princes used to live in this hotel. They lived well. So did we. The double windows are, as always in winter in Russia, sealed with tape, and fresh air comes by way of the little trap window called a *fortoshka*. In one corner stood a very large grand piano; it carried the mark "St. Petersburg," and so it predated World War I. Several times I heard that the one thing that the Soviet Union has not yet succeeded in producing is a grand piano, but this is not true. More than 43,000 pianos were manufactured last year, mostly in Estonia.

Part of our suite was cut off by a heavy red velvet curtain and a stained-glass window almost inconceivably Victorian, decorated with white flowers and bleeding topaz hearts. The sofa, an obvious relic of the *ancien régime*, was big enough for a gang of school kids to sit on. And the desk! It was immense, at least nine feet long, covered with green felt and bound with aggressive brass studs. Underfoot were no fewer than three Bukhara rugs. The lamps, hung with long, fringed silk shades, looked like what you might have seen in Grand Rapids fifty years ago, if you were having a bad dream. One wall held an enormous oil painting, not an example of "socialist realism," but crazily romantic, imaginative, and old-style; it was as big as a billboard, and had a gold frame seventeen inches wide. It portrayed, of all things, an emir in Central Asia, sipping coffee majestically and being saluted by obsequious underlings.

In the bathroom the oversized tub was cracked, but the shower gadget worked, and it was a perfectly good bath, if somewhat primitive. The tub had a plug. Sometimes Russian bathtubs do not possess this feature, and so it is impossible to take a bath. The story is that the plugs are carried off as souvenirs by visitors from Kazakhstan or some other remote province. A British friend of mine, when traveling in the Soviet Union, still carries with him half a dozen plugs of assorted sizes, in order to meet emergencies.

Not till later did I appreciate the interest of some other items in the National—the deep square glass ash trays made for Russian cigarettes with their cardboard holders; inkwells invariably holding purple ink, with wooden penholders; the state menu in the dining room, always the same; the wine, water and vodka glasses, made of tinted cut glass; the blue and gold china, very pretty; and the stout black brush in every armoire for dusting your shoes.[18] Such objects, and many like them, are identical almost everywhere in the Soviet Union. It is paralyzing after a while to encounter them again and again, always uniform. They are of course mass produced and mass

---

[18] Why these brushes do not disappear, by theft or otherwise, I do not know. Perhaps some do. But I never saw a hotel room without one.

distributed and the number of forks and spoons, as an example, that make up the national order every year must be prodigious. Of course the fact that everything of this nature is standardized to a simple pattern makes for cheapness and efficiency in production, but the aesthetic effect to the outsider is positively stifling.

Room service by telephone is unknown. You ring a bell for breakfast and sooner or later a waiter, in an antique black dress coat, arrives. Serving breakfast (I never knew this to fail anywhere in Russia), he spreads a white tablecloth over exactly *half* a circular table which is always in the living room, atop its big velvet cover with dangling fringes. Breakfast, in Moscow at least, is pretty good, but fresh fruit is rare in winter and citrus juices are unknown. As a substitute you can have a kind of weak diluted tomato juice or grape juice, known as *vinogradny sok*. Russian coffee is excellent, so good that we seldom used the powdered coffee we had brought with us.

The dining room in the National is small, with mustard-colored walls, and has a cozy atmosphere. Anybody can sit anywhere—at anybody's table—if space is scant. We had a table we liked and the waiters saw to it that we didn't have to double up—not out of any special consideration for me as such, but simply because we were foreign visitors. I have often wondered if a Russian couple would be treated with similar courtesy in a restaurant in New York. A five-piece orchestra, not in uniform, plays on most evenings. Old songs and American jazz are favorites; the first music I heard in Moscow was a Cuban rhumba, followed by the "Blue Danube Waltz." Once, late in the evening (but not very late—most restaurants in the Soviet Union close around midnight) a Russian guest lurched up from his table, advanced to the orchestra threateningly, and made an impassioned speech. He gave the impression of a bag of potatoes pouring open. He was very drunk. Also he was a flaming patriot. He was denouncing the orchestra for playing western music! A tough waiter dragged him back to his table presently by main force and the orchestra went on placidly playing its piece, which was none other than "South of the Border."

In state hotels the menu is an elaborate twelve-page booklet printed in four languages (Russian, English, French, and German). Here are a few prices for non-Intourist guests:

Fresh caviar ....13.35 rubles ($3.33)
Red caviar .... 5.60 rubles ($1.40)
Smoked sturgeon .... 7.30 rubles ($1.82)
White mushrooms in oil
(the cheapest hors d'oeuvre) .... 1.95 rubles ($0.48)

Fromage Sovietique .... 2.95 rubles ($0.74)
Solyanka (meat soup) .... 8.85 rubles ($2.21)
Vol au vent ....12.25 rubles ($3.06)
Wiener schnitzel ....10.05 rubles ($2.51)
Glacé à la plombière .... 2.30 rubles ($0.57)
Semolina Kasha with fruit .... 3.75 rubles ($0.94)
Café Noir .... 1.05 rubles ($0.26)[19]

You choose three or four courses for your main meal, which is usually served in the middle of the day, and two or three at supper, tearing out the appropriate coupons from your book. Intourist travelers do not, of course, pay in cash, since their coupons cover meals, and you can eat within reason all you want without extra charge. Sometimes a disorganized or capricious waiter will demand that you pay for your coffee and mineral water, which generally are thrown in free. Some soft drinks are oddly tinted, and taste strange.

Alcoholic drinks by the glass are charged by weight. One hundred grams of red Georgian wine costs 4.20 rubles, or $1.05. If you buy by the bottle, a fairly good light white wine will cost 20 rubles ($5.00). Champagne runs from 38 to 42 rubles a bottle, $9.50 to $10.50. Brandy is very expensive. A five-star brand from the Caves de Samtrust is 9.10 rubles per glass, and a variety known as Erevane des Caves de l'Ararat is not less than 22.35. The beer tastes like soap suds, and costs about five rubles a bottle, $1.25. Even vodka is expensive. The best variety is called Stolichny. Our normal ration for dinner was 100 grams of vodka each (about a quarter of a pint) and this cost 13 rubles or $3.25.

One curious point is that tea is served to a woman usually in a cup, to a man in a glass with a metal holder. For your wife to drink tea in a glass is nekulturny, not cultured. Tea, the skimpiest meal of the day, usually comes with a kind of cookie known as "English" Keks. Salt nowadays appears, not in saltcellars, but in cruets—for some reason saltcellars are not "cultured." Some things change fast in the Soviet Union. Cyrus Sulzberger of the New York Times found it difficult to get pepper a few years ago, but we had it on request. Fellow visitors play little games with their food coupons, offering to trade you five teas for one supper, and so on. If you have unused meal coupons at the end of your stay, these may be cashed in for wine or caviar. The caviar is almost always good but it is sometimes difficult to get the really

[19] Let me point out that I am converting these prices at the official rate, four rubles to the dollar, which was in force when we were there. The present tourist rate (ten to the dollar) makes everything very much cheaper in terms of dollars.

superlative variety, particularly after the round of celebrations accompanying November 7.

Tipping is a complex subject. In theory tips are forbidden, but in Moscow and the big cities most hotel servants accept them, except perhaps very young or new waitresses who do not know what a tip is. (They learn quickly.) In the washroom of one restaurant I even found a saucer laid out for coins, as in the lavabo of a French café. The gist of the matter is that a tipping "frontier" exists—the further you are away from Moscow, the less is tipping practiced. When we reached the Caucasus and Central Asia, most servants refused tips indignantly. The whole subject is one to which the Soviet soul is sensitive.[20] I mentioned casually to our interpreter one day that chambermaids at the National took tips. She was profoundly shocked and horrified, saying that foreigners must be "spoiling" the Russian people.

No mention of Russian food, no matter how brief, could be complete without a word about ice cream. The Russians call it *morozhenoye*, and it is a national craze. One Moscow factory makes it in thirty-six flavors, which beats Howard Johnson. Moreover, it is very good. Modern methods of ice cream manufacture came to the Soviet Union from the United States, and ice cream cones and confections like our Eskimo Pies are on sale at most street corners. Confectionery shops and ice cream parlors are numerous and are, in a sense, the Moscow equivalent of bars and coffee shops. Some are quite chic. A story is told, probably apocryphal, about Sir Winston Churchill. On a visit to Moscow during the war he saw a line of people shivering out in a blizzard. An icy wind blew gusts of snow across the city, and the streets were deep with frozen slush. What was the line of miserably dressed citizens, cringing in their rags, waiting for? Ice cream! Mr. Churchill is reported to have said, "Ah! These people *never* will be conquered!"

To sum up—food for the visitor in Moscow is plentiful and reasonably good, but monotonous and prepared with little art or discrimination. You can have any variety of jam for breakfast, provided it is strawberry. You can have any vegetable for dinner, provided it is a pea or a carrot. (Of course we were there in winter; during summer green vegetables and salads are much more plentiful.) The soups are almost always stoutly good, and so is the bread and butter. Meats and poultry are generally inferior, and such dishes as an American T-bone steak or a French *coq au vin* are altogether unknown. Well, so are they unknown in India or parts of the British Isles.

---

[20] John Reed quotes a waiter in Petrograd (1917): "Just because a man has to make his living waiting on tables is no reason to insult him by offering him a tip!" *Ten Days That Shook the World*, p. 14.

One cannot blame the Russians for cooking in their own way. A reason for the prevailing drabness is that so little initiative or incentive exists in the catering business. A man may suddenly be put in charge of a restaurant who has absolutely no interest in his job or the cuisine.

*

When you want a car, which is often, you telephone the Service Bureau from your room and tell the bright girl at the automobile desk where you want to go and when. This information she indexes in a log. She gives an order to the garage and, as you leave the hotel, hands you a slip on which she has written your destination in Russian. You give this to the driver. Few drivers speak English or any western language, and therefore written directions are necessary. Thus, without the necessity of any surveillance, the Intourist people know precisely where a person is most of the time. It is a simple and effective system. On the other hand, there is nothing necessarily sinister about it, and it serves to protect the visitor. Taxi drivers in New York write down every address they go to, although for a different reason.

The Zis, which resembles a Packard or big Buick of about five years back, and the Zim, which is slightly smaller, are very good cars indeed. We must have had two or three hundred rides in them, all over Russia, and I never knew one to snort, cough, snarl, stall, or have a flat. Most carry seven passengers, most are black, and most have small oriental rugs laid on the floor. All carry a small fire extinguisher and all have big clocks—which work. It is surprising, but the Soviet Union is extraordinarily time-conscious these days, and I never saw an automobile with its clock more than a minute off. (In the United States, I might add, I have scarcely ever known an automobile clock to run at all.) The big Zis is not for sale, but is distributed by the government to high-ranking bureaucrats and organizations. The Zim can be bought, if you have the money, but the waiting list is long. Only three other types of passenger car are made in the USSR, the Pobeda, which resembles a small outdated Chevrolet, another light car called the Volga, and the Moskvich, like a baby English car. A Zim costs $10,000 (at par) and the Pobeda about $5,000. The age of the automobile is just beginning in the Soviet Union. In all Moscow I saw only one filling station.

The "s" in "Zis" stands for Stalin ("Zis" means "plant named for Stalin") and, inevitably, the factory in Moscow that produces this car, formerly the Stalin Works, has been renamed the Likhachev Works. Ivan A. Likhachev was the engineer who built it. The joke in Moscow was that all the Zises would consequently have to be renamed Zils. But no! A *new* car, a two-tone hardtop to cost 70,000 rubles, is to be produced under the name "Zil." The Zim, manufactured in Gorky, was named for ex-Prime Minister Molotov, now in disgrace. What *it* will evolve into is unknown.

The Russians have intricate traffic rules, even though traffic is extraordinarily slight by our standards, and to get a driver's license is not easy. This means, among other things, that the foreign embassies are dependent in the main on Soviet chauffeurs. Very few Americans in Moscow have ever passed the Soviet driving test. Among other things you have to be approved by a *panel* of physicians, not merely one, including an eye doctor, a cardiologist, a back specialist, and one who tests reflexes in the soles of your feet. You have to work out traffic problems with model cars on something that looks like a parchesi board, and prove that you can take apart and mount an engine. Traffic accidents (for anybody) are a very serious matter, and offenders are punished with severity. Even if you scrape somebody's fender you can lose your license for a year, and if you accumulate three violations you lose it *for life*. In the interests of safety, no more than two persons are permitted on the front seat. Late in 1956 two hospital workers in Podolsk got drunk, ran off with an ambulance, and went on a joyride with their wives. The ambulance hit a bus, and later knocked down and injured two pedestrians. The ambulance driver abandoned his vehicle, and ran away. He was caught, and was sentenced to *twenty-five years* in jail.[21]

*

Interpreters are a whole long story in themselves. People often say, "How can you trust your interpreter?" But this question seldom arises—any experienced newspaperman can tell whether he is being interpreted accurately or not. A good interpreter, as ours was, can be a substantial asset, particularly in lining up interviews, and a bad one is a nuisance. Some will be loath to translate accurately *all* of a sensitive talk. But the visitor is at liberty to change his interpreter at any time. Intourist had no more than a round dozen interpreters five years ago; now it has hundreds, and hundreds more are being trained.[22] Mostly these are friendly young people fresh from the Foreign

[21] *Current Digest of the Soviet Press,* November 21, 1956.

[22] It is amazing that young men and women who have never been outside Russia can be taught to speak English, as an example, so well. Announcers on the Moscow Radio can mimic almost any kind of British or American accent, from Brooklynese to hillbilly. Some oddities may be noted, for instance that everybody has been taught to use the idiom "Don't mention it" in reply to an expression of thanks. Sometimes

Language Institute, but some are doltish; their salaries start at 800-900 rubles a month ($200-$225) and veterans can get as much as 2,000 rubles ($500). Most are phenomenally expert in the languages they choose, and many nowadays know Chinese. Very few, strange as this may seem, are members of the Communist party. Some are more politically interested than others. Our girl, Zoya Kurancheva, was a terrifically devoted and loyal Soviet citizen—an addict. She had some pungent observations to make about tourists she encountered. Most American businessmen, she assumed from the way they behaved in Moscow, drink too much, and people from California are particularly good-natured which, she thought, must mean that life in California is easier than elsewhere in the United States. Indians, she said, came to Russia to learn; Chinese to study; French and Italians to do serious sightseeing; Americans, just to look.

How to Meet Russians, If Any

Before we left the United States friends told us, "Oh, but you will never meet any Russians." We met hundreds of Russians, and had long talks with sixty or seventy, including some important people. True, we almost never met a Russian *alone*. Somebody else is almost always present, as a precaution, in addition to the interpreter. Only twice during our whole trip did we meet a Soviet official without somebody else from his office being present, ostensibly to assist in interpretation. And only twice did we see the inside of a Russian home. But this is par for the course. Russians simply do not admit foreigners to their homes as a general rule—partly out of fear and partly because they are ashamed of their cramped quarters and poverty. Lack of privacy makes entertainment at home almost impossible.

When, after laborious effort, we were received formally by a Soviet leader, the procedure was almost always the same. First, Russians are punctual. If a Russian gives you an appointment for 6:10, he means 6:10 and not 6:05 or 6:15. This, I must say, marks a great change from the Russia I knew before the war. Second, you are met at the outside door by an underling and whisked instantly to the official's room, so that opportunity to look around is limited. Third, interviews are taken very seriously, and are seldom interrupted. No secretary knocks, no phone rings. Fourth, talks are apt to be lengthy. If a Russian agrees to see you at all, he expects to keep you an hour and a half or even longer. Fifth, the visitor is usually served tea, fruit, and candy.

---

there is a confusion between idiom and accent. One girl we met used the Anglicism "Right you are" perpetually, but pronounced it in a very un-English way.

The easiest contact is on technical levels. An American physicist will have little difficulty in establishing a relationship with a Russian physicist. In general, the best way to approach Soviet citizens is to exploit their curiosity. Even if they don't admit it, they are burning to know more about the world outside. Suppose, talking with a psychiatrist, you drop the name "Freud" into the pool of talk, as if by accident. This will provoke a hostile reaction. It is the duty of the Soviet psychiatrist to denounce Freud. Or put in a little bait about abstract art in talk with a painter. He will bristle—at first. Then, however, as the interview proceeds, the psychiatrist or artist will begin to ask cautious questions about Freud or abstract art— what in our country do *we* think about them, and why? Soon, like as not, they will be talking about Freud and abstract art with animation. This game is fun to play, and we played it on all sorts of subjects.

I have said that we met a good many Russians, but this statement needs elaboration; it is easy enough to meet people in the realm of cultural exchange, but political Russians are very hard to meet, let alone become friendly with. I did a good deal of preparatory work before I left America, and sent letters to dozens of people enclosing a brief Who's Who of myself and explaining my mission. I got exactly three replies. Friends in England gave us small gifts for officials whom they knew well, together with letters of introduction. We dutifully sent these off when we arrived in Moscow, but no answer or acknowledgment ever came. It was as if we had dropped them into a well. I want to emphasize that my wife and I had no preferred status and were not given any red carpet or VIP treatment of any kind. What we got we got by patience and struggle. I never once gained entrance into the massive, ornate skyscraper that houses the Foreign Office, and I never even met officially the chief of the Press Department, whose business it is to take care of foreign journalists.[23]

*

Before we left the United States, friends told us, "Oh, but they will only show you what they want to show you." This is true to an extent. About 30 per cent of the Soviet Union, including most frontier areas, is closed to tourists. (Most Russian citizens are, incidentally, completely unaware

[23] Perhaps I should mention that we happened to arrive in Russia during the Hungarian and Suez episodes. Officials were reluctant to see us if only because they did not know what to say in a difficult and quickly changing situation. Suppose a Soviet journalist had arrived in Washington during Pearl Harbor week. I doubt if he would have had much access to the State Department.

of this, and flatly do not believe it when you tell them.) It should also be
pointed out that, reciprocally, large areas in the United States are strictly
closed to Russian visitors. Also the Soviet Union is opening up to a degree.
In 1957 for instance it became possible for the first time for motorists
to drive all the way from the Polish frontier to Moscow, and then down to
the Crimea.

The Baltic states were closed when we were there—except for airplane
passengers going through Riga—but Riga is now open. So is Lvov. But
large regions in the Arctic, the Far East, Kazakhstan, Central Asia, and
industrial Siberia are still closed except by special permission. The Russians
seldom admit that a formal ban exists on travel through these regions; they
say simply that no amenities or accommodations—hotels and so on—
are available. And, as usual, one Russian hand does not always know what
the other is doing. In Moscow, we were told that it would be impossible
to visit Armenia; on arrival in Tiflis with Armenia next door, we were told
that there was no ban on travel to Armenia at all. The reasons why substantial
areas of the Soviet Union are forbidden to travelers are obvious. (1) Russians
are sensitive about their frontiers and do not like visitors prowling around
in strategic areas. (2) Most Soviet work on thermonuclear weapons and
ballistic missiles takes place in remote areas in Central Asia, and American
visitors are no more permitted there than Russian visitors would be permitted indiscriminately at Oak Ridge or Los Alamos. (3) The most notorious
of the old forced labor camps were situated in the Arctic regions, Kazakhstan
and Siberia. Such camps as still exist are an extremely touchy subject in
Russia, and nobody is allowed to get near them.

All this being true, if you keep your eyes and ears open and use your legs
in Moscow and beyond, you can see a lot. Nobody will keep you from
strolling down the street, going to the theater, and visiting shops and
museums freely. I learned more about Russia in one evening at the Moscow
airport than I could have picked up in a month in Siberia.

*

Why is Russia so closed? First, fear of "capitalist encirclement," or to
put it in more contemporary terms, fear of the American policy of containment. Second, the fact that the living standard of the Soviet Union
is so much lower than that of the West, and consequent fear of "con-
tamination." Moreover the Russians have never acknowledged to their own
people that their standard of living is appreciably lower; hence it is neces-

sary to preserve the deception at all costs, and keep people from finding out the truth.[24]

We must become accustomed at outset to the most outrageous contradictions. Consider what we have already noted in these opening pages, that in some mechanical fields (e.g. airplane ladders) Russians are extraordinarily backward, whereas in others (e.g. the application of atomic energy) they are extraordinarily advanced. Priority goes to what *counts*; nobody cares if you break a leg hoisting yourself in an airplane, but to put an artificial moon in the sky is something else again.

Also Russians have, like many other people, a healthy taste for having their cake and eating it. A polite way to refer to this is to talk about Soviet "dichotomy" or "ambivalence." In the matter of relations to the West they show ambivalence to an almost schizophrenic degree. It will haunt us throughout this book. While walling themselves off from the West, the Soviets also want good relations with the West; while doing their best to protect themselves against foreign influences, they also purport to want to be good friends, and melt the Iron Curtain.

In the first issue of *USSR*, the Soviet picture magazine distributed in the United States, Prime Minister Nikolai Bulganin wrote, "We are deeply convinced that differences in ways of life and in political and social systems (as between USA and USSR) need not be an obstacle to friendship and fruitful cooperation between our peoples." This double point of view explains some manifestations in the Moscow press that are otherwise incomprehensible. On the same day I saw a magazine article recalling with fond wistfulness the first meeting of the American and Soviet armed forces on the Elbe (1945), and a poisonously slanted little paragraph in another periodical announcing that four million unemployed Americans were "starving" today in the state of Pennsylvania.

*

Why are Russians so afraid—even of the most casual contact with a foreigner? There are, of course, profound historical roots for this, that have little to do with the Soviet regime. Russian intellectual attitudes have often been marked by xenophobia; conflict between "Slavophiles" and "west-

[24] Stalin himself said back in 1946 that "the wall between the Soviet system and the West could never be broken down until the Soviet standard of life could bear comparison with the living standard elsewhere." New York *Herald Tribune*, August 4, 1956. Also see Isaac Deutscher, who has some pointed things to say about Soviet habits of deception in his *Stalin: A Political Biography*.

erners" dominated much of the nineteenth century. As of today, it is relevant to point out that, according to the State Secrets Act, no foreigner may approach any Soviet official except through the Ministry of Foreign Affairs or the Ministry of Foreign Trade. Of course this provision in the law is a dead letter for the most part. For instance, visitors often make direct contact with the Ministry of Culture. But the fact that the law is on the books makes *Russians* wary. Another provision in this act makes practically all statistical matter "classified" or secret. In theory, until recently, a Russian could be violating the law if he told a visitor what the population of a city was. Finally, Article 58, Section 4 of the Soviet Penal Code states that any Soviet citizen giving "assistance" to any "section" of the international bourgeoisie is subject to penalties ranging from three years in jail to death. Of course the word "assistance" is the operative word. Even so, the Russian citizen has good reason to be timid.[25]

The Gulf

There are times, no matter how friendly individual Russians may be, when it seems utterly impossible to reach them. How can you reach people who cannot reach themselves? If it is impossible, utterly impossible, to speak with a minor official of the Foreign Office on the telephone to discuss a visa matter, it will also be impossible to discuss disarmament at London. Moreover, even if contact is established, Russians talk an utterly different language. They never concede *anything*, and will distort and lie to a fantastic extent if necessary. We of the West, if we make a mistake, will usually admit it. The Russians never do, and are impenetrable.

The gulf, the chasm, the abyss, may seem too great to be bridged. But we must try to bridge it, because the world will have no rest otherwise.

[25] Khrushchev announced in May, 1957, that no action under this article had been taken against any Soviet citizen for three years. But—even so—it is still theoretically in force.

CHAPTER II

Moscow—Size, Shape, Qualities

Moscow: those syllables can start
A tumult in the Russian heart.
—ALEXANDER PUSHKIN

Moscow, the fifth largest city in the world, capital of both the Soviet Union and the RSFSR (Russia proper), has 4,800,000 people. It lies on the same latitude as the southern pocket of Hudson Bay, and is more to the east than is generally thought, on roughly the same longitude as Damascus or Jerusalem. We are not far from the Arctic here, and close to Asia as well.

Like several other cities—Rome, Lisbon, Kampala, Kiev—it is built on seven hills, which, however, are so low as to be hardly noticeable. With its golden spires and bulbous domes, Moscow has been called "an inland Constantinople, a Christian Cairo." In the last days of the Czars it had a nickname—the Calico City, because it was the seat of substantial textile manufacturing. Sometimes it is known as the "Third Rome" because, when Constantinople fell in 1453, it became the seat of the Orthodox Christian Church, and remained so for more than four hundred years. The word "Moskva," which is the Russian name of the city, is not Russian in origin, but Finnish.

Some cities, like New York, are built high; Moscow is built broad, although the new skyscrapers stick out like candelabra. It sprawls all over the place, as Los Angeles does, and covers about 125 square miles. Surrounding it are unending forests of pine and birch; if you arrive by train in summer the birches, with their piebald trunks, flash by the car windows colorfully. One fanciful friend of mine says that they always remind him of giraffes.

Moscow, like Paris, was built outward from its heart and center—the

26

Kremlin, which was originally an island. A map of the city today looks like a spider's web, or wheel, with broad spokes leading out to concentric boulevards. The first circle was the original wooden stockade around the Kremlin, built in 1156. The city steadily pushed out and other walls, which are the sites of several present-day circular boulevards, closed it in. The new boulevards are tremendously wide for the most part. Tchaikovsky Street, where the American Embassy is housed, can easily hold twenty automobiles abreast.

Three main characteristics of Moscow are strangeness, closedness, and a peculiar combination of drabness-*cum*-vitality. You may like it or not, but it can scarcely be denied that it is unlike any other city on earth. On most people it puts a spell they never forget, if only by reason of its weird, wacky Russian qualities. Life has been cut down to the very bone for most citizens, but this gives it a hardness, a raw push and drive, an intensity. It has an enthralling past, dramatically made real and splendid by the Kremlin and other monuments, and is, take it or leave it, one of the most tremendous cities in the world.

From a superficial point of view Moscow looks much better than it did in 1939, the date of my last visit. Queues in front of shops are rare. Bookshops are crowded, and people are avid for reading matter of any kind. Taxis are numerous. A lot of people have money, although there is extremely little to spend it on. Most citizens are still wretchedly, appallingly dressed, but clothes are better than before the war. Children are almost always well and warmly dressed nowadays, and look healthy. Perambulators exist; so do sleds and skis. And I found a good deal of relaxation in several fields. You can stroll around the Kremlin, which was forbidden in Stalin's day, and take photographs almost everywhere.

People grumble openly and, so long as it isn't about anything political, are astonishingly free with criticism. The overt terror has stopped, and political arrests are at the minimum. New urges are apparent—desire for privacy and mobility. But much remains the same. This is still a city—as well as country—in deadly earnest, wearing statistics like armor and obsessed by planning. It is still without freedom in our sense and without justice in our sense, and with precious little joy. Human values in terms of individuals—except in the case of children—are largely ignored. Why are children so favored? Not merely for their own sake, but because they represent the future.

Also the visitor must try to get used to Moscow's strangeness, its exoticism. The city has 4,800,000 people, but I never saw a girl with dark glasses or met a Russian with a cigarette lighter. Once I showed a waitress my pocket flashlight; she had never seen one and could not believe her eyes. No local citizen has ever seen a comic strip, read a gossip column, played Canasta, or gone to a cocktail party.[1] No one has ever seen a supermarket, a drive-in movie, or a motel. Nobody has ever shopped by mail, except through a single organization devoted to mail-order business, or paid a bill by check. (There are, however, savings banks which pay good rates of interest.) Probably not more than 10,000 privately or semiprivately owned automobiles exist in the entire city, and perhaps 25,000 movie seats. (But legitimate theaters outnumber those in New York.) No one has ever had a hamburger in a drugstore, or seen a juke box or an electric toaster. There are no cigar stores on the streets, no real estate agencies, no shoeshine stands, no employment offices, no restaurants with pretty marquees or plain little shops selling anything from paint to pets.

The Soviet Union covers 8,602,700 square miles and has not a single golf course. A serious country!

*

By legend, Moscow was founded in 1147 A.D. by Prince Yuri Dolgoruki. His name means "Long-Arm," and he was, of all things, the son of an English mother—Gytha, the daughter of King Harold II. His father was the illustrious Vladimir Monomakh, prince of Kiev. Prince Yuri built a fortress at the junction of the Moskva and the Neglinnaya, and this became a lively trading post, and then the capital of the rapidly expanding principality of Muscovy. It was burned down by the invading Tatars several times, and has seen all manner of bloody and challenging events, including some fancy murders. In 1713 Peter the Great transferred the capital to St. Petersburg, but Moscow continued to be, in most respects, the most typical and commanding Russian city. It did not become the capital again until March 10, 1918, after the Bolshevik Revolution.

Moscow is not only the seat of government today but incomparably the most important city in the Soviet Union, particularly as an industrial nexus, cultural center, and transportation hub. For the entire Soviet and Communist world, this is Mecca. In remote villages thousands of kilometers away, every ambitious eye turns to Moscow. Moscow has 870 architectural monuments preserved by the state, 116 museums, and 11 railway stations.

[1] A good Soviet citizen would say to this, "Thank goodness! Why should we import such trashy phenomena?"

Here are such organisms as the Institute of Nuclear Research, the State Institute for Civic Planning, and the Central Bureau for Abstracting Scientific Reports, which has thirteen thousand multilingual employees. Here are the Bolshoi Theater, the Moscow Art Theater, and the Central Polytechnical Library of the All-Union Society for Dissemination of Political and Scientific Knowledge, an organization ninety years old which has 1,800,-000 scientific books.[2] Khrushchev is eager to decentralize some of Moscow's activities. He asked in his celebrated Report to the Twentieth Congress, to be mentioned many times in these pages, why, for instance, two mining and three hydroelectric institutes should be located in Moscow, far from their domains. Also in Moscow are the State Publishing House for Political Literature (Gospolitizdat) which issues 70,000,000 books per year, and the State Publishing House of Literature (Goslitizdat), with an annual production of almost 50,000,000 books. More than 1,300,000 telegrams were sent in Moscow on New Year's Day, 1957, and Moscow citizens bought 2,700,000 bottles of Russian wine during the three-day holiday.

Moscow has the First State Ball-Bearing Plant, one of the most important undertakings in the country, and its candy factory, the Krasny Oktyabar, is well known. Not less than 8 per cent of the entire industrial production of the USSR comes from Moscow's 1,507 major industrial plants, which range from aviation to wood processing. Moreover Moscow is (or was until recently) headquarters of the immense pyramidal trusts covering medical supplies, perfumes, knitwear, road machines, and food products. Here too is a terminus of the Moscow-Volga Canal, one of the most vital of the nation's internal waterways. Canals play a large role in Russian transport and communications, and Moscow is a flourishing inland port.

The most conspicuous sights in Moscow are the Kremlin, the Red Square, and the Lenin-Stalin mausoleum. Let us explore.

The Kremlin and Red Square

Kremlin means literally "citadel," and there are Kremlins in the old cities all over European Russia. Few visitors, no matter how many photographs they have seen of the one in Moscow, are prepared for its brilliant, archaic beauty—the dark red wall with its swallow-tail battlements and nineteen soaring towers, as well as the palaces and churches with golden spires and domes within. Red stars flash from the towers at night, and the newcomer

---

[2] Names of many Soviet institutions are, as always, jaw-breaking.

staring at them may think that he is the victim of an optical illusion. They move. This is not an illusion. The illuminated stars *do* move, because— such a utilitarian country—they were put up not only for symbolism and decoration, but as weather vanes.

The Kremlin wall was built by three Italian architects imported for the occasion, Antonio Fryazin, Marco Ruffo, and Pietro Solario, in the reign of Ivan III late in the fifteenth century. Another Italian, Aristotele Fioravanti, built the Uspenski (Assumption) Cathedral in 1475-79, the largest and most resplendent church inside the Kremlin. The Czars were crowned here, and here Napoleon stabled his horses—not out of impiety, but because, after the great fire in 1812, few buildings with undamaged roofs were available.[3] Close by is Archangel Cathedral, also built by an Italian, Alviso Novo, in 1505, where lie the graves of Ivan the Terrible, of his son Ivan whom he murdered, and of another son, Czar Fyodor. The third church of this sumptuous and shining group, unmatched in the world, is the Annunciation or Blagoveshchenski; it was built, not by Italians, but by Russian architects from the ancient city of Pskov. It is interesting that the Italian authorship of these magnificent cathedrals, and much else, is freely acknowledged in the only good guidebook to the Soviet Union written since Baedeker in 1914—a *Pocket Guide* issued by Intourist in 1932. This has long been out of print, and is impossible to procure nowadays. The only guidebook available today, called *Moscow* and published in several languages by the Foreign Language Publishing House, carefully omits any mention of Italian or other foreign authorship of Russian monuments or works of art. Everything in Russia has to be Russian nowadays.

The Kremlin, after having been shut tight for many years, was opened to the public soon after Stalin's death—a suggestive minor example of de-Stalinization. But Stalin has not been altogether de-Stalinized in the minds of *all* Soviet citizens. Our guide made a remark that I thought was, while of no general significance, moderately revealing. We rounded one turn, near the Bell Tower built during the stormy reign of Boris Godunov, and I asked where Stalin's quarters in the Kremlin had been. The guide pointed to white-bordered windows in a butter-colored building and said with reverent awe, "*That* is where Mr. Stalin lived, worked, and died!"

Ten feet away stood a kiosk selling postcards, which certainly would not have been there while Stalin was alive.

The Museum houses fabulous and ornate treasures, like the ivory throne of Ivan the Terrible. The crown of Peter the Great is here, and numerous

[3] A *Picture History of Russia*, by John Stuart Martin, p. 117.

other crowns. One, split down the middle like a watermelon, contains no fewer than 3,800 large diamonds. And here one may gaze at the sledges that carried the imperial family from Leningrad to Moscow before the railway came (the journey took three days), and Polish carriages with windows made of mica, because glass walls would not survive the frost; a jeweled bridle presented to Catherine the Great by the Turkish sultan of the time, and horse blankets woven of orange parrot skins; the abnormally tall pair of boots which Peter the Great, who was almost seven feet tall, made for himself with his own hands—he was a master bootmaker; coronation robes, the trains of which spread out like wings of fallen angels, woven solidly of silver thread; and fascinating toys—for instance jeweled Easter eggs made by the court jeweler, Fabergé, and a miniature of the Trans-Siberian Express in gold and platinum.

Today's regime is eager to display these treasures to the people, and the museum is as crowded as Macy's basement. All Russian museums are jammed most of the time, by school children, delegations, and earnest peasants. The lesson is, of course, not lost to the crowds that the baubs and costly ornaments in the Kremlin and elsewhere, once the property of the imperial family, now belong (in theory anyway) to the nation as a whole. Nothing is thought of as being worth attention merely because it happens to be beautiful. Beauty for beauty's sake, art for art's sake, the appreciation of loveliness for the sake of pleasure—such "bourgeois" ideas went out of the window forty years ago. The imperishable works of art in the Kremlin are on display either as curiosities or because they teach Soviet citizens lessons from the past, emphasizing as the case may be the wickedness of the previous system or cultural continuity with what was worthy.

The Red Square, on which part of the Kremlin faces, is not a square at all but an irregular big oblong. It is paved with bricks the size and shape of large loaves of bread, and is called "Red" not out of any political connotation but because the root of the Russian words for "red" and "beautiful" is the same. The square was first named "Red," centuries ago, because it was so beautiful. Before that it was called "Fire Square." Part of the Kremlin wall is a pantheon where the great of the Soviet state repose after death. Sverdlov, Dzerzhinsky, Zhdanov, and other "heroes of the Revolution" are buried here. Not so well known is the fact that it also contains the ashes of several Americans, including Jack Reed, author of *Ten Days That Shook the World*; Bill Haywood, the IWW leader; Charles Ruthenberg, once the head of the American Communist party; and the writer Paxton Hibben.

Near the south end of Red Square is the Church of St. Basil the Blessed, one of the implausible wonders of the world. Correctly it is called the Pokrovsky Cathedral. It looks like peppermint candy sticks mixed up with pineapples. It has nine bulbous domes intricately convoluted and aglow with varied color; the tallest represents the Saviour, and those smaller are for various saints, in the familiar pattern of Russian church architecture. St. Basil's was built in 1554-60 to commemorate the conquest of Kazan by Ivan the Terrible; it has long been desanctified and is now a museum. The story is that as soon as it was completed Ivan ordered the builder to be blinded so that he could never again create such an extraordinary church. I mentioned this legend to our guide. Indignantly, he denied it. The Russian attitude toward historical figures varies sharply depending upon contemporary circumstances. Stalin decided that it should not be fashionable to think of Ivan as a monster. But no one can deny that he impaled courtiers who displeased him, and that the Red Square was the scene of public tortures and executions of unimaginable ferocity. Here Ivan's enemies, the boyars and others, were hanged, flayed, buried alive, roasted, and set afire in iron cages. "Counterfeiters were stretched on the ground, and molten lead was poured down their throats."[4]

On the western side of Red Square, standing out from the Kremlin wall, is the Lenin-Stalin Mausoleum, a flattish structure built of dark red porphyry. Its architect[5] studied in Paris, and it is almost the only example of modern— well, semimodern—architecture in all Moscow. Everybody knows that the bodies of Lenin and Stalin repose here, in a dimly lit and solemnly guarded chamber, preserved by an embalming process the methods of which are still secret. Lenin has lasted since 1924, and, as far as one can judge from the face and hands, has lasted pretty well. He looks waxier than Stalin. Various writers have put forward various reasons why Lenin, and Stalin after him, are so extravagantly exposed to public view. Nobody knows who took the original decision to keep Lenin, in the first instance, publicly displayed. One explanation, perhaps fanciful, is that Russian history is full of impostors (like the false Dmitris) and the authorities wanted to be in a position any time to demonstrate that Lenin was really dead.[6] Another is that the mausoleum is the "official shrine of a new religion," in the hierarchy of which Lenin and Stalin are demigods, and it is only fitting that they should be visible to all, even as were Christian saints in early days. A simpler explanation is that

---

[4] Arthur Voyce, The Moscow Kremlin, p. 94.
[5] A. V. Shchusev.
[6] This suggestion comes from Admiral Leslie C. Stevens, "The Russian People," Atlantic Monthly, May, 1952. Also see Walter Duranty, Stalin & Co., p. 52, and Bernard Pares, A History of Russia, p. 550.

Lenin, at least, was a revered figure, and Russians, who have an inordinate love for the spectacular, want to keep him around.

Millions visit the mausoleum every year; while we were in Moscow about fifteen thousand people a day were going through. For most citizens, the visit is a profound emotional experience. Some weep; some faint; once I saw a woman go into violent hysterics. From our hotel window we could watch the approaches, and toward noon mourners would gather four abreast, taking their position mutely between white lines painted on the street, and waiting hour after hour. Then, on the way out, the stiff columns would disintegrate and people in their black clothes would scatter, so that, against the blanket of snow, they looked like strands of a mop suddenly shaken apart.

Lenin may be holy and even Stalin has his holy points; but this doesn't keep people from making jokes about the mausoleum. When Marshal Tito of Yugoslavia came to Moscow, he is supposed to have saluted the structure with a hand over one eye, so that he could see Lenin but not Stalin. A familiar anecdote describes two peasants who emerge; one says to the other, "Just like us—dead but not yet buried."[7]

*

November 7, the anniversary of the Revolution, is a big day for Moscow. It was cold last year—about eight degrees above zero Fahrenheit—and the wind blew hard little clouds of snow across the square, against a backdrop of sharp green pines. The whole square—indeed the whole city—is festooned with stiff scarlet bunting. Mostly the portraits, on banners hung vertically, were of Marx or Lenin; I did not see Stalin once. The scene did not have the homeliness that a similar celebration would have brought forth in America. I saw no children hanging on roofs, or peeking from the yellow Kremlin windows. There was some bizarre Soviet snafu about getting tickets. You cannot get into Red Square on November 7 until your special pass is checked with your passport, and the militiamen, their cheeks shiny with the cold, were watchful. Hawkers sold coffee at a ruble a cup. Near us, where we stood stamping our feet in the snow, was a large omnibus. I wondered what it was for. Portable toilets!

A twenty-four-gun salute was sounded, and the chief dignitaries of the nation, in black coats, strode out on the roof of the mausoleum, which serves

[7] Toward the end of our stay in Moscow the mausoleum was suddenly, unaccountably, closed to visitors and the rumor at once spread that Stalin's body had been taken out. An American girl of my acquaintance said, "Oh! They wouldn't dare!" As it happened, the corpse of Mr. Stalin was not removed. But this was not because the authorities didn't dare remove it. They can dare anything.

as a tribune on these occasions. They seemed to be arranged in order of height, like a musical comedy chorus. Guns roared again; the heavy cobbles trembled, and an acrid smoke arose, till it met the snow coming down, tinting it blue. Soldiers, sailors, airmen, took their positions in solid phalanxes, and a small gray open car shot out into the square almost like a child's toy, but very chic and splendid; standing up in it, stout and erect, was Marshal Zhukov. He addressed each contingent of the parade while his car kept moving, and his voice, enormously amplified, rocked back and forth. One thing notorious about Russia is the drabness of most dress, but the parade this day certainly proved that Soviet manufacturers can produce colorful costumes if they want to. Young women athletes wore blue pants and yellow sweaters, purple gym suits and bright orange stocking caps.

In case anybody should make the grievous error of thinking that a demonstration like this is just for fun, I will append here some of the slogans used. *Pravda* and the other chief newspapers print suggestions for these slogans, which people dutifully inscribe on banners, or carry on huge floats. There were eighty-four this year.

Number 48 (I choose at random) was: "Soviet geologists! Explore our country's wealth more rapidly; discover new deposits of iron, coal, oil, gas and nonferrous and rare metals!"

Then consider Number 60: "Workers in agriculture! Strive for an over-all rise in labor productivity! Strive persistently for the full utilization of equipment, for the introduction of complex mechanization and electrification in all branches of agriculture!"

Nor are writers neglected. Number 72 read: "Workers in literature and art! Strive for a high ideological level in literature and art, tirelessly perfect your artistic skill!"

Youth is not forgotten, as witness Number 80: "Communists and Young Communist League members! Stand in the front ranks of the nation-wide struggle to fulfill the decisions of the Twentieth Party Congress! Persistently master Marxist-Leninist theory! Fight for technical progress in the national economy, for a rise in labor productivity, for the steady growth of the Soviet people's well-being, for the building of Communism in the USSR!"[8]

More Sights, More Scenes

Moscow is an exceptionally clean city—much cleaner than many in western Europe or America. Even after a sharp fall of snow, the streets are cleared

[8] *Current Digest of the Soviet Press,* December 5, 1956.

very quickly although little mechanical equipment is available. Most street-sweeping is done by old women in white aprons and black boots, wielding coarse brooms made of twigs. Militiamen posted at hotels, embassies, and public buildings are empowered to make you pick up a cigarette stub, if you toss it on the street instead of in a receptacle, but I never saw this happen. Also Moscow is an extraordinarily silent city. Automobile horns are forbidden, and in winter the carpet of snow serves to muffle traffic noises; the trolley buses, operating from overhead wires, are almost soundless, and, since the chief airport is sixteen miles away, airplanes are seldom heard directly over-head. Hardly ever in Moscow does anybody hear a loudspeaker, an ambulance siren, a fire engine, or even a police whistle.[9]

One thing no visitor to contemporary Moscow is likely to forget is that he, or she, must always check overcoat, hat, and galoshes at all public places such as restaurants, museums, and theaters. The reason for this is not security, but "culture." People don't think that you may be hiding a gun in your overcoat; they simply think that it is bad form to carry an overcoat indoors. Moreover Russian outer clothing is bulky in cold weather, and it is more comfortable for all concerned if coats are left outside. Having to check your things when going to the opera means, as a rule, a long wait in line both be-fore and after the performance, and this can be exasperating.[10] A book called *Little Golden America*, by Ilya Ilf and Eugene Petrov, which describes a visit to that barbarous country the United States, had a lively vogue in the Soviet Union some years ago. Two things, among others, piqued the authors —that Americans kept appointments on time, in contrast to Russian habits of the time, and that overcoats were not checked in offices or theaters. They describe with horror how "you put your overcoat on the floor [in the United States] or shove it under the chair in which you are sitting."

There are few big trees in Moscow, even on the handsome exterior boule-vards. The reason for this is curious. In the days before World War II, experts thought that leaves or foliage would retain poisonous fumes, in the event of gas attack; this was never proved one way or another but the Rus-sians, taking no chances, ruthlessly cut most of the trees in Moscow down. Also this made it easier to widen the boulevards. Replanting started in 1947,

[9] But in the small towns radio loudspeakers, blaring in the public square, make a strident racket. Moscow had radios of this type when I visited it before the war, but not now. The capital has passed beyond mass communication on such a primitive level, and the provincial towns will follow suit in time.
[10] One oddity is that, if you rent opera glasses at the ballet, you are entitled to come to the head of the line when the performance is over. Your clothes are security for the rented glasses.

but the work has gone slowly, and few of the new trees have reached substantial size. But Russians, like people elsewhere, crave the sight of something green and living, and as a result Moscow is a great city for plants. Even in the roughest districts, where tenements are scarcely more commodious than dog kennels, you see plants in every window. And there are flower shops all over the place; in winter they sell *paper* flowers. H. G. Wells, when he visited Leningrad in 1919, noticed that people in the most wretched houses still maintained plants behind shattered windows, although the city was a complete ruin and had almost ceased to function.[11] One other minor spot of color today—curious!—comes from the clusters of children's balloons on sale at occasional street corners. The story, possibly untrue, is that these are made of rubber left over from the contraceptive factories.

Gorkovo is Moscow's main street, the equivalent of Piccadilly. It was formerly known as Tverskaya, and leads into the Leningrad Chaussee, which in turn becomes the chief—in fact only—road to Leningrad. For most of its length Gorky Street is three times wider than Park Avenue. An astounding number of things in the USSR are named for Maxim Gorky. The old town of Nizhni Novgorod on the Volga is, of course, called Gorky nowadays, and the Moscow Art Theater is officially known as the Gorky Theater; the Institute of World Literature is named for Gorky, and so is Moscow's Park of Culture and Rest; there are innumerable Gorky factories, sanitaria, and so on everywhere. It is as if the city of Detroit, as well as Broadway, the Metropolitan Opera and Central Park in New York were all named "Sinclair Lewis." The odd thing about this is that Gorky's name was not Gorky at all, but Peshkov. Gorky adopted "Gorky," which means "bitter," as a nom de plume. So when we walk down Gorkovo what we are really walking on is "Bitter" Street, though this would be spelled differently in Russian—Gorkaya.[12]

Traffic signals on Moscow streets are for the most part operated manually, by an officer in a booth, and at many intersections the word "Stop" is painted on the street in large letters, as in American country towns. Some intersections carry pale bubbles on tall poles, like Belisha beacons, to mark pedestrian crossings. Jaywalking is a dangerous sport in Moscow, and people fly like frightened chipmunks as the big Zims charge down the streets. Trucks carry heavy padding on their hoods, which seems to indicate that Russian antifreeze mixtures are not satisfactory. Gasoline is evil-smelling.

---

[11] *Russia in the Shadows*, p. 13.
[12] Some Moscow streets were renamed temporarily in 1957 in honor of the Youth Festival. One, the Street of Love, has statues of Romeo and Juliet. Others are Friendship Street and Street of Happiness. Moscow *News*, February 15, 1957.

Kiosks with automatic telephones (fifteen kopecks a call) are abundant, and so are framed panels outside public buildings, with the day's newspapers spread out for passers-by to read. Another oddity in street scenes is that extremely few animals—pets—are to be seen. It costs too much to feed them. But once I ran into a dachshund on a leash made of grocery string.

The Metro or subway is a story in itself, and is the chief sight of the town, with the possible exception of the University. The subway carries more than two million passengers a day. The fare is not graduated by distance as it is on the buses, but is fifty kopecks, twelve and a half cents, for any destination. The trains are cleaner, faster, and better-looking than in New York, and carry special compartments for children and very old people. Escalators are very steep. In the cars, standing passengers hold on to overhead rails, which to my mind are more convenient than straps. But the main thing to say about the Moscow Metro is its luxuriousness. Stations, built of marble, look like palaces, and have dazzling chandeliers instead of strip lighting. A symbolic significance attaches to this opulence, of course. The Metro seems at first glance to be a perfect example of the Veblen theory of conspicuous waste come to full expression, but actually it was built extravagantly for a purpose, to represent a goal. Like some of the new luxury hotels, it is a kind of promissory note, a demonstration of what the rewarding future is going to bring. The Metro says to the people, "This is the kind of thing that everybody will have in every field someday."

Moscow is, among other things, full of literary monuments. Almost everything that has association to an important writer is carefully preserved. You may see the house where Herzen was born (25 Tverskoi Boulevard) and where Gogol died (7 Suvorovsky Boulevard). Dostoevsky was born in the Mariinsky Hospital for the Poor, at 2 Novaya Bozhedomka. His father, a physician, had quarters there. Turgenev wrote A Hunter's Sketches at 37 Ostrozhenka (Metrostroyevskaya Street) and Ostrovsky died at 14 Volkhonka. One of the principal squares on Gorky Street, Strastnaya Square, was renamed for Pushkin, whom present-day Russians revere above all other writers, to commemorate the centennial of his death in 1937. These lines are engraved on the monument:

> I shall be loved and long the people will remember
> The kindly thoughts I stirred—my muse's brightest crown.
> How in this cruel age I celebrated freedom,
> And begged for truth toward those cast down.

There are two Tolstoy museums. The first is Tolstoy's own house, on Lev Tolstoy Street, where the great man lived from 1872 to 1901, and which is carefully maintained in its original state. I wish I had space to describe it. One has the sense that a family lived here under the jurisdiction of an extreme tyrant, but was happy. Small jars of acid sit between the panes of the double windows, to keep the glass from cracking in wintry weather. There is no bathroom. Tolstoy himself went to a public bath once a week; what other members of the family did was not explained. Lenin set this home up as a museum in 1921. The second is the L. N. Tolstoy Museum in Kropotkin Street, devoted to such items as Tolstoy's manuscripts, medals, photographs, letters and the like. Both these museums have as curator one of Tolstoy's granddaughters, Sophie Alexandrovna; she is also in charge of the small museum in the provincial railway station where Tolstoy died.[13] Tolstoy is, as everybody knows, much respected in contemporary Russia, although his philosophical works are not published. A placard in the museum announces that *War and Peace* has sold 3,443,000 copies under the Soviet regime, and *Anna Karenina* more than two million. Several times in Moscow we heard about young bloods supposed to be descended from the prince who was the original of Prince Andrey in *War and Peace*, and granddaughters of Anna Karenina are all over the place, no doubt. This should not have been a surprise, but was. Everywhere in the USSR are phenomena showing continuity with what went before. Russia is still Russia, despite the Bolshevik regime.

The English Club, on Gorkovo, which readers of Tolstoy and Turgenev will remember, is now the Museum of the Revolution. Other notable museums are the Historical Museum on Red Square and the Lenin Museum close by, where 92,000 lectures on Lenin (so I am assured) are given every year.[14] Another "must" is the Lenin Library, which has two hundred kilometers of shelves and is said to contain seventeen million books.[15] Still others are museums in the realm of art, like the Pushkin and the celebrated Tretyakov.

Skyscrapers, like the Metro, give augury of the future. Moscow convention does not favor the word "skyscraper"—this smacks too much of foreignness and the bourgeoisie—and these structures are known as "multi-story buildings." As a matter of fact, they are not very high, running to

---

[13] News came of the death of this distinguished lady while these pages were in press. She was once married to the well-known poet Sergei Yesenin, who had previously been married to the American dancer Isadora Duncan.

[14] The Historical Museum is unbelievably hideous, but impressive. Russian guides stress that it was "a palace built by serfs," now put to good use. *USSR*, No. 11.

[15] The Library of Congress contains about 35,000,000 "items" (paintings, recordings, films, bound newspapers, et cetera), but only 10,800,000 actual books.

twenty or thirty stories as a rule, but they look high in comparison to other buildings. Their architecture is old-fashioned, and they resemble a combination of the Woolworth Building and an atrociously ornate wedding cake. But they make a brave show at night, because their façades are tricked out with red lights, and glowing red stars surmount the towers. Several are new blocks of apartments—complete with local shops, telegraph stations, post offices, and restaurants, in the manner of contemporary housing developments in the United States. The first time I inspected one of these monstrous edifices, the one on Kotelnicheskaya Embankment, I asked Zoya, our Intourist guide, what kind of people lived in it. She replied, "Workers." I expressed incredulity, and demanded to know how ordinary workers could afford such luxury. Zoya stuck to her guns and kept repeating stubbornly, "Only workers!" Then it dawned on me that she was using a special Soviet definition of "worker," and did not mean a worker with his hands, or laborer. In Russian two words for worker exist, *rabochy* (industrial worker) and *rabotnik* (worker in general), and a worker can be anything from an embalmist to a bookkeeper. In any case anybody who gets a place to live in one of these new buildings, whether he is a worker or not, is lucky. Housing is the worst thing in Moscow.

Every citizen, by terms of the Sanitary Code, is supposed to have nine square meters of floor space, but most do not have even half of this. Moscow has at least 25 per cent more population than it can hold, and people are crowded three, four, five, or even more to a room, with disastrous social consequences. Young people cannot marry, because they can find no place to live. Scarcely any Soviet family is without a covey of in-laws living on the premises, and it is rare for any family to have its own private bath and kitchen. These are shared by families. Sometimes a single doorway leads to a nest of stalls where a dozen people live; as a result private addresses are very complicated in Moscow, and citizens have their own doorbell rings, like users of a party-line telephone in the United States. If a Russian friend asks you to call, he may give his address as such-and-such a number on such-and-such a street, Block G, Entrance F, fourth floor, Number 17, ring two bells long, one short. The new flats going up are "functional," but heavily built, without grace or style. Kitchen equipment is scanty and of inferior quality, and shelves and storage space are lacking. Closets are unknown, and clothes, if any, have to be stored under the bed. No one ever dreams of having a "living" room. And of course the baby sleeps in the same room with the parents, or on a cot stuck somewhere.

Moreover, buildings deteriorate rapidly, and look battered almost as soon as they are up. Russians are proud of their mechanical skills and of the "technical society" they are creating, but just try, if you are a Moscow householder, to get a broken window pane repaired. Or try to replace the plaster already rotting in the building put up last year. The miracle is that, by and large, so many Soviet citizens accept household discomfort with such good spirit. Many are even cheerful, and have a vivid *élan*. Every time the visitor breaks out with some such sympathetic moan as, "Can't something be *done* for these poor, crushed, miserable, wonderful people?" he is apt to come across some episode or instance of life showing that the people are not broken, crushed or miserable at all.

But one reason why the streets are so thronged at night, even in winter, with crowds solidly marching down the boulevards in broad phalanxes and men and women carrying infants swaddled to the eyes, is that homes are so unbelievably crowded, squalid, and uncomfortable. People, even after a hard day's work, rush out of doors simply because the circumstances of life at home are so tedious, if not unbearable. Lack of "room" goes far beyond the housing shortage. There is little room in Moscow for what living should be about—but try to tell this to a good Soviet citizen.

Further Impressions of the Gray Giant

What contributes most to Moscow's superficial look of drabness is people's clothes. These have certainly improved in the last few years, as I have already said, but they are still revolting. Their positive shabby manginess, as well as cheap quality and lack of color, is beyond description. The black worn by almost everybody is not a shiny, sparkling black, but a doleful black— dead, dreary. Russians are, as a result, acutely conscious of the clothes foreigners wear, particularly their shoes, and people on the street will offer to buy your shoes off your feet. The whole country has a fixation on shoes. Moscow is the city where, if Marilyn Monroe should walk down the street with nothing on but shoes, people would stare at her feet first.

But clothes and the way people look are a subject requiring elaboration. One reason why people seem to be shabby and unkempt is that soap is expensive, and not of good quality; it isn't easy for a Russian woman to keep her hair, for instance, clean and shining. Another is that clothes are bought for utility, not for looks; pretty colors show dirt more than black, which is why black predominates. Clothes have no shape; but then neither have most Russian women. Moscow would look a hundred per cent better if every citizen lost thirty pounds.

Russians may be jealous of the clothes western visitors wear, but seldom admit it. This is a thoroughly indoctrinated country, needless to say, and the Revolution is forty years old. Some dedicated Russians are, I would say, actually proud of their plainness, even of their poverty. They *like* hardship. That mildewed suit is a badge of honor, because it proves virtue and sacrifice. And of course the government has been telling its people for years that we, the Americans, only achieve our luxuries as a result of evil and immoral processes, by "exploiting" labor and the like. The Russians seek to justify the shortages they impose on their own people by telling them that western living standards are not to be admired.

Men are short and squat, built like square corks. It is unusual to meet a Russian taller than five foot seven or eight, and most are broad. The Russian mode, for men, is to wear suits with very wide padded shoulders and trousers wide at the bottom, flapping almost like sailors' pants, which accentuate the prevailing impression of breadth, squatness, and solidity. When you see lines of men hurrying out of their offices at night, beating their arms and tearing down the streets, they almost look like short-armed ambulatory windmills.

Another point is the human toll brought by the war to Russia. This is a nation that has suffered much, and suffering shows in practically every face. Total Soviet casualties during World War II reached the astounding figure of 37,500,000; deaths were almost 12,000,000. More than 70,000 towns and villages were destroyed, and more than 30,000 factories wrecked; 25,000,000 people were made homeless. In one battle that most Americans have never even heard of, Kharkov, the Red Army suffered heavier casualties than *total* American casualties in the war against Japan.

Toughness—that is a characteristic everybody sees at once. Perceptible is a latent capacity for violence, running just below the surface. Hardly anybody ever visits Russia without seeing somewhere a sudden inexplicable fist fight. Also, let us repeat, life is extremely serious. A character in the novel *Not by Bread Alone* makes a revealing remark, "There are many weak spots in me, because I love life." Such puritanism! Some citizens break bonds if only on account of the strain imposed on them. People in the West have little conception of how mercilessly hard-working Russians have to be, in order to survive, as well as to put into efficient operation and protect what they call proudly their new society. These are a strong people, even if not free.

Shops, Prices, Wages

Shopping in Moscow is often an adventure. Shops are closed Monday, although Sunday, as in our society, is the holiday of the week. This is because shops are obliged to stay open on Sundays for the convenience of people who work the rest of the week, and then take Mondays off. One department store on the Red Square, a series of arcades known as GUM (State Department Store), is one of the biggest in the world, and has more than 130,000 customers a day. Macy's in New York has more, but even so the figure is substantial. GUM sells everything from fur coats to single hairpins. Modern cash registers are few, and the wooden abacus still predominates. Once when we were cashing some foreign money a girl repeatedly made mistakes on her abacus and we had to work out the transaction for her with paper and pencil; she was the most embarrassed person I met in Russia. Charge accounts are unknown. Sometimes, if small coins run out, you get change in postage stamps, or even matches.

Soviet stamps are, incidentally, remarkable for their variety and beauty; one set portrays, of all people, the Scottish poet Robert Burns. One thing puzzling is that some stamps have glue on the back, some do not. Licking postage stamps is considered "not cultured" and unsanitary, and if you buy your stamps in a hotel the girl selling them usually has paste on hand, with which she carefully affixes them to your letters. The following complaint from a citizen appeared recently in a Kiev newspaper:

> Once I had to send a letter air mail. It was already late, and after I visited several post offices I discovered that there is only one place in the Ukraine's capital where air mail letters are accepted in the evenings —the central telegraph office.
> The spacious room was almost empty. Only two customers stood at the window where I had to go. When my turn came I handed over my letter. The postal clerk weighed it and gave me several stamps.
> "Couldn't you fasten them on?" I asked.
> "That's not part of my job," she muttered, and turned away.
> "But I have nothing to moisten the stamps with. Am I supposed to lick them with my tongue?"
> "What sort of gentleman do you think you are? Everybody else licks them, so you lick them, too!". . .
> This is not an isolated instance. At Post Office No. 30 in Kiev I myself saw a woman messenger who had to stamp several dozen envelopes. She was licking the stamps; there was nothing else she could do. I became indignant and told the postmaster how humiliating and unsanitary such an operation was. The postmaster—as if he were in conspiracy with the postal clerk—also said contemptuously, "Never mind. Let her lick them!". . .[16]

Prices are fantastic. It is difficult to calculate what the ruble means to a Russian, but even so the cost of most commodities is outlandish, and there

[16] *Current Digest of the Soviet Press,* February 13, 1957.

are astounding discrepancies among values. An American jazz record can fetch 400 rubles ($100 at par) on the black market, and this is also the price of a pretty good radio. An automobile does not cost more than about a dozen times the price of a pair of shoes. Crazy! But again qualification is necessary. All luxuries are high, also clothes, but in general staple foods are comparatively cheap, as are items in culture—books and records. Household appliances, of mediocre quality, are not too expensive. Personal services are cheap—haircuts, permanent waves, and the like. You can get your hair cut for a ruble. And GUM has a machine which, when you put ten kopecks in a slot, squirts out perfume. Sometimes peasants come in, take their hats off, and put in one coin after another until their hair is doused. Incidentally, one story going around Moscow is that a perfume named for Stalin's daughter, Svetlana, and known as "Svetlana's Breath," will be renamed "Moscow Nights."

Here are some prices at random, calculated at the official exchange:

	Rubles	Dollars
Medium-sized chocolate bar	14.80	3.70
Nylon blouse	320	80.00
Man's felt hat	160	40.00
Set of Kremlin postcards	15	3.75
Pack of 20 cigarettes	3.50	0.875
Imitation leather traveling case	450	112.50
Can of salmon	5.80	1.65
Fountain pen	57	14.25
Cheapest grade women's stockings	14	3.50
Washing machine, clumsy and inferior small type	800	200.00
Large loaf of bread	2.18	0.54
Caviar (per kilo)	150	37.50
Decanter with 6 vodka glasses	132	33.00
Electric light bulb	2.10	0.52
1 Egg	1	0.25
Traveler's basket with fruit, candy and bottles	498	124.50
Bath powder	16	4.00
Fleece-lined boots	850	212.50

If you calculate rubles at ten to a dollar or less, these prices (in American terms) go down drastically. But Russians have to pay in rubles. If a Russian earns 1,000 rubles a month, it will cost him seven weeks' pay to buy a TV set—1,750 rubles. But—paradox!—a TV set is "cheap," if you think of it in terms of other commodities; it costs no more than two suits of clothes.

Prices constitute, to sum up, a form of rationing. The state authorities set the price depending on the amount of the commodity they wish to release to the public. The government knows perfectly well that the rank and file of people are yearning not merely for ordinary consumer goods—pots and pans—but for luxuries like cameras, electric iceboxes, bicycles, sporting guns and, a curious item, chandeliers. Because it will not, in the present phase, release enough productive power to manufacture such articles in quantity, the government deliberately prices them out of sight. Another reason why prices are so high is that retail shops are, of course, part of the general structure of government finance, and are expected to make money, if possible. All profits of state enterprises go into the common pot.

Most shops in Moscow are identified not by name but by number; there are innumerable *gastronoms* (food shops) and *aptekas* (pharmacies), known as Gastronom No. 17 as an example, or Apteka No. 56. Some names are more complicated, for instance "Children's Department Store No. 14 of Moscow Trade Trust." What goes on sale is not decided by the individual shop, but by the state; most shops have identical goods available at the same price on the same day. The customer has no choice. Very little is available in the way of foreign goods, but some gastronoms carry Icelandic perch and a variety of Mexican canned fruit called "Sweet Treat." Perfumery shops, of which there are many, sell cheap beads, ornaments, and the like, as well as cosmetics. In one shop I saw a series of large vials, rather like those in American drugstores, containing various fruit juices at prices ranging from 55 kopecks to 1.20 rubles a glass; trade was brisk. And in this same shop was the most pitiable specimen of food I encountered in all Russia—two ears of corn on the cob wrapped in cellophane and reposing in a kind of primitive deep freeze. Packaged frozen goods, in our sense, are virtually unknown. But wrapping paper exists nowadays, and so does string. Hams, cheeses and so on in window displays are always artificial, made of cardboard. This shocked me until I learned that the same practice was universal before 1917. Russians never put actual food in windows, because this was considered to be unsanitary.

One thing surprising to most visitors is that many buildings in Moscow carry illuminated signs at night—advertisements. But these do not advertise specific brands of goods, but are in the nature of public appeals, with slogans like "Put your money in savings banks!" and "Drink tomato juice!" One must always remember that the Russians, who want their country to be the grandest thing on earth, intend eventually to produce food and consumer goods in unlimited profusion, and at cheap prices. Utopia will come—tomorrow. Actually public service advertisements of the Soviet type are not uncommon in parts of the United States. All over Vermont one may see signs, "Drink more milk!"

How, considering prices, do people in Moscow live? The answer is that the majority lives poorly by our standards, very poorly indeed, but some special factors have to be considered. (1) Practically all women in Russia work, and hence most families have two earners. (2) Russians do not pay nearly so much as do citizens of western countries for basic services, like rent, and taxes are very light. The highest bracket in the Russian income tax is 13 per cent; most people pay only 5 per cent. Rent is calculated on the amount of space occupied, and usually comes to less than 4 per cent of income; the average rent of a small apartment in Moscow does not exceed the equivalent of $15 a month. Trade-union fees are 1 per cent of salary, and utilities are relatively inexpensive. Our interpreter paid 50 rubles a month rent, 25 for telephone, 15 for electricity and from 6 to 10 for gas. Her total expenditure in these basic categories was thus no more than $25 per month at par, or, at 10 rubles to a dollar, only $10, including rent.

Then too medical and dental care is free. But, if you choose, you may go beyond the regular medical panel and consult a professor or specialist on your own, in which case you pay a fee. Holidays are cheap, and you are guaranteed employment until retirement. Sickness and accident benefits are in force, and your old age is automatically taken care of. Above all, education for your children is scot-free.

Another point, not at all appreciated outside of Russia, is that a substantial number of Soviet citizens get large salaries. What might almost be called a millionaire class has grown up, composed mostly of writers who earn royalties, musicians, scientists, and inventors. The richest man in Russia is supposed to be a composer of popular music, whose earnings probably amount to 1,000,000 rubles ($250,000 at par) per year. Several well-known figures, like Galina Ulanova, the celebrated ballet dancer, and the novelist Konstantin Simonov, are supposed to have "unlimited" bank accounts; their balances are so large that they can draw without limit. There is in fact, plenty of *money* in the Soviet Union; the only trouble is that there is nothing to spend it on, except food, books, and alcohol. If you tip a taxi driver as little as 25 kopecks, he may contemptuously toss the coin out onto the street, as being too insignificant to be worth keeping. The best-paid people are intellectuals, like university professors. A full professor's salary is quite large by our standards, about 5,500 rubles a month, or $1,375. Then if you are a member of the Academy of Sciences you automatically receive a 5,000-ruble-a-month stipend in addition to your salary, and your earnings may be further augmented by royalties on textbooks, TV appearances, and lectures. The director of an important research institute will, as a rule, get several thousand rubles a month bonus in addition to his salary, if his work is good. Then intellectuals always have a chance of winning Stalin (now called Lenin) Prizes, which can run up to 200,000 rubles each, $50,000 at par. Finally, a man in a big position has special perquisites, like the right to have (or share) a motorcar, a *dacha* in the country, and an apartment in Moscow more comfortable than most.

Here are further salaries and wages:

	Rubles a Month	Dollars
President of the Academy of Sciences	15,000	3,750
Army colonel	4,000	1,000
Rector of an important university	8,000-12,000	2,000-3,000
Senior government official	6,000	1,500
Factory manager	3,000	750
Shop superintendent	1,200-1,600	300-400
Shop foreman	1,200	300

Earnings of those less favored are very low. Statistics are difficult to procure, and are seldom reliable. The guaranteed minimum wage is 300-350 rubles per month, a sum on which a worker is barely able to live; it can mean virtual starvation, although it is better than nothing. Incidentally wages are always paid fortnightly, and in cash. The *average* industrial wage is probably 650 rubles, though some calculations put it at 800. A skilled worker, like a pipefitter, may get up to 1,600. A taxi driver in Moscow probably earns 1,100 rubles a month, a waiter about 850, a cook anywhere from 500 to 800, and a nurse (with her keep) 300. Nor, it should be pointed out, are *all* intellectual workers well-off. It is quite true that a writer may earn several hundred thousand rubles with a successful book or play, but a country doctor will be lucky with 1,400 rubles a month. Curiously enough, doctors are not very well paid in comparison with members of some other professions, like architects. A run-of-the-mill doctor is considered to be a "repair" man, whereas an architect is a "creator." Most Russians, no matter what they earn, find it extremely difficult to save. That there should be such a fantastic disparity of incomes in Russia does not, of course, go well with the professed ideal of a classless, "socialist" society, on which more later. It is not a new phenomenon. When I did research in Russia for *Inside Europe* twenty years ago, a wide gap between wages high and low already existed. Lenin certainly believed in complete financial equality, but, as the regime found it more urgently necessary to employ and reward technical skills, discrepancies became inevitable. I have heard dedicated Communists deplore this. One writer told me that he would be perfectly willing to give back to the state anything he earned beyond an average income established in fairness for everybody, and he was quite sincere. In any case, the great majority of the people are sordidly poor.

Begging has become a minor problem, and gets considerable attention in the press. *Trud*, the organ of the trade unions and one of the most important Soviet newspapers, invited readers recently to contribute to a symposium on the evils of begging. Here is one letter, from a lady who signs herself Comrade Dolgopolova:

> An incident on the Number 20 Trolley especially shocked me. A drunken man got on at one of the stops, took off his cap, and walked through the car whining, "Little brothers, little sisters, help an unfortunate man with a large family who has lost all he owned in a fire." The passengers shrank from him in revulsion; there was a strong smell of wine on him. But in spite of this, some of them—and how deplorable it is!—tossed him 10 or 20 kopecks or even a ruble. When he had collected the money the "unfortunate man who had lost all he owned in a fire" went to the front of the trolley where two women were waiting for him. After a hearty laugh at the expense of the stupid passengers, they got off at the next stop.

Another comes from Comrade Kholodenko, a worker at the Belorechensk mine in Sverdlovsk province:

> Begging is a survival of the past. In Czarist Russia a person who was unable to work was often doomed to poverty and begging. There were no provisions for public support, so he was compelled to wander around from door to door with a cup, begging for alms. Our country now has a social security system that is predicated on the interests of the human being. Who are these mendicants then, and who forces them to beg? They are spongers and parasites . . . people without shame or conscience. . . . I think begging should be prohibited by law.[17]

Soviet newspapers are full of this type of thing, ranging from pious homilies to bitter letters of complaint.

The Girl with the Iron Teeth

I was astonished one evening in a Moscow restaurant to see a pretty girl. These are uncommon in Moscow. What is more, she was well dressed in a nicely cut gray suit, and, something very unusual indeed, she wore jewelry. I was more than astonished, I was dumfounded, because I saw that, in addition to being pretty and well dressed, *she wore make-up.*

Now this is almost unheard of among women in the Soviet Union. It is

[17] *Current Digest of the Soviet Press*, November 21, 1956.

not that lipsticks are forbidden, or hard to get; the fact is that, even if crude, they are quite cheap and easily obtainable. Some women use nail polish nowadays, and the government has indeed gone out of its way to encourage girls to prettify themselves, but lipstick is still rare. Mostly this is because conspicuous cosmetics are a symbol of the condemned external world, the bourgeoisie; also Russian women work too hard to care much about beautification, and want to be thought of on the same terms as men.

But this young girl had tinted eyebrows, mascara, purple eye shadow, and a great crimson rose of a mouth heavily painted on. Her blond hair was done in a pretty delicate puff, which, again, is something almost unheard of in Moscow, where most women wear their hair in heavy buns or deplorable-looking stringy braids. And she was *very* pretty. And then she opened her mouth to smile, and I saw that all her upper teeth were made of stainless steel.

*

Porcelain teeth are, for some reason, unprocurable in the Soviet Union. When members of the Bolshoi Ballet went to London in 1956, they wanted two things above all—knitting needles, also unobtainable at home, and porcelain for false teeth. A great many people in Moscow have tooth trouble, and conspicuous false teeth are common. And, when you need a complete dental job, steel is cheaper than gold, lighter, and less sensitive to heat and cold. When I mentioned this to my dentist in New York, he said that American dentists too are using steel to replace gold nowadays, but only in concealed bridgework. Another curious point is that iron teeth have been mentioned in Russian folklore.[18]

*

Most Russians have a marked quality of spontaneity; they are generous, informal, and love to give assistance. I could not make myself understood in a shop one day, and, within a minute, two or three people who knew rudiments of English sprang to my aid. One day my wife, with a friend, sought to buy a balalaika. They found one, but the salesgirl did not know how to play it and could not demonstrate it, nor could any other salesperson

[18] One folklore figure is the Witch Baby, which eats its parents with iron teeth. Geoffrey Gorer, "Some Aspects of the Psychology of the People of Great Russia," *American Slavonic Review*, October, 1949.

in the shop. At once a customer came forward, seized the instrument, and played a tune. On another occasion my wife went out to buy some phonograph records, and, in the crowded store, found herself next to a man who spoke a little English. He offered to help her, and started to talk about modern music. Like practically all Russians, he was crazy about American jazz. He thought that my wife was a member of a delegation. But, just as he was warming up, the fear that paralyzes most Soviet citizens in contact with foreigners overcame him, and with a sudden embarrassed gesture he stuck out his hand, muttered "Good-by!" and fled. Anecdotes similar to this could be told by the score.

CHAPTER III

More About the Third Rome

> No one can love or understand the Russian
> people who does not love orthodoxy.
> —DOSTOEVSKY

Moscow is a closed city, almost a secret city. To mention a minor instance
of this, in practically every world capital the existence of a foreign colony
is taken for granted; Americans or other westerners scattered throughout
the city are commonplace. But not in Moscow. The total American population in the entire Soviet Union, which means Moscow because Americans
are not allowed to reside outside Moscow, is only about 150, of whom
some 40 are children. Diplomats and their families, who live in an almost
completely isolated compound, a double structure holding both offices and
living quarters, form the largest segment of this small colony.[1] American
newspapermen—perhaps a dozen in all—live in hotels or are isolated in a
special apartment building for diplomats and correspondents of various
nationalities, nicknamed the "Diplomatic *Kolkhoz*" (collective farm).

The real point to make about closedness is not how closed off the Americans are, but the Russians. Things in the realm of communications that we
take utterly for granted in the United States or England simply do not
exist in the Soviet Union. Even such an item as the fact that Ulanova, the
most sublime of modern ballerinas, collapsed at the ballet one night is not
printed in the Russian press. She is a national heroine, but such an event
is simply not considered news.

The Voice of America and the BBC get through to many Russians, but

[1] A handful of embassy bachelors and members of the Marine Guard live in a
separate establishment, America House, but this is also isolated. The Ambassador
lives in Spaso House, his official residence.

these services are sometimes jammed. Music is seldom interfered with, but news and politics are apt to be blotted out by "selective jamming," if a controversial subject is involved. (On the other hand, once in a remote city I complained that there was utterly no way for me to learn what was going on in the world, and that I felt as isolated as if I were on Mars; the local Intourist man at once invited us to his office to listen to the Voice of America.) The main thing to say in this field is that the average Russian has no access whatever to a *free press*. Western newspapers are not allowed in, and news coverage in the Soviet press is, to put it mildly, slanted and inadequate.[2] Certain fields in particular are rigorously screened. For instance no ordinary Soviet citizen has ever heard of Klaus Fuchs or Alger Hiss.[3]

Of course secrecy, mystification, closedness, are traditional Russian characteristics, and censorship is an old, old story. Russians love secrecy for its own sake, and besides it served a purpose in conspiratorial and revolutionary days. The Soviet regime, by its atavistic accent on secrecy, sometimes creates more mystification than it wants. Secrecy has a nice habit of defeating itself. A former deputy prime minister, V. A. Malyshev, became ill in February, 1957. A German specialist was flown in to treat him, but the patient's name was not revealed. So all sorts of rumors flew; everybody tried to guess who the sick man was. When Mr. Malyshev died, his name was at last given out, but not before half a dozen more important Soviet leaders had been "named" as the person ill.

If one persists in asking *why* the Russians insist on closing themselves up, sealing themselves off from the rest of the world so completely, one can only reiterate an answer already indicated in these pages. The outer world is the enemy, and must be guarded against at all costs.[4]

Items in Surveillance

Everybody, even the most innocent visitor, knows that a prime essence of the Soviet regime is secrecy, and that Moscow is not going to be an easy city to crack open, but the reality exceeds the expectation.

[2] Satellite papers on the newsstands are eagerly snapped up, particularly those from Poland. The Polish press is infinitely freer than the Russian. Russian citizens have recently been given permission to subscribe to satellite papers, but few do.

[3] As to radio matters it is revealing that most Soviet listeners have much greater respect for the BBC than for the Voice of America. They say that BBC news is accurate and fairly presented, whereas the Voice defeats itself by its propaganda tincture and obvious distortion.

[4] But the Soviet regime does not concede that the *people* of any foreign country are an enemy—only hostile governments. See below.

Item. No maps of the city are available except small simplified maps showing the Metro routes.[5]

Item. No *Who's Who*, yearbook, statistical handbook, almanac, or other means of ready reference exists.

Item. No city directory or even telephone book is readily available, although one is promised soon. A phone book, six years out of date, does exist, but few people have ever seen it. If you want to telephone somebody from your hotel, you give the name to the Intourist Service Bureau, which will then produce the connection, if possible. But you cannot look up the number yourself. Nor does the Intourist staff itself have a book. Lists of numbers frequently called, such as those for hotels, embassies, and government departments, are on hand, but that is all. I was told that a phone book could be consulted in the post office on Gorky Street, but I do not vouch for this; I never saw it. And, let us be fair, a book called *Moskva 1956,* which contains a good many phone numbers, is available—if you can get your hands on one. But this was published in a small edition by Russian standards, 75,000 copies, and was quickly sold out. One curious point is that, whereas telephone service within Moscow is apt to be eccentric, the long-distance service out of Russia to points abroad is very good.

Were we followed? The answer is "Probably not," but this needs qualification; the whole subject of surveillance is mixed and thorny. If we left the hotel on foot in Moscow or elsewhere to go shopping or look around, I am certain that we were not followed. Actually there was no need to follow us because, as I have already explained, the Intourist system is set up to know what a foreign visitor is doing most of the time. Moreover, we were usually accompanied by our interpreter.[6]

If a person arrives in Moscow on an important mission, or to take up permanent residence, the chances of his being watched increase. A young Englishman whom I shall call Mr. X arrived in Russia early last year to do some scientific research. He knew Russian perfectly. On his first afternoon, he took a walk. He noticed at once that a man who had been waiting in the hotel lobby followed him. Mr. X walked hard and fast down one street and up another; his shadow stuck close behind. Mr. X took a bus. His shadow got on the same bus. Mr. X went to GUM and wandered through its corridors, but could not separate himself from his friend. He left GUM,

[5] A map for tourists has appeared since these lines were written, and a handbook listing factories and some other institutions has been published, but with a limited circulation.

[6] Tourists who speak fluent Russian sometimes manage to get permission to go about without an interpreter.

took a ride in the subway, and walked back. His shadow never left him. At last, exhausted, he stepped into the elaborate ice cream shop near the Red Square, and ordered some *morozhenoye*. His shadow sat down at the next table, and ordered the identical dish. Mr. X then turned to him with outstretched hand, grasped his warmly, and exclaimed, "We might as well be friends!" From that day he never saw the man again and, so far as he knows, was never shadowed or followed a second time.

Perhaps I may be permitted one more story in this field. Professor B., an eminent European philosopher, visited Leningrad last summer. In their apartment at the Astoria Hotel, he and his wife discussed their plans. They were alone. Mrs. B. said that she would go to the Hermitage Museum, while the Professor went to the bank and then to a cinema. They arranged to meet after their separate courses. So Professor B. set out for the bank in an Intourist car. He told the chauffeur, without any other word being said, "Go back to the hotel and take my wife to the Hermitage." Mrs. B. asked, when the car arrived, "Is Mr. B. still at the bank?" The interpreter replied, "No— he has gone to the cinema." In point of fact Mr. B had told no one but his wife that he *was* going to the cinema, to which as a matter of fact he did not go.

It is impossible to lose anything in the Soviet Union. If you forget a pair of rubbers in Minsk it will follow you to the Caucasus and eventually be delivered to your door in Moscow.

When we left Russia, we transshipped from a Soviet to a Scandinavian plane at Riga. During the flight to Riga I read a batch of English news bulletins that I had picked up in Moscow, and then stuffed them in the seat pocket, having no further use for them. When we stepped into the Swedish plane, up came a cop from the frontier police who politely handed me everything that I had thrown away.

Letters delivered in Moscow are, I should say, almost always opened. The clumsy ripple of new paste on the envelopes is ample evidence. The day I arrived in Moscow a friend left a note for me in the hotel. He delivered it at noon, by hand, but I did not get it until 4 P.M. the next day. Letters are intercepted and read; but they are seldom stopped. Why, it may be asked, should the Russians bother to scrutinize personal mail? Probably the answer lies in the general philosophy of espionage. Agents, no matter of what nationality, want to know *everything* about a suspected person; anything that helps to build up a complete portrait has presumptive value.

Whether or not routine telephone calls in Moscow are monitored I do not know. Probably yes. I am not sure whether our rooms were searched or not, for instance when the hotel people knew for certain that we were going out for a long lunch or spending an evening at the theater. Nor do I know whether our rooms were wired. It is possible. Restaurant tables are, I am inclined to think, not wired, if only because nobody knows at which table you are going to sit, and the mechanical arrangements would be onerous. But, if the Russians *really* want to listen in on you, there is no limit to the expenditure of personnel and technical know-how to which they will go. At non-Russian dinner parties in Moscow, the hostess may keep the radio on, playing soft music, during the entire evening, because this will make it harder for hidden microphones, if any, to pick up the conversation. All manner of bizarre stories may be heard about precautions taken by foreign embassies; perhaps some are apocryphal. In one embassy a junior secretary has an interesting if tedious duty—he sits in on every ambassadorial conference, and steadily rustles newspapers while his seniors talk, so that what they say cannot be recorded. An ambassador, conferring on an important confidential matter with a visitor, may take him for a walk through the garden (if the weather is warm enough) instead of talking in his office. Or, if something of supersecret nature is being discussed, the ambassador and his advisers may, while sitting together in a room, *write notes* to one another instead of talking.

All this brings up the vexing subject of relations between Russians and foreigners. Nobody wants to get an innocent Russian acquaintance into trouble. I did not know, when we arrived, whether it would be prudent to try to reach people on the telephone or not. Nothing would have happened to me; but something might well happen to them. There is, actually, very little possibility of embarrassing an official by reaching him on the telephone. After all, he can always refuse to talk. The experience of most correspondents permanently resident in Moscow is that they can have fairly close personal relationships with Russians, but not friendships in our sense. They may see a man every day for two or three months; then they will not hear from him for weeks on end. This depends largely on the international situation at the moment. During periods of relaxation, contact is easy; but when something arises like the Hungarian or Suez affairs, people become frightened, and avoid foreigners—*any* foreigners—like poison. One American youngster, courting a pretty Russian girl while we were in Moscow, saw her every day for months. Came Hungary. Without explanation, she refused to see him further. I wanted, after I returned to America, to send books to people we had met in the Soviet Union. After a good deal of thought, I cut several names from the projected list. They were not folk who, in the ordinary line of their activity, would be expected to have had any contact with foreigners, and I did not want to get them into trouble. In order to be able to receive foreign literature, a Soviet citizen has to be on an approved list. (As a matter of fact, conversely, an American in New York cannot be sure of receiving freely books or periodicals *from* Russia.) And, I was told, the chances of an American book getting through to a Russian—even if he is authorized to receive books from abroad—was only about 40 per cent.

Questions of Censorship

Years ago censorship was consultative in Moscow. You brought your copy to the censor, and could argue with him freely about what he might want to cut. Then for a brief period before World War II there was no censorship at all. I remember well this giddy interval. Nowadays, of course, censorship is in force again. It is not consultative, and in fact no one knows precisely who the censor is; the Russians maintain the fiction that the censorship bureau, under an organization known as Glavlit,[7] exists merely to deal with matters of language, and seeks only to improve the writer's "style." This is a nice Soviet touch.[8]

A correspondent sending a news dispatch by cable must take three copies to the telegraph office. One goes to Glavlit, one is for transmission, and one is returned to the correspondent after censorship. On this the correspondent sees what deletions have been made, if any. He is not allowed to see the censor or argue with him. The censor's decisions are final. If the whole story is stopped, which sometimes happens, the correspondent does not get a copy back. The process is run with reasonable efficiency, and, unless something special is going on, censorship of a dispatch takes only about twenty minutes.

Radio correspondents also have to submit copy, and their calls are monitored. If there is any deviation from the text, communication may be cut. Pictures transmitted by radio are subject to censorship, but *not* motion picture films or tape recordings. Tapes and movies may now be shipped abroad for processing without any interference at all, strange as this may seem.

What the censorship is most sensitive about is: (1) any speculation about

[7] Glavlit, if you want it in full, is the Main Administration for Affairs of Literature and Publishing Houses. It deals in the suppression of everything from pornography to works of "religious fanaticism."

[8] Actually if a correspondent makes a factual error in a dispatch—for instance if he says that Alma-Ata instead of Karaganda is the largest city in Kazakhstan—the censor, far from being helpful, will probably let the slip pass, not out of malice but because he does not consider this to be his business.

instability in the regime; (2) alleged rifts in the top leadership or changes in the assignments of members of the Presidium; (3) any *personal* criticism of leading Soviet figures.

Within certain circumscriptions the Moscow censorship, though irksome, is liberally applied. It is certainly more liberal than it was in Stalin's time. One curious point is that the censorship does not as a rule kill or mutilate dispatches describing the hard life of Russians, their poverty and suffering. In fact stories of this type are actually welcomed because (a) the Russian regime is proud, rather than the reverse, of the hardships its people endure, and (b) this kind of reporting carries the implication that Russians are indeed the undaunted, tough, and stalwart people that they claim to be.

The chief grievance of American correspondents against censorship is that it is so unpredictable. It is as if some imaginary rule book existed with the rules changing every day, without notification; a correspondent can never tell from any one experience what to expect from the next. As a result, all manner of crazy things happen.

It costs a great deal for an American (or British) newspaper, agency, or broadcasting company to maintain a correspondent in Moscow—say $50,000 a year to keep one man, exclusive of transmission tolls, which can easily amount to $5,000 per month. Three American correspondents have been expelled by the Soviet authorities within the last year. One motive for such expulsions is to frighten *Russians*; correspondents are painted as unscrupulous agents of foreign imperialism, who will get good Soviet citizens into trouble. Russians are thus indirectly warned to keep clear of correspondents. When a correspondent is expelled, the reason given for the expulsion is seldom the real reason. Welles Hangen of the *New York Times* was expelled ostensibly because he took photographs of a hydroelectric installation. The real reason was that the government disliked some hard-hitting and truthful dispatches he had sent from Rumania, and it used the dam incident as a pretext. When Charles H. Klensch, the correspondent of International News Service, was expelled in February, 1957, he was accused of "distributing anti-Soviet literature," and the press attacked him with extreme virulence not on grounds having to do with politics or journalism at all.

Censorship is, I have said, no new thing in Russia. Sir Bernard Pares, the eminent British historian, comments as follows on the "complete suffocation" of intellectual life during the reign of Nicholas I, in the middle of the nineteenth century:

> In 1851 a commission was appointed to examine all music for the discovery of possible conspirative ciphers. . . . Count S. Uvarov, himself

the reactionary Minister of Public Instruction from 1833 to 1849, was not allowed to use the word *demos* in his book on Greek antiquities, nor might he say that Roman emperors were killed, only that 'they perished.' From a scientific work the censor removed the expression 'forces of nature.'. . . The censor Akhmatov stopped a book on arithmetic because between the figures of a problem he saw a row of dots.[9]

Corps Diplomatique

When a new ambassador arrives in Moscow the procedure goes something like this. He is met at the airport or railway station by the *chef du protocol* of the Ministry of Foreign Affairs or one of his assistants, and, within a couple of days, is asked to call on one of the deputy foreign ministers. This is a purely courtesy call, and seldom lasts longer than five or six minutes. The ambassador sees nobody except the man receiving him, and severe precautions are taken to keep him from looking around in the Foreign Office skyscraper; he is under escort the whole time, and seldom even has a chance to crane his neck. There are no names on any doors, so craning the neck would not do much good anyway. Then, about a week later, the new ambassador formally presents his letters of credential to the Kremlin. He must wear full diplomatic regalia, although the Chairman of the Presidium of the Supreme Soviet who receives him is generally clad informally in what the Russians call a "commercial" dark suit. If this dignitary (at the moment Voroshilov) is out of town or too busy to receive the new ambassador, he may be received by a "president" of one of the other fifteen constituent republics of the USSR, provided that one happens to be in Moscow. The lower the rank of the country, the lower may be the rank of the man who receives its representative.

After presentation of his papers the new ambassador is in the hands of an organization known as Burobin, which is a kind of Intourist for nontourists; it serves the diplomats and permanently accredited journalists, supplying them with translators, chauffeurs and the like. Anything in this field must be handled through Burobin. This can be an exasperating organization. It took one European ambassador a month to get a secretary, and after a month he was still waiting impatiently for a Russian teacher. Burobin provides some services at a special diplomatic rate—for instance car hire is 150 rubles a day, or $37.50 at par. If any ambassador gives a big party in a hotel, the cost will be monumental but not quite so monumental as to a nondiplomat. A diplomat living in a hotel will pay around 170 rubles a day for his room, or $42.50.

[9] *A History of Russia*, p. 385.

Members of the diplomatic corps are pretty well isolated from any except official contacts. They are not permitted to have relations with any Russians except officially through the Foreign Office, and their social life is severely limited. If the wife of the British ambassador, let us say, wants to ask Russian guests even to an informal reception, the invitations must be transmitted through the Foreign Office. No direct contact is allowed. One ambassador asked sixty Russians to a recent party, and exactly three turned up. And, if a Soviet official accepts an invitation to lunch or dinner, it is never known whether or not his wife will accompany him; hence, the hostess is on tenter-hooks, and cannot set her table properly. The burdens of official life can be quite nerve-racking. New arrivals in the corps are expected to appear without fail at ceremonies which the Soviet government gives for visiting dignitaries, and these often include performances at the ballet. One new man who hates ballet, and is tone-deaf to boot, had to sit through *Swan Lake,* the chief demonstration piece in the Soviet ballet, three times in his first two weeks in Moscow. Another point in this domain is that no diplomat is allowed to travel further than twenty-five miles out of Moscow without per-mission. (Nor are Soviet diplomats allowed to travel freely out of Wash-ington.)

On the other hand, and this is an important item, diplomats accredited to the Kremlin see the top leaders of the Soviet Union with extraordinary frequency and at extremely intimate range at diplomatic receptions. This curious phenomenon we shall explore in Chapter V below. In *no* country are diplomats so close, in this special informal way, to high members of the government. It is as if an ambassador in Washington had casual drinks and chitchat with Eisenhower, Dulles, and the entire American cabinet two or three times a week.

A uniformed militiaman stands at the gate of every foreign embassy in Moscow. To have police outside embassies is a general practice throughout Europe, and is not a particular Soviet characteristic. What is a Soviet char-acteristic is that the militiaman will not permit any *Russian* citizen to enter the embassy, unless the citizen has been officially invited or is working there —say as a language teacher or governess.[10]

The foreign embassy most closely watched by the Russian authorities is probably the West German, and after that the Israeli. The foreign ambas-

[10] One day I had an appointment with the consul at such-and-such an Embassy. The telephone rang, and a Russian boy, a university student, began to talk. He told the consul that he wanted to come to the embassy and "talk things over." The consul's answer was a cordial invitation. The consul then turned to me and said, "Of course the militiaman will never let him in."

sador most respected was, by all odds, Charles E. Bohlen, who was American ambassador until early in 1957. Mr. Bohlen was not only respected, but sincerely liked—for his swift intelligence, bluntness, perfect knowledge of Russian, and uncompromising Americanism.

The following is an excerpt from a dispatch by the American Minister to Russia, Neill S. Brown, to the State Department on January 28, 1852:

The position of a minister here is far from being pleasant. The opinion prevails that no communication, at least of a public nature, is safe in the post office but is opened and inspected as a matter of course. Hence those legations that can afford it, maintain regular couriers and never send anything by mail. The opinion also prevails that ministers are constantly subjected to a system of espionage, and that even their servants are made to disclose what passes in their households, their conversations, associations and so forth. . . . If therefore I do not write as often as may be desired, this is my apology. And if I do not furnish matter of more interest, it must be attributed in part at least to the great difficulty of obtaining correct information. . . . Secrecy and mystery characterize everything. Nothing is made public that is worth knowing. You will find no two individuals agreeing on the strength of the army and navy, in the amount of the public debt or the annual revenue. In my opinion it is not intended by the government that these things should be known. . . .

Another dispatch from Mr. Brown:

Nothing is more striking to an American on his first arrival here than the rigor of the police. It would seem that the capital was in a state of siege.[11]

Not much change in a hundred years!

♦

Soviet diplomats in posts abroad do not, to understate the case, lead very free lives, intellectually or otherwise. Objective reporting on the western level by a Soviet ambassador is all but unknown. If he gave an impartial, truthful account of affairs in the United States, as an example, he would quickly lose his job, although it is not his *intention* to deceive his government. Similarly Soviet journalists stationed abroad never deviate from the party line, if only because this is also *their own line*. The slant comes from within; the censorship is altogether self-imposed. In Moscow, *Pravda* and *Izvestia* have

[11] Excerpts from the Brown dispatches appear in Walter Bedell Smith's *My Three Years in Moscow*, pp. 85 and 111, and in *America Faces Russia*, by Thomas A. Bailey.

no censor, nor is there any direct censorship any longer over literary magazines, theatrical productions, and the like, because there is no need for any. The editor of *Pravda* is his own censor, and so is the editor of the magazine. He would not have reached such a post unless his agreement with fundamental state policy was spontaneous, automatic, and complete.

Soviet diplomats get around little in cities like London or Washington. They live, as everybody knows, closeted in their own embassies, and even maintain their own schools. At a reception, the main Soviet dignitaries will always be flanked by KGB men; sometimes a Soviet ambassador does not even know who all the KGB men in his own embassy are.[12] The leading KGB man in each embassy or legation, who is known as the "Legal Resident," has his own private code for communication with Moscow, independent of the Foreign Office; he is autonomous, and may even be superior in authority to the ambassador. Also most Soviet installations abroad contain a *second* set of agents, representatives of the military secret service. These may, or may not, co-operate freely with the ambassadors and legal residents. Junior diplomats have scant freedom of motion. For a man to drop in Saks Fifth Avenue to do some shopping on the way home from the UN to the Soviet headquarters on Park Avenue would not necessarily be forbidden, but it might be considered "unusual." Some relaxations have accompanied de-Stalinization. Occasionally cultural attachés go to cocktail parties, and sometimes, but not often, senior members of a mission will favor some American or English friend with their company. Then they are apt to break loose in an almost comically exaggerated manner, bringing expensive gifts and cutting up like children on a lark, in the best old Russian manner.

The Defectors

The two best-known defectors from the western world are the former British diplomats Guy Burgess and Donald Maclean. They are not talked about much in Moscow, and are seldom seen.[13] Burgess is called "Jim Andreyvich" by his friends, and has a job in the Foreign Literature Publishing House; he has a small apartment in the Moskva Hotel, and is permitted a modest *dacha* in the country as well. Maclean, known as Mark Fraser, is believed to be one of the editors of *International Affairs*, the Soviet equivalent of the American quarterly *Foreign Affairs*. The two, although they profess friendship

---

[12] Differences between Soviet police organs like the MVD and KGB are mentioned in Chapter VII.

[13] The only defectors ordinarily mentioned in the Soviet press are scientists like the atomic physicist Bruno Pontecorvo.

and undertook their catastrophic adventure together, almost never see one another nowadays. Maclean has been ill, but still looks the perfect picture of a British diplomat.

There are several American defectors. One was a young woman, Annabelle Bucar, who worked in the United States Information Service office in Moscow; she married a Russian opera singer. Another, Professor Stephen Makar, born in the Ukraine, went to America and became a naturalized American citizen; he taught at St. Louis University. For a time he worked at the U.S. Air Force Base at Alamogordo, New Mexico, as a photo-map expert; he renounced his American citizenship and returned to the Soviet Union in December, 1956. He is believed to be working nowadays at the Polytechnical Institute in Lvov. Still another, Professor Alexander Kazem-Bek, who taught theology at the Connecticut College for Women, left his American wife and returned to the Soviet Union, in circumstances of considerable mystery, several years ago. His whereabouts and functions in Russia were for a time unknown. On January 16, 1957, however, he wrote an explosive letter to *Pravda*, in which he explained his disappearance. He said that he had enjoyed material security in Connecticut and would soon have been able to retire on pension, but that he could no longer live in a country "where anti-Soviet propaganda holds sway, where a constant offensive is waged against civil liberties." His letter, which is an odd document indeed, concludes with the words, "In 15 years of forced residence [*sic*] in the USA, I became convinced of the profound depravity and moral decay of every aspect of [American] public life from music to sports, from family life to the attitude towards science, from the understanding of religion to the approach to international affairs."[14]

[14] *Current Digest of the Soviet Press*, February 27, 1957. Mr. Kazem-Bek also attacked American culture. Interestingly enough the eminent Soviet writer and critic, Ilya Ehrenburg, replied to Kazem-Bek in what were, for Russia, unusual terms. Ehrenburg, who is as a rule bitterly anti-American, wrote an open letter of protest to *Literaturnaya Gazeta*, saying that Kazem-Bek's statement that the United States had not created its own indigenous and truly national culture was nonsense. "A. Kazem-Bek writes that 'millions of Americans may read Hemingway and Faulkner, but tens of millions of their compatriots never even heard their names.' I was very pleased to learn that millions of Americans read these writers; I had thought their circle of readers was narrower. But can one claim that a national culture does not exist because tens of millions of people have not been brought into contact with genuine culture? When I was a boy, tens of millions of people in our country did not know of the existence of Chekhov and Gorky. But even then I would have considered intolerable a statement by any foreigner that the Russian people had not created their own national culture. . . . Soviet people are brought up in a spirit of respect for the national culture of every people, large or small."

Soviet defectors—Russians who hop across the curtain to start life over again in democratic countries—are almost never mentioned in Moscow, unless this serves convenience. Recently came the case of Anatoli P. Barzov, a Soviet Air Force pilot who, with his navigator Peter Pirogov, flew out to the American zone in Austria in 1948, under sensational circumstances, and accepted American asylum. Then, after seven months in the United States, Barzov decided that he had made a mistake, and managed to make his way back to the Soviet Union. Everybody assumed that he must have been shot. But, as the phrase is, he "surfaced" in May, 1957, and the Russian authorities produced him at a press conference to prove that he was alive. Barzov said that he had not been badly treated, in spite of his defection, and that his only punishment had been a five-year sentence in Vorkuta, the Arctic labor camp, where he got paid for the work he did and where his family was permitted to join him. It all seemed quite cozy.

The Russians make, in fact, intermittent appeals to their defectors to return to the "glorious motherland," with the promise that all will be forgiven. Three main reasons exist for this policy. First, it is unbearably humiliating to the Kremlin that any Soviet citizen *can* defect, and for a defector to come back removes part of the stain of his departure. Second, to reinstate a defector shows the "forgiving nature" and "tolerance" of the Soviet regime. Third, defectors can be made to talk about how "horrible" the western democracies are, and thus serve a propaganda end. Also of course a defector on the loose abroad may become a spy for the West, which the Soviet Union naturally wants to avoid.[15]

Asians Are Everywhere

Not many Americans or western Europeans are to be seen in Moscow except perhaps in the tourist season, but all year around the Soviet Union swarms with Asians, particularly Chinese. Delegations come in and out incessantly—not only of Chinese, but of Burmese, Indonesians, North Vietnamese, Mongolians, and Indians of every category. Peng Chen, the Mayor of Peking, arrived in Moscow recently on an official visit, and the Shanghai company of the Peking Classical Opera opened its Moscow "season" a few weeks later. The second annual Indian film festival was a pronounced success in Moscow, Leningrad, and Baku, and a delegation of Indian cinema workers triumphantly toured the country. Work is beginning on a Soviet

[15] One curious item is that the Russians seldom give a *good* job to a defector from the West (except scientists), so that they cannot be accused of "bribing" them; they say that the Americans *et al.* only get Russian defectors to stay in America by overpaying them.

film to be made in India, describing the adventures of Aphansy Nikitin, a Russian merchant who penetrated there before Marco Polo.

The most dramatic—because spontaneous—demonstration I saw in Moscow was one for an Indian movie star, Raj Kapoor. The Soviet equivalent of bobby soxers descended from the galleries of the Bolshoi to seek autographs, almost like youngsters in a Broadway crowd, but more timidly. One night in Kiev we were unable to get to the ballet, because the opera house had been pre-empted for a mass meeting in honor of visiting North Koreans. In Tiflis, we ran into Indian technicians studying the machine tool industry, and I never went to a restaurant, theater, hotel, or other public place anywhere in Russia without encountering Chinese. The leaflets at Intourist hotels giving details about service are printed in French, German, and Chinese, and in our Moscow Service Bureau, Chinese newspapers were usually on hand.

Books too carry their message. The Russians distributed to readers in India no fewer than 1,410,000 books (sixty-two titles) in Hindi last year.[16] The most popular Chinese writer in the Soviet Union is Lu Sin, described as the founder of the new "democratic literature" in China. More than thirty-four editions of his work, with a total sale of a million copies, have been published in the Soviet Union in sixteen Russian languages. Much attention is also given to Moslem literature and books from (or about) Egypt, the Arab world, and the Middle East.

It certainly is not news that the Soviet Union is courting Asia, as well as Africa and the Middle East, but the extent and pace of this are startling. Two things assist the Kremlin. First, Russians have practically no color prejudice. The first Soviet picture magazine I ever opened had as frontispiece a spectacularly effective colored photograph of an extraordinarily handsome (naturally) African Negro embracing a white Russian girl. Second, they are partly Asian themselves.

The Russians know full well how stupid many Americans (and British) are about colonialism and the color bar. Every Russian school child has heard about Jim Crow and recent events in Little Rock. Samuel Marshak, a well-known Soviet poet, has invented a character for children known as Mister Twister. He is an American millionaire, with all appropriate trimmings, who arranges to visit Russia with his wife and daughter. When he orders hotel accommodation in advance Mr. Twister says:

> Be sure the crowd
> Isn't low-brow
> No Negroes
> Or Hindus

[16] *New Republic*, April 29, 1957.

Or riffraff.
Old Twister, he's touchy concerning
Dark faces.
He can't stand the sight
Of those colored races.

The Twisters arrive in Leningrad and go to their hotel:

All of a sudden
The Twisters stopped dead.
They gaped and they goggled,
"Lord help us," they said . . .
Along the hall
From a suite near theirs
Came a Negro
Calmly bound for the stairs.
"What's this?" roared Twister
"Does he live here?
I'd rather live with a racketeer—
Gangway!" roared Twister
And turned in his tracks,
"We'll find a place
Where there ain't no blacks."

For further adventures of Mr. Twister, which are well worth reading, consult *If You Were Born in Russia* by Arthur Goodfriend, from which these excerpts are taken.

Episode at an Airport

Russian airplanes usually take off punctually, and arrive at their scheduled destination on the dot. But, departing for Central Asia, our plane, which was supposed to have left at 1:50 A.M., did not actually get off until around 10 A.M. Bad weather. So we sat up all night in the Moscow airport.[17]

At about 2:30 A.M. a well-dressed, fresh, attractive boy came up to our table in the restaurant, bowed, and announced in English without other introduction, "I am very drunk." I said, "Good. Sit down." He said, "I could not possibly sit down. I am too drunk." Actually he had had nothing but a beer or two, and was not drunk at all. His manners were extremely

---

[17] Incidentally, my wife and I and our interpreter seemed to be the only passengers when we finally got aboard. But this was because, out of courtesy, we were put in the plane first. The stewardess heard us speaking English, and asked if we were Americans. She said, "How nice. I have never met Americans before. Thank God you are not English. I shall accompany you all the way to Alma-Ata." I asked where the other passengers were. She replied, confused, "Perhaps they are late!" And we had been waiting for eight solid hours!

good. I asked him where he had learned English. "Repeat please." I repeated my question. It was obvious that he spoke English better than he understood it, because of lack of practice. He told us that he was reading Hemingway's A *Farewell to Arms*. I said that I knew Hemingway. His face broke open with an astounded, sunny smile. "You *know* Hemingway? Then I sit down!"

He brought another boy over to our table, and we talked most of the night. These boys had come out to the airport because this was a holiday weekend, and they didn't want to go to bed. They had been in a beer hall on Pushkin Square, which closed at midnight, and there was absolutely no other place in all Moscow to get a drink at that hour, except the airport. So out to the airport they had come, by bus. Both boys were nineteen, and were studying to be interpreters. The mothers of both were doctors, and the father of one was also a doctor. First they wanted to know whether they spoke "American" or "English" English. They bickered gaily with each other about which spoke English better, and interrupted almost every sentence of mine with "Repeat please." Their questions and answers poured out. They were astonished that I scarcely knew the names of American musicians like the late Glenn Miller. They had heard of Theodore Dreiser, Howard Fast, and Upton Sinclair, but not Sinclair Lewis. They were very worried about the correct pronunciation of the word "Sinclair." They demanded to know who was the most "popular" writer in the United States, and why. They asked who was our best jazz musician, did we know the work of a certain producer on Voice of America, what was the difference between Harvard and Yale, and did we like vodka and mountain climbing. They burned with curiosity and could not believe all that we told them—for instance that a big American university could have as many as forty thousand students.

I went out to wash my hands; the first boy followed me. He said that he and his friend wanted very much to talk to us again when we returned to Moscow. I gave him my name, and told him to call us at the National. Then a peculiar, secretive look came over his face, and he blushed almost as if with shame, saying that there was no way for him to find out the telephone number of the Hotel National. I asked him if he knew where the hotel was, and he replied, "Of course." I told him to come without telephoning—to drop in at any time. An hour later I went to the refreshment counter. The second boy accompanied me and asked with eager determination if our invitation was "firm." I assured him that it was, and that we looked forward to seeing him and his friend again.

Of course they never came.

Jet Set and Partial Suicides

In the summer of 1956 a piquant little scandal made news in Moscow. Several young people of the fast set were arrested because they financed their high jinks by pilfering and selling clothes. Two of these youngsters were sons of a cabinet minister, no less, Ivan G. Kabanov, Minister of Foreign Trade. Arrested with them were daughters of prominent Red Army officers and police officials. Moscow is, by and large, a desperately puritan city, if only because few opportunities exist for defiance of the conventions. The case made a minor sensation, and brought into the open what a lot of ordinary citizens were whispering about, the activities of the so-called "jet set." This consisted, and perhaps still consists, of bright youngsters of the elite class who were bored with the drabness of their surroundings, had plenty of money to spend, and liked high living. They got black market recordings of hot jazz records, read smuggled copies of Vogue and The New Yorker, wore fancy clothes, and despised their less fortunate contemporaries.

The Kabanov boys were let off, but the girls each got a year in jail. This led to vivid criticism in the press. Komsomolskaya Pravda, the organ of the Young Communist League, insisted that the girls should have been given heavier sentences, and charged in a veiled way that the court had shown favoritism to the Kabanov boys, because of their father's high position.

On a different level are the Stilyagi, young hooligans, zoot-suiters, or juvenile delinquents. The word means literally "style-chaser." These youngsters, who are sometimes called "Teddy boys" or mitrofanushka, hang out at restaurants like the Praga, affect long sideburns or other eccentric dress, and dance to boogie-woogie and rock'n'roll. They consider themselves to be sophisticated and emancipated, and if they meet a foreign newspaperman with his Russian interpreter, they are quite capable of insulting the interpreter boldly, with contemptuous words like "How long have you been a government spy?" One reason for the rise of the Stilyagi is of course the unbearable frustration that smites youngsters in the Soviet Union, even as it smites youngsters in the United States. We have teen-age gangsters too. But in Russia much less opportunity for outlet exists than in America, and most young people have nothing to buy, nothing to do after school, nowhere to go. Frustration leads to exaggerated behavior, and in particular to alcoholism. The problem has become quite serious—again like juvenile delinquency in the United States.

The Presidium of the RSFSR issued a new decree (December, 1956) to "intensify the struggle against petty hooliganism" and "save Moscow's honor." Henceforth, any Teddy boy or zoot-suiter picked up for minor outrages is subject to immediate arrest and imprisonment for a period of three to fifteen days, without appeal. Listen to *Komsomolskaya Pravda*: "Who is not familiar with these utterly repulsive young men, with their ultramodish jackets, their ultratight and ultrashort trousers and their eccentric neckties in all colors of the rainbow, and with an air of self-satisfied stupidity on their faces? Or with the even more disgusting girls, with their . . . pitiful bristles of cropped hair, and their shoes that remind one of caterpillar tractors.

"Our people, healthy and sensible as they are, have nicknamed these wretched creatures *Stilyagi*, and ridiculed them on every possible occasion. But the wretched creatures turn up their noses and show little concern. You see, they imagine themselves to be the bearers of and—mind you—apologists for western culture. . . . But how surprised would the many *Stilyagi* of both sexes be, should they learn that they, the would-be bearers of western culture, look as ridiculous to western observers as savages who wear broken alarm clocks for earrings!"[18]

Still another variety of problem youth has arisen lately, the *Nibonichó*, or "nonbelievers." The word derives from the concept that they believe in neither God nor the devil *(ni boga, ni chorta)*. These are young men and women so completely disillusioned and inert that they despise all activity; in some respects they resemble strikingly nihilistic youngsters of the lost generation in Paris after World War I—"the youth without youth." They have been sapped of all convictions, even about patriotism. Some little poems describing them have appeared recently—with censorious comments—in *Literaturnaya Gazeta*:

> "If the world whistles and spins like a top,
> What's that to us?"—Everything on earth
> Seems nothing to these characters
> Because they are *nibonichó*.

> South or north, east or west,
> In ice or boiling water,
> He is neither cold nor hot
> Because he is *nibonichó*.

> Who, who is this young graybeard
> With the dashing air but just a rotten shrimp?
> Can it be that he is oppressed by age?
> No, he is young, but *nibonichó*.

[18] *Current Digest of the Soviet Press*, March 20, 1957.

One of these young men was interviewed not long ago, and asked why it didn't interest him to study, become a "brigade leader," and get ahead. Reply:

"Why should it? I have already bought an accordion in the second-hand store and soon I'll get a motorcycle. That's enough for me. I pull down nearly 1000 rubles a month. But the main thing is that I do my work and when I finish I'm free. Studying means getting stuck on a stipend of 300 a month at best. That is, if you do well. And you become an engineer and are appointed a chief. The money is about the same as I am making now and the responsibility is enough to send you to the grave. Why should I? No possible reason. Ridiculous."[19]

*

"He's had his hundred." This is a familiar phrase in Moscow, and means that a citizen is drunk. (Vodka is, as we know, usually measured in terms of grams, and although one hundred grams is not very much, it will, under certain circumstances, undeniably produce an effect.) Russian drunks are among the most vivid, sodden and uncompromising drunks ever known anywhere. This was true forty years ago, and it is still true today. Russians call vodka "a little ray of sunshine in the stomach," but many do not drink for fun or merely as an outlet; they drink to get *drunk*—to blot themselves out, obliterate themselves. Officially the Soviet government may deny that alcoholism is a serious problem, but it is. The article "Alcoholism" in the new edition of the Russian *Large Medical Encyclopedia* asserts that the per capita consumption of alcoholic beverages in the Soviet Union is substantially lower than the United States, Britain, or France. Even so, the country spent roughly seventy-six *billion* rubles on alcoholic drinks in 1955.[20] Nor do the Russians like to admit that some forty "cooling-off stations" exist in Moscow—places where drunks picked up off the streets are given rough-and-ready first-aid. One reason why the price of vodka is put so high is, of course, to discourage excessive drinking.

Vodka has been a state monopoly in Russia since the days of Count Witte, long before World War I. One thing the Bolsheviks did not have to nationalize was alcohol. An interesting example of modern Soviet terminology is that alcoholics are called "partial suicides."

[19] *Ibid.*, August 14, 1957.
[20] *New York Times*, May 26, 1957. I have read elsewhere, but cannot quite believe it, that in Czarist times alcohol provided *one-quarter* of all state revenue.

CHAPTER IV

Some Soviet Attitudes

*We are dealing with people who are unpre-
dictable and, at times, they are just practically
inexplicable, so far as we are concerned.*
— DWIGHT D. EISENHOWER

RUSSIA, even if sealed off, is in a state of flux—of transition. (It always has
been.) I had a talk with a French lady who has lived in Moscow for many
years and whom I will call Madame N. She commented on the insatiable
Russian thirst for knowledge, for education; talked about the mixed-upness
that comes to a people who are only separated from peasanthood by a
generation; described their yearning for bright colors and chromium furniture
and trips to the seaside; and said, "After forty years of privation, their sense
of fun is coming out." I said that I had just visited a housing project, and
could not understand how people could endure life without closets. "Oh,"
Madame N. replied, "they just haven't come to *closets* yet!"

Consider the following. It is not about closets, but felt hats. It comes from
a man named Galushko, and appeared in *Sovetskaya Kultura* recently under
the title "What Is a Cultured Person?" (Hats, it should be explained, were
taboo in the Soviet Union for many years, because of their bourgeois
symbolism, but are now encouraged.)

My friends consider me a cultured person. The basis for their opinion
is the several hundred books in my family library, my inability to drink
vodka or swear, and several other externals.

I think they are mistaken; I try to explain to them that I bought the
books out of a morbid passion for reading, that my weak stomach
accounts for the failure to drink, and as for swearing, my parents simply
didn't teach me to swear.

69

Comrade Galushko proceeds to explain that nevertheless he felt that it was necessary for him to prove that he was cultured:

So I buy a vacuum cleaner and a felt hat. My wife uses the vacuum cleaner according to the instructions which accompany it. But, as is known, instructions do not accompany hats. I turned to grandpa for advice. He is offended; coming of an old Cossack family, he has worn an Astrakhan [hat] all his life and "never indulged in foolishness." I seek something about hats in the library—and of course find nothing. I don my hat, go out on the street, and carefully observe all who wear hats. I meet a friend. He is wearing a hat! Now I will find out—"Greetings, Petya!" Petya doffs his hat with both hands and crushes it against his stomach. . . . I do not remove my hat; I simply do not know which hand to use, which part of the hat to hold, what to do with it when I raise it, and whether I should raise it at all. My aim in writing this letter is to hear the views of others and ultimately to see books appear which would teach people cultured behavior.[1]

The three main preoccupations of the man-in-the-street in Moscow today are education, peace, and consumer goods. It is almost impossible to meet a Russian without hearing excited talk about education. The very first Soviet citizen we met told us about the critical decision, as vital as any that could arise in his lifetime, confronting himself and his wife—what to do if their son failed in his entrance examination for the University. Without university education, the boy will be a helot all his life. As to peace, it is talked about all the time. No Russian wants another war. Time and time again people went out of their way to say, "We hope that you will be truthful, and tell your readers that we want good relations with your country and peace." Every toast includes a plea for peace. But, of course, *conditions* for peace are seldom defined. The attitude toward consumer goods may be expressed by a small joke. One Russian tells another that the Soviet authorities have perfected an intricate atomic bomb that will fit into a suitcase, and that this will one day be delivered to a target like New York. The second Russian replies, "Impossible. Where would anybody get a suitcase?"

. . . and Characteristics

At the risk of being rudimentary or even otiose, some obvious small generalizations should be made. First, *continuity*. The Russians spring from a mighty past, and much in their present behavior arises from deeply planted historical roots. More on this soon. Second, *puritanism*, based on discipline and self-sacrifice. This is a country where everything has a purpose, where

[1] *Current Digest of the Soviet Press*, November 14, 1956.

little is done for fun. Maybe that is why so many get drunk on the streets—to get away from the all-embracing, suffocating purposefulness of life. Third, *pride*. This country is precious to its citizens, which is one reason why they seek to guard its works so zealously. And together with pride goes touchiness. Fourth, *provincialism*, that is to say ignorance and uncivilizedness. Fifth, *hardness*. The Russians can, if they want, be as charming as any people in the world, but they are suspicious of charm these days, and eschew it, because in their view charm equals softness.

The following appears in Baedeker's *Guide to Russia*, last published in 1914:

> Their character [that of the great Russians] has been influenced not only by a long history of feudal despotism, but also by the gloomy forests, the unresponsive soil, the rigorous climate, and especially the enforced inactivity of the long winters. Even the educated Russian gives comparatively little response to the actual demands of life; he is more or less the victim of fancy and temperament, which sometimes lead him to a despondent slackness, sometimes to emotional outbursts. Here we have the explanation of the want of organization, the disorder, and the waste of time which strikes the Western visitor to Russia.

Baedeker was a shrewd old gentleman; after forty years, some of this still applies.

One could elaborate on the theme of Russian touchiness—even naïveté—almost without end. A British trade delegation took over one of the dining rooms in the Hotel Metropole for an Anglo-Russian function recently, and contrived to find and put up across a wall an immense Union Jack; it covered almost the entire area behind the speaker's table. Russian members of the committee helping to arrange the dinner saw this, rushed to the Kremlin, procured a Russian flag even bigger, and flung it across the other end of the room. Russians don't like to admit to being behind on anything. Marshall MacDuffie, the New York attorney who ran the UNRRA administration in Kiev after the war and who has written brilliantly on Russia, once asked for a Ukrainian exit visa rather than one issued by the Ministry of Foreign Affairs in Moscow. The Ukrainian Foreign Office had never, in its whole history, granted an exit visa before. MacDuffie looked at it curiously when it came through—it was numbered Ukrainian Exit Visa Number 100,001.[2]

You can win almost any Russian by speaking Russian, no matter how badly. When William Benton, former Assistant Secretary of State and Senator from Connecticut, visited Moscow in 1956 he told a group of

[2] *The Red Carpet*, p. 145.

officials that he hoped that his younger son would master Russian, saying that if things went well between the USSR and the United States Russian would be the most valuable language the boy could know, and that even if they went badly it would still be most important. His interlocutors, who were of cabinet rank, were gravely impressed and shook his hand "with enthusiasm."

Sensitiveness plays a role in policy little and big. One reason why Mr. Khrushchev does not like Mr. Dulles is that Mr. Dulles, in his view, does not think that the USSR is "an equal" to the United States. Descend to a different level. Nina Ponomareva, the champion discus thrower, was arrested in London last summer for shoplifting. Starved for pretty things, she had been unable to resist pilfering a few hats. The British, who were just as much embarrassed by this unfortunate episode as the Russians, had no recourse except to put the stout Amazon on trial. The response in the Soviet press was unbelievably explosive. If capitalist hyenas had dragged the corpse of Lenin from his tomb, the outcry could hardly have been more indignant. The case was called "blackmail," a deliberate attempt to hamper "the development of peace and friendship between peoples" and "a filthy provocation."[3]

Another well-known Soviet characteristic is to wear blinders. In his Twentieth Congress speech Khrushchev talked bitterly about "the bloody war launched in Korea." He did not of course mention by whom it was launched.

Russians have an appealing aptitude for adding two and two and getting three or five. Hamilton Fish Armstrong, of the Council on Foreign Relations in New York, was astounded some years ago when a Russian acquaintance told him quietly that he knew well that the distinguished quarterly he edits, *Foreign Affairs*, was subsidized by the house of Morgan. Mr. Armstrong, the most unsubsidized editor imaginable, could not believe his ears. Blandly, triumphantly, the Russian pointed out that Russell C. Leffingwell, who is indeed a Morgan partner, was a member of the editorial board of the magazine, and had his name *printed*—ah!—on the masthead. It was impossible to convince the Russian that this did not prove, beyond peradventure of a doubt, that the Morgans ran Mr. Armstrong's magazine.

Nobody can be more suspicious than a Russian. For a long time the Soviets refused officially to concede that Hitler was dead, and may even have thought that representatives of the American plutocracy had smuggled him out of the Berlin bunker at the last moment of the last hour, in order

[3] *Daily Telegraph*, London, October 15, 1956.

to keep him handy for mounting a new war against the Soviet Union some fine day. Ambassador Walter Bedell Smith records that until the war ended the Russians believed that the United States might make a separate peace with Germany, which the Germans—in a last-ditch effort to split the Allies —had several times offered. The Russians were, in fact, astonished that the Western Allies were decent enough to stick to their word, preserve unity, and resist Nazi temptations. General Smith adds dryly, "This causes one to wonder what the Soviet government would have done if the offer had been made to them instead of to us."[4]

Another characteristic is that most Russians, no matter what, have an answer to everything, and their stubbornness, as well as nice capacity for self-deception, can be dazzling. Everybody knows that hundreds of place names in Russia have been changed. St. Petersburg is Leningrad; Nizhni Novgorod is Gorky; Tsaritsyn is Stalingrad; and so on ad infinitum. A British tourist asked an Intourist interpreter not long ago to arrange a trip to the celebrated monastery near Moscow known for generations all over the world as Sergiyev and now called Zagorsk. He asked mildly why the name had been changed, and the Intourist girl looked puzzled. He mentioned then that hundreds, in fact thousands, of names had been similarly changed. "No!" the girl responded. "Sergiyev is the *only* name that has been changed in Russia!" The Briton protested, knowing that she *must* know that she was not being quite accurate, to put it mildly. She repeated stubbornly, "No other names have been changed!" Russians, if only because they do not always follow western channels of logic, can be vexing beyond speech, exasperating, and intolerable. Nevertheless we may repeat the cliché that, even under Communism, they are the most human human beings in the world, perversely attractive and fascinating without end.

Three Questions

Q. Why does not the Soviet government do more for its people?

A. An easy answer might be that it doesn't have to. Actually, however, the government hopes to do a great deal more in the future, but at the moment the day-to-day needs of citizens do not have priority, because of the accent on industrialization and technical advance, and there are not enough consumer goods to go around.

Q. Why do the people stand for it?

A. They have no choice. This is not to say, however, that discontent does

[4] *My Three Years in Moscow*, p. 22.

not exist, and this may become more boldly expressed in time.

Q. Will the Soviet government ever give freedom, civil liberties, to its citizens?

A. Probably this depends ultimately on large political and economic factors. If the government ever reaches a position when it considers itself to be absolutely secure internationally, it may relax at home. Moreover, in the Russian view, civil liberties have a close relation to standard of living and the economic "base." If the Soviet Union were to give freedom tomorrow, it might explode, if only because of economic grievances on the part of the people. First the standard of living must be built up, so that it will be altogether safe to give concessions.

Attitudes Toward the USA

First we must mention Soviet ignorances, which are formidable. Russians by and large think that only rich American boys go to college, and that the United States is totally run by big business. They honestly cannot believe it when you tell them that President Eisenhower's father was a railway worker, or that the brother of Harlow H. Curtice, the president of General Motors, is a paint and metal inspector, whose pension will be $63 a month when he retires. They cannot believe it that the New York Times prints verbatim the full texts of speeches by Soviet leaders, that the United States has an advanced and comprehensive social security system, and that you can buy a chocolate bar for a nickel. It stuns them to hear that Americans do not need permission to travel from city to city, or that you do not need to submit a passport at a hotel. They cannot believe it that city police have no connection with the national government, or that Yale and Princeton are not operated by the state. I have heard a Russian boy ask quite seriously, "Are there mountains in America?" and "Do you have oranges?"

The periodical Kommunist, organ of the Central Committee of the party and a towering ideological fountainhead, carried a choice little item lately. It was to the effect that American workmen are "permitted" to have automobiles only because this saved them from the strain of having to go to work by subway or train! In consequence they were less fatigued while on the job, and so made more money for their employers. The fact that TV is universal in the United States was explained by similar reasoning. The capitalist class has wickedly managed to get TV installations into the workers' homes, so they will not waste time drinking or going to parties at night, and consequently will be fresher for the next day's work, to earn more money for the capitalists.

Mr. Khrushchev said in his Report to the Twentieth Congress, "In America one man makes a profit by ruining another. . . . If the worker loses his health, the capitalist throws him out. . . ." In a recent interview he said, "In the United States there is freedom in the sense that everybody can go to work, but one may not find work and die from hunger. It is *freedom to die.*" (Italics mine.)

Russians are apt to be argumentative with Americans, down to the most trivial level. When, mentioning tourism, I said on one occasion that at least 100,000 Americans visit Paris every year, the girl to whom I was talking replied tartly, "That can only mean that you Americans do not like your own country!" When I offered Soviet citizens American cigarettes, the usual reaction was, "Ah, pretty good—but not so strong as ours!" Youngsters several times asked me about the difference between whisky and vodka, and I would reply that our bourbon was somewhat heavier. Answer: "Yes, but we drink more!"

One encouraging sign is that most Russians are intensely curious about the United States. This is one reason why publication of the magazine *Amerika* is so valuable, because it can nullify or ameliorate ignorances. The Soviet authorities limit its circulation to fifty thousand copies, but it could easily sell ten times that. Every issue disappears from the newsstands at once, and when we were in Moscow copies were being sold on the black market for several hundred rubles each. Readers tear out and sell single pages, and even copy them, passing them on to friends.[5]

The question asked me most by Russians was what political party did I belong to. Obviously it was known that Americans have a *choice* of parties, and it seemed to me significant that this lay close to people's minds, although I cannot say that anybody showed envy. The official Russian line is that political parties in America have no significance, in that both Republicans and Democrats are controlled by the propertied class, and have identical aims and policies.

The complaint that came up most in casual conversation was about fingerprinting. I tried to explain that, to Americans, fingerprinting was a fairly routine procedure which carried no stigma, and that *all* foreigners, not merely Russians, had to undergo fingerprinting in order to get visas for the United States. Also I agreed that the fingerprinting regulations were wrong and stupid, and should be changed.[6] One reply, from a friendly official in

[5] Distribution of *Amerika*, published in Russian by the American Government, began in 1956. At the same time a similar Russian magazine in English, *USSR*, started publication in the United States.

[6] Abolition of the fingerprinting regulations has lately taken place, but the Soviet public has not been told this as yet.

VOKS, the All-Union Society for Cultural Relations with Foreign Countries, was, "Ah, but you never change any of your laws!" I replied, "Ever heard of prohibition?" The VOKS man then suggested that the United States should exempt Russians from fingerprinting, but not members of other nationalities! This, he said, would prove the sincere interest of the United States in wanting good cultural relations with the Soviet Union. Other countries could apparently go hang.

Before long, in almost any serious talk, comes what I have called the Gulf. We talked in Kiev with the rector of the university there, an intelligent, co-operative, and earnest man, Professor Shvets. It was difficult to convince him that the New York Times was not an organ of the American government. We talked about freedom and I asked him if it did not bother him that he was not free. He denied vigorously that he was not free, and asked me what I meant. The first thing I thought of to say was, "Well, you are not free to go to London tomorrow morning." He was unshaken and replied that, by making arrangements with some delegation or other, he could visit London at any time. Once, in the Crimea, we had a particularly enlightening exchange with Zoya, our interpreter. She demonstrated, by some remark or other, her utter devoted faith in the regime, and I said, "Ah, Zoya, but you are an idealist." She became enraged. With bitter, flaming indignation, she replied that she was not an idealist at all, and that to call a person an idealist was the worst of all possible insults. "I am not an idealist, but a materialist!" she exclaimed. And then we had to explain laboriously that by idealism Americans and Russians meant two totally different things.

Most Russians, eager for co-operation with the United States, are also almost pathetically anxious for Americans to express a good opinion about things Russian. They pity us in their strange, fascinating way for not being Communist, but they want our praise. Our favorite girl in the Intourist office asked us with a kind of desperate wistfulness when we got back from Central Asia, "Were your impressions good?" When, in the summer of 1957, Moscow was preparing for the World Youth Festival, the press contained homilies telling citizens how to behave—not to be too excited about "women's jewelry, cigarette cases and lighters, and cuff links," and not to criticize foreigners for their "sharp color combinations in dress." Russian youngsters were told that "hospitality does not mean obsequiousness," and that, in order to be of assistance, they should know the names of the five gate towers of the Kremlin.[7]

During the festival, the Soviet press printed some revealing eyewitness

[7] Max Frankel in the New York Times, May 28, 1957.

stories of encounters between Russian and American youths. Consider this from *Trud*:

> On meeting Howard Leyman from California one cannot help observing that he has attentive and piercing gray eyes and a remarkable capacity to feel at home handling a car. . . .
> This strong, handsome, sunburnt fellow speaks a little bit haughtily and condescending about many things. He was talking with a group of workers near an old, low building on Sushchevsky Street; the windows and walls of the building had been festively and lovingly decorated with paper pigeons and bouquets of flowers. Howard made a critical remark. The listeners smiled, amused. A young woman in trim work clothes said to me softly:
> "He doesn't know much about real life. You can tell right away that he's a millionaire!"
> "But there's some truth in what he says—for example, that women should not have to do heavy work!" I answered.
> The young worker nodded her head.
> "Of course, that's right! But it's still necessary to understand life and not just to chatter away like that!"[8]

How Russian!

To recapitulate, the United States government may be thought of as an "enemy" by the Soviet regime, but not the American people. The line is that, everywhere, the people are all right, but are victimized by "reactionary" capitalists and "monopolists." On November 7, slogans appeared conspicuously in Red Square urging friendship with the American "people." Also, it is important to point out, the United States is thoroughly respected in some respects—in particular for its basic wealth, technological skills, and industrial energy. The Russians talk about our "savagery" to Negroes and describe our "thieving seizure" of Formosa, but admit some American virtues, and are even envious of them. A recent article in the Soviet Army organ, *Krasnaya Zvezda*, says, "Beyond doubt the American people are industrious and talented. They have made a great contribution to world civilization and culture in subjugating nature. . . . The American people have given to the world great political leaders, inventors, writers, and musicians."[9] One incidental historical point is that Lenin considered the war of the American Revolution to have been a "good" war.

Be this as it may be, I have never encountered anything more poisonous than some Russian attitudes to the United States. This is from a dispatch to

[8] *Current Digest of the Soviet Press*, September 11, 1957.
[9] *Ibid.*, July 17, 1957.

Izvestia, November 25, 1956, from a town in Transcarpathia. A community exists here of Christian Evangelical Baptists, which felt impelled to say the following:

> We . . . protest against the slanderous broadcasts of the so-called "free" radio, the Voice of America. This is the voice of Judas who betrayed Christ to his death.

Consider this excerpt from an article by a well-known journalist who was a Menshevik in older days, David Zaslavsky, in *Pravda*, January 26, 1957:

> They [the Americans] lost in Hungary and wanted to recoup their hand in Poland. Now they have lost in Poland too. Where will American imperialism stick its importunate nose now?

Komsomolskaya Pravda recently printed a ludicrous denunciation of the Rockefeller family and other American "billionaires," always "up to their knees in blood, always on the corpses of the people," and said that the American monopolists were responsible—a nice mixed bag!—for "the Hitler concentration camps, racial discrimination in America, the slave trade in Africa, and events in Jordan."[10]

*

One word on that well-known bugbear, Soviet propaganda. Americans are, unfortunately, apt to think that *anything* the Russians say is propaganda; to confuse, in a word, realities in Soviet accomplishment with fabrications, and to minimize or disparage genuine Soviet successes—a dangerous tendency. To dismiss something as "propaganda" may not invalidate the fact that it also may be true. It is Russian *policy* that we must watch and be on guard against, not merely propaganda.

Soviet propaganda over the air is particularly skillful and widespread. The Russians have a total of 147 short wave stations, and beam 2,000 hours of "news" to the world every week. About 112 hours are directed at the United States, particularly the Eastern seaboard. The American authorities make no effort to jam these programs. They are not much listened to by North Americans. Any reasonably sophisticated United States listener would laugh them off. But they can be effective elsewhere, and the Russians do their best to reach everybody, even in the most remote corners of the earth. For instance Radio Moscow is heard (in English) by Eskimos in the northern extremities of Canada. No other station reaches this distant part of the world, except a minor one in Greenland. Also the Russians miss no opportunity. It was no

[10] B. J. Cutler in the New York *Herald Tribune*, May 26, 1957.

accident that, when the first earth satellite was launched, their services made a particular point one day of the fact that it would pass over—Little Rock.

The Soviet broadcasts aim in particular to reach Asia, Africa, the Middle East, and even the Caribbean, and to exploit local prejudice. They stress and exaggerate mistreatment of Negroes in the United States, and in regard to things in Moscow describe blandly (in perfectly accented English) progress in education and opportunities in science for white, brown, and black alike. A typical program will make some sly reference to Eisenhower playing golf at some vacation spot in the segregated south, and then say that hardworking Soviet officials have just opened new schools in Moscow or Tashkent, and are welcoming African or Asian visitors. In particular, programs stress American complacence, lack of unity, and material selfishness.

One point more. Russians are certainly not generous (on the governmental level) about admitting any American generosities. Nobody in Russia ever hears that the United States gave the USSR Lend-Lease assistance to the amount of nine *billion* dollars during World War II, a sum which assisted massively in Soviet survival and reconstruction. Nor is the contribution of UNRRA ever mentioned. During the crisis over Suez in 1956, the Russian press completely eliminated any mention of American efforts to stop the Anglo-French-Israeli invasion, after the first days of the crisis. If you read nothing but *Pravda*, you would have no idea that anybody was on the side of peace except the Soviet Union, and you would have to assume that the cease-fire was purely a Soviet accomplishment.

Still another point. It is the official policy of the Soviet government to outstrip the United States in over-all industrial production, by some date not yet named. All Russians are taught that this is going to happen, and little, it seems, remains to be done except to pick the exact day. Moreover it is assumed that this will come about not only because of Soviet proficiency, but because the United States will collapse in time by reason of its own inherent contradictions and weaknesses, probably as a result of a profound economic depression.

Attitude to Eisenhower

It was interesting to try to estimate some Russian opinions during the last days of the American election campaign in 1956. So far as I could tell, the Kremlin bosses were strongly pro-Eisenhower, although cool to Nixon. They liked Eisenhower better than Stevenson for several reasons. He was a known commodity; Stevenson was unknown. He had a friendly association with Marshal Zhukov during the war. Above all, his reputation was that of a man who stood for peace, whereas Stevenson was the inheritor of the Truman-

Acheson "war-mongering" combination that put the Marshall Plan into effect, created NATO, and fought the Korean War. Eisenhower, on the other hand, was the man who made peace in Korea, assisted in the liquidation of the French position in Indo-China, came to Geneva to meet Khrushchev and Bulganin at the Summit Conference in 1955, and has pursued a generally conciliatory policy.

The Americans whom the Russians hate most are probably Mr. Truman, Mr. Dulles, and whoever is running NATO. MacArthur is called a "butcher," and Truman a "cannibal," but not because Truman ate him. Eisenhower, on the other hand, even if he is surrounded by "evil" and "unscrupulous" advisers, is a man of good will who is "responsive" to public opinion to an extent, and the Russians think that if they can "get through" to the President himself, questions at issue will be satisfactorily adjusted. One may assume that this will be news to Pennsylvania Avenue.

A Point in Counterpoint

Bad manners are frequent in the Soviet press; but so are they in ours. Only seldom, however, do the Russians attack any American on a strictly personal level any longer; this is now considered to be "noncultured" and undignified.

Following is a letter from a reader which appeared in the New York *Daily Mirror* on June 18, 1957:

KHRUSH-HIC VODKATORIOUS

There have been lots of complaints about Khrushchev's appearance on CBS-TV. Seems many think he pulled a terrific propaganda job on the American people.

Well, I was right there in my living room watching this Red Butcher, with a few million other Americans, and he left me cold!

Everyone knows a sneak and a liar can't look you straight in the eye, and while Khrushchev bantered the usual Commie yap-trap about peace and love, not once did he look directly into the TV cameras.

For my money Niki pork-barrel is a lousy salesman. The only thing he sold me on was that he was a sly, slippery liar who didn't have the guts to look his TV audience in the eye and a two-bit lush who wins all his victories in a shot of vodka!

No Soviet paper would ever print anything quite like that.

What Impressed Me Most

1. There has been so little change. Of course relaxations have come, industrialization has made tremendous progress, agriculture has been col-

lectivized, at indecent cost, the overt terror has stopped, and the accent on education is more pronounced. But, in some respects, this is still the same Russia I saw long before the war. I wrote news stories for the Chicago *Daily News* in 1928 that would apply virtually without change to conditions and affairs today. *Plus ça change, plus c'est la même chose.*

2. Conformity is not merely imposed from the top, but rises spontaneously from below. Lenin once said, "Give me four years to teach the children, and the seed I have sown will never be uprooted." Many citizens believe passionately in what the government stands for, and have ardent, patriotic pride in its accomplishments, which is one thing that gives the regime its force. They are not merely "deluded" by indoctrination and propaganda; they are indissolubly part of the system themselves, no matter how barbarous this may be.

3. Conflict will, it is possible, arise in time between the new class of technicians and industrial administrators now being trained, and the old-line party behemoths. Give a man scientific training, teach him the scientific method (even within Soviet limitations), and some possibility at least arises that he will seek truth and demand freedom of mind in other than academic or technical fields.

4. The vociferous outspokenness of the press on nonpolitical topics. The papers swarm with openly expressed complaints. Those Americans who think that the Soviet press never contains criticism of wayward trends or activities in general are altogether wrong.

5. The emphasis on intellect in top professional and political spheres. No anti-eggheadism in *this* country!

6. Coupled with this, the immense acceleration of education and in particular of technological advance, as copiously proved by the slick, exuberant launchings of the first Soviet "moons," as well as pregnant developments in supersonic missiles and much else.

7. "Culture" in the popular sense is still the magic word, and some earnest citizens give the impression of being bulls in dinner jackets. With a vehemence and determination almost inconceivable to us, they yearn and strive for self-betterment.

8. The extreme self-confidence of the regime, its implacable *élan*, its hardheadedness, shrewdness, long view, and fixity of faith. Certainly this country has important elements of weakness, but it is a strong country just the same.

*

So now we conclude this preliminary sketch. It is time to turn to government and personalities.

CHAPTER V

The Party Circuit

*They [the Russians] came to the court balls
dropping pearls and vermin.*
—THOMAS B. MACAULAY, *History of England*

WHAT runs the Soviet Union is, of course, the Communist party which, in addition, has formidable international power because it runs or is affiliated with other Communist parties elsewhere in the world. Within the USSR, its rule goes right through the structure of society, in a vast and intricately embedded network, all the way down to the party secretaries and local bosses in the smallest town or single farm. I will attempt to describe workings of the party in detail in Chapter IX. At this juncture I am dealing only with its executive arm, the Presidium of the Central Committee, which consists of twenty-three men—fifteen full members and eight candidates or alternates—since it was sensationally revamped by Khrushchev in 1957.

Certainly tiffs and disagreements occur in the Presidium as they may occur at a directors' meeting in an American corporation, but the idea, held in some European circles, that its members are perpetually at each other's throats is nonsensical. Nobody knows for certain if decisions of the Presidium are taken by an actual vote or show of hands. (Nor does this need to be particularly important; the British cabinet almost never takes a formal vote, nor does the National Security Council in Washington). On the other hand, the chief technical difference between full members of the Presidium and candidates is that candidates do not have the right to vote if a vote is taken. In any case it is known that discussion is encouraged at meetings of the Presidium these days, dissent is permitted, and minority opinions duly registered. The members meet; they argue; they take counsel; they come to some sort of decision; they function as a multiple-headed whole. Khrushchev is certainly the boss, as of the moment this book goes to press, but the other members have a voice.

82

During Stalin's day the procedure was very different, and went more or less like this. Stalin, presenting a problem, would invite ideas and recommendations, and listen with attention. But very little crossfire of discussion took place; each member spoke *to* Stalin. Then, at the end, he would turn to Molotov, say, and announce, "Let us adopt the position of Comrade Molotov." No argument or disagreement was permitted. Stalin alone decided. But, then, if things went wrong, *Molotov* (not Stalin) could be blamed.

I should perhaps interpolate a word about the term "Presidium." It is nothing more nor less than the old Political Bureau (Politburo) of the Communist party, which has existed since Lenin's day. Stalin, about six months before his death in 1953, enlarged the Politburo from its standard membership of about eleven to twenty-five, and changed the name to Presidium; his motive in expanding it was to reduce the power of the old members, for fear that they might combine against him. After his death, the new leadership retained the new name but cut the membership back to eleven, for the same reason in reverse—its members wanted to keep power close to their own chests, without diffusion. In the coup of June, 1957, to be described in detail later in these pages, Khrushchev expanded the full membership to fifteen. The old guard Stalinists and reactionaries Molotov and Kaganovich were dumped overboard, as well as Malenkov, Shepilov (a candidate member), and Saburov. Also Marshal Zhukov, the Minister of Defense, was advanced from being a candidate to a full member, and the gaps were filled with Khrushchev men. Then in October Zhukov was summarily dropped.

A certain amount of floundering and flubdub was inevitable after Stalin's death, if only because his power had been so unitary, exclusive, and overwhelming for so long. Probably not since the Middle Ages has any one man ever held such a position in any country. Ever since 1953, the main line of Russian politics has been to fill the prodigious vacuum he left. This is why political events today are so unpredictable and volatile. Khrushchev's first attempt was to *institutionalize* the dictatorship. Khrushchev may be the boss, but he is not the kind of boss that Stalin was, with unmitigated and merciless supreme dictatorial powers. There has been no reversion to dictator worship or "the cult of personality."

The question may well be asked—can collective leadership last indefinitely under a totalitarian system? To put it another way, can there be a dictatorship without a dictator? Can little Stalins maintain permanently collective rule? History does not afford many examples of enduring collective dictatorships. Of course, in the USSR it is the *party* that is the real dictator. But may not the party throw up some future Stalin, particularly if disagreements in the present leadership produce a split? It is certainly possible. Even in the immediate present a weighty reshuffling may occur at any time. One report is that Voroshilov will retire soon, to be replaced by Bulganin as head of state. But Bulganin is—at the moment—seemingly out of favor. Khrushchev is on top, but it is impossible to know how long he will last.

Be this as it may be, watching the Presidium when we were in Moscow was almost like watching a mutual aid society. At a reception you could see one member pass on the responsibility for a toast to another, with a gesture clearly meaning, "I'm tired of this—you catch the next one." You could see Voroshilov, say, looking in a somewhat befuddled manner to Molotov for enlightenment on what was going on, and then Molotov would come up close to him, very close, and whisper comfortingly in his ear, almost like an aged son to an even more aged father. (This was before the expulsion of Molotov, Kaganovich, and company.)

Once a certain western ambassador sought out Khrushchev at a party and engaged him in earnest conversation. This went on for a while—the western ambassador was highly interested in what he was saying—but then Khrushchev looked down the room and saw Bulganin talking to two other ambassadors, and he seemed to be hard-pressed. Khrushchev at once broke away from the first ambassador, saying lightly, "Forgive me, but I see that Bulganin is outnumbered, and I must rescue him."

It is all very cozy. One is tempted on occasion to forget that this group of men is not only probably the most powerful but also the most cynical, sinister, and extravagantly ruthless in the world, and that its chief aim is the conquest of *our* world.

I will never forget the expression on Kaganovich's face one afternoon when Khrushchev was making a rough, tough, off-the-cuff speech at the Polish Embassy. Kaganovich is a heavy-set man with a large head, hands like trowels, and fingers (if I may mix metaphors) hanging down like carrots. He was listening to Khrushchev with an air compounded of satisfaction, bewilderment, amusement, approval, and dismay. He put out his hands, palms up, with his head wagging, and you could almost see the words form on his lips, as Khrushchev kept on blasting away, "What can you do with a man like that? But what a man!"

Sometimes lively—even sharp—interchanges take place between members of the Presidium in public. During this same speech Mikoyan, with his dark Armenian face, kept interrupting Khrushchev, who did not seem pleased.

Khrushchev said that the western powers had done something "idiotic." Mikoyan muttered aloud, "Too strong, too strong!" Khrushchev quoted Lenin to the effect that, if a man was utterly convinced that he was right, not wrong, he should proceed to the limit in executing his views. Mikoyan interrupted, "But how do you know that you are not wrong?" On another occasion when I was present Khrushchev began his remarks with the phrase, "Comrades, Friends, Gentlemen." Mikoyan shot out, "Sometimes friends are also gentlemen!"

At one reception Khrushchev, talking about Egypt, said that the Russians respected Colonel Nasser for his fight against colonialism, but disliked him for putting Communists in jail. Kaganovich interrupted with his eyes rolling heavily and a mellifluous expression of pious protest, "We didn't like *that* very much!" Then Voroshilov broke in to say that Nasser had jailed Communists only because he had no other choice. Khrushchev turned sharply to him, saying, "Don't try to help me!"

The Top Leadership

These are the fifteen full members of the Presidium of the Central Committee of the Communist Party of the USSR:

Name	Age	Date of entry into full membership of Politburo or Presidium[1]
Averky B. Aristov	54	1957
Nikolai I. Belyayev	52	1957
Leonid I. Brezhnev	51	1956
Nikolai A. Bulganin	62	1946
Ye. A. Furtseva[2]	47	1957
Nikolai G. Ignatov	?	1957
Nikita S. Khrushchev	63	1938
Alexei I. Kirichenko	55	1955
Frol R. Kozlov	48	1957
Otto V. Kuusinen	76	1957
Anastas I. Mikoyan	62	1926
Nuritdin A. Mukhitdinov	52	1956
Nikolai M. Shvernik	68	1939
Mikhail A. Suslov	54	1955
Kliment Y. Voroshilov	76	1926

[1] The date is that of *re*-entry for several who were also members during the brief period when Stalin enlarged the body.

[2] Some Russian initials are in the form of two letters. "Ye" stands for Yekaterina in this case.

Candidate or alternate members are these, listed in apparent order of precedence:

Name	Age	Date of entry into full membership of Politburo or Presidium
Pyotr N. Pospelov	59	1957
Demyan S. Korotchenko	61	1957
Yan E. Kalnberzin	?	1957
Andrei P. Kirilenko	51	1957
Alexei N. Kosygin	52	1957
Kirill T. Mazurov	56	1957
Vasily P. Mzhavanadze	?	1957
Mikhail G. Pervukhin	53	1952[3]

Several observations are in order:

1. One woman is among the leading fifteen, Madame Furtseva. She is a close friend of Khrushchev's, and was the first woman in Soviet history to reach, first, alternate membership (February, 1956), and, second, full membership.

2. With Molotov gone, only one authentic "Old Bolshevik"[4] remains, Mikoyan, who has real power. Voroshilov and Shvernik are old in service, but were never close collaborators of Lenin, and do not carry much weight nowadays. Khrushchev and Bulganin are what might be called "Middle Bolsheviks"; they are in their sixties, but did not become prominent till the 1930's. In other words, the old generation of revolutionary leaders is dying out, and is being replaced by men who have lived all of their adult lives under the Soviet system. Several represent the new "technical aristocracy"— that is, they are trained managers, about as revolutionary (in the old sense of the word "revolutionary") as the directors of General Motors. The Old Bolsheviks were conspirators, men who suffered long years of imprisonment or exile, and who lived perilous lives underground; the new generation is far removed from such experience, and has a quite different point of view. A member is more likely to be an expert in thermodynamics or an accountant than a bomb-thrower.

3. With Kaganovich out, no Jews are present. For many years he was the only Jew in these elevated ranks.

[3] Demoted in 1957 from full membership.
[4] "Old Bolshevik" is used to denote men who played an active role *before* the 1917 Revolution.

4. Of the fifteen full members, all are Great Russians (i.e. men out of Russia proper) except Kuusinen, who is Finnish, Mikoyan, an Armenian, Kirichenko, who is from the Ukraine, and Mukhitdinov, an Uzbek. But Khrushchev has made an interesting precedent by bringing men in from outside to be *candidate* members, who may reach full membership in time. No fewer than five, in fact, of the eight candidate members at present are non-Russian—Mzhavanadze (Georgian), Korotchenko (Ukrainian), Kirilenko (Ukrainian), Mazurov (White Russian), and Kalnberzin (Lettish). Mukhitdinov, an able citizen, was the first Uzbek in Soviet history to reach national prominence. Also Brezhnev, a full member, although he is Russian, was boss of Kazakhstan for a period, and his appointment was something of a *beau geste* to the Kazakhs. Khrushchev's motives in all this are simple. His chief support comes from the party machine spread out all over the country, and it is consequently good sense for him to reward provincial leaders. Also he is genuinely eager to decentralize authority to a degree, and give recognition to the minority republics.

5. Average age of the group is around fifty-six. Probably it is the youngest aggregation of men of such illimitable power in the world.

6. Several rising stars are out-and-out "Khrushchev men," like Kirichenko, but as a rule an attempt is made, when a new member is chosen, to reflect broadly the interests and point of view of the party as a whole. When Kirichenko went in, his appointment was balanced by that of Suslov, a Stalinist who was not a Khrushchev man at that time. In matters like this, Soviet rulers are an extremely adroit and far-seeing group.

7. In the whole history of the Politburo from its foundation in 1917 to 1952, when Stalin opened the gates to enlarge it, *only twenty-eight men ever* achieved full membership.[5] Rule in the Soviet Union is an intensely concentrated phenomenon. Of the twenty-eight, five are members now (Khrushchev, Bulganin, Voroshilov, Mikoyan, Shvernik). The others died, or were purged. Stalin got rid of Trotsky, Kamenev, Zinoviev, Bukharin, Rykov, Rudzutak, Kosior, Voznesensky, and perhaps others; the triumvirate that took over immediately after Stalin's death got rid of Lavrenti P. Beria, Stalin's last police chief; the present Khrushchev regime got rid of Molotov, Kaganovich, and Malenkov.

8. Several members today, like Pervukhin, are not only expert technicians but are well educated generally. This marks a considerable difference from older days. When I first visited Russia in 1928, four out of eleven members of the Politburo had never been to school at all; several had been workmen

[5] Merle Fainsod, *How Russia Is Ruled*, p. 264.

with their hands, manual laborers, and not one had a university education.

9. It would be incorrect to assume that any of the present members are inexperienced, but none had much experience *without Stalin* until his death. Nobody was used to supreme executive responsibility. This is one reason for Khrushchev's rise, because he was bold and clever enough and enough of a gambler to make his way in and take over.

10. Today's Presidium is much more receptive to moods and opinions from below than during the petrifaction of the Stalin era, and takes advice on two levels. First, it listens to an extent to popular opinion, as reflected by local party secretaries and the like. Second, it pays close attention to professional counsel, as from the military and from scientists in various fields.

11. Partly by accident or force of circumstances, partly by design, the Presidium constitutes a complete interlocking net over almost all Soviet activity. No neater system of ramifying supervision and authority has ever been devised. Voroshilov is nominally head of state, and thus symbolizes the externals of governmental power. Bulganin is Chairman of the Council of Ministers or Prime Minister. Khrushchev holds no government job (except that he is a member of the Presidium of the Supreme Soviet), but he is First Secretary of the party. Kosygin is a deputy prime minister. Mikoyan has always specialized in trade, as well as being a trouble shooter at large, and Pervukhin in industry and atomic energy. Shvernik brings the trade unions into the picture. Kirichenko, an agricultural specialist, represents the Ukraine. Suslov is an expert in ideology and propaganda, and Furtseva and others represent the party.

The principal department not directly represented on the Presidium, now that Molotov has been shipped away to Outer Mongolia, is foreign affairs. The present foreign minister, A. A. Gromyko, has not yet reached Presidium level. Actually it is part of the Soviet tradition to exclude the foreign ministry from the Presidium; the foreign minister executes policy, but is not supposed to create it. Molotov was an exception. Other great Soviet foreign ministers, like Chicherin and Litvinov, never reached Politburo membership, although A. Ya. Vyshinsky was a candidate member for a brief time, as was Shepilov. As to the Army, it has never been the Soviet custom to include a military man on the Presidium. Khrushchev broke this rule by elevating Zhukov to membership, but Zhukov, as everybody well knows, did not last very long. Nor is any representative of the police on the Presidium at present.

12. These are all able men, but some of their ignorances, particularly about affairs abroad, are almost grotesque. Voroshilov met an American publicist at a party recently, and was astounded to hear from him that the works of

Lenin are to be found perfectly freely in American libraries and bookstores. When Khrushchev and Bulganin visited England they were much impressed by the behavior of the London crowds, which were respectful but altogether inert. Later Khrushchev congratulated an English acquaintance about this, saying that the British must have a phenomenally well-organized Ministry of Home Security, in order to be able to impose such a universal mood on large gatherings. Members of the oligarchy are inclined to see everything in purely *Russian* terms.

13. Khrushchev is certainly the Number One man as of the moment of writing, with Bulganin theoretically in second place, but after that it is not easy to assign order of precedence in these incandescent ranks. Until June, 1957, when Khrushchev and Bulganin were both out of the country, the man left in charge was Kaganovich. When a list of members appears in the Soviet press, the sequence is always alphabetical. Not long ago the Burmese Embassy asked the entire Presidium to dinner, and the invitation was, surprisingly enough, accepted. This meant that the members had to be seated in the correct order of protocol, and the Burmese hosts did not know what to do. There was no precedent. After prolonged hesitation, the Foreign Office gave a ruling. Khrushchev got first place, Bulganin second, Voroshilov third, and Mikoyan fourth.

At regular intervals Soviet leaders take jaunts out into the country to check up on what is going on, tune in on trends, allay criticism, and show themselves. Early this year the whole Presidium took to the sticks. Observers tried to work out, from the places where they went, relative degrees of priority, but it was difficult to draw a conclusive pattern. Khrushchev went to Tashkent, the most important city in Central Asia and the capital of Uzbekistan. Mikoyan went to Ashkhabad, the capital of a comparatively minor republic, Turkmenistan, while Bulganin visited Stalinabad, capital of Tadzhikistan, somewhat less important. Most of the others went to key cities in Great Russia, although Voroshilov turned up in Alma-Ata, the capital of Kazakhstan. Molotov went to the area southeast of Moscow, Malenkov to the Urals, and Kaganovich to Eastern Siberia. Suslov went to the Volga region, and Brezhnev took on Omsk.

14. It is exceptionally difficult to draw a line between the area of sincere belief and cynicism in these men. Most have high standards of individual integrity, on Soviet terms. It would be a signal mistake to think of them as vulgarly corrupt or irresponsible adventurers. On the other hand, what activates them most is faith and *power*, and, since they are Bolsheviks and hold to the thesis that the ends justify the means, they will go to almost any length

to achieve a purpose, particularly if something important for the party or regime is at stake. They will tell the most fantastic and monstrous lies, if this serves their end. Khrushchev knows perfectly well that it is just as transparently ludicrous to call Beria an "agent of the imperialists," which he did in his speech to the Twentieth Congress, as it was for Stalin to have called Voroshilov "a British spy."

Party Line

The tight little knot of men who run the Soviet Union and who represent the sharpest, densest concentration of political power known in the world, are, among other things, the hardest men in the world to meet—and the easiest.

Formal interviews across a desk, in the Kremlin or elsewhere, are somewhat rare. But—

I have a friend in Moscow.

I met him when we arrived in Moscow, and then I happened to see him again twenty-four hours later.

"How did your first day go?" he asked.

"Moderately well," I replied.

"What do you mean moderately?"

"Well," said I, pausing for effect, "I met, shook hands with, and had brief interchanges of conversation with Khrushchev, Bulganin, Zhukov, Molotov, Gromyko, and Shepilov. That's all."

My friend, who is Russian, came near to fainting.

And later I met Voroshilov, Kaganovich, Mikoyan, Shvernik, Pervukhin, Madame Furtseva, and others on what, in Moscow terminology, is called the "Team."

This did not happen because my wife and I were given special favors by the Soviet authorities. We weren't. We met these grandiose chieftains only because we had friends in the diplomatic corps, and went to parties. As a matter of fact, all the newspapermen in Moscow are invited to diplomatic receptions, or simply crash the gates. These parties were to me, an innocent outsider, an enthralling and unforgettable experience. Your car glides down a boulevard sheathed in ice, and, if you have timed it right, you arrive at your destination just before two, three, or even four long, black, shiny Kremlin limousines sweep up. Along the streets, open-mouthed passers-by shuffle fatalistically in the snow.

The Kremlin despots step out alertly, and are greeted by host and hostess inside. Overhead, pretty candelabra may be burning, and in one room will be a buffet, sometimes luxurious, sometimes plain. Champagne bubbles; uniforms sparkle; conversation sings. Then—like as not—you may find yourself in a secluded corner with Khrushchev, Bulganin, Mikoyan, and company not three feet away, talking to guests as if they did not have a care in the world.

And how do they look? My first thought was that they must be actors. It seemed almost inconceivable that the entire ruling body of the Soviet Union should be on such public display, so intimately, informally, and engagingly. Security precautions, if any, are inconspicuous, and although detectives may be stationed in the crowd, I never spotted one. There is no check of any kind of guests at the door.

My second thought was that, although real, these presiding bosses of the largest country on the globe *were* actors. They all looked healthily sunburned to the same ocher tone, as if they were using the same shade of theatrical make up. All wore dark business suits, white shirts, and pale gray ties (except Zhukov, who never appears except in uniform), exactly like Wall Street lawyers. The Hungarian crisis was in full angry flow at this time, and they had just made decisions about which there had probably been acrid disagreement—yet they stood there calm, bland, and united. Once a decision has been taken, they close ranks, and nobody shows signs of strain.

At a party at the Turkish Embassy the American Ambassador, Charles E. Bohlen, took me up to Marshal Bulganin.

People were packed as tight as caviar in a can, and conversation was not easy. Bulganin asked me if I knew Russian, and I replied that I knew only two words.

"One is enough," Bulganin said.

Bohlen, who misses nothing and who likes to give a twist to a lion's tail, said with a laugh, "And that word is 'No' "—referring to the well-known fact that Russians customarily say "No" to things, rather than "Yes."

Bulganin smiled blandly: "No. Yes." (Meaning that "Yes" rather than "No" was the word I ought to know.)

Toasts were flowing, and Bulganin with a courteous bow offered one to good relations between the United States and the Soviet Union. I didn't have a glass in my hand. Bulganin lifted his. Instantly, a well-trained servant wriggled through the solid mass of guests, like a quarterback doggedly severing a scrimmage line, and managed to get a full glass in my hand, without spilling, before Bulganin started to drink. It would have been a bad mark against me if I hadn't had a drink ready too.

Bohlen introduced me to Khrushchev, who was standing close by, and said that I was a writer and journalist.

Khrushchev gave it as his opinion, vividly stated, that journalists were an extremely low breed of cats. Bohlen's eyes, which are exceptionally mobile, flashed.

At that instant I saw Shepilov, who was at that time still foreign minister, a few feet away, giving a sort of press conference. For some years Shepilov was editor of *Pravda*.

I said to Khrushchev, "If you have such a low opinion of journalists, why did you make a journalist your foreign minister?"

Khrushchev replied with a peculiar dark, airy gesture, "He's the only good journalist in Russia, and so we had to give him a job!"

Not the least interesting thing about these parties is that they may occur several times a week. Moscow has more than forty foreign embassies and legations, and each gives a reception on its national holiday and perhaps on other special days as well; such days come thick and fast. Also foreign heads of state, kings, prime ministers, and delegations incessantly visit Moscow; each is, naturally, given a reception by its local representative, and, if the visitor is important enough, the Kremlin gives a reception in return. Kremlin receptions are somewhat more formal than those at the foreign embassies. Invitations come only from Bulganin's office, and the guest list is strictly checked and controlled—no crashing. Parties of this type almost never took place during Stalin's day, and are a striking minor example of de-Stalinization. One ambassador told me that, in seven years, no member of the Soviet government had ever crossed his doorstep; now, when he gives an official party, practically everybody comes.

But nobody, even the host, is ever sure who exactly will show up, and the suspense can be considerable. The Belgians, who are members of NATO, got only two ministers, Kaganovich and Shepilov, at their party for their visiting countryman, Paul-Henri Spaak. Turkey is a member of NATO, and hence damned, but the Turks got five, at their anniversary party. This was because the Russians are being particularly attentive to Turkey just now, in spite of its NATO affiliation. The Afghans, at their reception for the Afghan prime minister, got everybody. So of course did the Poles. When time came, early in December, for the annual Yugoslav party, people in Moscow were agog with curiosity—would any Russians arrive, or not? At that time relations between Moscow and Belgrade were particularly strained. Bets were made that not a single major member of the Team would appear; but all the giants came. Sometimes strange things happen. The Swedes, at almost the same time, got exactly one minister, and a minor minister at that, at their annual party; this was because, in Stockholm, they had sent only one member of *their* government to the Soviet party in celebration of November 7. The

Russians are devout believers in an eye for an eye, or if possible two. An out-landish fate befell the Mongolian People's Republic. This dreary, if worthy, little satellite had never had a party before. Its new embassy, a year in build-ing, was flung open proudly for a dedicatory housewarming. But not a single Soviet guest showed up! This was because of a misunderstanding—the Russians went instead to welcome the President of Syria, who happened to be arriving in Moscow that same afternoon. Only *three* persons, out of hun-dreds expected, appeared at the Mongolian party, all of whom were foreign journalists who had not been invited.

Exactly how accessible members of the Team will be, granted that they put in an appearance, depends on circumstances. Usually, on arrival, they are shunted into a room by themselves, and given a few moments in com-parative seclusion with host and hostess. Then other ambassadors have their innings. For the first half-hour or so, the press and general company are sup-posed to be segregated in a different room. Then some daring guest crosses the line, and a glorious melee follows. The smaller the embassy, the better is the chance for a free-for-all. One remarkable thing is the way interpretation is managed. No interpreters are conspicuous, but if you start talking to a Soviet official, an interpreter pops up out of the floor as if by magic. At the Afghans' I had a talk with Gromyko. He introduced me to Molotov. Gro-myko's English is excellent but in a second a little man—Molotov's inter-preter—appeared as if he had emerged from a puff of smoke, and stood by under Molotov's armpit in case Gromyko should get out of his depth.

Also at these parties appear nonpolitical luminaries. Mr. Petrovsky, Rector of Moscow University, is an occasional guest; so are distinguished musicians like Khatchaturian, painters like the academician Gerasimov, and ballet dancers like Lepechinskaya and the marvelous Plisetskaya. The Metropolitan of the Orthodox Church is sometimes seen, and so is the Mufti of Moscow;[6] at one party we even met the Chief Rabbi of Moscow. Television stars, theater directors, scientists, poets, are eagerly sought after. A well-known writer, Sergei Mikhalkov, acted as court jester at the Yugoslav party; for half an hour, the entire Team stood around him, enraptured with laughter. Some Russians drink a great deal at parties; some don't drink at all. The custom whereby guests were practically compelled to drink toast after toast, long after their capacity to enjoy them was exhausted, has lapsed to an extent, partly because so many Moslems, who don't drink, come to Moscow on official missions these days. The Russians first became accustomed to visitors

[6] Moscow has a fairly large Moslem community, made up mostly of Tatars (Tartars).

who do not drink when Mr. Nehru arrived. He demanded tomato juice or orange juice during the toasting, got it, and Moscow has never been quite the same since.

Minor diplomatic incidents sometimes occur at even the most orderly gala. On November 18, 1956, at the Kremlin reception for the Poles, Khrushchev became somewhat violent. Among other things he said that the British, who had just launched their attack on the Suez Canal, were "bandits." Sir William Hayter, the British Ambassador, did not like this, and the NATO ambassadors, conferring quickly, marched in a body out of the room. Bulganin, standing next to Khrushchev, was visibly upset by the withdrawal, and so were other Soviet leaders who thought this might presage a permanent rupture with the West. Next day the Poles gave a party in return. Again Mr. Khrushchev sounded off. He called the Israelis "lackeys," accused them of having tried to "cut the throats of the Egyptians" on foreign orders, and, addressing all the western representatives in the room, shouted, "Whether you like it or not, history is on our side. We will bury you!" Again the NATO ambassadors, standing only a few feet away, left the room in protest. But they did not leave the party. So as not to affront the Poles, whose guests they were, they withdrew merely into a room adjoining.[7]

Two or three members of the Presidium are seldom seen at parties—like Kirichenko, who is usually absent in Kiev, and Suslov, who is supposed to be too loftily intellectual for such frivolous pursuits. The rest of the leaders go day after day. It is a wonder that anybody ever gets any business done. But a good deal of business is done actually *at* these parties; they are the only convenient means for informal exchange between the government and the diplomatic corps, i.e., the world outside. Diplomats don't have much access to members of the Presidium otherwise. Sometimes the interchange is on the highest level. Also Russians assiduously attend parties in order to meet other *Russians* whom they might not see otherwise.

K. P. S. Menon, the Indian Ambassador, received an urgent message from Prime Minister Nehru for transmission to Marshal Bulganin on November 6. There happened to be a Kremlin party that night, for the Syrians, and Mr. Menon, to save time, took the message with him and delivered it to Bulganin personally at the party. Bulganin at once beckoned to Khrushchev and

---

[7] When Khrushchev makes remarks like this, they are usually cleaned up in the Russian press the next day. For instance there was no mention in Russian newspapers of the British being "bandits," and the remark about the Israelis became nothing more than a charge that they were "aggressive." *New York Times,* November 19 and 20, 1956.

Shepilov, and called them into a corner. All three read it, and Mr. Menon suggested that the message, urging peace, was of such importance that it should be disseminated by the Soviet press and radio at once. And the decision to do so was taken—by Bulganin, Khrushchev, and Shepilov—without further ado there and then. A strange way to run a government!

Also, these parties are useful because they often turn into press conferences. Twenty or thirty journalists, notebooks in hand, will surround Khrushchev like hounds bringing down a stubborn fox. When a member of the government gives a statement, the thirst of newsmen to hear may be so avid and the crowd so impenetrable that a *second* press "conference" has to be held at the same time, with one of the newspapermen briefing his colleagues. At the Belgian reception, two noisy conferences went on concurrently, amid exuberant confusion, with Shepilov addressing one group of journalists, and Spaak another.* At the Polish reception for Mr. Gomulka, photography was permitted. David Douglas Duncan, the well-known American photographer, took picture after picture of Khrushchev from two feet away. Khrushchev asked him after a time if he was an American, and Duncan said, "Yes." Khrushchev said, "We will be friends with you too [as well as the Poles] some day." Pause. "But it will take a little time."

Private Lives

Astonishingly little is known about inner relationships among members of the Presidium. As a matter of fact, very little is known about *anything* personal about them; nobody knows for instance what their salaries are. Probably, for senior members of the government, these range between 10,000 and 18,000 rubles a month, $2,500 to $4,500 at par. Not much is

---

* Such conferences are often the only mechanism by which correspondents can express grievances to members of the government. At the Yugoslavs' I listened in to this colloquy:
Journalist (speaking to Kaganovich): "How do you remember us all?"
Kaganovich: "I don't remember you all, but I remember you."
Journalist: "I am surprised, because you usually pay most attention to aggressors."
Kaganovich (laughing): "Oh, we know all about you all."
Journalist: "You don't know anything about us. The press department never answers our questions. You know nothing about our problems."
Kaganovich: "That's not right. We ought to do something about it." (He beckons to Gromyko.)
Journalist: "As I was saying—"
Kaganovich (To Gromyko): "We really must do something about arranging things better for the press."
Gromyko: "Yes. What I would suggest is—"
(Kaganovich and Gromyko are interrupted and saunter off. Curtain.)

known about their family life, and their wives are seldom seen, except at full-dress official celebrations or special performances of the ballet. Wives are a subject about which almost all Russians are reticent; the whole subject of family relationships is taboo, not because of security, but because the Russians take the line that this is none of the outsider's business, and anyway is of no importance. Correspondents may think that they know all about a man, and then will discover suddenly from a chance bit of printed matter something altogether new—that his wife died years before, or that he has had triplets.

Names of callers on members of the government are never made public, unless this serves a purpose, and, needless to say, no publication exists like Hansard or the *Congressional Record*. The utter secrecy with which the Soviet government operates is one of its cardinal characteristics. And, of all things secret, what goes on in the Presidium is most secret. No one even knows how often it meets, or exactly where. One minor item is that all members have, it is believed, the same doctor, who keeps them under careful scrutiny. Recently he is supposed to have asked all to cut down on their smoking, because of danger from cancer of the lungs. Ministers do not as a rule work much at night these days. Stalin, as everybody knows, did most of his work after dinner. Nowadays, Russian officials observe normal hours for the most part, working from midmorning till about 8 P.M. Every time I had a telephone call from a government bureau, it came at exactly 1:45 P.M.

No one even knows for sure where leading members live. When Malenkov was prime minister, the location of his house in central Moscow was known, and so was Khrushchev's next door, but Khrushchev lives elsewhere now. Once, when Admiral Alan G. Kirk was American Ambassador to Moscow, his wife was invited to the Molotov villa in the country; this was regarded as an utterly unprecedented event, if only because it made it known where the Molotovs lived outside the Kremlin. Ambassador Bedell Smith records that no one, in his days in Moscow, even knew where Stalin lived aside from his quarters in the Kremlin. Stalin did, however, spend a good deal of time at the *dacha*, some twenty kilometers out of Moscow, where Lenin died, and this may still be used, like Checquers in England, as the prime minister's country residence.

Today, near Moscow University in the Lenin Hills[9] district, five sizable houses, with copper roofs, stand between the embankment of the Moskva River and a broad two-lane highway, behind a long solid fence. Here several ministers live. But no one knows which ones are in which houses, or how

[9] The old Sparrow Hills that readers of Tolstoy will remember.

they are paired up. Probably nobody has a house all to himself. Sometimes traffic on the near side is cut off or diverted; sometimes not. Uniformed militiamen, who guard every important building in Moscow, are not there; but a few plain-clothes cops are usually strolling about. The idea is that the neighborhood should not be too conspicuous; if uniformed police were present, the rank and file of the population, which is in absolute ignorance of such matters, would catch on to the fact that something important was hidden here. Last summer, incredible as the fact may seem, the story is that a French tourist addicted to *le camping* arrived in Moscow with a bicycle, portable tent, and other paraphernalia. In some manner never explained, he penetrated to this embankment area by accident, climbed up, and, having no idea where he was, pitched camp on the lawn. Consternation. The authorities did not know what to do. If they asked him to move it would call attention to the sensitiveness of the site. But they wanted to get him out as soon as possible. He seemed to like the view, however, and showed no inclination to move. Finally—strange denouement—the police brought him a portable toilet, to preserve propriety, and let him be.

CHAPTER VI

Khrushchev at the Top

> *It is not true that we regard violence and civil war as the only way to remake society. . . . The Communist system must be based on the will of the people, and if the people should not want that system, then that people should establish a different system.*
>
> —NIKITA S. KHRUSHCHEV

> *Once you pledge, don't hedge.*
>
> —NIKITA S. KHRUSHCHEV

KHRUSHCHEV has been by far the most important man in the Soviet Union since 1955, and dramatically confirmed his dominance in June, 1957, when Molotov, Kaganovich, and company were dumped, but it would be rash to predict how long he will remain on top. His position could suddenly be made precarious by any of several factors, particularly since the ousting of Marshal Zhukov. At the moment, however, his hold on power seems reasonably secure.

His name is pronounced correctly "Crew-shove," with a light accent on the "shove." He is Russian, not Ukrainian (as is often inaccurately said); if he were Ukrainian, the pronunciation would be "Crew-*shef*." His nickname in the early days was the "Football"—no matter how hard you kicked him, he came up bouncing, or rolling all over the place. An acute observer once said, "Nobody will ever squash Khrushchev. He cannot be sat on. But he might be pricked."

His major sources of power are, first, the unquenchable, irrepressible force of his own personality; second, his control of the *party* apparatus, which controls the government apparatus, down to the lowest level; third, he sym-bolizes release from Stalinism—liberalization. Then too, if we may assume

98

that contact with the masses counts at all, Khrushchev has done a good deal to make himself popular. Early in 1957 came his announcement that the Soviet Union would within a few years pass the United States in per capita butter, milk, and meat production. This may or may not happen, and Khrushchev is certainly not going to sacrifice heavy industry and armament for dairy products, but his agricultural program will probably produce *some* increase in the amount of edible goods available to the consumer, which will in turn tend to augment his popularity.

In several ways Khrushchev has set out to make himself the antithesis of Stalin, even though (we must always remember) he himself is certainly tarred thickly with the Stalinist brush, and served Stalin faithfully for many years. Khrushchev has reformed substantially the administration of justice, has broken up most of the labor camps for political prisoners, and has, to a signal extent, modified the power of the secret police. He does not rule through the police, although they are at his command if he needs them. The police played no role at all in the 1957 coup, nor in the dismissal of Zhukov later.[1]

Khrushchev is infinitely more accessible and homely than Stalin ever was. He likes people. Years ago, when he was overlord of the Ukraine, he attracted attention by being the first leading Communist since Lenin who enjoyed mixing in crowds, and who was not afraid to rub against the man on the street. Today, still a gregarious man, he dislikes intensely being cooped up. Visiting Finland in the summer of 1957, he seemed to be trying to give the slip to his own bodyguards. He likes to be seen everywhere. On the other hand, photographs of him are comparatively rare—for every thousand portraits of Stalin on public display in the USSR before 1953, there is perhaps one of Khrushchev today. Here, too, he wants to differentiate himself from Stalin. No "cult of personality" is being allowed to lift its preening head, although his position steadily becomes more conspicuous.

The question is often asked, granting that Khrushchev will stay on top for some little time, whether he is more "dangerous" (to the free world) than Stalin was. The answer depends on definition. He is certainly less dangerous than Stalin in that he does not rule by iron caprice, and is more moderate, more flexible. Khrushchev (though it would be the worst of mistakes to call him a softie) is not likely to set off any such adventure as the Korean War. On the other hand, he is less cautious than Stalin, more indul-

---

[1] Purists might say that Stalin, at least in his last days, did not rule through the police either, but through a private secretariat. Khrushchev has no such mechanism for this purpose, although he could easily build one up.

gent. Also his very flexibility and moderation may, in the long run, serve to make the Soviet Union stronger vis à vis the United States, rather than weaker; relaxations may increase its power, not diminish it. Again the point might be made that by "respectabilizing" the Soviet Union, so to speak, Khrushchev is in a better position than Stalin to pull wool over the world's eyes, and delude neutrals and opponents.

Some Personal Qualities of Khrushchev

Photographs exaggerate his ugliness—he is certainly ugly, but not so gross, so porcine, as some pictures indicate. People who saw him on television missed something; the TV cameras took his mobility away, his pepperiness and color. He is one of those roly-poly stout little men—not really fat—who are fast on their feet, almost airy. He leans forward alertly, almost as if he were on tiptoe, when he talks, and his supple mouth is as a rule a tiny bit open, as if his eagerness to devour whatever experience is coming cannot be checked. He has a silver fringe of hair, an upturned nose, three small chins, and twinkling, very dark small eyes set widely apart and deep. It is hard to tell their color—probably deep brown. Two gold teeth shine when he smiles, and a gap is noticeable between the two upper front teeth; he has one mole, or wart, next to his nose in the left cheek, and another under his right eye.

Khrushchev wears as a rule pale suits and a peculiar sort of nylon-type shirt—off-white or cream in color, with a low-lying collar, almost like that of a sport shirt, but with full-length sleeves and cuffs, which are attached with formal links. He looks, even in winter, as if he had planned to go to a yachting party, and then changed his mind when half-dressed.

Khrushchev's manner is that of a rogue who, except when in one of his rages, enjoys being roguish. He is a kind of monster, but not an unattractive monster—what the British call a "card."

He speaks out as he pleases—straight out—and has been guilty of all manner of indiscretions. He is the only member of the Team who cares, or dares, to be indiscreet, and out of this arises his reputation not merely for bluntness, but for crudity. But he is good-humored as a rule, and anecdotes about him sound coarser than they really are.   Once he meandered amiably across a crowded room, went up to a foreign lady of great rank notable for her dignified aloofness, nuzzled her on the neck, and murmured, "My little white pigeon!"

He can betray truly horrible lack of taste. At the Yugoslav reception late in 1956 he called out to a French journalist in a loud voice, "I've just heard a good joke. Eden is sick. Do you know what he's suffering from? Inflammation of the Canal!"

At one party, when a member of a visiting delegation commented on the fact that so many Russian women work, Khrushchev horrified the guests by replying cheerfully, "Yes, our women work, and they are honest women —not like women in France, who are all whores!"

Khrushchev is a tough egg, and understands tough talk. He said to his host, after one particularly noisy reception, "This has been too crowded and confused." The host, who represented a quite important country, replied icily, "In that case don't bother to come again." Khrushchev was startled, but accepted the rebuff with good humor.

When arrangements were being made for the visit of Marshal Tito of Yugoslavia to the Crimea, correspondents at a press conference tried to worm details out of Khrushchev. Daniel Schorr of the Columbia Broadcasting System, a lively and penetrating interlocutor, fished around with various questions, trying to pin Khrushchev down as to the date, so that he could be there. Khrushchev turned to him finally with exasperated irony, "Mr. Schorr, I think that we will manage to have our meeting without you!" One cannot imagine any other figure in Soviet history indulging in conversation of quite this sort. Certainly it is impossible to imagine the Napoleonic Stalin doing so.

When he and Bulganin visited India he astonished the Mayor of Bombay, who met their plane, with his introductory remark. "I'm afraid, Mr. Mayor, that the first thing I've done on arriving here is to break one of your laws." The Mayor looked puzzled. Khrushchev went on, "So many people . . . they frightened me." Indeed, more than a hundred thousand men and women had met the Russian plane. "I felt uneasy and I took a bottle of vodka out of my bag and had a drink as we landed." And Bombay, be it remembered, is strictly prohibitionist.

The Mayor replied, "Mr. Khrushchev, do not be alarmed. You have not broken our laws. My jurisdiction applies only to the land and three miles out to sea, not to the air."

"What?" exploded Khrushchev, "You don't have air rights? What if the Americans send in propaganda balloons!"

But in making an estimate of Khrushchev one should not pay too much attention to the antics and the effervescence. The chief elements in his character are robust common sense, ruthlessness, a drive to get things done, and, above all, optimism and confidence. He is supple, wily, and enjoys his job. Another quality is quickness. In India he promised to set up in

Moscow a school for the study of Indian languages; it was done at once. He is peppery, practical, and likes projects. John Fischer, editor of *Harper's Magazine*, served on the UNRRA mission to the Ukraine, and had opportunity to watch Khrushchev in action there; he was much struck with the way he seemed "to get his main fun out of life out of conceiving and pushing through a variety of grandiose schemes."[2] Finally, his political canniness and intuition are advanced. When the Israeli attack on Egypt got under way, Khrushchev told K. P. S. Menon, the Indian Ambassador, that the British were certain within a matter of hours to deliver ultimata to *both* Israel and Egypt. He had the future moves worked out. And, an hour later, news came through that the British had indeed done just what Khrushchev predicted. Mr. Menon was so impressed by this that he wondered if Khrushchev could possibly have had secret information about it, but he had not.

Khrushchev is extraordinarily articulate, and well informed on an abundant variety of matters. In London he attended several conferences at 10 Downing Street, thrashing out issues with members of the British government. Most of those present were flanked with advisers, and had large stacks of printed matter before them. Khrushchev talked, and talked well, without ever referring to a single note, or asking advice from anyone.

On the other hand, largely because he is a prisoner of dogma and therefore crazily suspicious of western methods and institutions, he can be remarkably obtuse at times. He was convinced for instance that the British could not possibly have undertaken the Suez adventure without American foreknowledge and approval; he flatly refused to believe Ambassador Bohlen when Bohlen told him that President Eisenhower knew nothing whatever of the British invasion plans, and was much surprised when presently the United States insisted on the cease-fire.

During his TV interview to the United States on June 2, 1957, Khrushchev said two things that, unless he is completely blind, a zealot beyond reason, he must know are not true. One was that the Kadar regime in Hungary had the support of the Hungarian people; the other was that there are no "contradictions" between the Russian government and Russian people, i.e., that no manifestations of dissent exist in the Soviet Union. This passage was cut when the text of the interview was published in Russia.[3] If Khrushchev really meant what he said, the inference can scarcely be avoided that

---

[2] *Harper's Magazine*, April, 1955.
[3] Partly because Khrushchev did not want to make a public issue with Mao Tsetung, the Chinese Communist leader. Mao had recently talked about contradictions in China. See Chapter XXIII below.

he knows little, if anything, of what is going on in Russia; if he did not mean it, one must assume that he thinks that everybody else in the world is an idiot, to accept such a misstatement. Of course the question about contradictions took him off base, and he could not easily have answered otherwise without confessing to the entire world that discontent *did* exist in Russia, something he would be loath to do. In any case, willful denseness, self-deception, and unwillingness to make any concession to reality (assuming that Khrushchev thought that he was telling the truth) are among the most disconcerting and dangerous of all Soviet characteristics. Why dangerous? Because self-deception may lead to blunders, and blunders are what may lead to war.

Another factor in Khrushchev's hold on power is that he has packed high positions with his own men. All leaders do this, of course, or try to. Most of the younger men in important party and government posts are ardent Khrushchev followers, like Kozlov, Kuzmin, and of course Kirichenko, proconsul for the Ukraine. Madame Furtseva is close to him. Luminaries like Aristov, Brezhnev, Belyayev, and Pospelov were his long-time subordinates in the party secretariat; ministers like Matskevich served under him in the Ukraine, and Serov and Dudorov, the bosses of the police, have for a long period been associated with him. Also, as we have just seen, Khrushchev is being pointedly attentive to representatives of the outlying nationalities —Kazakhs, Uzbeks, and the like.

It is somewhat premature to list Khrushchev's accomplishments, but already—since early 1955—he has changed Russia irreversibly. Two paramount events, the anti-Stalin speech to the Twentieth Congress and the ouster of Molotov, Malenkov, Kaganovich, and subsequently Marshal Zhukov, we shall allude to in later chapters. Meantime, whether he survives as top man or not, Khrushchev has given a new course to Soviet history by repudiating to an extent at least two basic Marxist tenets—that parliamentary government is never anything more than a mockery and that violence is essential for the transformation of society. Also, in rough summary, consider other points: (a) By enunciating the policy that countries can find their own individual ways to socialism Khrushchev indirectly released the Polish explosion. Of course he did not know that Poland would explode; he took a calculated risk.[4] (b) The Virgin Lands agricultural project, which may vastly augment Soviet farm production, and which has already brought 87,500,000 new acres to cultivation. (c) The decentraliza-

---

[4] I once heard him compare Sovietism to sausages. "You go to a shop. . . . Everybody wants his own kind."

tion of industry program, which, if it works, will transform the face of
Soviet economy. (d) The tentative return, after the Stalinist terror, to what
is known as "socialist legality."

                                    *

Much talk attends Khrushchev's drinking habits, and, indeed, he drinks
a lot. Once at a reception I saw him sip eleven glasses of champagne; then
he switched to tomato juice. But it is certainly not true that he is drunk
most of the time, or has to be carried out feet-first from parties. He is
convivial and, like most Russians, enjoys alcohol and has a robust capacity
to absorb it; but he is not an alcoholic.

He had too much to drink, and no mistake about it, during the festivities
in Moscow attending the visit of General Nathan F. Twining in July, 1956,
and when, after a banquet with Tito in Yugoslavia, he promised the American correspondents visas to Russia "the next day"; he was *not* drunk, contrary to most talk, when at a celebrated dinner party in London he was
scandalously rude to his Labour party hosts. One story is, however, that
he had never had Scotch whisky before, and underestimated its authority.
All in all, alcohol is not so much of a problem to Khrushchev as it is to
several of his colleagues on the Presidium, notably Bulganin.

Khrushchev likes to live well, by Soviet standards, and John Fischer, in the
article cited above, mentions that when he was running the Ukraine he had
four houses at his disposal—one in Kiev, one in Moscow, a *dacha* in the
country, and a vacation place in the Crimea. When he gave a dinner
party, it was elaborate, with each guest being served individually by a waiter
in livery; dinner would last from eight in the evening until two the next
morning, with toasts aplenty. On outdoor occasions, Mr. Fischer records, Khrushchev wore a workman's cap to symbolize his fellowship with
the proletariat, but this was specially tailored, out of cream-colored linen,
to match his suit. A factor intensifying his provincialism, peasant outlook,
and rude *hetman* manners was that, until he reached the top, he had never
traveled, and knew nothing at firsthand of the world outside Russia. Ignorance of the external world is, let me repeat, probably the most menacing
as well as exasperating of contemporary Soviet qualities. Since 1954 he has
traveled widely, but whether his sojourns have broadened him may be
doubted; travelers with an *idée fixe* do not as a rule see much beyond
their *idée fixe*. But at any rate Khrushchev (usually in company with Bulganin) visited Czechoslovakia and China in 1954, Yugoslavia, Switzerland,

East Germany, Afghanistan, Burma, and India in 1955, Poland several times, the United Kingdom in 1956, and Finland, Czechoslovakia, and East Germany again in 1957. He would dearly like to be asked to visit the United States.

His wife, a pleasant-faced, plump short woman, is seldom seen. She did, however, appear in Moscow recently as a guest at, of all things, a British fashion show. She was well dressed and looked like the kind of nice retiring woman whom one might meet at a garden party at an English rural vicarage. The Khrushchevs have several daughters and had two sons, but one was killed in the war. This boy had been severely wounded and broke out of the hospital against orders to rejoin the front, and then lost his life at Stalingrad Khrushchev's other boy, Sergei, about twenty-two, is studying at Moscow University. Khrushchev took him to London with him. He keeps company with the daughter of the celebrated airplane designer, A. N. Tupolev.

Jokes about Khrushchev have wide subterranean currency. Most are variants of the standard jokes one always hears about totalitarian leaders. For instance when a theater is named for Khrushchev in Leningrad, its repertory will consist exclusively of *Much Ado About Nothing*. Stamps bearing his portrait have been withdrawn from circulation ostensibly because the glue won't stick; the real reason is that people affixing them to letters spit on the wrong side of the stamp.

Life Line of the "First Equal"

In most respects Khrushchev's career follows the familiar—even blatantly trite—Soviet pattern. Peasant stock; little formal education; worker with his hands; then party activity and advance by slow stages. Nikita Sergeyevich Khrushchev was born on April 17, 1894, in Kalinovka, a village near Kursk, one of the oldest towns in southern Russia. His father was a miner and shepherd, and he himself, after working on a farm as a boy, became a pipefitter in a Donbas mine. This was before the October Revolution (1917), and, years later, he told a Chinese delegation in Moscow as a matter of casual interest that as a young man he had "worked at capitalist enterprises, participated in strikes, and negotiated with capitalists."

He joined the Communist party in 1918, immediately after the Revolution, and was quick-witted enough to gain attention; party officials took him off manual work, and saw to it that he got some schooling. In 1922, after the civil war, he was sent to the Workers School at the Donets Industrial

Institute and in 1929, aged thirty-five, he entered the Stalin Industrial Academy (now known as the Moscow Industrial Academy) in Moscow, for further study. This—picking out promising men, even when over thirty, and giving them opportunity for specialized adult education—happens all the time in the Soviet Union, and is a noteworthy characteristic.

We have not the space to trace his political career in detail. Again, the pattern is familiar. He rose in the party hierarchy and in the mid-1930's, as a Kaganovich protégé, became Secretary of the Moscow District Party Committee and, very important, a member of the Central Committee of the Party. In 1939 he reached the top, and became a full member of the Politburo (Presidium), a position he has held ever since. He was the first man ever to be admitted to the Politburo who came into the party after the Revolution, and, as such, symbolized the new generation of leaders who had no record of pre-Soviet conspiracy or activity. He is "totally a product of the Soviet era."[5]

For a time he was party headman in the Ukraine, and also in Moscow; he was commissioned as a lieutenant general on the outbreak of World War II and took active part in the defense of Stalingrad after fighting against the Germans in the Ukraine; he helped, in the Soviet idiom, "to quell discontent" in the Ukraine after the war, when the retreating Germans left drought and famine in their wake. What this means in fact is that he superintended the infamous purges that wiped the Ukraine clear of opposition to the Stalinist regime. He moved on to Moscow in time, and played a leading role in its restoration. But his major interest, aside from politics and the party, has always been the peasantry; his talk is full of quaint peasant phraseology, and the saying is that he never makes a speech without referring to wheat or corn.

These are extracts from remarks Khrushchev made to a conference of "farm personnel" in Gorky early in 1957, when it might be thought that he would have other things to think about. That he should lecture peasants about potatoes is very typical:

> I would advise you all to sow corn by hand . . . Mark off the land, and put fertilizer on it. . . . Two or three grains of corn should be put in a hill and a handful of decomposed manure added. If you have no decomposed manure, add regular manure. . . .
> Potatoes should, of course, be planted by the square cluster [checkrow] method. . . . How was the square of 70 cm. by 70 cm. decided upon? I will disclose this secret to you. The square of 70 cm. by 70 cm.

[5] Fainsod, *op. cit.*, pp. 270-271.

was settled on because all our machines for the row planting of potatoes were designed for a distance of 70 cm. between rows. There is your scientific foundation. (*Stir in the hall.*)

I consider that for potatoes the square could be reduced to 60 cm. by 60 cm.

Voices: Correct.

In short, we must experiment. Whatever is advantageous, whatever gives the highest output is good. (*Applause.*) . . .[6]

In the speech at Leningrad (May 22, 1957) in which he promised that the Soviet Union would overtake the United States in meat, butter, and milk production by about 1960, he took time out to tell his audience:

I think it is wrong for the northwestern zone to cut down the planting of clover and timothy grass. Yours is a flax growing zone but you will not have good flax harvests if you do not first sow clover. Clover is good fodder. It improves the structure and increases the fertility of the soil. Therefore the planting of clover must not be cut down arbitrarily. You know that even Chekhov's trouble maker[7] unscrewed one nut and left the other, but some among you unscrew all the nuts at once. (*Laughter.*)

I would recommend that in your zone you plant potatoes, corn, lupine, clover, vetch and other crops. More grasses should be stored. Look, in Northern Ireland meadow grass is put in silos and the silage fed to cattle and even to horses. Yours is a humid zone and you find it difficult to dry hay. By the time you dry it, half has been lost and half has rotted away. Would it not be better to cut the grass and put it in silos? Then you can keep all that you raise and feed it to cattle when it is in the best condition.

But politics were not neglected:

The imperialists have now thought up the following theory. They say: The Soviet Union now has the hydrogen bomb, so does the U. S. A., and so also now does Britain. Since the hydrogen bomb is a weapon of extraordinary power, neither side will use it, but they will scare each other with it, wage a cold war, and live on the principle of "neither war nor peace." We Soviet people are against this principle. We are for peace and the banning of atomic and hydrogen weapons. We appeal to the U. S. A. and Britain to join us in this. We do not intend to blow up the capitalist world with bombs. If we catch up to the U. S. level of per capita output of meat, milk and butter we shall

[6] *Pravda*, quoted by the *Current Digest of the Soviet Press*, May 22, 1957. Corn is a favorite preoccupation of Khrushchev's. Once he called corn the "queen of plants," a "sausage on a stalk."

[7] The troublemaker is a peasant who, in a Chekhov story, causes a railway wreck by taking a nut from a car and using it as a fishing sinker.

have shot a highly powerful torpedo at the underpinnings of capitalism. (*Applause.*)[8]

Khrushchev has never been a cabinet minister or head of administration in a government department. He is First Secretary of the Party and a member of the party Presidium, theoretically a *primus inter pares;* that is all, but it is enough.[9] Officially his correct mode of address is "Hero of Socialist Labor Nikita Sergeyevich Khrushchev, First Secretary of the Central Committee of the Communist Party of the Soviet Union." He has offices both in the Kremlin and the Central Committee headquarters on Kuibyshev Street near the Red Square; if you want to reach him quickly, this latter is the place to send a message. A bust of Gandhi stands on his desk.

One of the things that struck Americans most in Khrushchev's television interview on CBS was his remark that the grandchildren of his listeners would be living under socialism. This is an old line of his, and he really believes it, devoutly. He said the same thing to the British in London. In other words he expects the socialization of the world within about fifty years. After all about a third of it is socialized already. But this marks a recession in his thinking; a few years ago, he was wont to say that the *children,* not grandchildren, of present-day citizens of the West would be socialists. Even so, he is a passionate optimist, and his utter confidence in the future, not merely in himself, is what gives him his chief quality.

Khrushchev believes in peace and coexistence, if only because such concepts, in his opinion, favor his ultimate goal; he has even offered to negotiate the withdrawal of Soviet troops from eastern Europe, if United States troops withdraw from western Europe. But let no one think that he will withdraw one inch from several elements in Marxism. Some time ago a newspaperman asked him if the "new look" of Soviet foreign policy was genuine. He replied that he wanted peace, co-operation, and good relations with the West, yes, and then added what has become the most famous of all his off-the-cuff remarks: "If you think that peace means giving up socialism, you can wait until the shrimp learns to whistle."

A Look at Bulganin

Bulganin is an altogether different type of character. He is suave—almost courtly; his manners are graceful, and he bows to people like a courtier; he

---

[8] *Current Digest of the Soviet Press,* July 3, 1957.

[9] He was asked about future plans for the development of the Sputnik in October, 1957, and blandly replied that he could not answer because "he was not a member of the government."

acts as a Kentucky colonel might, and even looks like one, with thick silver hair parted far on the left side, tawny eyebrows, a silver mustache, and a small silver pointed goatee. That he should wear a beard is of some interest, if only because he is the only leading member of the hierarchy who does. Beards have been more or less taboo for Bolsheviks since the Revolution, although Lenin, as everybody knows, had one.[10] The reason is that the Communists, taking power, wanted to differentiate themselves as far as possible from the conventional look of Russian conspirators. To be clean-shaven was their badge.

I have heard it said that the dominant note in Bulganin's character is that he is not ambitious. I have also heard him called the most "ruthless" man in Russia, which is to say a lot. His main function is to be a kind of co-ordinator. He is not exactly a front man or greeter, despite his somewhat bourgeois exterior, but is "the chap who guards the machinery," an operator, a kind of business manager for everybody. A British politician who has met him several times says that, in organizing capacity, he resembles Lord Woolton, the well-known Conservative party leader.

He loves to drink, drinks a lot, and has a lively sense of humor, which is one reason why, until recently at least, he and Khrushchev got along so well together. They were as cozy as twin peanuts in a shell, but he has little of the occasional nastiness of Khrushchev. Their relations became knitted during the war, when Bulganin, Khrushchev, Zhukov, and another Soviet soldier, Marshal Konev, were all close collaborators in the defense of Moscow. Also Bulganin has a nice ironical touch in conversation. An American correspondent accosted him at a reception recently, saying that his permit to stay in Moscow expired that night, and that, if his visa were not extended, he would be in serious trouble. Bulganin interjected mildly, "You mean that after midnight you will be a criminal?" "Yes." Bulganin patted the correspondent on the cheek. "You have a nice criminal face," he murmured amiably, and walked away.

Bulganin is franker than many of his colleagues. For years the Swedish government was exercised over the disappearance of one of its diplomats, Raoul Wallenberg, in Hungary in 1944. The presumption was that he had been kidnaped by the Soviet police. The Wallenberg issue became a *cause célèbre* severely straining relations between Sweden and the Soviet Union. When the Swedish Prime Minister, Tage Erlander, visited Moscow in 1956 he brought up the matter to Bulganin personally. Bulganin spread out his hands

[10] As a matter of fact Lenin, in his earlier years, wore his beard intermittently. He was clean-shaven when he arrived in Petrograd to take charge of the Revolution.

and said, "If I knew what happened to Wallenberg, I would tell you. If he is alive, I will gladly deliver him to you. But I do not *know* what happened to him." Probably Bulganin was, as of that date, speaking the truth.[11] It is not uninteresting in this connection that Bulganin himself did not feel easy under the Stalin terror. Khrushchev mentioned in his speech to the Twentieth Congress that Bulganin had said to him, "It has happened sometimes that a man goes to Stalin on his invitation as a friend. And, when he sits with Stalin, he does not know where he will be sent next—home or to jail." It is also worth mention that Bulganin was himself a minor official of the secret police early in his career. He served for a time as chief of the transportation board of the Cheka, the execrable forerunner of the GPU, NKVD, and MVD.

Marshal Nikolai Alexandrovich Bulganin was born in Gorky, which was at that time Nizhni Novgorod, on the Volga, in June, 1895. The official story is that his father was a workman in a flour mill, and that young Nikolai, graduating from high school, worked for a time in the same mill; unofficial sources have it that his family was moderately wealthy, and of the middle class. In any case Bulganin joined the party in March, 1917, when he was twenty-two. He is no theoretician. Almost all his work has been strictly on the practical side. He has been a party organizer in Central Asia, director of the Electrotechnical Trust, a member of the Supreme Council of National Economy, Mayor of Moscow, President of the State Bank, Premier of the RSFSR, Minister of the Armed Forces of the Soviet Union, Minister of Defense, and, finally, Chairman of the Council of Ministers of the USSR, that is to say, Premier or Prime Minister, the post he holds today. He is the sixth prime minister in the forty years of Soviet history. I can think of only one other country—the Union of South Africa—that has had so few prime ministers in so long a period.

He held important military commands during the war, rose to be a full general, and was promoted to be a marshal in 1947.[12] He has been a member of the Central Committee of the Party since February, 1934 (he and Khrushchev came in on the same day), but he did not become a full member of

---

[11] Wallenberg was an official of the International Red Cross, who aroused local Soviet enmity by his work in Hungary getting destitute Jews out of the country. The mystery of his disappearance was finally cleared up in 1957. He had been kidnaped, and was held under secret arrest in Moscow till July, 1947, when he died in Lubyanka prison of a "heart attack." As a result of investigations ordered by Khrushchev and Bulganin, the police officers responsible (for this and other outrages) were shot.

[12] One source of his power is that, for some years, he controlled promotions in the army, and many Soviet officers in the middle ranges owe their ranks to him. Philip E. Mosely, *Russia After Stalin*, p. 10.

the Politburo until 1948, nine years after Khrushchev. One story is that Bulganin and Khrushchev became close when they worked together building the Moscow subway. But this could be said of almost everyone. *Everybody* built the Moscow subway.

Bulganin had some—but not much—firsthand experience of things abroad in the pre-Khrushchev era. One persistent rumor is that, as a boy, he worked for a time in a Swiss watch factory. He visited Germany, France, and England in 1936 as a member of a commission studying urban economy.

A large iron-gray building on Sverdlov Street, opposite the Hotel Moskva and near the Bolshoi Theater, houses the Council of Ministers. But Bulganin's own office is in the Kremlin. He does not, it is believed, live in one of the apartment-villas out in Lenin Hills, but has a five-room menage of his own in central Moscow, with a private elevator. His wife, Yelena Mikhailovna, is a schoolteacher, and still keeps up her classes in a Moscow secondary school; they have two children, Lev, a lieutenant colonel in the Air Force, and Vera, who is studying to be a doctor.

Bulganin's position has been gravely compromised since the shakeup in June, 1957, and his days as prime minister may be numbered. He made the piercing error of taking sides against Khrushchev when it appeared that Khrushchev was going to be beaten. For years the two were paired as equals when they traveled abroad or exercised official functions, but nowadays Khrushchev takes clear priority.

Five Who Fell

We must now, to fill in the record, inspect briefly the careers and personalities of the five men, three of whom were titans in the Soviet scheme of things, whom Khrushchev got rid of in June, 1957.[13]

The chief of these was Vyacheslav Mikhailovich Molotov. Until the moment of his fall, he was a personage of commanding prestige and influence. This was, in part, because of his tremendous experience and organizational gifts, in part because, aside from Kaganovich and Mikoyan, he was the only powerful Old Bolshevik left. Molotov was a revolutionary way back in 1905; he was a member of the original Petrograd Military Revolutionary Committee, and began to edit *Pravda* in 1912; he was the youngest man ever to become an alternate member of the Politburo (in 1921 at the age of thirty-one). Consequently, his word carried formidable weight in the party rank and file.

But, as the acknowledged leader of the Old Guard and a "Stalinist," his

---

[13] For the coup itself see Chapter XI.

power had waned as Khrushchev's grew. He was still a First Deputy Prime Minister when Khrushchev fired him, but his two administrative jobs were minor. Both derived from the crisis that gripped the Soviet Union after the Hungarian bloodbath. The Presidium decided (this is to foreshorten greatly a subject of touchy difficulty) that something must be done (a) to check discontent among students and intellectuals, and (b) to loosen up the bureaucracy. So to deal with the first point Molotov took over a supervisory function in the Ministry of Culture; to deal with the second he became Minister of State Control. This ministry may, or may not, be a dead letter, depending on who is running it (Stalin ran it once). Its main business is to see that the bureaucracy carries out directives from the government without fumbling or delay. It was abolished shortly after Molotov's dismissal. Previously Molotov had got himself into ideological trouble. He was careless or honest enough—grievous sin!—to say in a public address that "the *foundations* [italics mine] of a socialist society had been built in the Soviet Union." Of course this is the truth, inasmuch as the Soviet Union has by no means achieved full socialism. But it is the worst of heresies to admit this, since the official party line is that socialism, as a prelude to Communism, already exists. Molotov was forced to recant and apologize, but he stuck stubbornly to the truth as he saw it, and conceded only that "a socialist society has already *in the main* been built in our country."

Talking to him for a moment before the June coup, I felt that he was the most agreeable of all members of the Presidium. His appearance is chilling— the bulging round forehead, cold eyes blinking behind pince-nez, and the mustached mouth turned down almost in the shape of a fingernail—but not his manner, which is courteous, dignified, and even charming.[14]

Sir Winston Churchill wrote of Molotov once, "In the conduct of foreign affairs Mazarin, Talleyrand, and Metternich would welcome him to their company if there be another world to which Bolsheviks allow themselves to go." John Foster Dulles has stated, "I have seen in action all the great international statesmen of this century. . . . I have never seen such personal diplomatic skill at so high a degree of perfection as Mr. Molotov's." Another view is that of Governor Averell Harriman, who said, when Molotov was dismissed, "I have been looking forward to it [the dismissal] for sixteen years," adding that as long as Molotov had any influence in the Kremlin

---

[14] Also he has considerable wit. Once, early in the war, Molotov visited Berlin and had to take refuge, with Ribbentrop, in a shelter during a heavy raid by the Royal Air Force. Ribbentrop had just told him eloquently that Great Britain was "finished." Molotov turned to him dryly with the words, "In that case why are we in this shelter?"

"there was no possibility of agreement with the Soviet Union on political questions."

Molotov's wife is Jewish, by name Pauline Zhemchuzhina; she has one brother living in Israel, and another in Bridgeport, Connecticut. Mme. Molotov had a busy career as a business woman—first in the cosmetics trust and then the fish industry; the little story was that she made the fish smell like cosmetics, and vice versa. She came into disfavor in the last days of Stalin, and was exiled to Central Asia. Personal items of this kind make astonishingly little difference in the Soviet Union. The fact that his wife got into trouble did not, so far as anybody knows, damage Molotov's prestige with Stalin, nor did it even faintly tempt Molotov himself to leave the government. This is a regime, we know, almost totally devoid of individual human values, as the West understands the term. A cabinet minister can still hold his job after his brother has been shot. (This happened under Stalin.) A man can still work for the secret police after the secret police have executed his own father. (This happened, too.)

Nineteen towns and other places in the USSR were named for Molotov in the course of his long career, including Perm in the Urals, which has a population of more than 500,000. Laboriously, the names are being changed. Even the passenger liner *Molotov* has been renamed the *Baltika. Sic transit gloria.* As a result of the confusion attending such changes the Soviet government decreed late in 1957 that henceforth no towns or institutions shall be named for living personages, a sensible decision.

＊

Lazar Moiseyevich Kaganovich, another titan and one of the most picturesque of old-line Bolsheviks, was the only Jew on the Presidium. He has— or had—impressive force, animation, and volubility. When I met him, before his fall, he lectured me roundly about the "lies" of the American press, and then asked if I knew George F. Kennan, the former American Ambassador to the Soviet Union. He added, with a florid gesture, that it was Kennan's grandfather who had made him a revolutionist. Actually Kaganovich was referring to a George F. Kennan who was not the present Kennan's grandfather, but his grandfather's cousin. This elder Kennan did indeed visit Russia before the Revolution and wrote a book about the Czarist terror, *Siberia and the Exile System,* that had a strong influence on Russian youth at the time.

Kaganovich, who had the reputation of being the best administrator in the Soviet Union, never had much time for purely intellectual pursuits but, like almost all Communist leaders, thinks of himself as a good theoretician. Recently a British student of philosophy called on him, and was astonished when Kaganovich reeled off the names of obscure philosophers of various breeds and schools. The Englishman asked about contemporary Soviet philosophers, and said casually that he would like to meet some. "I will bring you twenty—thirty—forty!" Kaganovich boomed with enthusiasm. The British student, having a vision of dozens of elderly savants being rounded up and produced for display in an open truck or something of the sort, politely declined the offer.

Many years ago, Kaganovich read that, during the American depression, city streets after a heavy snowfall were cleared by men with shovels, instead of machines, in order to give employment. His comment: "Why not remove the snow with teaspoons, and thus employ thousands more?"[15] For years, Kaganovich was given the toughest, hardest jobs. He has at one time or another been in charge of transportation, heavy industry, the oil industry, and the building materials industry. When he was deposed in 1957, he was a first deputy premier in charge of no fewer than twenty-four different industrial ministries.

Kaganovich came up from nothing. He was born in 1893 in a village near Kiev, and never had any education beyond two years in a primary school. He worked as a tanner in a shoe factory, and became a shoemaker. And now he is down to nothing.

*

The next most important of the Khrushchev victims, Georgi Malenkov, was, or is, pre-eminently a creature of the bureaucracy, a manipulator, a specialist in party affairs. He was Stalin's principal private secretary for years, and as such had unexampled access to the party apparatus. He was also a chief intermediary between Stalin and much unpleasant business; he worked closely with Nikolai I. Yezhov, chief of the secret police during the purges of 1936-38, when the Stalin terror reached its most fantastic, grisly intensity. During this period fifty-five of the seventy-one members of the Central Committee of the Party disappeared, and no fewer than six members of the Politburo.

Subsequently came the so-called "Leningrad Case." One of Malenkov's closest rivals in the hierarchy, and the man who, on points, seemed to be

[15] *Duranty Reports Russia,* p. 356.

the most likely successor to Stalin, was Andrei A. Zhdanov, party boss in Leningrad. Zhdanov, a fantastic character, was the son of a priest; he died (a natural death) in 1948. Soon Zhdanov men, vulnerable now that their leader was dead, began to disappear. Two of these were among the most important men in the Soviet Union at that time, Nikolai A. Voznesensky, a brilliant and promising young man who was a member of the Presidium and chief of Soviet planning, no less, and A. A. Kuznetsov, a secretary of the party. They left their homes for their offices one fine day, and were never seen again. The equivalent in America would be the disappearance, without warning or trace, of, let us say, Harold Stassen and Sherman Adams. No announcement was ever made about Voznesensky's fate. He never had a trial, not even a bogus trial. Stalin's police chief at the time, Beria, of course had a hand in this. Khrushchev and Malenkov managed, with help from the army, to get rid of Beria after Stalin's death. Then the Leningrad case was pried open and, in 1954, several important police officials were shot, charged with having conspired to put leaders of the "Leningrad group" to their death. Now Khrushchev accuses Malenkov of having been party to the whole affair whereby Voznesensky and others were wantonly liquidated.

When Malenkov visited London early in 1956, he was asked frankly at a press conference "if he felt any sense of guilt" for his part in the Stalin purges. He replied, "Under collective leadership we always feel responsible for the shortcomings and errors we have made." At this same time a British political personage was bold enough to tell him that he was an object of particular interest to the British public, if only for the fact that he was a Soviet prime minister who lost his job and yet survived. Malenkov replied seriously, "I represent the new Russia. We do not shoot people any more." This sentence has an odd ring today. Mr. Malenkov has not been shot—at least at the moment of writing—but he is not representing the new Russia in the Kremlin any longer.

Malenkov was all odds the Soviet chieftain best liked and most admired by the foreign diplomatic corps in Moscow, during the period of his prime ministership and after. Khrushchev, people said, was a checkers player; Malenkov was a chess player. Khrushchev led with a fist; Malenkov with his mind. He had a broad range of thought, did not seem to be blinded by ideology, and was sophisticated; I heard observers in a good position to know say that he was the *only* leading Russian who comprehended the western point of view, and with whom Europeans could talk on European terms.

He is certainly an odd-looking character, short and fat, with a face like a three-quarter moon under a flat cloud of black hair. He is somewhat sensitive about his weight. Usually, like Stalin but unlike anybody else at the top, he wore a Russian blouse buttoned to the neck, rather than conventional western dress. He almost never went to the diplomatic parties in Moscow, and had never set foot outside the Soviet Union until a visit to Poland in 1947, when he helped set up the Cominform. Russians admire the purity with which he speaks Russian. One odd point is that he is a passionate admirer of the poetry of Robert Burns.

Georgi Maximilianovich Malenkov was born in 1902 in Orenburg, which was renamed Chkalov in honor of the Soviet airman, V. P. Chkalov, who flew to the United States (1937) by way of the North Pole. Orenburg is in the lower Urals, in the heart of the old Cossack country, and has a strong romantic tradition.[16] Nobody knows for sure, but Malenkov probably came from a middle-class family; he went to a technical school, and studied to be an electrical engineer. His wife, whom he met as a student, *is* an electrical engineer; in fact, she is (or was) director of one of the largest electronics institutes in Moscow.

After Stalin's death Malenkov was the only person in Soviet history except Lenin and Stalin to be both prime minister and party boss. But he did not hold the secretaryship of the party for more than a few weeks; later Khrushchev took it. He remained prime minister for almost two years, until February, 1955, when Bulganin replaced him, and he became Minister of Electric Power Stations. Malenkov lost the prime ministership partly, at least, by reason of a dispute over consumer goods. He wanted, with certain reservations, to give the people substantially more in the form of pots and pans and the like, whereas Khrushchev at that time insisted on keeping most emphasis on heavy industry. Malenkov's chief achievement as prime minister, in which Khrushchev shared, was the evolution whereby Russia is no longer overtly ruled by terror, although terror certainly still exists. He put the old-line cops out of business, even though his own history was inextricably mixed up with them.

*

Shepilov's days of grandeur did not last long. Outside the party, he was almost completely unknown until he succeeded Molotov as foreign minister in June, 1956; he held the post only until February, 1957, when he was replaced by Gromyko. Then, in the June coup, he lost whatever other jobs

[16] Edward Crankshaw in the *New York Times*, June 19, 1949.

or position he may have retained, and disappeared into limbo. But he was dismissed "without condemnation," and may come back. Even while he was foreign minister, there were those in Moscow who called Shepilov a "torrential false alarm." He loves to talk. He is a big, dark, tousle-haired man, and has been nicely described as a "St. Bernard without the brandy flask."

Nobody knows much about the beginnings of Dmitri Trofimovich Shepilov, except that he was born in the Caspian area in 1905. He may have Asian blood, but he looks like an Italian poet. His history is that of a fantastically doctrinaire intellectual, who worked largely in propaganda fields. Shepilov's first big job came in 1949, when he was made director of *Agitprop*, the propaganda division of the Central Committee of the Party. Then, like a good many other Soviet leaders major and minor (Molotov, Radek, Bukharin, Suslov, Pospelov, Ilyichev) he became editor of *Pravda*, and thus was the chief propagandist of the realm.

His opinion of the United States reflects the general view of Soviet leaders, but is perhaps more sharply expressed: "In that bastion of the capitalist world, the United States of America, prominent government leaders and their spiritual armor-bearers are compelled to cover up the senile and rotting body of capitalism with a 'popular' toga."

I shall risk another paragraph about Shepilov, even if he is out of power today, to demonstrate once more how extraordinarily versatile as well as industrious Soviet leaders have to be. Usually, perhaps because there are not enough men to go around, they hold two or three jobs at once. Shepilov was a specialist in agricultural economics, ran a collective farm, and was an editor of the Great Soviet Encyclopedia. He wrote an official textbook on political economy, taught at the Soviet Agricultural Academy, and became—a big jump—Deputy Public Prosecutor for Siberia. Also he served as an official of the old People's Commissariat of Workers and Peasants Inspection, became a director of the Academy of Sciences, and was made a major general during the war. As chairman of the Foreign Affairs Commission of the Soviet of Nationalities, he led several important missions to China and Yugoslavia, and meantime served as a deputy to the Supreme Soviet and was one of the six party secretaries. He is the author of more than fifty books. Even so, his mind is nailed tight shut.

*

Maxim Z. Saburov was also a First Deputy Prime Minister, one of the big planning despots, and a full member of the Presidium. Indication came, however, that all was not going smoothly with him when, in a shakeup in December, 1956, he was dismissed from his post as chairman of the State Economic Commission, in charge of short-term planning. Saburov, a mechanical engineer by profession, started work for the old *Gosplan* (State Planning Commission) as far back as 1938, and was its chairman for several terms. He was the only member of the old Presidium who spoke tolerable English, and has visited the United States. His personality is somewhat dim. He was born in 1900 in the Ukraine of a worker's family, and started life as an agricultural laborer and apprentice locksmith, finally becoming a graduate engineer at thirty-three. His rise then was swift, as has been his fall.[17]

Zhukov Dethroned

On October 26, 1957, as these pages went to press, the sensational news came that Marshal Georgi Konstantinovich Zhukov, boss of the Red Army, had been deposed as Minister of Defense. A week later he was removed from his membership in both the Central Committee of the Party and the Presidium. Zhukov's dismissal came without warning, immediately after his return from a brief official visit to Yugoslavia and Albania, and was totally unexpected. Very complicated elements enter into this story. One theory is that Khrushchev got rid of Zhukov because the stout Marshal had become too big for his boots. Another is that a cabal within the Soviet Army itself had for some time been building up against him. In any case the decision to remove a personage so massively important as Zhukov could not have been taken lightly, and must have been made with extreme suddenness. His prestige when he left Russia for Yugoslavia a few weeks before was, according to good evidence, as high as it had ever been. As of the moment of writing his subsequent fate is unknown, but Khrushchev has announced that he is in good health, is taking a holiday, and will be given some job commensurate with his abilities.

Zhukov, sixty, robust, and young for his years, was called the "best" man in the Soviet Union when we were there. One diplomat told me, "Zhukov is the only man high up who tells the truth. He may evade a question, but he will not lie." He had the friendliest, heartiest smile of any of the leaders we met, and otherwise looked as blunt as a bollard in the Venice lagoon. On his thick chest reposed eight solid ridges of decorations, below no fewer than three of the squat scarlet-and-gold medals that are the supreme Soviet

[17] But he was not accused of antiparty conspiracy, as were the other deposed leaders, and presently he re-emerged in a minor job.

badge of distinction. Zhukov was, at that time, the only man in the USSR with three.

As Minister of Defense, he was in charge of the Soviet Air Force and Navy as well as Army, and was generally thought to be the most powerful personage in Russia after Khrushchev. Some people thought that he was *more* powerful than Khrushchev. They were wrong.

Zhukov became a candidate member of the Presidium in February, 1956, and a full member in June, 1957, the first professional soldier in Soviet history to reach this position. (Voroshilov and Bulganin are not military men by career.) Even before he was admitted to full membership, his counsel counted for a great deal. It is doubtful if Khrushchev would have been able to survive the challenge to his leadership in June if Zhukov had not stepped in and thrown the weight of the army on his side. This makes it all the more remarkable that, four short months later, Khrushchev should have found it necessary to get rid of him.

Zhukov was accused of "antiparty" maneuvering within the army. But he was, and is, an ardent and convinced Communist; he became a party member when he was a boy, back in 1919, and has been a good party man ever since. He may—possibly—have been guilty of "antiparty" tendencies, but this does not mean he was not loyal to the regime. Anybody disgraced in the Soviet Union is always accused of being "antiparty"; this is the sin of sins, which justifies any punishment. Also Zhukov was charged with "adventurism" in foreign and military affairs, and even of having encouraged his own "glorification."[18] These alleged derelictions are probably what broke him. He did not show the "Communist modesty" now demanded of everybody—in other words he was making trouble, although the story that he was actively plotting against Khrushchev is probably not true.

Zhukov took Khrushchev's side in June because he much preferred Khrushchev's progressivism to the Molotov-Kaganovich stand-pat line. Also he liked Khrushchev because he hated Stalin, and Khrushchev was the man who unmasked Stalin at the Twentieth Party Congress. Stalin, who was jealous of Zhukov, humiliated and exiled him after the war. It was Khrushchev who brought Zhukov back. And now it is Khrushchev who dismisses him—the greatest military hero in the Soviet Union, its "savior," and the most popular man in Russia! It doesn't seem to make sense. But it does—if it is firmly kept in mind that under Khrushchev, as under Stalin, *nobody* who gathers too much power or glamour on his own is likely to survive. If the October episode proves anything, it is that the *party* still runs the Russian

[18] Max Frankel in the *New York Times*, November 5, 1957.

state, and that Khrushchev runs the party.

Zhukov was born in a village near Moscow, of peasant stock, on December 2, 1896; he was an apprentice furrier by trade. He was drafted into the Czarist Army in 1915, and served as a cavalryman in the Novgorod Dragoons. Came the Revolution and civil war, and he at once jumped camp and joined the Red Army. He was picked to get special education at the Frunze Military Academy[19] in Moscow, and spent some time in Germany as a student officer, in the period when the Red Army and Reichswehr were collaborating closely. What he learned of German methods served him well later. He saw something of the Spanish Civil War as a Russian "observer," and distinguished himself in a war nobody ever remembers these days, the one fought between the Soviet Union and Japan in Mongolia in 1939. Luckily for the Soviet Union, he survived the prewar Stalin purges. No fewer than 350 of his fellow Red Army generals were not so lucky. Zhukov's great days began when Hitler attacked the Soviet Union. He helped save Moscow in the first onslaught in 1941, and after that his advance was rapid; he fought at Stalingrad, and was commander-in-chief of the forces that took Berlin in 1945.[20]

General Walter Bedell Smith said about Zhukov in *My Three Years in Moscow* that he "would be a great man in any country." General Eisenhower said of him, "To no one man do the United Nations [that is, the western allies] owe a greater debt than to Marshal Zhukov." A more critical view is that of Sir David Kelly, a former British Ambassador to Moscow, who wrote recently, "He incarnates the military doctrine of the Red Army which is based on territorial expansion, the necessity of a despotically planned economy, the explicit conviction that military art is the application of the party line in military matters, and the certainty that all wars spring from class war and are therefore totally unavoidable until the last capitalist society has been liquidated."[21]

Zhukov gives the over-all impression of being a reasonable man, but, like most pillars of the Soviet regime, he talks wild nonsense on occasion, and

[19] Named for Mikhail Frunze, an Old Bolshevik who succeeded Trotsky as War Commissar in 1925 and died shortly thereafter.

[20] In several characteristics, particularly his taciturn, bull-like quality, the Marshal resembles the Russian general Kutuzov, whom readers of *War and Peace* will remember. Like Kutuzov, he is of the earth earthy. In fact, Stalin during the course of the war grumbled about one of his predilections, saying scornfully that before each battle Zhukov was wont to take up a handful of earth, sniff it, and say, "We can begin the attack," or, on the other hand, "The planned operation cannot be carried out." This story, which was told by Khrushchev to the Twentieth Congress, has the authentic Kutuzov touch.

[21] London *Observer*, July 7, 1957.

may even believe in what he is saying. It is, for instance, his firm opinion that, during the Suez crisis, "reactionary American imperialists stood behind France, Britain, and Israel and incited the aggressors and supported them in every way." Also Zhukov was largely responsible for the Soviet decision to intervene in Hungary.

Eisenhower and Zhukov

Eisenhower and Zhukov got on well during the war, and the American President on several occasions expressed a high opinion of the Soviet Marshal, before his fall. Eisenhower found Zhukov to be a "confirmed Communist" but a sincere and "honest" man, and said that they had seen "eye to eye" in their administration of Berlin in 1945, when he was convinced that Zhukov was "intensely devoted to . . . good relations between the United States and the Soviet Union." For a period the two men exchanged personal letters, and met again at the Summit Conference in Geneva in 1955.

Zhukov, when he was visiting India early in 1957, was asked by Indian journalists his opinion of Eisenhower. He replied bluntly, "Eisenhower is my old friend—as a soldier. I do not know what is left of him . . . whether he is the same man."[22]

On July 17, 1957, at a press conference in Washington, Edward P. Morgan of the American Broadcasting Company asked President Eisenhower if, in view of the changes in the Kremlin leadership, he might invite Zhukov to visit the United States. Eisenhower's reply deserves quotation at length:

> Certainly, the changes in the Kremlin are the result of some fundamental pressures within the country. Now, apparently the group that went out were those that were, could be called, the traditionalists. They were the hard core of the old Bolshevik doctrine, whereas those that stayed and seem now to be in the ascendancy are apparently those who have been responsible for decentralization of industrial control, all that sort of thing.
>
> Therefore, the idea that they are trying to be flexible, to meet the demands, the aspirations, requirements of their people, I think seems to be sound. Now, you referred to General Zhukov, and I must say that during the years that I knew him I had a most satisfactory acquaintanceship and friendship with him. . . .
>
> We had many long discussions about our respective doctrines. I think one evening we had a three-hour conversation. We each tried to explain to the other just what our systems meant, our two systems

[22] A. M. Rosenthal in the New York Times, February 10, 1957.

meant, to the individual, and I was very hard put to it when he insisted that their system appealed to the idealistic, and we completely to the materialistic, and I had a very tough time trying to defend our position, because he said:

"You tell a person he can do as he pleases, he can act as he pleases, he can do anything. Everything that is selfish in man you appeal to him, and we Russians tell him that he must sacrifice for the state."

He said, "We have a very hard program to sell." So what I am getting at is, I believe he was very honestly convinced of the soundness of their doctrine and was an honest man.

A few minutes later James Reston of the *New York Times* asked the President, "Do you want to leave the inference that it is difficult to defend the proposition that democracy is a more idealistic system than Communism?" Mr. Eisenhower's reply did not seem, in the view of many, altogether adequate:

I said when you are talking with the Communists you find it is a little difficult, for the simple reason that you say a man can earn what he pleases, save what he pleases, buy what he pleases [in the United States]. . . . Now, I believe this, because I believe in the power for good of the, you might say, the integrated forces developed by 170,-000,000 free people. But he says that "We say to the man 'You can't have those things. You have to give them to the state,' " and this is idealistic because they ask these people to believe that their greatest satisfaction in life is in sacrificing for the state, giving to the state.

In other words, he takes the attitude that they don't force this contribution, they are teaching a people to support that contribution. So, when you run up against that kind of thing, look, Mr. Reston, I think you could run into people you would have a hard time convincing that the sun is hot and the earth is round. I don't say that I don't believe it. I am merely saying that against that kind of a belief you run against arguments that almost leave you breathless, you don't know how to meet them.[23]

It became known later that, as a result of these and other remarks by Eisenhower, the Kremlin sounded out Washington as to the possibility of a visit by Marshal Zhukov to the United States. Mr. Dulles rejected the idea.

Malinovsky and the Army

Marshal Rodion Ya.[24] Malinovsky, who succeeded Zhukov as Minister of Defense, is a tough, squat, pug-nosed man of fifty-nine, who has been a

[23] *New York Times,* July 18, 1957.
[24] For Yakovlovich.

professional soldier since the age of sixteen. He is certainly the only minister of defense in Soviet history, or for that matter the only officer of consequence in the whole Soviet military establishment, who ever (a) fought beside Americans at Château-Thierry and elsewhere in France in World War I, and (b) served a term in the French Foreign Legion. When the Czarist forces fighting the Germans on the eastern front collapsed in 1917, Malinovsky, who had run away from home to join the army, managed to get all the way from Odessa to France—via Siberia, Singapore, the Indian Ocean, and the Mediterranean. His motivation was simple: he wanted to keep on fighting the Germans. At that time a Russian brigade was in service in France. Malinovsky, now aged nineteen and a corporal, joined it. He fought in France till the Armistice in 1918, and then joined the French Foreign Legion. Meantime, news came of the Bolshevik Revolution in Russia. Malinovsky decided that it was time to return to his own country. He made his way back to Russia, overcoming obstacles almost inconceivable, and joined the Red forces fighting the Whites in the civil war. Almost at once he made a name for himself, rose to be an officer, joined the Communist party, and became a violently dedicated Communist.

Malinovsky, like so many of the men who count in the Soviet Union today, comes from the Ukraine. He was born in Odessa in 1898. He had no education beyond primary school, and began to work for a living as a farm laborer at the age of twelve. He is a Hero of the Soviet Union, and has been decorated with the Order of Lenin (not the chief Soviet decoration, but an important one) no fewer than five times. Little is known of his personal life, except that he was married in 1925, and has two sons.

After the civil war Malinovsky decided to make the Red Army his career. He became a machine gun instructor and battalion commander. His superiors saw that he was a youngster of exceptional grit, courage, and resource, and pulled him out of the ranks, to give him special training at the Frunze Military Academy. Then—the Russians always try to give their officers as varied an experience as possible—he was transferred from the infantry to the cavalry, and advanced rapidly. By 1940 he was a major general, and when the Nazis attacked the Soviet Union in 1941 he was a corps commander on the Bessarabian frontier. He acquitted himself well, and served in various capacities during the rest of the war—at Kharkov, Stalingrad, and elsewhere. Malinovsky, promoted to be a marshal in 1944, was commander of the Soviet forces which tore through the Balkans and took Budapest. He first came to Khrushchev's attention when the Germans were forced out of the Ukraine.

In the closing days of World War II Malinovsky served mostly in the Far East. He commanded the Sixth [Far Eastern] Army, which occupied Manchuria during and after the six-day war between the Soviet Union and Japan in August, 1945.

*

The question often asked, "How important is the army in running Russia?" is somewhat unreal. The Soviet Army, under Malinovsky or under anybody else, is part and parcel of the state, and has never been an independent source of power; it is a conscript army, composed of Soviet citizens who have been brought up under Communism, and is of course thoroughly indoctrinated. There is no officers' corps or clique like that in the old German Army that played politics on its own—maybe against the government. That could not happen in Russia unless an actual counterrevolution occurred, something almost inconceivable. On the other hand, if the Khrushchev administration should collapse or seem at any time to be on the point of disintegration, the army (or parts of it) might well step in to save the regime, or reconstruct it to its satisfaction.

Malinovsky is a member of the Central Committee of the Party, as are almost all army officers of exalted rank, but not of the Presidium. He may rise to this height later. The main thing to keep in mind is that, as of the moment at least, the party controls the army, not the opposite. If a military dictatorship should develop, it will probably be a military dictatorship *within* the party, made by party members.

CHAPTER VII

More Demigods and Thanes

The true leader must submerge himself in the
fountain of the people.
—VLADIMIR I. LENIN

... A night in Russia,
When nights are longest there.
—Measure for Measure, II, i

ALMOST everything about Mikoyan seems excessive—the sharpness and
glitter of his dark eyes, the flash of his clenched teeth, and the arch in his
nose, which looks like a small twisted club. He has an emphatic character,
with a famously barbed tongue, independence of mind (within limits), and
a disputatious manner. He dresses with a certain flamboyance, and one
visitor to Moscow, taking a good look at him, said, "A gangster in *two* silk
shirts!"

Mikoyan's chief quality is his glistening shrewdness. He is an Armenian,
and all Armenians are notoriously expert traders. He was, in fact, in charge
of the foreign trade of the USSR for many years, and had the reputation of
being the best negotiator in the country. Nobody has ever doubted his alertness, tenacity, and acute intelligence. Sometimes he is thought of as a kind
of court jester, or even clown, because he likes to kick up his shiny heels, and
it has been said that he manages to be on all sides of any given question, but
both these statements are misleading because they do not take account of his
essential deadly seriousness. Of course, all Soviet leaders have to be deadly
serious. Mikoyan is fascinating to watch at a reception—controlled, almost
sinister, but vibrant at the same time, with suppressed flashes of energy
rippling across his face. Before Khrushchev became well known for candor,
Mikoyan was supposed to be the only top-flight man who would answer

125

questions frankly. He knows all the double-talk, but sometimes cuts through it. When an Italian journalist asked him once why there was no freedom in the Soviet Union, Mikoyan snapped: "Because we cannot afford to give it."

He certainly has courage. Khrushchev told a little anecdote about him in the Twentieth Congress speech. Khrushchev had telephoned Stalin from the Kharkov front during a critical battle in World War II, appealing for a change of tactics and giving advice which Stalin rejected. The result was a very serious Soviet defeat. After the war, at a meeting of the Politburo, Mikoyan directly taxed Stalin with this, mentioning how unfortunate it was that Khrushchev's suggestions had not been adopted, and thus underlining Stalin's blunder. Stalin was furious. As a matter of fact, Mikoyan delivered at the Twentieth Congress a speech that paved the way for Khrushchev's, in which he was bold enough to say that there had been no vestige of socialist legality in the Soviet Union for twenty years. No such attack on the Stalin record had ever been voiced before.

Anastas Ivanovich Mikoyan had (like Lenin) an elder brother who was executed in his youth for revolutionary activity; this influenced him strongly. The two Mikoyans were members of a Communist group, known as the "Twenty-Six," leading Red forces in the Caucasus during the civil war. They were forced out of Baku and made their way across the Caspian to Krasnovodsk. Here they were caught by British contingents who had intervened on the white side. Mikoyan was sentenced to death by the British as a revolutionary agitator, but for some reason the sentence was not carried out. His brother was, however, with the rest of the Twenty-Six, shot. Mikoyan was born on November 25, 1895, in Sanain, a village in Tiflis province. He got a good education and, of all things, was graduated from the Armenian Theological Seminary in Tiflis in 1915; he intended to become a priest in the Nestorian Catholic faith. Stalin, too, a fellow Caucasian, was educated to be a priest. But theological works did not hold young Mikoyan long, and he joined the Communist party after graduating from the seminary. He rose swiftly, and, by 1917, when the Revolution broke out, was secretary of the Baku Party Committee. He is one of the few surviving Bolsheviks who joined the party before the Revolution and fought actively in the civil war.

After the war, his career follows the standard pattern. As a party organizer, he worked in Transcaucasia and the Volga regions. One of his biographies says, without elaboration, that he "took part in the elimination of Menshevik and Kulak elements" between 1922 and 1926. Mikoyan reached the Politburo as a candidate member in 1926, and became a full member in 1935. He has at one time or other been minister in charge of foreign and domestic trade, supplies, the food industry, agriculture, and grain and stock breeding. He was appointed Deputy Premier in 1937, and has been on the top leadership ever since. His importance is probably greater today than ever before, if only because the Khrushchev shakeup in 1957 brought in several unknown quantities to the Presidium, and broke its texture down. Old-timers like Mikoyan, who survived, are doubly counted on.

Mikoyan knows some English, and gets along well with westerners. Some years ago he led a Soviet mission to study food production and distribution in the United States. He has worked hard to introduce American techniques into the food and catering industries, sought to encourage canning and frozen foods, and is called "the father" of Soviet ice cream. He would like to have an automat, or at least a cafeteria, on every street corner. He likes women, and loves to dance.

Old-Timers in the New Guard

Kliment Yefremovich Voroshilov, the chairman of the Presidium of the Supreme Soviet of the USSR, has little serious importance these days, and is a figurehead. He is, in fact, close to being senile, but is affectionately regarded. He drinks. Once I saw him inadvertently get in the way when a photographer was trying to take a picture of Bulganin, and Bulganin gently pushed him aside, as one might push away a child.

Marshal Voroshilov has had a distinguished and honorable career. He went to work in a mine at the age of six, and the story is that he did not learn to read until he was twelve.[1] His father was a night watchman. He was born on February 4, 1881, in a village near Yekaterinoslav, now known as Dnepropetrovsk, and is partly Ukrainian. He became a fitter in a factory, and joined the old Social Democratic Labor party back in 1903. Legend says that he was arrested for the first time when he refused to take off his cap to a Czarist officer. For a time he was a mechanic in a locomotive works at Lugansk (now called Voroshilovgrad in his honor), and then in an arms factory at Tsaritsyn, a town known better under its present name of Stalingrad. He was imprisoned and exiled for revolutionary activity several times, volunteered for the Red Army after the Revolution, and rose fast. His military career was remarkable during the civil war, and he was a brilliant divisional commander. He became a member of the Central Committee of the Party in 1921, was named War Commissar in 1925, and has been on the Politburo uninterruptedly since 1926. He is the only contemporary Bolshevik in a high position who played

[1] "Voroshilov," by Glyn Roberts, London *News-Chronicle*, November 19, 1935.

an active role in the Revolution of 1905, when he was chairman of the Soviet of Workers' Deputies at Lugansk. He met Lenin for the first time at a party meeting in London in 1907. Stalin is supposed to have been there too.

One fantastic story is that, inadvertently, he caused Stalin's death. *France-Soir* recently published an article by its well-informed Russian specialist, Michel Gordey, to the effect that Stalin "died of a fit of rage" after a fierce encounter with the old, doughty Voroshilov. This was at the time of the notorious "Doctors' Plot." Nine prominent physicians, most of them Jewish, specialists at the very top of their profession, were arrested by Stalin's police in January, 1953, charged with attempts to poison members of the Presidium, whose regular medical attendants they were. Two were beaten to death. Nothing more shocking has been known in Russia since Ivan the Terrible. The charges were of course fraudulent, but Stalin took them seriously, and to punish the Jewish community and teach it a lesson, drew up a plan to banish *all* Jews in European Russia to Siberia. At a meeting of the Presidium Voroshilov was so enraged and revolted by this proposal, after Kaganovich and Molotov had been too timid to speak up, that he is supposed to have pulled his Communist party card out of his pocket, slapped it on the table before Stalin, and called out, "If such a step is taken, I would be ashamed to remain a member of our party." Stalin, black with rage, then shouted to Voroshilov, "It is I who will decide whether or not you can keep your card!" Came an uproar. Pandemonium spread. Stalin collapsed and crashed to the floor. The *France-Soir* story proceeds to say that Beria, who was present, danced around Stalin's prostrate form, crying gleefully, "We are finally free!" Then Stalin's daughter, Svetlana, forced her way into the room, and threw herself on her father's body. At this dramatic point Stalin opened one eye, "but could not speak." Beria, fearing that the dread dictator might recover, then dropped to his knees and hysterically kissed Stalin's hands. Doctors (presumably non-Jewish) arrived in haste, and Stalin was removed to his chambers. He never regained full consciousness.[2]

Blond, blue-eyed, with a tiny pursed mouth, Voroshilov looks like a cherub. He also resembles astonishingly the plasticine dolls, or puppets, which once adorned the cover of the magazine *Esquire*. His wife is, of all things, supposed to have been a countess, and for many years was an ornamental, stately leader of the Kremlin "aristocracy." One romantic legend is that Voroshilov, during the civil war, saved her in the nick of time from a firing

[2] *New York Times*, June 8, 1957, quoting *France-Soir*. Original source for this anecdote is supposed to be none other than Panteleimon K. Ponomarenko, a former Presidium member and Soviet Ambassador to Poland.

squad, whereupon their romance began.[3] One of his brothers-in-law, Alexander M. Gerasimov, is the dean of contemporary Soviet painters, responsible for many of the adulatory portraits of Stalin once seen everywhere.

Voroshilov may be old and befuddled, but he still represents his country on important ceremonial occasions. He went to China in the spring of 1957, and then made a state visit to Indonesia.

*

Another veteran is Nikolai M. Shvernik, boss of the trade unions for many years. He was chairman of the Supreme Soviet of the USSR before Voroshilov. Shvernik was born in Leningrad (then St. Petersburg) on May 19, 1888, the son of a doorman. He was orphaned as a child, and had only four years of schooling. Most of the men who run Russia, we hardly need point out, come of humble origins. Men who were workmen with their hands make this country work. Shvernik joined the Bolsheviks at seventeen, when he was a laborer in a metallurgical factory. For fourteen years, from 1930 to 1944, he was Secretary General of the All-Union Council of Trade Unions, and, close to Stalin, was the *only* member of the Trade Union secretariat to survive the great Yezhov purges. He has been an alternate or full member of the party Presidium since 1939, and also was for some years chairman of the Central Committee, a commanding post.

I saw Shvernik only once; he looks like a man who has gone through too much. His forehead and nose are parallel, as in a Greek head, but both are curiously short, or blunted. Shvernik knows a good deal about labor organization abroad, and is, like almost all Soviet leaders, a thoroughly able character.

*

Otto V. Kuusinen, born in 1881, is one of the last surviving members of the Bolshevik Old Guard. He is a Finn, and was formerly chairman of the Presidium of the Supreme Soviet of the Karelo-Finnish Soviet Socialist Republic. Of all the Soviet "presidents" he was the best known, after Voroshilov. When the Karelo-Finnish Republic was absorbed into the RSFSR in 1956 he was still allowed to keep his title as chairman of its Supreme Soviet, although this no longer existed. There were only fifteen Union republics, but sixteen chairmen.

Kuusinen is one of the "internationalists" of the old Communist move-

[3] Edward Crankshaw, *Russia Without Stalin*, p. 212.

ment and for eighteen years, from 1921 to 1939 when it ceased to exist, he was a secretary of the Comintern, or Third International, the first world-wide organization set up by the Bolsheviks with the aim of conquering the world for international socialism. As such, he was close to such celebrated Communist chieftains as Togliatti in Italy, Grotewohl and Ulbricht in Germany, Manuilsky in the Ukraine, Dimitrov in Bulgaria, Thorez in France and the malevolent Rakosi in Hungary. During the Soviet war against Finland in 1939, Kuusinen set up a short-lived "workers" government in Finland. A vivid glimpse of his harsh, implacable quality may be had from Ignazio Silone, in *The God That Failed*. All men in the Soviet Union of the rank of Kuusinen, no matter how doctrinaire, have force.

Furtseva and Pervukhin

Furtseva is the first woman in Soviet history to be a member of the Presidium. She is also a leading member of the party secretariat, and since 1954 has been first secretary of the Moscow city party committee, the first woman ever to hold this vital post. Madame Furtseva resembles nothing so much as a really first-rate YWCA secretary, or leader of some female military organization like the WACs. She is, however, burningly, blindingly intellectual. Her looks are pleasing, though she is stout; she has rich yellow blond hair done in a big twisted bun, apple cheeks, and fine, candid blue eyes. Every time I saw her she wore the same costume—a severe suit, with a neat white shirtwaist and a black string bow tie—and radiated euphoria and energy. Her husband is Nikolai Pavlovich Firyubin, a former Soviet Ambassador to Yugoslavia; they are believed to have two children.

Only three other women have, so far as I know, ever reached a rank equivalent to Madame Furtseva's in the Communist world. One is Ludmila Jankovcova, a member of the top-policy-making body in Czechoslovakia, and the other Madame Belishova, sometimes called the "empress" of Albania. Ana Pauker had a position in Rumania even more important, but has long since been stricken off the rolls.

Yekaterina Alexeyevna Furtseva was born in Kalinin province, near Moscow, in 1910; she came of a family of textile workers, and during the 1920's went to a factory school. Her career has been varied. Most Soviet careers are. For a time she was a student of aeronautics, and taught in the aviation technical school of the Civil Air Fleet. Also she was an instructress in the student youth section of the All-Union Komsomol Central Committee, and then, aged twenty-seven, went into the Institute of Fine Chemical Technology in

Moscow,[4] and was graduated in 1941 as a chemical engineer. Her party work has, however, been so arduous and continuous that she has had little opportunity to practice her profession. From the beginning, Furtseva was a passionately dedicated Communist. She joined the Komsomols at fourteen, and, before she was twenty, worked as a youth organizer in the Crimea, Kursk province, and elsewhere. She was received into the party in 1930, and, after twenty-two years of the hardest kind of work, became in 1952 a candidate member of the Central Committee.

On May Day, 1955, came an event in the Red Square which, for the Soviet Union, was spectacular. Madame Furtseva stood dutifully at the foot of the mausoleum, together with hundreds of other dutiful party members, as the annual parade got under way. Khrushchev, on top of the mausoleum, saw her in the crowd, and then publicly summoned her to join him and the inner core of the party elite, in their privileged position. She has been reviewing the parade from a privileged position ever since. Another thing sensational for the Soviet Union is that Madame Furtseva drives her own sports car, a fast little Zis-112, round and about Moscow. One of her recent public appearances (though not in this vehicle) was to dedicate Moscow's new skyscraper hotel, the Ukraine, in her capacity as head of the Moscow party committee. Her most important recent job has been to superintend the reorganization of Moscow industry.

After the Hungarian uprising, labor in Moscow showed a certain restlessness. Attempting to tranquillize the workers at one plant, Madame Furtseva made a speech and asked for questions. A worker rose from the floor and asked what her salary was—not the kind of question that is often asked. She did her best to avoid answering, but the heckler was persistent. Thereupon she admitted frankly that she got 18,000 rubles a month salary, plus "other emoluments" amounting to 12,600 rubles.[5] The worker asking the question probably got 800. Furtseva has traveled a good deal outside the Soviet Union, and has visited both London and Paris. She led a woman's delegation to Sofia, Bulgaria, in 1947, and in 1954 went with Khrushchev to Czechoslovakia. She accompanied Khrushchev, Bulganin and Mikoyan when they visited Mao Tse-tung in China, and was a member of subsequent Soviet delegations to Italy and Yugoslavia.

Pronouncements on theory by Communist leaders are often paralyzingly dull, and can be wearisome beyond belief; nevertheless, it is important to try

[4] We do not have to point out again that Soviet names of institutions are usually a mouthful.
[5] Frank Kelley, Paris Edition of the New York *Herald Tribune*, December 26, 1956.

to digest them from time to time, because Soviet orthodoxy, a bedrock source of strength to the regime, cannot be understood otherwise. Here is Madame Furtseva on democracy:

> The ideologists of imperialism are doing their utmost to blacken our system of government. . . . They have recently revived the old line, long since exposed by Marxism, that the dictatorship of the proletariat allegedly excludes democracy. Lenin has shown them that there is and can be no democracy pure and simple, no freedom pure and simple, but that there is bourgeois democracy and proletarian democracy. In countries where the principal means of production . . . are in the hands of capitalism, democracy and freedom have always been and remain to this day a reality to the exploiters and a deception to the exploited.
>
> Defenders of the capitalist order usually reduce democracy to a few formal aspects—the number of parties in the country, the existence of parliamentary opposition, etc. But the main aspect of democracy—the conformity of government policy with the interests of the masses—they prefer to disregard. Why do they act in this fashion? . . . Policy is determined not by the interests of the majority of the people, but by the interests of a puny handful of billionaires using the State apparatus for their enrichment. . . . Under a bourgeois democracy . . . the masses unfortunately are not in a position to give true expression to their will through state agencies.

Also:

> The reactionary forces of the capitalist world fear peaceful competition and international cooperation like the plague because they do not believe that they can win in such a competition. By following the policy of militarism in war, the arms race and preparations for military adventures—which fabulously enrich the capitalist monopolists while bringing the people privation and poverty—they hope to check the processes of historical development.[6]

All Soviet leaders take this line, wrapped around by clouds of fustian and mythology.

*

Another consequential dark horse, or white hope, is Mikhail Georgiyevich Pervukhin. Fishing around for potential candidates for top leadership in the Soviet Union is not easy; there are hosts of secondary figures almost completely unknown who may turn out to be important at any moment. The dynamics of succession is always through the party; when a person starts to

[6] *Current Digest of the Soviet Press,* May 22, 1957.

move up, this is not necessarily by reason of merit or pressure from below, but because he is the protégé of someone higher. Moreover the Soviet Union is a country where title, as such, does not necessarily mean power, and this makes it doubly difficult to assay the coming men. Also shifts are abundant, the turnover is prodigious, and secrecy is the prevailing rule. Recently a western government prepared a list of Soviet officials in important posts in October, 1952 whose present jobs, if any, are absolutely unknown, and it ran to no fewer than 294 names.

Pervukhin is at present a candidate member of the Presidium. Interestingly enough, he was demoted, not promoted, to this post. Until the 1957 coup he had been a full member and Khrushchev, so to speak, *half*-purged him; he was removed from various jobs and dropped to candidate membership, but he was not forced all the way out, and was not rebuked.

Pervukhin looks like a typical American small-town professor, with gold-rimmed spectacles, clean-looking wavy ginger hair, and one of the few good sets of teeth I saw in Russia. He has an academic manner, and is a pre-eminent example of the new "technical aristocracy" thrown up since Stalin's death. Born in 1904 in the Urals near Chelyabinsk, he was the son of a blacksmith. He joined the Bolshevik party at fifteen, became a news paperman in his youth, and, reaching Moscow, studied electronics at the Plekhanov Institute of National Economy. He has degrees in both chemical and electrical engineering, advanced to be a specialist in power supply, and rose quickly in the party, becoming a member of the Central Committee at the early age of thirty-five.

As a lieutenant general of the Engineer-Technical Service and Minister of Medium Machine Building, Pervukhin was in charge of Soviet atomic development for some years. He was also Minister for Electric Power Stations, the Electrical Industry, and the Chemical Industry at various junctures, a deputy to the Supreme Soviet, and leader of delegations to Finland and East Germany. What chiefly distinguished him, however, was his close association with national planning.

The story of Pervukhin's half-fall is complicated. We must go back to May, 1955, when the State Planning Commission (*Gosplan*), a body of supreme importance, was split into two halves, dealing respectively with short- and long-term planning. Saburov, mentioned in the preceding chapter, took the short-range job. Then in December, 1956, Pervukhin superseded him, becoming in effect Russia's economic "czar." But then came another shakeup, the *Gosplan* was reconstituted in something like its original form, and a man virtually unknown, by name Kuzmin, became its chairman, in charge of all planning operations. Concurrently came other intricate developments. Against Khrushchev's will a scheme for industrial reorganization was put forward by the Presidium which would have given very advanced powers to planner-technicians like Saburov and Pervukhin. This was at a time when Khrushchev's prestige was somewhat low. In March, 1957, on top again, Khrushchev reversed the December decisions and put into motion his own scheme for economic reorganization, which envisages complete decentralization of industry on a regional basis, with the old Moscow planners out. So Pervukhin lost his power.

Before his half-fall Pervukhin had generally been mentioned as a future successor to Bulganin as prime minister. As of today he is in charge of the Soviet foreign economic aid program.[7]

In the Cabinet

The Council of Ministers of the USSR, that is, the cabinet, is an altogether different body from the party Presidium, although several Presidium members are also ministers. In general, the cabinet has nothing like the prestige and authority of the Presidium.

Outside Russia, the best-known member of the cabinet is probably Andrei A. Gromyko, the Minister of Foreign Affairs. He is in fact, better known outside the Soviet Union than in. He is a distinct junior so far as party rank in the hierarchy is concerned, and did not become a full member of the Central Committee, that is, one of the people who really count, until as recently as 1956. He is not yet a member of the Presidium.

He was born in a village called Gromyki in White Russia, which was named for his family, on July 18, 1909. He studied at the Institute of Economics in Moscow, and planned to be a teacher; after holding a minor job in the Academy of Sciences for several years, he turned in 1939 to the foreign office, where he became a specialist in things American. He went to Washington as one of Litvinov's assistants; then Litvinov was recalled to Moscow and Gromyko, when he was only thirty-four, succeeded him as Soviet Ambassador to the United States. This, however, was not so much a tribute to his own powers as an attempt to snub the American government. Stalin was angry that the United States had not yet opened a second front

[7] At least a score of other conspicuous Soviet leaders deserve mention, in particular towering theoreticians like Suslov and Pospelov, but I do not include them here because, by and large, their careers follow identical patterns, and repetition becomes tedious. A brief account of some will be found in the Appendix on Personalities at the end of this book. Several have considerable interest as human beings.

in Europe and, to demonstrate his displeasure, gave the Washington Embassy to an inexperienced underling, as one might send a deliberately inferior gift to humiliate a host.

Gromyko has a reputation for dourness, which probably arose because he gave voice to no fewer than twenty-six vetoes during his tenure as chief Soviet delegate to the UN. Actually he has a marked—if somewhat rough—sense of humor. More than any leading Russian, he understands the United States, as far as any Soviet citizen can understand it. Once he was asked to comment about an article about his personality in the *New York Times*. His dry reply was: "Half true, half false. Since the *Times* is a balanced newspaper, this is to be expected." He is stubborn, tenacious, and above all, patient in negotiation. Any diplomatic negotiation with the Soviet Union is likely to be agonizingly tedious. Gromyko made the process even more tedious than usual. On one occasion, during the tussle over international control of atomic energy, Gromyko and Frederick Osborn, the American representative on the Atomic Energy Commission of the UN, came to an exhausting deadlock. Mr. Osborn suggested that, since he and Gromyko were both sincere, a little quiet tête-à-tête might lead to a solution. Gromyko replied, "Mr. Osborn, you may be sincere, but governments never are."

In Gromyko's stable are some competent men. One is Valerian A. Zorin, a former Soviet Ambassador to both Czechoslovakia and West Germany. He is in his middle fifties, and for long months represented the Soviet Union in the interminable disarmament negotiations in London in 1957. Several Soviet ambassadors have considerable party rank, and are full members of the Central Committee. Closest of all to the Kremlin is probably P. K. Ponomarenko, the former Ambassador to Poland. Men of his caliber go as a rule to posts most sensitive from the point of view of party relations, like China, North Korea, North Vietnam, and the European satellites. Vladimir Semyenov, well known to western diplomats when he was High Commissioner to West Germany, is now one of Gromyko's deputy foreign ministers.

G. N. Zarubin, Ambassador to the United States until recently, is regarded as an able and responsible technician; others are A. A. Sobolev, Ambassador to the UN, and V. G. Yakovlev, who recently went to Ceylon. Yakovlev was formerly head of VOKS, the All-Union Society for Cultural Relations with Foreign Countries. Yakob A. Malik, the Ambassador to Great Britain and, like Zarubin, a candidate member of the Central Committee, is another well-known figure, partly by reason of his career at the UN. Malik comes from White Russia, near the Polish border, and derives from a family long established there. A colleague in Moscow asked him one day if Russian fear of attack from the West was genuine. Malik replied quietly, but with bite, that his family village had been destroyed by invaders no fewer than 17 times in 270 years.

Among other cabinet ministers, an important man is Vladimir Vladimirovich Matskevich, Minister of Agriculture and formerly a deputy chairman of the USSR council of ministers. He is a Ukrainian, with long experience in party affairs, and close to Khrushchev. Born in 1909, he was educated to be an agronomist; he was director of the Kharkov Zootechnical Institute, and has also been a practical dirt farmer out in the field, in charge of various state farms. He visited the United States in 1955 as chairman of a Soviet agricultural mission. As many Americans discovered, he is an energetic man, likes to laugh, and looks surprisingly like a younger Winston Churchill. Until recently the USSR had two ministries devoted to agriculture on the All-Union level, one for state farms, one for everything else. The two are now consolidated, with Matskevich in command—an extremely important post.

The Minister of Culture, N. A. Mikhailov, is an old party hack, but of high rank. He has been in the top leadership since 1939, and ran the huge Komsomol organization for a period; in other words he was in charge of the Soviet youth. What he does not know about culture is a good deal, but he runs his ministry with vigor. He is supposed to have summoned recently a conference of leading Soviet composers, including Shostakovich. He asked them to write more popular music, and, pounding the table, wanted to know indignantly how long the Soviet Union would have to wait before producing its own Yves Montand, a French singer much admired in Moscow. A member of the conference murmured dryly, "Two Five-Year Plans."

The Ministry of Culture is new, having been put together since Stalin's death, as a consolidation of various former commissions and agencies. Mikhailov covers a lot of ground. His ministry has, among much else, sections dealing with books, circuses, folk-dancing, "cinefication," film production, cinematography, radio, theaters and musical institutions, TV, printing and publishing, and the arts. About Mikhailov's predecessor, Georgi F. Alexandrov, who founded the ministry, there are many tales. He was a former head of *Agitprop*, a member of the Academy of Sciences, a philosopher by profession, and a much respected historian. Also he had a lighter side. In fact, something unprecedented for a politician of his rank, he was supposed to have given wild parties in his office, where ballerinas and other pretty girls were brilliantly—even scandalously—entertained. Once, in a brawl over a movie star in Leningrad, Alexandrov was actually arrested. He lost his job as minister, and was shipped out to Siberia forthwith, to be, of all things,

Rector of Tomsk University. But the students there, having got wind of his fondness for high jinks, refused to have him, and went on strike. Such things *can* happen in the Soviet Union, though they do not happen often. Now Alexandrov is on the teaching staff of a minor institute near Leningrad, cooling his heels or lips.

The Cops

Serov runs one branch of the police, Dudorov the other. This demands explanation, and let us go into details for a moment. There have been a good many mutations in the development of the Soviet police. First, under Lenin, came the establishment of the Cheka, which took its name from *Chrezvychainaya Komissiya*; its full title was "Extraordinary Commission for Combating Counter-Revolution, Sabotage and Speculation," and its first chief was an extraordinary Pole, Felix Dzerzhinsky, in whose character sadism, idealism, and fanaticism were peculiarly mixed. After his death in 1926 he was succeeded by another Pole, a man less interesting but still formidable, V. R. Menzhinsky. He was in turn succeeded (after the Cheka had assumed other names) by G. G. Yagoda, a grisly bureaucrat who, after two years of power, was neatly executed; his successor was a criminal madman, the unspeakable N. I. Yezhov. He superintended the great purges, and his period in office got a special name, the *Yezhovshchina*, as a synonym for horror. Yezhov in turn disappeared, good riddance to put it mildly, and was in time succeeded by Lavrenti P. Beria.

But to return to the Cheka. It was modeled on the Committee of Public Safety in the French Revolution, and had the powers, not merely to arrest, but to punish; it was cop, prosecutor, judge, jury, and executioner all in one. As such, it came close to being a state within a state. The Cheka engaged in punitive terror—indeed that was its main business—but, at the beginning at least, it was not quite so despicable and fearsome an organization as is commonly thought. It was abolished (in 1922) to make way for something that *was* fearsome, the GPU or State Political Administration.[8]

For a variety of reasons Stalin decided ten years later, in 1934, to do away with the OGPU as such, and reorganize it under a different name, the NKVD or People's Commissariat of Internal Affairs. "NK" means "People's Commissariat," and "VD" means "Internal Affairs." This was when the Popular Front phase of Soviet policy was getting under way, and perhaps Stalin wanted the USSR to appear more respectable to the external world;

[8] The initials denote *Gosudarstvennoye Politicheskoye Upravleniye*. Later this became the OGPU; the "O" indicates All-Union status, which came under the new Soviet constitution of 1924.

also there were internal considerations. Powers of the organization, including its right to impose the death penalty, were—briefly—curtailed. Twelve years later, in 1946, when Stalin was "Russianizing" Russia full blast, the locution "Peoples' Commissariat" was replaced by "Ministry," and the NKVD became the MVD, Ministry of Internal Affairs.

What follows is complicated. We must go back a bit. One of the subordinate organs of the NKVD was the Administration for State Security, and in February, 1941, shortly before the Nazi attack on the Soviet Union, this was converted into an independent commissariat, called NKGB, or People's Commissariat for State Security. After the German attack, in July, 1941, NKVD and NKGB were reunited, but later they were again set up as separate entities. The NKVD, renamed the MVD, Ministry of Internal Affairs, and MGB, Ministry of State Security, as the NKGB was renamed, worked side by side for seven years, from 1946 to 1953. Then, after Stalin's death in 1953, both were combined again under Beria. After Beria's downfall, they were separated once more, which is the position today, except that the MGB is now called the KGB, or Committee of State Security. It no longer has the rank of a ministry.

The differences between the two are as follows. The MVD is a full ministry, the Ministry of Internal Affairs, under Dudorov, and its members are, for the most part, uniformed. It is much larger than the KGB. It has very wide powers and functions, altogether aside from routine police work; for instance it is in charge of frontier troops, convoy troops, traffic cops, highway patrol, and the militiamen or patrolmen seen on every street. It also handles registration activities, like birth certificates, marriage licenses, and even driving licenses; also it controls all passport and visa work, both for foreigners and Russian citizens. Also, an odd point, the fire department in every Soviet city belongs to the MVD.

The KGB, on the other hand, is the *secret* police. When a person in Russia talks—or whispers—about the secret police, it is almost always the plain-clothes men of the KGB who are meant. Outside of Russia, the term "MVD" is often used inaccurately as a synonym for "KGB" or as a blanket term meaning *all* the police. The KGB under Serov does not have cabinet status, but is a commission attached directly to the Council of Ministers. General Serov has, however, ministerial rank, and is much more conspicuous a personality than Dudorov.[9]

Of course KGB and MVD overlap to some extent, but the particular

---

[9] When I use the various designations above in the course of this book I try, perhaps not always with success, to use whichever name is correct as of the given period.

domain of the KGB is counterintelligence, espionage, and security. The "legal residents" in Soviet embassies abroad, already mentioned, are KGB men, and so are Soviet spies all over the world. The KGB has its own codes, ciphers, and means of communication, about which other agencies of the Soviet government know nothing. It fulfills, *mutatis mutandis*, the same functions as the Central Intelligence Agency in the United States, in gathering and evaluating information, and in addition has police powers like those of the FBI. The budget of the KGB, its personnel and so forth, are among the most closely guarded secrets in the Soviet Union, like similar details about the CIA in Washington. The KGB is, in the fancy manner of espionage organizations everywhere in the world, devoted to tricks and gadgets. One new KGB weapon is an electronic pistol the size of a cigarette lighter, and at first glance indistinguishable from one.

General Ivan Alexandrovich Serov, boss of the KGB, is a military man by career, who has been active in police work for many years. A professional security man, he had big jobs under Beria, but he could not have been too closely associated with him, or he would have been liquidated along with Beria; all overt Beria people have disappeared. Serov, according to Soviet sources, was born on August 25, 1905, in the village of Afinsky, and was the son of a peasant. He joined the party when he was twenty-one, and after working in the Komsomol organization entered the army. He was graduated from the Frunze Military Academy, the Soviet equivalent of West Point, and, as a career officer, rose rank by rank. He became a full general in 1955, and, except for Beria who was promoted to be a marshal in the last days of Stalin, was the first Soviet police chief to achieve such a high military rank. Apparently Serov first got into police work in 1941, when he became deputy commissar of the NKVD; by 1947, he was first deputy minister of the MVD. He did not become a member of the Central Committee of the Party until 1956. He is, needless to say, close to Khrushchev, and personally handles most of the security arrangements on the Khrushchev-Bulganin trips.

Much of his early work was in the Ukraine, where he first came to Khrushchev's attention; he was, in fact, a member of the Ukrainian Politburo under Khrushchev. During the war, he fought at both Moscow and Stalingrad. He took part in the siege of Berlin (1945), worked for a while as a deputy to Marshal Zhukov in Berlin, and for his services there got the Order of Lenin and was named a Hero of the Soviet Union.

Serov was, it is generally believed, the responsible officer in charge of liquidating opposition in the Baltic states, and superintended the deportation of tens of thousands of Letts, Estonians and Lithuanians from their homes, one of the most barbarous episodes in contemporary history. Probably, too, he played a sinister role in the Polish and Ukrainian deportations, and he won a second Order of Lenin (1952) for his "work" on the Volga-Don Canal; in other words he contributed to it the necessary forced labor. Also Serov is a member of the Soviet of the Union, and for a time represented a White Russian constituency on the Supreme Soviet; he is a deputy to the RSFSR Supreme Soviet from Stalingrad, and a member of the Moscow City Council. General Serov is, as a human being, perfectly suave and presentable. A seventeen-year-old girl, the daughter of a European diplomat, told her horrified parents after a party in Moscow recently that she had met the most "charming" man. It was Serov.

Nikolai Pavlovich Dudorov, the head of the MVD, is, not inappropriately, a specialist in construction matters. He is a civilian, and was born in May, 1906, near Moscow. He got a good technical education, went into the building industry, and by 1945 was—an odd-sounding job—chief of the Main Administration of Thermal Insulation in the People's Commissariat of Construction. Later he became a member of the Moscow Soviet, and then went into the MVD as a building expert. Little else is known about him, except that he is a newcomer to high party rank. Dudorov's predecessor as head of the MVD was a notorious character, Colonel General S. N. Kruglov; his whereabouts are unknown nowadays, but he ran the MVD for ten full years. Kruglov, one of whose early jobs was that of being a bodyguard to Molotov, handled the security arrangements at the Yalta, Potsdam, San Francisco, and London conferences.

Another important personage in these dank, malignant realms was Sergei Yaklovlevich Zhuk, who died in 1957. He was an engineer, who "designed and directed the construction of the greatest forced labor enterprises since the building of the Egyptian pyramids."[10] The MVD, under Stalin and then Beria, was by far the most powerful body in the Soviet Union, next to the Politburo. It had its own army, which took precedence in some respects over the regular army, and its own airplanes, tanks, communications system, and supply services. During the worst years of terror, when monsters like Yagoda and Yezhov were on the loose, it dominated every life in the Soviet Union, except perhaps Stalin's. Above all, it ran the slave labor camps, like Vorkuta above the Arctic Circle and Karaganda in Kazakhstan, and at the peak of its infamous potency probably employed, if employment is the correct word, at least ten million prisoners as forced laborers. During the war, when Soviet affairs in general got a lot of whitewashing in the United States,

[10] Harrison E. Salisbury, New York Times, March 9, 1957.

there came some curious transvaluations of values; for instance in a special number devoted to the USSR the magazine *Life* called the NKVD a "national police similar to the FBI."[11] It was a great deal more than that. By its fantastic command of wholesale labor power, the NKVD and MVD played a stupendous, overwhelming role in Russian economy. In 1941, as an example, the NKVD was responsible for more than 10 per cent of all Soviet lumber production, over 20 per cent of the production of railway ties, 40 per cent of chromium ore, more than five million tons of coal or about 3 per cent of the national total, one-sixth of all new construction, and an immense output in other fields, from silkworms to gold to oil.[12] The labor camps were run by an organization known as Gulag, which maintained at least forty major "colonies." Some authorities gave the total number of forced laborers at fourteen million. In the last Stalin years, the budget for MVD and MGB together exceeded that of all other organs of the government combined. Several Gulag administrations, especially those in the extreme far east of Siberia, like the Dalstroy center (State Far East Construction Trust) near Magadan, became so powerful that they were virtually autonomous.

Out of Terror, Terror

A final word about these ugly matters. Terror is certainly no new thing in Russia; Peter the Great cut off heads with his own hand, and the country has had a ministry of state security from 1811. Actually in the *very* early days of the Bolshevik Revolution terror, as an instrument of policy, was at the minimum Then, in August, 1918, Lenin was seriously wounded by an assassin; at once five hundred prominent citizens of the *ancien régime* were taken out and summarily shot, both as a matter of vengeance and to frighten malcontents. Under Stalin the processes of terror were, of course, vastly intensified.[13]

The GPU was certainly conspicuous, as well as detestably malign, in the years that followed, and its headquarters in Moscow, at No. 22 Lubyanka Street, the former offices of an insurance company, symbolized national dread. Even so, things went on smoothly for most ordinary citizens until

[11] March 29, 1943, p. 40.
[12] Harry Schwartz, *Russia's Soviet Economy*, p. 570.
[13] Nothing can palliate the wanton horrors that occurred, but bare mention at least should be made of the fact that the Bolsheviks discovered, after reaching power, that several of their own most trusted colleagues had, right to the very end, been police agents of the Czar. The most conspicuous was a confidant of Lenin's of many years standing, by name Malinovsky. Hence, fear and suspicion of everybody, almost without exception, became rife.

December 1, 1934, when Sergei Mironovich Kirov, the boss of Leningrad, who at that time was supposed to be Stalin's closest friend and heir presumptive, was assassinated. This was the first political *attentat* of consequence in the Soviet Union since the attack on Lenin, sixteen years before. Instantly mass revenge was taken. More, the Kirov murder unleashed in Stalin a mad lust to clear from the boards any surviving remnants of opposition. Thus began the series of extraordinary treason trials that stunned and mystified the outside world for years, and made Russia tremble to its foundations. One theory is that people close to Stalin himself may have had something to do with engineering the Kirov murder; people in high positions in Leningrad were shot to cover up traces of those who organized the killing. Khrushchev talked of the Kirov murder at considerable length in his February speech, and some of its motives and circumstances are still a mystery. Mixed up in it were several factors. The murderer had personal motives; Kirov was his wife's lover. The case may be made, whether Stalin was involved in the affair or not, that at about this time he became insane—insane, at least, on certain subjects. Insanity, temporary or otherwise, is no new thing among Russian rulers.

There were four major treason trials. They were distinguished, as the world well knows, by the spectacle of party chieftains of the highest rank "confessing" to conspiracy with foreign powers, plots against Stalin's life, and so on. Leaders who did not play ball and "confess" were simply shot out of hand, like S. V. Kosior, boss of the Ukraine. (1) *August, 1936.* The chief defendants were the celebrated old-timers Zinoviev and Kamenev, who with Trotsky had led the "Left Opposition." A. Ya. Vyshinsky, who before long was to represent the Soviet Union at the UN, was the prosecutor. (2.) *January, 1937.* Yuri L. Pyatakov, one of the four leaders mentioned by name in Lenin's testament, and a round dozen other veterans were executed; Karl Radek, the most brilliant Soviet journalist since the Revolution, got off with ten years. (3.) *June, 1937.* Marshal Tukhachevsky and seven other high officers in the Red Army were tried by secret military tribunal, and forthwith shot, on charges of espionage and high treason. (4.) *March, 1938.* The old "Right Opposition" was liquidated, including Alexei I. Rykov, who had been Lenin's successor as prime minister, and Nikolai Bukharin, the leading theoretician of the party and Lenin's best friend for years. Thrown in to boot was the unspeakable Yagoda, who, a quaint little point, had been in charge of gathering "evidence" at the previous trials.

The trials are to be carefully distinguished from the purges, which began concurrently, and swept Russia like an evil subterranean fire, consuming probably *one-third* of the best brains in the nation. Defendants in the trials did at least get a trial, fraudulent as these were; the great mass of people purged got no trial at all, and were simply shot or put away. Victims were of two groups. First, important officials of government and party, whom Stalin wanted to get rid of, or who were victims of denunciation by rivals, or who were swept away into the phosphorescent maelstrom without any cause at all. Of the Central Committee of the Party, numbering seventy-one at that day, only sixteen survived, as has been mentioned above. Khrushchev himself has stated that more than seven thousand party members were shot, who have subsequently been found "to be innocent of the crimes charged." But worse was the fate meted out to little people. Now the *real* terror got under way. Tens of thousands of citizens in no way accused of any crime or misdemeanor were plucked from their homes or jobs and tossed into the labor camps. Quotas were established for towns, farms, and even apartment buildings; such-and-such a number of people from each were chosen—moreover, chosen *at random*. Sometimes the police went along a city block and arrested one person here, another there—utterly innocent of any wrongdoing—ringing doorbells by whim and carting people off with no object except (a) augment the labor force, (b) terrorize the neighborhood.[14]

In 1938 Beria came to power, ended the *Yezhovshchina*, and tried to restore some semblance of legality to police procedure. Stalin, from about this time, did not use Beria for private police matters, but tended to concentrate them instead in the hands of the chief of one sector of his secretariat, an odious creature named Poskrebyshev. The purges dwindled off but isolated outrages continued to occur for a long time, some of them so macabre as to be startling even for the Soviet Union. I have in a passage above mentioned briefly the "Leningrad case" and the fate of Nikolai A. Voznesensky, the ablest economic planner in the Soviet Union, a member

[14] I have indirect knowledge of one case; it was quite unimportant except to the individuals concerned, but the details are revealing. A classic Bolshevist hero is Erostratus, who, defying constituted authority in 356 B.C., burned down the Temple of Diana at Ephesus. A Russian boy stood outside the Bolshoi Theater late in 1947, and said jokingly to a friend, "Do you think I would be remembered for two thousand years if I burned down the Bolshoi?" Six months later he was arrested on the charge of conspiring to burn down the Bolshoi Theater, and was sentenced to five years in a corrective labor camp. His parents appealed—the result was that the sentence was increased to ten years! The boy was sent to Vorkuta and, because his family was well known, the case was reopened and went all the way to the Supreme Court. The boy's sentence was thereupon extended to twenty-five years, the maximum permissible (except death) under Soviet law. Came de-Stalinization in the 1950's, and the boy was freed, with profuse apologies.

of the Politburo, and head of the *Gosplan*. To this day, no specific details have ever been revealed about what happened to him, beyond the bare fact that he was shot. This happened as recently as 1949. Then came the crazy episode of the Doctors' Plot, also mentioned above. Even more recently, in February, 1953, a few weeks before Stalin's death, came the remarkable disappearance of General S. M. Shtemenko. He was chief of the general staff of the Soviet Army, no less—a position analogous to that once held in the American Army by General Marshall, also by General Eisenhower. Somebody picked up a phone one day, and that was the end of Shtemenko. His name, inexplicably, did not appear on the invitations for an annual army function in Moscow; then he was seen, for the last time, at a Soviet reception in Berlin. He was superseded in his post, and from that day to this nothing has ever been heard of him, and nobody even knows whether he is alive or dead.[15]

As of today, under Khrushchev, things like this no longer happen. Mass purges are a thing of the past, and overt terror has long since stopped.

*

We must pause now to take account of things which, even if well known, we have perhaps taken too much for granted, and have a chapter or two about the history, government, and shape of Russia.

[15] Harrison E. Salisbury, *American in Russia*, p. 181. General Shtemenko suddenly "surfaced" late in 1957 after his long years of obliteration.

CHAPTER VIII

A History of Russia in Half an Hour

> When a great social revolution shall have mastered
> the results of the bourgeois epoch . . . and sub-
> jected them to the control of the most advanced
> peoples, then only will human progress cease to
> resemble that Hindoo pagan idol, who would not
> drink the nectar but from the skulls of the slain.
> —KARL MARX IN 1853

> I have seen the future, and it works.
> —LINCOLN STEFFENS IN 1919

> You cannot make a revolution with silk gloves.
> —JOSEF STALIN IN 1934

RUSSIA came out of shadows—primordial hosts of Scythians and other pre-Slavic invaders who flowed upward from Asia into the European steppe in the eighth century B.C. These are portrayed nowadays as fierce warriors, but it is more likely that they were simple nomads, a restless and hungry folk seeking new horizons; they have left some remarkable works of art, in the shape of golden ornaments, which show Greek influence. They crossed and recrossed the Russian plain, and prodded into the dark forests. Eventually, after being tinctured by various elements for centuries, Russia became filled with a people known as the Slavs. Who these were in the first instance we do not know exactly. But we do know that they were a European people, not Asian, who rose about A.D. 600 from the Danube Valley or the Carpathians, moved east, and settled along the great Russian rivers. These Slavs were (and are) a signally tenacious people; they have not yet been displaced from Russia or eastern Europe, and their languages are still the voice of mankind all the way from the Adriatic and Black Sea to the Arctic Circle and the Pacific.

145

Soon came invasion by a northern people, the Varangians (Vikings), who established themselves at trading posts and forts which became flourishing towns, like Pskov and Novgorod, and flowed southward to mingle with the Slavs. They were what has aptly been called "land sailors," who took full advantage of the Russian network of rivers; you could cross Russia by boat in those days, even as you can today. It is a striking phenomenon that the Vikings, branching out in two enormous streams from their Norse homelands, should have not only discovered America, but, in a manner of speaking, Russia too.

Even the derivation of the word "Slav" is obscure. "Slave" comes from it, because many Slavs became slaves, but "Slav" does not mean "slave." On the contrary, its original meaning was "glorious," and probably it derives from a root, *slovo*, meaning "word" or "language." "Russia" comes from "rus" or "ros." The Finns called the Varangians "Rus," apparently because the first Viking invaders came from an area in Sweden known as Roslagen. For centuries Russia was called "Rus," until the name expanded into *Rossiya*, or Russia. Another theory is that "Russia" stems from *Ruotsi*, the Finnish name for the Swedes, which in turn was suggested by the Swedish *rothsmenn*, or seafarers.

In any case the Norse leader Rurik founded the first Russian dynasty at Novgorod, not far from the Leningrad of today, in A.D. 862, and Russian history begins. He is the equivalent of William the Conqueror, another Norseman. Rurik entered Novgorod (New City) by invitation; the Slavic inhabitants of the region summoned him with the words, "Our land is great and fruitful, but there is no order in it; come and reign and rule over us." This he did.

Southern Russia had a somewhat different development, although here too invaders like the Sarmatians, Goths, Huns, Avars, Khazars, and other folk, coming mainly from the Caucasus, Persia, and Central Asia, preceded the entrance of the Slavs. Along the Black Sea Greek and then Roman settlements flourished. Then the Slavs poured in from the west, and a great city, Kiev, was founded in the Ukraine. Rurik's successor, a prince named Oleg, took Kiev in 878, and the two Russias of the day, centering on Novgorod and Kiev, began to merge. Kievan conquerors set up a sturdy empire, stretching from the Danube to the Volga, and sought to beat back nomadic barbarians like the Bulgars and Pechenegs.

Kievan Russia lasted for almost four hundred years, from roughly A.D. 860 to 1240. (During all this time, Moscow was little more than an obscure trading post. The chief city of central Russia was not Moscow, but Vladimir.)

We shall treat of Kiev in a later chapter. Suffice it to say now that its importance to pan-Russian development was monumental, because Kiev brought Byzantium into Russia. A prince of Kiev was baptized into the Orthodox Christian Church in 988, and the conversion of Russia to the Greek form of Christianity began, with results copious and striking to this day. For centuries, the unity of Church and Czar dominated Russia. The Greek Orthodox faith, with its sinuous theology, emphasis on dogma, and ceremonial orthodoxy, gave a unique pattern to Russian affairs and attitudes, and not merely in ecclesiastical realms. From Byzantium came the Greek alphabet, Byzantine art and culture, and above all the Byzantine habit of mind, with its stress on autocracy, deceit, and hair-splitting for the sake of the true cause.

So, on a Slavic pedestal sunk deep into a substratum of wandering Asian or semi-Asian peoples, were added Norse moodiness and phlegm and a glittering, messianic Byzantine overlay. Now came the Mongols, who are called in Russian terminology Tatars (Tartars). They have left traces even more marked than those of Byzantium. The Mongol conquest began in 1237, and was led by a nephew of Genghis Khan. The Mongols extinguished Kievan Russia, and marauded far into the north; their ruthless dominion lasted for 250 years, until 1480. They are responsible for several characteristics that we call "eastern" or "Asiatic" in the Russia of today, like cruelty, fatalism, and sloth. The servile position held by Russian women for centuries dates from Mongol conceptions, and so, in a way, do serfdom and the totalitarian structure of the state. The Mongol capital was at Sarai, on the Volga near the site of Astrakhan today, and its government was called the Khanate of the Golden Horde.

Russian rulers during the early Khanate, like Alexander Nevski (1236-63) had troubles on other fronts as well. Alexander beat off the Swedes on the Neva (1240) and the Teutonic Knights (1242) on Lake Peipus, in a great battle fought on ice. Later came troublesome incursions from Lithuania, and perennial warfare with the Poles. Meantime the principality of Moscow expanded vigorously, both in geography and power, and presently absorbed its neighbors.

Ivan to Peter to Catherine

Out of all this, the concept "Russia" rose. Ivan III, the Great, (1462-1505) was the first "national king," and claimed descent from Rurik; he was also "international," and performed the extraordinary feat of marrying the Eastern Roman Empire. That is, in 1472 he married Sophia Palaeologue, the niece of Constantine XIII, the last Greek emperor of Constantinople. So, in theory at least, Russia and Byzantium became united. Ivan assumed the title of Czar (Caesar), although he was not crowned as such, and took over the Byzantine double-eagle as a symbol of the new imperium. The court ceremonial in Moscow, with its bizarre extravagance, became patterned on that of the decadent Byzantine emperors. It was Sophia, incidentally, called by the Russians Zoya, who imported from Italy the architects who built the Moscow Kremlin. Ivan introduced firearms to Russia, extended his domain to the Urals, and wept for the souls of those he slew. During this reign, the Mongol or Tatar suzerainty over Russia broke apart. The link that connected Moscow with Peking, which had become the Mongol capital, was broken and did not come into history again until the 1950's.

Ivan III was an interesting man, but he cannot be compared for interest to his grandson, Ivan IV or the Terrible (1533-84). Here was a great man, who also happened to be a monster; now absolutist Russia really began. He inherited the throne at the age of three; at thirteen, in a fit of temper, he had his principal adviser torn apart by hounds. He chose a bride, whose name was Romanov, out of a covey of fifteen hundred virgins assembled from all parts of Russia for his inspection, in imitation of a Tatar custom. In time he was crowned Czar and Autocrat, a title subsequently assumed by all Czars till the end of Czardom. The institution of the secret police, a curse of Russia ever since, dates from Ivan. He turned Novgorod into a Lidice, and spent the last three years of his life, under the name Jonah, as a monk, seeking to expiate his wickednesses. But the most noteworthy thing about him is probably something else; he turned to the south and east, and captured Kazan (1552) and Astrakhan (1556), thus rolling the immensity of Russia eastward, and opening the way for subsequent advance into Central Asia and to the Pacific. He was called the "great gatherer of the Russian land."

During all this time, Ivan struggled incessantly with the boyars, or feudal lords, and to control them better set up a vestigial national assembly, the first in Russian history, and the last until 1905.

Ivan's reputation has undergone severe revision in the Soviet Union lately. Under Stalin, he was glorified. Stalin thought that he was a "great, wise, and progressive ruler," who first united Russia and, among other things, was "the first man to introduce a state monopoly of foreign trade into Russia," the next being Lenin. Ivan's chief mistake, Stalin thought, was that he did not wipe out *all* the feudal families, but let a few survive. "Ivan would destroy one family of boyars, and would then spend a whole year repenting, while he should have acted more resolutely," Stalin is reputed to have said. In 1956 the Soviet Academy of Sciences appointed a commission of historians to give a new estimate of Ivan and other royal rulers. Ivan is now considered to be a tyrant and a hangman, "coldly wearing the ugly mask of a humble and penitent sinner . . . but at the same time a notably shrewd statesman." Following this ukase, Soviet history books are laboriously being rewritten.[1]

We should now define a few terms, like *Streltzi* and *Cossack*. The Streltzi were a kind of imperial bodyguard of chosen troops at the sovereign's personal disposal. Ivan used them as an instrument to beat down provincial warlords, and establish national unity. Cossacks are not, as often thought, people of a distinct racial stock, although most came in the first instance from the river valleys of the Ukraine and the Volga steppes. During Ivan's time they were frontiersmen, who acted as scouts for his armies penetrating the "Wild East" of Europe, and who became in time hardy settlers in the frontier zones. Later, they evolved into a "cavalry militia."

I do not have space for Ivan's successors and "the time of troubles," though it is difficult to omit mention of Boris Godunov and the two false Dmitris— such a dark, confused extravaganza! Michael Romanov, a grandnephew of Ivan, took the throne in 1613, and established the line that ruled for three hundred years, until 1917. The main thing to say is that, as reign followed reign, the major characteristics of the Russian scene as we knew it later became fixed. Steadily—to mention just one example—the gap widened between rulers and people, between the privileged and nonprivileged, between a fantastically rich and ornate upper class and a peasantry downtrodden, miserable, and unspeakably poor.

Serfdom, the cancer of the old Russia, became as time went on a force debasing the entire moral structure of the community. It injured irreparably both parties, landowners and serfs alike. In some ways, the position of the serfs came to resemble that of Negroes in the United States; an entire community was submerged. But there were many more serfs in Russia than Negroes in America, they were spread all over the country, and their economic importance went deeper. In fact it was the submerged iceberg of serfdom that supported the rest of the population. The land, to which the serfs were attached, became the basis of practically all Russian wealth. The serfs were emancipated in 1861, two years before the Emancipation Proclamation in the United States, but emancipation did not stop further exploitation, any more than emancipation of the Negroes did away with continuing exploitation and discrimination in America. The Bolshevik Revolution did

[1] *New Statesman*, December 1, 1956, and *New York Times*, September 23, 1956.

not occur till 1917, more than half a century after the serfs were liberated, but serfdom was its fundamental root and cause. A cancer will destroy a body, unless cured. However, this is to get ahead of our story. After Ivan laws were progressively made stricter, and the serfs became the virtual equivalent of slaves. They were forbidden to move, migrate, or work for other landlords than their own. Holdings in serfs by noblemen, like shares on an expanding stock exchange, became steadily more lucrative; one aristocrat under Catherine, as an example, owned 300,000 serfs, and the concept became intensified that these human beings were no more than "baptized property."[2]

It should be emphasized, at this juncture, how different Russian development was in most respects from that of western Europe at approximately the same time. Russia missed the Crusades, the Renaissance, and the Reformation; it had no middle class to speak of and few stout communities of burghers, and, except in the most rudimentary way, the expression of popular will in government was unknown. Russia never had a Magna Charta, any more than it ever had a Spinoza, a Luther, or a Michelangelo.

But it had Peter I, the Great (1689-1725), with whom modern Russian history begins. His impact was such that everything before him in Russia is sometimes lumped together and dismissed as "pre-Petrine." He was six feet nine inches tall, and the master of an inordinate number of crafts; he could bend a silver coin in his hands, and was a shipbuilder, sailor, dentist, astronomer, engraver, bootmaker, and artillery expert. His character and life were shot through with violence, and he committed atrocities as heinous as those of Ivan IV or Stalin, although perhaps not quite so many. The more "romantic" details of his career need not concern us, such as that he was taught in his youth by the court fool, and put his own son, Alexis, to death by torture. Peter moved the capital from Moscow to St. Petersburg, had twelve thousand Streltzi executed in one batch, created the Russian Navy, was the first Russian monarch to travel abroad, reformed the alphabet, reorganized the civil service, founded the first Russian newspaper, and intensified the serfdom of the serfs. But two other items outrank all of this. First, the industrialization of Russia, such as it was, began under Peter. Second, he tried to make Russia European, and not merely by shaving off the beards of nobles. His dearest ambition was to break Russian isolation, and get a window to the West. Russia was, at this time, still landlocked, and had no warm seas; it had not yet reached the Black Sea. It was the Baltic that interested Peter most. He beat Charles XII of Sweden at the celebrated

[2] Incidentally until the eighteenth century all land in Russia was considered to be the property of the Czar.

battle of Poltava, in 1709, and after that Russia was a European power.

Peter also changed the laws of succession, so that the reigning czar had the right to *appoint* his own successor. Inheritance by the normal procedure of primogeniture went by the boards. Absolutism could go no further. Like Stalin two hundred odd years later, he had a compelling drive to go forward, to get things *done*. The cost did not matter. Ends justified means, then as now. Peter would have understood very well the Five-Year Plan.

Among rulers following Peter were several extraordinary women. Catherine I, his widow, ruled for only two years (1725-27), and died just in time to keep a palace revolution from unseating her. She was not popular. It revolted the court nobles to have a woman ruler foisted on them.[3] She had a love affair with her chamberlain while Peter was still alive; Peter had the man beheaded, pickled the head in juice, and set it beside his Queen's bed table, without further ado. She took the hint, and apparently behaved well thereafter.

Under Anna of Courland (1730-40), the daughter of Ivan V, the court was dominated by a coterie of German advisers. Anna once had two midgets married and then, presumably for fun, had them frozen to death in an ice palace. Elizabeth (1741-62), Peter's youngest daughter, reached the throne after melodramatic interruptions. Now the Petersburg court reached full fancy flower, with strong French influences, and the "golden age" of the aristocracy began. Elizabeth, whom we shall meet later in these pages, was a fantastically extravagant character, but a worthy patron of the arts. She established the first Russian university (Moscow, 1755), and encouraged the work of the first great Russian scientist, Mikhail Lomonosov, who founded the Academy of Sciences, and was the son of a fisherman.

In 1762 came Catherine II, known as the Great. She ruled for more than thirty years, until 1796. The Communists of today have never quite decided what to think of her; she "crushed the peasantry and encouraged a reactionary foreign policy," but nevertheless had some good points, from the Soviet point of view. Of course Catherine was a German, and Russians, by and large, have always had a low opinion of Germans; the very word for "German" in the Russian language, *nemets*, means "stupid." Catherine did not have a drop of Russian blood in her veins, and had no lineal right to the throne at all. She married the Grand Duke Peter, a nephew of Elizabeth's, who became Peter III. The ambitious Catherine soon managed to get

---

[3] Catherine's real name was Martha Skavronska; she was a Lithuanian servant girl, taken prisoner after a battle and sold to a Russian prince, in whose household Peter encountered her. He married her after divorcing his first Czarina.

rid of him, and he was conveniently disposed of. Under Catherine occurred the first three partitions of Poland; for the fourth we had to wait till 1939. Catherine, as everybody knows, had multitudinous lovers, corresponded with Frederick the Great and Voltaire, wrote plays and poems, and pushed Russia to the Black Sea and the Caucasus. She gave new privileges to the nobility, and distributed immense tracts of land, with their serfs, to her favorites. During her reign occurred a serfs' revolt, led by a man named Pugachev, who, after being beaten down, was brought to Petersburg in a wooden cage, and publicly executed.[4]

By this time certain emancipated members of the intelligentsia had come to recognize the evils of serfdom, and some were bold enough to protest against it. Catherine arrested and sent to Siberia a writer named Alexander Radishchev, who was one of these, and thus established a precedent which carried over into modern times.

What Catherine hated most was the French Revolution. Partly because of her dislike of republicanism, she refused to recognize the United States government after 1776, and, indeed, the Czarist regime did not give recognition to the United States for thirty-three years, until 1809. (Bolshevik Russia had to wait for American recognition from 1917 to 1934, not quite so long.) One odd historical point is that, except for an accident, the British would have employed *Russian* mercenaries, instead of Hessians, in the American Revolutionary War. Russia was willing to sell troops to Britain, but in exchange wanted the cession of the Balearic Islands; the British did not relish the idea of having Russia in the Mediterranean, and so hired German troops instead.[5]

Catherine's son, who became Paul I (1796-1801), was, most historians think, not the child of her short-lived husband Peter III, but of one of her early lovers, probably a courtier named Saltykov. If this is true, the conclusion is inescapable that no "Romanov" since Peter III ever had an ounce of Russian royal blood.[6] Paul was a madman. Even so, to him belongs the honor of being the first Czar who tried to do something for the serfs; in 1797 he put through a ukase limiting the amount of work the landowner could demand of his slaves. Also Paul countermanded Peter the Great's law whereby the sovereign was empowered to appoint his own successor.

Of the nineteenth century we need say little. The pattern became more pointed. Repression, extravagance, incompetence, top-heaviness, even more

---

[4] This was the second serf revolt. The first occurred in 1671, led by a Don Cossack named Stenka Razin.
[5] Paul Scott Mowrer, New York *Post*, April 18, 1946.
[6] R. D. Charques, *A Short History of Russia*, p. 124.

than before, were characteristics of the ruling elite. But a profound stirring, a groping toward illumination, arose in the giant body of Russia. The cry for reform, no matter how much suppressed, could not be stilled. This century was, above all, the epoch of bad conscience. Aristocrats scrutinized themselves painfully about the evils of serfdom, while still living on the serf's labor. Nihilism began, and insurrectionary secret societies grew out of the Populist movement. Intellectuals were inflamed. Noblemen like Alexander Herzen became revolutionaries, and, as all readers of Dostoevsky know, a neurotic, cumulative, explosive sense of guilt, a turmoil rising out of misery and aspiration, shook the country.

To conclude: Alexander I (1801-25), the architect of the Holy Alliance, was a sinuous character. He liked to think of himself as a kind of representative of Christ on earth, but one mutinous officer was, during his reign, spared the indignity of the knout and given six *thousand* strokes of the rod instead. Under Nicholas I (1825-55) there took place no fewer than 556 localized revolts. Also, as one may read in the memoirs of the Marquis de Custine, Nicholas once gave a ball at Peterhof to which guests were brought by 6,000 carriages, while 1,800 serfs tended 200,000 illuminated lanterns. Alexander II (1855-81), a progressive ruler, emancipated the serfs and set out to establish other reforms, but was assassinated. Alexander III (1881-94) reverted to a policy of extreme stultifying reaction. He died in the room at Yalta used fifty-one years later by Franklin D. Roosevelt, and was followed by the last Czar, Nicholas II (1894-1917). He was a "nullity," almost a placebo, a kindly man cursed by tragedy, and with no pith or will. His mother was a Dane, and he was reputed to have been the richest man in the world. One-third of his empire had to be put under martial law after 1905, and, during one period lasting seven years, he never once visited Moscow out of fear of assassination. The dynasty was finally pinched out, like a guttering candle, on July 16, 1918, by Bolshevik executioners in a dark, forlorn cellar in a Siberian provincial town.

*

Some remarkable precursors of things to come may be noted in the old Russia. Terror, as an instrument of punitive assault on an entire class, began with Ivan the Terrible. Boyars=kulaks. The local councils called zemstvos, which go back to the earliest times, are clearly forerunners of today's soviets, and the collective farm of today borrows much from the old *mir*, or village commune. The keynotes of Russian policy in the nineteenth century were, in the words of one historian, "orthodoxy, autocracy, and nationalism"; what better words could describe the Soviet Union today? Khrushchev and company are still, like Ivan and Peter, attempting relentlessly to "impose cohesion on the fluid Russian state."[7]

In foreign policy there are some suggestively close analogies. The tactics of Alexander I vis-à-vis Napoleon were, for a period, almost exactly those of Stalin vis-à-vis Hitler at the time of the Russo-German Pact. Russian intervention helped put down a popular revolution in Hungary in 1849, and we all know what happened in Budapest 107 years later. Above all, Russian satellite policy today is an obvious inheritance from the Pan-Slavism of the Czars; Russians have been playing politics in Belgrade and Sofia, as an example, for at least eighty years. Finally, the cultural isolation of Russia from the mainsprings of western thought, so marked in the Middle Ages, is doubly marked today.

Marx

There were several peculiarities about Marx. Take merely the fact that no man in history has ever contributed more to the destruction of bourgeois ideals, but Marx himself was a devoted, affectionate husband and father, believed sternly in sexual puritanism, and adored his wife, Jenny von Westphalen. Again, no man ever did more to modify conventional attitudes toward aristocracy, but his wife came of an aristocratic Rhenish family, and on her mother's side was descended from the Earl of Argyll. Still again, Marx became God of the proletariat, but his own manner of life was bourgeois in the extreme. He let loose the most devastating revolution ever known, but he disliked conspiracy, abhorred violence, and never in his life had a serious brush with the police. He lived, not on the barricades, but in the British Museum, which he called "an ideal strategic vantage point" for the study of society.[8] He transformed utterly the ideas of mankind about property, and his conception that economic considerations underlie history is his most lasting contribution to social science, but he had practically no interest in money himself, except to have a pittance to live on. For some years he supported himself as a London correspondent of the old New York *Tribune,* and got two pounds an article.

One word about his life. Karl Heinrich Marx, whose family name was originally Levi and who was known to his friends by the nickname "the Moor" or "Old Nick," was born in Trier, Germany, on May 5, 1818. He was

[7] Charques, *op. cit.,* pp. 48 and 77.
[8] Isaiah Berlin, *Karl Marx,* p. 17.

descended from a line of rabbis, but his father, a lawyer, became a Christian shortly after he was born, the family was baptized, and Karl was brought up as a Lutheran. A brilliant student, he went to the University of Bonn, also Berlin. Lenin in a famous passage noted that he was a product of German philosophical idealism, French rationalism and belief in the rights of man, and British political economy. Hegel (whom he never met) was a strong influence, and so was the British socialist Robert Owen.

He became a journalist, and was a pamphleteer of indisputable genius; some of his early articles—e.g., on India—are, to an amazing degree, packed with prescience as well as analytical power; they read as if they had been written yesterday. Marx moved on to Paris in 1843, and plunged into the socialist movement. His lifelong association with Friedrich Engels dates from this period. He became a Communist, and moved to England. In 1848 the *Communist Manifesto* appeared, written in collaboration with the effervescent Engels, and was followed in 1867 by the first volume of *Capital*, which might never have been written except for the encouragement, nagging, and financial support that came from Engels, the son of a rich manufacturer. Meantime (1864) Marx became leader of the International Workingmen's Association; this body moved to New York after a time, and went out of existence in, of all places, Philadelphia. Marx immersed himself in polemics, study, and further writing. In old age, he was a cantankerous and disappointed character. He died in London in 1883, and was buried in Highgate Cemetery.

One paradox is that he was a ferocious anti-Semite; if he had lived under Hitler, he could quite possibly have been a Nazi. His Jewishness, even if he never thought of himself as a Jew or admitted that he was of Jewish origin, had a profound influence on his thinking, and probably contributed both to the grudge he felt against society and his dictatorial, righteous quality. One item of curious interest is that Marx is *never* described as Jewish in the Soviet Union today.

A paradox even more startling is that Marx was also profoundly Slavophobe and anti-Russian. It is, indeed, one of the most sensational accidents of history, which contravenes all Marxist doctrine, that Marxism should have had its first tryout in, of all unsuitable places, Russia. There were several reasons why Marx disliked Russia. (He disliked most other countries too, and often gave vent to such opinions as "the French need a thrashing.") For one thing, he never got over being a German, and feared Russia on nationalist grounds; for another, he abhorred the Czarist autocracy. Russia was, to his mind, a kind of exasperating savage irrelevance, not part of the body of Europe at all, and of no consequence in putting his theories to proof. Marx staked all his hopes for proletarian revolution on Germany, not Russia, where there was no proletariat to rise.

Another paradox might be that Marx, anti-Semite and anti-Russian, was also anti-Marxist, in the light of what goes on in the USSR today. He could, at any rate, have little relish for the stupendous state-capitalistic structure that identifies itself as "Marxist" under Khrushchev and company. If he should be brought back to life and deposited in Moscow today, I do not think he would be happy at much that he saw, particularly in the line of Soviet betrayals of his original egalitarian ideals. Marx irremediably changed the face of Russia, but also Russia changed the face of Marx.

*

This is not a book for the expert and we do not need to define here, except in the most elementary and cursory way, what the theory of Marxism is. It is dangerous to oversimplify, but the Marxist concept includes, among much else, the following basic elements:

1. "Scientific" socialism, in contrast to the "Utopian" socialism of his predecessors. Marx founded "scientific socialism," and borrowed for it the name "communism," which he thought would lead to a society without poverty. Moreover he thought in terms of action and immediacy on a world-wide basis. "Workers of the world, unite." By scientific socialism he meant *attainable* socialism, as soon as possible.

2. The Theory of Surplus Value. All wealth, Marx says, derives in the first instance from man's labor; but labor has been cheated of its fair share of reward, because the capitalists, or employing class, take away from labor its "surplus value," by low wages and other mechanisms. This is to put into almost comically simple terms a statement that Marx wrote hundreds of thousands of inordinately complex words about, and which has been the core of millions of disputatious words ever since. In any case, he preached that "government and society in every age are controlled by the class which possesses the chief sources of wealth."[9]

3. Class War and the Dictatorship of the Proletariat. Class conflict, according to Marx, is inevitable, because the proletariat is bound to rise and the bourgeoisie will not surrender its power without a struggle. The bourgeoisie is certain, however, to lose, and be replaced by a new society, just as feudalism was replaced by capitalism. To safeguard the new society after the proletarian revolution is successful, Marx proceeds, there must be a temporary

[9] Carl Becker, *Modern History*, p. 534.

dictatorship of the proletariat. After that, government will no longer be necessary (since governments are based on class, and by this time classes will have disappeared) and the state will "wither away."

4. The Fall of Capital. One reason why the "democratic" proletarian revolution is predestined to be victorious is that it is in the nature of the capitalist system to destroy itself, through excessive competition, the runaway growth of monopoly, and other "contradictions."

5. Above all, Dialectical Materialism. This concept, on which Marx's philosophy of history rests, falls into two divisions. Marx saw history as a process of ebb and flow, of a continuous struggle between opposites, of integration, disintegration, and again integration. To explain this, he used the Hegelian doctrine of the dialectic (*thesis, antithesis, synthesis*), and added to it the theory that the prime motivation in all human affairs was economic, i.e., materialistic. He also held, however, that man created his own destiny, within the great curve of historical development which, he thought, could be accurately and scientifically "determined" or plotted out.

All this was, for the middle of the nineteenth century, extremely heady stuff. Some of it still is, to some. Few people, except professed Communists, take the theory of surplus value seriously any more, but the impact at the time was startling, and Marx had profound cumulative effect. Not many men have left such an imprint on human thought, no matter how fallacious, prejudiced, and tediously dogmatic much of his teaching was. The reasons are not far to seek. There were, at that time as now, more poor people in the world than rich, to whom the Marxist system inevitably appealed; moreover the capitalism of that day, bristling with painful evils and abuses, was glaringly vulnerable to attack. Laborers worked in factories in shameful conditions for twelve or even sixteen hours a day, and their wages were minuscule. On such tinder, Marx was a lively spark. But the basis of his appeal was not purely economic. Communism denies religion; but it became one. It gave millions a passionate, distorted faith. Also it appealed to lazy dissatisfied folk who did not like to think for themselves, and to cynics and careerists who admired the doctrine that the ends justify the means. Above all, Marx brought the individual into acute realization of his own association with the historical process; every good Communist is taught to believe implicitly that he is an agent, not merely of a party or a system, but of the larger forces of history, and that history is *on his side*.[10]

[10] Much in Marx is not original with Marx. The debt to Hegel is manifest, and it was the poet, Heinrich Heine, of all people, who helped win him to the "practical" idea of Communism. He was massively influenced by several French

How did Marx reach Russia? The story is complex. He himself, of course, never set foot on Russian soil, and he must be one of the few characters in history who was a major determinant in the life of a country without ever having been in it. He did, however, sufficiently get over his aversion to things Russian to begin the study of the Russian language, when he was nearing sixty. This was because his work was beginning to have influence there, and he modified his original view that proletarian revolution could not be successful in Russia without an intervening period of bourgeois capitalism.

Das Kapital was first translated into Russian in 1872; this was its first translation into another language.[11] This should certainly go down as one of the seminal dates of modern times; it is a good joke on somebody that the Czarist censorship permitted its publication on the ground that it was unreadable, and too dull "to do anybody harm."[12] Of course Marx had been known in Russia long before this, through intellectuals like Herzen and Bakunin, who had translated the Communist Manifesto. Moreover Marx, by way of the First International, was in close touch with Russian colleagues, and numerous revolutionaries shuttled back and forth between Russia and western Europe. Russian revolutionary thought steadily became more socialist. At first the ogre had not been capital, but the Czar; now it became both. Most of the early revolutionaries were not proletarians at all, however, but came of the middle class; the first Marxist leader in Russia was an intellectual and the son of a nobleman, G. V. Plekhanov. Year by year the movement gained momentum, but slowly, and if it had not been for Lenin it is not at all certain that Marx would ever have conquered Russia. But he did, and the impact is with us yet.

In the Soviet Union today, Marx is of course more alive than he ever was in life. In a recent issue of Pravda chosen at random his name appears twenty-seven times. But oddly enough no important city has ever been named for him. There is an Engels, but no Marx.[13]

---

thinkers, like Proudhon, who coined the slogan "Property is theft," and apparently the concept Dictatorship of the Proletariat came from a French revolutionist, Babeuf. Nor did Marx invent the doctrine of the class struggle, though he was the first to apply it to economics. His contributions as a synthesizer as well as prophet were, nevertheless, prodigious. See Edmund Wilson's brilliant study, To the Finland Station, p. 144.
[11] It did not appear in English until after Marx's death.
[12] Frederick L. Schuman, Russia Since 1917, p. 5, and Berlin, op. cit., p. 254.
[13] A smallish town does exist, however, named Marks on the Volga northeast of Engels, in the former Volga German Republic.

Lenin and the Revolution

Vladimir Ilich Ulyanov organized and led the October Revolution, and was the founder of both the Communist party and the Soviet Union, enough revolutionary achievement for one lifetime. He also created the Communist International. Marx was a theoretician; Lenin was also a theoretician of some weight, but more than that a man of action. What Marx put into words, Lenin, by reason of his extraordinary capacity for leadership, was able to put into deeds. By crude definition "Marxism" is a philosophy; "Leninism" is Marxism applied to government in Russia.

What Lenin did, in effect, was to cut through millions of words of Marx to reassert and achieve a series of simple propositions, based in part on the *Communist Manifesto.* First, the creation of a party; second, the overthrow of bourgeois supremacy; third, setting up of the dictatorship of the proletariat; fourth, the introduction of socialism; fifth, the conquest of political power. Lenin was direct, pragmatic, logical—such un-Russian characteristics!

His life story may be told briefly. He was born Vladimir Ilich Ulyanov in Simbirsk, now called Ulyanovsk, a small city on the Volga, in 1870; Simbirsk was also the birthplace of the novelist Goncharov and of Alexander Kerensky. Kerensky's father was, in fact, one of Lenin's teachers. Lenin took the name "N. Lenin" in his early revolutionary days. The "N" does not represent "Nikolai," as is commonly thought; it was simply part of his pseudonym, and, like the "S" in Harry S. Truman, stands for nothing. Authorities differ as to why Vladimir Ilich adopted this particular name, and the matter has never been cleared up to total satisfaction. One theory is that it was suggested by the Lena River, near which he spent his Siberian exile. (He was exiled only once, for three years.) But he had several *noms de révolution* in those days, and quite possibly hit on "Lenin" by accident.

Lenin's father, Ilya Nikolaevich Ulyanov, was a member of the minor nobility, having reached a rank in the bureaucracy corresponding to that of major general in the army; he was inspector of schools in the Simbirsk district, a consequential post.[14] He was of sound middle-class Russian stock, in which there were probably old Tatar admixtures. Lenin's mother, Maria Alexandrovna Berg, was the daughter of a doctor, and had German blood. She was a devout Lutheran. Even today, a remnant of Americans brought up on early inaccurate renditions of the Bolshevik Revolution think that Lenin was Jewish. Several of his early coadjutors were Jews, like Trotsky

[14] Bertram D. Wolfe, *Three Who Made a Revolution,* p. 46.

(whose real name was Bronstein), Zinoviev (Apfelbaum), and Kamenev (Rosenfeld), but Lenin himself did not have a drop of Jewish blood. Lenin's family was upstanding, well-off, and intellectual. Young Lenin wore an Eton collar to school, and, of all things, read *Tom Sawyer*. By this time youths all over Russia were being swept headlong into the revolutionary movement. Lenin's elder brother, by name Alexander, joined a terrorist society, and, in a juvenile feckless way, became involved in a plot to murder Czar Alexander III; although the plot failed and although he had only the most peripheral connection with it, he was executed. This broke his mother's life, and was, not without reason, a puissant influence on Lenin's subsequent development. Vengeance! On the other hand Lenin was too hard-headed to think much in terms of personal outrage, retaliation, or "romantic" violence. His ruthlessness took larger, more abstract forms. He had, in the words of Hamilton Fish Armstrong, "grandiose visions of the betterment of mankind" plus "total contempt for human life."[15]

Lenin was expelled from the University of Kazan for revolutionary activity, moved to St. Petersburg, and studied law. He became a barrister, and practiced law for a time at Samara. In about 1890 he discovered Marx. This was the controlling event of his life. Back in St. Petersburg, he went into revolutionary work in earnest. He was arrested in 1897, spent a year in prison, and was shipped off to Siberia. He wrote several books, and, in 1900, was allowed to leave Russia and became an *émigré* in Switzerland, where he helped to found and edit the important revolutionary paper *Iskra*, or *Spark*. He moved to London in 1902. When he returned to Petrograd in 1917 to lead the Revolution, he had not been in Russia for ten years.

Lenin was an extraordinarily intricate character, although Soviet idolaters today say that "he was as simple as the truth." The contemporary hagiography obscures much. He had several homely traits and characteristics, loved children and pets, and was wont to make mild little jokes, such as that no woman could understand chess, a railway timetable, or dialectical materialism.[16] He lived in austere simplicity, did not smoke, refused to have easy chairs in his office, disliked cut flowers, and, a curious point, always kept his watch fifteen minutes slow. He had a passion for reading, and, among Russian classics, particularly admired Turgenev. The main elements in his character were a piercing realism, pertinacity, and magnetism. He could meet a man once, and win him for life. Maxim Gorky records that he read a newspaper as

---

[15] *Foreign Affairs Reader*, p. 170. A Leninist would reply to this to the effect that Lenin did *not* have contempt for human life at all as a whole—only for the lives of those who attempted to thwart his plans for making a better life for all.

[16] David Shub, *Lenin*, p. 65.

if his eyes were "burning holes in it"; also that his mind had "the cold glitter of steel shavings." Marx was neither a fanatic, a demagogue, nor even an orator; Lenin was all three, and, besides, loved facts, a combination that can be terrifying.

The story of the Revolution we shall interpolate later. Let us first round out the bare details of Lenin's life. Before the October Revolution was a year old, on August 30, 1918, he was shot and seriously wounded by a young woman Social Revolutionary, by name Fanny Kaplan. He recovered his powers fully, but was shaken. He suffered a severe stroke in 1922, had several other strokes, and died on January 21, 1924. His funeral was one of the supreme events in Soviet history, and, among other things, proved that the Revolution had been won. Even the blindest of observers, suffocated by their hatred of Bolshevism amid the passions of that time, could not but be impressed at the demonstration of mass devotion that occurred. "Three quarters of a million people waited an average of five hours in the Arctic cold of 30 degrees below zero, night and day alike, before passing through the hall where Lenin's body lay in state."[17]

Today, needless to say, Lenin is gospel in the Soviet Union, much more so than Marx. More than 7,300 editions of his works have been printed, and a new edition in fifty-five volumes has just been prepared, to be issued to 200,000 subscribers. He is seldom referred to by name alone, but is called "great Lenin," or something of the sort. He is not only used as a stick to beat opponents with, but is quoted affirmatively on every known variety of topic. He wrote abundantly, and said some things that were contradictory; hence, every time a Soviet writer or speaker quotes him, which is about once every five minutes, a footnote or parenthesis is inserted giving, with a pedantry almost stifling, the exact source and text cited. The most banal observations are preserved; he is quoted, and the relevant authority established, even for such remarks as "Imagination is a quality of great value." It would not be surprising to find him meticulously spitted on the record with some such statement as, "A man has two eyes," or "Three and three make six." In argument he can, of course, be referred to in support of almost any thesis. At the moment the Leninist line is used to support two main considerations: (a) socialist legality, and (b) the necessity for collective leadership.

*

Now to go back. Lenin reached his position as leader of the Revolution in this manner. In 1898, when he was still in Siberia, the Russian Social

[17] Walter Duranty in the Encyclopaedia Britannica, "Russia," p. 742.

Democratic Labor party, father of the present-day Communist party, was organized. It worked underground in Russia, overground abroad. Then it split into two wings. Lenin, arriving in Switzerland, took over the left wing. In 1903, at a party congress in London, the split was formalized, and two rival groups of Social Democrats emerged—the *Bolsheviks* under Lenin, and the *Mensheviks*. The division came more out of considerations of tactics than philosophy. Meantime another party, the Social Revolutionary party, had come into existence (1901). The SD's (both Bolshevik and Menshevik) and the SR's detested each other, and for years fought bitterly. The SR's were much less disciplined than the SD's, and believed overtly in assassination and terrorism.[18]

In 1905 came an astonishing event, the first Russian revolution. It followed the defeat of Russia in the Russo-Japanese War, just as emancipation of the serfs followed the Crimean War, and as the February and October revolutions to come in 1917 were indissolubly connected with Russia's defeat in World War I. Foreign wars always seem to shake Russia up: perhaps this is one reason why its present rulers do not want one.[19]

The 1905 events caught most SD and SR leaders by surprise. Bolsheviks and Mensheviks had been arguing heatedly in cold garrets all over western Europe about how to manage the impending revolution—when it came! Lenin at once contrived to return to Russia for a brief interval.

From 1905 to 1917 Russia had, for the only time in its history, quasi-representative government. But the Czar was still an autocrat, without whose consent fundamental laws could not be changed, the country still had no constitution, and the powers of the Duma (parliament) were rudimentary. Even so, this was an advance. The year 1905 was important for two other reasons. Until "Bloody Sunday" (January 22, 1905), when Czarist troops wantonly fired on a procession of workers in St. Petersburg, and subsequent indiscriminate bloodletting in Moscow after a general strike, the Czar himself, most historians tell us, was genuinely loved by the broad mass of the Russian people. He was the "Little Father." After Bloody Sunday the fiction that he was a father, little or not, was difficult to preserve. Second, the word "soviet" became consequential for the first time. This word, which merely means "council," now became invested with an entirely new sig-

[18] The Bolsheviks did not strike out and form a party entirely of their own until 1912, and did not adopt the official name "Communist party (Bolsheviks)" until much later.

[19] During the Russo-Japanese War a Russian liberal said, "The Japanese will not enter the Kremlin, but the Russians will." Bernard Pares, *A History of Russia*, p. 485.

nificance. Strikes were organized by the St. Petersburg Workers Soviet, and it came to mean revolutionary *workers' power*. Lenin decided that armed insurrection against the Czar was feasible, and set out to prepare the way for it.

In 1917 there were, as everybody knows, two more revolutions. The one known universally today as the "February" Revolution occurred on March 8. Russia used at that time the Julian calendar, thirteen days behind our Gregorian calendar.[20] Factors which played a role were disgust with the course of World War I, which was eating the life of the nation away; mass desertions in the army; a severe breakdown in domestic economy; moral, ethical, and social dissatisfactions; disintegration in the court, culminating in the murder of the Czarina's favorite Rasputin. Riots broke out in St. Petersburg (since 1914 called Petrograd) which Czarist troops refused to put down; in fact they fraternized with the strikers. The Duma declined to accept an imperial decree ordering its dissolution, and, on March 12, established a provisional government. There was practically no resistance, and very little bloodshed. Nicholas II abdicated on March 15, and, a few days later, the dynasty ended. The monarchy was not forcibly wrenched off the throne; it fell of its own torpid weight. In the following months the provisional government, under Alexander Kerensky and others, vainly sought to hold power.

The Bolsheviks had little, if anything, to do with the February Revolution, which was almost completely unorganized, or with the fall of Czardom. The chief Bolshevik leaders were abroad or underground, and litanists of the party today contemptuously dismiss the events of February as the "bourgeois-democratic revolution."

But the October Revolution was quite a different story. With this the Bolsheviks had a great deal to do: they made it, although they were a minority among the revolutionaries. Lenin, on the outbreak of war in 1914, was living in Galicia; the Austrian authorities arrested him as an undesirable alien, and deported him to Switzerland. In 1917 the German general staff conceived the idea that this corrosive revolutionary could be of signal value to their arms. He might provoke a new revolution in Russia, which in turn might reverse the pro-Ally policy of the provisional government, or even seek a separate peace and take Russia out of the war, which would immensely serve German ends.[21] Lenin and a handful of companions were shipped across

[20] To be precise, the Julian calendar is thirteen days behind in the twentieth century: it was twelve days behind in the nineteenth century and will be fourteen days behind in the twenty-first, if anybody cares. Charques, *op. cit.*, p. 22.

[21] Peace *was* signed with Germany, on terms disastrous for Russia, at Brest Litovsk on March 3, 1918, but by the Bolsheviks.

Germany in a sealed train, and arrived in Petrograd on April 16, 1917. It is of the utmost interest that Lenin, although revolution in Russia was what he had hoped and worked for all his life, was not exclusively interested in Russia by any means. He represented the *international* Communist conspiracy. The October Revolution was made by *émigrés*, by a handful of outsiders. Moreover, let us repeat, they were a minority. Only five Bolshevik deputies had been in the Duma. They were also a distinct minority in the first All-Russian Congress of Soviets of Workers and Soldiers Deputies (June 16), and, as everybody who has read John Reed knows, were fanatically opposed by elements in the army, the trade unions, and even the Central Committee of the Party.[22]

How, then, were Lenin and his men able to reach and hold power? The chief weapons were three. First, he converted the *party*, even if small, into an extremely effective and sharp instrument, the elite "vanguard" of the proletariat. Second, he was a masterful political manipulator, who did not hesitate to use force brutally. Third, and above all, he promised peace, and the people were mortally sick of war. Also consider the "technological" aspect of the Revolution, for which Trotsky was responsible. He invented the technique of the modern coup, in which extensive military effort is avoided, and effort concentrated on seizing key points of power, like the telegraph office and other means of communication.

In any case, the Bolsheviks duly seized power on October 25 (old calendar); the Revolution is always called the October Revolution (or in Russia simply "October" or "Great October") although, since the adoption of the western calendar by the Soviet Union, it is celebrated on November 7. Slogans like "Peace! Land! Bread!" and "All Power to the Soviets!" reverberated through the country. Before long these became transmuted into other slogans, like "He who does not work, neither shall he eat," and, not quite so menacing, "From each according to his abilities, to each according to his needs." The means of production were seized by the state, and the land nationalized; banks were taken over, and the public debt repudiated. Not the least astounding thing about this revolution was that it was almost bloodless. Total casualties were probably not more than a few hundred. What sober historians have called "the greatest event in human history since the

[22] Russia has had only one moderately free election in its entire history. This occurred immediately *after* the Bolshevik *coup d'état*, on November 25; it had been set up before the Revolution in order to choose a constituent assembly, and could not be easily called off. The Bolsheviks won only 175 out of 707 seats. The SR's won by far the biggest representation. Of course the Bolsheviks subsequently saw to it that the constituent assembly never functioned.

Reformation" duly occurred, and, except for a good deal of oratory and noisy scratching of pens, it was as if a button had dropped.

*

More than buttons dropped, however, in the civil war that followed, and which tore Russia apart until 1920.[23] From the perspective of today what counts most about the civil war period, or, as the Bolsheviks called it, "the period of militant Communism," was foreign intervention. British, French, Czech, Polish, Japanese, and other foreign troops entered the field, to help suppress the horror of Bolshevism. Great Britain intended to take the rich Baku area, and France the Crimea.[24] The White leader, Admiral Kolchak, out in Siberia, became briefly "Supreme Ruler of Russia," and the Bolsheviks lost for a time something like two-thirds of their total territory. The United States put several thousand troops into Siberia. All this confirmed the Communist thesis of the time, that, by Marxist doctrine, the capitalist world could not possibly afford to let a socialist state survive. It did, however, manage to survive. The Reds won. Intervention was bitterly resented by the Communists, and still is. No wonder. Imagine, if the United States were fighting for its life in a civil war, what the American attitude would be if Soviet Russia and other powers invaded and occupied large areas of our territory.

In March, 1921, following a mutiny of Soviet sailors at the Kronstadt naval base, Lenin introduced the New Economic Policy, or NEP. This was a "strategic retreat," made necessary because of economic breakdown. Communism seemed to be a chaotic failure. One story is that, outside the main headquarters of the electrical industry, a sign was posted next to the doorbell, "Bell not working." Famine struck the Volga regions. Private trading was restored to an extent under NEP, agricultural policy was modified, and the banking system was reorganized. A return to a modified, reformed capitalism was in full swing. This produced, among other things, a splendid rhetorical passage from Mr. Churchill: "Lenin was the Grand Repudiator. He repudiated everything. He repudiated God, King, Country, morals, treaties, debts,

[23] Don Cossacks loyal to the old regime started the civil war, but it is interesting to note that, in Russia as a whole, four-fifths of the officers of the Red Army, as it sprang into being, were former Czarist officers. Also the Orthodox Patriarch took the Red side. Another point is that this fierce, bloody struggle could not have been won by the Communists had it not been for the genius, courage, and vivacity of Leon Trotsky, vilified nowadays as a "traitor."

[24] Vera Micheles Dean, The United States and Russia, p. 32.

rents, interest, the laws and customs of centuries, all contracts written or implied, the whole structure—such as it is—of human society. In the end he repudiated himself. He repudiated the Communist system." When death seized him "the Russian people were left floundering in the bog. Their worst misfortune was his birth; their next worst—his death."[25]

The *effect* of Lenin's accomplishment, no matter what Mr. Churchill says, is that he created a new kind of state, on "foundations new to the world's experience." He set into motion what has been called "the greatest social experiment in history," and, although his original premises and promises have been abused and distorted beyond recognition, the challenge he laid down is still strongly with us. The world has never been the same since his advent, and whether you like him or not it is indisputable that he was a great man, one of the greatest of modern times.

As to NEP it lasted till 1927, when Stalin killed it.

The Stalin Aftermath

Stalin, whose real name was Josef Vissarionovich Dzhugashvili, was born in the Georgian town of Gori, near Tiflis, in 1879. His father was a cobbler, his mother a peasant woman; he was the first ruler of Russia whose background was authentically proletarian. From 1898 to 1917 he was a professional revolutionary living an almost totally submerged life. He came to Lenin's attention, and Lenin wrote to Gorky in 1913 about the "wonderful Georgian" in his entourage.[26] Later Lenin did not think him quite so wonderful.

Stalin had an utterly closed mind, and told an interviewer once that he believed in one thing only, "the power of the human will." His other qualities included concentration, remorselessness, cunning, an almost inhuman patience, and, above all, durability. "Stalin" is derived from the Russian word meaning "steel," and the legend is that comrades in the early days gave him this name in tribute to his iron durability. He cared nothing for human life. He curdled the blood of a Polish plenipotentiary once by asking him *why* he bothered to wonder if several thousand Polish officers in Russia were dead or alive. It was written of him by a youthful journalist visiting Russia many years ago, "He is about as emotional as a slab of basalt. If he has nerves, they are veins in rock."[27]

In exile above the Arctic Circle when the October Revolution occurred, Stalin took no part in events of the first days. But he became active and im-

[25] Winston S. Churchill, *The Aftermath*, p. 65.
[26] Wolfe, *op. cit.*, p. 398.
[27] But a former American Ambassador wrote of him once, "His brown eye is exceedingly kind and gentle. A child would like to sit on his knee."

portant soon; he was, in fact, one of the seven members of the first Politburo, which Lenin set up in October; the others were Trotsky, Zinoviev, Kamenev, Bubnov, and Sokolnikov. Because he was a Georgian and had always been interested in national questions, Lenin made him Commissar of Nationalities in his first cabinet, or Council of People's Commissars, and he was the man largely responsible for transforming Russia into the USSR, a difficult task and a vitally important development. It is often said that, until he chose to make himself prime minister in 1941, Stalin had never held a government post, but had always ruled from behind the scenes in his role as party secretary; this is not quite true, and he did not become party secretary till 1922.

Stalin's rule, which lasted almost thirty years, can be divided into several clearly marked periods, which, however, overlap to an extent.

1. The struggle for power with Trotsky and the "Left Opposition," after Lenin's death in 1924. Stalin and the temperamental, aristocratic Trotsky were deadly rivals. Moreover, each personified a radically different approach to the most pressing problem of the time, on which the very existence of the new Soviet Union depended. Trotsky, an intellectual who had lived most of his life outside Russia, believed passionately in the doctrine of the "permanent revolution," and held that socialism could not succeed in a single state. Stalin took the opposite view, as everybody knows, and insisted that the first task of the party was to build up *Russia*. Trotsky, too restless and individualistic to be a good politician, was no match for Stalin; he was ousted from leadership in the party in 1926, and expelled from the Soviet Union in 1929.[28] His murder in Mexico followed.

2. The period of the Five-Year Plans, beginning in 1928. Industrialization on a major massive scale began, and transformed utterly the face of the nation. Along with industrialization, during the first plan, came the collectivization of agriculture, which has been called the biggest event in all Russian history. Collectivization (socialization) was completed by 1933, and, at frightful cost, some 25,000,000 individual peasant holdings were concentrated into the present fabric of collective and state farms.

A great many kulaks resisted this unpleasant process, which was held to be necessary because the old agriculture was so disorganized and wasteful, and killed their livestock rather than co-operate with the government. Almost *fifty* per cent of farm animals in the country were slaughtered, and, even

[28] Stalin's technique in this struggle, which he also used in liquidating the "Right Opposition" later, was simple enough. The Right Opposition, led by Lenin's devoted disciple, Nikolai I. Bukharin, believed that under Stalin the socialization of Russia was proceeding at too *rapid* a pace. Stalin got rid of his enemies by (a) ruthless manipulation of the party machine, and (b) interpreting Leninism in such a way as to make all his opponents heretics, and therefore punishable.

today, production of livestock has not yet made up for all of this catastrophic loss. Next the peasants attempted to sabotage the government by passive resistance, and refused to harvest their grain. They gambled that Stalin would not let them starve. They gambled wrong. He did let them starve, and something like five million peasants died. "First the peasants killed their animals. Then they killed themselves."

3. In 1934 began the purges, a period of blight and terror. Millions went into forced labor. Stalin consolidated his power, installed a new constitution (1936), announced that the exploiting classes had been liquidated and socialism "in the main" achieved, and became deified.

4. In the realm of foreign affairs came the Popular Front period, then the Russo-German Pact, and then the Nazi invasion of Russia and its aftermath, what Soviet citizens always call the Great Patriotic War. Russia, after a bad start, beat off the German attack, with Stalin as Generalissimo. After the war the Yalta Conference gave him what was probably the greatest triumph of his life, although Mr. Roosevelt and Mr. Churchill did not mean this to be so. Nor did he get all he wanted at Yalta. Meantime, the Third International languished and was put to death.

5. The black despotism of the later years, during which the Cold War got under way. Stalin died on March 5, 1953. It is possible that he was murdered, although no evidence has ever come to light.

It is the fashion to criticize Stalin these days, and minimize his achievements, but these, in some respects, bordered on the colossal. *He made the Revolution a success.* More than any man since Peter the Great, he was the enemy of Russian backwardness. He said in 1931, "The history of old Russia is of defeats due to backwardness. She was beaten by the Mongol Khans. She was beaten by the Turkish Beys. She was beaten by the Swedish feudal lords. She was beaten by the Polish-Lithuanian squires. She was beaten by the Anglo-French imperialists. She was beaten by the Japanese barons. All beat her for her backwardness, her military backwardness, her cultural backwardness, her governmental backwardness, her industrial backwardness, her agricultural backwardness." Stalin resolved, with a mighty concentration of will and utterly ruthless imposition of this will on the body of the largest nation on earth, to end this backwardness once and for all, wipe it out, extirpate it, abolish it, so that never, never, never, no matter how long history lasted, would Russia ever be defeated again.

It is also necessary to point out that Stalin was probably responsible for more deaths than any man in history, with the possible exceptions of Hitler and Genghis Khan.

CHAPTER IX

The Soviet Union Has Fifteen Republics

*Who rules East Europe commands the Heartland;
who rules the Heartland commands the World-
Island; who rules the World-Island commands the
World.*

—SIR HALFORD MACKINDER

Russia is not a State, but a World.

—CZARIST PROVERB

Now we must tackle geography. Russia did not get the name "Union of Soviet Socialist Republics" until 1923, when, largely as a result of Stalin's work on the nationality problem, the present federal union was set up. The four original republics were Russia proper, the Ukraine, White Russia, and the Transcaucasian Soviet Federated Socialist Republic, composed in turn of Georgia, Armenia, and Azerbaijan. Soviet writers sometimes compare the first four republics to the original thirteen states of the United States, in that they were the nucleus for further growth. The Transcaucasian Republic was in time broken up, and its three members duly entered the USSR as separate entities. By 1936, the date of the new "Stalin" constitution, there were eleven republics. The number rose to sixteen, and then, when the Karelo-Finnish Republic, which had been admitted to the Union in 1940, was demoted to the status of an autonomous republic within Russia proper, it dropped to fifteen, the number that obtains today.

The nationality problem was, from the beginning, given extraordinary priority by the builders of the Soviet system, if only because the population of Russia was not less than 57 per cent non-Russian in 1917; Russians were, though the fact is hard to believe, an actual minority in their own country. Lenin knew full well that something must be done, as soon as possible, to recognize the position and claims of the non-Russians, and build a cohesive multi-

169

national structure, if only to make Russia itself stronger. Besides, in those days, the principle of self-determination was an overriding slogan; Lenin borrowed much from Wilson. Also, of course, Lenin was not merely head of the new Russian state, but of an international Communist network that had surface tracings, if not roots, almost everywhere. His conception of a Soviet "Union" was strictly in accordance with his basic hypothesis. He thought in terms of gradually expanding concentric circles of Communist power, with Russia as the core. The creation of various Soviet republics, their progressive "admittance" to the Union, and the fiction that all this was voluntary, rose inevitably out of the master plan.

To this day, every Soviet apologist not only clings to the myth that membership of the various republics in the Union is voluntary, but stresses it vigorously. "This is a voluntary union of nations, united for the joint building of socialism," Madame Furtseva stated recently. Moreover, it is repeatedly pointed out that every member republic, by terms of the 1936 constitution, is free to *secede* from the Union at any time; this principle goes back to Lenin himself. We do not need to elaborate on what would happen if one of the republics ever *should* try to secede.

The fifteen Union republics are these:

Name	Area (square miles)	Population April, 1956	Capital
RSFSR			
(Russia proper)	5,593,909	113,200,000	Moscow
The Ukraine	232,604	40,600,000	Kiev
White Russia			
(Belorussia)	80,154	8,000,000	Minsk
Armenia	11,506	1,600,000	Yerevan
Georgia	29,498	4,000,000	Tbilisi (Tiflis)
Azerbaijan	33,089	3,400,000	Baku
Uzbekistan	156,640	7,300,000	Tashkent
Kazakhstan	1,062,242	8,500,000	Alma-Ata
Turkmenistan	187,181	1,400,000	Ashkhabad
Tadzhikistan	54,826	1,800,000	Stalinabad
Kirghizia	76,718	1,900,000	Frunze
Moldavia	13,050	2,700,000	Kishinev
Lithuania	25,174	2,700,000	Vilnius (Vilna)
Latvia	24,903	2,000,000	Riga
Estonia	17,413	1,100,000	Tallinn (Reval)

By Soviet tenets, each Union republic is an independent, "sovereign" state, with its own supreme soviet, flag, council of ministers, and party structure, but anything vital to the Union as a whole is of course decided by Moscow. Most republic leaders of consequence, in addition to holding local posts, are delegates to the Supreme Soviet of the Union; this is as if the governor of an American state, say, should also be a Senator or Congressman in Washington. There are no passport or customs examinations at republic frontiers within the Union, and citizens of each republic are also citizens of the Union as a whole. The ministerial structure is inordinately complex, and includes what are known as Union, Union-republic, and republic ministries; in general, each republic has a ministerial apparatus that parallels the central structure in Moscow, as well as "independent" ministries. A political scientist could amuse himself for a long period by comparing the Russian federal structure with that of the United States.

Each of the fifteen republics, as we shall see later in this book, is encouraged to preserve and emphasize its own culture, languages (with qualifications), folklore, and the like. The Moscow government will let the minorities do anything they like, provided it is harmless.[1] I was reminded several times, while traveling in the exterior republics, of Dr. Albert Schweitzer. Once Schweitzer, in an attempt to reconcile his belief in human equality with the backwardness of the Africans with whom he was working, and who were only too manifestly not his equals, remarked with asperity, "I am their brother, yes, but their *elder* brother." Much the same attitude may be observed in the behavior of Moscow toward the republics. And, of course, if Moscow wants to crack down, all it has to do is do so. In the great purges of the 1930's, no fewer than seven republic presidents and six republic prime ministers were shot.

To become a Union republic, a Soviet area has to fulfill three conditions—constitute an ethnic unit, have a self-sufficient economy, and lie on a frontier. This last stipulation is curious, and derives from the stoutly held, but fictional, assumption that each republic has the right to secede. Obviously, if a republic lay imbedded in the center of the Union, its "right" of secession would be compromised. So every republic touches a *foreign* area, strange as this may seem; White Russia fronts on Poland, Turkmenistan on Iran, Georgia and Armenia on Turkey, and so on.

This rough summary by no means exhausts the nationality picture. Many peoples in the Soviet Union—dozens—do not have the geographical position or economic development necessary for the status of full republics. Yet, in accordance with Soviet nationality principles, these must all be duly recog-

[1] Walter Kolarz, *Russia and Her Colonies*, makes this point, and is a thorough and indispensable guide to these matters.

nized, with their cultural identity protected and opportunity for autonomous advance assured. Hence, within the full Union republics, a number of secondary republics exist; some are enormous, bigger than the smaller full republics. These are known as "Autonomous Soviet Socialist Republics," and carry after their names the abbreviation "ASSR." Seventeen of these exist in all, of which most are in Russia proper, like the Yakut, Bashkir, and Dagestan ASSR's. Below these in the scheme, but separate from them, are other national regions less advanced, which are known as "Autonomous Regions"; of these there are ten. One is in Georgia, one in Tadzhikistan, one in Azerbaijan; the rest are in the RSFRS. Finally, for people still less developed, but who nevertheless have their own distinct national characteristics, there are ten "National Areas."

The Immense Mass of Russia Proper

The *Russian Soviet Federated Socialist Republic*, or Russia proper, which includes Siberia, is by far the largest of the fifteen Union republics, and contains more than half the total population of the Union. It stretches all the way from East Prussia to the Bering Strait, and from points far above the Arctic Circle to the borders of Manchuria and China. Not only is it the largest and most populous of the republics; it is by far the most important culturally, economically, and historically. This is the great mother republic, to which most of the others are attached, like piglets suckling on a monstrous sow.

The word "Federated" appears in its name because its immense mass contains an immense variety of peoples, who live in no fewer than fourteen autonomous republics, seven autonomous regions, fifty-four provinces or lesser regions, and six national areas. Just like the Union of which it is a part, the RSFSR is an amalgam of different parts, and carries out, on a subordinate scale, the same principle of nationalist subdivision.

The European area of the RSFSR, roughly a quarter of the whole, is what people instinctively think of as "Russia," and is the epicenter and "basic national element" of Soviet power. Moscow is, of course, the capital— both of the Union and of the RSFSR. The "central industrial region" surrounding Moscow accounts for not less than 25 per cent of all Soviet industry.[2] In the RSFSR as a whole are commanding cities like Leningrad, to be described in a subsequent chapter, the Volga regions, the rich agricultural area in the north Caucasus known as the Kuban, the Urals and their

[2] Theodore Shabad, *Geography of the USSR*, p. 97.

RUSSIA IN EUROPE

prodigious concentration of mineral wealth, the great industrial complexes in the Urals and Siberia, and multitudinous other elements in the broad Soviet picture. It contains two-thirds of the Union's total crop area. Also the Soviet polar regions—the Arctic Belt—fall within the RSFSR. Russia is to a pronounced degree Arctic-conscious, if only because the Arctic has lately become so important in world strategy and aerial communications. The intimidating quality of these frigid areas may be gauged from the fact that the island of Novaya Zemlya, between the Arctic Ocean and the Kara Sea, stretches a distance equivalent to that between Maine and Florida, and has a population of exactly four hundred. But Soviet research into Arctic regions, under their eternal mask of ice, is pertinacious and incessant. Much work has been done on the study of ice, for instance on floe movements, and on mapping coasts and currents; also geologists are on the lookout for strategic minerals. Not till 1932 did any ship ever sail across the closed polar seas from Archangel to Vladivostok, along the extreme northern rim of the Eurasian continent. Today this remarkable voyage is routine, at least in summer, and ships cover the distance, eleven thousand nautical miles, in nineteen days. A voyage between the same points around the Scandinavian coast, the Atlantic, the Mediterranean, the Indian Ocean, and the Pacific takes more than three months.

Of the autonomous republics imbedded in the European section of the RSFSR, several have marked interest. On the precipitous northern slopes of the Caucasus is *Dagestan*, with its capital at Makhach-Kala; this is an ethnological crazy-quilt, and has thirty-odd different racial groups or tribes—some of them extremely primitive mountain people—who speak no fewer than seventeen *main* languages. Nearby is the important oil-producing center of Grozny. Along the middle Volga between Gorky and Ulyanovsk, where Lenin was born, is a cluster of small autonomous republics—*Mari, Mordovia, Udmurt*, and *Chuvash*—populated by peoples of Finno-Ugric origin, who are probably related to the ancient Huns. Below, centering on Kazan, is the *Tatar* ASSR; the Tatars have lived here since the Golden Horde.

To the East, and reaching close to Siberia, is the noteworthy *Bashkir* ASSR. The Bashkirs, a Turkic survival, have a picturesque identity. The capital, Ufa, dates from 1596, and the Bashkir people recently celebrated the four-hundredth anniversary of their "voluntary" entry into Russian dominion. They were nomads at the beginning, whose specialty was raising half-wild horses. The well-known Russian drink kumiss, fermented mare's milk, is a Bashkir contribution. A writer less recognized than he should be, S. F. Aksakov, author of A *Family Chronicle*, lived in Bashkiria for many years.

The Bashkir steppes lead up to the rich Ural foothills. Bashkirs are a spirited people, and can complain vociferously on occasion. In May, 1957, Z. N. Nuriyev, a Bashkir deputy to the Supreme Soviet, said that departmental disputes in Moscow and "artificially erected barriers" have severely hampered Bashkir production of copper, and impeded the development of the local petroleum-chemical industry. "Development . . . is lagging inadmissibly."

Far to the north is the *Komi ASSR*, which stretches deep into Siberia and almost reaches the Ob. This is a very large area, covering 156,200 square miles, the size of California. The capital is Syktyvkar. Komi in 1917 had seven hospitals, one pharmacy and no doctors; today it has 2,000 doctors and 365 medical institutions. The Komis are an offshoot of the Finns. The notorious labor camp Vorkuta lies near the extreme northeastern tip of Komi, just above the Arctic Circle. Coal and oil are the principal elements in the Komi economy, along with furs and timber. The republic has 150 industrial enterprises described as "large," employing 150,000 industrial workers, up in the freezing Arctic. No fewer than thirty different ministries and departments in Moscow had a finger in Komi affairs until recently, and gave contradictory directions to its economy. As a result of the Khrushchev decentralization of industry scheme, if it works, a single Economic Council of the Komi Republic will try to make order out of this bureaucratic chaos.

A Calendar of Cities

Any attempt to list even a few of the principal cities of the RSFSR will make these pages look like a gazetteer, and no writer wants his pages to look like a gazetteer, particularly a Russian gazetteer. But anyway let me try. Most Russian cities, particularly those new, are as alike as tenpins or mothballs, but some still preserve a bright individual quality. Ringing Moscow in a broad circle are several whose historical associations, at least, have colorful interest. SMOLENSK, near the border of White Russia, commands the western entry into Moscow; Napoleon knew it well, and so did Hitler.

On the headwaters of the Volga is KALININ, known for centuries as Tver. This, one of the oldest towns in Russia, started life as a fort, built by the Suzdal princes to ward off invasion from Novgorod; like Ryazan nearby, it was a rival dukedom to Moscow for many years. It is pierced by the old railway, laid straight as a needle, which connects Moscow with Leningrad. Also it was, and is, well known for specialized industries—bamboo furniture and boots in the old days, and textiles and railway carriages today.

Eastward on the upper Volga is another historic town, YAROSLAVL, which has the prettiest church I ever saw in Russia and which, despite its contemporary conversion to all manner of industry, still retains something of its medieval character.[3] Not far away are VLADIMIR, founded in 1116, once famous for icon making and now for tractors, and, in a different category, IVANOVO, a vital textile center under the Czars, and still the same today. It is called the Russian Manchester. Here the first Soviet of Workers Deputies in Russia was set up in 1905.

Many central Russian towns were identified with particular crafts, out of which grew the early co-operative movement. Whole towns specialized in such articles as saddlery, axes, locks, and toys.[4] For several generations TULA, south of Moscow on the Upa River, was noted for the manufacture of (a) firearms and (b) samovars; also strangely enough for the quality of its gingerbread. Peter the Great established the Imperial Small Arms Factory at Tula in 1712, under the superintendence of a British expert, by name Trewheller. This plant still exists, and has recently produced a new and sensationally superior type of pistol, invented by a man named Margolin. But Tula is no longer the "armaments capital" of Russia, if only because styles in armament have changed.[5]

Leningrad too is surrounded by historic cities, like NOVGOROD and PSKOV. The former dates from 862, and in the Middle Ages was a famous city-state, like old Italian cities or even Nuremberg; it had an art-loving merchant class, the wealth of which was based mostly on furs.[6] Novgorod sided with Lithuania in the fifteenth-century wars, and as punishment, Ivan IV killed sixty thousand of its citizens, and then prayed for their souls. It has a wonderful old Kremlin. To the northwest of Leningrad is VYBORG (Viipuri), which was Finnish until 1940; the Finns would like to have it back. Here Lenin spent some months in 1917, between the February and October revolutions, when the provisional government put a price on his head, and he wrote here, although one would think that he would have had more immediate things to think about, the best-known of his theoretical works, *The State and Revolution.*

In the extreme north are MURMANSK on the Kola Peninsula, and ARCHANGEL (Arkhangelsk), where the Great Northern Sea Route begins. Mur-

[3] Incidentally the first recorded use of the knout came in Yaroslavl.
[4] For details of towns like these under the *ancien régime* a most valuable source is Nevin O. Winter, *The Russian Empire of Today and Yesterday.*
[5] The Margolin pistol has won awards for Soviet marksmen in several international competitions. A remarkable point is that the inventor is blind. USSR, No. 7.
[6] D. S. Mirsky, A *History of Russian Literature*, p. 17.

mansk, even though it is in the polar regions, is flicked by the tail of the Gulf Stream, and is consequently ice-free all year. Here are Lapps and reindeer. Mineral reserves that are described as "spectacular" have recently been discovered in the Murmansk hinterland. Archangel is important as a lumber center as well, but the lumber industry has been in trouble recently. A recent report in *Izvestia* says, "The tremendous losses of the Archangel lumber combine continue to grow. . . . The lumber enterprises not only make poor use of equipment but in general they take poor care of it as well. . . . Repairs are neglected. . . . Lumber is often loaded by hand while cranes and other loading equipment are unused. . . . Branches are trimmed in the old way with axes. Nowhere is there any equipment except buckets for pouring fuel."[7]

Next, the constellation of great cities along the middle and lower Volga. GORKY, the old Nizhni Novgorod, the sixth biggest city in the Soviet Union (population 876,000), was founded in 1220, and has been a lively trading center for more than five hundred years. It lies at the junction of the Volga and Oka; when I visited it in 1928, arriving by boat from Tver, I thought it was the most attractive city I saw in Russia. During the years that it was Nizhni Novgorod, its annual fair, the Nizhnegorodskaya Yarmarka, founded by Ivan III, was the most celebrated of all European commercial fairs, with the possible exception of that of Leipzig. The fairs are no longer held. In contemporary times, the sinister A. A. Zhdanov was boss of Gorky for many years, and built his reputation here before moving on to Leningrad. Today Gorky is par excellence the citadel of heavy industry—locomotives, heavy machinery, rolling stock. Newsprint for *Pravda* comes from a near-by town, Pravdinsk. Gorky's automobile plant, where the Zim is made, was built by engineers sent over by Henry Ford in 1932.

Further east along the Volga is KAZAN, the Tatar center. It has a famous university, where Tolstoy and Lenin studied. In Czarist times, few Tatar students were admitted; today, they are all over the place. Kazan has a watch factory which is said to turn out a wrist watch every two seconds. To the south, still on the Volga, is KUIBYSHEV, the old Samara, with 760,000 people. Here the Soviet government set up its temporary capital in 1941, when it seemed that the invading Germans would capture Moscow. It was founded in the sixteenth century, and today has one of the largest hydroelectric stations in the USSR, with a capacity of two million kilowatts.[8] SARATOV, further

---

[7] *Current Digest of the Soviet Press*, January 9, 1957.
[8] The city was renamed in honor of Valerian V. Kuibyshev, a party stalwart of the 1920's. The trade-union leader Shvernik was its boss for many years.

south, with half a million people, is another important point. An immense dam and hydroelectric plant are under construction nearby. The lower Volga, like the Dnieper, is bridged by a formidable succession of dams. Saratov stretches for thirty miles along the Volga, and taps a fantastically rich agricultural area.

Southwest is the pivotal industrial city STALINGRAD, population 525,000. Here too a prodigious power station is being built; when the dam is completed in 1960 the Volga water will be backed up almost all the way to Saratov, and a huge sea formed which, Soviet experts say, will be the largest man-made body of water in the world, covering more than six thousand square miles. Also Stalingrad is the eastern terminus of the Volga-Don Canal. Stalingrad's record during World War II is well known, and it is officially one of the four "Hero Cities" in the Soviet Union.[9] Practically nothing was left of Stalingrad, and the completeness of the work of reconstruction is remarkable; it might even be considered handsome, with its "Avenue of Heroes" and "Fallen Fighters Square." An entirely new city, Volzhski, has been built across the river, primarily to house workers on the hydroelectric project. Always, when a development like Stalingrad-Volzhski gets under way, one of the first buildings to be erected is a House of Culture; that of Stalingrad is probably the most sumptuous in the Union. Several other sights are notable here. One is the very large bronze statue of Stalin, almost as big as the Statue of Liberty, that commands the city; it is still undecided whether to tear it down or not. Another sight, if smaller, is splendid—the magnificent jeweled sword presented by the British royal house to the Soviet government during the war, as a token of its admiration for the defense of Stalingrad.

The Volga reaches the Caspian at ASTRAKHAN, the sturgeon city.[10] The population is 276,000. The peculiar people known as Khazars, nomads who adopted Judaism in about A.D. 800, came from the Astrakhan area, and comprised one of the first migrating waves of Asian peoples invading European Russia.

Finally, ROSTOV-ON-DON, (population 552,000) the capital of the North Caucasus. It is not a particularly attractive city, but its airport, I will attest, has an admirable restaurant; its industrial undertakings include everything from agricultural machinery to food products, from airplanes and cement to shipyards and cigarettes. Not far away, in its fertile agricultural hinterland,

[9] The others, which were all subjected to long sieges, are Leningrad, Odessa, and Sevastopol.
[10] The first Englishman ever to see the Caspian was an explorer named Sir Anthony Jenkinson, who reached it in 1557.

is Gigant, the biggest farm in the world. The Rostov area is the heart of the old Cossack territory.

*

Strikingly enough, political leaders of the RSFSR are as a rule inconspicuous, in fact practically unknown. Take A. M. Puzanov. He was till recently chairman of the Council of Ministers of the RSFSR, and as such, was chief executive of one of the largest administrative units in the world, with an area almost twice that of the United States and a population of more than 100,000,000. But not one person in a hundred thousand either outside Russia or in has ever so much as heard his name.[11]

Siberia and Alaska

The concept "Siberia" automatically suggests coldness, loneliness, immensity, and exile. Much of it is, indeed, quite cold. Large regions are under "permafrost," and what geographers call the "cold pole" of the world lies in Siberia, east of the Lena River; the lowest temperature ever recorded in the world, ninety degrees below zero Fahrenheit, was registered in Siberia back in 1892.[12] And certainly Siberia is still lonely, immense, and full of exiles. But Siberia is not what it used to be; what it symbolizes today is industrial development, change in the center of gravity of the Soviet Union, and a vast movement of population, although in large areas the density of population is still only one person per square mile.

Siberia is an arsenal, "the inner bastion of Soviet defense." Here is 75 per cent of the Union's coal, 80 per cent of its water power, 80 per cent of its timber, 65 per cent of its tin, in terms of potential reserves, as well as incalculable other mineral resources and raw materials. Here new cities have sprung up like metal dandelions. The atmosphere resembles, to a degree, that of the American West in frontier days; pioneers build cabins with their own hands and "town warmings" take place as new urban clusters become habitable. The emigration from western to eastern Russia is one of the most significant phenomena in the Soviet Union today; some three million new workers will, it is planned, settle in Siberia by 1960. Industrial development has, of course, been incessant. Events in World War II helped to prompt this: multitudes of factories were moved bodily west to keep them out of German hands. The chief industrial complexes are the Mag-

[11] Puzanov was recently succeeded by a former mayor of Moscow, Mikhail Yasnov. Then Yasnov was succeeded in turn by Frol R. Kozlov. The premiership of the RSFSR is usually a tryout post or stepping stone.

[12] The lowest temperature ever recorded in the United States was seventy degrees below zero Fahrenheit, at Rogers Pass, Montana, in 1954.

nitogorsk iron and steel areas in the Urals, and, deeper in Siberia, the Kuznetsk Basin, which has the largest coal reserves in the world. Siberia is booming—that is the long and short of it. Moreover the boom, the planning authorities say, is just beginning. As of today, the Magnitogorsk and Kuznetsk areas, which are 1,250 miles apart, have to feed each other to an extent, with iron ore going from the former to the latter, and coal moving in the opposite direction, a laborious and expensive process. But now, following major discoveries of iron ore near the Kuzbas, and with the development of the coal industry in European Russia, each area is to become independent. In addition a third great "power" center is in process of erection, centering on hydroelectric installations further east, between Krasnoyarsk and the Angara River, with huge new power stations at Bratsk and near Irkutsk. "Central Siberia is being opened up to form what will be virtually a new country the size of Europe."[13] Until the current Five-Year Plan was modified, total Soviet industrial production was scheduled to be 65 per cent over the 1955 level by 1960; the target for Siberia was 120 per cent. Above all, the new Siberian enterprises will specialize in industries consuming large amounts of fuel and power, like aluminum.

One should also point out that Siberia has disadvantages. The great rivers flow north, and lead only to the Arctic. A vast amount of land is frozen and useless. Communications are still primitive in the extreme, and the only east-west link across the immensity of the country is the thin, brittle line of the Trans-Siberian.[14]

Russian expansion into Siberia is, we know, an old story. Movement across the Urals began with Ivan III, and colonies of frontiersmen sprang up along the cold river valleys. The conquest of Siberia was largely peaceable, and what little resistance came from Siberian aborigines was put down by the Cossacks. The country was largely empty, a no man's land. Russians reached Tobolsk in 1587, Tomsk in 1604, Chita in 1658, and the Kamchatka Peninsula in 1697. By the end of the reign of Peter the Great (1725) all of Siberia, at least nominally, was part of Russia, and it assumed for the most part the frontiers it has today. In the 1890's came a great and fruitful development; the Trans-Siberian Railway was at last built. As a result it became possible to reach Vladivostok from Moscow (5,800 miles) in nine days. Before that the journey took a year.

Two autonomous republics and several autonomous regions are embedded in today's Siberia. The *Yakut ASSR* is an enormous area still largely under-

[13] Edward Crankshaw in the New York *Herald Tribune*, March 21, 1956.
[14] See "News from Siberia," by George B. Cressey, *Harper's Magazine*, July 1938.

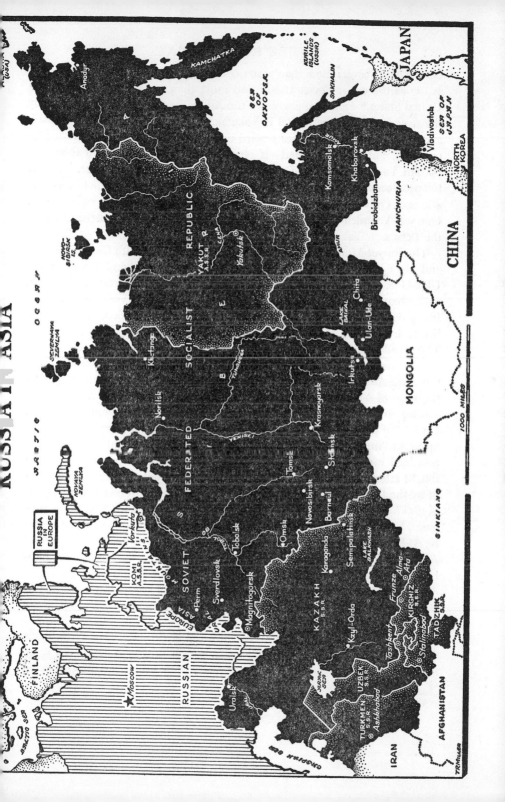

developed; it covers more than 1,100,000 square miles, and is thus one-fifth as big as the entire Soviet Union and more than one-third the size of the United States.[15] Half of it lies above the Arctic Circle; the area is bisected by the river Lena, and the capital is Yakutsk. This is unserved by any railroad, and the highway leading south toward the Amur River is seldom traversed by outsiders, but it has a proud—if remote—new university. Gold is an important Yakut industry, and so are diamonds and reindeer culture. Most of the people are primitive folk of Turkic origin, and the total population is only 480,000. Only five Americans have been in Yakutsk since the early 1940's. One was Wendell Willkie. Lenin spent his brief period of Siberian exile on the Lena near Yakutsk, and was married there.[16]

The *Buryat-Mongol ASSR* lies along Lake Baikal in South Central Siberia, and faces Mongolia. The people are Mongol offshoots, and the capital is Ulan-Ude. The Trans-Siberian passes through this picturesque little town, and a branch line penetrates down into the Mongolian People's Republic. Industrial development is beginning, although the chief occupation is still livestock breeding. Along Lake Baikal are important petroleum deposits. The population is only 650,000.

One geopolitical oddity with a special status is *Tannu Tuva*, now known as the *Tuva Autonomous Oblast.*[17] Like its Buryat-Mongol neighbor, it lies on the edge of Mongolia proper, and has 168,000 people. They resemble the Kirghiz, but are a distinct subnational group. Tuva has a unique history. Under the Czars it was a Russian protectorate; then the Communists set it up as an "independent" People's Republic, under Soviet tutelage, which it remained until 1944. Its postage stamps were triangular, and were much sought after by philatelists. Eventually the Tuva people "asked" to be taken in by the USSR, which means that the USSR decided to take them in. The capital has the curious name of Kyzyl, meaning "red," and, even more curiously, has borne such former names as Belotsarsk, Krasny, Khem-Belder, and Kyzyl-Khoto.[18] Adjoining Tuva on the west is another oddity, the *Gorno-Altai Autonomous Region.* Here live the Oyrots. The capital, Gorno-Altaysk, once bore the euphonious name Oolala. So far as I know it has been visited by only one American in the last twenty-five years, the late Junius B. Wood of the Chicago *Daily News,* who managed to reach it in the 1930's. There are

[15] The first Soviet atomic bomb was detonated at an inaccessible town in the Yakut area, Olekminsk.

[16] His wife, Nadezhda K. Krupskaya, whom he met in revolutionary circles in St. Petersburg, followed him into exile. Incidentally both her parents were of noble birth.

[17] *Oblast*=province.

[18] Shabad, *op. cit.*, p. 295.

handsome mountains here, and the plan is to develop the area as a holiday ground for workers in the industrial cities immediately to the north, like Biisk and Stalinsk.

Finally among these curiosities we must include the *Jewish Autonomous Oblast*, a small unit far to the east near Khabarovsk, and on the border of Manchuria. Years ago, in 1928, this inaccessible and utterly forlorn little segment of territory was set aside by the Soviet government as a "national home" for Russian Jews, and the region was given an autonomous administration. The capital is BIROBIDZHAN. As a so-called national home, the experiment was a failure; few Jews liked it when they got there, and during the period of Stalinist anti-Semitism, none were permitted to go. About half the total population of 157,000 is, however, still Jewish.

*

At least twenty key cities in Siberia, some of them brand-new, deserve a word. SVERDLOVSK, the former Yekaterinburg (population 707,000), is the Pittsburgh of the Urals, and commands an area bursting with gold, platinum, tungsten, copper, and asbestos. Seven railways serve it, and it has a large industrial development; surrounding it, in the Soviet manner, are satellite cities in a rapid process of growth. It has an important university, and is a fecund center for scientific research. More than five thousand research workers are employed by the Urals branch of the Academy of Sciences, and the Urals Polytechnical Institute is one of the biggest in the country. Sverdlovsk province has 1,230 industrial enterprises, employing more than a million men; the gross output, worth 35 billion rubles in 1956, was 7,000 per cent higher than in 1913, 600 per cent higher than in 1940.

Sverdlovsk itself, founded in 1720, goes back to Catherine the Great; the poet Pushkin spent some time in exile here, and here the last Czar, Nicholas II, and his family were brutally put to death. The city's name was changed to honor Jakob Sverdlov, a close associate of Lenin's and the first chairman of the Central Executive Committee of the new Soviet government, who died of typhus in 1919. Like most Siberian cities, Sverdlovsk is off the Intourist circuit, and, except to members of delegations and occasional enterprising newspapermen, is closed. The excuse given is that hotel accommodation is not sufficient; the real reason is that the Russians do not like to have foreigners wandering about anywhere in Siberia, particularly in critical and sensitive industrial foci like Sverdlovsk.

South of Sverdlovsk is another major city, CHELYABINSK, known as the "Gateway to Siberia." Its tractor plant, next to that of Stalingrad, is probably the most important in the Soviet Union, and its population has jumped from 60,000 in 1928 to almost 700,000 today. Gross industrial output has increased 140 times since 1917. Near by is the renowned steel city MAGNI-TOGORSK, which has the largest iron foundry in the world, and also the largest steel mill. A mountain made of solid iron gives Magnitogorsk its name; it was discovered, according to the local legend, when airplane pilots flying over the region discovered that their compasses wouldn't work, so powerful was the magnetic pull from ore below. Magnitogorsk was founded in 1931, and its population is already 284,000. American engineers helped build its first factories.

A thousand miles to the east is NOVOSIBIRSK, the capital of Siberia; it lies on the Trans-Siberian beyond Omsk, and is called the "Chicago" of Siberia. A fast-growing metropolis, its population has risen from 5,000 in 1897 to 76,000 in 1923 and an estimated 731,000 today. It is situated on the Ob, and is the terminus of the Turk-Sib Railway coming up from Central Asia. The temperature sometimes reaches fifty-five degrees below zero in Novosibirsk. During the NEP period it had tough little night clubs and a gambling casino that operated twenty-four hours a day. The first new building in the city completed after the war, when thousands of workers were still living in wretched wooden hovels, was the imposing Opera, bigger than the Bolshoi in Moscow; it has a repertory of forty-seven operas and seventeen ballets. Novosibirsk has the largest plant in the USSR making electric light bulbs, and no fewer than sixteen different research institutions dealing with minerals. The new sports stadium, now being built, will hold eighty thousand people, and the House of Culture is elaborate. Nevertheless Novosibirsk still gives the impression of being violently raw.

Southeast of Novosibirsk is the Kuzbas (Kuznetsk Basin) which is now believed to contain coal reserves amounting to 900 *billion* tons, twice the former estimate. Here are comparatively new cities like STALINSK, which has one of the biggest steel factories in the world. BARNAUL, a thriving but dreary city, is the capital of the Altai Kray, a province which, because of its potentialities for industrial and agricultural development, has been called the "Canada of Siberia." Twenty years ago, in the entire Altai, there was exactly one university graduate; today there are hundreds. Also in the Kuznetsk Basin are KEMEROVO (chemicals) and BELOVO (zinc).

OMSK (population 505,000) and TOMSK are both old cities. Stalin passed one of his periods of exile near Omsk, and Dostoevsky spent four years in jail in Tomsk, and called it a horrible little town. It had one hospital in 1913, and has sixty now. Dostoevsky was, incidentally, married at Kuznetsk. Near Tomsk are iron ore deposits believed to be greater than any other in Russia.

Here was the first—and for decades the only—university in Siberia. Some nine hundred miles north of Tomsk, at a point well above the Arctic Circle, is a new city NORILSK, which Russian geographers say is the largest northerly city in the world. It is a nickel center. Norilsk (population 92,000) has been built from nothing in the past few years and, like Vorkuta, was the site of a notorious labor camp.

Descending again to the line of the Trans-Siberian, we must make note of KRASNOYARSK on the Yenisei, established by Cossack detachments in 1628, an important fur center, and CHITA, which was capital of what was called the "Far Eastern Republic" until this was joined to Russia in 1922. Between them is IRKUTSK, founded in 1652; it had about 100,000 people in 1928, and now has three times that number. Trotsky, a scarlet tanager among robins, spent a period of exile here under the Czars, and here Admiral Kolchak, the White leader in the civil war, was executed by the Bolsheviks in 1920. Irkutsk was headquarters for the gold mining industry for many years, and calls itself the "proudest" city in Siberia. It has an important new university.

At last we reach the Soviet Far East. KOMSOMOLSK, on the Amur, was built from scratch as a kind of patriotic stunt by members of the Young Communist League in 1932, and is called the "Youth City"; it has 169,000 people now. KHABAROVSK, close to the Manchurian border, with 280,000 people, is a vigorous transportation center and military headquarters. VLADIVOSTOK, the biggest Russian port on the Pacific, is a beautifully situated city, shaped like an amphitheater; the name means "Lord of the East." It is an important canning center for fishing products, especially crabs, and is the headquarters of the Second Far East Whaling Fleet. Also in this area, it is believed, are important sites for development in ballistic missiles; this is why Vladivostok was cut off recently to foreign shipping. More than a thousand miles to the north is the Chukchi Peninsula, the extreme eastern extremity of the Soviet Union, abutting on Bering Strait. Two small towns perch at its very tip, and face Alaska; one is Uelen, and the other bears the remarkable name Providence.

In the middle of the Bering Strait are two little islands, Big Diomede, which is Russian territory, and Little Diomede, which is American. They are only three miles apart. On a clear day, if your eyes are good enough and it isn't raining, you can see easily from American territory to Soviet, or vice versa.

*

Alaska belonged to Russia, as everybody knows, for about 150 years. The Russian explorer Vitus Bering crossed the strait named for him in 1728, and

Russian colonists and traders followed. Another explorer, Shelekhov, is called "the Russian Columbus." From 1799, the territory was administered by the Russian-American Fur Company, under a governor appointed by the Czar. As a matter of fact the Russians penetrated well below Alaska, and made substantial settlements in what is now California. Traders arrived near San Francisco in 1812, built a fort not far from Sacramento, and maintained their own territorial enclave there for a generation. The Russians withdrew from California, peaceably and of their own will, in 1841. How different history might have been if they had stayed!

Alaska was in those days called "Russian America." In 1867 the Czar's government sold Alaska to the United States for $7,200,000. Secretary of State Seward, who helped negotiate the purchase, was bitterly criticized at home because Alaska, despite its gold resources, was thought to be worthless; newspapers called it "Seward's Icebox" and "Walrussia." Russia gave up Alaska for at least four reasons. The company running it was badly managed, caused trouble in St. Petersburg, and lost money; the Russian Navy was weak, and could not defend Alaska in case of need; the Russians thought that the United States would grab it off anyway; and Russia, in a period of diplomatic tussling with Great Britain, wanted cordial relations with the United States.[19]

The Russians have no particular interest in Alaska today, but a startling proposal was put forward by a writer named Vasili Zakharchenko, in the December, 1956 issue of the magazine *USSR*. He suggests building a dam, no less, across the Bering Strait, which would be a permanent land bridge between Siberia and the American continent. The Bering Strait is narrow and only about 150 feet deep; such a dam, although expensive, would not be impossible to erect. What a thought! One could go all the way from Moscow to Miami Beach, or vice versa, without crossing water. This, however, is not the idea behind this fanciful proposal. Its proponents say that such a dam could block off icy water from the Arctic Ocean, make the Pacific warmer, free Far Eastern ports of ice, and even permit the cultivation of oranges in Kamchatka, if pumping stations were to be established and powered by atomic energy. Simple!

The Lost Peoples

Even now, we have not exhausted the illimitable copiousness and variety of lands and peoples within Russia. There remain to be discussed the "Lost Peoples." These are, or were, the seven nationalities which were expunged

[19] Paraphrased from *America Faces Russia*, by Thomas A. Bailey, pp. 95-108.

during the 1940's, and which are now being rehabilitated—minority groups like the Crimean Tatars, Kalmuks, and Karachays. Their governments were destroyed and their places of being obliterated from the very maps; they were picked up bodily, uprooted, and deported into exile thousands of miles from their homes. The accusation against them was that they had collaborated with the Nazis during World War II, or were pro-German. Altogether, about 1,700,000 people were involved.

Typical of the experience of all seven was that of the Chechen and the Ingush. These are Circassian peoples, Moslem by religion, who had their own autonomous republic in the north Caucasus. The Nazi invaders did not quite reach the Chechen-Ingush area, but came close. Whether the Chechen-Ingush actually collaborated with the Germans is not clear; the Russians say that they "wanted" to collaborate, and did not "oppose collaboration." The Chechen-Ingush are a stubborn, pugnacious folk, proud of their independent mountaineer tradition, and they certainly did not like Stalin. Their history goes far back. They had their own kings before the Russians came, and fought Catherine the Great. They were not finally crushed till 1859 and recurrent revolts against Czarist authority came in 1867, 1877, and 1905.

After the Revolution, Chechen-Ingush history continued to be stormy. Some details are worth recording, if only to show in microcosm the extreme factionalism of people in this part of Russia, as well as their yearning for free political institutions. A revolt was beaten down in April, 1930. (Yes, there *have* been minor revolts against Soviet rule since the Revolution.) The Chechen-Ingush resisted collectivization, and in 1931 the GPU arrested some 35,000 of them as "Counterrevolutionary Kulaks and Nationalist-Moslem Ideologists." In 1936 they were given full autonomous status, and their own republic was established. Then, when the German invasion of the Caucasus began, the Chechen-Ingush became restive once more, and a revolt broke out in 1941-42, led by a young poet named Khasan Israilov.

The beaten Germans were in time forced out of the Caucasus, and Stalin struck against the Chechen-Ingush on February 23, 1944. These naughty rebels were to be punished. The word "punish" is mild. The Chechen-Ingush Autonomous Republic was liquidated as an administrative unit, and, more than this, every Chechen and Ingush in the entire Soviet Union was rounded up and sent to exile or put to forced labor. Individual Chechens, perfectly patriotic citizens, who had left their homeland years before and worked in Moscow or elsewhere, were seized and deported. The entire nation of 500,000 people was destroyed.

A good deal of evidence has come to light recently about the manner in which the deportations from the Chechen-Ingush home area were carried out. In charge of the operation as a whole was General Serov. NKVD troops moved into the district in January, 1944, and made themselves at home. They were billeted in schools and hospitals, on the pretext that they were resting after front line duty. Thus, they became familiar with local conditions and the terrain. On February 23, mass meetings were ordered in the public square of each village; brass bands played, and the populace turned out. Some even brought gifts. They were cruelly betrayed. Loudspeakers blared out the news, without warning or explanation, that the entire Chechen-Ingush people were to be resettled; each family was given an hour to get ready. At the end of the hour men, women, children were marshaled into fields near the villages, and piled onto trucks; then they were transferred into freight cars at the nearest railhead, and sent off to exile. The trains were unheated, and food was scant. The journey to Central Asia lasted at least two weeks, and thousands died.

All members of the Chechen-Ingush government, party organization, and Komsomols were arrested, and anybody of substance was, of course, shot. A minor irony is that the NKVD used new American automobiles and trucks, part of Lend-Lease shipments to Russia, in some districts, which led the dazed Chechen-Ingush to think that the United States had something to do with the deportations. Not a single Chechen or Ingush was left in the whole territory, a region as big as Connecticut, twenty-four hours after the operation started. Then new inhabitants—Russians from Kursk and Orel provinces— were promptly moved in. They did not want to live in the Caucasus any more than the Chechen-Ingush wanted to leave it. Concurrently a program began to wipe out every element of Chechen-Ingush culture. Museums and archives were destroyed, and place names Russified. Nor, for many years, was any reference ever made to the Chechen-Ingush in the Soviet press; the name was even removed from standard works of reference. This was genocide with a vengeance. All traces of these people were to be obliterated.

The Soviet authorities insist that the Chechen-Ingush, together with other dispossessed peoples, were "given allotted land and necessary state aid for their economic arrangements," in Kazakhstan and elsewhere in Central Asia. In practice, they were simply dropped in a locale utterly alien to them, and left largely to fend for themselves. Within each area, they were allowed a certain freedom of movement, and those not assigned to labor camps could get jobs—if any—of their own choosing. Generally, deportees were sent to labor-deficit areas, or places where no one else would volunteer to come, because of remoteness, poor living conditions, or wretched climate. All over Central Asia, these miserable outcasts are still to be seen. Not a single one is ever known to have escaped to the West.

The Karachays, a refractory highland people who lived near Mount Elbruz, suffered the same fate as the Chechen-Ingush; so did another mountaineer group, the Balkars. The Karachays openly collaborated with the invading Germans, and greeted them as liberators; they even sent Hitler a white pony, and some Karachays fled with the Nazis when they started to retreat. The Karachays who stayed were duly deported by the Russians, every man, woman, and child, and have been lost ever since—forgotten. No decree about them was ever published, and their deportation, unlike that of the Volga Germans and Crimean Tatars, was never officially admitted. Their whereabouts today, if any survive, is unknown; some are believed to be in Kirghizia. The very word "Karachay" was expunged from the Great Soviet Encyclopedia, except as the name of a river, and the Karachay autonomous region was stricken off the map.

The Kalmuks, another liquidated people, have a fascinating history. There were about 130,000 of them, and they had their own extensive autonomous republic on the lower Volga and near the Caspian. They are Buddhists of Mongol origin. They erupted into Russia from their homeland, northern Sinkiang, in 1630, led by their national hero, Khan Kho Urlyuka. About fifty thousand families made the long trek. Generations later many Kalmuks returned to China. Those who stayed led an independent, largely nomadic existence, raising sheep and cattle, until 1771, when Catherine brought them under Russian rule. A "Kalmuk Office" was established in Astrakhan, and the people given a "Guardian."[20] But the Kalmuks were, for some reason, almost always badly treated by the Czars. They were forbidden during one period to live within ten versts of Russian settlements, which cut them off from access to water; time and time again their cattle died. Nor did they get along well under the Soviets. Lenin talked about the "uninterrupted chain of suffering" undergone by the Kalmuks, and promised to do something for them, but little was done. Soviet administrators tried to break down their adherence to Buddhism, and, under collectivization, their nomadic mode of life became impossible. Came the German war. The Nazis overran the western half of the Kalmuk republic, and took its capital, Elista. Some Kalmuks, serving in the Red Army, were loyal; some openly collaborated with the Germans, and, when the Germans left, about 25,000 Kalmuks left with them. So, when the Soviets resumed control, the Kalmuks were punished en masse in the familiar pattern. Their country was abolished, and Kalmuks are not mentioned in the Soviet Encyclopedia. Nobody knows for sure where the Kalmuks were sent— probably western Siberia. Some have been seen on collective farms near Tomsk.

[20] Kolarz, *op. cit.*

A much more advanced and important people, the Crimean Tatars, were likewise liquidated. These were descendants of the original Tatar conquerors of the Crimea, who set up a colorful, sturdy civilization there. They comprised about 25 per cent of the population of the Crimea. They too were charged with collaboration, and many, hating the Soviet regime, did in fact welcome the Nazi invaders. So, as punishment, the whole nation was destroyed by the Soviet authorities, and the Crimean Republic was absorbed administratively into the RSFSR. (Now it is part of the Ukraine.)

Finally, the Volga Germans. Their fate has been hardest of all. The Volga German Autonomous Republic was liquidated as far back as August, 1941. About 400,000 Volga Germans were deported, including every inhabitant of the region who was of German descent, even if these were Red Army officers or soldiers. History of the Volga Germans goes back a long way. Catherine II issued two manifestoes—in 1762 and 1763—inviting foreign settlement on the "freelands" of Russia. Germans were promised full religious freedom, and were exempted from military service; they received financial aid, and were let off taxes. So prosperous German colonies grew up all over Russia. Germans settled in Bessarabia, the Odessa area, the north Caucasus, Orenburg province, and in particular, the lower Volga region centering on Saratov. The Volga community was progressive, industrious, and rich. But, even under the Czars, the Germans were suspected of being more German than Russian, and during World War I, plans were drawn up—but never executed—to exile the entire German community to Siberia. The Bolsheviks, seizing power, rescinded this plan, established a commissariat for Volga German affairs, and came to the Volga Germans in the guise of deliverers. But during World War II they did exactly what the Czars had threatened to do. Almost at once, when Germany attacked Russia in 1941, the Soviet government decided to take no chances with the Volga Germans. To catch spies and agents among them, the NKVD used aircraft disguised as German planes, which dropped bogus pamphlets. When members of the population rose to this bait, reprisals began; hundreds of Volga German leaders were caught and shot. Then came liquidation of the whole republic. Its territory was divided between the Saratov and Stalingrad provinces of the RSFSR, and the population was deported.

Today the Germans appear to be scattered over wide areas in Central Asia, Siberia, and the northeastern reaches of European Russia. One large concentration is in the Altai Kray, and a German language newspaper is published in Barnaul; others have been seen in Vorkuta, and in the Kolyma region in the Arctic. Little, incidentally, has ever become known of the fate of hundreds of thousands of other Soviet citizens of German descent who lived in the

Crimea, the Urals, and elsewhere. But at least fifty thousand Germans in the Ukraine joined the Nazis, and thousands more, who did not cross the lines, were punished by deportation or otherwise. Also, Germans were moved out of the north Caucasus, and a "partial deportation" took place in Moscow, Leningrad, and other cities. But there are still plenty of Soviet citizens of German descent in the big cities, particularly Moscow, who have never been molested at all.

*

On May 17, 1955, occurred something sensational. A small item appeared in the *Kazakhstanskaya Pravda* announcing, like a whisper from a long-forgotten grave, that a newspaper in the Chechen-Ingush language, to be called *Banner of Labor*, was to begin publication. So there were still enough Chechens and Ingush alive to support a newspaper; moreover, they were to be allowed to have one! Then a complete reversal of policy toward the liquidated minority groups was announced. Khrushchev went out of his way in his February, 1956, speech to announce that the liquidation of the Chechen-Ingush, among others, had been a major Stalin crime, that collective punishment for individual actions was not good Leninism, and that amends would soon be made. So rehabilitation is the order of the day, except in the case of the Volga Germans, who are apparently still considered to be beyond the pale. All other of the liquidated national groups are to be restored, and given their previous status; the survivors will, by terms of a Kremlin decree of February, 1957, be repatriated as soon as possible, and returned to their ancestral homes.

Baltic States and Moldavia

Estonia, Latvia, and Lithuania are Union republics and have the same general background, but differ from one another strikingly. All, however, fell victim to the same historical process. They broke off from Czarist Russia, which had held them submerged for generations, in 1919, refused to associate themselves with Bolshevik Russia, set out on their own, and lived as independent entities until 1940. Then, after this brief—pitiably brief—period of national independence, their freedom was brutally seized; the Soviet rape of the Baltics is as evil a tragedy as any that has defaced modern times.

Russia and Germany, by terms of the Russo-German Pact of 1939, divided eastern Europe into spheres of influence; then, in June, 1940, the Russians moved bodily into the Baltic regions, and forcibly installed Communist regimes in all three countries. These—conveniently—then "applied" for admission into the Soviet Union and were, needless to say, promptly "admitted." Subsequently when the Russo-German partnership was broken by the Nazi attack on Russia (June 22, 1941), the Baltic regions were overrun by advancing German troops. When the Germans at last withdrew, the three Baltic states—totally helpless—reverted to Soviet authority.[21]

The Russian pretext for the conquest of these three countries—in which the Communist element was infinitesimal, except perhaps in Lithuania—was to "save them from German Fascism," the Fascism with which the Soviet Union had made a treaty only ten months before. The real reason goes back to Peter the Great. Russia, now as then, likes windows on the Baltic. The Soviet annexation was accompanied by mass terror. In Estonia alone 1,178 leaders were executed. Some of those shot were, no doubt, representatives of the old "Baltic Baron" aristocracy, and some were certainly pro-German. Even so, the Russians made a clean sweep of the political and cultural elite of the nation. More than sixty thousand Estonians were rounded up and deported bodily into Russia, sixty thousand Letts, and around thirty thousand Lithuanians.

The *Estonian Soviet Socialist Republic*, with its capital at TALLINN, is completely closed off today, out of bounds to all outsiders. Once it had a pleasant individualist tradition and a spirited intellectual life; Tallinn, with its golden beaches and graceful Hanseatic architecture, was as charming as any small capital in Europe. To imagine what it must be like today, try to conceive what Copenhagen would be like if Denmark had been forcibly Communized, and Danish farmers dragooned into collective farms—moreover forcibly Communized to the tune of a tyrannical hypocrisy which holds that the people themselves invited this wretched fate.

Moscow milks Estonia to its own advantage, and gives little in return. Complaints are frequent—particularly about discrimination in economic fields. Estonian factories are starved for raw materials, and the quality of the goods the people get from elsewhere in the Soviet Union is unspeakably shoddy. The whole area is depressed economically as well as otherwise.

The *Latvian Soviet Socialist Republic* is probably more favored, if only because its capital, RIGA, is the largest port on the Baltic after Leningrad. Riga, founded in 1200, has an illustrious history, and the Letts are tougher people than the Estonians. One point to reiterate is that Latvia and Estonia, although they had feudal characteristics, maintained high standards of social services before the war. Hence, the descent to conditions that

---

[21] The United States government has never recognized the annexation of Estonia, Latvia, and Lithuania by the Soviet Union.

prevail today is the more striking. Soviet activities in areas like Kazakhstan or Yakutsk, which have never known civilization at all before, are one
thing, and include much that is commendable; Soviet activity in countries
like Estonia and Latvia, which have had a spirited indigenous culture for
centuries, is something else again. Instead of being built up, society is broken
down.

The *Lithuanian Soviet Socialist Republic* has, or had, a strong Roman
Catholic population (which makes it unique in the Soviet Union except for
areas taken over from eastern Poland), and is grossly poor. The Lithuanians,
despite their inflammatory history in pre-Soviet days, were less fine-grained
than the Estonians, and the country was largely a peasant state. All remnants
of its former sturdy nationalism have been ground out. In the old days the
Lithuanian capital was Kaunas (Kovno); it is now VILNIUS or Vilna, which
has a famous university. Vilna was, for a great many years, a contested city
between Poland and Lithuania, and it was the birthplace of the Polish
dictator Pilsudski. Napoleon campaigned through Vilna once, and a
monument here has two inscriptions, one on each side: "Napoleon Bonaparte
passed this way in 1812 with 400,000 men," and "Napoleon Bonaparte passed
this way in 1812 with 9,000 men."[22]

*

The *Moldavian Soviet Socialist Republic* need not detain us long. This consists mostly of the old Rumanian province of Bessarabia, together with parts
of northern Bukovina, which Rumania was forced to cede to the Soviet Union
in 1940. It lies along the Dniester, and is one of the most densely populated
areas in the country; the capital, a predominantly Jewish city, is KISHINEV,
the former Chisinău. Pushkin spent three years in Kishenev, "detesting the
filthy barbarity of the Moldavians."[23] A vicious pogrom took place here in
1913. Some recent Moldavian complaints: "The collective farms of our Republic are in great need of such building materials as lumber, cement, iron
and roofing. . . . Large numbers of livestock pile up at delivery points; their
feeding is poorly organized and cattle cars are not provided in time. As a
result of this the cattle are exhausted and in the end the consumer gets low
quality meat." The hops industry is in a bad way, a vitamin factory is in
trouble, and, in Kishinev, school buildings are so short that several schools
operate in three shifts.

[22] Winter, *op. cit.*, p. 206.
[23] Mirsky, *op. cit.* p. 81.

CHAPTER X

Government and Party

An anthill Utopia.

—ANDRÉ GIDE

How is all this complex vastness governed? The simplest answer is to say that the Soviet Union is governed by a duplex system in which government and party interlock. Lenin once said, "The party is the brain, the government is the body."[1]

Let us take government first. In theory, political authority derives from the local soviets, which exist in every rural area or town, and which represent workers or peasants in a particular cell, factory, or collective farm. Deputies to the soviets are—again in theory—elected by direct, free, and secret ballot. Anybody over eighteen may vote, without regard to race, sex, nationality, job, social origin, or residential qualifications. Approximately 1,536,000 citizens—a lot—have been thus elected to local soviets. Soviet propaganda makes much of the "freedom" of these elections. Actually, in our sense, they are not remotely free, although 99 per cent of people entitled to vote do vote; more than 120,000,000 people voted at the last elections. But all candidates are nominated by the local Communist party or allied organizations, and opposition, once the nominations have been made, is unknown.

Power flows upward, and each higher body is elected directly by the people, through town, district, province, and republic levels, until the Supreme Soviet is reached. This, the highest legislative body in the country, corresponds to Congress or Parliament, and is elected, on the basis of the single party ticket, every four years.[2] It meets twice a year, and sessions usually last about a week. There are two houses, which have equal authority: the Soviet of the Union,

---

[1] As quoted by Karl Radek, in turn quoted by Walter Duranty, *Stalin & Co.*, p. 12.
[2] But "multicandidate" elections, on a local level, are promised soon. Harrison E. Salisbury in the *New York Times*, June 29, 1956.

more or less analogous to the House of Representatives in Washington, to which deputies are elected on the basis of population, one for each 300,000 people, and the Soviet of Nationalities, corresponding to our Senate, which represents "national" interests. Each Union republic has twenty-five deputies, each autonomous republic eleven, each autonomous region five, and each national area one. Anybody is eligible for election to the Supreme Soviet at the age of twenty-three, and any deputy may, in case of dereliction, be recalled by his constituency at any time. The total membership at present is 1,347, with 708 members in the Soviet of the Union, and 639 in the Soviet of Nationalities. Of the total, 348 are women. Deputies—like members of the House of Commons until comparatively recent times—are not paid salaries, but get an allowance of a thousand rubles a month for secretarial help, and a small *per diem* payment while they sit in Moscow. Free debate, in our sense, does not take place. Deputies simply give reports. There has, however, been a distinct "democratization" of procedure since Stalin's death. Today, very lively talk may be heard, including much criticism, as deputies describe their local problems.

The Supreme Soviet, at the very top, has a presidium—not to be confused with the Presidium of the Communist party. This consists of thirty-three members (including the president of each Union republic) and it sits in permanent session, representing the Supreme Soviet. But actual day-to-day executive authority is in the hands of the All-Union Council of Ministers, or cabinet, which the presidium appoints. The chairman of the presidium of the Supreme Soviet (at the moment, Voroshilov) is nominally the chief of state, like the President of the United States. The chairman of the Council of Ministers (Bulganin at the moment) is prime minister or premier.

Ministers were once called People's Commissars. The fiction is always maintained in the Soviet Union that ultimate authority belongs to the people. The phrase was an off-the-cuff invention of Trotsky's, which Lenin enthusiastically accepted. In 1946 the commissars became ministers, as part of the general Stalinist trend toward nationalism. Much old-style Communist terminology was discarded at this time. Former Czarist decorations, like the Order of Suvorov, were restored, and army officers, as insignia of their rank, started to wear shoulder boards, similar to those worn in Czarist times. The "International" was dropped as the national anthem, and replaced by one stressing the concept of *Russian* patriotism.[3] Even the term "Bolshevik" was thrown overboard. Dozens of similar details might be cited.

The All-Union Council of Ministers was, until the Khrushchev reforms in

[3] The "International" was, however, retained as the *party* anthem.

1957, an extraordinarily large and unwieldy body, with no fewer than fifty-one full ministerial posts and dozens of affiliated organs. Thirty-six of the fifty-one were industrial ministries; it was as if, in the United States, automobiles, electric machinery, timber, shipbuilding, food processing, and multitudinous other industries were all run exclusively from Washington by members of the cabinet. There was (in the Soviet Union) a Ministry of Meat and Dairy Production, a Ministry for Construction of Oil Industry Enterprises, a Ministry for Instrument Making and Automation Equipment, ministries for fish, road machine building, wood processing, and so on almost without end. Khrushchev threw out most of these industrial ministries, and the Council of Ministers today resembles cabinets in western Europe. There are at present twenty-four ministers instead of fifty-one. Some oddities remain. Geology and Conservation of Resources is still a ministry, as are Medium Machine Building (which handles nuclear affairs), Grain Products, and Electric Power Stations.

Turn now to the party. This, too, is organized on a pyramidal basis. At the bottom is the local party unit, which can consist of as few as three members, in a factory, farm, or office. These units elect delegates to larger party units in towns, provinces, districts, and so on up, in theory by secret ballot, until the All-Union Party Congress, the highest party organ, is reached. This, between sessions, delegates its powers to the Central Committee of the Party, which it selects. In turn, the Central Committee chooses (a) a secretariat, and (b) the all-important Presidium (formerly Politburo) at the very top. Khrushchev is, at the moment, first secretary of the party as well as the dominant member of the Presidium; other members of the Presidium, several of whom also hold important cabinet posts, are, or should be, known to us by now.

The Central Committee contains 133 full members and 122 alternates. It meets in secret, and no public announcement about a meeting is ever made until it is over—if then. Its members are the real rulers of the Soviet Union, and it represents the supreme height of Soviet power.

As to the All-Union Party Congress, this is supposed to meet every two years, but in fact is likely to be convened at somewhat irregular intervals. It has 1,355 delegates, one for each 5,000 party members. As in the case of the Supreme Soviet, procedures have been a good deal relaxed since Stalin. Members of the party Presidium are, by tradition, welcomed by standing ovations from the floor each time any member enters the hall. At the Twentieth Congress Khrushchev walked up to the tribune informally and asked the delegates not to applaud in this manner but "to behave in the Communist way and show that you are masters of this Congress." Delegates to the Congress include many more factory workers and dirt farmers than in Stalin's day; Khrushchev, as always, wants to knit his organization into the people on as wide and deep a base as possible. Leading Communists from abroad are, as a rule, invited to attend Congress sessions as honored guests; they came from forty-four different countries to the Nineteenth Congress (October, 1952) and from fifty-five at the Twentieth (February, 1956). Verbatim reports of the proceedings are issued, and the leading speeches appear in *Pravda* the next day, except in the case of special secret speeches; during the last Congress a few sessions were televised. Foreign correspondents representing the bourgeois press are not admitted.[4]

It is of course obvious, both as regards government and party, that nothing remotely like our democracy exists. The pyramids may rise from the bottom, but it is the top that has the power. Everybody knows this, but the point is worth stating if only because Soviet spokesmen boast so vehemently and dogmatically about their "democratic" procedures. In plain fact, no mechanism is permitted whereby the will of the people, the essence and *sine qua non* of democracy, can exert itself or be registered in a political sense. Representative government simply does not exist. The constitution itself, which boasts in its first sentence that the USSR is a "socialist state of workers and peasants," can be amended by the Supreme Soviet at will.

More About the Party

In 1956 the CPSU, as the Communist Party of the Soviet Union is called for short, and the only political party in the country, had 7,215,505 members; about 6,700,000 of these were full members, and about 420,000 were candidates. It is often said, on the basis of such statistics, that the party makes up less than 4 per cent of the population of the USSR, but this does not give a quite fair picture, in that it refers only to adult party members; a truer percentage would arise if the party membership was set against the total *adult* population. If members of the Communist youth organizations are included in the party total, the membership will be 45,000,000, or more than 25 per cent of the population of the country. Two points are in any case clear. One is that the party has grown very substantially in recent years. It had only 240,000 members in 1917, and only about 2,500,000 at the time of the Eighteenth Congress in 1939. The other is that, even though getting larger steadily, it still represents a minority.

[4] Welles Hangen, *New York Times*, February 19, 1956.

Membership is restricted for the simplest of reasons. Keeping the party small means that power is concentrated in relatively few hands. It makes membership a privilege, encourages ambition, creates an elite, and makes government easier to manipulate. It makes dictatorship of (that is, over) the proletariat workable.

Curiously enough, plenty of good Russian citizens who are sincere addicts of the regime are *not* party members, and moreover do not wish to be. To be a party member is an arduous business, a militant sweat. Membership means total submission to discipline, brings on hard and thankless work, takes a great deal of time, intrudes on personal life, and may entail grave risks and danger. There is no professional stigma attached to not being a Communist, in most ranks of society; on a university faculty, a science laboratory, or even in the management of a big industry, party and nonparty men work side by side. In a way, not to be a member of the party corresponds to not being a member of a really good club in New York society. A New Yorker can reach a perfectly respectable status, earn a good living, and enjoy most of the privileges and favors of metropolitan life, without dreaming of ever becoming a member of the Knickerbocker Club or the Century.

On the other hand, extremely few non-Communists reach the very top. Among exceptions are the Rector of Moscow University, Ivan G. Petrovsky, who is not a member of the party, and Nikolai S. Tikhonov, head of the Soviet Committee for the Defense of Peace. Also, an interesting point, no fewer than 297 members of the Supreme Soviet, between a fifth and a quarter of its total membership, are *not* party members, strange as this may seem.[5] But of course they are Communists in attitude and sympathy. Multitudinous figures in the world of music, the theater, ballet, literature, and the arts, are not Communists, particularly if they are of the older generation. The most eminent living Russian poet, Boris Pasternak, would no more become a member of the Communist party than would John Foster Dulles. Then there are some nonparty members, like the writer Ilya Ehrenburg, who hew closer to the party line than do most members. It simply suits their convenience to stay outside party ranks, and may serve to make them more—rather than less—valuable to the regime.

How does a young man become a member? First, three party members must vouch for him, and he must be passed by the local party unit; there is no formal initiation ceremony. A probation period lasts for a year. Dues must be paid,[6] and, in the early days, all good party members were supposed to

[5] Schuman, *op. cit.*, p. 229.
[6] Ranging in amount from one-half of one per cent to three per cent of salary.

give back to the party anything they earned more than the equivalent of a skilled worker's wage. Character, rather than intellect, is what is looked for. Similarly, men in the lower ranks who are expelled from the party suffer this fate not as a rule for ideological deviation, but because they have been mixed up in a scandal, do their work badly, or get drunk in public. Spartanism, sacrifice, discipline, are the keynotes. I called one day at the editorial office of an important newspaper, and talked with two of its editors. One was a party member, the other not. The party member said, discussing these matters, "When we find a bright young man, we try to get him in. We want new blood. But some people do not qualify, even if they are exceptionally intelligent. They are lax, and will not mend their ways."

How are new members among workers in a factory, or members of a collective farm, trained, given faith, and taught their onerous responsibilities? This, perhaps oddly, is one of the most difficult questions to answer in the Soviet Union. The inner workings of the party machine, how it is administered, what means of education are available, and so on, are still closed subjects. Probably this is because the old tradition of subterranean and secret revolutionary conspiracy still weighs heavily on the party leadership. Some details are, however, known. I asked a party organizer in Central Asia how his cadres were trained, and got this answer. Suppose a worker shows promise. He will, after admission to the party, be sent to a party school where he may spend as much as three years, learning Marxist theory. During this interval the equivalent of his salary is, assuming that he is married, paid to his family; his own keep is provided by the school. He is, in a word, completely subsidized. Such party schools do not take men over forty. Also, a Marxist-Leninist evening university exists in almost every Soviet town, where a worker of any age can take free courses at any time. Also available are special advanced and secret institutes in Moscow for exceptionally promising members. Contrary to most opinion, the standard universities no longer give specific courses in Marxism-Leninism. This is a new development. They do have chairs in the history of Communism, but this is not quite the same thing. The Rector of the University of Kiev told us, "It is not the function of a university to teach Communism. Students should learn Communism from life, not from teachers."

Indoctrination of the whole population begins in childhood, without regard to whether or not the child will ever reach party membership. Youngsters in nursery schools become "Little Octobrists," and then, at the age of nine or thereabouts, go into the Young Pioneers. There are some twenty million Pioneers.[7] Next, at about fourteen, favored children enter the Young Communist League, the Komsomol organization which has around eighteen million members. This is a very important organization indeed. Only about 40 per cent of the boys and girls available are taken in; it is at the Komsomol stage that the first extensive and detailed screening of the population at large takes place. Normally a young person remains a YCL member until he is twenty-six. The program includes everything from political instruction to competitive sports, from military exercises to cultural activity of every sort. A sharp eye is kept for potential leaders. But not all Komsomols by any means become adult members of the party; at this juncture, too, there is a widespread winnowing. The party takes only the best.

Party members not only have the right to criticize their associates, if they are derelict, but a specific duty to self-criticism; also, as everybody knows, they are supposed to be volunteer watchdogs, looking for failings even in their superiors. What really makes scandal in the Soviet Union is a report by somebody that (to cite a recent example) only 211 out of 3,300 students eligible showed up at a party indoctrination course in a provincial town. The nation rocks. It is as if, in Hollywood, some celebrated movie star were to be found in bed with a horse. When individual criticism reaches the press, the story is apt to carry the peculiarly sanctimonious but devil-may-care inflection characteristic of Soviet journalism. For instance, covering the last session of the Supreme Soviet, *Izvestia* mentioned with obvious relish a minister, Comrade Sheremetyev, who was severely rebuked by another minister. *Izvestia* said heartily, "It is to be assumed that . . . the minister, who was right there in the hall, did not feel very cheerful. And not he alone. Several other ministries, agencies and enterprises were justly and impartially criticized for uneven work and for failing to meet their duty to the country. The voice of this . . . criticism sounded forth freely and loudly under the arches of the Great Kremlin Palace. . . ."[8]

This same *Izvestia* report provides a good example of another party charac-

[7] We visited the "House of Pioneers" in Odessa, and this was a challenging experience. Toy railroads and sailboats filled one room, and in another, for children slightly older but still very young, were model dams and turbines, as well as a sizable power station built by the youngsters themselves. One chart, equipped with buttons which flashed with different colored electric lights, showed agricultural conditions in various countries. The stress toward technological education was obvious, and brilliantly achieved. Pioneers go to establishments like this for six hours a week, on Saturdays and after school, as an earned privilege; children with bad marks in school are penalized by being kept out. The whole thing was an extremely impressive and effective demonstration of Soviet methods in education.

[8] *Current Digest of the Soviet Press*, March 27, 1957.

teristic, the wholesale giving of decorations, medals, and so on to deserving members. Not merely persons, but factories, cities, regions, and even entire republics may be given such an order as the Order of Lenin. Careful tabulations are kept, and, without fail, every eminent personage in the country receives some sort of decoration on his fiftieth, sixtieth, and later birthdays. The terminology is sometimes imposing. Recently, to give one instance out of thousands available, the Order of the Red Banner of Labor was awarded "to Russian Republic Honored Worker in Science and Technology Konstantin Vladimirovich Chibisov." And consider this tidbit from a story describing lobby scenes at the last session of the Supreme Soviet: "Not far away three women are talking. Let us make their acquaintance. They are Hero of Socialist Labor Yelizaveta Nikolayevna Yegorova, Field Brigade Leader of the Streams Collective Farm, near Leningrad; Team Leader Yekaterina Nikolayevna Avsiyevich of the May Dawn Collective Farm, Moscow province; and Orel province milkmaid (sic) Yefrosinya Ivanovna Tazenkova."

*

Agitprop, the party apparatus dealing with agitation and propaganda, is "keeper of the sacred flame." It does not create the party line, but disseminates it, and is responsible for what one astute and knowledgeable observer, former Senator William Benton, calls the "most stupendous psychological manipulation in history." It maintains more than 6,000 schools, and has 375,000 full-time propagandists and agitators in the field. Each is armed with "scripture"—an 824-page book, called Guide for the Propagandist and Agitator. This publication appears at regular intervals, and is revised from time to time to expunge previous material that is no longer in fashion, keep up with the convoluted twistings of the party line, and in particular make actual happenings fit into the ideology, which they often contravene.

When Khrushchev makes an important speech, the gist of what he says passes down at once through newspapers and the radio. After Malenkov and company were ousted, hundreds of speeches were delivered all over the Soviet Union denouncing these villains and miscreants, who had been heroes the day before, in practically verbatim language. The switch occurs almost instantaneously. Previously, Khrushchev had made his celebrated references to butter, meat, and milk. Within a matter of days, virtually identical speeches about butter, meat, and milk appeared, as if by magic or conjuration, on the lips of ardent speakers everywhere in the Soviet Union. Agitprop really does a job.

We should, however, point out again that conformity is not merely imposed from the top, but, as a result of forty years of indoctrination, rises from below. People obey not merely out of fear, but because they think in uniform terms. General Augustin Guillaume, who was the French military attaché in Moscow for a period, and who certainly has no sympathy for the Soviet regime, felt impelled to write recently, "The Soviet Union is essentially the country of *unity*." I will draw a minor item from my own experience. In various widely separated places, from Leningrad to Alma-Ata, we asked people of widely varying stations what their first reaction had been to Khrushchev's speech to the Twentieth Congress, and how they had heard of it. I do not believe that *Agitprop* or anything else could possibly have known just when, where, and to whom we would put this question, or could have worked out in advance the hypothetical contingency that it would be asked in the way I asked it. Yet all to whom we talked replied in almost identical terms, as follows: "We felt a mixture of shock and relief, when the speech was first read to us. The fact that the leadership was courageous enough to make severe criticism of what had gone before shows our strength, and the vigor of the regime. The speech has relaxed the atmosphere, and helped speed the way to socialism."[9]

To conclude: almost everything in the Soviet Union still has to be done in the name of the party and its "monolithic unity"; the worst thing that can happen to a man, jail or banishment aside, is to be accused of being "antiparty." The party secretary in any community has formidable power, as has the local *aktiv* or group of leaders. The truly dedicated, indoctrinated section of the population believes fervently in the party. Let me provide an illustration. A Polish magazine, *Polsha*, is published in Russian in the USSR, so that Soviet readers may keep in touch with things Polish. A Russian critic recently inspected the first twelve issues of *Polsha*, and gave an anguished report to the *Literaturnaya Gazeta* in Moscow; he was outraged, as well as bewildered, by what the Poles are interested in—modernist art, political deviations, and a recent comedy on classical themes in which the hero, Achilles, "with complete composure makes mothers out of all five of Sappho's daughters." The Soviet critic wails in horrified protest, "But where is the true life of Poland? . . . How does the worker live? What does he dream about? What are his aspirations? . . . What does the Polish peasant think about? . . . What kind of *party life* is there in the country?"[10]

---

[9] One bright young man replied, "How did I hear of it? I was there!"
[10] *Current Digest of the Soviet Press*, March 6, 1957.

On the other hand, it is important to make a distinction carefully between party and regime. There are probably not ten thousand men, zealots all, in the entire Soviet Union who would die for the party *as such*, even though millions would probably die willingly for the country and system. Leaders belong to the party, yes, and an elaborate dovetailing structure combines party, system, and state; nevertheless few citizens, except the most dedicated or sanctified Communists, have much interest in purely party affairs on a purely party level. They pay respectful lip service to its mechanisms, but what they care about is something else. It is the *regime* that counts—jobs, government, power, the regime.

The Bureaucracy

The Soviet bureaucracy is compartmentalized to an extraordinary extent, and the liaison is vertical rather than horizontal. The ministry of finance may, as an example, run smoothly from top to bottom; but section heads in the ministry are apt to have little idea of the work of men in parallel posts in other ministries. One reason why the bureaucracy is so cumbersome is that, because of the duplex system, there are two bosses in every town, no matter how small—the party secretary and the chairman of the local soviet.[11]

Bureaucracy is, of course, no new thing in Russia; the petty bureaucrat in his pigeonhole has been an obstacle to progress for a century or longer. The pigeonhole becomes a bottleneck; ten thousand pigeonholes become ten thousand bottlenecks. Everything must be continually referred to the next higher authority, which may be inordinately stubborn and slow-moving. Trotsky once made a little joke to the effect that the dictatorship of the proletariat had become the dictatorship of the secretariat.

Moreover a minor official in a ministry may, for example, decide that doors in a new housing project should be so many inches wide, and ceilings so many feet high. Once that decision is made, and it may have been made on totally inadequate premises, those doors and windows are fixed forever. All Soviet leaders have, for at least thirty years, understood how the bureaucracy has spun out red tape and smothered initiative. Lenin talked about the evils of bureaucracy; so did Stalin; so does Khrushchev. But the Soviet

---

[11] The party secretaryship is not, in small towns, necessarily a full-time job, and the secretary, quite without regard to his power in the community as secretary, may have almost any kind of other occupation. A British friend of mine, vacationing in the Caucasus recently, asked his Intourist guide to lead him to the local secretary. He did not have to go far. The secretary was the manager of the hotel.

system itself serves to make bureaucratic top-heaviness inevitable. Take the budget. It is not, like our budget, devoted merely to government finance; it must, in all its ramifications, include the budgets of every industrial enterprise in Russia, of which there are at least 200,000. Or take publishing. The state is, under the Soviet system, responsible for every single bit of printed matter that appears in the entire country, which is a lot of reading matter. Or go further: the state is, after all, the sole employer of labor in the Soviet Union. Imagine what a bureaucracy there would be in the United States if *every* job in the country derived from authority in Washington.

Last Words on Marx

That Marx was a man of profound seminal and magnetic influence cannot be doubted; as a pioneer he ranks with Darwin, and no history of human thought could possibly omit his name. Nevertheless, he made mistakes. The conception that, even today, he is infallible is one of the most preposterous of Marxist myths. Mostly Marx's errors derive from his *idée fixe* about class, and consequent romanticizing of the proletariat. He thought that only the proletariat could truly represent the interests of a suppressed people, but much in the history of contemporary Asian and African nationalism refutes this thesis. Marx gravely underestimated the power of nationalism; he assumed that, as class antagonism declined, so would the hostility of nations. He thought that the workers of the world *would* in a time of crisis tend to unite; this they certainly do not do. For example—to mention no more than one obvious point—German workers by the million fought Russian workers during World War II. Moreover, Marx believed firmly that capitalism was bound to effect a progressive pauperization of the working classes, but almost the exact opposite has taken place. Count the number of American workers who have TV sets and luxurious automobiles. Marx thought that wages would, by some kind of eternal process, always tend to be forced down, as capitalist processes expanded, but they have steadily gone up. Also, he did not anticipate a great many developments in the field of capital and government, like wide public ownership in corporations and the necessity, now granted by almost everybody, for the state to insure full employment. He had no intimation of the way social democracy would come to function in Scandinavia for instance, and such concepts as "welfare state" would have bewildered and enraged him. Finally, to pick and choose among a multitude of items available, he thought that the apparatus of the state would, under Communism, "wither away," which is one thing that certainly has *not* happened in the Soviet Union.

Why, one may fairly ask, has Marxism caused so much misery, such pervasive and widespread suffering? Marx and Lenin did not want men to suffer; they wanted them to be free of chains. Communist apologists today, assuming that they grant the fact of suffering at all, seek to explain this with several familiar clichés—that the new Soviet republic had to defend itself against intervention from the West, which made an extensive arms program necessary, that industrialization and collectivization necessarily forced the standard of living down, and that stringent police authority was necessary to remove the dangerous possibility of counterrevolution. Another factor is more fundamental, and lies close to the heart of Marxist-Leninist doctrine. It is the fact that dedicated Marxists believe in the future, almost to the exclusion of the present. It is the duty of this generation to make sacrifices for the next because, as seen by Marx, history is to an extent predetermined and a "good" future will inevitably emerge from the turmoil of the present. Further, it is the masses that count, "humanity" as a whole and its larger good, not individuals. People as such do not matter, and are expendable, if only because Communism is an expression of the ineluctable "will of history" itself, which is larger than any personal constituent.

*

One curious paradoxical point is that few citizens of the Soviet Union, except zealots, have much interest in Marxist theory. Marx underlies the whole structure of the state and many people have a vague over-all Marxist view, but Marxism is accepted mostly as a kind of fact of life—often a boresome, dreary fact. Not many people talk about dialectical materialism, even if they have been taught to think dialectically. Milovan Djilas, the Yugoslav Communist and author of *The New Class*, now serving a long jail sentence because of his so-called heresies, makes the point (which is so obvious to a non-Communist that it would never need stating) that "Communist power, having overthrown the old tyranny of landlords and capitalists, inevitably imposes a new class of oligarchs on the people it promises to liberate." The man in the street in Moscow would shudder if you said this to him aloud, but (zealots aside) in his inner heart of hearts he would probably agree. Ideological fervor, like loyalty to the party itself *as such,* is running out.

Some Lies and Broken Promises

Soviet officials distort; also they lie, if lying serves their purpose. The constitution itself contains outright lies, for instance the impudently bland statement that freedom of the press, speech, and assembly is assured (Article 125), and, reading the Soviet press over a long period, it is difficult for an outsider to efface the impression that the whole life of the people is based on falsity. Of course a great many Soviet citizens, having no experience of a free press, think that if something is *written*, and exists on paper, it is therefore true; perhaps they do not realize quite how much is fabrication. This, to put it mildly, does not keep members of the government from telling lies, which are held to be justified if they are in the interest of the higher "good." We shall inspect soon some really dazzling, monumental lies about Hungary. But examples can be found on every level. Comrade Mukhitdinov said lately, in reference to a statement about Moslem affairs, "Mohammedans of the Soviet Union maintain unobstructed ties with Mohammedans all over the world." This, clearly, is fantastically untrue.

Lying is, of course, not considered improper or unethical in the Marxist *mystique*; not only have most Communists no respect for objective truth, but they do not even concede that this exists. The Russians do not, like some children, lie for fun or because they don't know better, but because all ethical and moral considerations are considered to be subordinate to the class struggle, as Lenin himself has said in so many words; the concept of truth is subordinated to the concept of proletarian victory; truth does not count, unless it serves an end. This is why so much of what goes on in the Soviet Union appears to be so utterly topsy-turvy. Shortly after arriving in Moscow, I asked a veteran diplomat if the Soviet attitude was, on a certain subject, "genuine" and "sincere." He answered dryly, "Of course the Soviet attitude is genuine, but that has nothing to do with whether it is sincere." He went on, "The most menacing thing about this country is that its leaders are the most sincere liars in history. When uttering the basest lies, they are at their most sincere." This trait is, of course, not only baffling to the visitor with good will, but infinitely perturbing; it is no easy thing to listen to a man tell you, with a straight face, that Trotsky had nothing to do with winning the civil war, or that hostilities came in Korea because of unprovoked American aggression against the Korean people, or that the "volunteers" on call in the early days of the Suez crisis were really "volunteers."

One more word on Soviet hypocrisy. A writer in *Izvestia* on July 9, 1957, exhorting the faithful to party unity, leads off with the phrase, "Who does not know Lenin's famous testament?" But this testament, which contains Lenin's outspoken criticism of Stalin, had been suppressed in the Soviet Union for more than thirty years, and was never published until 1956.

To list examples of Soviet broken pledges and promises would be tedious; they range from the invasion of Poland in 1939 and the occupation of the Baltic states in 1940 to violations of more recent agreements, including several made at Yalta. Contrariwise—it is very curious—Soviet commitments in business and commercial affairs, including foreign trade arrangements, are almost always carried out with punctilious correctness, without fail. This has been true since the beginning of the Soviet regime, and probably derives from the fact that, once it was decided to do business with the bourgeois world, the Russians felt that it was a matter of prestige for them to out-West the West in respect to business conventions. It isn't easy to get a Soviet signature on a contract but, once it is signed, the contract will be honored to the letter.

Playful Work by the Historians

The way Soviet publicists distort history is enough to make the hair crawl from the scalp. Sometimes the distortion cleverly contains a grain of truth; sometimes the grain of truth is, to understate the case, not included. For instance it is a fixed and incontrovertible fact, disputed by no one, that the Soviet Union entered the war against Japan on August 8, 1945. This was two days after the United States dropped the first atomic bomb on Hiroshima, and six days before the Japanese surrendered (August 14). In other words, the Soviet Union was in a state of war with Japan for less than a week. During this period Russian troops, it is true, flooded across the Manchurian border, but resistance from the demoralized Japanese was of the slightest, and casualties very few. But there are Russian historians who, today, make the unbelievable assertion that the Soviet Union *won* the war against Japan. Consider the following passage from a recent article in *Krasnaya Zvezda* (*Red Star*), the official army organ: "The American atomic bombs which destroyed Japanese cities and took 200,000 human lives were dropped for political, not military reasons. The main purpose of this move was to deprive the Soviet Union of the advantages which victory had brought to it. . . . The atomic bombing of [Hiroshima and Nagasaki] was not dictated by military necessity. The military necessity was eliminated after the Soviet

Union's entry into the war against Japan."[12] Yet the Soviet Union did not enter the war until *after* the first bomb had been dropped!

Bolshevik,[13] the organ of the Central Committee of the Party, printed an article in June, 1951, to commemorate the anniversary of the German attack on the USSR. Listen: "Hitlerite Germany, *instigated by American and English imperialists* [italics mine] suddenly and faithlessly attacked the Soviet Union. . . . The English-American refusal to fulfill their obligations as allies was the main reason for the radical military deterioration of the Soviet Union in summer 1942. . . . The leading groups in the U.S.A. and England continued to refuse to fulfill their obligations concerning the second front throughout 1943 and the first half of 1944. This policy was openly calculated to destroy completely the Soviet state and to strengthen the world hegemony of the Anglo-American imperialists. . . . This is why the disembarkation of the Anglo-American troops in Europe took place only in June 1944, when it had become obvious that the Soviet Union was able to end the war victoriously by its own forces. . . . Our victories resulted in the withdrawal from the war of the main ally of Hitlerite Germany—Fascist Italy. . . . In 1945 . . . Fascist Germany capitulated."

It might be thought that the Russo-German Pact of August, 1939 would be difficult for Soviet apologists to cover up. Not at all. Here are excerpts from a primary school text, published under the editorship of Professor E. A. Shestakov, approved by the Ministry of Education of the RSFSR and published with a circulation of one million copies: "Germany seized Norway, Denmark, Holland, Belgium, Yugoslavia, Greece. It was helped by Italy, Hungary, Rumania, Bulgaria, and Finland. France and Britain opposed Germany, and later the United States of America joined with them. . . . Almost the whole of Europe fell under the power of Hitler. The Soviet Union was against war, and all the time fought for peace. Hence, our government completed with Germany a treaty of non-aggression." Then: "But the Fascists did not keep their word. They concentrated a big army at our border, and perfidiously attacked the USSR."[14]

So perfervid is the local chauvinism that, an interesting point, Soviet historians have on occasion been rebuked for attacking nineteenth-century

---

[12] *Current Digest of the Soviet Press*, July 17, 1957.
[13] Now renamed *Kommunist*.
[14] For this passage I am indebted to William Benton. Other material secured by Mr. Benton points up the fact that Soviet school children are given a picture of World War II in which the United States plays only a belated secondary role in Europe. That the Japanese surrender took place on an American battleship is, incidentally, *never* mentioned in the Soviet press or history books.

Czars indiscriminately. For instance, it is now the accepted line that the Czarist conquest of Central Asia was commendable, because it expanded Russian power, had "correct" and "progressive" elements, and led to "national unity."

Better than the Czars?

Sometimes people say that the Bolshevik regime started from nothing, and was built from scratch. This, of course, is quite untrue, though it may be freely granted that Czarist Russia was undeveloped. Its agriculture was hopelessly backward, and its industry was, to a considerable degree, controlled by foreign interests, which meant that profits flowed out, not in. But it is nonsensical to assert that the Communists started with an altogether empty slate. Russian science produced some extremely distinguished figures under the Czars, like Mendeleev. According to the 1914 Baedeker, conscripts drawn into the Czarist Army were only 50 per cent illiterate; this is a long way from being 100 per cent, but it is also a long way from zero. In particular, the Bolsheviks had a good deal of industrial development from which to draw. Russia never experienced an industrial revolution comparable to that of western Europe, but its industrial advance was considerable in the last half of the nineteenth century. "In the 20 years between 1877 and 1897, the production of textiles doubled and the production of metals trebled."[16] By the turn of the century, Russia was the second biggest oil producer and second biggest cotton producer in the world. Also there was considerable intervention by the state in private enterprise. Sixty per cent of the railways were state-owned, and the state was both the largest employer of labor and the largest landowner in the country. One well-informed writer, Bertram D. Wolfe, goes so far as to say in his *Three Who Made a Revolution*, "What the Bolsheviks really took over in 1917, even before they had nationalized a single industry on their own, was the largest state economic machine in the world."

On the other hand, Russian railway mileage in 1912 was less in proportion to territory than in any country in Europe, except Norway; the country only produced 2.6 per cent of the total world industrial output, and industrial workers comprised only 3 per cent of the population; there were only thirty-three cities with a population of more than 100,000; and only 26.2 per cent of cultivable land was under tillage. Not more than one-third of the peasantry had any land at all, although the peasants made up four-fifths of the popula-

[16] Edmund Wilson, *op. cit.*, p. 362.

tion. Of 1,084 towns with a population exceeding 10,000, only 182 had an organized water supply, only 105 had gas or electric lighting, and only 55 had tramways. Three hundred and twenty had no paved streets. (These statistics are not from Soviet authorities, which might be slanted, but come from the old Baedeker and other sound sources of the day.)

Another question is whether or not people are by and large better off today than they would be if the Bolshevik Revolution had not occurred. First of all, we have no right to assume that there would not have been *some* progress in Russia between 1917 and the present day, no matter what type of regime prevailed. No matter who governed Russia, even if it had never become Sovietized, it would almost certainly have been bound to march in step, to some extent at least, with modern times. Russia might not have become as progressive as Scandinavia, but it could not have remained what it was under the Czars. The temper of the people forbade that. Revolutionary impulses were too strong. Even if Russia had succumbed to counterrevolution, and a regime grew up like, let us say, that of Pilsudski in Poland, some technical and economic progress would have been inevitable.

If, without regard to such qualifying factors, we attempt to make a straight-out comparison between Czarist Russia and the Russia of today, some results are these. Heavy industry is roughly ten times more productive today than in 1913; light industry three times more productive. The production of pig iron has increased 900 per cent, coal 1,500 per cent, and electric power 10,000 per cent. Output of machines is 181 times greater. Czarist Russia, with 160,000,000 people, produced 60,000,000 pairs of shoes a year; Soviet Russia, with 200,000,000, produces 314,000,000 pairs.[16] By 1960, according to Soviet statisticians, each nine days will see as much production of consumer goods as the entire *year* 1913. Real wages are hard to calculate, and are probably not so much higher than in 1913 as might be imagined, but certainly the average industrial worker or peasant has more purchasing power than his grandfather, and in several other respects is better off. The urban citizen has, it is true, less living space. However, he has a very broad paternalistic system at his disposal, and a wide variety of free, or nearly free, services, such as medical care, social security, pensions, education, rent, and utilities. He is assured of sustenance and employment.

The best Soviet record is in education, public health, technological advance, and the development of science. The death rate has been cut 75 per cent, and every child goes to school; literacy is universal. Under the Czars *illiteracy* ranged up to 70 per cent for the country as a whole. And, even if the Soviet

[16] Paul Wohl, in the *Christian Science Monitor*, March 15, 1957.

system has not produced an egalitarian society, class barriers have been broken down, women emancipated, popular culture encouraged, social discriminations abolished at least in theory, vivid interest in such fields as sport stimulated, and immense opportunity provided for individual advancement within the system. Time and time again—it was a challenging experience—we came across people who, rising out of illiterate peasant families, were carving out (by Soviet standards) successful lives. Above all, the country today has vitality, discipline, and *direction*, in contrast to former slipshodness, decay, and contemptible lack of social vision and conscience. In the realm of politics and civil liberties, there is not so much to choose. Russian citizens under the Czars did, however, have substantially more personal freedom than Soviet citizens have today; if, in fact, the Czarist government had not been lax enough to allow émigrés like Lenin and Trotsky to leave the country, the Revolution might never have occurred. The Czars had censorship, secret police, and the concomitant paraphernalia of autocracy; but their regime was not so dictatorially cruel, totalitarian, and arbitrary as the Soviet regime.

Finally, we must mention points in the realm of emotion. The great mass of Soviet citizens feel that the Soviet Union, however good or bad it may be, *belongs* to them; peasants under the Czars had no such feeling. They belonged to the country—or to the nearest landlord—not vice versa. A famous passage in Tolstoy depicts a country gentleman proudly displaying one of his wolfhounds—a splendid beast which cost only one hundred serfs. Russia will never go back to that.

CHAPTER XI

What's Going On—De-Stalinization

Russia—a freak of nature . . . —DOSTOEVSKY

WE RETURN now to the contemporary scene. Since Stalin's death in 1953 the major element in Soviet affairs and policy has been a profound readjustment, that is to say de-Stalinization. Several phases and events belong to this period: (a) emergence of Khrushchev to top place, the execution of Beria, and the dismissal of Malenkov as prime minister in 1955; (b) the Khrushchev speech to the Twentieth Party Congress in February, 1956, formal repudiation of the Stalinist cult of personality, and re-expression of the policy of collective leadership; (c) explosion in the satellites; (d) the shakeup of June, 1957, and the removal from power of the "antiparty" group of Molotov, Malenkov, and Kaganovich. The dismissal of Zhukov followed. Let us take each event in turn.

The Khrushchev speech is often thought to have been the opening note in the de-Stalinization process, but this is not so. Actually it was the climax. In blunt fact, de-Stalinization commenced within half an hour of Stalin's death or even before, when Marshal Zhukov, who had been exiled by Stalin to the provinces, was brought back to Moscow. Then, before Stalin's body was fairly cold, occurred a signal occurrence—the disappearance without trace of Alexander N. Poskrebyshev who, for some years, had been head of Stalin's inner council and who did most of his really gruesome work—work too private or too dirty even for Beria. No explanation for his summary liquidation has ever been given. By one and all, he was detested. There is something fascinating, if revolting, about this macabre episode— the picture of the Kremlin oligarchs who took over from Stalin pooling their efforts and forgetting their differences to jump, as one man, on Poskrebyshev and extinguish him utterly and at once, like self-righteous and indignant tigers.

Malenkov became both premier and secretary of the party on March 6, 1953, the day after Stalin died. But, as we know, he was replaced as party secretary by Khrushchev soon and it became clear that the triumvirate or *troika* (Malenkov, Beria, Molotov), which sought to monopolize power would not last long. Malenkov was forced to resign as prime minister in February, 1955, to the tune of public groveling in the best Soviet manner. He confessed his "guilt and responsibility" for the "unsatisfactory state of affairs in agriculture" and to errors, caused by "insufficient experience," in the guidance of the national economy. Bulganin took over as prime minister. During these two years, Khrushchev was little known to the public at large. Most people outside the inner circle, as well as a majority of observers abroad, had in fact scarcely ever heard of him. The first indication that he had cogent influence, as well as party rank, was that he was chairman of the committee making the arrangements for Stalin's funeral. The only three speakers at the funeral were Malenkov, Molotov, and Beria, but it was Khrushchev who superintended the proceedings.

Meantime Beria met his fate, and joined Yagoda and Yezhov in the remarkable community of Soviet police chiefs who do not die a natural death. Even today, full details of what happened to him are not known. Beria was an interesting man. He was a Georgian, and an architect by profession. He looked like a bookkeeper, and was not at all incendiary in character. It was announced (July, 1953) that he had been dismissed some weeks before, and was being held for trial. A secret trial did take place, with Marshal Konev as the presiding judge, and he was executed on Christmas Eve, 1953. Marshal Zhukov is also supposed to have played a piquant role in Beria's transposition from the earthly scene. Beria had his own armed forces in the MVD, which naturally caused friction with the army. Beria was, according to one story, accused at a meeting of the Presidium of various derelictions, and was ordered to give up his personal control of the police, and put it under collective administration. He refused. One version of what happened is that Zhukov, Konev, and other high officers were waiting outside the door, when this meeting took place, and personally arrested Beria on the spot; another is that the arrest took place in a more regular and leisurely manner, and that he was simply picked up by army officers in his quarters at Lubyanka. In any case, there is no doubt that Beria did consider the police to be his private domain, superior to both party and government, and this had produced an intolerable situation.

As I heard it put by a somewhat cynical Englishman, "Communism had to be made safe for the leading Communists." That is, rule by arbitrary police power had to be modified, because otherwise the point could have been reached where "everybody would be killing *everybody* off." Nobody wanted any maniacal revival of the Yezhov witch-hunt, and everybody feared and hated Beria. Before his death Stalin apparently had the intention, sooner or later, of liquidating *all* surviving members of the old leadership with Beria's connivance or assistance. Not only did the terror have to be kept from starting again, but some explanation had to be made as to why it had gone on for so long, with such nightmarish results. On both counts Beria was doomed.

The Khrushchev Speech

Actually Khrushchev made two speeches or reports to the Twentieth Congress. It is the second that I am dealing with in detail below. The first (February 14) was his presentation of the Report of the Central Committee to the Congress. This was about fifty thousand words long, and was full of dynamite. Khrushchev announced that "the Leninist principle of coexistence of states with different social systems" was not a tactical, but a fundamental, principle of Soviet foreign policy, that war between capitalist and Communist states was not "fatalistically inevitable," and that socialism can be reached in a country by parliamentary means, without civil war or violence. Backtracking from former precepts could scarcely go further. On the other hand Khrushchev still stressed the "revolutionary militancy" of Communism.

As to the second speech, I have mentioned it so often in passing that it may seem anticlimactical to treat of it at length. But it is the key to much, and is a most remarkable human as well as political document; one authority calls it "the most important document ever to have come from the Communist movement."[1] It isn't every day that the leading figure in a government calls his immediate predecessor, and a predecessor who had been deified to boot, a "criminal murderer," a purveyor of "moral and physical annihilation," a "fabricator of dirty and shameful cases," and a brutal, despotic, capricious, irritable "slanderer." Moreover the speech gave dramatic emphasis to the new direction of Russian policy.

The circumstances were these: Khrushchev spoke for approximately six hours, on February 24 and 25, 1956, before a closed session of some fourteen hundred members of the Twentieth Party Congress; apparently he began near midnight, talked for several hours, and resumed the next day. Much of the speech had been carefully prepared, and documents were ready for

---

[1] Bertram D. Wolfe in *Khrushchev and Stalin's Ghost*, p. 67.

distribution to the audience. However, internal evidence suggests that Khrushchev, carried away by his own eloquence and the turmoil of the occasion, probably did a good deal of ad-libbing. The speech has never been published in the Soviet Union, and in fact is seldom even referred to in print; but practically every Soviet citizen knows about it. First, leading party members were ordered to disseminate it in their own circles; second, it was systematically read by party organizers to closed groups all over the country in party cells, factories, and collective farms; third, it was relayed to nonparty listeners in wholesale number.

The text was leaked out of Russia probably by the Poles, and in time reached the State Department. The State Department text was published in Washington on June 4, 1956, and its authenticity is indisputable.

Two questions pose themselves at outset. First, what in the immediate course of the Congress impelled Khrushchev to speak in exactly the way he did? The conclusion is inescapable that, even though the speech was carefully prepared, this was done in a hurry, and was a result of strong, insistent pressure from the Congress itself. Mikoyan broke the ice first. Congress delegates then demanded to know more. Having made a slit in the bag, the leadership had to tear it open the whole way. Second, why in view of the fact that the speech was widely disseminated at once, has it not been published in the Soviet Union? The answer is not altogether clear, but one element is that the Presidium must have felt that forthright, complete publication would be too much of a shock. It was wiser to let the document penetrate into the body of Russia slowly, drop by drop, with only a chosen few hearing it at first, moreover a chosen few who, since they read it to audiences aloud, were in a position to explain its unprecedented meaning.

Khrushchev starts off bluntly with his main theme:

> Comrades . . . Quite a lot has been said about the cult of the individual and about its harmful consequences. After Stalin's death the Central Committee . . . began to implement a policy of explaining . . . that it is impermissible and foreign to the spirit of Marxism-Leninism to elevate one person, transform him into a superman possessing supernatural characteristics . . . infallible in his behavior.
>
> Such belief about a man, and specifically about Stalin, was cultivated among us for many years.
>
> The objective of the present report is not a thorough evaluation of Stalin's life and activity. Concerning Stalin's merits an entirely sufficient number of books, pamphlets and studies had already been written in his lifetime. The role of Stalin in the preparation and execution of the socialist revolution, in the civil war, and in the fight for the con-

struction of socialism in our country, is universally known. . . .
At present we are concerned with a question . . . how the cult of the
person of Stalin has been gradually growing, the cult which became
at a certain specific stage the source of the whole series of exceedingly
serious and grave perversions of party principles, of party democracy,
of revolutionary legality.

Khrushchev proceeds to mention Lenin's modesty, in contrast to Stalin's
avaricious glory-seeking, and points out that the classics of Marxism-Leninism
denounce "every manifestation of the cult of the individual." Lenin never
tried "to impose by force his views upon his co-workers. He tried to convince." Then Khrushchev describes how Lenin, eager for "the application of
the ideas of scientific communism to life," wrote to the Party Congress in
1922 warning delegates against Stalin and suggesting that he be removed
as secretary general of the party. This is the celebrated Lenin Testament.
Never till this moment had the existence of this document been made known
publicly in Russia. Next Khrushchev read two letters, one from Lenin's
widow to Trotsky, complaining of Stalin's wanton rudeness to her, and the
other from Lenin to Stalin, sternly rebuking him for this. These had never
even been heard of before, inside the Soviet Union or out. They made a
"commotion in the hall."

Khrushchev proceeds:

We have to consider seriously and analyze correctly this matter in
order that we may preclude any possibility of a repetition in any form
whatever of what took place during the life of Stalin, who absolutely
did not tolerate collegiality in leadership and in work and who practiced
brutal violence not only toward everything which opposed him, but
also toward that which seemed, to his capricious and despotic character, contrary to his concepts.

Stalin acted not through persuasion, explanation, and patient co-
operation with people . . . but by demanding absolute submission. . . .
Whoever opposed [him] . . . was doomed to removal . . . and subsequent moral and physical annihilation. . . .

Worth noting is the fact that, even during the progress of the furious
ideological fight against the Trotskyites, the Zinovievites, the Bukhar-
inites, and others, extreme repressive measures were not used against
them. . . . Some years later, when socialism in our country was fun-
damentally constructed . . . when the ideological opponents of the
party were long since defeated politically—then the oppression directed
against them began [when the revolution was already victorious and
it was no longer necessary].

Lenin, had he lived, never would have taken "extreme measures" against
his old comrades, Khrushchev is convinced. Nor was it necessary to an-

nihilate such people. He quotes Lenin to the effect that senior officials of the party had a duty to establish "a deep, individualized relationship with, and sometimes even a type of therapy for, the representatives of the so-called opposition—those who experienced a psychological crisis because of failure . . . in their career." Had this been done, "thousands of people would not have fallen victim to the methods of terror."

> Stalin originated the concept "enemy of the people." This term automatically rendered it unnecessary that the ideological errors of a man engaged in a controversy be proven. . . . In the main, and in actuality, the only proof of guilt used, against all norms of current legal science, was the "confession" of the accused himself, and as subsequent probing proved, "confessions" were acquired through physical pressures against the accused. . . . The formula "enemy of the people" was specifically introduced for the purpose of physically annihilating such individuals.
>
> Mass arrests and deportations of many thousands of people, executed without trial and without normal investigation, created conditions of insecurity, fear and even desperation.

Stalin, Khrushchev proceeds, allowed year after year to go by without deigning to summon party congresses, and, using his unlimited power, began the process of rule in secret. Not only did he ignore the Central Committee, but the Presidium as well. "Stalin was a very distrustful man, sickly suspicious; we know this from our work with him. He could look at a man and say: 'Why are your eyes so shifty today?' He had a general distrust even toward eminent party workers, and everywhere saw 'enemies, two-facers and spies.' "

Khrushchev raises a question that for many years profoundly puzzled observers of the Russian scene. "How is it possible that a person confesses to crimes which he has not committed?" He gives the answer: "Only in one way—because of the application of physical methods of pressuring him, tortures, bringing him into a state of unconsciousness, deprivation of his judgment, taking away of his human dignity." Men who had never been enemies, spies, or wreckers, but who had always been honest Communists, were no longer able "to bear barbaric tortures," and so "charged themselves with all kinds of grave and unlikely crimes."

Of the 139 members of the Central Committee elected at the Seventeenth Congress, no fewer than 98, that is 70 per cent, were arrested and shot. (Indignation in the hall.) Of the 1966 delegates to that Congress, elected in 1934, no fewer than 1,108 were subsequently arrested on charges of anti-revolutionary crimes, decidedly more than a majority. (Indignation in the hall.) "This very fact shows how absurd, wild, and contrary to common sense" were Stalin's charges. But Stalin believed that "the closer to socialism we are, the more enemies we will have."

Khrushchev proceeds to tell the story of Comrade Robert I. Eikhe, a candidate member of the Politburo and an Old Bolshevik who entered the party back in 1905. He was arrested on April 12, 1938 "on the basis of slanderous materials," without the sanction of the Public Prosecutor of the USSR, and was "forced under torture" to sign a confession implicating himself and others in anti-Soviet activity. This was an "odious falsification." Eikhe then sent a declaration to Stalin categorically denying his guilt and asking for an examination of the case. "There is no more bitter misery," he wrote, "than to sit in the jail of a government for which I have always fought." Then he sent a second letter to Stalin:

> Had I been guilty of only one hundredth of the crimes with which I am charged I would not have dared to send you this pre-execution declaration; however I have not been guilty of even one of the things with which I am charged and my heart is clean of even the shadow of baseness. I have never in my life told you a word of falsehood and now finding my two feet in the grave I am also not lying.

He asks Stalin again to examine his case, not out of hope of saving himself, but to clear the reputation of those others who, under torture, he had been forced to incriminate. "My broken ribs have not mended properly and have caused me great pain. . . . I have never betrayed you or the party. I know that I perish because of vile and mean work of the enemies of the Party and of the people who fabricated the provocation against me."

Khrushchev interjects:

> It would appear that such an important declaration was worth an examination by the Central Committee. This, however, was not done, and the declaration was transmitted to Beria while the terrible maltreatment of Comrade Eikhe continued.
> On February 2, 1940 Eikhe was brought before the court. Here he did not confess any guilt and said as follows:
> "In all the so-called confessions of mine, there is not one word written by me with the exception of my signatures under the protocols. . . . I have made my confession under pressure from the investigative judge, who from the time of my arrest tormented me. After that I began to write all this nonsense. . . . The most important thing for me is to tell the Court, the Party and Stalin that I am not guilty. I have never been guilty of any conspiracy. I will die believing in the truth of party policy as I have believed in it during my whole life."
> On February 4 Eikhe was shot. (Indignation in the hall.)

It has been definitely established now that Eikhe's case was fabricated; he has been posthumously rehabilitated.

One wonders how Bolsheviks more intellectually eminent than Eikhe, but perhaps not so uncomplicated and tough-minded, like Zinoviev, Kamenev, Sokolnikov, Bukharin, Rykov, behaved in their last grim moments. Did they, too, have courage enough, faith enough, if guiltless, to repudiate their fraudulent confessions, and defy their judges? What were their last messages to Stalin? What indignant or despairing words, if any, did they pass down?

Stalin, Khrushchev insists, must have been personally responsible for cases like that of Eikhe, since the police could not possibly have arrested men of such exalted rank without his knowledge. "The vicious practice was condoned of having the NKVD prepare lists of persons . . . whose sentences were prepared in advance. Yezhov would send these lists to Stalin personally for his approval of the proposed punishment." There were 383 such lists in two years, and Stalin approved them all. Cases, one by one, are now being reopened, in an investigation by the Military Collegium of the Supreme Court that began in 1954. So far, Khrushchev says, 7,679 innocently convicted persons have been rehabilitated. This, however, does them little good, since they are dead.[2]

Khrushchev now turns to a new theme and describes how accumulation of power in the hands of a single person, Stalin, led to grave consequences in World War II. Stalin, according to Khrushchev, completely ignored repeated warnings that Hitler was about to attack Russia, and refused to permit any defense measures to be organized, on the ground that this might give the Nazis provocation. Spies even told him the exact date of the attack, but he did nothing. Yet, in the postwar years, he was extolled as the hero "who had foreseen everything." Actually when war came in 1941 not only were tanks and artillery short, but even rifles. "I recall that in those days I telephoned to Comrade Malenkov from Kiev and told him, 'People have volunteered for the new army and demand arms. You must send us arms.' Malenkov answered me, 'We cannot send you arms. We are sending all our rifles to Leningrad and you have to arm yourselves.' " (Movement in the hall.) As a result of lack of preparation, the USSR lost *half* its industry in the early days of the war. Moreover the Stalinist purges had decimated the army. "Repressions were instituted . . . literally at the company and battalion commander level and extending to the higher military centers; the cadre of leaders who had

---

[2] But it may substantially help their families, if these survive. Often relatives of those unjustly purged receive pensions or monetary grants.

gained military experience in Spain and the Far East was almost completely liquidated."

Khrushchev proceeds:

> After the first severe disaster and defeat at the front, Stalin thought that this was the end. . . . He said: "All which Lenin created we have lost forever."

Then for a long time he did not direct military operations and in fact "ceased to do anything whatever"; he did not resume active leadership until persuaded to do so by other members of the Politburo, in view of grave reverses at the front. But:

> Stalin was very far from an understanding of the real situation. . . . This was natural because, during the whole Patriotic War, he never visited any section of the front or any liberated city except for one short ride on the Mozhaisk highway during a stabilized situation. . . .

In 1942, Khrushchev relates, an exceptionally serious military situation developed near Kharkov. This news was communicated to Stalin with a request for a change in operational plans. Stalin rejected the suggestion, although the Red Army on the Kharkov front was threatened with encirclement. Khrushchev goes on:

> I telephoned to [Marshal] Vasilevsky and begged him, "Alexander Mikhailovich, take a map and show Comrade Stalin the situation which has developed." We should note that Stalin planned operations on a globe. (Animation in the hall.) Yes, Comrades, he used to take the globe and trace the front line on it. I said to Comrade Vasilevsky, "Show him the situation on a map; in the present situation we cannot continue the operation which was planned. The old decision must be changed for the good of the cause."

Vasilevsky, who was present in the hall while Khrushchev spoke, and who is now Deputy Minister of Defense, told Khrushchev at the time that Stalin refused to hear any arguments on the subject, and that therefore he (Vasilevsky) would not try to see him.

> After my talk with Vasilevsky I telephoned to Stalin at his villa, but Stalin did not answer the telephone and Malenkov was at the receiver. I told Comrade Malenkov that I was calling from the front and that I wanted to speak personally to Stalin. Stalin informed me through Malenkov that I should speak with Malenkov. I stated for the second time that I wished to inform Stalin personally about the grave situation which had arisen for us at the front. But Stalin did not consider it convenient to raise the phone and he again stated that I should

speak to him through Malenkov, although he was only a few steps from the telephone.

After "listening" in this manner to our plea, Stalin said: "Let everything remain as it is!"

And what was the result of this? The worst that we had expected. The Germans surrounded our army concentrations and consequently we lost hundreds of thousands of our soldiers. This is Stalin's military "genius"; this is what it cost us. (Movement in the hall.)

Khrushchev alludes to novels, films, and "scientific studies" which stress the role of Stalin in the Patriotic War. "They make us feel sick."

Then:

> Not Stalin but the party as a whole, the Soviet government, our heroic army, its talented leaders and brave soldiers, the whole Soviet nation—these are the ones who assured the victory in the Great Patriotic war. (Tempestuous and prolonged applause.)

Khrushchev passes on to Stalin's "monstrous" violations of Leninist nationality principles, and mentions the mass deportations of the Chechen-Ingush and other peoples, which were not dictated by any military considerations. "The Ukrainians avoided meeting this fate only because there were too many of them and there was no space to which to deport them. Otherwise Stalin would have deported them also." (Laughter and animation in the hall.)

Next come some harsh references to Beria in connection with the Leningrad case,[8] which was "fabricated." Beria, says Khrushchev, cleverly took advantage of Stalin's suspicions and persecution mania, which reached "unbelievable dimensions." Beria "murdered thousands of communists and loyal Soviet people." Then:

> The question arises: Why is it that we see the truth of this affair only now and why did we not do something earlier during Stalin's life in order to prevent the loss of innocent lives? It was because Stalin personally supervised the "Leningrad Affair" and the majority of Politburo members did not at that time know all of the circumstances in these matters and could not therefore intervene.

Now Khrushchev mentions briefly the conflict with Yugoslavia, and Stalin's "shameful" role in this:

> The Yugoslav affair contained no problems which could not have been solved through party discussions among comrades. . . . It was completely possible to have prevented the rupture of relations. . . .

---

[8] Mentioned above in Chapter VI.

This does not mean, however, that the Yugoslav leaders did not make mistakes or did not have shortcomings. But these were magnified in a monstrous manner by Stalin, which resulted in a break of relations with a friendly country.

I recall the first days when the conflict between the Soviet Union and Yugoslavia began artificially to be blown up. Once when I came from Kiev to Moscow I was invited to visit Stalin who, pointing to the copy of a letter lately sent to Tito, asked me, "Have you read this?"

Not waiting for my reply he answered, "I will shake my little finger —and there will be no more Tito. He will fall."

We have paid dearly for this shaking of the little finger. . . . You see to what Stalin's mania for greatness led. He had completely lost consciousness of reality.

Next comes the Doctors' Plot.[4] Khrushchev says that there was no plot whatever, but that Stalin was incited by a letter from an *agent provocateur*:

> Such a letter was sufficient for Stalin to reach an immediate conclusion. . . . he issued orders to arrest a group of eminent Soviet medical specialists. He personally issued advice on the conduct of the investigation. . . . He said that the academician Vinogradov should be put in chains, another one should be beaten. Present at this Congress as a delegate is the former Minister of State Security, Comrade Ignatiev. Stalin told him curtly, "If you do not obtain confessions from the doctors, we will shorten you by a head." (Tumult in the hall.)
>
> Stalin personally called the investigative judge, gave him instructions, advised him on which investigative method should be used; these methods were simple—beat, beat, and once again, beat.
>
> Shortly after the doctors were arrested, we members of the Political Bureau received protocols of the doctors' confessions of guilt. After distributing these protocols, Stalin told us, "You are blind like young kittens; what will happen without me? The country will perish because you do not know how to recognize enemies."

Khrushchev cannot keep off the subject of miscarriage of justice. His explanation that he and his colleagues could not intervene because they did not know what was going on obviously does not hold water; the real reason he stood aside must have been that he knew full well that his own head would fall if he raised a whisper. Anyway he tells the story of the Kedrov case. Kedrov was an Old Bolshevik like Eikhe, who suffered a similar fate. Here is what Comrade Kedrov wrote the Central Committee:

> I am calling to you for help from a gloomy cell of the Lefortovsky prison. Let my cry of horror reach your ears; do not remain deaf; take me under your protection; please, help remove the nightmare of interrogations and show that this is all a mistake.

[4] See Chapter VII above in the section about Voroshilov.

I suffer innocently. Please believe me. Time will testify to the truth. I am not an *agent provocateur* of the Czarist Okhrana; I am not a spy; I am not a member of an anti-Soviet organization of which I am being accused on the basis of denunciations. I am not guilty of any other crimes against the party and the Government. I am an old Bolshevik, free of any stain; I have honestly fought for almost 40 years in the ranks of the party for the good and prosperity of the nation. . . .

. . . Today I, a 62-year-old man, am being threatened by the investigative judges with more severe, cruel and degrading methods of physical pressure. They [the judges] arc no longer capable of becoming aware of their error and of recognizing that their handling of my case is illegal and impermissible. They try to justify their actions by picturing me as a hardened and raving enemy and are demanding increased repressions. But let the party know that I am innocent and that there is nothing which can turn a loyal son of the party into an enemy, even right up to his last dying breath. . . .

Everything, however, has its limits. My torture has reached the extreme. My health is broken, my strength and my energy are waning, the end is drawing near. To die in a Soviet prison, branded as a vile traitor to the Fatherland—what can be more monstrous for an honest man? . . . Unsurpassed bitterness and pain grips my heart. No! No! This will not happen; this cannot be, I cry. Neither the party, nor the Soviet Government, nor the People's Commissar, L. P. Beria, will permit this cruel, irreparable injustice. I am firmly certain that, given a quiet, objective examination, without any foul rantings, without any anger and without the fearful tortures, it would be easy to prove the baselessness of the charges. I believe deeply that truth and justice will triumph. I believe. I believe.

Kedrov was found innocent by the Military Collegium. Nevertheless, on Beria's order, he was shot.

Khrushchev proceeds now to discuss aspects of Stalin's ego. "Stalin himself, using all conceivable methods, supported the glorification of his own person." Khrushchev refers to the *Short Biography*, published in 1948, in which Stalin is presented as "an infallible sage, the greatest leader, sublime strategist of all time and nations." Not only, Khrushchev says, is this book filled with such "loathsome adulation," but, unbelievably enough, Stalin added to the proofs passages in his own handwriting, making the adulation even more extreme. (Movement in the hall.) Next Khrushchev deals with Stalin's ignorances about what was going on.

All those who interested themselves even a little in the national situation saw the difficult situation in agriculture, but Stalin never even noted it. Did we tell Stalin about this? Yes, we told him, but he did not support us. Why? Because Stalin never travelled anywhere, did not meet city and *kolkhoz* workers; he did not know the actual situation in the provinces.

He knew the country in agriculture only from films. And these films had dressed up and beautified the existing situation in agriculture. Many films so picture *kolkhoz* life that the tables were bending from the weight of turkeys and geese. Evidently Stalin thought that it was actually so.

Stalin separated himself from the people and never went anywhere. This lasted ten years. The last time he visited a village was in January, 1928.

Khrushchev comes to his peroration, and states that, even if Stalin made contributions to Soviet power in his thirty years of rule, the major credit belongs to the party and, above all, to the people. "The socialist revolution was attained by the working class . . . under the leadership of the Bolshevik *party.*" Then: "The Soviet state is strong because of the awareness of the masses that history is created by the millions and tens of millions of people."

At the very end:

Comrades! We must abolish the cult of the individual decisively once and for all. . . . We are absolutely certain that our party, armed with the historical resolutions of the 20th Congress, will lead the Soviet people along the Leninist path to new successes, to new victories. (Tumultuous prolonged applause.) Long live the victorious banner of our Party—Leninism! (Tumultuous prolonged applause ending in ovation. All rise.)

An Attempt to Clear Up This Puzzle

What, aside from the desire to clean house, are the major reasons for de-Stalinization?

1. "Stalin himself made de-Stalinization inevitable," one of the wisest men in Moscow told me. By this epigram, which contains much truth, he meant that the enormous educational process now operating in the Soviet Union, by which millions of people are being turned into literate citizens (within limits) and for which Stalin himself was partly responsible, must necessarily in the long run give citizens more consciousness of their role in the state, more influence, more curiosity. To prepare the way for this, various relaxations were decreed, and in order to convince people that this new policy (such as it was) was genuine, a sharp and dramatic break with the past had to be made.

2. Robots, slaves, cannot possibly create or run efficiently a technical society. Therefore, to some degree at least, people had to be released from

slavery. The prime Soviet aim, to overtake the United States as an industrial power, cannot possibly be fulfilled, in a period when mass education is also being pushed to the utmost, without a greater measure of assent from the people. Of course the "assent" sought is hedged in firmly by the whole totalitarian apparatus.

3. Nuclear developments and other factors convinced the Kremlin that war was not, in the immediate future, likely. Therefore this was a good time to mend fences and create strength at home.

4. Yugoslavia played a role. So long as Yugoslavia and Moscow were at daggers drawn, it was impossible to hide from the Russian people the fact that a Communist state was not merely an enemy of the Kremlin, something almost inconceivable, but, even worse, was living at peace with the United States and the West as a whole, and getting substantial American aid to boot. The easiest way to explain this was to put the blame on Stalin, and add some such injunction as "Now we are back on the right Leninist track after Stalin's mistakes."

5. Also, by putting a curse on Stalin, Khrushchev certainly hoped to improve relations with the United States, tone down the Cold War, enhance Soviet prestige with leftist parties in western Europe, and mollify criticism in India and China.

This analysis does not by any means explain everything. Several other questions rise. Long before the Khrushchev speech de-Stalinization was in full swing, and Stalin himself was scarcely ever mentioned in the Soviet press. Why did not the Soviet leaders simply let things go as they were going? Why was it necessary, not merely to repudiate Stalin, but trample on his grave? Why was Khrushchev so extraordinarily, sensationally explicit? The main reasons would seem to be five. First, Stalin had been so fantastically venerated that, in order to clear the record and make it convincing to the average man that he had made mistakes, he *had* to be presented as a monster. To make the new policy convincing, he had to be not merely discredited, but pilloried. *Second*, Stalin's writ had penetrated practically every textbook in the Soviet realm, every work of history, every law. To change all this was going to be an immensely laborious task, and a good excuse was needed. *Third*, it became clear that many people who had spent long years in labor camps would soon return to normal life, and would have to be rehabilitated and absorbed into society. They had endured frightful hardships, and yet were totally innocent of the "crimes" for which they had been put away. Simply to blame Stalin for this was not enough; he had to be portrayed as an overt criminal. *Fourth*, one must take into account emotional considerations. Khrushchev spoke in honest rancor, and, it seems clear, was carried away by years of pent-up anger, frustration, and revulsion. *Fifth*, the terror had to be terminated because citizens could no longer endure the tension, the inhuman strain of Stalinism; the country might blow up. But the new regime, in relaxing tension, did not want it to be thought that its ameliorative policy was a result of weakness. It was urgently necessary to convey the impression that it was just as strong as Stalin's government; therefore, it felt that it must annihilate his memory.

Still more questions rise. Why, since Khrushchev and his company had for years known what was going on, and had certainly themselves taken part in much highly unpleasant and bloody business, had they not risen in protest before? One of several reasons was, as explained above, that they could not possibly have done so with success. Another goes to the roots of the Marxist conception of history and life, namely that no sacrifice is too great to make for the cause. If Khrushchev and company had sought to interfere with Stalin, not only would they have lost their jobs and lives, but the safety of the Revolution itself might have been imperiled.

Madame Furtseva is, so far as one can judge, the only member of the present leadership who has had courage enough to deal with this matter frankly. All of Stalin's close lieutenants were, she has stated publicly, guilty to some extent of Stalin's crimes. "We are all guilty in various degrees, for when we voted for the expulsion of a party member in those days we knew very well what it meant. But some people are guiltier than others, and only time and careful investigation will reveal this."[5]

Interestingly enough *Pravda* printed on June 27, 1956, an article by Eugene Dennis, General Secretary of the Communist Party of the United States, which originally appeared in the New York *Daily Worker*, and which specifically raises this awkward question—had not Khrushchev and his own intimates been accomplices in Stalin's guilt? This was, incidentally, the first time that a statement by an American Communist criticizing the Kremlin ever appeared in a Soviet newspaper, and was also the first open reference permitted in the Soviet press to the Khrushchev speech. There was a good reason for this. By this time the Kremlin had become severely perturbed by the violent commotion caused in Communist ranks all over the world by Khrushchev's disclosures, and it was necessary to prepare the way for a reply. For instance, Communist leaders like Togliatti in Italy asked publicly, "Why did these things happen? Were they inevitable? Are they inherent in socialism, in communist philosophy? Could not the past evils have been checked

[5] *New Statesman*, July 20, 1957.

earlier?"[6] The Moscow reply came in the guise of a resolution by the Central Committee, broadcast by the Moscow radio on July 2. This statement tones the Khrushchev speech down, raises ancient clichés such as that the Soviet Union after the Revolution stood "like a besieged fortress situated in capitalist encirclement," and reiterates lamely that it had been impossible to remove Stalin from leadership because he was too strong, although "outstanding Soviet commanders made independent decisions" during the war.

Some further results:

1. Communists and Communist sympathizers all over the world suddenly found that what they had staked their careers on for thirty years, Stalinism, was abolished; their whole past was cut from under them, and the ensuing turmoil wrecked the party structure in several countries. Innocents had to face the fact that Stalin *had* indeed been an outright monster.

2. If Khrushchev's motive was to pull wool over the eyes of the West, he succeeded in part. Sir Winston Churchill said, "A new question has been raised by the recent Russian repudiation of Stalin. If it is sincere, we have a new Russia to deal with, and I do not see myself why, if this be so, the new Russia should not join in the spirit of this solemn agreement [the North Atlantic Treaty]. We must realize how deep and sincere are Russian anxieties about the safety of her homeland from an invasion. In a true unity of Europe Russia must have her part."

3. Khrushchev's own position and power were certainly enhanced.

4. The loosening-up produced by the speech within Russia is, from one point of view, advantageous to the western democratic world, if only because it gives us more opportunity to penetrate into the Russian mass, by means of cultural exchanges, tourists, and the like.

5. On the other hand, the case might be made that international Communism has been markedly strengthened, since, particularly in the neutralist and uncommitted countries, it will appeal to more people with the dead weight and deathly pall of Stalin removed.

6. The Soviet Union itself becomes more unpredictable than before. Stalin was a known quantity, a ham in a sack, and so, to a degree, was Stalin's Russia. Now all manner of new vistas and possibilities are opened up. We do not know what we are dealing with.

7. Profound emotional results may, in time, make themselves apparent within the Soviet Union. People were taught to believe in Stalin with fanatic and idolatrous devotion; then he was suddenly removed from them, cut down. And so citizens are inevitably impelled to ask questions, if only to

[6] *Time*, July 9, 1956.

themselves. If everything was a lie before, what is it now? How can anybody ever trust or believe in anything again? Of course most Russians have had their minds so bent and twisted, so distorted and positively deformed, by years of didactic dictatorship that they have become automata—they tend to believe anything they are told. Nevertheless, the Khrushchev revelations did, beyond doubt, produce a stir. Sharp proof of this is that there has been so much discontent among students. If students, an elite class, are troubled, others are troubled too. Perhaps in time a true public opinion may arise. If so, that will show the real and lasting importance of de-Stalinization, even if the leaders did not anticipate this result.

There Was a Good Stalin and a Bad Stalin

As if this general picture were not confused enough, soon came further confusions. Eleven months after the speech, in January, 1957, Khrushchev said at a reception that Stalin was "a great fighter against imperialism" and "a great Marxist." The opening paragraphs of the Twentieth Congress speech made the same points, but even so the fact that Khrushchev now seemed to be rehabilitating *Stalin* was a shock to many. The explanation is simple enough. We must always keep in mind that Stalin has never been *completely* de-Stalinized. He is never criticized or condemned for liquidating Trotsky in the old days, or for the Five-Year Plans, or for the deaths of millions of kulaks during collectivization. The gist of the matter is that there was both a good Stalin and a bad Stalin. Stalin has been dethroned, but not all of Stalinism. Even though his methods were wrong, his goal was right. Or, to put it somewhat differently, the cult of Stalin is condemned, but not some accomplishments of the man himself.

Quotations confirming this view may be found in the Soviet press without end. The magazine *Voprosy Istorii* (*Problems of History*) said recently, "Despite the gravity of J. V. Stalin's mistakes we cannot view his activity solely through the prism of these mistakes. This would be a distortion of actual party history, in which J. V. Stalin figures as an outstanding Marxist-Leninist."[7] Of course this is an extremely mild way to praise Stalin, compared to what went on effusively before. Russian writers, like men tiptoeing among eggs they dare not break, have to regard their steps with delicate, wary circumspection. Editors who a few months ago were criticizing Stalin too harshly, too zealously, are now being obliged to recant. Overzealousness is as great a felony in the Soviet Union as underzealousness. One

[7] *Current Digest of the Soviet Press*, August 21, 1957.

writer, not long ago, was so indiscreet as to declare that "he was proud of the fact that Stalin's name was not mentioned in a single work of his." He has been made to eat these rash words.

Perhaps the last word should come from Khrushchev, who has summed the situation up as follows:

> We criticize Stalin not for having been a bad communist. We criticized him for certain deviations, negative qualities, for having made serious errors. . . . However . . . the chief and most important matter is the defense of the interests of the working class, the cause of socialism, and the struggle against the enemies of Marxism-Leninism—in this main and most important respect, may God grant, as the saying goes, that every communist will be able to fight as Stalin fought.[8]

The use of the word "God," even though qualified, is strange on the part of an official atheist, but Khrushchev has several times done this. In a different connection he said recently, "If you live among dogs, keep a stick handy. Rely on God, as the saying goes, but don't you yourself fail."

Some Items in De-Stalinization

At any rate, de-Stalinization is the clue to most of what is going on. I have already mentioned several of its manifestations, all the way from the fact that photographs may be taken in Red Square to the rehabilitation of the "Lost Peoples." Innumerable other instances may be noted on all sorts of levels. The atmosphere is freer, though still not free. Police no longer line the Arbat when ministers drive out to their country villas, and people *dance* at Kremlin receptions. Can one imagine Stalin dancing? Youngsters hold hands in cafés, and kiss in movies. The day I arrived in Moscow I asked an official how the New Look had affected the little people, the man in the street. Reply: "You will soon find out."

The last anniversary of Stalin's death passed completely unnoticed in the Soviet press. But there still are countless pictures of him in hotels and even in government offices, some of them showing with revolting hypocrisy the elder Lenin handing over to him the baton of power, and countless silver-painted statues of him in the bleak, threadbare little parks and gardens all over the Soviet Union. The names of cities like Stalingrad, Stalinabad, and Stalinsk have not been changed. The smart, shiny locomotives on the big express trains still carry resplendent plaques showing Lenin and Stalin, in a halo of stars. Khrushchev made it quite clear in his speech that the trans-

[8] *Ibid.*, August 21, 1957.

formation of names, emblems, and the like would have to go slowly, and that most old names would not be affected, which was reasonable enough. To take Stalin out of everything would be an Augean job. To mention just one item—if his name were to be absolutely obliterated, millions upon millions of books would have to be scrapped, including children's books, poems, and songs.

But a good deal has been done, if not actually to erase all evidence of him, to play down his role. Surviving members of his family are seldom seen, and in fact are ostracized. For years a group of galleries in the Pushkin Museum was stuffed with gifts he had received, particularly those which arrived from all over the world on his seventieth birthday; these have been relegated inconspicuously to back rooms in the Museum of the Revolution. He has been cut from the name of the Marx-Engels-Lenin-Stalin Institute (also for some reason Engels has been dropped) and, even if actual cities have not been renamed, many lesser entities like factories and institutes are now known by some other name. In at least one airport, where enormous frescoes of Lenin and Stalin stood on opposite walls of the reception hall, that of Stalin has been ripped out; nothing replaces him, and the whole wall is an angry scar. Perhaps most interesting of all, the Stalin Peace Awards have been renamed the International Lenin Prizes for Strengthening Peace Among Peoples. It was also announced in September, 1956, that the Lenin Prizes for achievement in science, literature, art, and so on would be "revived." They had not been awarded—under the name of Lenin—since 1935. But the decree embodying this decision did not mention the fact that from 1935 to 1956 thousands of Soviet citizens received these identical awards, and that during all this time they were called Stalin prizes. How extraordinary it is that the authorities should bother to go through with such obscurantist false-face! Nobody is fooled.

Next, take the realm of civil liberties and allied subjects. Russian citizens are now allowed to travel within limits, and can buy a railway or airplane ticket to all but a few closed areas in the Soviet Union. On arrival at a new city, however, registration is compulsory, and nobody without a job is allowed to stay for longer than a month in certain big cities like Moscow, because of the housing shortage. Soviet citizens are now permitted to marry foreigners. This reform went into effect in November, 1953. But if a Soviet citizen married a foreigner years ago and the husband or wife is outside the country, permission will almost certainly not be granted for the Soviet citizen to get out, or the husband or wife to come in. In the realm of law, there have been substantial ameliorations and reforms. As to politics, certain alterations in the structure of government are supposed to be impending whereby the

Supreme Soviet will get some vestige of legislative power, and more freedom given to the Union republics. Stalinist contributions to economic theory are being attacked and revised, and his foreign policy revamped. American statecraft is still bitterly attacked, but anti-Americanism as such is played down. Mr. Truman, if he were President of the United States today, would not be called a "mad haberdasher," and it is inconceivable that the Moscow stage should specialize, as it once did, in virulently anti-American plays.[9] Historical judgments are of course being altered constantly. Five years ago Gandhi was attacked for "advocating class peace," and was sneered at as an agent of the Indian bourgeoisie who "sided with the imperialists against the people." Such arrant and disgraceful nonsense no longer sees print, and Gandhi is given credit for his fruitful, history-making accomplishment. Above all, Soviet history itself is being revised. The army in particular has insisted on describing events during World War II more truthfully, and scarcely a day passes without news of some historian or other being given the sack for clinging, despite the contemporary enlightenment, to Stalinist hallucinations.[10] Trotsky is still beyond the pale. In the end, the Soviet revisionists may even get around to him.

Things are stirring, too, in fields like literature and drama. We shall go into this in detail in a chapter following. For years Russians have had a positive mania for western "popular culture," and this is now being let in to a limited extent. It fills a vacuum, as the Soviet authorities see it, and does no harm.[11] Recently permission was granted, after years of waiting, for the publication of the sheet music of *Oklahoma!* Foreign films are trickling in, but none from the United States. The imported films are selected with care, and nothing is ever presented that will embarrass the Soviet attitude; what is regarded with most approval is some picture showing in a particularly grisly light such a phenomenon as, let us say, the slums of Glasgow. However, some good foreign pictures do arrive. Gina Lollobrigida is a hot favorite. Take music. Composers like Shostakovich, who have been under wraps for years, are now freely played again, and Prokofiev has been posthumously brought back.[12] The taboo has been lifted from Soviet plays that have not been per-

[9] No fewer than twenty-eight of these reached the Moscow stage between 1945 and 1950. *The Mad Haberdasher* was actually the title of a play.

[10] On the other hand there has been a severe tightening up of revisionism in Soviet history lately.

[11] But see below. Western jazz, though wildly popular, is often attacked in high party circles. The Russians want to develop their own style of jazz.

[12] Recently Prokofiev was honored (posthumously) for his Seventh Symphony, composed in 1951, and his heirs received a 100,000 ruble ($25,000) award. London *Times*, April 23, 1957.

formed since the 1920's—satires critical of government. Audiences go, somewhat frightened and bewildered, to plays like *Wings*, by the well-known Ukrainian playwright Korneichuk, which actually dares to attack the secret police. In books too, horizons are becoming somewhat freer. European and American works are being translated again after a blackout of twenty years, but, as we shall see, this does not mean that *many* foreign books are available. As to Soviet writers, dozens who have been under a cloud, or who could not be published at all under Stalin, are emerging and some who came into such disfavor that they had to be executed during the purges have come to life again, in their works. For instance Boris Pilnyak has been rehabilitated.

To an extent, new horizons have come to art as well. Moscow saw some nudes this year—and was shocked.

Also science has felt a certain relaxation. Freud has as we know been under the strictest of bans for a generation but, soon after Khrushchev's speech, one journal was bold enough to publish an article, "Why Should We Be Afraid of Psychotherapy?" Dr. Peter L. Kapitsa, one of the world's most renowned physicists, spent several years under house arrest in Stalin's day, but is free today, and so is A. N. Tupolev, the foremost Soviet airplane designer, who actually drew his first blueprints for his first jet while in confinement. Stalin's attempt to give a new—and totally unscientific—basis to the science of linguistics has been mercifully allowed to die. Most important of all, Trofim D. Lysenko resigned in April, 1956 as head of the All-Union Academy of Agricultural Science. He is still close to Khrushchev and a conspicuous figure, but his word is no longer law. It was Lysenko, as everybody knows, who evolved a new anti-Mendelian theory of genetics, which held that acquired characteristics in a plant (or man) could be handed down by heredity. This, naturally, played exactly into the Soviet hand, since it implied that human nature could be conditioned. Education on the Communist model could "create a new species of human being," which would then transmit Communist characteristics to ensuing generations.[18]

*

All this is, however, relatively minor. What counts is the lightening up, such as it is, in political, police, and security fields. A diplomat told me in Moscow, "Yesterday a functionary in the Ministry of Foreign Trade got a telephone call while he was out to lunch from a member of the Central

[18] Professor Nikolai Vavilov, a celebrated geneticist who paid the penalty for his opposition to Lysenko by dying in a labor camp, has been posthumously rehabilitated.

Committee of the Party. He did not bother to return the call for two hours. That is the most important thing that has happened in Russia since 1924!"

First, as to the rehabilitation of political prisoners. Scarcely a day passes in Moscow now without the return to his family, if the family has survived, of a man who may have been locked up beyond the Arctic Circle for ten, fifteen, or even twenty years—during which period, quite possibly, no word was ever heard from him. Khrushchev in his February speech mentioned the return to society of Comrade Snegov, who had been imprisoned for seventeen years. Another Old Guard Leninist, I. G. Petrovsky,[14] about whom not a word had been heard since he disappeared in the early 1930's, suddenly came back to life with a long article in *Pravda!* People could not believe their eyes. Andrei S. Bubnov, who was a member of Lenin's first Politburo, no less, came back into circulation in 1956 after nineteen solid years of penal servitude. A professor of classics has resumed his chair in Moscow University after twenty-two years away—as if nothing at all had happened!—and one case I came across concerns a youth who, arrested at the age of eighteen for no reason whatsoever except that he was the son of an anti-Stalin editor, has been released after no fewer than twenty-six years of obliteration.

The dead cannot come back, but their reputations can. The army is particularly interested in this. Marshal Vasily K. Bluecher, who commanded the Far East Army after the Revolution, and who was executed on Stalin's orders in 1939, was formally rehabilitated in April, 1957, and is now a hero again. A few weeks later the newspaper *Komsomolskaya Pravda* listed Marshal Mikhail N. Tukhachevsky, who was shot in 1937, as a Soviet "hero." He had not been mentioned in the Soviet press for twenty years, except as a spy and traitor. Of the physicians in the Doctors' Plot arrested just before Stalin's death, all were released except two who could not be released for the simple reason that they had been beaten to death. One who survived, Professor M. S. Vovsi, the leading heart specialist in the Soviet Union, was given the Order of Lenin in July, 1957. Widows of the two doctors murdered are receiving today very handsome special pensions—a way to make amends.

One case I heard about has to do with a man whose name, even now, had better not be mentioned. I will call him W. He was British by origin, and had a conspicuous record in the British Communist party. He moved on to Russia in the 1920's, and became thoroughly Russianized. During the siege of Leningrad in 1942 he left the city on an official mission to address Soviet sailors in Archangel. Somebody denounced him, and he was picked up off

[14] Not to be confused with the Rector of Moscow University, who has the same name.

the train. But the authorities did not want to admit that Mr. W. had been arrested and kept sending his wife, for months and months, fabricated telegrams from Archangel, as if from Mr. W. himself, saying that he was ill and could not return. He was tortured, and then sent to a camp in the Kola Peninsula in the Arctic. This was one of ten special camps, holding fifteen thousand prisoners each, which were called "Beria Camps for Enemies of the People." It held prisoners so unspeakably "contaminated" that, as punishment, they were not even allowed to listen to the *Moscow* radio. In their mess hall, posters like "Dig Coal for the Fatherland" had the word "fatherland" blacked out, because monsters incarcerated here must not even *see* such a healthy word as "fatherland." Mr. W. was amnestied after serving fourteen years, and has now returned to Moscow. He is still a loyal member of the party, and has been given a responsible position. Moreover he is receiving 1,200 rubles ($300) a month pension, plus additional allotments, because the place where he "worked" was a "hardship area" above the Arctic Circle, which entitles workers to special extra benefits!

A serious effort is made, as political prisoners are released, not merely to give them jobs and otherwise fit them for resumption of life, if any life is left, but to punish those who, by bearing false witness, incriminated them. There have been dozens of cases—particularly of young men who were sent away for short terms in the last Stalin years—in which freed prisoners are brought face to face with their accusers. The accusers, if found guilty, are tried and punished. In some cases no clear case can be made and the released prisoner and his accuser may find themselves back at work in the same factory or office again, side by side. What a people! Recently one young man was asked by the authorities investigating his false arrest if all the "implements of torture" that had been used against him were on display in the courtroom. "No," he replied, "lacking are the instructions from Moscow that sent me away."

The labor camps, as of today, have been largely done away with for political prisoners. This is a major expression of de-Stalinization. Forced labor certainly still exists, but it plays nothing like its former role in Soviet economy and otherwise. Ordinary convicts—thieves, racketeers, bandits, embezzlers, what you will—may still be sent to "correctional labor camps," but the camps have been to a large extent depopulated of inmates who were put there without cause, or for political offenses.

Reasons for this are several. First, the Khrushchev group genuinely thought that forced labor for political misbehavior was iniquitous, and should be stopped. Second, the use of forced labor had reached the point of diminishing returns, much as did the use of child labor after the Industrial Revolution in England. Forced labor simply was not efficient enough. Third, to keep the labor camps going at full capacity necessitated an intake of approximately one million new men per year, and such a regular inflow of "criminals" was, it is only too obvious, difficult to set up under "socialist legality." Once you commit yourself to a regime of law, it is impossible to plan in advance how many forced laborers shall be utilized. Fourth, there were grave shortages in labor power elsewhere in the Soviet Union, and it was more important to have free labor working at machines in Stalingrad than slave labor digging coal in the Arctic.

A general amnesty was proclaimed in March, 1953, immediately after Stalin's death. This applied to petty criminals, those who had been sentenced to terms up to five years. In 1954 came another amnesty, which was broader and which applied mostly to those who had been found guilty of collaboration with the Germans. The sentences of most of these began in 1945 and were for ten years; hence, most would be out of confinement by this time anyway. Finally, winnowing of the politicals began. Jurisdiction was taken away from the police and turned over to the Ministry of Justice. The process is still going on, because so many politicals were in confinement that it has been impossible to deal with them all expeditiously; about fifty to sixty cases are handled every day.

One reliable estimate is that, in the four years since Stalin's death, 70 per cent of all prisoners in confinement in 1953 have been released, and two-thirds of all labor camps abolished. Of those still confined, only about 2 per cent are classified as politicals; of these, most are convicted wartime traitors.[15]

One peculiar point is that, although discipline in the camps was terrifyingly severe, actual strikes took place at Vorkuta and other camps in 1953, which worried the authorities. Another is that a good many prisoners, on being released, have—incredible as the fact may seem—volunteered to remain in the locality of their confinement. A man may in other words be released from the compounds at Vorkuta or Karaganda, and then elect to stay there as a free worker. Several reasons exist for this. For one thing, better wages are paid in these "hardship" posts. For another, housing is difficult in the big cities, and permission to reside in Moscow is often difficult to obtain. Again, men have become accustomed to life out in the wilderness, and like it.

Above all, the main result of the de-Stalinization process is that the *overt* terror has stopped. There is still plenty of terror in Russia, but nobody's door-

[15] Professor Harold J. Berman of the Harvard Law School, a leading American expert on Soviet law, as reported in the *New York Times*, May 16, 1957.

bell is likely to ring at 3 A.M. with the secret police outside the door. So far as is known, no political arrests, let alone political executions, have taken place since March, 1956. At that time a few surviving remnants of the Beria apparatus were caught and liquidated, and some students in Georgia—who ironically enough were protesting at the de-Stalinization of Stalin—were arrested. (Of course if you sailed into the Red Square and called out that Khrushchev was a criminal or an idiot, you would be arrested promptly enough.)

Nor is anybody likely to get into trouble through unsubstantiated private denunciation. An attempt is being made, on the broadest scale, to make judicial processes more judicial; for instance the doctrine of "guilt by analogy" has been abolished. (Even if you did call Khrushchev a criminal or an idiot you would probably get a trial, though it might not be public.) Rule by arbitrary police power, has, in other words, been pretty well terminated, and wholesale purges are a thing of the past. Moreover, it is difficult, in view of Khrushchev's speech, to see how they could ever occur again under the present leadership.

Is the New Look Genuine?

Yes. The reforms that have occurred so far are perfectly genuine, if limited, but this does not mean that Khrushchev is a liberal or a democrat. The system is still the same in principle, and is still a tyrannical dictatorship; the motive for de-Stalinization has not been merely humanitarian, but lies in the desire to create a more efficient, modern state. What is going on, as George Kennan has said, is transition from the black Stalin nightmare to a state more orderly and reasonable, but still oligarchical.[16] De-Stalinization is an experiment, nothing more. Russian citizens, well aware of this, are apt to take its mercies with a grain of salt, even if they are grateful. One comment I heard was, "Yes, things are better now. When we die, we will be buried in a coffin."

All this being said, it is impossible not to concede that there have been tremendous changes for the better since Stalin's day.

[16] "Overdue Changes in our Foreign Policy" by George F. Kennan, *Harper's Magazine*, August 1956, a brilliant, sensible and authoritative comment.

CHAPTER XII

Hungary and After

> The Czarist government holds not only our own
> nation in slavery, but tends to subdue other
> nations which rise against their own slavery—as
> happened in 1849, when Russian troops suppressed
> the revolution in Hungary.
>
> —LENIN IN 1920
>
> An adversary in good faith is inconceivable to the
> Russian Communist.
>
> —IGNAZIO SILONE

The satellites are not part of this book, but I must try to describe some reactions I heard in Moscow during the Hungarian—and Suez—crises. First,
some bare bones of chronology. On June 20, 1956, Khrushchev and Tito
made up—for the time being—and issued a joint declaration stating
that it was possible for different countries to pursue "different roads to
socialism." This, on the part of Khrushchev, completely reversed previous
Soviet policy toward the satellites, and, in effect, cut the moral strings of
Russian control. Explosion in Poland and Hungary would have come anyway,
whether or not Khrushchev had made this statement, because the passion for
release from Moscow's iron hegemony could no longer be contained. On
June 28 came the Poznan riots in Poland. On July 18 the Hungarian party
boss, Matyas Rakosi, the most sinister and menacing of all old-line international Stalinists, was unhorsed. By this time Moscow was thoroughly
alarmed, and a split in the Presidium developed; Molotov and Kaganovich
thought that Khrushchev had gone too far, and was responsible for these
loosening developments. On October 21 Wladyslaw Gomulka, in spite of
extreme Soviet pressure, was able to take over power in Poland, and make
his own special kind of Communist regime. Two days later, on October 23,
the Hungarian Revolution began. Budapest blew up.

There were two separate Soviet interventions in Hungary. The first came at once. It was invited by Hungarian ministers themselves, who could not cap the boiling bottle. The Kremlin, most good observers in Moscow think, took the decision to use Russian troops reluctantly at this time. A marked difference of opinion was voiced in the party councils. Intervention would be dangerous—Marshal Tito called it a "fatal" mistake later. Some Kremlin ministers must have had the foresight to see what fierce resentment it would inevitably cause in the western world, and how much good will would be lost in neutralist and even Communist circles abroad as well. But could Russia afford *not* to intervene?

The Hungarian revolt was, let us remember, not officially anti-Communist at this stage, although it was certainly anti-Russian; it was a civil war between two breeds of Communists. Imre Nagy, the new prime minister, was a Communist, if of the Tito persuasion. But as the fighting went on it took on unmistakably the character of a genuine national uprising, against the Soviet Union and Communism both. The struggle went on fiercely for most of a week, and, as everybody knows, the freedom forces won. Russia on October 29 announced that it would withdraw Soviet troops, and for five breath-taking days Hungary was close to being free. Then the position rapidly changed. Having won much, Hungary yearned for more. On November 1 Nagy, propelled irresistibly by popular forces, renounced the Warsaw Pact (which binds the satellites to Moscow), declared Hungarian neutrality, and asked protection from the United Nations. If Nagy had been a Gomulka and had had greater personal subtlety and command, things might have gone differently. But he was not. The facts of the evolving situation were too much for Moscow, and, on November 4, the second Russian intervention took place. The Hungarian patriots were, for all their magnificent bravery, beaten down. Soviet tanks crushed without mercy as splendid and stubborn a display of courage against impossible odds as the world has ever seen.

Moscow intervened on November 4 because, given the circumstances and from its own point of view, it had no other choice. The decision was military more than political, and Zhukov played a key role in making it. His line was that if the Hungarians were allowed to wrest themselves free from Kremlin control, the whole Soviet position in eastern Europe would collapse, and Poland and the other satellites would be lost. Repercussions in Russia itself would also be disastrous.

Meantime, the Israelis attacked the Sinai Peninsula on October 29 and the Anglo-French invasion of Egypt got under way on November 4, the same day that Soviet troops began their all-out assault on Budapest. The Russians would have attacked Budapest anyway, but the Anglo-French invasion of Egypt certainly gave them good propaganda cover and, in their view, complete moral license. The cease-fire in Egypt came quickly. The fighting in Hungary persisted, as the free world watched in agony, for several weeks. On November 22 Nagy was kidnaped by the Russians, an infamous episode, and deported to Rumania. During this whole period Poland was astir, and on December 17 Gomulka won very important concessions from the Russians. Millions of Poles ardently hoped that the Hungarian Revolution would be successful, but could do nothing about it. One bitter Warsaw joke of the time was, "The Hungarians behaved like Poles, we Poles behaved like Czcchs, and the Czechs, as usual, behaved like swine."

Two Comments

If any summary of the Soviet attitude is necessary, the following two quotations will serve. We have in this book given the reader ample opportunity to savor and torment himself with Moscow terminology. Even so, these passages should be read with care.

This is from L. I. Brezhnev, a member of the Presidium, speaking at Omsk on January 20, 1957. Distortion of truth could not go further, or be more blatant:

> Recently international reaction has . . . attempted to launch an open offensive against Socialist countries. The dark forces of international reaction provoked a counter-revolutionary rebellion in Hungary, which had as its aim the overthrow of the people's regime, the destruction of Socialist gains of the Hungarian working people, and the establishment of a fascist regime, thus creating a hotbed of new war in Europe. This imperialist adventure . . . failed shamefully. The Hungarian people, led by the Revolutionary Workers' and Peasants' Government and the Hungarian Socialist Workers' party, with the aid of the Soviet Union routed the forces of counter-revolution within a short period of time.[1]

This is from none other than Marshal Zhukov, speaking on Egypt at a conference on March 16, 1957:

> You know how events unfolded. The Egyptian people showed stubborn armed resistance to the aggressors. . . . The Soviet government came out resolutely in defense of Egypt and issued a serious warning to Britain, France and Israel. Hundreds of thousands of volunteers from various countries, especially from the Soviet Union, China and other people's democracies, expressed the personal desire to fight against the

[1] *Current Digest of the Soviet Press*, February 27, 1956.

marauders. The Soviet Union's firm stand played a decisive role in bridling the imperialist aggressors. Anglo-French troops were duly repulsed by the Egyptian army and the Egyptian people (sic!).

Not a word about the contribution of the United States, the UN, the Commonwealth, or British public opinion at home to the cease-fire. Then:

> The U.S. imperialists are hastening to replace the British, French and Israeli aggressors in the Near East. A new imperialist plan for seizing this region known as the "Eisenhower Doctrine" has appeared.[2]

Statements like these do not represent idiosyncratic views of individuals, but express a consolidation of *basic* Kremlin doctrine, and are fed wholesale and without interruption to the Russian people.

The Moscow Angle

Now let us survey the Moscow press reaction in some detail. The successive evolutions are illuminating, if exasperating. The first news of the Hungarian revolt appeared in both *Pravda* and *Izvestia* on October 25, in the form of a Tass report from Budapest. The headline was "Downfall of an Anti-Popular Venture in Budapest" and tucked away in the fifth paragraph was the inconspicuous announcement that Soviet troops had intervened. "Soviet armed divisions stationed in Hungary under the Warsaw Pact assisted the armed forces of the Hungarian Republic in the restoration of order in Budapest." Then: "The Central Committee of the Hungarian Working People's Party is receiving telegrams from all sections of the country" . . . which "expressed the angry indignation of the Hungarian working people toward the criminal acts of the counter-revolutionaries."

On October 26, the Soviet press announced without much elaboration that the counterrevolutionary forces had been "destroyed." However, small armed bands were still operating "here and there." Then, on the twenty-seventh, came a longer report which, to any Russian capable of reading between the lines, indicated that the business was still serious. Hence some explanation is necessary. A writer in *Izvestia*, on October 28, connects the entire course of events with a conspiracy that "can be traced to transatlantic centers." The article admits freely that a certain amount of dissatisfaction existed in Hungary, which arose because of "supply difficulties, serious shortcomings in the work of the State apparatus, and recent violations of revolutionary legality." However, foreign manipulators have been at work. "In the west, reactionary emigre organizations are active, which are richly financed at the expense of

2 *Ibid.*, May 1, 1957.

the American taxpayers. Out of the notorious $100,000,000 approved by the U.S.A. for destructive activity against the Socialist states, the amount spent on the Hungarian counter-revolutionary underground is by no means small." Also: the Hungarian counterrevolutionaries "get their slogans from the American broadcasting station, Radio Free Europe." So—the Hungarian uprising becomes an American plot!

By October 30, again according to *Izvestia* and *Pravda*, the situation has become "more complicated." The antipopular underground has interested "young people" in their "reckless venture." "The buildings of several institutions were destroyed." And, although workers and employees are still being paid their wages, the "majority of industrial enterprises are not functioning." Then on November 1 comes the abrupt announcement, "Soviet troops have withdrawn from Budapest."

What is the Moscow reader to think? At once something is provided for him to think about. A few days before, to make the impending withdrawal palatable, the Kremlin had announced plans for a satellite "commonwealth." This was clever propaganda, and the Moscow press suddenly became full of news of this projected "commonwealth" development. "Hundreds of millions of people with faith in a better tomorrow, in the triumph of democracy and socialism, will greet the new charter." Satisfaction is, however, premature, because news comes from Budapest that "various anti-Socialist elements are emerging and gaining strength." Moreover the "American incendiary center in Salzburg is operating at full capacity." By November 4, it is announced that Nagy has denounced the Warsaw Pact, and "chaos reigns in Hungary." "Various anti-Socialist elements are emerging and gaining strength," and "the danger threatening the Hungarian workers' movement from these reactionary forces cannot be underestimated."

After November 4, the date of the second Soviet intervention, the situation "improves." The fact of action by Russian forces is, however, much played down. A Tass dispatch says simply, "The Socialist forces of People's Hungary, together with the units of the Soviet army requested by the Revolutionary Workers and Peasants government of Hungary, have selflessly carried out their tasks." Then: "The forces of reactionary conspiracy against the people's democratic system in Hungary were smashed this morning."

"Bloody Crimes of Fascist and Horthyist Bandits Exposed to World." This headlined an eyewitness story in *Pravda* (November 9) reprinted from Czechoslovakian newspapers. The Soviet public learned for the first time that Hungarian Communist leaders and members of the security police had been lynched and hung by their heels:

Counter revolutionary ringleaders organized an attack on the peaceful population, terrorized it, and murdered all progressive workers. . . . The government was powerless to prevent these criminal excesses from continuing and spreading. . . . Counter revolutionary bands dragged Hungarian patriots through the streets, kicked and tortured them until these defenseless victims of terrorism died in horrible suffering. . . . The fascists prepared for fratricidal slaughter. . . . Everything reminiscent of Socialism, the party, or friendship of the Soviet Union was destroyed with fury. . . . Boys of 16 and 18 were given weapons and reduced to a state of frenzy by the fascist elements, and murdered everybody they encountered.

The American "role" is reiterated. *Somebody* has to be blamed. On November 11, in a dispatch from Bonn, *Pravda* says that Radio Free Europe was the "virtual headquarters" of the revolt. Then a *Pravda* correspondent cables from New York: "The American press has been waging a furious campaign against the U.S.S.R. and the peoples' democracies in connection with the events in Hungary. The purpose of this campaign is to divert attention from the failure of the Anglo-French-Israeli aggression in Egypt, and to encourage the defeated fascists in Hungary with promises of U.N. support. Now, more than ever before, the responsibility of the U.S.A. for the counter revolutionary *Putsch* in Hungary is obvious. Irrefutable facts testify that it was indeed American reactionary circles who incited and activated the Horthyist underground which unleashed the bloody events in Hungary."

Meantime (November 6) came Bulganin's message to Great Britain over Egypt, which contained a veiled threat to attack Britain with atomic weapons. Also occurred demonstrations in Moscow against the British, French, and Israeli embassies. This was something unprecedented in Soviet history. The Russians have always prided themselves on the fact that foreigners on legitimate business in the Soviet Union were never embarrassed or molested. If Russian delegations visiting the United States, say, were ever subjected to some such minor annoyance as picketing, this was always piously held up in the Soviet press as an outrage, in contrast to Soviet behavior toward foreigners in Russia. But now, thousands of Moscow citizens gathered on the streets to demonstrate "spontaneously" against the British and French. Of course these demonstrations were deliberately organized by the authorities. A public demonstration of any kind in Moscow is inconceivable unless organized. But listen to *Pravda:*

The Anglo-French and Israeli aggression against the freedom-loving Egyptian people has aroused the wrath and indignation of the Soviet people. On November 5th, thousands of Moscow working people gathered spontaneously . . . near the British Embassy to express their protest against the criminal actions of the aggressors. Many brought with them placards with phrases in Russian and English such as these: "Down With War!" "Shame On the Aggressors!" Students, workers, employees, and housewives were among the groups who moved past the Embassy. . . . They sang songs of peace. . . . A similar demonstration took place near the French Embassy. . . . Angry shouts of "Down with the Aggressors!" "Down with Imperialists!" and "Suez for Egypt!" were heard in the crowd.

That Russians should complain about "imperialist" aggression in Egypt at the self-same moment that they themselves were being much more heinous aggressors in Hungary, is, of course, typical of Soviet hypocrisy, braggadocio, and insolence.

By November 19 Budapest was described as "speedily returning to normal," but on the twenty-second came news of the general strike. "Budapest enterprises stopped work today. . . . The situation is the result of a 48-hour strike declared yesterday by an arbitrarily formed workers council." On November 23 the kidnaping of Mr. Nagy is dealt with. In the *Pravda* version, he "asked permission of the Hungarian government to depart from Hungary to the territory of another socialist state." By this time it became necessary for the Russians to explain again why so much resistance in Hungary was continuing so stubbornly. The reason (*Izvestia*, November 25) is that "thousands of criminals" were released from prisons by the Nagy forces, and had to be rounded up.

The Soviet government was now well aware of the revulsion and disgust aroused everywhere in the civilized world by events in Hungary. This too had to be explained. *Literaturnaya Gazeta* published on November 22 a letter from Jean-Paul Sartre and a group of left-wing French intellectuals, which asked for enlightenment. The Russian answer is suggestive. It admits that what happened in Hungary was "grave and tragic," and that "we were partly responsible for this." But then it lapses into nonsense even more mendacious than usual about fascism, Horthy, and the international "forces of reaction." The truth, namely that the Hungarian insurrection was a genuine popular revolt against Soviet institutions, obviously could not be admitted. But signs of uneasiness are apparent. On December 1 the same journal carried a report from one of its correspondents describing a meeting of Hungarian writers in Budapest which he had attended. He is outraged by what he hears. One Hungarian "dabbler in literature," on whom contempt is thrown, said that "the threat of counter revolution did not exist at all," and others present, with their "extremely free and easy manners," even appeared to agree with the "filthy slander" being poured out at the U.N. Also:

> One of these writers, who calls himself a Communist, mumbled something about the "crisis of Marxism." A certain young literary dabbler began to shout about his "hatred of the Russians." The atmosphere of the meeting was by no means that of a friendly discussion. But the shouter was taken away [sic!] and the conversation was resumed.

Now a striking new element enters the Soviet attempts at self-justification —uranium. It is said that the western exploiters and imperialists made the counterrevolution in order to seize Hungarian uranium deposits!

Finally, the refugee question begins to absorb Soviet commentators. Blandly, it is assumed in the Soviet press that Hungarian refugees who escaped from Hungary should be assisted to *return to Hungary*. An article in *Trud* (December 8) even suggests that funds allocated in the United States to help Hungarian refugees escaping from Hungary should be used to *send them back*:

> Funds will be spent . . . for mass forced deportation of these refugees across the ocean for cheap labor. . . . The American merchant in live goods intends to transport 1,000 persons a day in the future. The Latin Americans are not lagging behind the U.S.A. They have also been included in this foul, speculative trade. . . . Under the guise of aid to Hungarian refugees, the western powers led by the United States are committing foul deeds. They are actually realizing on a mass scale the forced deportation of Hungarian citizens to other countries.

At last comes something really staggering. *Izvestia* explains on December 19 why Hungarian refugees are being welcomed particularly in Canada. The reason is that Canada has 160,000 unemployed, and the refugees will, in the event of strikes, be useful as strikebreakers.[3]

Notes in Aftermath

All this reflects the official line. There is no other line. This is what the Russian people were fed, and, what is more, many believed it. Of course the Kremlin itself knows better, and was perturbed. The three elements in the population upon which Communist hopes have always rested most surely— army, workers, students—had all been proved "unreliable" in Hungary, and

[3] Most of the above quotations are from *Current Digest of the Soviet Press*, issues of November 14, 1956 to January 23, 1957, inclusive.

this was news disconcerting in the extreme. Moreover Kremlin propagandists began to wonder how they could ever successfully approach neutralist states like India again, with the myth of their "peaceful intentions toward all peoples," or talk about "people's democracy" in the satellites. Nor did Communists in Moscow relish seeing photographs of Communists in Budapest hanged upside down. A correspondent in Moscow wrote to the London *New Statesman,* "You can hear many attempts to draw the lesson from the Hungarian events and apply them to the Soviet Union. . . . The photographs of Communists hanging head downward from Budapest lampposts have brought home to people here how rough a justice awaits those who leave the correction of 'mistakes' too late. Are we going fast enough ourselves? That is the question that many responsible Communists are asking now."[4]

One communication of interest appeared in the *New York Times* on January 25, 1957. It was in reply to a dispatch from Budapest to the effect that the Russians "have searched their scriptures . . . and found no explanation for what happened in Hungary." It stated in rebuttal: "Lenin gave a clear explanation for the Hungarian events 40 years before they happened. Writing in 1916 he warned that 'revolutions against the Socialist state' are possible, justifiable and indeed inevitable if that state follows wrong policies. Later, after the Soviet state was established, Lenin warned its leaders that 'their doom is certain' if they lose their ability to reflect . . . and dispassionately ascertain when 'revolution' must give way to 'reform.' 'Not that they will be defeated from outside,' he said, 'but that their affairs will suffer internal collapse' if they abandon their sober outlook." The writer of this communication was none other than Earl Browder, former head of the Communist party in the United States.

Something out of the ordinary occurred on February 10 when *Pravda* printed in full the text of a letter signed by five prominent members of the British Labour party. This letter, much sharper than the earlier one from the French intellectuals, contained some extremely pointed questions. It tries to pin *Pravda* down on its definition of "counter revolutionary," and asks if the Nagy government had "disintegrated," or was forcibly overthrown. The British questioners proceed to ask if *Pravda* seriously believes that the uprising was planned long in advance by the West, and if it can hold seriously to its view that the Hungarians really aimed at restoring the power of feudal landlords and capitalists. *Pravda's* answers are, of course, the straight party line. But the fact that a Soviet newspaper like *Pravda* could

[4] December 1, 1956.

print questions like these, thus putting them before millions of Russian citizens, was an interesting development. One should be careful about drawing optimistic inferences from this, however, since it indicates complete confidence by the Kremlin that its own propaganda will carry more weight with the Soviet masses than questions from outsiders, no matter how penetrating or embarrassing these may be.

The fact remains that many Soviet citizens, particularly students, were violently upset by the Hungarian bloodshed. Students have a keen nose. They knew that something must have gone gravely wrong, and their demonstrations were, while minor, a serious annoyance to the authorities. Hand-picked youngsters were brought forward to testify that they had *not* become "restive," as alleged, and the newspapers sought to minimize demonstrations of disaffection by saying that only a "negligible handful" of people had become "contaminated" by "demagogic statements" and non-Communist ideas.

What happened mostly, as anybody who was present in Moscow at the time could hardly help from finding out, was that students persistently refused to swallow the official story. For instance—to cite one instance typical of several—when a speaker at a public lecture on international affairs at Leningrad University attempted to explain the Hungarian events, Hungarian and Polish students in the audience rose to contradict him—something almost unprecedented—and then addressed the audience themselves. Wall newspapers appeared in factories, some mimeographed, some even handwritten, asking for enlightenment. Lecturers at the Lenin Library in Moscow were interrupted by listeners who said that they did *not* believe what they were being told. Most important of all, Moscow University had to expel something like one hundred students, and was obliged to give up several of its courses, because persistent boycotts emptied the halls. One student dared to ask a well-known professor, by name Syroyetkovich, how it was conceivable that a general strike had taken place in Hungary, since a general strike is of course not a weapon used by capitalists, fascists, or reactionaries, but only by the working class. The learned professor had no answer.

Khrushchev took a characteristic line on this, dismissing all of it as youthful effervescence. Then he dryly reminded students that "if they did not approve of the regime they had no right to be studying at the expense of the factory workers." He told them that there was plenty of room for them in the factories, and that others were ready to replace them in the classroom.[5] Khrushchev's major effort has been to try to minimize the significance

[5] *New Statesman,* November 24, 1956.

of Hungary. Speaking in Moscow in April, 1957, he said, "The Hungarian affair was a rather sharp affair, sharp like Hungarian paprika. And added to this Hungarian pepper was Egypt. But things now are settling down." On his visit to Czechoslovakia in July, he said that "stupid mistakes" by the former Hungarian Communist leaders, Rakosi and Gero, had permitted a "handful of counterrevolutionaries, with help from abroad, to make a blood bath in Budapest." In a remarkable interview with a Japanese journalist at about the same time he concluded, "The main thing is to heed the voice of the people, and not make mistakes which . . . break down relations between the leadership and the people. . . . We are convinced that it is impossible to rule the people by force alone, by terrorizing the population."[6] He proceeded, interestingly enough, to cite the example of subjugated Europe under the Nazis during World War II; it was impossible for the Gestapo to keep the people down, and guerrilla warfare resulted; popular resistance could not be crushed. Of course he will not admit that discontent or resistance in the satellites can be "popular."

Palace Revolution Quelled

We come now to events in Moscow in June, 1957, when Khrushchev, aided by Zhukov, at that time his close supporter, put down the "antiparty" effort to supersede him. We have mentioned this episode often in passing, but the full story deserves a word. There is no doubt that, as 1956 merged into 1957, Khrushchev found himself in a compromised position. Hungary had weakened his prestige, and there were bitter seesawing disagreements over developments in policy toward industry at home. Under a western system of government, with authority vested in a parliament, Khrushchev would probably have been forced to resign. He managed to hold on, however, for at least three reasons. First, everybody in the Kremlin wanted at all costs, in view of the situation in the satellites, to preserve the appearance of stability. Second, Khrushchev's control of the party rank and file gave him substantial power under the surface. Third, Mao Tse-tung in China, closely in touch with the situation, is believed to have put in strong words on his behalf.

Thus Khrushchev rode out the preliminary storm, but opposition to him hardened, led by Molotov. On June 6 Khrushchev, with Bulganin, was scheduled to make a state visit to Finland. They went on the day set,

[6] This interview, with Tomoo Hirooka, editor-in-chief of the *Asahi Shimbun*, has so far as I know never appeared in the British or American press. It contains much. *Current Digest of the Soviet Press*, August 7, 1957.

which seems to indicate that they were not aware of the conspiracy being organized, or were confident that it would come to nothing. It is also remarkable that the Molotov group, with a whole week free for action, did nothing while the two leaders were away. Either the general temper of the times made it impossible for Molotov and company to think in terms of an outright *coup d'état*, or they did not dare to risk one. They made no attempt to seize power forcibly. Their maneuvers all took place within the party structure, and, although conspiratorial, were "legal."

Apparently events went something like this. First, while Khrushchev was still away, Molotov spoke against him at a meeting of the Council of Ministers, of which Khrushchev is not a member, demanding that he be ousted for various reasons. Molotov denounced him as a "peasant lover" and deviationist. This caused so much commotion that a special meeting of the Presidium was called. Khrushchev returned to Moscow on the fourteenth, and the meeting took place on the seventeenth. It was extremely agitated, and Khrushchev was not able to hold the chair. It seems that Molotov had engineered this meeting for a time when he knew that several outright Khrushchevites would be away from town, vacationing. Only seven members, aside from Khrushchev himself, were present. The lineup to remove Khrushchev was four to three—some versions say five to two. Apparently Bulganin deserted Khrushchev when it appeared certain that he was beaten, and then came back. Only Mikoyan stood by his side right through.

So, it seemed, Khrushchev was out. Malenkov was to become prime minister again, and Shepilov party secretary. Khrushchev would be relegated to the comparatively minor post of Minister for Agriculture. But Khrushchev did not admit defeat. He did two things. First, he got in touch with Marshal Zhukov. The doughty Zhukov and a group of generals refused to countenance what was going on, and put the army firmly on Khrushchev's side. Second, Khrushchev sent out an emergency call to his supporters in the hinterland, and demanded a full plenary session of the Central Committee. This, an appeal from a decision of the Presidium to the much larger Committee, was a technique that Stalin had used in the early struggles against Trotsky, but the precedent had not been followed for many years. Under Stalin, the Presidium became more important than the Committee, although the Committee was always, in theory, superior. Now Khrushchev restored the old position holding that the Committee as a whole was—or should be—master.

Khrushchev got 70 out of the total membership of 133 on the Committee to agree to his request for a plenary session; this was a clear majority, and the Molotov group, which was in no position to use strong-arm methods after the Zhukov intervention, had to accede. It was thereupon doomed. But the meeting lasted eight full days, from June 22, and was stormy. Suslov was in the chair. There were 309 delegates present, including alternates and others. The Soviet account of all this, which does not by any means tell the full story, stresses above all the extraordinarily "democratic" nature of the proceedings. Two hundred fifteen of those present asked to speak; sixty did make speeches, and the others submitted written memoranda. Molotov, Kaganovich, and Malenkov each spoke twice, defending their attitude. At the end the vote was unanimous in favor of Khrushchev, with one abstention. Molotov—considerable tribute to his inflexibility and courage—refused to go through with the usual hypocritical business of agreeing to his own condemnation, and abstained. A sanctimonious bleat came later from his old comrades: "Miserable is the leader who stands alone."

Not till July 4 was any of this made public. The Russian people were not informed until the Moscow radio had first disseminated the news to most of the rest of the world. Then came the official communiqué, to the effect that Molotov, Kaganovich, and Malenkov had been removed from the Presidium and Central Committee, and Shepilov, Pervukhin, and Saburov ousted from their posts or demoted. None, however—an interesting point which presages much for the future—was dismissed from the *party*, although they represented "antiparty" forces. At the same time announcement came that Zhukov, Furtseva, and company had been elevated to full membership in the Presidium. It was a clean sweep for the Khrushchev-Zhukov team.

Revelations came that were, for the Soviet Union, extraordinarily revealing. The antiparty group, according to the communiqué and material that followed, was not merely "obsolete" and "inert," but "shackled by old notions and old methods." It failed to see new conditions, didn't realize that the world had changed, and had a "narrow, lifeless attitude toward Marxism-Leninism." The conspirators stood against an extension of rights to the Union republics, opposed the Leninist principle of "democratic centralism," and resisted any attempt to find new, better forms of industrial management. Molotov, it was revealed, had not only opposed the Virgin Lands scheme, but fought the Khrushchev butter and meat program. Moreover, he had "obstructed with all available means the implementation of measures for the relaxation of international tension and consolidation of the peace of the world." He made the split with Tito, opposed the peace treaty with Austria, and did not believe in coexistence. Malenkov had been guilty of "adventurism" when he was prime minister, i.e., he sought to ingratiate himself with the peasant and worker by fallacious means. A few days after the first condemnation Malenkov was also accused openly of complicity in the Leningrad case, and was described by Khrushchev as being "one of the chief organizers" of this nefarious plot. He "exploited and incited Stalin," and was guilty of "grave violations of Socialist legality during the period of mass repression."

As for Shepilov, Khrushchev called him a careerist and "most shameless double-dealer." Kaganovich was denounced for having mismanaged the Soviet railways, and for an attitude of "aristocratic contempt" for Khrushchev's plans.

In other words, the masses of the Soviet people were, without preparation and with precious little explanation, told that their leadership had been bitterly divided, that the "monolithic unity" of the party hierarchy was a fiction, that their foreign minister for a long period (Molotov) had not worked for peace, and that Malenkov was a murderer. And they took it all like lambs. Or, if they did not take it like lambs, they shut up. "Spontaneous" mass meetings took place all over the country, demanding further punishment for the miscreants, who had been exalted heroes the day before. The Molotovs dropped off the maps as if by magic, and the only sensible thing for a man of the West to do was read George Orwell.[7]

Khrushchev had to get rid of Molotov and Kaganovich because, otherwise, they would have got rid of him. Saburov and Pervukhin went because Khrushchev wanted to remove from influence in Moscow the surviving "technocrats" who opposed his plans for decentralizing industry. The reasons for Malenkov's ouster are also clear—Khrushchev knew that he was the only man in Russia youthful, able, and popular enough to take the leadership away from him.

Perhaps the most significant thing about the whole affair was that none of those dismissed were shot. This, needless to say, marks a momentous change in Soviet techniques. The culprits, far from being executed, were given jobs, and, although disgraced, were still made use of and in fact allowed to play roles in the national activity. True, they were put in posts a long way from Moscow.[8] Molotov became ambassador to Outer Mongolia—not an unimportant post. Malenkov was made manager of a hydroelectric installation,

---

[7] Two towns—Molotovabad and Kaganovichabad—in the Tadzhik Republic in Central Asia were renamed on July 3, *one day before* the news of the shakeup was made public. Somebody must have had advance notice, and made a slip.

[8] Except Pervukhin and Saburov, who are still in Moscow.

one of the biggest in the Soviet Union, at Ust-Kamenogorsk, in Kazakhstan. Kaganovich is supposed to be running a cement factory in the Urals, and Shepilov was appointed to the faculty of an institute in Kirghizia. As always, the Soviet people were not told about these developments for a considerable time, and even now have not been told everything. That Molotov could be guilty of the sins with which he was charged and *not* be shot was, obviously, too unusual a pill for citizens to be allowed to swallow all at once.

Another remarkable thing is that Khrushchev and Bulganin went to Czechoslovakia on July 8. This was by far the most sensational shakeup in Soviet history in twenty years or more, but Khrushchev had no hesitation about leaving the country almost at once. Speaking in Prague he summed up the business with the light remark, "We had some black sheep in a good flock. They thought they would seize power and you know how it ended. We took the black sheep by the tail and threw them out." It was more than that. It marked the end of one phase of the new era. A last remnant of overt Stalinism went out. This was a coup in which force and terror played no role, and which worked itself out within a constitutional framework, insofar as anything is constitutional in the Soviet Union, although Khrushchev assigned punishment to his opponents in an arbitrary manner. Many observers dismiss Khrushchev as a "moujik," or, on the other hand, cling to the myth that he is "the same as Stalin." One answer to this second charge is the reminder that Stalin sent his enemies to a place further away than Ust-Kamenogorsk.[9]

Most foreign comment took a moderately pro-Khrushchev line after these events. Mr. Nehru said, "What is happening seems to be a natural, desirable toning down," a return to "relative normality." Even Mr. Dulles took a somewhat optimistic view. Behind the shakeup was a "rising irresistible demand of the people for more enjoyment of the fruits of their labor." The "fundamentalists" who wanted "absolute centralized power in the Kremlin and rule with a rod of iron" have given way to "modernists" who give "an appearance at least of flexibility" to the Soviet system.

Then, in October, 1957, came the dismissal of Marshal Zhukov, to which we have already alluded in Chapter VI above. This abrupt development confounded all the experts, but was probably less significant than it seemed to be. The main thing to keep in mind is that deep and various currents have

[9] On the other hand, it might be well to remember that Beria was removed from power in July (1953) and not tried and executed till five months later. Perhaps Malenkov is not out of the woods yet. But Malenkov was not arrested, as Beria was, and in several other respects the cases are not analogous.

been let loose in the USSR since the Twentieth Congress, and almost anything may happen. But everything seems to be going Khrushchev's way at the moment; apparently he was able to get rid of Zhukov without prejudicing his own position to the slightest degree, and with no dangerous repercussions from the army or other elements.

*

Now we drop politics for a time, insofar as politics can ever be dropped in the Soviet Union, and move on to other aspects of the contemporary scene—science, education, literature, with a word or two about women, religion, and youth, and a glance at economic affairs, the armed forces, and aviation.

CHAPTER XIII

New Worlds in Science and Education

> There are at the present time two great nations in
> the world, which started from different points, but
> seem to tend toward the same end. I allude to the
> Russians and the Americans. . . . Each of them
> seems marked out by the will of Heaven to sway
> the destinies of half the globe.
> —ALEXIS DE TOCQUEVILLE IN 1835

> The Soviet Union has changed the entire men-
> tality of the Russian people in a single generation,
> an accomplishment . . . without parallel in history.
> —DOROTHY THOMPSON

> Soviet rule has bestowed on science all the author-
> ity of which it deprived religion.
> —ÉDOUARD HERRIOT

THE most interesting person I met in Russia next to Khrushchev was a lady,
by name Thais Khadarovskaya—interesting as a type, and for the work she
does. She was pleasant-looking, about forty, a trifle reserved in manner but
serene, with her hair parted severely in the middle and twisted into a big
soft chignon; she was placid of eye, used no cosmetics, and wore an old
sweater. Madame Khadarovskaya is a schoolteacher. She is, in fact, the director (principal) of Public School No. 151, in an outlying district of Moscow;
it has forty-five teachers and a thousand children. The three or four hours
we spent talking with her and visiting her school were a valuable—and sober-
ing—introduction to the field of primary and secondary education in the
USSR.

I thought first that this school must be one specially picked out for show.
It seemed too good to be true. Its physical plant would put to shame nine
out of ten public schools in New York City. Maybe the most impressive thing

253

about it was that it was *not* picked out for show. Of course Intourist does not deliberately choose the worst school available for visitors to inspect, but this one was average, although fairly new; it was built four years ago. "How could we pick out something special to impress you with?" protested Zoya, our indefatigable interpreter, with her bright button eyes and albino-colored hair. "All the schools are exactly alike." Indeed they are all almost frighteningly standardized—with identical curricula, books, and pedagogical techniques everywhere in the Soviet Union—and this is done with a purpose, not merely for the sake of economy and efficiency but so that the children, if their parents move from one city to another, suffer no interruption or alteration in their studies.

Then I thought that this school, even if average, must be one of only a few. But driving back to our hotel we picked a route at random, and in twenty minutes saw seven more of these schools, tit-for-tat alike. There are, in fact, eight *hundred* of them in Moscow, the majority of which have been built since 1946.

The total school population of the USSR as a whole is around thirty million. Roughly four million seven-year-olds enter the schools every year. Education is, of course, free and compulsory. There are two main types of school, the seven-year schools that carry children from the ages of seven to fourteen, corresponding to American primary schools, and the ten-year schools, for children from seven to seventeen, corresponding to American primary-plus-secondary schools. There are also some special experimental schools; in several of these *all* instruction is carried on in a foreign language. After the age of seventeen children go to the universities—if they pass the required examination, which is stiff. About 1,500,000 are graduated into institutions of higher learning every year. As of today the ten-year course applies to all children in towns with a population of more than ten thousand. Out in the smaller towns and villages, seven years is still the rule. But, the Russians say, the ten-year system will become universal within the next few years, as soon as enough new schools are built. There is no teacher shortage, in strict contrast to the situation in the United States. There can, in fact, never be a teacher shortage in the Soviet Union, at least in theory, because the planning schedule is set up so that the correct number of teachers will always be available to satisfy the need at any moment.

The Soviet child must absorb in ten years much more than an American child gets in the equivalent twelve under the American system. Also he works a good deal harder than the average American child; for instance he goes to school for six hours six days a week, and attends classes for roughly 213 days a year, as against 180 in the United States. Homework adds other hours.

This is, in fact, so grueling in Russia that a Soviet medical commission, investigating the health of students, their predisposition to worry, eyestrain, and the like, has urgently recommended that homework requirements be cut down. As of the moment children in the fifteen-to-seventeen age group are expected to do from ten to twelve hours of work a day, roughly half of this at home.

As to teachers, the Soviet Union has 1,811,000, as against roughly 1,300,-000 primary and secondary school-teachers in the United States. A Soviet teacher in the first four grades starts at a salary of 580 rubles ($145 at par) per month; this is raised automatically by 10 per cent every five years; those in the higher grades start at 700. All are eligible to retire after twenty years, with a pension of 350 rubles per month ($87.50). Seventy per cent of teachers in these schools are women. Overcrowding is a problem, as it is in the United States; most schools are full to bursting, and many operate in two shifts; one reason for this is a conscientious effort to keep the size of classes down.

Soviet educational techniques are in full evolution, and advances have been rapid. As always, it is the *pace* of Soviet development—in this and other fields—that is particularly striking. For instance, compulsory schooling in rural districts did not go beyond the fourth grade until 1949. Tuition had to be paid in the last three years of the ten-year schools until 1956. In other words, if a parent wanted his child to go beyond the seven-year course, he had to be able to afford it. Now this requirement has been eliminated. There has been an interesting controversy over coeducation. This was abolished under Stalin in 1943 except in some rural communities; boys and girls were split up and sent to separate schools. Then coeducation was reintroduced in 1954, and is now in force everywhere. Recently came something sensational for the Soviet Union, the introduction of boarding schools. Some two hundred of these are now functioning, with seventy thousand selected students. No child is (the authorities say) picked for these schools without consent of the parents, and tuition is charged according to capacity to pay. Khrushchev made a considerable point of the inauguration of these boarding schools in his report to the Twentieth Congress. Two reasons for them are adduced. First, they reduce pressure on the existing system, and make it more elastic. Second, they give better opportunities for training an *élite*.

We Visit a Public School

Madame Khadarovskaya took us around Public School No. 151. The halls and public rooms were full of plants like philodendron, and there were busts of Lenin, Tolstoy, the poet Mayakovsky, and Krylov, the celebrated writer of fables. Some classroom equipment was old-fashioned compared to ours; for instance children sit on fixed benches instead of movable chairs. Russians seldom care much about chromium plating or the external appearance of things, and building and other materials are apt to wear out quickly, so that the gymnasium, laboratories, and so on have a somewhat dowdy look. The children were entrancing, bright as firecrackers. The youngest boys wear white soft Eton collars and have dark gray or brown suits; those older are in a kind of uniform, with a belted tunic. The girls wear black pinafores and, if they have been admitted to the Young Pioneers, have bright red kerchiefs around their necks (boys too). Most of the boys have their hair closely cropped; the girls are pigtailed. In one class little tots were making bookmarks out of cardboard, with colored paper stars. One seven-year-old girl, agog with excitement, demonstrated what she had produced: it was totally unlike all the others, which had obviously followed a specified pattern. One of our escorts scowled. Such nonconformity was not to be commended!

Tuition is free, but the children have to pay for their textbooks (I was told that they were very cheap) and for their hot lunches, which cost 1.50 rubles (37½¢). A kind of canteen is available, selling sweets and weak coffee; strangely enough, most Russian children are given coffee from an early age. A doctor (usually a woman doctor) is a member of the school staff, and is in permanent attendance; so is a nurse. Once or twice we ran across aimless-looking groups of parents; they are the Soviet equivalent of members of the Parent-Teacher Association, and visit the schools which their children are attending, to see that all goes well. This school draws most of its children from three large apartment blocks in the immediate vicinity; each school in Moscow is, in theory, designed to serve a particular source of supply, and is thus "bound" to the community. Very few children need transport to get to school, and school buses like ours are unknown. In the first four grades classes number forty to forty-two, and thereafter average thirty-five.

I asked what happens if a child showed some particular or extreme talent, say for the ballet or painting—would he be drawn out of the mass, sent to some special school, and given a chance for advanced training? As with so much else in the Soviet Union, the answer is both Yes and No. *Every* child in a ten-year school is obliged to finish his ten years, no matter what. But a youngster who shows special aptitude or genius will be encouraged to take outside instruction elsewhere, provided his basic work remains up to par. I asked what happened to students who flunked out. Madame Khadarovskaya told us that, out of her total enrollment of a thousand, there had been forty-seven failures in one class or other this year. Those who fail are obliged to take the course over again, as in the United States. Only one student in the history of the school has ever been expelled. Expulsion is an extremely serious matter in the Soviet Union, because there are no private schools to which an errant child can be sent.[1]

What interested me most was the curriculum, especially its extraordinary stress on science. Herein lie the greatest factors of challenge in comparison to our system. Every Russian child takes two subjects for all ten years—arithmetic, evolving into mathematics, and the Russian language. In this latter, the courses run all the way from the alphabet to Pushkin and up to books of the present day. Also every child must study a foreign language for five years, as for instance English, beginning with the fifth grade; choice of this language is the only elective course in the entire curriculum. Everything else is uniform and obligatory. About 70 per cent of students choose English as their foreign language; the second choice is German. History starts in the fourth grade; one year is assigned to the history of ancient Russia, the next four go to the rest of the world, and the last year is devoted to contemporary Russia and the Soviet state. There are no specific courses in Marxism-Leninism. Geography gets six years, two for Russia, four for the rest of the world. Art is taught for six years, and music for seven; gymnastics and sport are obligatory for all ten.

But the main emphasis is on science and technology, for both boys and girls. In addition to ten solid years of arithmetic and mathematics, every child is obliged to take four years of chemistry, five of physics, and six of biology. Training with tools (or needle and thread) begins in the fourth grade, carpentry in the fifth, and other handicrafts in the sixth. But handicrafts are subordinated to more serious types of endeavor. There are shops for everything from metalworking to simple electronics. In the ninth grade boys learn to take an automobile engine apart (and put it together again), with an actual automobile in the classroom, and in the tenth some are taught to drive. Comparison to the United States is highly pertinent in these fields. Many American high schools, particularly those in country districts, have no physics or chemistry courses at all. An American authority told me that the Soviet child graduating from the tenth grade (our twelfth), aged about seventeen, has a better scientific education than most American *college* graduates. In particular Soviet students are far ahead in mathematics. For instance the average Russian boy or girl, taking the normal course, gets

[1] Dorothy Thompson, "The Soviet School Child," *Ladies' Home Journal*, February, 1956.

more than *five times* the amount of science and mathematics that is stipulated for entrance even into such a specialized American institution as the Massachusetts Institute of Technology.[2]

We stayed a while in the fifth-grade English class, for twelve-year-olds. Children had been learning English for about two months. The teacher uttered phrases like "What is your name?" and "Come to the blackboard and wipe it off." There seemed to be a great deal of difficulty with the word "sledge," which was used for "sled." I managed to get a quick look at a textbook. One story was called "Black Jimmie," and described the adventures of a Negro boy in the American South. Black Jimmie lives in Niggertown. His father is out of work. Jimmie is very hungry, and he is not allowed to go into the "white man's city." He shivers, sleeping on the floor. One passage was: "Jimmie must be out in the street at eight o'clock. At that time the workers' demonstration against the factory will begin. Jimmie's father was the first in line." Et cetera, et cetera. Let no one ask *how* Soviet children are conditioned to some of their attitudes to America.

At Public School No. 151 about 145 students were graduated last year, and of these 60-70 per cent passed their entrance examinations to the University. All over the Soviet Union, such boys and girls become the superior class of the country. The unfortunates who do not gain entrance into institutions of higher learning are damned. Out to the mines with them! Some, of course, manage to rise in society, and get good jobs, but many, when they are old enough, are simply *assigned* to a particular type of manual or clerical work and are shipped off to a farm or factory, partly because their primary and secondary schooling has been so expensive and the authorities want to cash in on it. A hard world.

We Visit the University

Moscow University, an imposing structure done in "Russo-modern" architecture, is known officially as the M. V. Lomonosov State University, and is the proudest skyscraper in the city.[3] It rises to a height of 787 feet; only seven buildings in the entire United States are higher, and it is the highest structure in Europe except for the Eiffel Tower. The Rector, with whom we had a long and vigorous talk, is Academician Ivan G. Petrovsky, a physicist of great distinction whose specialty, aside from university admin-

[2] Homer Bigart in the *New York Times*, November 11, 1957.

[3] It is named for Mikhail V. Lomonosov, Russia's first great scientist who founded the Academy of Sciences in the early eighteenth century.

istration, is crystallography. He is an alert, compact, and energetic small bald man, with a nice sense of humor. His father was a peasant; he came up from nothing. He is, of course, a loyal Soviet citizen, but is not a member of the Communist party. He was too busy ever to get around to joining, and anyway has small interest in politics. He is, however, a member of the Supreme Soviet of the USSR.

A dutiful guide took us around, and smothered us with statistics. Mr. Petrovsky's reception room, which measured 120 feet by 70, with a ceiling 40 feet high, was by far the most imposing and resplendent room I saw in the Soviet Union. The University has 1,900 laboratories, 15,000 rooms, 113 elevators, and 110 kilometers of corridors. Physics and chemistry each have large buildings of their own, wings of the main structure. There are eight candelabra overhead in the assembly hall; each weighs five tons. When I mentioned mildly that several universities in the United States are bigger establishments even than this, and that New York City has five large universities, not merely one, with a total of well over 110,000 students, our guide looked perturbed. The skyscraper division of Moscow University was built between 1948 and 1953, and cost three billion rubles, one billion of which was for equipment. This, at the official exchange, is $750,000,000, more than the total endowments of Harvard, Yale, and Princeton put together, and is about five times the total value of the plant of the University of Chicago. Money, as they say, is no object in the Soviet Union; when the government wants to spend something, it spends it. Moscow University's annual budget is 250,000,000 rubles, without counting new construction, a very tidy sum.[4]

Rector Petrovsky told us something about his problems. The University has a teaching staff of about 1,800 in all, for approximately 17,000 students, not including 6,000 correspondence and night school students and 1,500 graduates working for advanced degrees. Those in the main building, about 13,000, are *all* science students—in the faculties of physics, chemistry, biology, geology, and geography (which includes such fields as oceanography and meteorology). A student can spend his entire five years here majoring on a single aspect of geography. The emphasis is on pure science and research. The aim is to train specialists, moreover specialists in *theoretical* work. The University does not deal with engineering at all, and has no engineering courses. Nor is there any medical school; boys and girls studying to be

---

[4] Some of these details come from William Benton, former Senator from Connecticut, in a private memorandum recording his conversation with Professor G. D. Vovshenko, the Pro-Rector of the University.

physicians go to different institutions. This division of the University is purely an institution for producing pure scientists. Liberal arts are dealt with by a quite different division, which has about four thousand students and is located at a different site in an old building near the Kremlin; here are six faculties in the humanities—philosophy, philology, economics, history, law, and journalism. All science students must, incidentally, take courses in philosophy and economics, and one foreign language is obligatory; students are encouraged to take a different foreign language from the one studied in high school.[5]

Professors and teachers at Moscow University are "elected," not appointed, with the decision in the hands of the Council of the University, a group of its highest officers. One of these, the Dean of the School of Mathematics, sat with us as we talked. Men who do not actually teach at the University, but who represent some such institution as the Academy of Sciences, are also members of this Council. Teachers seeking jobs apply to the Council, and await decision; if accepted, they serve for five years, and then may be renewed. There is no such thing as permanent academic tenure in the Soviet Union. Every appointment is reviewed at the end of each five-year period, and, if a man's work is satisfactory, his term will be extended. This system serves to keep teachers on the *qui vive*. I asked Mr. Petrovsky what kind of men he looked for; his simple reply was "Good scientists!" A member of the faculty is supposed to divide his time equally between teaching and research. A teacher starts with a salary of about 3,300 rubles ($825 at par) per month, and a full professor, who has served ten years, gets 5,500 ($1,375). But many earn a great deal more than this, up to 20,000 or even 30,000 rubles. About two hundred leading professors live in apartments in the University skyscraper itself, and about six hundred in flats provided in the neighborhood.

The curriculum is established by the Ministry of Higher Education, and is identical in universities all over the Soviet Union. The course lasts five years, carrying the average student from the age of seventeen to about twenty-two; three more years are necessary for reaching the degree comparable to our Ph.D. Sixty-five per cent of all students aim for science degrees, as against 10 per cent in the U.S. Fifty-one per cent are women—the same ratio of women to men that obtains in the population of the USSR as a whole. Students are accepted up to the age of thirty-five (of course the great majority are much younger), and represent more than sixty different Soviet nationalities and twenty-two foreign countries. Of the foreigners most are Poles, Hungarians,

[5] A student submitting a thesis for an advanced degree is obliged to do so in duplicate; he writes it in Russian but also must provide a précis that he has prepared in a foreign language.

Indians, and Chinese, with a handful of French and Norwegians; there are no Americans at the moment (the University would be glad to have some) and no British. The University takes in about three thousand students every year, out of ten to twelve thousand who apply; about 15 per cent flunk out before their five years are up. Students whose homes are in Moscow live at home; the out-of-towners live in dormitories for which they pay twenty-one rubles rent a month. The rooms we saw, in the main University building, looked simple, practical, and well cared for; every boy or girl has a room to himself, with a closet, a sizable desk, and good light, and shares a bathroom with the occupant of the next room; the standard pattern is a double cubicle, with toilet and bath between.

Some comparisons to higher educational processes in the United States are relevant. For one thing, entrance into college is, by and large, pretty much of a routine phenomenon on the American scene, but not in Russia. Whether or not a Russian boy or girl passes into the University is, in fact, probably the single most important event to take place in his or her whole life.[6]

For another, a considerable number of American young men and women, even today, cannot afford to go to college. This is a factor worrying in the extreme to American educationalists, particularly because the costs of education in the United States are rising more steeply all the time. But, as I mentioned in the Foreword to this book many pages past, every Russian student is *paid* to go to college. There is no economic problem for him or his parents. He receives a stipend, or salary, from the state. This starts at 300 rubles ($75) per month, and rises to 500 ($125) in the fifth year. In addition, particularly good students are rewarded with substantial bonuses.

Again, most Russian university students are exempted from military service. The Soviet authorities would not dream of taking a promising young physicist away from his studies and interrupting his education by service in the armed forces.

Still again, Russian standards are, it goes without saying, severe. The number of hours of instruction is between a thousand to thirteen hundred per school year, many more than in the United States.[7] In contrast to the pampering that goes on in a great many American schools, the regime is Draconian. The emphasis in the United States is, only too often, to push the youngsters through somehow, no matter how indifferent their work, if only to satisfy the trustees and taxpayers with a good over-all record of "success." Few

[6] A Russian diplomat stationed abroad received the news recently that his daughter, after a period of doubt, was admitted to the University. He immediately asked for permission to return all the way to Moscow to assist in the family celebration of this great event, and permission was duly granted, with huzzas.

[7] New York *Herald Tribune*, November 11, 1957.

American schools would dare to flunk out as many students as do Russian schools. No such fear exists in the USSR, although it should be pointed out conversely that a Soviet teacher is considered to be doing an unsatisfactory job and is subject to reprimand if too high a proportion of his students fail.

One pressing problem in Soviet universities, as in the primary and secondary schools, is overcrowding. As I heard it put in good Moscow phraseology, "Our intake into the colleges has not expanded sufficiently to meet the increased output from the schools." This has led to a certain amount of minor corruption. Nobody would dare to bribe the rector of a big university to obtain admittance for his boy or girl, but officials with big political power have sought on occasion to exert "influence" on minor educationalists, and some pungent scandals have resulted and reached the press.

Finally, the university graduate in the Soviet Union is, of course, assured of a job at once, and his prestige and earning power will, like as not, bring him substantial economic rewards more quickly than these come to run-of-the-mill university graduates in the United States. The standard salary for a youthful scientist entering industry in Russia is 2,000 rubles ($500) per month; if he has an advanced degree, 3,000 rubles per month. Moreover, an intellectual in the Soviet Union is envied, not scorned, and has an honored place in the community from the moment he gets out of college. In the United States a bricklayer or plumber may, as is only too well known, earn more than an assistant professor at a university. But an assistant professor in Moscow is paid roughly three times what a skilled laborer gets.

Superfinally, there are 767 institutions of higher learning (of which thirty-three are full universities) in the Soviet Union today, and more than 3,500 *tekhnikums* (vocational schools), agricultural schools, and the like. One question often asked is why so many students choose scientific courses. There are several answers: (a) the government plans it this way because it needs scientists; (b) science is fashionable, pays well, and is a good career; (c) a good many Russian boys and girls have the intelligent idea that, as scientists, they will be under less political pressure than members of other professions, and will have more opportunity to live comparatively free lives, although this does not always necessarily follow.

About Education in General

Points to add or recapitulate:

Item: The main thing to say about education in the Soviet Union, next to its stress on science, is that it is universal. Illiteracy has been wiped out, except among a few surviving old people; since the beginning of the Soviet regime, more than one hundred million people have been taught to read and write. There are 213,000 schools in the country today, and they operate in more than *sixty* different languages.[8] The government has fulfilled its promise to give education to the entire nation, where little education existed before. The factor of advance is most remarkable in the outlying republics. Consider what has been going on in Tadzhikistan, as an example. Here, in 1919, a total of seven schools with 124 students existed; today, the Tadzhik Republic has 350,000 students enrolled in 2,500 schools. Or take Uzbekistan. Here only 2 per cent of the people could read and write forty years ago; today, there are eighty-one Uzbek college graduates for every ten thousand of population, a percentage seven times greater than that in Turkey, and twice as high as in France.

Item. But what, we may well ask, is all this education good for, in our terms, if it does no more than teach citizens to become obedient robots? The purpose of education, as we see it, should be to make minds free. What good is education if people do not have the right of fundamental inquiry? Immense areas of the world's knowledge are cut off from the Russian people, and they are fed lies incessantly. One might also add another point, that the Soviet system of education does not, to put it mildly, produce a well-rounded human being. A young man may know everything there is to know about marine biology, but this does not mean that he is educated. The Russians have the most formidable educational machine in the world, but they are also the most ignorant people in the world about affairs outside their own country.

Item. Still, it would be unwise to minimize the Soviet accomplishment. All that has happened so far is the result of education in a little more than one generation; the thought of what the Soviet Union may be like after two or three more generations is staggering. Let me revert once more to science and technology. The USSR graduated in 1956 about seventy thousand engineers; the corresponding figure for the United States is thirty thousand. Moreover, the Russian curve is going up; the American is going down. The USSR, by official statistics, produced 1,120,000 trained "specialists" of all kinds during the last Five-Year Plan (1951-1955), and is at present training more young people in applied science every year than "the United States and western Europe put together." Since the Sputnik, the United States has sought to

[8] *Moscow News*, November 14, 1956.

assay its critical comparative position, and no doubt will set about catching up. Experts say that we cannot possibly catch up in number of engineers until the 1960's, and will be lucky to manage it even then. One unpleasant little joke is: "We have either got to learn physics and mathematics—or else Russian."[9]

I have amply mentioned that, in the universities, the emphasis is on pure science and theory; the situation in the *tekhnikums* is the exact opposite. More than two million students are enrolled in the *tekhnikums*, and every graduate of a *tekhnikum* is obliged by law to spend three years at practical work in his specialty, out in the field, immediately after graduation. One recent proposal is to the effect that high school students, *before* they enter the university, shall be obliged to spend two years at work on some job. Behind this is the feeling that many students are, at seventeen, not mature or hardened enough to withstand the full rigor of university life.

Item. The case may be made, but is disputed by some American authorities, that the immense proliferation of educational activity in the Soviet Union may, in the long run, serve to loosen up the regime, and perhaps even change its structure. Stalin, talking to Wendell Willkie during the war, told him about Soviet educational plans and projects. Willkie replied amiably, "Careful, Mr. Stalin, or you will be educating yourself out of a job someday." Indeed the argument is plausible that if people become educated, even Soviet citizens, they may in time become reachable; once a class is created that is taught to think, particularly in scientific terms, it will sooner cr later begin to think for itself in other fields, glimpse broader horizons, learn about the free world in spite of all efforts to keep knowledge out, and demand various healthy satisfactions. Mr. Nehru said recently that the prodigious educational process now in operation in the USSR, as well as the liberal reforms that accompanied de-Stalinization, will "almost inevitably" produce in time a government in which the "democratic expression" of popular will must prevail.

Item. Occasionally Americans, even well-informed Americans, ask *why* the Soviet government should put such an extreme emphasis on education, despite risks. The answer is simple enough—a modern technical society cannot be operated by helots. Without education the USSR cannot fulfill its most pressing ambition, which is to become the first power in the world. Also there are "idealistic" factors.

[9] *New Statesman*, September 8, 1956.

We Visit the Academy of Sciences

This, after the Presidium of the CPSU and the Council of Ministers, is probably the most influential body in Russia. It directs, supervises, and stimulates the work of some 250,000 Soviet scientists. The Academy of Sciences was founded in 1726, imported its first students and professors from Germany, did interesting work for a time, and then languished, becoming largely an honorary body. The Soviet government revitalized it in the 1920's, and put it back on its original course—research and the propagation of new discoveries. The Academy of Sciences is not, like the universities, responsible to the Ministry of Higher Education, but is autonomous, being attached directly to the Council of Ministers, and has vital ramifications throughout the entire country.

My wife and I drove down Kaluzhskaya Street, and stopped at an old baroque palace once occupied by a family of the nobility. Its marble halls contain antique statuary and other relics of the past that no one, seemingly, has ever bothered to remove. It no more resembles the sleek modern building of Moscow University than an old-fashioned plum pudding resembles a frozen dessert with fancy spun sugar and illuminated caves of ice. But it is more important than the University. This is only one of a dozen or more buildings that house various agencies of the Academy in Moscow. We were told that we were the first nonscientific foreigners ever to be admitted to this particular building. The scholars receiving us were Professor Noraier M. Sisakyan, a biochemist who is a secretary of the institution, and Professor Anatole Khmelnitsky, who represents technical science. They told us about their work and gave us the kind of tea customary on such occasions—pears, grapes (rarities in the Soviet Union in winter), candy, and delicious little petits fours. No drinks.

The Academy of Sciences is a small body, as far as its leadership is concerned, with fewer than two hundred full members and about three hundred "corresponding" (candidate) members. These are the elite of the elite among scientists and scholars in the Soviet Union. To become a full academician is the very top. Members are chosen by invitation, and tenure is for life. "We do not take a man in," said Mr. Sisakyan with understatement, "unless we are sure that he is going to contribute." Members are altogether free to work as they like in their special fields, under the general circumscription of Soviet activity. There are no rules or regulations about duties or the time spent at a task. A good many foreign scientists are honorary members. Einstein was, and Niels Bohr is. Full members in Russia are paid an honorarium of 5,000 rubles ($1,250) a month, in addition to their professorial salaries; many hold more than one chair, and are also consultants to industry. Some members, I was told, get up to 200,000 rubles a year or more. Women make up 40 per cent of the total staff of 37,000. The top membership is deliberately designed to give a spectrum of the best research minds in the nation. The oldest man, a specialist in terrestial magnetism, is eighty-four; the youngest is twenty-three. His name is Yuri Knorozov, and he has worked out a system of translation for the Maya languages. (Another youngster has devoted himself to the birch bark writing used in Russia in the period before the foundation of Novgorod and Kiev.) The budget is six hundred times greater than in 1917. "If we need money for development, there is no limit to what we can have, but we must prove our need."

By Russian definition, history, philosophy, and even literature (at least the linguistic base of literature) are considered to be sciences, and the Academy exists in eight main divisions—the physical and mathematical sciences; chemistry; geology, geography, and astronomy; biology; technical science; history; literature and languages; philosophy, law, and economics. Art, music, and medicine are excluded (although the Academy does a great deal of work applicable to medicine); these branches of knowledge have their own academies. Physics is the biggest division; biology next. Then each division exists in various subdivisions. Biology has sixteen, including biochemistry, microbiology, physiology, genetics, hydrobiology, and so on. Russia is predominantly an agricultural country, and pronounced attention is given to research on soils. Technical science includes machine building, mechanics, automation, metallurgy, nuclear technology, power production and transmission, electronics, and radiology.

The range of activity is, indeed, astonishing. The aim is to give a centralized, systematized approach to all scientific and associated problems in the Soviet Union. At the moment, as an example, the Academy has out in the field no fewer than 117 expeditions. They range from prospecting teams looking for mineral resources in the Turkmenistan desert to icefarers investigating what goes on underneath the Arctic ice cap. The Antarctic has high priority as well; some 23,000 square miles of the Antarctic have been mapped near the Soviet base at Mirny in Antarctica. More than a hundred different research institutions work under the supervision of the Academy. It has an active Oriental Institute, which among other things is preparing books on Syria and Turkey. In scientific realms, the Academy is doing work at the moment (I choose a few examples out of literally hundreds available) on the structure of the Milky Way, acoustics, applied geophysics, digital control machines, varieties of marine life at very low depths, virus pathology, ichthyology (resistance of fish to disease in polluted waters), and geothermal research toward the possibility of using heat stored deep in the bowels of the earth as a source of power. An expedition is working in Kamchatka to this bizarre end. In another area, biologists summoned a conference recently on the origin of life. In the humanities field the Academy is working on a new twelve-volume history of Russia and a study of the origins of the Russian theater, and has just published a new textbook on political economy and is issuing two new historical magazines. (The Academy publishes something like 28,000 papers a year.) One recent job has been the preparation of a new and exhaustive ethnological map of India, and activity in Sinology is strong. Soviet maps are, incidentally, probably the best and most accurate in the world.

The President of the Academy of Sciences, Professor Alexander N. Nesmeyanov, is a biochemist. He is a leading specialist in the theory of metallic-organic compounds, and has written more than 250 original scientific papers. It was Nesmeyanov who, on June 1, 1957, announced that the Soviet Union was on the point of launching its first earth satellite. Few in the western world paid attention. The satellite, he said, would move in an orbit comparatively close to the earth, so that it could send back useful information about phenomena in the upper strata of the atmosphere. He also talked about a new branch of theoretical physics —magnetohydrodynamics—which may open up secrets of the ionosphere. Russians are apt to be full of surprises, and love experimentation. Mr. Nesmeyanov also got into the news last summer by almost losing his job. One faction in the Academy, while respecting his research work, wanted to get rid of him when he came up for re-election as president. (He holds his position as an academician for life, but officers of the Academy must be elected or re-elected every five years.) A split came in the governing council of the Academy. Many eminent academicians, though no doubt perfectly loyal to the regime, are not members of the Communist party, and the Academy has a long tradition of making its own decisions. Several of these thought that, under Nesmeyanov, it was losing what independence it had to choose and develop its own areas of research, and was giving way too much to excessive government dictation. This was all thrashed out in a spirited session, which even reached print, and in the end Nesmeyanov—against strong opposition—was re-elected. Flurries like this occur more often in the Soviet Union than one would think.[10]

*

Not far from the center of Moscow is the large site (five hundred acres) of the Agricultural Exhibition, resembling a world's fair. Forty-six pavilions house agricultural exhibits here, and some twenty are devoted to industry. We headed, like most first visitors, for the building given over to atomic energy. As always in Soviet museums, the emphasis is educational; expertly worked-out panels and pictorial displays explain the background and function of each exhibit. The casual visitor can learn a good deal about atomic energy here. Then we saw it! That is, we saw an actual atomic pile in operation, creating energy through a chain reaction. This is a "swimming pool" type of pile, and has only a very small capacity (150 kw.); distilled water fills a pit twenty-five feet wide and ten or twelve feet deep, and consumes the heat released by fission in the uranium below, which glows in a blue light, and is there for all to see.

This pile has no practical use; it is purely a stunt, and resembles one that American authorities set up as an exhibit in Geneva, during the Atoms for Peace conference three years ago. But the Russians have their toy pile on permanent display, and millions of Soviet adults and children gape at it every year. They lean over the railing on top of the sinister-looking tank, ask questions, and go away thrilled and impressed. The pile may be a stunt, but it is an effective stunt, and seems to popularize and make tangible the new and challenging scientific forces now let loose in the universe. So far as I know no similar atomic pile is on display anywhere in the United States or the western world. It would be easy enough to set one up in New York or elsewhere, and to do so might be a good idea.

Halls leading out from the atomic pile show various applications of atomic energy, particularly in the conquest of disease. Here are cobalt "guns" and tracer mechanisms. Then I saw something that did really surprise me— a mechanical man. Perhaps we have something of this fantastic sort in America, but I never heard of it. The mechanical man, a kind of puppet operated by a puppeteer, does work in a room or laboratory, say, where the extent of radioactivity would be deadly to a human being. The man has metal arms which break off at the steel wrists, and can pick out of a hand bank, or finger bank, whatever type of artificial hand he needs for a specified

[10] *Current Digest of the Soviet Press*, February 13 and July 10, 1957.

task. An operator (human) manipulates this creature by remote control. The creature drops off one set of hands, dips its wrists into the bank, and pulls out new metal hands or fingers which are attached magnetically. One type of finger is in the shape of a pair of pliers; another is a forceps. I saw the creature, with immaculate precision, use its different steel hands to pull a cork out of a test tube, pour fluid from one beaker to another, screw two links of pipe together, and delicately tap a wad of cotton into the neck of a small bottle.

Some fifty-five miles from Moscow is the town of Obninsk, where the Academy of Sciences has another interesting installation. Here, a few years ago, Russian engineers set up the first atomic station in the world for the industrial production of electricity. (The British built an experimental plant before the Russians did, but Obninsk was the first plant to feed actual atomic power into a grid, through which electricity is distributed to consumers.) This station is small—5,000 kw.—and serves only a handful of communities in the neighborhood, but it may be an important augury. It consumes about thirty grams of uranium a day, an amount the size of a walnut; an ordinary fuel-driven plant would need about a hundred tons of coal per day to produce the same amount of electricity. Meantime the Russians have gone ahead with other atomic power projects. One major station, with an estimated power rating of 420,000 kw., has been completed and is scheduled to go into operation early in 1958; four others are to follow with capacities even greater, the output of which will, Soviet authorities assert, be integrated into the existing electric power system, and will give fuel and light to whole cities. Localities of the four have not been revealed, but different experimental types of reactors will be used in each, according to official Soviet announcements.[11]

Also near Moscow, about seventy miles to the north, is Dubno, nick-named "Atomgrad." This is the seat of the Joint Nuclear Research Institute of the Academy of Sciences, in which all the satellite countries are repre-sented. Here the Russians have their new ten-billion electron-volt proton-synchrotron, or atom smasher, by far the largest in the world. The supercyclotron at the University of California, the biggest in the free world, has three-fifths of this capacity, or six billion electron-volts. The Russian apparatus has a magnet which contains more steel than an aircraft carrier,

[11] The United States has as yet no full-scale atomic power plant for commercial use, but one with a capacity of 60,000-100,000 kw. is being built at Shippingport, Pennsylvania, and is scheduled to be ready soon.

36,000 tons. Meantime the Russians are pushing along with a project for an atom smasher even bigger—in fact, five times bigger. The U.S. Atomic Energy Commission had plans in 1955 for building a really big machine of this same type, which would be highly useful for atomic research work, but the American government canceled the project for reasons of economy; it would have cost $100,000,000, which is peanuts to the Russians if they really want to spend money.

A third nuclear research city is being built, reports say, near Pyatigorsk in the North Caucasus. It has been put up from scratch in the past few years, and reached official status as a city in June, 1956; before this even the fact of its existence was unknown. It has been named, inappropriately enough, for the nineteenth-century Russian poet Lermontov. He wrote marvelous lyric verse (and urged freedom for the Caucasus among other things) but had little association with atomic energy. He was, however, killed in a duel near the site of today's brand-new city; hence the name. The Lermontov installations are believed to deal mostly with practical applications of atomic energy. Population and other details are unavailable.[12]

*

One scientific field in which the Russians are particularly strong is abstracting. Their service in this regard is admitted to be incomparably the best in the world, even by people who hate to admit it. Years ago in the United States students of chemistry were obliged to learn German, in order to read scientific papers and keep up with German chemical literature, which was without peer. Similarly today a great many students in the free world, particularly of physics, biology, and mechanics, wish that they knew Russian, even if they are not obliged to learn it. Russian abstracting is so copious and skillful that a point has been reached where American scientists have found out about new developments in their fields by fellow Americans in *Russian* scientific journals.[13] While I was in Moscow a visitor there was the well-known New York ear specialist, Dr. Samuel Rosen. He was astounded, visiting the Ministry of Health, to be shown abstracts of much of his own most recent work, including illustrations of new instruments he has invented for a pioneer deafness operation. (Certain other things astonished Dr. Rosen too. At the Institute of Acoustics he

---

[12] Theodore Shabad in the *New York Times*, May 31, 1957.
[13] Eric Sevareid of the Columbia Broadcasting System in the New York *Herald Tribune*, November 8, 1957.

saw equipment of unbelievable sensitiveness, including an apparatus for measuring impulses emanating from a single nerve of hearing in a rabbit one day old. But when he demonstrated his deafness operation in Moscow hospitals doctors were deeply impressed by the efficiency of the ordinary surgeon's forehead lamp he used, which is commonplace in America and much superior to the Soviet equivalent. The Russians, as always, do startlingly advanced work and are backward at the same time. They can build a ten-billion electron-volt cyclotron, but a good, simple flashlight seems to be beyond them.)

The Russian abstracting service was set up in 1953, after Stalin. The aim is to make *everything* of any interest or value on a scientific or medical subject published in the world available in Russian within a few months of its first appearance—abstracted, translated, and published. This goes far beyond anything ever attempted by any other government or private institution in the world. In the United States abstracts of important *American* medical material, coming from right next door, and for use by American doctors, are often a year late. The Soviet mechanisms are two. One is the All-Union Institute of Scientific and Technical Information; the other is the Institute of Scientific Information. Both operate under the Academy of Sciences. The first publishes a periodical of abstracts called *Express-Informatsia*, which appears forty-eight times a year and costs from 180 to 360 rubles per year to subscribers. (Expensive!) The subscribers are laboratories and institutions everywhere in the USSR. The second publishes material which is equivalent in bulk every year to thirty-five volumes of the *Encyclopaedia Britannica*, and contains 400,000 abstracts. The two organizations between them take in eight thousand foreign periodicals from eighty countries; of the eighteen hundred scientific journals published in the United States, they subscribe to fourteen hundred. The cost of subscriptions to American magazines alone has been estimated at one million dollars per year.[14]

Comparable American effort in this field seems puny. The Russians are in a position to know about everything we do; but we are not in an analogous position to know everything that they do. Through an exchange process, the United States receives about twenty thousand scientific documents from the Soviet Union every year. But few Americans know Russian, and no mechanism has been set up for translating these and making the

[14] But Russians don't know everything, and are quite capable of lapses. Lapses are, in fact, a famous Russian characteristic. Plenty of libraries and institutions have only a very few foreign periodicals available, and these are often years out of date.

translations generally available. The USSR publishes roughly twelve hundred scientific journals; two hundred of these are estimated to be of "major importance" by American scientists, but only thirty are regularly received and translated under United States government sponsorship. A very large proportion of the Russian material is untranslated and not abstracted, and goes to waste on library shelves.[15] American scientists as a result remain woefully ignorant about what is going on in their fields in Russia. This can have practical consequences. I quote the following from John W. Finney in the *New York Times*, November 25, 1957: "The radio frequencies to be used in the Soviet satellites were described in the June and July issues of *Radio*, a Soviet magazine for radio amateurs. The magazine articles were not translated and relayed to United States scientists. As a result, our scientists were caught by surprise by the frequencies of the Soviet satellites and had to work frantically to convert their stations to track them."

*

Americans, like Russians, have their little provincialisms, and it has been difficult for us on occasion to admit to the fact that the Soviet Union produces some extraordinarily accomplished scientists, in particular theoreticians. Europeans are, it would seem, better generally at theory than we are; for instance the great physicists who contributed most to American work on nuclear fission, from Einstein to Teller, were European born. A few names of contemporary Soviet scientists might be mentioned; they are men to be reckoned with. Academician I. V. Kurchatov is probably the foremost Russian physicist. He has predicted that energy from the fusion of hydrogen will, within twenty years, be harnessed and put to peaceful use, because of a method he has discovered for transforming hydrogen into helium at ordinary temperatures. Kurchatov is youthful, and has a flamboyant double-spade beard. He is a dedicated Communist. Another physicist of renown is Academician L. D. Landau, only forty-three, a specialist in elementary particles of matter, and another is an older man, Igor E. Tamm, known everywhere in the world in his field. A pure mathematician, N. N. Bogolyubov, visited the United States in 1956, and was described by Dr. J. Robert Oppenheimer as "the hottest thing out of Russia I have seen yet." Academician Nikolai N. Semyonov won the Nobel Prize in chemistry last year. One of the foremost mathematicians in the country, who has paid special attention to statistics, is Andrei N. Kolmogorov.

[15] But four thousand Soviet medical abstracts per year are made available to American doctors through a private agency, the Pergamum Press.

The Lenin Prizes awarded in 1957 gave interesting indication of the range of Soviet activity in science and technology. Among winners: Yevgeni K. Zavoisky (discovery of paramagnetic resonance); Konstantin Ivanovich Skryabin (completion of a twelve-volume work on *tremadota*, flatworms); Valentin A. Dogel (general protistology); Alexander Bakulev (heart surgery); Pyotr S. Novikov (algorithmic problems in mathematics); Georgi A. Melikishvili (ancient history of the Transcaucasus); Dmitri Nalivkin (completion of a new 1:2,500,000 geological map of the Soviet Union); Vladimir Fyodorovich Shishmarev (morphology of the French language); Andrei N. Tupolev (designer of the TU-104 jet airplane); Alexander Burov (discovery of diamond deposits in Yakutsk); Bagrat Ioannisiani (optics and work on a new large telescope); Boris Yevgenyevich Paton (new method of electric slag welding); Dmitri I. Blokhintsev (operation of an atomic power station); Serafim N. Vlasov (automated production of ball bearings); and almost fifty others.[16] The prizes range up to a value of 200,000 rubles ($50,000).

Soviet science is good; there is no reason to get panicky, and assume that it is better than American science. The Russians probably have a lead in theoretical physics and certain areas of mathematics, also possibly in oceanography and certainly in the development of missiles and satellites; the Americans are probably far ahead in chemistry, bacteriology, genetics, electronics, most engineering procedures, agricultural science, and almost all branches of medicine, including pharmacology in particular. The chief distinguishing marks of Russian science are (a) boldness, and (b) unlimited access to money. Most of us have forgotten, as an instance of boldness, Russian experiments with artificial penises during the war, for the use of men wounded by fragmentation mines or otherwise. As to money, it is never easy to translate Soviet budget figures into American terms, but one authoritative estimate is that the Russians spent last year the equivalent of seven *billion* dollars on "research and development." These terms are, however, not precisely defined or broken down. Of course the Russians are able to spend money with such grandiose abandon only by ruthlessly depriving their population of material benefits, and by keeping the standard of living down. But if the United States is to keep up with Russian advance we too will have to spend a great deal of money, and will perhaps be obliged to sacrifice some of the comforts and luxuries of life.

[16] Some winners in the realm of the arts were the ballerina Ulanova, Leonid Leonov (author of a novel, *Russian Forest*), and the eighty-two-year-old sculptor Sergei Konenkov.

Another important factor in the USSR is, of course, the indissolubly close link between science and government. When Khrushchev and Bulganin visited London in 1956 they took with them the physicist Kurchatov, and proudly showed him off. It would probably startle Americans if President Eisenhower should take Dr. Teller or Dr. Rabi with him on some trip, but it might not be a bad idea.

*

I never met a Soviet scientist or worker in technical realms who did not ask eagerly for better relations with the United States, and who did not urge closer scientific co-operation and exchange of information. Most Soviet scientists feel that they are being snubbed by the United States. The Academy of Sciences two years ago sent an invitation to the Smithsonian Institution in Washington, suggesting that an American delegation come to Moscow and look things over. It never got an answer.

Some Soviet "Firsts"

An American friend in Moscow told me, "Russian scientists don't claim false priorities any more, and they have de-invented the airplane and penicillin." He was half right, half wrong. It is quite true that exaggerated patriotic claims are no longer put forward in scientific circles, but the Russians still cling tenaciously to some outlandish claims made in the Stalin era. Perhaps, however, these are not so outlandish as they sound. Establishing true priorities in science can be a touchy matter, because it is always possible for two scientists or inventors in widely separated parts of the world to hit on the same idea at the same time. Anyway the Russians are resolute in their faith that Alexander S. Popov, an inventor and instructor in the Czarist navy, discovered radio and successfully demonstrated radio transmission and reception in 1895, a year before Marconi. Similarly the Russians say proudly that a professor named Boris Rozing was the inventor of television. In 1907 Rozing took out a patent for the use of a cathode-ray tube in telescopy. An academician named V. P. Goryachin was recently described in the Soviet press as the "founder of the science of agricultural machines," and work on the curative power of molds, the basis of modern antibiotic therapy, is said to go back to Russian research in the late nineteenth century. Above all, Soviet citizens salute today the memory of a man who was utterly unknown except in limited circles a year or two ago, Professor Konstantin E. Tsiolkovsky. He was born in 1857 and died in 1935; his centenary was celebrated in Moscow this year, and it is now said that it had been hoped to fire Sputnik I on September 17 instead of October 4, because September 17 was his birthday. Why? Because, according to the Russians, Tsiolkovsky was the first man to envisage creation of multistage rockets for penetrating beyond the earth's atmosphere, and did valuable theoretical work to this end, back in 1911 when the project seemed to be totally in the province of Jules Verne.

I came across this recently in *Krasnaya Zvezda*, the organ of the Soviet Army: "Numerous documents in the archives irrefutably prove that the world's first airplane was built in Russia in 1882 by our own Captain, First Grade, A. F. Mozhaisky. From 1882 to 1885 Mozhaisky carried out tests of his airplane." Anybody who says that this is moonshine is, according to *Krasnaya Zvezda*, "a bourgeois libeler and falsifier," who tries to efface "our motherland's unquestionable priority in building and testing the world's first airplane" and who seeks "to belittle the outstanding contribution of our country's scientists" and "cast a shadow over the creations of our people's genius."[17]

Some Soviet Ingenuities

Nonsense aside, the Russians, who have always been an ingenious people, have produced lately some remarkable inventions. The Soviet Union is, one American authority suggests, at the crest of a technological curve; out of each device or invention comes another; momentum is on its side. Nor does the USSR ever forget its basic concept of economic determinism; inventors are encouraged by handsome rewards. For instance anybody who creates something that will save the country nine million rubles or more per year is granted a 200,000-ruble ($50,000) award. Lesser inventions draw prizes running from 50,000 rubles up.[18]

One effective new Soviet invention is a turbodrill for use in oil wells. A motor is connected directly with the bit deep down in the well, sometimes thousands of feet underground, replacing the former rotary system whereby the whole column of pipes leading down into the well had to be put under power. American specialists treat this invention with considerable respect. Another series of developments is in the field of computers. The Russians have machines which, they assert, go beyond the range of most American

[17] *Current Digest of the Soviet Press*, July 31, 1957.
[18] Walter Sullivan in the *New York Times*, November 21, 1957. Also it should be noted that a Committee for Inventions and Innovation operates directly under the Council of Ministers.

business machines; for instance they can translate books automatically, as an experiment, and even play chess. (But, let me point out, most shops in Moscow do not even have simple cash registers as yet; watch that salesgirl manipulate her wooden abacus with flying fingers.)

Weather is, of course, a permanent Soviet preoccupation; it has to be, in a country a large part of which is made useless by ice and snow for long months every year. Of all Soviet technical projects I heard about the one that seems most fanciful is a scheme for painting snow black at certain strategic points along Siberian rivers, to hasten the thawing process, break up ice, and thus produce an "artificial spring." In several other fields too Soviet scientists are seeking to "control" weather.

Power, too, is a steady preoccupation. All sorts of mechanisms are projected to bring the old-fashioned windmill back to life in new forms, and thus utilize "blue" (wind) power, of which a great deal is freely available in Russia. Sunshine, too, will be tapped if experiments work out. The Academy of Sciences has recently built what is called the world's biggest "solar reactor" in Armenia. This consists of a large flat-sided tank of water, surrounded by twenty-three concentric railway tracks. Trains of flatcars circle steadily around these tracks, equipped with more than twelve hundred giant mirrors which focus the sun's light on the boiler, and thus create heat and steam.[19]

The Russians have a new camera which, they say, can take 32,000,000 photographs per second, an atomic engine that will fit into an airplane, and, wonder of wonders, a "hydrofoil-equipped" ship which skates on the surface of the Volga River at seventy miles an hour. In more homely fields, they are demonstrating (and selling) a new type of camera for the individual consumer with an automatic winding mechanism (ten exposures can be made one after another without winding the film), and a neat little machine, devised by the Soviet Institute of Experimental Surgical Apparatus, which induces sleep electrically. A rubber helmet, with electrodes reaching the eye sockets, is placed over a person's head, and sleep is automatically induced by a series of weak electrical impulses passing through the cerebral cortex.[20] Try it for your next bout of insomnia. Seriously, prolonged electric sleep is widely used in the USSR in the treatment of mental disorders.

Medicine and Public Health

As stimulating and pleasantly informative as anybody we met in the Soviet Union was Professor V. M. Zhdanov. A distinguished doctor of medicine,

[19] London *Daily Telegraph*, October 9, 1956.
[20] London *Times*, May 17, 1957.

he is a Deputy Minister of Health. He wears a round fuzzy beard, speaks shy English, and has a bright sparkle in his eye; his manner was courtly and precise. I asked him what his own specialty was, outside of administration, and he replied that it was difficult to say—both epidemiology and virology. Zhdanov is quite eminent. Earlier in his career he "discovered" a new disease, related to Japanese scrub typhus. He is a graduate of the University of Kharkov, and spent some years as the director of a bacteriological institute in Central Asia. Except for the fact that he spoke English with a furry accent and has some engaging Russian characteristics, I felt after two hours with him that I might have been talking to an official of the Rockefeller Foundation in New York. Scientists all over the world have pretty much the same characteristics.

Dr. Zhdanov gave us a briefing about Soviet medicine. He was proud of what has been accomplished, but modest. Mostly he talked about preventive medicine. Malaria has, for one thing, been virtually wiped out in the Soviet Union; the country had ten million cases ten years ago, and today has scarcely any. Plague has been altogether wiped out, although it was endemic for generations. Tuberculosis, too, is a "conquered" disease, although it has not yet been eradicated by any means. The venereal diseases are very much on the way out, not merely because of the use of antibiotics but because prostitution is disappearing. Social measures, not medical, have ended the venereal scourges, Dr. Zhdanov affirmed. Then he told us about new work in virus diseases. The Russians have just begun use of the Salk vaccine for poliomyelitis; monkeys (necessary for production of the vaccine) have been scarce, but are now being imported from China and India. Work is proceeding on vaccines for mumps, undulant fever, and Mediterranean fever. Above all, the Soviet Union has developed a vaccine useful in certain types of influenza; about ten to twelve million people were immunized last year. The virus is "attenuated by passage through human embryo tissue culture and egg culture," and is introduced, live, into the patient's nose in minute quantities. There have been some difficulties with it, because of its lack of stability. Still, results have been "moderate to good," and there have been no serious influenza epidemics in the Soviet Union for the past two years.

There are 344,000 doctors in the Soviet Union today, that is to say 165 for every hundred thousand of population; this is said to be the highest ratio in the world. In Czarist Russia there were only about twenty thousand doctors. The United States has 218,522.[21] About 70 per cent of all Soviet doctors are women, including most practitioners. The U.S. has substantially

21 Figures for 1953.

more hospital beds, something over 1,600,000 as against 1,290,000 for the USSR. The general mortality rate in the United States is 9.3 per thousand of population; in the Soviet Union 7.7. We asked Dr. Zhdanov how physicians were trained in the Soviet Union. Medical education is under the jurisdiction of the Ministry of Health, not the Ministry of Higher Education; the universities and medical schools (of which there are seventy-eight in the Soviet Union) are separated. Nor are physicians, as such, represented on the Academy of Sciences; they have their own Academy of Medical Sciences. A boy or girl wanting to be a doctor goes through the ten-year schools, and then has six years in a medical school. He is thereupon given a diploma and is entitled to practice, but is known (it is difficult to translate the terminology exactly) as a "physician," not as a "doctor." Postgraduate work is necessary for receiving the "full" doctorate.

About one per cent of the entire population of the Soviet Union, more than two million people, work in one way or other in the field of public health, including nurses, laboratory attendants, inspectors, and sanitary technicians. All medical services in the Soviet Union are, of course, free.[22] I asked Dr. Zhdanov where all the money for his ministry—administration, research, etcetera—comes from. He replied, "We ask for it." For instance the funds he needed for research to produce his influenza vaccine were granted without question or limit. Recently delicate new instruments were necessary for advanced techniques in surgery of the blood vessels and heart. A new institute was at once set up for the specific purpose of manufacturing them.

*

American medical experts in a good position to know think that Soviet medicine, on the high level, is quite good; on the medium level, not so good. Treatment for minor complaints is apt to be rough and ready, nursing is inadequate, and instrumentation and drugs distinctly poor by

[22] But, as mentioned above in these pages, citizens who want care beyond that provided by the state can have it. Doctors are permitted to treat "private" patients and charge fees. One Russian young woman we know went to a regular clinic to have a child recently, and paid nothing; but subsequently she consulted a specialist, who charged fairly steep fees for postmaternity complications. A Russian chauffeur I know had a severe neuralgia, refused to go to the medical panel in his neighborhood, and paid for private treatment. Foreign diplomats in Moscow go to a special clinic. The charge for consultation is twenty-five rubles. The Soviet doctors work in teams— one for nose and throat, one for cardiac complaints, and so on—and are seldom individually identified to the patient. One British lady I know was crazy about an internist, but was never able to learn his name.

our standards. Still, if you need an appendectomy at two o'clock in the morning, the Soviet emergency service will probably turn out to be all right. One American doctor told me, "They are about five years behind us, but catching up very fast."

Russian doctors, like almost all Russians, love the spectacular, and go in for sensational experiments. David Douglas Duncan, the photographer, told us about a "shock clinic" he visited where dogs are killed (painlessly), and then brought back to life. They remain "dead" by any known test for six or seven minutes, but can be revived. The idea is, of course, to learn from this how to save lives in the case of human beings hurt in accidents or otherwise suffering from severe shock. Then too the emphasis of Soviet medicine, like most other things in Russia, is utilitarian. The legend, not to be taken too seriously, is that the Russians paid comparatively little attention to cancer when it was thought that this was a disease mainly afflicting old people, who would die soon anyway; when it became clear that cancer also took multitudinous valuable *young* lives, the Soviet researchers got busy. Cancer research is, at any rate, imaginative, incessant, and heavily supported.

Dr. Maria D. Kovrigina, the Minister of Health, urged recently that special attention be paid to minor illnesses like mild respiratory and throat infections, because these cause one-fifth of *all losses in working days* (italics mine) due to temporary indisposition. Also Soviet medical authorities have their share of the national touchiness and chauvinism. Any time that the visitor thinks that, at last, he has come across some branch of Soviet activity not slicked over with the usual nationalist buncombe and suspiciousness, he is apt to be quickly disillusioned. Madame Kovrigina, in a recent speech, made great play of the fact that the British medical journal *Lancet* had quoted Soviet specialists to the effect that endemic syphilis still exists in some parts of the USSR. This, she said hotly, was "a slanderous fabrication." She added, "It must be remembered that peaceful coexistence of states with different ways of life . . . does not mean at all that our struggle against bourgeois ideology should be weakened"—a typical and significant remark.

Finally, mental health and psychiatric therapy. These subjects could be written about for pages, but this chapter is getting to be uncomfortably long. My wife and I visited one well-known psychiatric institute in Moscow. I thought that it compared quite favorably with any I have seen in the United States. Some of its equipment may be crude. On the other hand consider the fact that this institution, one of four in Moscow (the others are much bigger), receives from the state three million rubles per year for research *alone*, although it has only 110 beds. Mental illness is a serious problem in the USSR, as it is in the United States; there has been in particular a disconcerting rise in schizophrenia since the war. In all Russia there are about 100,000 hospital beds available for psychiatric cases. The main form of treatment for those seriously ill is insulin shock, but tranquilizing drugs are also used, as is "electric sleep." Electric shock therapy, which is widely practiced in the United States, is frowned upon as being too dangerous for the patient, and lobotomy (surgical penetration of brain tissue) is forbidden.

About neurotic illnesses one could also write much. In theory, no such thing as a neurotic exists in the USSR, since it is held that mixed-up people and misfits with personal conflicts cannot arise in a "classless" society.[23] Life—in theory—is so conditioned that the anxieties which produce most conflicts in western society are eliminated. No one needs (again in theory) to worry about employment, old age, or security. Dr. Freud is a creature of the devil, for holding that conflicts may have a *personal* basis. The Russians ignore altogether the fact that Freud and Marx are, in a way, closely allied, in that both stress "exculpatory" reasons for misfortunes in human behavior; Marx blames economic factors for breakdowns, and Freud blames the subconscious. Anyway psychoanalysis (at least as of the moment) does not exist in the Soviet Union, and Freud has no place in the Soviet scheme of things.[24]

More about the Sputniks

The processes described earlier in this chapter form the background out of which the Sputniks rose. Russian technical and scientific skills are not only proficient and advanced; they are harnessed to a centralized control and have a unified aim. One of the most remarkable (and from the American point of view) disconcerting aspects of Soviet success is that, so far as is known, the Russians never had a failure or misfire in their moon launchings. As of the moment of writing, they have made only two tests, and a successful Sputnik went into orbit out of each. An official communiqué says (and on this type of subject the Russians usually speak the truth), "There have been no unsuccessful attempts to place a satellite in orbit." Another factor is that

[23] Victor Erlich in *Continuity and Change in Russian and Soviet Thought*, edited by Ernest J. Simmons, p. 416.

[24] On the other hand enlightened members of the literary (not scientific) intelligentsia do not take such an extreme view. They think, as do many people in the United States, that Freud is old-fashioned, but recognize his value as a pioneer.

this unprecedented feat does not represent an "isolated breakthrough," but, on the contrary, is the result of "solid mastering of a new branch of science and engineering." Finally, one might mention the somewhat casual way in which the Russians themselves greeted their accomplishment at first, although their emotion was by no means unmixed with pride and nationalist delight. One of Khrushchev's early pronouncements was, "Our satellites are circling the earth and are waiting for the American and other satellites to join them and found a commonwealth of Sputniks."

Academician A. A. Blagonravov, one of the scientists responsible for the Sputnik, happened to be in Washington in the first week of October, 1957, when the first satellite went up. He was attending a conference having to do with the International Geophysical Year, and he appeared on an NBC-TV program called "Youth Wants to Know." Several young people interrogated him and his two colleagues:

Q. Was this satellite meant to be a strictly scientific achievement or one of political and propaganda importance? Will that be entering into it too?

Dr. Blagonravov: Not only this satellite but all the future satellites will have scientific meaning.

Q. What about political and propaganda importance? Will that be entering into it too?

Dr. Poloskov: I don't think so. On the contrary the satellite will promote ties between scientists of different countries.

Q. I would like to address this to the panel. Is there any influence from Moscow or from the Russian government as to how these scientists answer their questions on this program?

The Interpreter: Will you repeat your question, please?

Q. Is there influence from Moscow or from the Russian government as to how the men answer the questions on this program?

Dr. Blagonravov: There is no influence at all. While being in the United States I have not received a single telegram or message from Moscow.

Such blandness! But the Russians had a right to be bland, because they were sure of themselves. As early as June, four months before the first Sputnik, officials of the International Geophysical Year announced on the basis of information received from Soviet scientists that a Soviet earth satellite would soon be launched, and gave information about its size, speed, and orbit which the subsequent launching exactly confirmed. A dispatch outlining all this appeared in the New York Times on June 23 (buried on page 12). Few Americans heeded it. This was Soviet craziness, visionary boasting. Immediately after Sputnik No. 1, many Americans, still refusing to concede Soviet prowess, insisted that the Russians must have succeeded in their accomplishment through "espionage," or that their "Germans" must have done the job for them. Maybe espionage and captured German scientists did play a role, but most responsible American experts do not think so. After all the United States had German scientists at its disposal too— better Germans than the Russians have—and even so failed dismally in its first attempt to launch a satellite.

Other items from the NBC-TV panel interview are perhaps worth quoting:

> Q. May I ask Mr. Kasatkin [another Soviet scientist present], then, what his personal view as a scientist is, toward the problem of reducing arms in the world?
>
> Mr. Kasatkin: I personally have nothing to do with and am very far from producing armaments. This is not the question to be addressed to me.
>
> Q. I would just like to know his opinion, as a scientist and as a representative of his country.
>
> Mr. Kasatkin: I am just one of the Soviet scientists, but all the Soviet scientists, including myself, are for disarmament, and our hope is that disarmament will bring more friendly relations between our countries, not only for the present generation but for the generations to come.[25]

This is not hypocrisy; it is the view implanted in all Soviet scientists by the Soviet system. But do not think that the Russians are not fully aware of the military implications of their cosmic vehicles.

*

Who did build and launch the Soviet moons? On October 17 an official of the Academy of Sciences gave out a list of about thirty names, of those who worked on theory and basic research. One was the renowned physicist Professor Kapitsa, a Russian who worked in Cambridge, England, for many years, and is the world's foremost specialist on magnetism at low temperatures. He was invited back to the Soviet Union in the 1930's, accepted the invitation, and subsequently was never permitted to leave Russia again. This "kidnaping" made a bristly cause célèbre. Among others cited are several named in the pages above, like Landau (who contributed work on theoretical thermodynamics) and Kurchatov, "the first man ever to produce heat reaching 1,800,000 degrees Fahrenheit under laboratory conditions." Others were the well-known Academician V. I. Veksler, who helped develop the big atom

[25] New York Herald Tribune, October 7, 1957.

smasher at Dubno, M. V. Shuleikin, who solved problems connected with radio transmission in the ionosphere, and L. I. Mandelshtam, who invented tracking devices. Others represented work in chemistry (fuel study), meteorology, thermoelectrical phenomena, metallurgy, and optics.

How much did the Sputnik cost? The Soviet Minister of Finance, Arseny Zverev, was asked recently if the cost had been greater than that of the Manhattan Project in the United States, which developed the atom bomb and spent two billion dollars. Zverev replied, "A great deal less. If it had cost that much I would have protested it."

What is going to happen next? The Russians announced publicly in June, 1957, that they intended to launch no fewer than 125 rockets from three sites in the next few years. But these are to be merely high-altitude rockets, not Sputniks. The three sites lie approximately on the 56th meridian of longitude, a line running through Novaya Zemlya, the Urals, and Ashkhabad in Turkmenistan. The most northerly is in the Franz Josef Archipelago, in the extreme north of the Arctic on the 80th degree of latitude; the second is presumably in the Urals or Turkmenistan; the third is a ship, no less, operating near Mirny in the Antarctic, the chief Soviet research station for Antarctic affairs, latitude 56 degrees south.[26] As to developments further in the future, the Russians say that they will reach the moon with a radio-guided reconnaissance rocket in the early 1960's, and they expect to have a space station on the moon, manned by human beings, "five or ten" years thereafter.

Lessons deriving from Sputniks and missiles should not be ignored, to put it mildly. It is possible, although not at all certain, that the United States has for the moment lost command of the air, moreover lost it in a period where world supremacy depends on command of the air. Clare Boothe Luce, former ambassador to Italy, said recently, "The beep of the Soviet satellite is an intercontinental outer-space raspberry to a decade of American pretensions that the American way of life was a gilt-edged guarantee of our material superiority." Such an expert as Dr. Edward Teller, creator of the hydrogen bomb, has said that it may take us ten years to catch up to the Russians. The lesson of Soviet science is that the Russia of today is a strong country, even if not free, and that the democratic world must acknowledge this fact, wake up, and face the future with a hard, imaginative new look.

[26] New York Times, June 23, 1957, a dispatch from Uccle, Belgium. Also see Chapter XVIII below for military developments.

CHAPTER XIV

Writers under Socialist Realism

The writer is an engineer of the human soul.
—J. V. STALIN

I accept all; just as it is, I take it.
I am ready to travel the newly broken road.
I give my whole soul to October and May,
Only my beloved lyre I will not give.
—S. A. YESENIN

THE main characteristic of Soviet intellectual, literary, and artistic life is fermentation—even turbulence. In no other field has the process of de-Stalinization let loose so much confused excitement. Free literary expression was crushed—exterminated—during the Stalin period, and it goes without saying that it is still held down; nothing even approaching true intellectual freedom exists, or will be permitted to exist. Nevertheless a good many Soviet writers, dramatists, artists are seeking to express themselves with more individuality, and, within circumscriptions of the regime, are conveying plainly the profound urges that the post-Stalin era has released. All this was well symbolized by the case of Vladimir Dudintsev, the author of *Not by Bread Alone*, but before discussing this savory episode we should go back a bit.

Most Soviet literature, today as well as during the Stalin period, is excruciatingly dull. Very few good writers have come up in recent years. A really big dramatic scene in a novel will have to do with the faulty operation of a valve in a cement factory, and dialogue seems to consist mostly of small talk about nuts and bolts. To read Soviet fiction is, in fact, a good way for the bourgeois reader to begin to appreciate the almost insane Soviet preoccupation with industry. The last three novels I picked up were all about factories. Industrialization has replaced the Great Patriotic War as the favorite theme. One critic suggested perfectly seriously a few months ago that "a love story should be written about the Lenin Metallurgical Works." There is, of course, no reason why a good novel should not be written about a factory, but good ones are few and far between.

Quite aside from choice of theme, several reasons exist for the wearisome flatness of most Soviet writing. One is that the government controls all publishing. A writer is supposed to be a servant of the state, whose only function is to give expression to what will serve the state best—obviously a concept lethal to creative activity. A good writer cannot write to anybody's prescription. Another is something that goes deep into the Russian past, puritanism, which can make for tedious writing. If a hero and heroine so much as hold hands in a Soviet novel, it is an event.[1] We must also have a word about socialist realism, colloquially called in Russia *sotsrealizm*, the doctrine that has dominated most Soviet creative activity for the past twenty years or more.

Socialist realism is not so much a doctrine as a kind of platform, embracing much, and it is not altogether easy to define. In essence, it means art in the service of the community. A writer or artist is supposed to depict things as they *are*, with special emphasis on social significance. This does not necessarily mean that socialist realism forbids the use of imagination or fantasy or humor. If a poem makes a child laugh, then that poem has social significance, according to Soviet definition. Perhaps the easiest way to describe art under socialist realism is to say that it is representational. To a Russian observer most covers on the *Saturday Evening Post* would appear to be excellent examples of "socialist" realism; on the other hand most *New Yorker* covers would not. The opposite concept in the Soviet scheme of things is "formalism," a term used to describe heretical works of art in which *form* is stressed at the expense of content. Rembrandt and Dickens are, to the Soviet mind, good examples of "socialist" realism; Picasso and James Joyce are "formalists."

Soviet writers are obliged to take these concepts quite seriously, but they manage to be light about them too, at least among friends. Once at a literary meeting I attended, an elderly author came in late; he was a poet, and was greeted by the others with good-humored taunts, "Formalist! Formalist!"

[1] One Soviet writer, grimacing, told me as an illustration of puritanism that a Russian dictionary defines "kiss" as the "conjunction of two organs used for the intake of food into the body." I am not sure that I believe this. Also—another indication of puritanism—many good Soviet citizens were shocked by the outspokenness of *Porgy and Bess* when it played in Moscow.

An analogy in a foreign political field might be a meeting of some Labour party group in England to which a popular dissident penetrates, to be welcomed with affectionate shouts of "Tory!" On the governmental level, ferocious polemics attend most literary discussion. A big literary debate is big news in the Soviet Union, practically like the World Series in the United States. Ministers make impassioned speeches hours long, laying down the correct literary line and fervently urging authors and readers to be faithful to it. On the other hand, ordinary audiences are apt to be bored by such demonstrations. The attitude is something like that in America to a pep talk on foreign affairs by John Foster Dulles. Listeners may show respect, but not what you would call fierce enthusiasm.

One story is that socialist realism was invented by Maxim Gorky, to please Stalin, or on Stalin's orders, and that the doctrine was trumped up as a semipolitical device. But the general conception that art should have a utilitarian aspect and purpose is inherent in the Soviet ideal, and this is what counts. I remember a talk I had with Sergei Eisenstein, the greatest movie director that the USSR has ever produced, back in 1928, when he said, "Anything purely beautiful is useless."

What most contemporary Soviet writers object to is not socialist realism as such, but what happened when the ruthless Stalin dictatorship was super-imposed on top of it. For almost a generation nothing could be printed without the Stalinist imprimatur; the result was complete stagnation, the smothering of almost all genuine creative talent and the production of literature and art fit only for "dead souls."[2] One of our writer friends told us, "The point is not whether socialist realism is correct or not. The point is whether a man is a good or bad artist. Socialist realism doesn't mean bad art necessarily, but it gave an excuse for bad artists to be *accepted*, which is what we resent."

Came de-Stalinization. Socialist realism still rules, but with a certain difference. Ilya Ehrenburg wrote *The Thaw*, which sought to draw human values out of the contemporary scene and had some sharply critical over-tones, and several other distinguished writers, like Vera Panova, broke new ground by stressing individual (rather than collective) problems and trans-actions. Also books in other fields which had been suppressed for many years, like John Reed's classic *Ten Days That Shook the World*, were re-

[2] Mikhail Sholokhov, author of *The Don Flows Home to the Sea*, in a speech to the Twentieth Congress. Sholokhov, a party member, is probably the most popular author in Russia, but he has not written much lately. The whisper is that he is "on strike"—against socialist realism and much else. An author of Sholokhov's reputation can afford to go on strike. Others cannot.

stored to circulation.[3] Love scenes are permitted in movies, and kissing even takes place on the stage, something strictly taboo in Stalin's day. People yearn for romantic (also satirical) books, and even get some; there has been a revival of the works of Sergei Yesenin, the imagist poet who was blacked out for twenty years or more, and brilliant dramatists like Vladimir Mayakovsky, whose satirical works had been off the boards since the 1930's, are now being widely played again.[4]

In 1956-57 came the fiery controversy over Dudintsev's Not by Bread Alone. This is not a particularly good novel, but the issues it provoked reach very deep roots indeed. Some curiosities should be reported. It was the rage among the illuminati—before anybody had ever seen a copy! For a time it was something unique in literary history, a book translated before it was even published in book form.

To explain: Not by Bread Alone appeared first in the well-known Moscow literary magazine, Novy Mir, edited by Konstantin Simonov, in three long serial installments. Serialization is a customary procedure with new Russian novels. But it created such a glistening furor that the authorities became nervous, and publication in book form was held up. Then news about it got out, penetrating the Iron Curtain, and enterprising publishers in West Germany and elsewhere published it in various translations. Then, after almost a year, Moscow relented, and it was finally permitted to be issued as a book, in Russian. But the edition was only thirty thousand copies—a trifle for the Soviet Union, where book sales are counted by the million. The authorities took the decision to let Dudintsev's book appear, but imposed censorship on it in a different manner, by holding down on circulation.

Why was Not by Bread Alone allowed to come out in Novy Mir in the first place? This is a complicated question. Magazine editors have a good deal of leeway in the USSR these days, especially a man like Simonov. Censorship does not apply to magazines, because the editors are supposed to be their own censors, as has been noted in an earlier passage in this book. The same thing is true of the theater, and, to a certain extent, of books. Moreover, a significant point, most authors have been so thoroughly indoctrinated and taught to conform automatically that it is only seldom that anything "doubtful" is even submitted to a publisher. Little comes

---

[3] Stalin suppressed it because it did not mention him. The book describes the October Revolution, and it was unthinkable that Soviet readers should be allowed to get the impression that he did not take a leading part in the events of the first few days, even though he was not even in Petrograd at the time.

[4] See the chapter following.

up that needs to be censored. Not only is the editor, publisher, or theatrical manager his own censor; so is the author himself.

All this makes the case of the Dudintsev novel even more remarkable. Why did it provoke such a vivid storm? Easy! *Not by Bread Alone*, although its author is a good Soviet citizen perfectly loyal to the Soviet apparatus as a whole, pokes a finger into several sensitive areas. Why, then, did the authorities reverse themselves in the end and permit its publication as a book? Probably because they are intensely proud of the general loosening up now going on, and did not want to turn the clock back in this particular instance.

Perhaps, although the novel has become widely known in America, I should outline its plot. A schoolteacher turned inventor, by name Lopatkin, invents a new method for casting drain pipes. How romantic! But do not laugh. Lopatkin, a lone wolf, is frustrated at every turn in trying to get his invention adopted, although it will save the government millions of rubles. His bureaucratic boss, Drozdov, blocks his way, as do the ministries involved. But Drozdov's wife falls in love with Lopatkin and helps him; so does an elderly crackpot individualist inventor. Lopatkin almost starves, but against a variety of gross obstacles pushes doggedly ahead with his invention. He is eventually accused of betraying state secrets, and is packed off to a labor camp in Siberia. But one of the judges on the military court that convicted him is an honest man, and helps to clear his name. He is released from imprisonment, and at last his invention is adopted and put to use, after a rival machine, supported by Lopatkin's bureaucratic rivals, is proved to be a failure. Happy ending? Not quite. Lopatkin and the former Madame Drozdov marry and presumably live happily ever after, but Drozdov, the villain, becomes a vice minister. Even so, this ending is apt, artistically effective, and true to Soviet life.

The plot alone, unconventional as it is by Communist standards, would not have led to so much uproar. The book really reflects what the Soviet Union is *like* these days, with its fantastic combination of the idealistic and the uncivilized; people held it up like a mirror and saw themselves in it. Moreover it cuts straight across some prime concepts of the orthodox. The hero is an individualist, who, when down on his luck, calmly lives on borrowed money instead of working. Moreover (horror of Soviet horrors) he sleeps with another man's wife, and other women express interest in his person. The thesis that a good Communist has no room for a personal life is challenged, and the hero wins through in the end, without being forced to give up his principles. One of the most significant lines of the book is spoken by Lopatkin toward the end, when he emerges from incarceration, "Somebody who has learned to think can never be deprived of freedom." Also the presentation of Drozdov shows up a familiar Soviet type for what it is—the man who makes unscrupulous use of Communism to satisfy and expand his own ruthless ego and ambition.

Hundreds of literary meetings took place to discuss *Not by Bread Alone*, and thousands of agitated words were printed about it. In the end Dudintsev was rebuked, but was not otherwise punished so far as I know. Simonov was rebuked as well, with the words that he had committed a "grave error" in publishing the book in *Novy Mir*. Dudintsev, who must be a resolute character, refused to accept rebuke.[5] One report of the meeting condemning him said that "he brushed aside all criticism in a demagogic speech." People *can* (sometimes) express themselves in the Soviet Union. Then an astonishing thing happened. No other personage than Mr. Khrushchev leaped into the struggle, and attacked the book for being "slanderous." This is as if Mr. Eisenhower should take time out to take part in a literary debate and to pillory a new novel that had appeared originally in the *Partisan Review*. It should be added that Khrushchev also said that he hoped Dudintsev would find the right path again, "with our help."

This type of literary affair is taken seriously in the Soviet Union for a good reason. The issue is an extremely sensitive one: whether or not a totalitarian society can tolerate free creation. The future position of the intellectual is at stake. Moreover events in these realms, even if they begin with words, may end in deeds and have disastrous political consequences; the Soviet authorities have not forgotten that the Hungarian insurrection had its birth in a writers' club. The decision at the moment is that free creation shall not be tolerated. Several important writers have lately been obliged to withdraw or rewrite works, and Khrushchev has announced that authors shall not be permitted to indulge in the luxury of "emotional self-expression." Even so, things are freer than they were under Stalin. Writers are frightened and made to conform, but they do not go to jail.

*

One of the best and possibly the most influential of writer-editors in the USSR today is Konstantin Simonov. The circulation of *Novy Mir* is only about 140,000, but it reaches everybody who counts. Simonov is a

[5] One of Dudintsev's critics said that the book did not represent "truth" and, moreover, if writers were seeking truth they should seek it in the Soviet struggle "to overtake the United States in milk, meat, and butter production." (*sic!*)

devout Communist, but his career has had ups and downs. He is a strong and vivid personality, packed with ego. One old joke is that when Stalin had *real* moments of megalomania, he thought that he was Simonov.

During the war, when Simonov was fighting on the Stalingrad front, he scribbled a poem and sent it back to his wife; a friend set it to music, and it became enormously popular as a song. The language will, to most westerners, seem indescribably banal, but this may be the fault of the translation; even so, Simonov was severely criticized for having given such public display to private emotions; Stalin himself said that this was the type of poem of which only two copies should be printed, one for the author, the other for his loved one. But all it says is:

> Wait for me and I'll return,
> Dear one, only wait;
> When the leaves of autumn burn
> 'Round our garden gate;
> Wait, when winter winds blow free,
> Wait, through summer's sun;
> Others may forgotten be
> Ere the fight is won. . . .
> Dear one, wait for me.
> Safely through the fire you bring me,
> Waiting there for me.[6]

Simonov regained his position (if he had ever lost it) as a serious writer when his magnificent novel about Stalingrad, *Days and Nights*, was published. Also he has written a number of successful plays. I can say several other things about him. He serves vodka with sharp red pepper in it, and his cook makes a superlative variety of *kasha*. Moreover, no matter what the jokes say, he is a man of quality, with deep human and artistic integrity.

*

One day my wife and I had a session at the Moscow headquarters of the Writers Union of the USSR. This was a scintillating occasion. The Union is housed in a sprawling old building on Vorovkego, with creamy yellow walls, facing a semicircular court. It has a marked old-fashioned aristocratic style, and I found out later that it was the town house of the family which was the original of the Rostovs in *War and Peace*. I would have liked to have seen Natasha's room. But we were concentrated on the present. Half a dozen of the best-known writers in Russia met with us.

[6] Arthur Goodfriend, *If You Were Born in Russia*, p. 81.

We sat around a big table, nibbled chocolates from a box that must have cost a hundred dollars, and talked about everything from Balzac to socialist realism; most of the conversation was on a sophisticated level, and was very Russian. Questions were asked like, "Is so-and-so a *Catholic* writer, or merely a Catholic who writes?" and, "Is the Venus de Milo beautiful because the model was beautiful, or by reason of what the sculptor added?"

The Writers Union is an important organization, nothing less than the intellectual fountainhead of the USSR. All professional groups in the country—musicians, artists, architects—have unions of this sort, which are not merely unions in our sense, but clubs. The Writers Union, with branches all over the country, has 3,900 members; the membership, like that of the Academy of Sciences, is divided between members of the Communist party and nonmembers in a ratio roughly of two to one. It was split right down the middle on the Dudintsev affair—and savagely. Its president, Konstantin Fedin, is not a member of the Communist party, strange as this may seem, but the secretary, A. A. Surkov, is, and Surkov runs it.[7]

I might interpolate a word about Alexander A. Fadeyev, a former president of the Union. He was considered to be the foremost Soviet writer, and was a fervent Communist. This did not, however, keep him out of trouble; once he was forced to withdraw a novel, *The Young Guard*, after it had sold a *million* copies; he took three years to rewrite it, whereupon it was published all over again, and again sold an enormous number of copies. Party behemoths attacked it because it did not emphasize sufficiently the role played by the party, as apart from the military, in the civil war. For a decade Fadeyev ran the Writers Union with a hand of iron, and came near to throttling it. He was an alcoholic, who committed suicide in 1956. He got a state funeral. Suicide is not, to put it mildly, looked upon with favor in the Soviet Union; the official Soviet attitude toward suicide is much the same as that of the Roman Catholic Church, but of course for a different reason. Fadeyev's suicide was one of the very few in the Soviet Union that were ever frankly acknowledged to be suicides. Several conflicting stories have arisen to account for his action. One is that he was drunk; another has it that he was despondent about the prolonged illness of one of his children; a third explanation is bad conscience. Fadeyev did a good deal of unpleasant literary purging on Stalin's behalf, and dozens of his colleagues went off to the labor camps as a result. With de-Stalinization, some came back, and it was not comfortable for Fadeyev to see them around.

[7] I met one writer on another occasion, not of this group, who told me with bluff heartiness, "I have NOT been a member of the Communist party since 1906!"

The Writers Union has its own important newspaper, the *Literaturnaya Gazeta,* maintains a big publishing house, publishes a family of magazines, encourages talent, scouts out the literary scene, and takes care of old and indigent authors. Writers—successful writers—make a great deal of money in the Soviet Union, but some are not successful. The royalty system is complex. Royalties on a novel are calculated partly on the length of the work, or even on the number of characters it contains. Royalties are *reduced* as sales go up, in contrast to our system. The standard royalty for a playwright is 1½ per cent of box office receipts (after certain deductions) *per act;* the author of a play in four acts gets twice as much as one who writes a two-acter. Maybe this is why most Soviet plays are so inordinately long. The fee for translation of a foreign play is a fixed sum, sixteen thousand rubles. Poets appearing in magazines are paid a flat rate by the line— fourteen rubles. Maybe this is why most contemporary Soviet verse is written in very short lines. For instance here is a part of a recent poem on Lenin:

> He was
> he is
> he will always be with us.[8]

Mayakovsky wrote:

> I want pens
> listed with bayonets;
> The output of poems
> listed with iron and steel.
> Let there be items
> on the labor of poems
> In Stalin's reports
> from the Politburo.[9]

Simeon Kirsanov, one of the best-known contemporary poets, got into trouble recently for his *Seven Days of the Week,* and it was withdrawn after publication for "revision." Kirsanov wrote about tearing out his heart, and substituting a mechanical heart for it, "always ready to take orders." This is from another poet of considerable reputation, Yevgeny Yevtushenko:

> It offended my eyes to see
> The improper writing on a fence

[8] Quoted by Avraham Yarmolinsky in the *New Republic,* June 11, 1956 in an article on recent Soviet verse.
[9] Goodfriend, *op. cit.,* p. 158.

And the drunk sprawled out in front of the tearoom,
And the argument in the queue by the district store,
And a drayman cursing the city Soviet. . . .
The artificial limbs of the beggars banged on the stones,
And a boy with a stick chased after a cat.[10]

Other writers of distinction aside from Dudintsev and Kirsanov who have been rebuked lately are the poetess Margarita Aliger, Alexander Yashin, a novelist, and in particular Emanuel Kazakevich, another novelist.[11] The government cracks down, but the ferment keeps on bubbling.

Several successful writers, like Simonov, live in an enclave of their own, called the "Writers' Village," set up by the Union about forty minutes from Moscow by car. In their close-knit little colony they exist comfortably, but not luxuriously. I mentioned in an earlier chapter that Simonov is one of the wealthiest men in the Soviet Union, but his house is modest in the extreme by American standards, and certainly shows no ostentation. How well individuals in this covey of writers plucked out of Moscow and planted in the wilderness here get along with each other I do not know. One of the oldest of literary definitions is that a literary movement consists of two writers who live in the same community and hate each other.

Purely *literary* criticism in Soviet letters is much spicier and more vigorous than most outsiders are apt to think. Critics assault writers and dramatists with ferocious verve, usually in connection with political and ideological factors. Any number of examples are to hand. Just read a few issues of *Literaturnaya Gazeta*; it makes the *New Statesman* or *Saturday Review* seem mild. This is from a review in *Sovetskaya Kultura* of a new novel, *Yellow Metal*. "This book deals with the Soviet militiamen who ensure the observance of socialist law. The author's intention was certainly praiseworthy. But . . . it is simply a piece of libel. The author presents Soviet life in a grossly distorted light. . . . The author resorts to completely inadmissible devices in depicting the negative characters. The novel is full of vulgar expressions." It is also "alien," "chauvinist," and "negative."

Good or bad, dull or lively, Soviet writers and artists are, like scientists, regarded as important instruments of the state, and have an honored place in the community. Writers are frequently decorated with some such order as the Red Banner of Labor, and receive titles like "Honored Worker

[10] *Current Digest of the Soviet Press*, August 7, 1957.
[11] "Writing in Russia," by Harry Schwartz, *New York Times*, and an article in the London *Times*, "Soviet Authors under the Flail," May 17, 1957.

in the Arts." Of the 8,470 Stalin Prizes given between 1939 and 1952, about 2,340 went to workers in the field of literature, music, drama, and the arts. Soviet political leaders are, on their side, supposed to be *au courant* with artistic events; a cabinet minister unable to discuss the newest book or play at the drop of a hat will be thought to be uncultured, a fate worse than Siberia.

Books, Books, Books

Soviet appetite for reading matter is, we should know by now, boundless. There are good bookshops in almost every sizable town; they are almost always crowded, and a new novel, even if published in a substantial edition, will sometimes be sold out on the day it is published. Western authors may well envy this refreshing phenomenon. People have a thirst and enthusiasm for books almost unbelievable by our standards. In the Moscow subway I noticed passengers reading *books*—not magazines or newspapers, but actual books—while going up or down the escalators; I thought later that I must have imagined this sight, so outlandish did it seem; then I saw photographs of it in a Moscow magazine. Why do people read so much? For the same reason, among others, that they drink so much—to blot themselves out, and enter for a few blessed moments a different world—but also because they have a genuine passion for self-education. Most books are non-fiction. Recently a group of poets held an autographing party in a Moscow bookshop. The mobs were so great that, within an hour, all their own books were sold; the poets then seized any book off the shelves, biology texts or dictionaries or engineering manuals, and wrote their names in these too, with gay and robust abandon; all were madly snatched by the insatiable customers.

Once more, we must gulp some statistics down. More books are published in the Soviet Union than in any other country in the world. There are 213 different publishing houses (of which 109 operate under the Ministry of Culture), which issue books in 122 languages. Total book production in 1956, a record to date, was 1,100,000,000 copies. There were 54,732 different titles.[12] Fifty-nine per cent of the total Soviet output was in the realm of the exact, natural, and applied sciences; the comparable figure for France, as an example, is 29 per cent, and for Britain 22 per cent. Textbooks appear in huge editions.[13] Children's books also have a very wide sale; in fact more

[12] As against 12,589 in the United States.
[13] One reason for this is of course that texts are standard and uniform throughout the whole country. Also texts are constantly being revised (in some fields) to meet changes in the party line, and so must be republished periodically.

than a billion and a half of these, not including schoolbooks, have been published since 1918; forty-five million came out in 1956. Also the Soviet Union leads the world in translations, 480,000,000 volumes of which have been published in the last forty years. This is about twenty times the output of translated literature in the United States.[14]

Children's books have, by and large, a great deal of charm and appeal. The best Soviet poets, like Samual Ya. Marshak, devote large amounts of time to writing for children; here, as an example, are several stanzas from a Marshak poem:

In the Van

A lady sent in the van:
A bag,
A box,
A divan,
A hamper,
A sampler,
Some books,
And a wee little doggie named Snooks.

At the station in Red Banner Street
She was handed a yellow receipt
That listed the things for the van:
A bag,
A box,
A divan,
A hamper,
A sampler,
Some books,
And a wee little doggie named Snooks.

Snooks gets mislaid, and:

Just then an enormous black hound
Came over the rails at a bound.
It was caught and put in the van
Along with the bag and the box,
The hamper,
The sampler,
The books,
Instead of the doggie named Snooks.

In the end, after a dozen more stanzas, Snooks is found, the big dog is returned to its owner, and all ends happily.

No fewer than three hundred editions of the works of Nikolai S. Tikhonov,

[14] *Current Digest of the Soviet Press,* June 12 and October 16, 1957.

poet, essayist, and head of the Soviet Peace Committee, have been published (in forty-four Russian languages), totaling eight *million* copies.[15] I was told that, next to a popular composer of music, the richest man in the USSR at present is a comparatively obscure Kazakh poet, a recent volume of whose work was a sudden smash hit and earned one *million* rubles in royalties. Soviet critics sometimes severely rebuke the publishing houses for the amount of paper they "waste" on books not considered intellectual enough, particularly translations. *Kommunist* expressed outrage lately that Conan Doyle's *The Hound of the Baskervilles* has been printed by three different houses in a total edition of 925,000 copies, and that more than 2,500,000 copies of Alexandre Dumas have been issued in the last two years.

"Errors" occur in other types of books as well. For instance it became known that the Agricultural Publishing House planned last year to publish a book called *The Food and Pastures of the Northern Reindeer*, of interest only to "zootechnicians in the northern reindeer-raising countries," in an edition staggeringly large—100,000 copies. Scandal! The publishers ate humble pie, and said that there had been a clerical slip in the announcement; the correct number of copies to be issued was ten thousand. Still too much! Finally it came out in an edition of three thousand copies.

Despite all this, bookstores in the Soviet Union are apt to be somewhat dreary. Books do not have bright jackets, and shop window display in our sense is unknown. Some bookshops carry prints—reproductions of Russian and other art—and people stand in line avidly to collect these, even at fancy prices. One big bookstore on Gorkovo that specializes in foreign literature displays its Chinese books in the most conspicuous position; next comes East Germany with a profusion of German art books, texts, and technical manuals; behind Germany are Yugoslavia and Hungary. One of the books I saw in German was *Tom Sawyer, Detektiv*. Books in English are few, and the range of titles is distinctly limited. Most are little items like *English Ships Correspondence* and *First Talks on Ceramics*. In one secondhand shop on Kuznetsky Most, the first three English books to catch my eye were H. G. Wells' *First Men in the Moon*, a work by Mrs. Gaskell, and a novel about the Australian gold fields, *The Roaring Nineties*; there were also some scattered classics, like Scott and Thackeray. But if I were stranded in the USSR for a couple of years and my reading was restricted to English or American

---

[15] Books published in the Soviet Union carry on the last page all technical details about their production and distribution, including the number of copies in the edition. This is a sensible procedure which American and British publishers might well follow.

books I could find in *English* in Russian bookstores, death from starvation would come very soon.

The ten most popular Russian writers are held to be Pushkin, Leo Tolstoy, Turgenev, Chekhov, Gogol, Goncharov, Gorky, Ostrovsky, Sholokhov (the only one living), and Alexei Tolstoy, in this order.[16] One day in a good Leningrad bookshop it occurred to me to ask what Russian classics were actually on sale, and this proved to be a somewhat embarrassing question to the saleswoman. Not much was available, nothing comparable to the rows of English classics in inexpensive editions that are to be found in most good bookshops in England or America. There was plenty of Tolstoy, but no collected or pocket edition (*War and Peace* cost 11.25 rubles), only two volumes of Chekhov, and very little Turgenev; of Gogol only *Taras Bulba*; a good deal of Pushkin and Maxim Gorky; only one minor book by Dostoevsky. Dostoevsky has, in fact, until recently been hard to get at all. He was not officially banned, but he was strongly disapproved of, ostensibly because he was too "neurotic," and his works were deliberately allowed to go out of print. In the House of Pioneers in Odessa we saw a large chart of Russian authors prepared for the guidance of school children; Dostoevsky was not included, although the exhibit contained a number of minor names. But, following de-Stalinization, Dostoevsky has been to some extent resurrected; busts of him are being unveiled in libraries, a new series of postage stamps carries his image, and his plays are being revived. It is still, however, impossible to buy *The Possessed* (except possibly in secondhand shops); *The Brothers Karamazov* is sometimes available, but *The Possessed* is still considered to be too "dangerous" for contemporary Soviet readers, no doubt because it deals with political conspiracy.

An Item about Things Translated

With certain exceptions, the Soviet authorities translate nothing that does not serve a utilitarian or propaganda purpose. I have just seen a list[17] of the 550 foreign books which are to be translated into Russian and published in the USSR next year (total printing, 7,500,000 copies). Of these 208 are from Great Britain, Canada, and the United States. Only a handful on the English list are examples of belles lettres; one is the autobiography of Sean

[16] Ernest J. Simmons, *Continuity and Change in Russian and Soviet Thought*, p. 416.
[17] Courtesy of Morris Ernst.

O'Casey. As for the rest, five are mathematics texts, seventeen are works on agriculture, six deal with military history, fourteen are on biology, and sixteen on chemistry. Some sample titles:

> Shaukross and Bumont (sic), Air Law
> Hunt, The Ascent of Everest
> Doob, Processes of Probability
> Kucheman and Weber, Aerodynamics of Airplane Motors
> Lyuis and Wells, Millimicrosecond (sic) Impulse Technology
> Robertson, The Origin of Christianity
> Rosen, Tropones and Tropolones

Also included are Harvey Matusow's False Witness and Fahrenheit 451, a novel by Ray Bradbury. Titles like these, out of the whole rich and magnificent range of books published in England and America during the past year or so, with its unparalleled catholicity, variety, and capacity for intellectual enlightenment, are the only ones the Russians choose for 1958. Nothing else! The conclusion cannot be avoided that they simply do not wish to give any serious or fair representation of contemporary Western culture.[18]

However, two big hits in Moscow last year were The Quiet American, by Graham Greene, and The Old Man and the Sea, by Ernest Hemingway, translated by the journalist-dramatist-critic Boris Izakov. Friends in Moscow insisted to me that both these books met such wide response because they are beautifully written, and are indisputably genuine works of art. Possibly there are other reasons. Mr. Greene's novel attacked colonialism and is profoundly anti-American in a subtle and effective way, and the Hemingway book was obviously a perfect choice for translation in that it shows what happens to an old fisherman in a bourgeois society who does not have social security.

While we were in Moscow the best-regarded contemporary American novelist was Howard Fast. I do not know what the rank and file of Russian readers will be permitted to think about him now. Mr. Fast dramatically severed his relations with the CPSU early in 1957, and this was made known to the high literary authorities in Moscow in no uncertain terms. Losing Fast will be a blow to them. He was a prized object. Two other American writers (not Communists) are well known. One is a lady named Ethel Voynich, who wrote a novel called The Gadfly back in 1897; its theme is socially useful revolutionary conspiracy, wrapped up in a good, exciting spy

[18] See "Glimpse Concluded" in Chapter XXIV below.

story, and it has had a tremendous vogue in the Soviet Union. The other is Mitchell Wilson, author of *Live with Lightning* and *My Brother, My Enemy*. Time and time again I heard Mr. Wilson described as "the foremost American writer." I had, to my shame, never even heard of him, although *Live with Lightning* had a considerable success when it was published in the United States in 1949. *My Brother, My Enemy* sold out its Russian edition (390,000 copies) in five weeks. *Live with Lightning* is a kind of latter-day *Arrowsmith*; its hero is an idealistic young American physicist, who struggles against academic inertia and prejudice, pressure from big business, and wrongheaded government. No wonder it struck such a chord in the Soviet Union![19]

Arthur Miller is another writer well regarded, although little of his work is known as yet to the public at large. Boris Izakov is translating *Death of a Salesman* for *Novy Mir*, and it will go into production next year. I was asked wistfully if I thought that there was any possibility that Mr. and Mrs. Miller would attend the première. No one in Moscow I met had ever heard of Mr. Miller's troubles in Washington. What happened to his literary work in Russia in former days is somewhat peculiar. *All My Sons* was produced about ten years ago, and, after appearing for three weeks, was suddenly pulled off; this was during the worst of the Stalin "anticosmopolitan" period, when anything foreign was under a nasty cloud. Later, *The Crucible* was put on in Leningrad, but passages were added to it without Mr. Miller's knowledge or permission, and the Russians even stuck in a few characters whom he had not thought of inventing. Moreover, the translators got the title wrong, and produced it as *The Man Who Had All the Luck*, Miller's first produced play and a totally different work.[20]

Some American writers, when mentioned at all in the Soviet Union, are mentioned in severely uncomplimentary terms. Clifford Odets is thought to be "outside the ranks of cultured mankind," and T. S. Eliot is a "hyena." Eugene O'Neill is merely "degenerate," but Thornton Wilder is a "fascist."[21] Changes in the mode occur unpredictably. Critics formerly hurled every opprobrious adjective at William Faulkner, but nowadays he is treated with respect, even though his views on segregation are deplored.

[19] I have had the pleasure of meeting Mr. Wilson since returning from Russia. He is one of the few American authors who has managed to extract royalties from the Soviet Union. This came about as a result of a series of bizarre and even spectacular circumstances, too long to go into here. Anyway the story is Mr. Wilson's to tell, not mine. I hope that he will someday. It is a wonderful little story.

[20] *New York Times*, July 21, 1957, an article by Mr. Miller.

[21] W. W. Kulski, *The Soviet Regime*, p. 26.

Russian poets are incidentally marvelous translators of English verse. Both Boris L. Pasternak, the most distinguished living Russian poet, and Samuel Marshak have done wonders with Shakespeare, and Marshak has also made brilliant translations of Burns and Byron. Kornei I. Chukovsky, predominantly a children's poet, is celebrated for his translation of Walt Whitman, and Ivan Bunin's Longfellow has been called "better than the original."[22] Longfellow is having a big revival at the moment. Dozens of Soviet scholars occupy themselves by poring through classic foreign verse, in order to discover sentiments that may be valuable today in giving support to Russian aims. Longfellow, it seems, was against war and slavery.[23]

Jack London, Mark Twain, and Edgar Allan Poe have always been enormously popular in Russia, and so is O. Henry. (I do not know if the Soviet Union has ever heard of Damon Runyon.) Then, until the Stalin blackout in the middle 1930's, Theodore Dreiser, Sinclair Lewis, and John Steinbeck were widely translated. Some authors well favored at the moment seem somewhat old-fashioned, like John Galsworthy and J. M. Barrie, but there is a reason for this; the Russians are systematic people, and, after the long Stalin period, they are determined to miss nothing, and want to pick up where they left off. It should also be added that several present-day Soviet critics in the field of belles lettres make incessant appeals to the authorities to establish a better and more representative translation program. One recent request is for more Feuchtwanger, Mauriac, Maugham, Moravia, Priestley, and Remarque.

Libraries and the Encyclopedia

No fewer than 392,000 libraries exist in the USSR, containing 1,351,000,000 books.[24] Many Russian libraries are, of course, so minor as to be scarcely worth considering; a shelf on two in a school, factory, or collective farm may be called a "library." Nevertheless the over-all figure is impressive. Several Soviet libraries are very large institutions indeed, like the Saltykov-Shchedrin State Library in Leningrad, which is probably the best in the country; it has twelve million books, roughly twice as many as the New York Public Library.

[22] Robert Magidoff, "American Literature in Russia," *Saturday Review of Literature*, November 2, 1946. Whitman was taboo under the Czars, and in the pre-Soviet days Chukovsky got into trouble for popularizing him.
[23] In 1957 the Soviet Union actually held celebrations to honor the 150th anniversary of Longfellow's birth. An oratorio, *The Birth of Hiawatha*, was specially written for the occasion by the Soviet composer Boldyrev, and was performed by the USSR Radio Symphony Orchestra with heady fanfare.
[24] A great many more than in the United States.

One interesting point is that more than *forty* of the big Soviet libraries receive by law every book, magazine, and major newspaper printed in the entire USSR. In the United States only one library, the Library of Congress, receives automatically all American books published.

William Benton, the American publicist, visited the Leningrad library recently; let me quote a paragraph from a memorandum he prepared of his impressions:

> We visited two reading rooms, and every desk seemed to be filled with busy students, most writing industriously in note books. The quiet was absolute. I have never seen such a concentrated zeal on the part of such a big group, applied to studying. . . . We were told that all of the students had jobs, most of them at night. They were working in order to get degrees, or to take examinations so that they could get ahead in their profession. . . . The sight is impressive, almost terrifying. I gather that the library runs day and night so that the people who work during the daytime in their turn occupy and fill these same study halls at night.

What is also terrifying is something else, that neither this library nor any other in the Soviet Union can be called a true library in our sense. They do not give free range to a researcher, scholar, or simple reader because *nothing is in them except books that the government wants to be there.* Special students may be given permission to make use of foreign books and journals, but even these are, with certain exceptions, limited in number and carefully hand-picked. Under Stalin librarians regularly received lists of titles, both Russian and foreign, to be removed from circulation for political reasons. Probably this kind of thing does not go on so much nowadays. Even so the fact remains that it is not only the books in a library that are slanted; so is the library itself.

*

The Great Soviet Encyclopedia, which contains more than 100,000 entries and which, when complete, will fill fifty volumes, includes some distortions so flamboyant as to be beyond belief. These are an old story. But such distortions have importance, because the Encyclopedia is the supreme Soviet work of reference, and its word is law; its editorial staff works directly under the Council of Ministers, and its two chief editors are full members of the Academy of Sciences. Each new volume goes to 300,000 subscribers, and the books are serviceably bound and well illustrated. Publication of this vast work began in 1949, and the last volume received in the United

States is No. 48; an enticing point is that No. 40, covering entries from SOKI to STILTON, has never appeared. The reason is not far to seek; the editors have not decided as yet how to handle Stalin. People waited with considerable curiosity to see what would happen to Khrushchev. His fate was not known until a few months ago, because "Kh" comes toward the end of the Russian alphabet, and the volume containing Khrushchev has only just appeared. He gets a modest, factual biography, quite brief and not laudatory in tone. No more cult of personality!

Almost everybody has heard about what happened to Beria in the Encyclopedia. After his liquidation subscribers were notified, with full instructions, that they should snip out the article about him, and insert in its place substitute articles which were duly enclosed, about the Bering Strait and an obscure eighteenth-century statesman named Berholtz. These were the best available substitute names beginning with "Ber." During Stalin's day when the party line changed on some matter so important that the Encyclopedia itself had to be changed, subscribers were obliged to turn in the volume affected to the local party secretary; it was pulped and a new whole volume, cut and patched, was then sent out to the subscriber. Nowadays the reader is allowed to keep the book, and trusted to make the proper emendation himself. Progress!

Another person recently "expelled" from the Encyclopedia was a Chinese Communist leader, Kao Kang. To replace him, a substitute page went out dealing with a city in Tibet.[25] Molotov, Malenkov, and company, have not yet been honored with razor-and-paste exclusion. There are times when piquant hocus-pocus of this sort makes it almost impossible to take Russians seriously, but take them seriously we must.

Newpapers and Magazines

Of all dull things in the USSR the dullest are the great newspapers. Literate (and even not-so-literate) Soviet citizens realize this to the full; I heard one journalist say, "Your American newspapers are too sensational and irresponsible; ours are suffocating; what each of us ought to have is a cross between the two." Russian newspapers are much smaller than ours in size (*Pravda* runs to six pages), and are printed on wretched paper compared to that which, for instance, is used by a good British newspaper; the cuts, as Robert Benchley once said of illustrations in newspapers in France, look as if they

[25] Harrison E. Salisbury in the *New York Times*, July 12, 1956. In their haste to make the revision, the editors overlooked the fact that the same Tibetan city also appeared elsewhere in the Encyclopedia, spelled differently.

had been "etched on dough." There are no comic strips, advice to housewives or the lovelorn, features in our sense, or financial news, few want ads or other advertisements, and very little news of accidents or sex. Editorials can be ponderously long, often running to six or seven solid columns; news, on the other hand, is often handled with disconcerting brevity, for which there may be a good reason. The "Doctors' Plot" got ten lines in *Izvestia*. Sometimes a newspaper will do something startling by way of innovation; for instance *Pravda* once gave nearly the whole of an issue to the full text of a play by Alexander Korneichuk called *The Front*, much as *The New Yorker* once gave a whole issue to *Hiroshima*, by John Hersey; this was during the war, and the authorities wanted to get before the people some lessons of the battle of Stalingrad; Korneichuk pilloried old-style military commanders, and demanded new blood at the front.

The Soviet Union has 7,246 newspapers, with a total circulation of about 53,000,000 in sixty languages.[26] There are more than two thousand different magazines, with a circulation of 361,000,000. In Leningrad alone at least a hundred magazines and small periodicals are published. Most sell at a fabulous rate. Never once, as an example, was I able to find a copy of *Ogonyok (Flame)*, the Soviet equivalent of *Life*, on a newstand anywhere in the USSR. Like many other periodicals, it is sold out the moment it appears. People will read *any*thing.

Editors do not, obviously, have to compete for reader interest but it would be a mistake to think that they do not concern themselves with popular appeal; they do, except in the case of the official newspapers. Russian editors are human, even as are editors in the United States, and like to keep ahead. Censorship is not applied directly by the government, but is self-imposed. Some newspapers are little more than bulletin boards. The level to which they go to print minor personal news, if this serves a social purpose, is astounding. And names are named. *Pravda* will publish a complaint from a reader that Comrade So-and-So in Such-and-Such a ministry does not answer his telephone. Headlines almost always convey a political note, if this is at all possible; for instance *Pravda* headlined its first story about the Sputnik, no less, with the words, "A GREAT VICTORY IN THE PEACEFUL COM-PETITION WITH CAPITALISM."[27]

The principal newspaper is, of course, *Pravda (Truth)*, the organ of the

[26] The United States has 2,301 daily and Sunday newspapers, with a circulation of 102,000,000.

[27] One curious point is that, reporting a speech, Soviet papers sometimes intersperse the text with exclamation points and question marks as a guide to the reader, in order to achieve editorial emphasis or to cast doubt on what is being reported.

Central Committee of the CPSU. It is printed simultaneously in various cities, from mats flown from Moscow, and has a circulation of 4,900,000 all over the Soviet Union; its editors say that this could be expanded at will to 12,000,000. *Pravda* has no fewer than forty *thousand* correspondents, mostly amateur watchdogs, scattered throughout the country, and is the supreme arbiter about political affairs. The next most important newspaper is *Izvestia (News)*, the organ of the Soviet government, with a circulation of 1,400,000. I have often mentioned in these pages such other consequential papers as *Trud (Labor)*, organ of the trade unions, *Komsomolskaya Pravda*, organ of the Young Communist League, and *Literaturnaya Gazeta*, which appears triweekly. The liveliest and most "popular" newspaper in Moscow is *Evening Moscow*; it prints neighborhood items, news of what will be found in the shops, announcements about movies, and the like. Most branches of Soviet activity have their own special newspaper. Both *Gudok*, the railroad newspaper, and *Red Star*, organ of the Defense Ministry, are dailies; *Soviet Culture*, *Soviet Sport*, and a newspaper for medical workers are triweekly, as is an agricultural paper with a huge circulation. *Radioprogrammy* comes out weekly. One revealing point is that, among provincial newspapers, only those published in the capitals of the various Soviet republics are allowed to be exported from the USSR. Presumably this is because other provincial papers contain news of local events which are not checked and might give away too many small straws in the wind, if they were closely read by Soviet specialists abroad.

The official Soviet news agency is Tass. We went to see its director, N. G. Palgunov. His graying hair is cut in the stiff pompadour favored by Russian officials, and, with a neat blue suit, pale blue shirt, and red bow tie, he was the best-dressed man I met in the Soviet Union; he might have been a movie actor dressed up to play an American tycoon. Palgunov worked for many years as Tass correspondent in Paris. Also he underwent one period of severe official disfavor in Moscow, and even passed some time in jail. Today he is top of the top. He told us about Tass. About five thousand Soviet newspapers take its service; they pay according to circulation, from 100,000 rubles a month down to five. Tass correspondents are scattered all over the world, with eight hundred in Russian cities; some forty foreign correspondents work abroad. Three-quarters of its men are university graduates. Tass has exchange agreements with the Associated Press, United Press, and other western agencies, and disseminates their services (if this suits a purpose); once I was startled to hear the UP being quoted in an official Soviet radio broadcast. Tass is said to be the largest news service in the world, with a daily file reputedly exceeding that of Reuters or the AP. It receives no subsidy, supports itself, and turns over its profits to the government.

Journalists in the USSR have their own union, like the Writers Union. Most are well paid, but Mr. Palgunov told us that the "spread" between those best paid and those on the moderate level was much less pronounced than in the United States. A senior editor in the Soviet Union gets the equivalent of anything from $1,250 to $2,500 per month. One highly accomplished Soviet journalist is Yuri Zhukov, formerly the foreign editor of *Pravda*, who now heads a special committee under the Council of Ministers for liaison with foreign countries. Another is Boris Polevoy, author of *A Story About a Real Man*, who led a recent delegation of Soviet newspapermen to the United States.

As to magazines, they have considerable variety. I have several times mentioned *Novy Mir* (*New World*) but this is only one of several important and influential literary monthlies, like *Oktyabr*, *Znamya* (*Banner*), and the Leningrad *Zvezda* (*Star*). Music, ethnology, theater, economics, education, Orientology, philosophy, history, all have their own learned magazines. One of the most interesting is *Inostrannaya Literatura* (*Foreign Literature*). This, comparatively new, is devoted entirely to translations into Russian of foreign literary works, with comments, and is currently printing much more representative examples of literature from the West than would have been thought possible a few years ago. The Russians go in strongly for magazines published simultaneously in a multiplicity of non-Russian languages. *International Affairs* is printed in both English and Russian; *Soviet Literature* appears in English, French, German, Spanish. The *New Times*, published by the trade unions and devoted to foreign affairs, appears weekly in no fewer than ten different non-Russian languages, mostly of the satellite countries; *Soviet Woman*, an illustrated monthly, appears in twelve, including Chinese; another, *Soviet Union*, which features illustrations in color, comes out in no fewer than thirteen.

Finally, we must mention *Krokodil*, the humorous weekly. This does not resemble *Punch* or *The New Yorker* as much as the old German *Simplicissimus*, particularly in its illustrations—line drawings of pert pretty girls which come as near to being titillating as anything ever printed in the USSR. On most topics *Krokodil* is outspoken, even daring, and both its artwork and humor are on a fairly sophisticated level; its best cartoonist, Leonid Soifertis, is the Soviet equivalent of Saul Steinberg or Charles Addams. One recent *Krokodil* cartoon depicts the way women have done their hair throughout the course of history; the first panel (a cave dweller) and the last (a contemporary fashion model) are identical. Another shows a married couple sleeping; the wife murmurs, "Just imagine, my dear, I dreamt that we were stripped of everything," as a burglar makes off with a sackful of their possessions. Still another presents a crowded government office. One man says, "We are not overstaffed. We have seven bosses and one worker."

*

Soviet visitors to the United States, when they glance for the first time at an American newsstand, are apt to be profoundly shocked. Such a medley of cheap obscene trash, sensational exposé magazines, naked bosoms with exaggerated cleavage, and other vulgarities and outright examples of bad pornography would not, to put it mildly, be permitted in the Soviet Union.

CHAPTER XV

Ballet, Theater, and Entertainment

I'm fed
to the teeth
with Agitprop,
I'd like
to scribble
love ballads—
But I mastered my impulse
and crushed underfoot
the throat of my
very own songs.
— VLADIMIR MAYAKOVSKY IN 1930

FOR other aspects of Soviet intellectual and artistic life we have little space. But there must be a word at least about such glittering institutions as the Bolshoi (Great) Theater, the central citadel of culture in Moscow and one of the most magnificent theaters in the world. It gives as a rule four or five performances a week of opera, and two or three of ballet; the program for one typical week when we were there was *Lohengrin*, *Boris Godunov*, *Sadko*, the ballet *Swan Lake* (twice), *Prince Igor*, and *Eugene Onegin* (twice). This makes a score of four Tchaikovskys, one Rimski-Korsakov, one Moussorgsky, one Borodin, and one Wagner. All the great Russian operas are standard in the repertory: foreign operas are played less often. Not far away, however, is a smaller opera affiliated with the Bolshoi, where one may hear Mozart, Verdi, and most operas of the classic western repertoire.

Most productions of the opera at the Bolshoi are extraordinarily sumptuous and palatial, with a strong accent both on realism and the spectacular; to western eyes and ears, they may seem a bit old-fashioned. The orchestra is almost always good, and the singing superb. Stage effects are splendid. If

307

five hundred tons of water are necessary to simulate a flood, they will be there. Every effort is directed to putting on a resounding *show*.

The Bolshoi is certainly impressive—also beautiful—as a building, with its graceful classic exterior and glow of red and gold within; there are no fewer than six tiers of balconies and boxes, and seats in the stalls are fixed, gilt-and-crimson armchairs. The best seats cost 33 rubles ($8.25 at par), and there is a flourishing black market in them, because the theater is always sold out. Between the acts—intermissions are interminably long in any Russian theater—you can buy champagne for 6.75 rubles a glass, and eat caviar. A small sign in the buffet says NO SMOKING—the only sign in English I saw in all Moscow. The audience, even on gala occasions, looks pretty much like that in the top gallery in Carnegie Hall, and is equally vociferous. In Russia as a rule people clap to time. This marvelous theater dates back to 1776; it has occupied its present building since 1825.

Showpieces in ballet are *Romeo and Juliet* (music by Prokofiev and first produced in 1940), *Don Quixote*, old stand-bys like *Giselle*, and some ballets comparatively new, such as *The Bronze Horseman* and *The Red Poppy*. The well-known Armenian composer Aram Khachaturian has recently written the music for a new ballet based on the life of a standard Communist hero, Spartacus; Mr. Khachaturian endured a period of disfavor under Stalin, but is now "back." The Russians are, of course, prouder of their ballet than of any single phenomenon in the realm of the arts in the entire country. The history of the Ballet Russe goes back more than two hundred years, and its tradition is fostered with assiduous devotion. Some thirty-two Soviet cities have their own ballet troupes which, by any standard of comparison, is a fantastic number. Imagine thirty-two American cities having their own permanent ballet schools, theaters, and companies! The Soviet ballet is, however, likely to seem old-hat to a sophisticated western observer. Performances are magnificent, yes, with a *corps de ballet* incomparably skilled, well trained, and edged with fire, but most are put on in a manner unchanged since 1910. The repertoire is restricted to classic ballet, and experimentalism is virtually unknown; there are few new ballets, and even in these the choreography is apt to be dated. No Anthony Tudor here, or even Balanchine![1]

One night we encountered something extraordinary. Ulanova was to play in *Giselle*, her first performance in Moscow after her triumphant visit

[1] One troupe, however, the Moiseyev Dance Company, is devoted to ballet based on folk dances and uses contemporary themes. One of its successes is called *Soccer*. It is scheduled to visit the United States in 1958.

to London in the autumn of 1956. (It is the Soviet custom not to announce in advance what performers will be in any given play, opera, or ballet, but in this special case the news leaked out.) The spacious square in front of the Bolshoi was not only jammed with people, but filled with open trucks on which TV cameras and lights were mounted, something unusual for Moscow. Roughly the scene was comparable to that attending a special Broadway opening, but was bigger, more fluid, more "Russian" and improvised, with excitement passing like electricity through the crowds, and an air of thrilled expectancy making everybody tense. People passionately offered us twice, three times, four times, what we had paid for tickets. Early in the second act Ulanova collapsed. She fell, however, so gracefully that few in the audience could tell for certain whether this was part of the action of the ballet or an accident. Then one could see from the shocked, horrified faces of the other ballerinas that it was indeed an accident. A line of them, maintaining their dance, almost floating, formed an oval around the prostrate Ulanova, as if to protect her in this moment of profound agony, and bowed to her, again still as if this were part of the dance, and then made a long sweeping bow to the audience. With a swish, the great curtain rang down. Utter silence for a second. Then pandemonium. People caught on to what had happened, and loud murmurs were heard, and then puzzled cries. "Ulanova! Ulanova! What has happened? Ulanova!" people whispered, in a kind of muffled horror. The emotion was intense; one woman near me groaned, and I thought that she would faint; another put her head in her hands, sobbing; another stuffed a handkerchief in her mouth as if she were about to be sick. "Ulanova! Ulanova!"

An official of the theater quickly slid out on the stage, and announced that what had happened was nothing—Ulanova had merely sprained a leg muscle, but would be unable to resume. Blandly he announced that the performance would proceed, with another dancer taking over Ulanova's role: this was none other than Raisa Struchkova, one of the foremost ballerinas in the country. It was as if Margot Fonteyn, say, had collapsed in a ballet in London, and within a few moments was replaced by somebody almost as celebrated as herself. From the audience came a long sibilant rustle of relief. It sounded as if the amphitheater itself was giving voice to a profound, prodigious sigh. After the performance my wife and I walked back to our hotel, pushing our way through cold, wet, sticky blobs of snow. This had been a long, grueling day for us before the Bolshoi performance; the Soviets had announced a new H-bomb test, and the western ambassadors had walked out of a reception at the Kremlin. We tottered into the dining room of the National, exhausted, and ordered a drink. What piercing anticlimaxes occur in Russia! The miserable little orchestra was sadly playing an American song called "Melancholy Baby"!

Galina Sergeyevna Ulanova, People's Artist of the USSR and *Prima Ballerina Assoluta*, was born in Leningrad (then St. Petersburg) in 1910. She was to the ballet born; her father was a ballet master, and her mother, Maria Romanova, was a soloist in the *corps de ballet* of the Mariinsky Theater, also a teacher. By most critics, Ulanova is thought to be the greatest dancer in the world. This is not merely because of her magical technique. Like Greta Garbo, she gives forth something intangible beyond the normal limitations of art—an aura, an essence, an incomparable communication of romantic ecstasy. Like Garbo too, she is an extremely shy woman, pleasant to meet, and serious. Ulanova made her debut in *Swan Lake* in 1929, and became famous immediately for her performance as the Princess Aurora in Tchaikovsky's *Sleeping Beauty*. She was elevated to the rank of People's Artist in 1940, and has won Stalin (or Lenin) Prizes no fewer than four times. One of her supreme roles is in *The Fountain of Bakhchisarai*, from the Pushkin poem. She lives modestly, and contributes regularly to civic activities. Recently for instance she participated in a public forum on Anglo-Soviet relations. In Russia they make *every*body work.

Great ballet dancers are important assets to the Soviet regime, and their conduct is supposed to be impeccable politically and otherwise. One illustrious ballerina, only slightly less illustrious than Ulanova, was not permitted to go to London. It seems that on a previous trip abroad she had behaved with mild scandalousness. The Minister of Culture himself called on her to break the news. "My little one," he purred, "our ballerinas have to be pure, like Soviet ice cream."

*

Moscow has more than thirty legitimate theaters; four of these are exclusively children's theaters. There are several peculiarities about theatrical life in Moscow. One is that (except in special circumstances) a long continuous run is impossible; each theater gives as a rule four or five different plays a week, since all are repertory theaters. If a new play is a success, however, it may stay in the repertoire of a given theater for a long period; one new play, first produced in 1954, is still a hit. Another peculiarity is that there are no stars, at least officially, and certainly no star system.

Instead prominent performers become in time "Honored Artists of the RSFSR" (or other republic), rising to be "People's Artists" on the republic level, and then, the supreme honor, are promoted to be "People's Artists of the USSR," like Ulanova. These titles always appear with the cast of characters on the program.[2] In *Anna Karenina* at the Moscow Art Theater were no fewer than three People's Artists of the USSR (Alla Tarasova as Anna, M. N. Kedrov as Karenin, and B. Y. Stanitsky as Anna's brother), seven People's Artists of the RSFSR, and twelve Honored Artists of the RSFSR, out of a total cast of forty-two.

The Intourist offices have large broadsheets printed on rough, flimsy paper on display each week, listing what is playing. So you can order tickets about a week ahead. However, a complicated Russian touch, these broadsheets are useless if, for instance, you want to know on a Saturday what will be available on Monday; the *new* broadsheet does not come out till Monday morning. What to do? The Intourist girl, in her mysterious way, has a little booklet secreted in her drawer, which, if persuaded, she will fish out and consult. In this, programs are listed for a month ahead. But on the *last* day of the month it is impossible (or at least difficult) to choose anything to see in the first week of the month to come, because the little booklet has become out of date and the new one isn't ready. One curiosity—in the realm of theatrical architecture—is that theater auditoriums do not have exit signs.

All theaters are, of course, agencies of the state, but most do not get financial support from the government, and have to make their own way.[3] It is not merely in Moscow that the theater is wildly popular. There are no fewer than seven hundred legitimate theaters in the Soviet Union, and 350,000 theatrical "groups." Every provincial capital or town of consequence has its legitimate theater or theaters. It would be inconceivable in the Soviet Union for a city the size and rank of, let us say, Montpelier, Vermont, not

[2] Until I got on to them some programs puzzled me, because they contained not the name of one actor or actress for a given part, but several. This indicates that *all* of these are equipped to play this particular role; the actor or actress who actually does play may not be chosen until the last minute, and so all the names are given. The usher checks off the correct name as she hands you the program, or sometimes another name is put in with a rubber stamp.

[3] The Bolshoi and the Maly (Little) are the only theaters in Moscow to be subsidized. A curious point may be mentioned in connection with this. The 1914 Baedeker mentions that most Russian theaters are "subventioned" by the government. If it is true that more received state support then than now, the theater must be the only field in Russia in which there was more "nationalization" under the Czars than under the Soviets today.

to have its own permanent theater and stock company. But try to find one in Montpelier, Vermont. A new play by a Russian dramatist of renown may be playing simultaneously in as many as three *hundred* theaters. This happened, at least, in the case of Konstantin Simonov's *The Russian Question*.

Citizens are mad about the theater for the same reason that they are mad about books, but more so. Ballet, opera, and drama give them the glamour they lack in their daily lives; they have no beauty at home, and so seek it on the stage. Moreover—a most important point—the authorities do their best to see that the ravenous thirst is satisfied. (But standing in line at the Bolshoi one evening we talked to a high school teacher who said that he could afford to take his family to the opera only once a year.)

The Moscow theater can, and often does, provide marvelous entertainment, but it is not, needless to say, a frivolous theater; the emphasis is altogether serious. No Folies Bergères, no leg shows, no burlesque, no bedroom comedy! The theater is supposed to reflect the highest interest of the nation; here is classic theater in the grandest of grand manners. There is, at the present time, no direct censorship, contrary to most thought; censorship of the theater was dropped a few years ago, a suggestive minor example of de-Stalinization.

Of course the situation is much the same as in publishing; every theater director is a responsible person, who would not dream of producing anything *overtly* offensive to the regime. If a dramatist writes a play, he is at liberty to submit it to any theater. It may be accepted; it may not. If not, the dramatist has further recourse; five or six magazines and one publishing house exist primarily for publishing plays not yet produced, an innovation other countries might well imitate. The effect of publication is to make the text of the unproduced play available all over the Soviet Union, and some producer in the provinces may like it and produce it. *Then*, if a success, it may have another chance in Moscow.

Most show-business people in Moscow have little interest in politics. I will not forget the wry grimace on a dramatist's face when I asked him if most of his fellow dramatists and producers were members of the Communist party. His response was very Broadwayesque, uttered with ironic, complacent piety: "Our party cannot have *too* many members. If everybody joined the party, there wouldn't be any party!"

Dramatic criticism can be very sharp in Moscow, and even such revered temples as the Bolshoi and Maly are not spared. Moreover actors and actresses are privileged—indeed encouraged—to write letters to the papers, expressing their countercriticism, if any, to the critics. One remarkable practice is the well-known Soviet institution of *public* criticism; it might be fun to follow this in our world, although to do so would cause chaos on Forty-second Street or Piccadilly. Each Moscow theater, once or twice a year, holds a mass meeting, which is widely advertised; the public is invited to turn out and, if so inclined, heckle and ask questions of producer, director, author, and actors, who are assembled on the stage. Speeches from the audience are limited to three minutes, and hundreds of people speak. One play recently discussed in such a session was Lillian Hellman's *Autumn Garden* which has been a pronounced recent success in Moscow. Several of the amateur critics said that it reminded them of Chekhov; some said generously that they did not think it could be really representative of conditions in the United States. Americans simply could not behave like that!

The tremendous sting and push and bite of the old Moscow theater has pretty much dwindled away; Stalin killed it, and there has not been time for a new generation of dramatists and *régisseurs* to arise.[4] Practically no revolutionary impulses are discernible in the Moscow theater of today. In fact, there are few new Russian plays of any kind, revolutionary or not, and most are mediocre. Innovation and experiment are at the minimum. The greatest of the old revolutionary producers was Vsevolod E. Meyerhold, a former actor in the Moscow Art Theater who founded and managed the Revolutionary Theater. He was a good Communist, but was arrested in 1938 and was never heard of again; presumably he died in a prison or labor camp, or was shot. He was posthumously rehabilitated in 1956. Several old plays have now been revived in the manner in which Meyerhold put them on, like *Klop*, and it is possible that a new Meyerhold "period" may begin. Certainly most Soviet dramatists hope so.

Now as to what a visitor to Moscow may see. The range of fare is circumscribed (as is everything in the Soviet Union, as we should know by now), but nevertheless quite wide. I will pick a sample week as of the time we were there. Among Russian classics *The Three Sisters* (Chekhov), *The Lower*

---

[4] Stalin's writ did not kill plays only out of basic political impulses but because of mere whim. If Stalin happened not to like a new play, it was doomed. He sent word out to one of his hatchetmen on *Pravda* or in the Writers Union; the play was then publicly attacked, and had to be taken off. (*Pravda* still sometimes attacks plays, but this does not mean *necessarily* that they are taken off.) One Soviet actor told me a little story about Stalin, in contrast to Lenin. Lenin, who was a voracious reader and liked almost anything, hated Dickens because he thought that Dickens was too sentimental. But *The Cricket on the Hearth* played in Moscow for year after year, and it would never have occurred to Lenin to interfere with it. "But when Stalin said that he didn't like a play, it was suppressed," my friend went on. "As a result we have had no theater for twenty years."

Depths (Gorky), and an Ostrovsky comedy were all playing at the Moscow Art Theater; so was a play by Alexei Tolstoy and one written some twenty years ago by Nikolai Pogodin and now being revived to frantic success, the *Chimes of the Kremlin*.[5] It is about Lenin and electricity. At other theaters Shaw was available (*Mrs. Warren's Profession*), Wilde (*An Ideal Husband*), and Sartre (*The Respectful Prostitute*, retitled *Lizzie McKay*).[6] There were multitudinous Russian plays, including three different Chekhovs and one well-known modern satire, *Aristocracy*. Scarcely any week ever passes in Moscow without some Shakespeare; hundreds of Soviet actors have done Hamlet, or "Gamlet" as he is called in Russian. One night we could have seen *Othello* in no fewer than three different forms!—at the Opera, in the theater, and as a movie. Instead we went to a *Macbeth* at the Maly. This was the most stunning *Macbeth* I have ever seen, even though it was disconcerting at first to hear good Scottish names surmounted with Russian declensional suffixes. For a moment I did not know who "Mok*doof*-a" was. The acting was marvelous, but, as in most Russian theaters, somewhat heavy; scenery and costumes are old-fashioned as a rule, and, no matter what the play, almost always reminded me of *Siegfried* at the Metropolitan.

The most famous theater in Russia is, of course, the Moscow Art Theater, known as the Mkhat. It is a very small theater by our (or Russian) standards, and much run-down nowadays, but it still has considerable elegance. It was founded in 1898, and has a powerful tradition; it is the only public place of its kind I saw in Moscow which does not use the hammer and sickle as an insignia; instead it has its own symbol, a dove. Here Konstantin Stanislavsky and Vladimir Nemirovich-Danchenko created the modern realistic theater, with results well know the world over. Perhaps the acting is not so stupendous as it was in the days of Kachalov and Moskvin, but it is certainly unsurpassed elsewhere in the world on a group level; performances, especially of the ensemble, are so perfect as to be mesmeric. The repertory consists of about thirty plays. Maybe *Anna Karenina* and *Uncle Vanya* are old-hat as performed here, because of the relentless accent on realism, but they are very good old-hats. One play recently put on by the Moscow Art Theater for the first time, with dazzling effect, was Schiller's *Mary Stuart*. Oddly enough it had its New York première at about the same time. Alla Tarasova, the foremost Russian actress of the older generation, played the role created in

---

[5] It was a bad mark against me when, asking for tickets for this, I made a fluff and said *Crimes of the Kremlin*.

[6] And played by a lady considered to be the Soviet equivalent of Brigitte Bardot, and the "sexiest" actress in Moscow. She is, however, fifty-three.

America by Irene Worth. Somehow this reminds me that it has been a great many years since any Soviet play has been produced in New York. The last was, I believe, Simonov's *The Russian Question*, put on during the war.

The play I liked best in Moscow was *Klop* (*The Bedbug*). Mayakovsky wrote this in 1929, a year before his suicide. It was suppressed for many years, but has now been revived in *two* versions. An odd story hangs on this. *Klop* is a satire about a Soviet bumpkin, indescribably coarse, who becomes imprisoned in a block of ice; he wakes up fifty years in the future, which gives opportunity for some shattering satire about what the USSR will presumably be like at that time. Also *Klop* contains one of the most deliciously ribald and in fact depraved scenes I have ever seen in a theater, a wedding that is a kind of Trimalchio's feast. It was decided to revive *Klop*, and the Satire Theater put it on. It was a great hit. The authorities did not, however, like it a bit. But, proud of de-Stalinization, they did not want to crack down on it. Somebody had the fantastic idea of putting on a *rival*, cleaned-up version of *Klop* while the first was still running; this was done, and the second *Klop* duly had its première at the Mayakovsky Theater. The authorities hoped that good Soviet citizens would snub the indecent *Klop*, and favor the emasculated, whitewashed version. Wacky Russians! What happened? Both versions play to huge audiences!

To conclude: the Moscow theater, like so much else in the Soviet Union, gives a picture of vivid conflict, frustration, argument, aspiration. Russia is not all a ham in a sack.

Perhaps the theater is not what it once was, but even so it is the ballet and theater, perhaps more than anything else, that give Moscow its peculiar haunting quality, its aroma of wild, exotic stimulus and fascination. As I have said before in this book, this city is apt to put a spell on you never to be forgotten, and what you see on the stage is one of the reasons why.

*

Now a last word in this field. Moscow has what is by all odds the finest puppet theater in the world, run by Serge Obraztsov. We had a rewarding long talk with this exuberant, gay, and determined character. He is full of idiosyncrasy. In twenty-five years, no one has ever kept him from producing exactly what he wants. He was the son of an academician, who wanted to be a painter; he drifted into acting, visited the United States in the 1920's as a member of the *Lysistrata* troupe, and eventually became interested in puppets. Pre-Revolutionary Russia had no puppet theater, and Obraztsov set out to create one in 1931. The Chinese (also the Czechoslovaks) had full-dress puppet theaters; why not Russia too? Today his staff numbers 214, and his Central Puppet Theater has a repertory of forty different puppet plays, of which there have been eighteen thousand performances so far. Some of the best dramatists in the Soviet Union write for Obraztsov. He is a People's Artist of the USSR, and is both producer and director of his theater. "So then I have to argue only with myself!"

Repertory is about equally divided between plays for children and grownups. The puppets are marvelously articulated, and can convey almost any action or emotion; they are not marionettes or hand puppets, but are operated deftly from long sticks. The concentration on puppetry is so intense that several of Obraztsov's veteran associates even *look* like puppets. If I had only one evening in Moscow, I would spend it at the puppet theater. The visitor should not give way to the thought that there is something symbolic about this; it would be easy to write a nice ironic sentence to the effect that, even in the theater, Russia has abolished the human being, and that everybody, on stage as well as off, is a puppet under the Soviets. As a matter of fact Obraztsov's theater has more life in it than most live theaters. This is one of the few institutions in the USSR where things are done purely for the joy of it, for fun. Obraztsov took his company to London last year, and it was fabulously well received. New York should see it.

One favorite item in the repertory is *Unusual Concert*, a wildly delicious parody of performers doing a series of turns in a concert hall. The performance I liked best was *The Girl with the Fluttering Eyelids*, a satire on Hollywood. It is like a Disney film in three dimensions, gone slightly crazy. Every Hollywood type you ever heard of is there, from the fat cigar-smoking agent measuring the bust of a pretty girl to bewildered, frustrated writers and yes-men. In one scene, depicting a writers' conference, seven stenographers simultaneously take down seven different versions of what the producer wants. The plot deals with *Carmen*. The scene shifts violently to the Soviet Union for a time, because the company has trouble finding a satisfactory bull, and searches for one on a collective farm. Results: hysterical.

Uproar in Art and Music

For art this is an agitated and exciting time in the Soviet Union. As in the world of books, the basic conflict is what to do about socialist realism. Many artists, like their writer colleagues, are mortally sick of the stereotyped "calendar art" produced by the ruling dogma, the dry-as-dust representational or propagandistic stuff that has passed for art during the past decades. They cannot do much about it but, even so, certain changes have come to the atmosphere. For instance the dean of contemporary Soviet painters, Alexander Gerasimov, was forced to resign recently as President of the Artists Union. His successor, B. V. Ioganson, is no flaming insurrectionary by any means; his best-known painting, strictly in the genre of socialist realism, is called "At an Old Urals Plant," and looks it, but he is probably more modern-minded than Gerasimov.

Background to this is peculiar.[7] In the very earliest period of the Revolution artists were pretty much allowed, without overt nudging, to paint what they liked. Before this several Russian painters, like Kandinsky and Chagall, had become world-famous as pioneers in modern art. Both Kandinsky and Chagall lived abroad; after October, 1917, they returned to Russia with high heart, hoping to share in the artistic fruits of the Revolution. Other modernists like Pevsner, Gabo, Malevich, and Tatlin did the same thing. They were quickly disillusioned. The Soviet Union, as soon as it was ready to lay down the party line in re the arts, would have nothing of them.[8]

Why should the Soviet rulers, then as now, have such fierce vituperative antipathy to modern art, particularly abstract art? By Marxist doctrine, art forms are supposed always to reflect the basic economic structure of society. But the western world is full of the most violently revolutionary art, which is widely appreciated, whereas art in the Soviet Union is fantastically puritanical, old-fashioned, and conservative. One British critic has said that the net result of socialist realism has been to set Russian painting back forty years. Yet the Soviet Union likes to think of itself as always being in advance of the West in every intellectual field. There are several other paradoxes. The struggle over art crosses party lines altogether. For instance it might be thought that Picasso, a Communist, would be revered by Communists in the Soviet Union; he is one of their own, they need prestige badly, and he is not only a great revolutionist but one of the most distinguished men in the world. But academic and government circles in the USSR think of him

[7] See "Is Modern Art Communistic?" by Alfred H. Barr, Jr., New York Times, December 14, 1952.

[8] Chagall and Kandinsky got back to western Europe, with their souls singed but still alive; Malevich and Tatlin stayed. Malevich was the first artist ever to paint complete abstractions based on geometric designs, squares and circles; Tatlin, the founder of what is called "constructivism," designed a new building for the Comintern in Petrograd seemingly made of loops of wire. Malevich took one trip out of the USSR, returned, and died. Tatlin is believed to be still alive, but nothing has been heard of him for years.

as Satan incarnate, or even worse. I met Mr. Gerasimov, who is one of the most delightful of men, at a party, and asked him about Picasso. He chuckled, "We approve of him as a Communist, but not as a painter!" An American friend with me replied, "Our attitude is exactly the reverse!" Another Russian said, "Picasso is a Communist and a capitalist at the same time! Ha-ha!"

Probably there were three main reasons why the Soviet line turned so vehemently against modern art, which is called "pathological delirium." (1) It was "useless"; it did nothing for society. (2) The entrenched academicians didn't like it, and the public could make no sense of it. (3) Lenin himself, although he rarely troubled about matters of this nature, could not bear impressionism, expressionism, cubism, and the like, and said so in no uncertain terms. As to the second point, it should certainly be emphasized that the Soviet attitude paralleled that of many quarters in the West. The Russian line was identical with that of, let us say, the Royal Academy in London at the same time. Vested interests in the world of art are likely to have the same view everywhere. Even today, there are plenty of Americans and Britons who think that modern art is demented. But the social aspect of the question was what counted in the USSR. Under socialist realism, the Soviet authorities could not countenance anything outrageous or bizarre or even unconventional, anything that opened up new vistas, made people think, jolted them out of complacency toward accepted norms, or gave them stimulus.

Another provocative and revealing point is that, until the late 1920's or early 1930's, Russian citizens at large, not merely students of art, had opportunity unparalleled in the world to see examples of impressionist art—Manet, Monet, Renoir, Matisse, Van Gogh, Cézanne, and so on. Great collections of these masters are now commonplace all over the world; they were not so commonplace a quarter of a century ago. Moscow was unique in having such a magnificent concentration. The history behind this is well known. Two Russian men of wealth, by name Morozov and Shchukin, set about collecting French impressionists at the turn of the century. Year after year they brought cargoes of sublime and priceless works of art back from Paris to Moscow. Matisse visited Moscow as Shchukin's guest, and did two incomparable murals for his house there. Steadily the two collections grew. Came the Revolution. I do not know what happened to Mr. Morozov and Mr. Shchukin, but their paintings were forthwith nationalized, and duly became the property of the Soviet state.

At the beginning, if my memory is correct, both collections were lumped together, and put on display (in the Shchukin house) as the Museum of Modern Western Art. I saw it in 1928. It was a breath-taking collection.

There were something like twenty Cézannes, a round dozen Renoirs, and one of the greatest Van Goghs in the world, the prison courtyard at Arles. Moreover many of these had never been reproduced in the form of prints, and were virtually unknown to the world outside. (Later, the Russians did prepare and publish a folio of prints, but this is a volume scarce and hard to lay hands on nowadays.) But the Soviet authorities, far from being proud of this superlative collection, talked of it with derision. It was "bourgeois" and "decadent." Then the museum was closed down, and the paintings disappeared into the stacks of the Hermitage in Leningrad. Now they are on the point of being permanently shown again. A jurisdictional fight is in progress as to what museum shall have them, the Hermitage or one in Moscow, and how they shall be divided. We saw some in Leningrad.[9] That these masterpieces are, after all these years, going to be permitted to see the light of day once more is, of course, not merely an interesting example of new perspectives in the world of art in the USSR, but of the de-Stalinization process as a whole.

One day my wife and I visited the Moscow State Institute of Art (our chauffeur had a hard time finding it in a remote, derelict area of the city), and were courteously received by its director, Arkadi M. Kuznetsov. This is the principal art school in Moscow, and has 340 students. Several sat with us as we talked. Students take a six-year course, and are paid a stipend ranging from 280 to 800 rubles a month. (Models get ten rubles an hour for posing in the nude, eight rubles otherwise.) All students are certain of a job immediately after graduation; the Soviet Union needs artists. Factories, schools, and offices are full of pictures. Also the government subsidizes art quite heavily; appropriation of 35,000,000 rubles ($8,750,000 at par) came in 1957 for the purchase of art works to celebrate the fortieth birthday of the Revolution. But an artist who sets himself up in a studio of his own and depends on exhibitions of his own work to earn a living will have a hard time, unless he is a strict conformist. Even conformists can have a hard uphill time. We heard one story of a painter who did nothing but portraits of Stalin; he had a big backlog of these in his studio, which, since the coming of de-Stalinization, he cannot sell, and he has been ruined. We inspected

---

[9] See Chapter XX below. We had an exciting experience in connection with this. An exhibition of some of the Morozov-Shchukin works had been held in the Hermitage, and was being dismantled on the day we visited it. Pictures were standing against the walls all over the place. So we had the unique privilege of picking up priceless Cézannes and Renoirs and carrying them from wall to window and back again to see them in the best light, with nobody present except the museum authorities.

carefully the work of the young artists with whom we talked. Nothing, to our eyes, had spark or originality. Most of what we saw looked like rejects from the Grand Salon in Paris, or the kind of thing one would have seen on Washington Square twenty years ago. I asked one young man what he specialized in—landscapes, portraits, or what. Reply: "Anything you like." So are Soviet artists made!

The director and his associates defended socialist realism warmly. They wanted to make it clear to us that this concept did not mean that bad art was countenanced; one of them said, "After all, if a picture is bad it can't be any kind of realism!" The main thesis presented was that a painter should not paint subjectively, to give joy to himself, but to give joy to others. Art should serve a purpose, to improve the nature of man. Abstract art has no roots in life. Art has no mission, except to assist in *unification* of the people. Art must be useful to socialism. If the common man does not understand a work of art, it is worthless. And so on ad infinitum.

Then a few days later—startling contrast—we went to an unprecedented Picasso exhibition being held in Moscow. We had to force our way in through crowds of people almost beside themselves with excitement (and who paid three rubles each for tickets). This was the first opportunity Soviet citizens had had in a generation to see something akin to abstract art, although the Picassos exhibited were not abstractions. That the authorities should have allowed so many examples of Picasso to be assembled and shown is a striking demonstration of new forces at work, even if they are not puissant as yet. The pictures came from several sources, including the private collection of Ilya Ehrenburg, the writer; Picasso himself sent two or three things from Paris. Fierce controversy could be overheard. We listened to an excited group before a portrait of a woman in green, with hair like exploding streams of confetti. An oldish, respectably dressed lady turned in exasperation to a young man behind her, and pointed to the picture with the indignant words, "What's that?" The young man replied, "Hair." The lady became furious: "You call that hair? And look at this!" She stuck her finger at a nipple on the painting, protruding from the subject's blouse. "I have never seen anything so disgusting. Indecent! Shameful!"

Before another picture we overheard this colloquy:

Boy: "This is wonderful. This shows true freedom of expression!"

Man (interjecting angrily): "Freedom! Do you want freedom to act as you please? That isn't good Marxism!"

Boy: "Nonsense, you don't even know what Marxism is."

Man (doggedly): "Marx has no room for things like that!"

(Man disappears. Boy turns to another boy): "That old codger was a funny one, wasn't he? Lots of people don't understand what all this means here. They don't realize what is going on. But it's all right—they'll come back again. Look at these pictures three or four times and you begin to understand them."

Such phenomena as the Picasso show do not, of course, mean that art is going to be revitalized in the Soviet Union, or that socialist realism is on the way out or even that the criteria of appreciation will be changed. Socialist realism is going to hang on for a long, long time, and the academicians will continue to fight nonrepresentational art tooth and nail, for artistic as well as social reasons. But a conflict has arisen, and it has extraordinarily deep implications. The Russians do not (as Hitler did) think in terms of autarchic culture; they want their art to be known and admired everywhere in the world, not merely in China, India, and the satellites, but in the West. Several reasons exist for this. First, Soviet imperialism takes many forms, and the Russians realize that culture is a highly valuable article of export. Second, they would like to be able to report at home successes of their artists (also musicians) abroad. Third, they want to refute the thesis that they are uncivilized barbarians.

But how—and here rises the dilemma—can they establish cultural prestige abroad if the work they produce at home is ridiculously archaic and mediocre? To be accepted internationally, they must begin to recognize and train artists who will win international recognition and approval on world terms. But this is impossible under socialist realism. They want prestige, yes, but they cannot get it abroad without repudiating, at signal cost, all that they stand for in the world of art at home. It is difficult, as always, to have your cake and eat it too—even in the Soviet Union. So tussling and struggle are inevitable, and are hopeful signs.

*

Socialist realism has, of course, been applied to Russian music too, as well as to books and art, and a certain amount of ferment is discernible in the musical world. Intelligent creative people cannot endure the prevailing grayness and monotony. The official Kremlin attitude has always been that music should be something you can whistle; music is nothing if not a tune. Here, too, strikingly enough, Soviet artistic standards are almost exactly those of Philistine, illiterate, and old-fashioned elements in the West. The run-of-the-mill Soviet official has the same opinion of Hindemith, Bartok, or some similar composer as the run-of-the-mill businessman or shopkeeper in St. Louis; he finds it incomprehensible or worse. Soviet and *conservative* bourgeois attitudes are, in these and several other fields, identical.

Shostakovich and Prokofiev, who are modern composers, are however widely played in the Soviet Union; in fact the première of Shostakovich's latest symphony was held simultaneously in *thirty* Soviet cities. The Russians, as always, like to do things in a wholesale way. Shostakovich has considerable autonomy and prestige; it is unlikely that he would be asked these days to write a composition to celebrate a reforestation project. (This actually happened, and an oratorio, *Song of the Forests*, was the result.) For a long time Shostakovich lived under a bitter cloud. His period of disfavor began, it seems, when Stalin took a heated dislike to *Lady Macbeth of Mtsensk*, and ordered *Pravda* to attack it.[10] Perhaps music lovers in the West will wonder about the Communist attitude to another illustrious Russian composer, Igor Stravinsky. He is (so far as I know) never played in the USSR, but this is probably because he lives in the United States and is considered to be a defector, not by reason of his music per se. He is occasionally mentioned in the Soviet press, with respect, and probably Russia would like to get him back.

*

Music, almost any kind of music, is a passion to most Russians. These people are starving for more music. Members of the Boston Symphony Orchestra, which made a brief Russian tour in 1956, said that they had never known such vociferously (as well as sensitively) responsive audiences; men like the American violinist Isaac Stern report the same thing. On a different level, try to force your way into a Moscow shop selling phonograph records. Such shops are crowded to the seams. Also recordings of American jazz bring bizarre prices on the black market, as much as 400 rubles ($100 at par) for a single record. These recordings are taken on tape from Voice of America or other broadcasts, and then reproduced on, of all things, discs made of discarded X-ray plates salvaged from the hospitals. A marked

[10] Later came the so-called Zhdanov decrees of 1948, when the attempt to harness all Soviet artistic activity to socialist realism became official. Shostakovich was accused of "bourgeois formalism" and other heinous crimes; appeals were made to him to write music that "the people could understand," instead of "deformities." Excitement over this reached such a point that the poet Sergei Mikhalkov wrote a play about it, which the Moscow Art Theater put on and which won a 100,000-ruble Stalin Prize.

favorite at the moment is Elvis Presley; others are Louis Armstrong, Rosemary Clooney, Frank Sinatra, and Patti Page.

A good deal of controversy attends jazz. The highest cultural authorities do not want the craze for American jazz to get out of hand, and are inclined to be critical of milder forms of foreign popular music as well. The Moscow Operetta Theater recently put on *Ball at the Savoy,* and the critics took it severely to task for doing so. "The very choice of this work testifies to a certain infatuation on the part of this theater with superficial performances of a *purely entertaining nature*" (italics mine). Instead, the directors are sternly urged to devote themselves to performances dealing with "our Soviet reality."[11] Everything to the service of the state!

The Second All-Union Conference of Soviet Composers took place in Moscow early in 1957, and was addressed by Comrade Dmitri T. Shepilov, who at that time was still a secretary of the Central Committee of the party. One passage in his speech, which was hours long, dealt with boogie-woogie and rock 'n' roll, which are compared to the "wild orgies of cavemen," and are "hysterical" and "raving." Also Mr. Shepilov paid his respects to aspects of music in the United States, and had a point:

> The U.S.A., this rich imperialist country, has less than a dozen opera houses, which keep their heads above water with great difficulty. They are open from one to five months a year. . . . In the very heart of New York, surrounded by huge skyscrapers finished in marble or aluminum, which belong to oil, steel and other monopolies, stands an old building covered with smudges. This is the Metropolitan Opera. I was told that this opera house (Washington has no opera and ballet theater at all) is maintained on music lovers' donations, which save it from bankruptcy. The question of selling the building at auction arises almost every year.

Then after a description of the Soviet composer's "social duty" comes a truly remarkable bit of balderdash: "Individualism is the worst enemy of freedom of creation."

*

The following is an extract from the lyric of a popular Soviet song of the moment. It is only fair to add that Mr. Shepilov has a low opinion of ditties of this type.

[11] *Current Digest of the Soviet Press,* August 21, 1957.

> A Negro is kissed ardently
> By two Italian girls
> Only he, in all Moscow, seems embarrassed;
> Everyone else cries, "More!"

Another:

> Marusya's lover is a locomotive engineer;
> Anyuta's lover builds wonder towns;
> Arina's friend plants new gardens;
> But Dunya's friend feeds pigs.
> I did wrong to send him packing;
> We have not seen the swineherd since.[12]

One afternoon I visited the Scriabin museum, and this was an enchanting experience, a glimpse of what Moscow must have been like before everything was sacrificed to the Moloch-state. Scriabin, one of the most romantic of modern composers, lived for many years in the building that now houses the museum. It has the aroma of old lace and frangipani. Then one day we had tea with Emil Gilels, the pianist. He looks like a tough, amiable woodchuck. I asked him how musicians were trained in the Soviet Union. Moscow, it seems, has no fewer than twenty-six junior schools for music students, as well as the great Conservatory.[13] Particularly talented children are allowed to go to other special music schools after regular school hours if their parents can afford them. All children must finish the ordinary ten-year school course before being admitted to a conservatory.

For an artist of the rank of Gilels concert tours are arranged much as in western countries, by contracts with the philharmonic societies. Two thousand rubles is the highest fee for a single concert. An artist is entitled to keep royalties from phonograph records, even if these are made abroad, as well as fees for performances on the radio or TV. Gilels and David Oistrakh, the violinist, are the two Russian virtuosi of the present day best known in America and Europe. But several others are almost as well regarded at home, like Mstislav Rostropovich (cello), Leonid Kogan (violin), and Sverdeslov Rikhter (piano). Kogan was scheduled to visit the United States in 1958.

Movies, TV, and the Popular Arts

Most present-day Soviet movies are pretty terrible. The note of stirring experimentation and freshness they once communicated has altogether dis-

[12] *Ibid.*, May 8, 1957.

[13] Students at the Conservatory are now obliged to study three courses which for a time had been dropped from the curriculum—political economy, history of the Communist party, and *diamat* or dialectical materialism. Even in the realm of music the regime takes no chances, and plays things safe.

appeared. Nothing is being produced even remotely comparable to the early Eisenstein and Pudovkin films, like *October* and *The End of St. Petersburg,* or of subsequent good movies like *The Road to Life* (1930), the first Russian sound film, which dealt with the *besprizorniki,* "wolf-children" who roamed city streets after the Revolution, or even *Chapayev* (1935), a classic picture about a hero in the civil war. Eisenstein was purged. (After many years, his name and that of his cameraman, Tisse, are sometimes mentioned nowadays in the Soviet press, so the presumption is that he will be rehabilitated; from being an "unperson" he will become a person again, even though dead.)

One reason why the current crop of Soviet films is so dismal is that most really bright people in the movie business were, as in other countries, Jewish. These fell into disfavor during the Stalin "anticosmopolitan" campaign and, even if not actually shot or purged, lost their jobs. Some have come back, but the quality of films has not. Socialist realism rules, and nobody dares to make pictures with artistic zeal or point.

For one new picture, the first Soviet wide-screen movie in color, the producers have gone all the way back to medieval Kiev, with the life of Ilya Muromets, a legendary hero, as the safe theme. The most widely acclaimed film of the moment is *The Forty-First,* which has a neat Hollywoodish plot with an even neater Soviet overlay. The heroine, Maryutka, is a fighter with Red Army partisans in the civil war; after furious adventures she is marooned on an island with an officer of the White Guards, her hated enemy. She falls in love with him and when, following a romantic interlude, a rescue party finds them, Maryutka not only decides that she must give up her Czarist lover, but shoots him to boot. He is the forty-first man whom this valiant Amazon has killed—hence the title.[14]

Visitors from the West are not the only people who find Soviet films slatternly; so do Soviet critics, who are outspoken in their demand for better films. But appeals in the press do not merely ask for better entertainment, but for more ideology as well. One such appeal, asking for truthful portraits of the Soviet man as "builder and creator of the new world," goes on to say, "Comrade workers in the film industry! Give us films in which a true Soviet

[14] Not all plots are so noisy. One recent picture, *She Loves You,* describes the mixups that occur when Kostya, the director of the local zoo, falls in love with Olya, a schoolgirl athlete; complications are provided by letters getting into the wrong envelopes, and similar almost sensationally tedious banalities. Nor are all themes so light; great things are expected of a new production of *Don Quixote,* starring one of the foremost Soviet actors, Nikolai Cherkasov. One popular current film is *Gospodin 420,* featuring the Indian star Raj Kapoor. Article 420 of the Soviet Penal Code deals with cheating, and the subject of the picture, a satire, may be readily imagined.

family is shown, in which the parents love and respect one another and bring up their children in Communist fashion, films in which the children enter upon life with a firm step!"[15]

One remarkable communication appeared in *Literaturnaya Gazeta* recently in the form of an open letter to the American producer, Michael Todd. It suggests that Mr. Todd, well known for his abortive attempt to make *War and Peace* in Russia, should demonstrate his continuing interest in cultural collaboration between the United States and the Soviet Union by arranging for a joint Russo-American film about *American* history in the Civil War period. The author of the letter, a well-known Soviet dramatist named Yury Krotkov, outlines his plot, and suggests that the characters include a Russian seaman, an American infantryman, Lincoln, Czar Alexander II, Lord Palmerston, a Russian admiral named Popov, the great Russian pamphleteer Chernyshevsky, and Napoleon III. The letter concludes cheerfully, "So now it's up to you, Michael Todd!"[16]

Eighty-five Soviet films were produced in 1956, as against an annual average of seven or eight during the Stalin blackness. Most stars are developed through the theater, and have fanatically devoted fans. There are said to be 58,000 cinema theaters in the country, many more than in the United States, but the average daily attendance is only about three million. In small towns (or even big) the film often breaks during a performance; audiences scream and shout, even as did American audiences many years ago.

*

The age of TV, like that of the automobile, is just beginning in the Soviet Union. There are only thirteen or fourteen regularly functioning TV stations,[17] and probably not more than 1,500,000 sets. On the other hand more antennae are sprouting on the roofs of buildings in Moscow and the other big cities day by day; very large expansion of the industry is hoped for.[18] We called one morning on Ivan I. Inozemtsev, director of the Moscow TV station, and he told us something of his problems. The tower of his station is only 160 meters high, and the studios (it isn't his fault) are amateurish-looking and shabby. The Moscow station has a range of less than a hundred kilometers; even so, Mr. Inozemtsev calculates that he reaches four million

[15] *Current Digest of the Soviet Press*, August 14, 1957.
[16] *Ibid.*, November 13, 1957.
[17] The United States has 496.
[18] The goal for 1960 is seven million sets. A new TV tower to be built in Moscow will (the authorities say) be five hundred meters high, the world's tallest structure.

people. One reason why the range is so limited is that there are only two coaxial cables in the entire Soviet Union, Moscow-Kalinin and Leningrad-Novgorod, short distances both. But Moscow will be connected with Leningrad quite soon.

The Moscow station transmits programs for four hours a day as a general rule: from 7 P.M. till 11 on weekdays, 8 to 12 on Saturdays, and 2 till about 6 on Sundays. This may not seem like much, but is average for continental Europe. Telecast times are not always adhered to strictly, and programs can go on or off at almost any time. The Moscow station has two channels, but one is still experimental. No telecasting takes place during the daytime (except on Sundays), not because of lack of material, but because almost everybody works in the Soviet Union, and there are no audiences to reach at home by day. The largest screen now being manufactured for home users is fourteen inches. One Soviet practice, which the western world might well imitate, is to release new feature movies to TV ten days after the first performance in a theater. In the United States, one may wait for ten years.

There are no commercials, unless government announcements can be considered to be commercials, no cheesecake, no disc jockeys, no soap operas, no adventure stories, no news shows like *See It Now*. Sixty per cent of all programs are live, and between 40-50 per cent originate in the studio. Programing is carefully worked out on a yearly basis. Ten per cent of annual telecast time goes to sport, 12 per cent to theater, 20 to music (whole operas are often presented), and 40 per cent to films. Children's programs get 10 per cent, news 4 per cent, and industry and science (including education) 2 per cent each.

*

One immensely popular and homely Soviet institution is the circus. All the big cities have circuses, and, like theaters, these have their own permanent buildings; all performances (so far as I know) are indoors, and there is no such thing as our big top. One ring is the rule. Some circus characters are national figures, like Karandash, who is one of the most accomplished clowns in the world. On occasion Karandash is too peppery for the authorities, and he goes out of circulation briefly. One of his most festive routines is to announce that a competition will be held for the best political joke from the audience. "First prize—twenty years." More recently he has been convulsing his audiences by coming into the ring with a small balloon, which explodes.

"What's that?" he is asked.

"A Sputnik." Pause. "You do not understand," he tells the audience. "That is the American Sputnik."

*

Some visitors to Moscow, even those well informed, think hopefully that they will see entertainment in the lavish old Russian manner—the "Volga Boat Song" sung by a chorus, or Circassian dancers in belted tunics crossed with cartridge pouches, bending their knees sharply in the familiar athletic movement known as the *vprisyadku*. Nothing of this sort exists. Everything of this sort has been exterminated. No bar, night club, dance hall, or music hall in our sense of the term is allowed to operate, and even dance orchestras are unknown except in a few hotels.

CHAPTER XVI

Some Social Patterns

Russia . . . an alien planet.
—LESLIE C. STEVENS

The nature of the true revolutionist excludes all romanticism, all tenderness, all ecstasy, all love.
—NECHAYEV AND BAKUNIN

Our teaching is not dogma. . . . Life will show us.
—LENIN

IN SOCIAL affairs, attitude toward the family, and similar matters a substantial reversion to conservatism has taken place in the Soviet Union, as in artistic affairs. The days when people talked about "nationalization" of women are as remote as those when orchestras tried to give concerts without a conductor. One illustration of this is the feeling about abortion. Years ago abortions were perfectly legal and, so to speak, free as air. They were outlawed in the late 1930's, partly as a measure to keep the birth rate up, but became legal again in 1956. A principal motive for legalization was to keep women from patronizing black market abortionists, who often performed the operation without proper safeguards, endangering health. Some women still go to the black market for abortions, in order to keep their names off the records, but doctors practicing illegal abortions are, if caught, severely punished, exactly as in bourgeois countries. Nor is abortion encouraged, even if it is legal. Moreover, although medical services in general are free in the Soviet Union, abortions must be paid for and the price is fairly steep for Russia, about a hundred rubles or twenty-five dollars.

There is incidentally no such thing as illegitimacy in the USSR. The concept is, in fact, entirely alien to Soviet law and morals. An unmarried girl with child gets exactly the same medical and maternity care (free) as does

329

a wife, with no stigma whatever attached.[1] Girls are, however, strongly encouraged to marry. One reason for this is the desire to recoup losses in population suffered during the war. On the other hand, contraceptives are legal in the Soviet Union, and can be bought anywhere; people say that they are of indifferent quality. The government wants more babies, but does not go out of its way to discourage birth control. Men and women are urged to marry and have a healthy, normal family life; if they do not want to have more children than they can comfortably support, that is their own affair, although special taxes are imposed on childless couples, also bachelors. If a woman *does* produce a great many babies, she is rewarded by bonuses (beginning with the fourth child) and a monthly stipend from the state ranging from 40 to 150 rubles; any who has ten children or more receives the Order of Motherhood Glory, and others are known as "Mother Heroines," First, Second, or Third Class.[2]

Casualties in the war caused—and still cause—profound human dislocations. So many men were killed that women in the middle thirties outnumber men of the same age today by a ratio of almost seven to one. I met a young woman, a widow, with a child aged fourteen, whose husband was killed at the front; it is practically a mathematical certainty that she will never remarry, and her case illustrates the fate of hundreds of thousands of women. No country has a greater man shortage than the USSR today in certain age groups. Also the birth rate fell sharply during and immediately after the war.

Another illustration of the prevailing mood of conservatism in social relations is divorce. This, as everybody knows, was in the old days granted automatically in the USSR. The old quip was, "Just marriage is grounds for divorce in Russia." The early revolutionaries prided themselves on the contempt with which they held the marriage relationship. In 1928 I knew a Russian girl, in her early thirties, who had been married seven times. Not only was divorce (in those days) granted at the simple request of either party, without notice having to be given and in a procedure that did not take more than three minutes, but a husband or wife could get a divorce without even informing the partner. All this has long since been supplanted, and the divorce rate in the Soviet Union is substantially lower than that in the United States. Marx predicted that the bourgeois family would "vanish as a

---

[1] Not only is hospitalization free but mothers with jobs receive 124 days' maternity leave with full pay. An unmarried woman having a child is known as a "single mother."

[2] About fifty thousand women hold the Order of Motherhood Glory.

matter of course," but nowadays the whole emphasis of Soviet legal and other procedure is to protect marriage and the family.

The situation at present is that, if a man or woman wants a divorce, he or she must go to a people's court (not merely a registration bureau) and make application in person. *Both* parties must appear; the procedure is laborious and expensive, with a sizable fee attached. This court has no power to grant a divorce, but only hears the preliminaries of the case; the usual practice, especially if children are involved, is for the judges to insist that the estranged husband and wife go through a "cooling-off period," during which time they will be expected to adjust their differences. If, however, reconciliation fails, the case may then be brought to another, higher court, and divorce will be granted, but only if the cause of dissatisfaction is adjudged to be "real" enough. Alimony may be substantial. Casual infidelity is not grounds for divorce, nor is mental cruelty. This procedure is so stringent that many Soviet sociologists and jurists are urging its relaxation, largely out of consideration for children. Easier divorces will enable more persons to remarry, and produce more children; moreover children of an unhappy marriage, in which parents are forced to continue to live together against their will, are likely to grow up unhappy and badly adjusted, a situation which the state authorities deplore.

Divorce is complicated; marriage is very simple. Young people who want to marry file an application at ZAGS, the registry office, and then wait ten days. The license costs 15 rubles ($3.75), and the ceremony is performed as a rule by a civil magistrate. The bride may, if she wishes, keep her own name, and bridegroom and bride are given three days' holiday from their jobs. Church weddings still occur, and in fact are increasing in number, as we shall see below.

Puritanism and Prostitution

Prostitution has virtually disappeared in the USSR, but surviving remnants may be seen. No call girls, brothels, or organized vice traffic exist, but streetwalkers still manage to do business along Gorkovo in Moscow, and in similar neighborhoods in other cities. Streetwalkers are, however, much less conspicuous than in many western cities, for instance London. One factor severely hampering prostitution is the housing shortage. Girls have no place to take customers; sometimes they use taxis, which circle a block or drive elsewhere for the period of time necessary. This repellent practice is not a Soviet invention; it was once quite common in parts of Asia, particularly Japan.

Trud recently published the following under the title "A Delicate Subject":

The visitor who came into the editorial offices was obviously upset. "I'd like to talk about a delicate subject," he said. "I don't know how you feel about it, but it can't be kept quiet—we can't just close our eyes to it in shame and pretend it doesn't exist. We stigmatize vices we inherited from the past, we prosecute hoodlums and thieves, we re-educate parasites. But as soon as this subject comes up we shame-facedly fall silent. You've probably guessed already what I'm talking about—the so-called women of easy virtue. Of course I can be told that they aren't typical of our society, that it's merely a matter of isolated instances. That's true—they are few in number. But they exist for all that, and we can't ignore the fact. Indeed, they are a shame to us, to our people. But we pass by unconcernedly, pretending that we don't notice this disgusting scum. Is this proper? Of course it isn't. We must speak out loudly about this."

Trud proceeds to expatiate on the subject. Nadezhda M. has just been picked up for soliciting. "She is not at all bashful; she is brazen, free-and-easy. And why did they [the militiamen] take her into custody? It isn't the first time. They give her a talking-to, then let her go. She isn't put in jail, isn't sent away; there is no law that covers her case. Investigation discloses that Nadezhda has a good profession—she does artistic needlework. She used to work, and made a good living, but she became enamored of restaurants and carousing, and it landed her on this dangerous and shameful path."

Then consider the case of Galina G. An illustration shows her in an automobile, half-hiding her face. The article says that she does this out of shame, but in fact she is cupping her chin and gazing at her captor in what seems to be friendly curiosity. "It wasn't so very long ago that Galina finished secondary school. She might have followed the example of other girls her age, who have gone off to develop the Virgin Lands in Siberia or to build cities or power stations or to study at institutes. But Galina chose a different path—streetwalking. . . . What has brought [these young girls] here? Hunger? Want? Nonsense! The very thought is ridiculous. All of them could earn an honest living if they wanted to. . . . How is it that Nadezhda, Galina, and their like go unpunished? Isn't it true that they flout the basic law of socialist society—that he who does not work does not eat?" And so on for more indignant words, ending with a stern demand for punishment.[3]

Soviet puritanism, Victorianism, is always a factor to be reckoned with, in these and other matters. Everything must have a purpose; nothing is to be done for joy. The moral concept extends even to language, and swearing is

[3] *Current Digest of the Soviet Press*, May 22, 1957.

supposed to be taboo, although the Russian language is extraordinarily rich in picturesque oaths and epithets, which are widely popular. *Izvestia* not long ago opened up on the use of bad language and said that it was not enough merely to rebuke foul-mouthed people. "We must seize them . . . and drag them to the militia, in accord with the law on petty hooliganism. And without any kind of kid-glove treatment."

Russians are a strongly sexed people, but sex is not supposed to be seen in public. Petting in a parked car, in the American manner, is almost unknown. (A recent Soviet visitor to the United States expressed outraged horror at the "deafening whistling and hooting" that takes place on American university campuses, when boys see a pretty girl stroll down the street.) Despite all this, the fact cannot be denied that a great deal of love-making goes on in the USSR, and that this starts at an early age. One day I had a festive, vivacious lunch in a hotel with a professor of engineering from the University and his wife. The professor spoke excellent English; his wife, an amiable woman, not a word. We had a considerable amount of vodka, and our talk became somewhat ribald. I asked the professor if he thought that any pretty girl in the Soviet Union over the age of sixteen was a virgin. Absolutely dead-pan, without comment, he translated my question to his wife. She gave a horrified shriek, and whacked him on the head with a napkin; otherwise the question went unanswered.

Homosexuality is, so far as the casual visitor can tell, practically unknown in the USSR. There may be a few homosexuals in the theater and ballet (it would be an odd ballet which did not have them), and probably a certain amount of homosexual practice goes on in Georgia and in the Moslem areas of the country. But there is no homosexual problem on a national basis even remotely comparable to that in several western societies. Homosexuality between males is a criminal act by Soviet law, and convicted offenders get stiff punishment.

Further Word about Women and Children

As is well known, almost all women in the Soviet Union work. I do not mean merely that they work in offices, schools, and hospitals; they do heavy manual work as well. Forty-five per cent of *all* jobs in the Soviet Union are held by women; women comprise more than 40 per cent of all industrial workers, and 30 per cent of all building workers, which means that they are construction laborers, steam fitters, crane operators, riveters, welders, what not.[4] Women do not, however, serve in the Soviet Army.[5] In theory, a woman can reach any political position in the state, but comparatively few achieve the highest posts. Still, 348 of the 1,347 deputies to the Supreme Soviet are women, and there are 8 women on the Central Committee of the party, which numbers 133. Some 205,000 women were engineers and 414,000 were technicians in 1956 (as against 600 in both categories in 1917), and 741 women have won Stalin or Lenin Prizes in science or the arts. Every convenient opportunity is taken to salute women and their doughty prowess. One of the few nonpolitical holidays in Russia is March 8, Woman's Day, when all women workers get off two hours early, which, when you come to think of it, does not make it much of a holiday.

Women, within the circumscriptions of Soviet puritanism, are being encouraged to prettify themselves; a good many primitive beauty shops exist in Moscow, and courses have even been set up to teach women how to use mild cosmetics, clean up their skin, and so forth. (Incidentally, very few Russian women smoke.) One extraordinary sight is the Dom Modeli, or fashion house, on Kuznetsky Most. This is the Soviet equivalent of Balenciaga or Christian Dior. Admission costs five rubles. There are three or four shows a day, with the mode demonstrated by four models—a child, a youthful girl, a woman of matronly proportions, and a man, who demonstrates male clothing. GUM, the biggest department store, has similar exhibitions, at which an orchestra plays. The procedure is for the prospective customer to watch, note down the number of whatever creation suits his or her fancy, and then go to another division of the shop and buy the appropriate pattern, price one ruble. This you take to your dressmaker, and the job is done.

It isn't easy for the designer to make something dashing, because of course there can never be any such thing as a partly exposed bosom or even a bare shoulder. The following is the text for a recent fashion illustration in *Soviet Woman*. The designer represents the Experimental Laboratory of the Moscow City Clothing Trust:

> Dress-and-jacket team. The dress is of unfigured wool and the jacket of a heavier, checked material (the checks matching the color of the dress). The dress is a narrow, form-fitting and sleeveless sheath, uncut at the waist, with zipper fasteners in the side seam and on the shoulder. It has tailoring folds at the waist in front. The scarf is trimmed with fringe. The loose jacket tapers slightly. The sleeves are stitched into the square armholes. A narrow strip of the dress material is inserted

---

[4] The authorities feel shame to an extent for the fact that women are still obliged to do heavy manual labor, and it is a paramount item in the contemporary creed that this will, in time, be eliminated.

[5] The only army I know in which women serve equally with men is the Israeli.

in the sleeve from shoulder to cuff. Slit and flapped pockets. Fastens with wooden buttons the color of the dress.

Soviet Woman also gives warnings to mothers of teen-agers as follows:

High heels have an adverse effect on the development of girls during this period. These bring the center of gravity forward and backward, which may affect the form of the pelvis and the position of the uterus.

Soviet children are, as has been pointed out several times in this book, well taken care of and favored; this is basic, bedrock policy if only because it is the coming generation which, in time, will rule the country; hence, youth must be healthy as well as disciplined. Children are the future of the nation; no wonder so much attention is paid to their gratification in fields all the way from books and theaters to medicine. Eyeglasses are—a curious small point—not often seen among adults in the Soviet Union, or at least appear to be much less common than in Great Britain or America; but I noticed many children wearing them. One peculiarly Russian characteristic is swaddling. From birth till about the age of nine months, an infant is as a rule kept completely swaddled, almost as if he were in a strait jacket, bound by strips of cloth that keep his legs rigid and his arms fixed to his sides. You can pick a baby up as if he were a log of wood. The reason, one must assume, is that this procedure makes children easier to handle.[6]

When a child is born, the father is allowed, by Soviet custom, to see him only once immediately after birth; then visits are forbidden for a week or longer, presumably to reduce the possibility of infection being brought to mother or child. If the mother lacks milk, the infant is fed from a "milk bank" provided by the hospital; formulas in our sense are unknown. One point of considerable bizarre interest is that diapers are not used. No Soviet mother has ever seen a diaper. When my wife visited a nursery school with Zoya, our interpreter, a mother herself, and asked about diapers, Zoya and the nurses were thunderstruck, and the conception and philosophy of diapers had to be explained to them. Russian infants are, we were told, expected to be toilet trained by the age of one, and similarly are supposed to be able to eat by themselves at this early age.[7]

[6] The well-known British sociologist Geoffrey Gorer suggests that swaddling plays a large role in the subsequent development of the child's character, and markedly influences the Russian temperament. Subconscious resentment at the confinement and frustration imposed by swaddling leads in later life to exaggerated impulses toward violence, guilt feelings, destructive rages, and tendencies toward "confession, atonement, and revenge." It would be interesting to know the reaction of Soviet psychologists to this theory.

[7] Favorite names for boys are Yuri and Alexander; for girls, Tanya, Anna, and Natasha. Recently protests have been heard in the Soviet press against the choice by

At about three months, when the mother is back at work, most Soviet infants are sent to a nursery school. Such schools are obviously a necessity, since nobody is at home to take care of a child, except in the comparatively few families which can afford a nurse or servant or where grandparents or other elderly relatives are available. The mother deposits the child at the nursery early in the morning, and picks him up in the evening, six days a week. A child is completely undressed on arrival at the nursery each morning, and wears clothes provided by the school during the course of the day; on going home he puts on his own things again. Children of women who work at night sleep at the nursery. These nursery schools are, almost without exception, clean, well serviced, and well equipped, at least in the bigger cities. At the age of three comes kindergarten, which takes the child until he is ready for regular school at seven. Children in kindergartens pay a tuition fee, ranging from twenty-five to a hundred rubles per month, if the parents can afford it.

Children are encouraged from the earliest days to respect their fathers and mothers. The practice of a generation ago, when this was not the case and dutiful youngsters were even supposed to have the duty of informing on their elders, has been altogether given up. Until about 1928 a child, on reaching the age of eighteen, was at liberty to disown his parents and change his name if he wished, and adopt any new name he liked. All such radical innovations have been dropped.

A Line about Religion

We attended church services several times in the Soviet Union—in Kiev, Tiflis, and at the great Bogoyavlensky Cathedral[8] in Moscow—and visited several other active churches. The main thing to say is that churches are crowded, but filled chiefly with very old people, mostly women. I had a feeling that people came to several partly to get out of the cold; in their miserable black shawls and ragamuffin boots they sat huddled on the floor, dazed, inert, and derelict. There was, however, strong evidence of devout worship in the bigger churches. Women prostrated themselves, and kissed icons greedily; old men wept as the magnificent choirs sang.

There were more than four hundred churches in Moscow alone before the Revolution; today, about thirty. The Orthodox Church was, of course,

---

parents of fanciful names. Children have been named "Ballerina," "Brillianta," "Unit of Society," and the Russian words for "I Didn't Want" and "I Didn't Expect." *Current Digest of the Soviet Press*, September 18, 1957.

[8] Sometimes known as the Yelokhovsky Cathedral.

disestablished soon after the Soviet government took power (on January 22, 1918, to be exact), and all church property was nationalized. The churches that survive today are supported by their own congregations, and must pay taxes. Religious instruction for anybody under the age of eighteen is forbidden in schools or institutions; it may, however, be carried on at home. The Soviet government is an atheist government, but, paradoxical as this may seem, Article 124 of the constitution guarantees "freedom of religious worship." It also guarantees "freedom of antireligious propaganda." A person is thus, in theory, equally free to go to church or join an atheist group.

Politically the situation is that the government has, so to speak, moved in on the church, but active persecution does not take place any longer. The regime tolerates the church for two main reasons: (a) to extend its hold on the people, many of whom are still profoundly religious, and (b) as an arm in foreign policy, because the Orthodox Church still has substantial power in several satellites, particularly Bulgaria. Khrushchev formalized this position in a statement in October, 1955, which to a degree extended the de-Stalinization process to religion. His general line was that religion is nonsense, alien to Marxism, but that if people wanted to worship it was their own business; plenty of good, sound religious believers are also good, sound Russian patriots, and should not be attacked on religious grounds.

The church, on its side, has had no option but to accept this *modus vivendi*, and it behaves with appropriate docility. Its head is His Holiness Alexei, Patriarch of Moscow and All the Russias. He was elected to this post in 1945, and, a very old man now, has little power. He is, however, treated with respect, and is occasionally seen at government receptions; when he issues a statement, it is duly printed in *Izvestia*. On New Year's Day, 1957, he managed at one and the same time to preach a text drawn from Corinthians, attack Israel for the invasion of Egypt, and talk about the "antipopular forces" which disturbed "peaceful life in Hungary." I wish I had the space to quote the entire message; it is really something. Except for its scattered references to God, it might well have been written by Bulganin. (Maybe it was.) More important than Alexei is the Metropolitan Nikolai, the second-ranking churchman in the country. He is Lithuanian by birth, and, even if he is not a member of the Communist party, certainly talks like one. He called Stalin "our dearly beloved leader," and says that Pope Pius XII is not merely "anti-Christian" but an "agent of American imperialism."[9]

So much for the church leadership. As to popular sentiment, it is clear that something akin to a religious revival is going on in the USSR, despite all

[9] *New York Times*, June 4, 1956.

obstacles. Religious impulses in people, like impulses toward political liberty, cannot be permanently, totally thrust down in any country. If any spark of protest survives at all, it may seek religion as the outlet. One authority states that the number of baptisms has doubled since Stalin's death in 1953. There were 46,000 churches and 50,000 priests in Russia before the October Revolution; by 1935, only 4,000 churches and 5,000 priests were functioning, but the figures for 1956 were 20,000 churches and 35,000 priests.[10] Several academies and seminaries have been permitted to reopen, where young men study for the priesthood in limited numbers. A picturesque point is that more and more young people in country villages (but not in the big towns) demand church weddings, if only because these are festive occasions, and serve to give the community a chance to break away from the prevailing monotony and take a holiday. The whole village celebrates. A recent note in *Komsomolskaya Pravda* says that Lvov province, in the Ukraine, had four thousand church weddings last year, as against only forty-five performed under the auspices of the Young Communist League. On the other hand, almost all youths of the intelligentsia think of the church with open contempt.

Party zealots hotly resent the revival of religion, such as it is. When a new industrial city is built, no provision is made for churches. Editorial writers give forth grave warnings to the effect that religious celebrations lead to "violations of labor discipline," and urge that the Society for the Dissemination of Political and Scientific Knowledge increase its atheist propaganda. One newspaper said recently, "We do not use the radio to propagandize atheism; this is a mistake." Another points out sternly that, as an example of laxness prevalent all over the country, "No scientific lectures on atheism were given during 1956 in the villages of Staraya Sol and Sushitsa in the Staro-Samborsk district of Drogobych province, and the Palace of Culture of the October Revolution Mine in the town of Shakhta did not give a single lecture on atheism in all of 1957."[11] One thing is certain: the church will never be permitted to regain the prodigious economic power it once had. The Zagorsk monastery was at one time the largest landowner in all Russia. People still feel about this kind of thing deeply, whether they are Communists or not. One young man in Leningrad, who was certainly not a Communist, told us, "The church robbed the people in the name of the landlords; it was the right hand of the Czar."

One could continue on this subject, with its various paradoxes and com-

[10] "Religion Will Survive in Russia," by Dr. Walter W. Van Kirk, *Collier's Magazine*, June 8, 1956.
[11] *Current Digest of the Soviet Press*, September 4, 1957.

plexities, almost without end. It was interesting to see that the Chapel of the Iberian Virgin, near Red Square in Moscow, has been torn down; after the Revolution it bore Lenin's famous inscription, "Religion is the opium of the people." It was also interesting to learn that Stalin's wife, along with a surprising number of other Soviet dignitaries, is buried in the courtyard of the Novodevichy Monastery in Moscow, no less. A large portrait of Lenin stands behind the desk of the chief religious functionary at Zagorsk, the holiest place in Russia. His fellows of older days would have turned in their graves at this; but so would Lenin. Bibles are now being printed again by the Patriarchate, but, so far as I know, they are not on public sale in Russia, although some are exported to the United States and other countries to serve Russian communities abroad. One thing that struck me is that Christmas, even if it is not an official holiday, is widely observed; Christmas trees, decorated in the western manner, appear all over the place, but are known as New Year's trees; a robust red-cheeked, white-bearded Santa Claus, indistinguishable from ours but called Grandfather Frost, is to be seen on ornaments and "Christmas" cards.[12]

*

Czarist Russia in 1914 had approximately 6,200,000 Jews, which was roughly half the Jewish population of the world at that time; it is difficult to calculate the number of Jews in the USSR today, but a reasonable estimate is 2,500,000. The Soviet government is not responsible for this immense shrinkage. For one thing half the Jews in the Russia of the Czars lived in what is now Poland, and became Polish subjects after World War I. For another, hundreds of thousands of the Jews remaining on Russian territory inhabited areas occupied by the invading Germans in World War II, and were exterminated in Nazi gas chambers.

Russian history has, it must be said, had an ugly, persistent streak of anti-Semitism for generations. Pogroms and outright massacres, like those in Czarist days, do not, of course, occur any longer, but the position of most Jews in contemporary Russia, in particular those of the older generation who have Yiddish roots, is very far from being comfortable. In 1948-52 came the Stalin "anticosmopolitan campaign," which was directed in theory against

[12] Several Protestant churches and one Roman Catholic church still survive in Moscow. If an American or other foreign clergyman happens to visit one of the Protestant churches, he will almost certainly be requested to preach, and will get a warm reception. In fact visiting Americans who are not ministers at all are often asked to preach.

all "rootless foreigners," but which was aimed at Jewry in particular. Yiddish newspapers and theaters were closed down, and evidences of Yiddish culture wiped out; Jewish editors, writers, and artists were purged wholesale, and fierce discrimination was exerted against Jews in a multitude of other fields. Anti-Semitism was, in a word, open, active, and virulent.

The situation is not so bad today, but is still bad enough. Jews are frightened and feel discrimination and the threat of oppression, except the comparatively small number who have reached important posts in science, the bureaucracy, or the arts. The Orthodox community is, it would seem, better off than the proponents of Yiddish culture, although very few synagogues are open, and Moscow, which has a total Jewish population of about 300,000, has only one Kosher butcher shop. The Russian authorities pay little attention to Orthodox Jews. Hebrew culture has never been conspicuous in Russia. Khrushchev hopes apparently that all Jews will gradually lose their identity, and be assimilated. The Jews are, it is significant to note, the only nationality in the Soviet Union not permitted to use their own language in education and culture. The Yiddish movement was very strong in the early days of the Soviet Union, and Yiddish schools and theaters flourished. Since about 1955 Yiddish concert artists, folk singers, monologists, and the like have been permitted to perform again, but the Yiddish language remains outlawed so far as education and the printed word are concerned. The ban on Yiddish newspapers still holds. Yiddish books are being published again, but only in Russian translation.

On the other hand, a few ameliorations have come lately to the Jewish community. The Chief Rabbi of Moscow, Solomon Shliffer, worked closely with the government, as indeed he had to, and won several recent concessions, for instance the establishment in Moscow of a Yeshiva, or school for Jewish religious education, and permission to publish the first Jewish prayer book to be issued in Russia since the Revolution.[13]

Israel is an exacerbating factor. The Soviet authorities are strongly anti-Zionist, which adds to the general anti-Semitic picture. No Russian Jews are permitted to go to Israel, not even as visitors.[14] The USSR government would, of course, deny categorically that it is guilty of anti-Semitism. Mr. Khrushchev told Mrs. Eleanor Roosevelt that "if a member of the Com-

[13] *New York Times*, April 2, 1957. Rabbi Shliffer died in 1957.
[14] The Russians do not, however, concede that they have always been anti-Zionist. The Soviet government voted for the establishment of Israel as an independent state. What it dislikes is that Israel is, in its view, a "cat's-paw" of the "imperialistic" powers. Also of course the Soviet Union takes these days a pronounced pro-Arab line.

munist party were known to be anti-Semitic" no other Communist would even shake hands with him.[15] He mentioned that Jews had high rank in the Soviet Army, that a Jew was buried in the Kremlin wall, and, interestingly enough, that his own son, who was killed in the war, was married to a Jewish girl. Despite statements of this sort, Khrushchev is generally thought, on good evidence, to have a marked personal anti-Semitic tinge, which dates back to his days in the Ukraine. Once in Warsaw he is supposed to have warned Gomulka about having too many "Rabinoviches" (Jews) in his circle. He told one interviewer, not Mrs. Roosevelt, that the Jewish community, being international, could not be considered trustworthy in the event of war, and that the only three Soviet tourists who had ever failed to return to Russia after trips abroad were Jews.

Shortly after the Suez crisis Jews in Bukhara, deep in Central Asia, signed a manifesto "Hands off Egypt!" expressing their "profound indignation" at the Israeli invasion of the Sinai Peninsula, and saying that such an action was contradictory to holy Scripture and religious ethics. Even the Buddhist priesthood in the USSR was requested to give similar expression to its "profound indignation" at the "treacherous invasion of Egypt" by the Israeli forces, which contravened *Buddhist* principles. Everybody in the Soviet Union is mobilized to serve the end in view; everybody is put to use in this cold inferno of a country.

Bits and Pieces about Crime and Law

The Soviet Union has plenty of crime, but most is petty. Arson (a favorite Russian crime in the old days), robbery with arms, rape, and even burglary are rare; the crimes that occur most often are embezzlement, black market operations, speculation, hooliganism, and minor swindling. Punishment, no matter what the crime, is apt to be severe. The death penalty for murder, after having been abolished for some years, was restored in 1954; some very fancy murders of the *crime passionnel* type are committed in the Soviet Union from time to time, as well as plain murders arising out of violence. The longest term of imprisonment ("deprivation of freedom") is twenty-five years. In Kazakhstan not long ago a drunken driver who killed a man was given the death penalty. This is believed to have been the first instance in Soviet history of a man being sentenced to death for a crime committed in connection with an automobile.[16]

[15] *New York Post*, October 8, 1957. The Jew in the Kremlin wall must be Sverdlov.

[16] New York *Herald Tribune*, April 5, 1957.

Crime news gives much oblique revelation of Soviet character and circumstances. Stories are never sensationalized, and seldom get big headlines. The following, from *Sovetskaya Rossiya*, is an example:

"Do you have fancy shoes?"
"Of course."
The customer looked the shoes over and thought they were rather crude.
"Don't you have anything better?"
"This, dear citizen, is a first-class product," the saleswoman said without batting an eye. "Better take it while you can."
Store No. 40 of the Workers' Supply Division of the Moscow Coal Combine, where this conversation took place, is at Uzlovaya Station. It is a busy place and the store was doing well. In the evening saleswoman Ye. Nikiforova would come to store manager A. Sverzhin and say:
"Well, Alexander Ilyich, today hasn't been bad. We made 50,000 on shoes. Here's the money. I've kept a few thousand for myself."
These swindlers selling at exorbitant prices were extremely lucky for a long time. Sverzhin waxed bolder and took 400,000 rubles from the store, hoping he could cover the shortage from the returns on the sales. He was unable to do this, however, because he and saleswoman Nikiforova were arrested.
An investigation showed that the store received shoes from a sporting goods *artel* [co-operative] in the village of Sadovniki, in Lenino District of Moscow Province. This . . . provided the store with mass-produced shoes but had an agreement with Sverzhin:
"Sell the shoes as fancy, give us 75% of the difference in price and keep the rest for yourself."
The criminals will soon go on trial.[17]

Sometimes sentences unduly severe are reduced by higher courts. Two men in Belorussia stole nineteen geese (value 529 rubles) in March, 1957. Because they had performed this theft together, which made the crime a "conspiracy," they were given fifteen years and ten years respectively. On appeal, the sentences were modified.

Youngsters get into trouble too:

There lived in Kiev two friends; both were novitiates at a seminary. One day they walked into a bar and decided to slake their thirst—with vodka. . . .
Subsequently the novitiates, wandering from bar to bar, blundered . . . and walked straight into the borough dispensary. . . .
The friends shoved aside the people who were waiting and made their way up to the doctor's door. But the door was shut. The novi-

[17] This and the following items are from the *Current Digest of the Soviet Press*.

tiates, incensed, broke down the oaken door and burst into the doctor's office.

"Clear our heads, doctor—chase the devil away," the tipsy novitiates begged the physician.

The people's judge of the Second Precinct of Podolsky Borough "cleared" the novitiates' heads for them; they were both given 15 days in jail for petty hooliganism.

Herewith a story from the Lithuanian-language newspaper *Tiesa*:

Vilnius [Vilna] residents who happened to walk down Gorky Street were sometimes astonished to see a queue of people at one of the stores. Jadvyga Stefanaviciene was often among them. Like the others, she was waiting her turn to buy a sewing machine. When this experienced speculator finally managed to buy a sewing machine, she immediately sold it to someone in the same queue . . . at double the price.

The people's court, having heard the case of Jadvyga Stefanaviciene, sentenced her to three years' deprivation of freedom.

The following item from Latvia might have been raw material for Dostoevsky:

On the night of Feb. 6 several people were drinking on the upper landing of the stairway at 24 Leona Paegle Street. They were Konstancija Ermanis, born in 1914; Velta Berzins, born in 1920 (both had been tried before); Stanislav Novik, born in 1924, a sanitary technician of the Moscow Borough Construction Repairs Office in Riga; and an unidentified man.

A little later Lev Ivankovsky, born in 1939, and George Novoseltsev, born in 1936—both without regular jobs—joined the group. Novik, Ivankovsky and Novoseltsev threatened the stranger with violence and robbed him. Later they were all still drinking together in Apartment No. 2, where the superintendent of the house, Rolans Aizpurs, lived.

The drinking and arguments, and also motives of robbery, led L. Ivankovsky and G. Novoseltsev to inflict mortal knife blows on the unidentified man and on K. Ermanis and the superintendent, R. Aizpurs, and to wound V. Berzins gravely.

Thanks to energetic measures on the part of the criminal investigation workers, the murderers were arrested at four o'clock on the same day at the Riga railroad station. Railroad tickets to Moscow and a suitcase with the belongings of the unidentified murdered man were found on them. . . .

The murderers and robbers will soon stand trial.

The unidentified man killed by Ivankovsky and Novoseltsev was 170 cm. tall and black-haired, with gray streaks in his hair and a small bald patch. His left index finger has no nail. On the left leg there is a scar resulting from an old bullet wound. He was dressed in a blue double-breasted suit with white stripes, a dark gray cap, black cloth topcoat, and boots, the tops of which had been cut off.

One could go on indefinitely. A currier in a Vilna fur plant stole twenty-nine calfskins; he got seven years. A girl in charge of a lunchroom in Georgia embezzled fifty thousand rubles; sentence was thirteen years. A gang in a shoe factory at Zaraisk got away with "stacks of high-quality hides"; twenty-five years. A doctor in Riga performed a criminal abortion, and the patient almost died; two years. A sawmill operator behaved like a "feudal lord," and sold three thousand rubles' worth of state timber for private profit; ten years. A boy in Frunze stole a bicycle; five years. A Moscow chauffeur had false license plates; four years. A lawyer in Minsk sought to bribe a police official; three years. A boy in Kiev picked a worker's pocket, and got ten rubles; six years. A Lithuanian carpenter beat his landlady to death with a hammer; death.

The Soviet police, interestingly enough, do not catch everybody—at least not right away. A newspaper in Turkmenistan announced recently that a young woman cashier who absconded with the payroll of an oil-drilling trust in 1952 had finally been caught, after four years of search. Another point is that wartime traitors and collaborators are still being sought and rounded up. A man named Ivanov joined the Nazis in 1942, betrayed the motherland, and tortured and killed Soviet citizens. After the war he sought to escape detection by enlisting in the Soviet Army. He was not found out and caught till 1956, when he was promptly tried and executed.

For larger realms in Soviet law we have, unhappily, no space. De-Stalinization has brought substantial reforms; for instance the All-Union Ministry of Justice was abolished in 1956, and its functions taken over by ministries in the various republics, in an effort to decentralize the administration of justice. A strong effort has been to regularize judicial procedure, and to divorce the courts from the secret police. Nobody is apt to be arrested nowadays unless he breaks some *law*. Moreover fundamental changes in Soviet law, while not yet in full effect, are being worked out. The process of "trial by confession" has, in theory at least, been eliminated, and arbitrary powers of the public prosecutor reduced. *Izvestia* has even got around to urging that the principle that a man is innocent until proved guilty, something basic to all western ideas of law, should be "guaranteed" by Soviet law.

Americans should not be too self-righteous in their attitude toward Soviet law, crime, and public morality. More than 2,700,000 *major* crimes were committed in the United States in 1957, the highest number on record and one that vastly exceeds the analogous figure for the USSR. Nobody has ever bribed a traffic cop in the Soviet Union, or fixed a parking ticket. There is no such thing as a numbers racket, labor unions are not contaminated by criminal goons, and nobody has ever, like Mr. Anastasia, been removed from the earthly scene by being shot by persons unknown in a barber's chair.

One should also point out that, in our sense, the USSR has no civil liberties. The right of free protest on basic issues fundamental to the operation of a good society does not exist in the Soviet Union, and the Soviet Union cannot be considered to be an adult, civilized country until it does.

Sport

Sport, like everything else in the Soviet Union, is made to serve the national interest. Patriotic and utilitarian factors are always stressed. Physical culture, athletics, games, and sport are not merely popular for their own sake—the country is sport-crazy—but are assiduously fostered by the government. All sport affairs in the nation are directed by a commission attached directly to the Council of Ministers; this is as if the United States had a cabinet post devoted to sport in Washington, with complete authority over every athletic endeavor in the country. The reason for the intense Soviet preoccupation with sport is double. First, athletic training makes healthy citizens, who are therefore capable of more and better work, the most important of all desiderata in the Soviet Union. Second, prowess in athletics is effective propaganda abroad. Also games like chess sharpen wits.

The two games most popular in the USSR are football (soccer) and chess. Golf is unknown, because it is considered to be effete, and tennis is not widely played as yet. If, however, Russia should ever enter such a competition as the Davis Cup, it would learn to turn out good tennis players quickly enough. Enormous numbers of young people—in fact, people of all ages— go in for sport in the Soviet Union. More than nineteen million athletes belong to various clubs devoted to competitive outdoor sports; of these no fewer than 2,900,000 are good enough to hold medals. Of course local standards are not necessarily very high. There are two million active football players, organized on a pyramidal basis; the leading clubs, like Dynamo and Torpedo, have a prestige like that of pennant-winning baseball teams in America, with rabid fans and followers. The Ukraine alone has more than sixty *thousand* soccer teams, of which five thousand are said to be "of good quality."[18] The country as a whole has 3,900,000 chess players good enough

[18] "I Must Admit—Russian Athletes Are Great," by Avery Brundage, *Saturday Evening Post*, April 30, 1955.

to belong to organizations, 3,500,000 track and field athletes, 2,500,000 skiers, and no fewer than 900,000 trained gymnasts and 600,000 swimmers.

The Soviet Union won the 1956 Olympics, both at Cortina and Melbourne, more or less for the same reason that it was the first country to put Sputniks into the sky—by fixity of aim, zeal, and a rigorous concentration of national effort imposed on good raw material. Several *million* Soviet athletes took part in Olympic tryouts—first in local athletic organizations, which exist in the remotest farms and villages, and then on the district and republic level. Of these, 9,224 were chosen to take part in a Moscow tournament, a kind of pre-Olympic tryout, called the Spartakiad of the Nations of the USSR. Then, after further careful winnowing, the best were selected to get intensive and exhaustive Olympic training. Of course, by our standards, these athletes can hardly be considered to be amateurs; the Russian government denies that any are subsidized directly but certainly their upkeep and training are provided for by the state while they are in competition.

Soviet athletes are classified into divisions, the highest being "Master of Sport." To get into this category a man must be good, and no mistake about it. Qualification for the 100-meter sprint, is, for instance, 10.4 seconds, just short of the world's record; for the 800-meter, 1.49 minutes; for the pole vault, 4.40 meters; and for the decathlon, 7,500 points. Curiously enough the Soviet Union, before it became interested in sport, sneered at records as being "bourgeois," and attacked the "disease of record-breaking"; physical culture was held to be an end in itself. But times change, even in the USSR, sport has become an implement of national policy, and winners cannot be an asset unless they do break records. Another odd point is that sport is called "active rest," a nice Soviet neologism.

Vox Populi

Protests and complaints, as I have several times pointed out in these pages, are incessant and vociferous in the USSR. Here are a few culled from the Soviet press within the past year or so, out of literally thousands available. Can Russians yell!

Author of Complaint	Object
Official of Highway Division No. 17, Semipalatinsk	Not enough snowsweepers, trucks, and tractors.
Izvestia correspondent, Voroshilovgrad	*Blat* ("pull") in assignment of workers to housing space.

Author of Complaint	*Object*
Art Student, Moscow	Inferior quality of clay in sculpture class.
Deputy from Latvia to Supreme Soviet	Absurdly excessive demands by Moscow for production in Riga Machine Repair plant.
Deputy from Estonia to Supreme Soviet	Pitchforks and spades received from Gorky so inferior as to be useless.
Central Committee of Kazakh Communist Party	"Formalistic," "bureaucratic," and "inhumane" behavior by local newspaper editor.
Housewife, Dnepropetrovsk	Delays in putting children's playground into shape.
Topographer, Leningrad	No time to go to movies or enjoy life. ("But perhaps I do not know what real life is.")
Letter writer, Frunze	Bureaucratic bungling and critical breakdown in school and hospital building program.
Writer in *Kommunist*	Dull methods in teaching Marxism-Leninism in party schools.
N. S. Khrushchev, speech to Party Congress	"Seat-warmers" among executives, inefficiencies in transportation; "intolerable" conditions in agricultural colleges.
City officials, Yalta	Medicine in short supply.
Letter writer, Tula province	Wages of miners spent on liquor; obscene ditties sung in restaurant.
Letter writer, *Sovetskaya Pechat*	Journalist was sent from Moscow to study at an institution in Alma-Ata which did not exist.
Letter writer, *Izvestia*	Dull uniformity of labels on vodka and other bottles.
Editorial writer in *Meditsinsky Rabotnik*	Only 20 per cent of pregnant women entitled to leave get full amount of leave as provided by law.

Author of Complaint	Object
Correspondent to *Pravda* from Turkmenistan	Flagrant violation of party democracy in meetings of Ashkhabad party committee.
Lawyer, Lvov	Unprincipled behavior by public prosecutor.
Izvestia correspondent in Krasnoyarsk	Scandalous mismanagement in construction of oil industry enterprise; broken promises on housing.
Specialist on folk art	"Intolerable indifference" by the authorities to training of folk song choruses in villages.
Writer in *Literaturnaya Gazeta*	Splendid airplanes like TU-104; no power-driven armchairs for invalids.
Deputy from Yakut ASSR	Administrative bungling. ("It is incomprehensible why this . . . has not penetrated the consciousness of Comrade Averev, the Minister of Finance, in the course of decades.")

One reason why such widespread criticism is permitted—in fact encouraged—is that it acts as a safety valve. Criticism seldom, if ever, touches politics, basic policy, or the fundamental concepts of the regime, but is directed against particular shortcomings, especially against red tape and inefficiency in the bureaucracy. The party sees to it that it does not become antiparty. Even so, protests reach a high level on occasion. The following is from a statement to the Supreme Soviet by D. A. Kumayev, Chairman of the Council of Ministers of Kazakhstan:

The Kazakh republic produced more than three-fourths of the lead, forty per cent of the zinc, and more than forty per cent of the black copper produced in the Soviet Union in 1956. . . . However, success in exploiting this wealth . . . is blocked to a large extent. . . . Clearing of plans among the ministries concerned are dragged out for many years.

A ton of ore costs two-thirds to one-half as much at the Dzhezkazgan deposit as at other deposits, and yet extremely little is being done to develop this major deposit. The Ust-Kamenogorsk lead mill . . . produces a considerable part of its lead from raw material hauled in from other republics, and meantime the Zyryanovsk deposit is practically right alongside this enterprise. However, work did not start on building a Zyryanovsk mine for a long time. And why was that? Simply because of bureaucratic delays in planning . . . and red tape. . . .

The Kirov Chemical Combine at Aktyubinsk processes costly raw materials brought in from the Kola Peninsula when a wealth of local resources is not being used. . . . The situation [elsewhere] is even worse.

The Karaganda Metallurgical Combine has been under construction for ten years now, with only 12 per cent of the work . . . completed in that time. How many more years will it take before this plant is put into operation?[19]

The Human Equation

So much in the Soviet Union is barren, sour, and grim that one forgets on occasion how profoundly, incorrigibly human most Russians are. Anything "human" comes as a relief, and the newspapers are full of personal stories, anecdotes of good fortune or bad, tidbits about ways of life, instances of generosity and humor, that strikingly reflect lighter aspects of the national mood. One I saw recently describes an eagle that was poisoned by eating insecticide in a gopher trap, and the grief this brought to a community. It would have been a front-page feature in almost any American newspaper. Another tells the story of a father who buys his ten-year-old daughter a pair of expensive shoes; but they are made of cardboard, and fall apart in three days. The father trudges laboriously out to the factory that made them, to register a complaint. The manager gives him a new pair, decorated in gilt, to help assuage his daughter's disappointment. But these fall apart as well!

Time and again I have come across incidents in Soviet newspapers that would make perfect Chekhov stories, or characters that seem to step straight out of Gogol. The following from Sovetskaya Rossiya should be reproduced at length:

> Excitement reigned in the railroad station restaurant in Novosibirsk.
>
> Chabanova, manager of the dining room, breathlessly ran up to one employee after another and whispered some startling news in his ear.
>
> "Are you sure?"
>
> "It can't be!"
>
> "Sensational!"
>
> When the news reached Rukhman, assistant manager of the restaurant, panic broke out.
>
> "Make a general cleanup immediately," Rukhman thundered out. "Have the chefs change their caps. More fat in the soup! We're being visited by—"

[19] Current Digest of the Soviet Press, quoting Pravda, March 20, 1957.

Who had come to the Novosibirsk restaurant? The examiner? The trade inspector?

A middle-aged man dressed in good taste and carrying a large leather briefcase was already sitting at one of the tables in the restaurant.

Beckoning to the waitress, he said to her with injured dignity:

"How is it, my dear, that you serve the ordinary passengers while I, the Deputy Minister of Trade, have to wait?"

These words echoed like thunder on a still night.

The assistant manager of the restaurant, and behind him the entire retinue of helpers and waiters, ran up to the exalted guest, apologizing, bowing and scraping.

"You're the—Please don't be upset," Rukhman spluttered. "Wouldn't you like to move to a separate, official table?"

"I would," grumbled the exalted guest in reply.

But, heavens, the Deputy Minister, it seems, wanted to jot down some notes on the [conduct of the] assistant manager. He unearthed his notebook and took a whole stack of papers out of his pocket. An imposing document with a gold stamp and a used TU-104 ticket could be seen among them.

The situation was saved by the opportune arrival of Usatyuk, the manager of the restaurant.

"We are honored by this attention—Please try the caviar—I venture to beg you to speak to our staff on the tasks of the moment. Trade in the light of the general world situation, so to speak."

Meanwhile the news of the Deputy Minister's arrival quickly spread beyond the bounds of the restaurant. He was suddenly given a separate room at the railroad station hotel. A car spun him now to the tailor's, now to the department store, now to the theater. The Deputy Minister, it turned out, was a most endearing fellow. What an education! What manners! He made friends quickly, displaying a special predilection for the ladies.

"Ah, Anna Andreyevna! Ah, Maria Antonova! Don't you like your job? Why don't you say something about it, then, my dear?"

Or:

"Your daughter didn't get into the institute? It will be arranged. I can do anything! You know, I have 30,000 messengers alone!"

What a bustle there was around the Deputy Minister of Trade in Novosibirsk! Only yesterday he gave an official address. . . . Now he is expected at a conference of railroad restaurant employees. Usatyuk, the manager of the restaurant, and Rukhman, his assistant, have arranged things: the hall is filled to overflowing. Usatyuk, applauding expectantly, officially announces:

"And now a word from Deputy Minister of Trade—pardon me, your last name?"

"Ragmm," the excited guest murmured indistinctly.

There was more applause, enthusiasm, bowing, and scraping.

"It would be advisable for us to be cautious," said Pugacheva, the restaurant's secretary and typist. "This Deputy Minister seems very suspicious to me. Have you seen his documents?"

"What documents?" Rukhman interrupted her. "You can recognize a man like that without documents!"

But Pugacheva insisted.

The "Deputy Minister" was hauled before the railway militiaman on duty. He reached for the imposing document with the gold stamp and took out—a certificate of release from prison![20]

Factors of Assent and Discontent

There are beyond doubt thousands of Soviet citizens today who would be delighted to see Khrushchev and company hanged upside down by their heels. On the other hand, the possibility of actual revolt or counterrevolution is almost inexpressibly remote.

To analyze this situation, we must first consider elements of *assent.* One of the most difficult of all questions to answer in the Soviet Union is whether or not the regime has the passive assent, if not actual support, of a majority of the people. I have talked to specialists who have devoted their lives to Russian studies; one will answer a flat "yes," another a flat "no." The subject must be approached from at least three different levels—age, nationality, and occupation. Surviving older folk, who knew Russia before the Revolution, probably still hate the regime as much as they ever did, although they may be grudgingly proud of some of its achievements. Among national groups, the Georgians are probably the most dissatisfied; next the Estonians and Letts. No adult citizen of the Baltic states before World War II, unless a Communist (and there were extremely few Communists in the Baltic area at that time), can possibly view the Soviet Union with anything but bitter distaste; this derives not only from hatred of Communism, but hatred of Russia. Also there are almost certainly islands of dissatisfied Ukrainians, Belorussians, Armenians, and Azerbaijanese, particularly among the in-telligentsia.

The bureaucracy as a whole is, so far as one can tell, loyal, and so are the industrial managers and the army. An immense number of citizens have, it must always be kept in mind, a strong vested interest in the regime; moreover these comprise the most important and influential elements of the population. An immense number of others, even if their vested interest is small, have, if they are under sixty, never had any adult experience of any other regime; also, except in the lowest category of industrial workers, they

[20] *Current Digest of the Soviet Press,* October 2, 1957.

are probably better off than their fathers were. Probably, all in all, the most disaffected section of the population, from the point of view of occupation, is the peasantry.

Of course discontent has always existed in the Soviet Union, without question; if not, millions would not have fled or attempted to flee during the war, and there would never have been any need for an elaborate secret police. One factor today is that, up to a certain level, citizens have more opportunity to *express* discontent than they have ever had before; hence discontent may not be as lively in reality as it appears to be at present. Russians are, strange as it may seem, to some degree a docile people, apathetic and inert. Many have an ingrained tendency to obedience, and many, especially those in technical jobs, are not too badly off. Children of illiterate families have, as we know, been given unexampled opportunity to live productive lives. And one must always remember Russian pride, a characteristic so basic that it can even include support of unpopular institutions, so long as these are thought to be Russia's own. A prevailing mood is of nonactive resentment, skepticism, and, to an extent, disassociation with what is going on.

Hungary was a stiff jolt to the Kremlin, if only because it indicated that two elements in society on which the Communists counted most—youth and the working class—proved to be unreliable. But the Soviet Union is not Hungary, at least not yet. Recently, but before events in Hungary, a group of specialists at Harvard University conducted a comprehensive, acute, and fair-minded analysis of Soviet attitudes. What the Russian people want most, it seems, is new clothes. What they dislike most is (a) the police and (b) collectivization of agriculture. They approve in general of industrialization, military achievements, and the welfare-state aspects of the Soviet system. The report says, "For the average citizen, political loyalty to the regime is a strange compound of apathy, passive acceptance, and cynicism." Dissatisfaction and discontent exist, but there seems to be only a relatively small amount of active "disaffection and disloyalty." In conclusion, "There is scant evidence for the view that more than a very tiny part of the population would, except under circumstances of extreme crisis, take appreciable risks to sabotage the regime or aid western democracy."[21]

Students are a question mark. The youth, it would seem, contains both the most conformist and most nonconformist elements in the nation. The Harvard Report says that the youth, along with the white-collar class, is the "most satisfied" group, but this situation may have changed substantially by now. In any case examples of student unrest have been conspicuous lately.

[21] Harrison E. Salisbury in the *New York Times*, July 29, 1956.

Mostly this is based on the desire of young people to know more about what is going on in the world, as in Hungary, and to find out things for themselves, about everything from Pavlov to Picasso, rather than be told. Recently at a Leningrad institute seven different teachers had to be hired one after another within a few months, because students simply would not listen to teachers who they thought were not telling them the truth. Whether student unrest has reached the point of actual conspiracy is unknown. No means of political organization exist; there may, however, be a few scattered secret societies, which circulate handwritten "newspapers" or even rudely printed poems and pamphlets, as in Dostoevsky's day.

One of the most astute observers I met in Russia said, "The Soviet Union will collapse, if it ever does collapse, of boredom." This is, of course, an overstatement, but it contains a spark of truth. People want variety, novelty, more access to outside knowledge, freedom of will, free inquiry—in a word, change. They want to be free even if they do not know what freedom is. How far the Khrushchev government will go in the future to meeting such impulses and fermentations is unpredictable—probably not very far. When Marshal Tito visited Stalingrad something happened that was extraordinarily revealing. Thousands of people broke through the police lines to see him better, and gave him a tumultuous ovation. He was almost mobbed —something that does not happen often in the Soviet Union. Tito is, of course a Communist. But also he symbolized revolt from the Kremlin, nonconformity, freedom, and the urgent excitements, mysteries, and wonders of the unknown external world.

CHAPTER XVII

Aspects of the Economic Picture

Soviet Russia equals socialism plus electrification.
—LENIN

ONE thing surprising to most American and western European visitors to the Soviet Union is that taxes are so low. Basic income tax is only 5 per cent, and the highest bracket, applicable to the relatively few citizens who have, by Soviet standards, comparatively large incomes, is only 13 per cent. Moreover, those in the 13-per-cent category are favored as a rule with substantial exemptions. The very lowest income group, comprising men and women who earn 380 rubles a month or less, pays no taxes at all. All told, not more than about 8 per cent of the total revenue of the USSR comes from income tax or from other direct personal taxes. The point need not be labored that this is in violent contrast to the situation in most bourgeois countries and in particular the United States, where income tax rates go up to 77 per cent, and personal income taxes contribute not less than 52 per cent of total national revenue. Fifty-two per cent is a lot more than 8.

How, then, does the Soviet Union support itself? Where does it get the money from? What is the basis of public finance? The fundamental answer is, of course, that the state owns and operates all the land, industry, transportation, and means of production in the country. There are 206,000 industrial enterprises in the Soviet Union, as well as about 100,000 in the course of construction; 92 per cent of these are owned by the state outright, and all profits from them go to the state; the other 8 per cent are co-operatives. Factories, mines, farms, mills, workshops, apartment buildings, turn their revenues over to the state, and the state alone determines to what use these shall be put. Moreover, the proceeds of retail trade pour enormous sums into the coffers of the government. The country has, after all, 200 million customers, and the total value of its domestic trade is the equivalent of 120 *billion* dollars per year or more.[1]

What all this means is, in effect, that the ordinary Soviet citizen, no matter how light his direct taxes may be, pays through the nostrils otherwise. Any time he buys anything in a shop, the government makes a profit; in fact, the markup on goods sold in the shops gives the state not less than 60 per cent of its total revenue. This markup, which includes the so-called turnover tax, can amount to several hundred per cent, and is indistinguishable from a general sales tax. The government sets its prices with the deliberate intention of absorbing as much of the consumer's purchasing power as possible; the amount of goods released to the public depends not merely on production, but on the amount of money estimated to be in the hands of the public. In order that there shall be enough to go around, the government imposes scarcity in certain lines. High prices, as I mentioned earlier in this book, are nothing more nor less than a form of rationing.

The current Soviet budget is around 560 billion rubles, or $140 billion at par, roughly twice the American budget. But, as always, it is impossible to translate rubles into dollar terms accurately. According to Soviet figures, 52.8 per cent of Soviet revenue is plowed back into the national economy, 31.2 per cent goes to social services, and 16 per cent is spent on national defense. The surplus for 1956-57 was calculated at approximately 12 billion rubles, a tidy sum. But, even though its operations show a handsome profit, it is impossible for the lay outsider to accept easily the contention that the USSR is a rich country, if only because of the simple fact that so many of its people are so miserably, grotesquely poor. As a matter of fact, the Soviet government is undergoing at the moment a period of severe financial stringency, partly, of course, because it continues to spend so much on industrial expansion. The United States consumes roughly 73 per cent of its own total national production; the USSR reinvests more than 50 per cent of USSR production, mostly in new plants for the production of heavy capital goods—a tremendous lot. Ever since 1928 the country has been in the position of a man who is constantly putting a new wing on a factory, and the peasants and wage earners foot the bill.

Early in 1957 the Kremlin calmly repudiated 260 billion rubles of its internal debt, or $65 billion at par. For many years, citizens had been en-

[1] Foreign trade is much less, but is not to be ignored. The USSR is the sixth largest trading country in the world; foreign trade amounted in 1956 to about $6.5 billion, an increase from $2 billion in 1948. Trade with the USA is no more than a trickle, but is going up. Foreign trade is, of course, a state monopoly in the USSR. Chief purchases from the world outside at the moment are rubber and copper wire.

couraged to invest in state bonds, which include lotteries; in the case of many, a proportion of their pay was deducted automatically, and put into state loan certificates. These certificates paid 4 per cent interest, allowing for the lottery factor, and could be (such was the promise) cashed in after twenty years. The decision to repudiate them came as many were reaching maturity, and would have to be redeemed by the government. Perhaps "repudiation" is too strong a word. But repayment was postponed for "twenty or twenty-five years," and interest payments were "frozen," that is, stopped. So the investor gets no return, and cannot regain his capital until 1978, if then. The life savings of hundreds of thousands of citizens have been wiped out. The cruelest thing in the Soviet Union, which helps to make it the cruelest country on earth, is the grisly economic toll it extracts from its citizens.[2]

Planning

Essential to all Soviet economic activity is the planning concept. The basic object of Soviet planning was, in the first instance, to industrialize a largely feudal and agrarian country, in other words to produce the means of production; also to create a viable "socialist" system and to collectivize agriculture. What planning meant, in essence, was creation of nothing less than a new nation under systematized, calculated, long-range government direction and control. The First Five-Year Plan, or *Pyatiletka*, was not from one point of view a Five-Year Plan at all; it merged inevitably into the Second Five-Year Plan, which in turn merged into its successors; the successive plans were spaced into quinquennial terms for convenience, and also in order to keep sharp watch on periodic accomplishment, but basically they have been, and are, parts of a single program which is supposed to be continuous.

The First Plan was not the invention of any single man, but grew out of the nature of the Soviet system; the concept goes back to Lenin, and Stalin was certainly the man who made it work, at unimaginable cost to human values at the time. The First Five-Year Plan was launched in 1928; it was not put into effect dramatically, with a blow of a whistle, but in fact started out so gradually that well-informed correspondents in Moscow did not know its full implications until it was under way. Not till a year or two later did Soviet planning inflame the imagination of the entire world. The tasks of the First Plan (1928-32) were accomplished in four years instead of five, and, by Russian claims, it was 93.7 per cent successful. Industrial output of the

---

[2] But, to be fair, let us point out once more that the Russians seek to justify the deprivations of the present on the ground that these are strictly necessary now in order to ensure a "glorious" future for everybody in days to come.

country increased by 118 per cent, an extraordinary feat. The production of steel went up 40 per cent in four years, of pig iron 80 per cent. Automobile, engineering, machinery, and aviation industries were created out of nothing, and totally new industrial cities like Magnitogorsk in the Urals were built from scratch. Unemployment ceased. Moreover, all this occurred during the period of the Great Depression in the world outside, when the capitalist powers were afflicted by an economic crisis of unprecedented severity and depth.

The Second Five-Year Plan (1933-37 inclusive) continued to broaden the industrial base, but not at quite such an intensive pace, and completed the collectivization of agriculture. The Third Plan (1938-42) was made largely inoperative by the war, and the Fourth Plan was not put into operation until 1946; it was devoted mainly to the recouping of war losses and the rebuilding of shattered industry. The Fifth Plan (1951-55) continued to emphasize heavy industry, in particular steel, paid strong attention to military preparation, and opened the door somewhat on housing and consumer goods, for which the need was crying—everything from garden tools to wrapping paper, from sleds to chandeliers. The Sixth Five-Year Plan (1956-60) was supposed to pay particular note to hydroelectric installations of vast scope, mines, petroleum, fuel supply, automation, textiles, and atomic energy. Capital investment by the state was to exceed that of the Fifth Plan by a substantial amount, and six thousand new industrial plants were to be built. But the Sixth Plan has been running into all sorts of trouble. It was revised early in 1957, with drastic curtailment of its aims, and was then suddenly scrapped in September, 1957—an unprecedented event, presumably because it could not reach its target goals and because of the strain and dislocation caused by the new industrial reorganization scheme going into effect. It is being replaced by a Seven-Year Plan covering activity from 1958 to 1965. Nevertheless the general level of Soviet economic advance continues to be spirited.

We Visit a Collective Farm

This was near Odessa, in the Ukraine. We were greeted by the director, a tall man of ampular shape, with arms like joists. He turned us over to the agronomist, Benedikt Gavrilkevich, who told us that his father had been a railway worker. (It astonished him when I mentioned that the father of the President of the United States had also been a railway worker, but, as almost all Russians do in similar circumstances, he sought to dissemble his surprise; Soviet citizens do not like to be surprised.) This farm, known as the Karl

Liebknecht Collective Farm, lies close to the Black Sea. The earth is deep black soil, very rich. The farm, 4,110 acres, is small for a collective; there are about 700 workers and 250 children who, of course, have their own school. Some members of the collective work in Odessa factories, but at least one person in each family must be an active, full-time farm worker. This farm grows vegetables, fruit (plums, apricots, cherries), grapes for wine, and corn, and has three to four thousand head of dairy cattle. About half its income comes from wine. This we tasted, and it was good. What impressed me was, first, the inordinate primitiveness, crudeness, and rawness of most equipment, coupled with use of the most advanced techniques. If you want to see really pungent contrasts, go to rural Russia. The village street was nicely paved with asphalt; the telephone in the manager's office was an instrument obviously built in 1890, and was operated by a battery. For the most part, conditions seemed archaic. It is only when you get out of the cities in Russia that you see the "big drop." Second, planning. We walked through the cowsheds with their damp dirt floors. But a "nurse" is in attendance for obstetrical work. Each cow is numbered and named—Lustra, Duma, Palima, Doli—and a placard outside each pen gives neatly not merely her age, weight, daily yield, and so on, but her projected annual yield. Then at the end of the corridor is a large sign listing all the milkmaids. They too have their names on display, just like the cattle, together with a tally sheet showing exactly how many hours they have worked, what milk production they have been responsible for, what percentage this is of their planned goal, and how much more they have to produce daily to keep up. Accomplishment and goal are set side by side, for both animals and human beings.[3]

There are around 80,000 collective farms in the Soviet Union, with a total membership that comes close to being half the population of the country. The collectives (*Kolkhozy*) account for roughly 80 per cent of all Soviet agricultural production. Average size of a collective is 14,200 acres, of which perhaps 4,000 are under cultivation. Formation of the collectives was, in theory, "voluntary" at the beginning. Actually most were, as we know, pounded together by brute force out of the 25,000,000 individual farm units which existed in Russia in the 1920's. After 1935, when collectivization was accomplished, the tendency was to keep the collectives somewhat small, and 254,000 of them existed by 1950. Now they have been consolidated, for reasons of efficiency and otherwise, to the present 80,000, and are bigger. What is a collective? Essentially, a village. It is a community of farmers in a stated area, with shops, schools, a library, a hospital, theaters—even a church

[3] Milkmaids who do well get bonuses paid in milk.

in some cases. How are the members paid? This is complicated. The land belongs to the state, but is leased (perhaps "lease" is not the correct word technically) to the collective in perpetuity. Each collective is required to turn over to the state a certain percentage of its produce, either through "obligatory deliveries" or by "contract purchase." The state sets the price. This is higher for contract purchase than for the obligatory deliveries. Then the state sets another, higher price, when it sells the product to the consumer in the towns; this may be several *thousand* per cent more than what the collective got—another instance of the formidable markup that helps the USSR to finance itself. On the other hand, prices paid by the state to the farmer-producer have lately been going up.

Payment to the individual farmer on the collective depends on the number of "workday units" he earned during the year. The number of workday units depends in turn on the type of work done. The collective pays out of its surplus a certain sum to each worker, according to his work, after certain deductions and after the state has taken its percentage, which is usually in the neighborhood of one-third. Part of the payment by the collective as a whole to its individual members is in cash, part in produce. The theory is that everybody shares. If a harvest is good, members of a collective may be fairly well off; if bad, they suffer. The director of each farm is elected by the collective itself, not chosen by the government.

Two other factors must be mentioned. First, the Machine Tractor Stations, known as MTS's. The collective does not have its own heavy machinery or mechanical equipment, but obtains this, at need, from the nearby MTS. There are eight thousand MTS's in the USSR today, roughly one for every ten collectives. (Thirty years ago there were only six.) The collective pays the MTS in produce, not in cash, and this produce also goes, of course, to the state, since the MTS's are state owned, and forms an important element in the profit of the government on agricultural operations in general. MTS stations carry out roughly 90 per cent of all mechanized agricultural field work in the country. Technicians in each are the equivalent, more or less, of county agents in the United States, and are at the service of the collective for advice regarding fertilizer, irrigation, crop rotation, and kindred subjects. MTS workers are paid a fixed salary by the state, which runs to an average of nine hundred rubles a month, and sometimes groups of technicians are assigned semipermanently to a given farm.

Second, every family on a collective has its own private or "garden" plot, ranging in size from about half an acre to an acre. Here the farmer is entitled to grow vegetables for his own consumption, and keep livestock as well.

He may own one cow and two calves up to two years of age, one sow and a litter of pigs, ten sheep or goats, and unlimited poultry. Incredible as the fact may seem, about half of all livestock in the Soviet Union is still privately owned. Also the family is not only entitled to feed itself by what it grows on the private plot but may sell what is left over, if anything, on the free market, after the government takes its share.[4]

That free markets for agricultural produce still exist in the Soviet Union is not generally known. They are the last remnant of "capitalist" enterprise left in the country. The government calls them, however, "collective farm markets." Let me explain. There are two principal types of food shops in the USSR. First, the majority, are the government stores owned and operated by the state like the *gastronoms* in the big cities, where prices are fixed by the government. Second, the free markets, which absorb leftover produce from the collectives or private plots. The collective itself, as well as the individual farmer, may sell on the free market. After the collective has made its deliveries to the state, paid the MTS, set aside necessary supplies (seed, feed, and so on) for its own use, and distributed produce to its membership in accordance with the number of workday units involved, it is at liberty to sell on the free market for profit, if any goods remain. Prices on the free market depend on supply and demand, and are likely to fluctuate widely; for instance, the price of a liter of milk in Moscow can vary by two or three rubles in the course of a single day. In the small towns, the free markets are in effect bazaars, and in many localities they operate on only two or three days a week. Even so, and although free market prices are substantially higher than government store prices, about 22 per cent of the total food supply of the USSR is sold to the consumer through the free market.[5]

The farm we saw near Odessa has an average annual income of 9,700,000 rubles ($2,825,000 at par.) The cash proceeds of an individual member amount, in a good year, to 10,000-12,000 rubles. Also each family gets 450 kilograms of grapes, 600 kilograms of vegetables, a ton of forage, and as much wine as it can drink. Later we visited another collective near Tashkent, a show place called Red Uzbekistan, much bigger, and devoted largely to cot-

---

[4] The private plots have been an angry political issue lately. In June, 1957, following the Malenkov-Molotov ouster, the government made a play for peasant support by exempting the private plots from state collections. But in October new taxes were levied on collective farms which seemingly wipe out the benefits of the earlier concession.

[5] Bread, the basic food of the country, is like vodka a state monopoly. Bread accounts for roughly 70 per cent of all calories consumed in the Soviet Union, and potatoes for another 10 per cent. No wonder so many Russians are pudgy. The comparable figure for bread and potatoes in the United States is 25-26 per cent.

ton, but growing cattle, onions, cabbage, melons, and silkworms as well. The private "sector," that is, the garden plots, covers 480 acres out of 8,910, and the total membership is 1,170 families, with 1,650 workers. The work on cotton is 90 per cent mechanized. On this collective, 16-20 per cent of income goes to the capital fund, 2 per cent to culture (library, clubs, lectures), 10-12 per cent for capital needs (fertilizer, seed, and the like), and 8-9 per cent to taxes. The rest is divided between government and the collective. The state supports the hospital, pharmacy, and other items in the realm of public health; the collective supports the schools. Cotton and silk are marketed exclusively by the state; vegetables and fruit go mostly to the free market. The director gets a salary of four hundred rubles a month in addition to his share in the proceeds, and serves a ten-year term. Men and women work ten to twelve hours a day in summer, four in winter. I asked the direc-tor, a tired, dark, unsmiling man, Moslem by religion, if he had any problems or complaints. Like practically all Russians asked this question by a foreigner, he at once closed ranks within himself, and replied that there were none. One of the most pronounced of Soviet characteristics is that most citizens, in talk with an outsider, always say that *everything* is perfect, although they complain without end among themselves.

*

State farms (*Sovkhozy*) form the second great category of agricultural enterprises in the Soviet Union. These are quite distinct from collective farms. If a collective farm is a village, a state farm is a factory. The state farm is an exclusively state enterprise, without profit sharing; its workers are straight-out state employees, like factory workers; they are paid a salary, and are guaranteed a minimum wage no matter what the harvest. Pay ranges from 700 to 1,100 rubles a month. The state farmer is given a dwelling, works as a rule a forty-six-hour week, and is paid for overtime. There are no MTS's associated with state farms, which have their own permanently available mechanical equipment. State farms are in general much bigger than collec-tives, averaging about 37,000 acres, of which perhaps one-third are under cultivation. Approximately 5,800 state farms exist in the country (as against 80,000 collectives); they cover roughly one-fourth of the total cultivable area, and account for about 20 per cent of Soviet agricultural production. Employees on state farms are, like members of collectives, permitted to till their own garden plots and to sell the surplus.

The Kremlin oligarchs much prefer state farms to collectives, and would like to see them supplant the collectives in time. The number of state farms has increased steadily in recent years. State farms are easier to administer, are more "socialistic," and produce more profit; also the director is appointed by the state, not chosen by members of the farm. But replacement of all the collectives by state farms would be an utter impossibility politically; this is one thing that the Soviet government could not dare do. Peasants do not like collectivization, but they like state farms even less, and an attempt to dragoon everybody into state farms would almost certainly cause such an uproar that it would be more trouble than it would be worth.

*

Agriculture is by far the sorest spot in Russia. The USSR lives, just as Czarist Russia did, predominantly on the land; at least half the total population is engaged in agriculture in one form or other; the peasant, not Khrushchev, is king. Industrialization, scientific power, military strength, education, all depend basically on what wealth the "dark masses" on the land will, or will not, produce.

How to curry the good will of the peasant, how to persuade him to produce more without pressures too overt, is the most fundamental, persistent, and gravid of all Soviet problems.

Difficulties lie in three principal dimensions:

1. Natural limitations. The country lies far to the north; even the Odessa region, with its rich black earth, stands on the same latitude as northern Minnesota. The growing season is short almost everywhere, and rainfall scant; even counting snowfall, average precipitation is only marginal, about fifteen to twenty inches a year. Immense regions are locked up forever and unreachable under permafrost, and other immense regions are covered by taiga, forest, or desert. Soviet statisticians do not claim that more than 20 per cent of the total area of the country is arable; neutral observers put the figure closer to 15, and some experts even say 11. Another point is that, as you go north, you get more rainfall, but in the north the growing season is shorter. Crops have to be got out in a hurry.

2. Waste, primitiveness, inefficiency. The MTS's have done much, but do not have a fraction of the mechanical power available to American agriculture. Almost all Soviet farm equipment is old-fashioned, if not downright obsolete, by our standards, and the average productivity of the Soviet farmer is probably only one-quarter of that of a farmer in the United States. Following is a paragraph from a report by Senator Allen J. Ellender of Louisiana,

who, on a recent visit to the Soviet Union, paid particular attention to agricultural themes. "I saw much waste, particularly with respect to food grains. For example, huge piles of grain lay in the open, on the roadways and the farms, without covering of any kind. Russian workers turned this grain frequently by hand, in order to facilitate drying. Buckets, trowels, dishpans, in fact all sorts of utensils were used in the operation. (Because of the short growing season, and the lack of equipment, much grain must be cut before maturity. It is windrowed in the field when the kernels are milky and thereafter thrashed after the kernels harden.) South of Moscow, one-half of the hardsurfaced roadway we traveled over was covered with grain for a distance of about 500 kilometers to permit it to dry. It was raining and I know there was much loss sustained. Much human power was in use to save the grain."

3. Human factors. Hundreds of thousands of peasants partake steadily in what is a kind of passive revolt against the collective system. They concentrate on their private plots, at the expense of the work of the collective as a whole, sabotage procedures, and are careless of equipment and state property. They resent the rigidity of the system, taxes, and the prices they get for obligatory delivery quotas, and hence produce just enough to support themselves. Some say that they are worse off than their grandfathers, who were serfs. Above all they lack incentive. The peasant does not produce more because, even if he gets a substantial cash income, as many do, he has no "spending power." Nothing worth buying is in the shops. This brings up one of the dramatic paradoxes of the Soviet economy. The government must, in order to improve the standard of living of the country as a whole, get more out of the farmer, but at the same time is unwilling or unable to release more consumer goods to the farmer in order to stimulate him to more production. Soviet industrial production rose by 230 per cent between 1940 and 1952; agricultural production by only 10 per cent.[6] The Soviet Union is the second industrial power in the world; but many of its rural districts look like a sour, destitute area in some such country as Bulgaria fifty years ago.

*

The Khrushchev regime pays incessant anxious attention to agriculture. One preoccupation is livestock. The country today has less livestock than it had in 1917, partly because of the slaughter of animals during collectivization in the early 1930's. But Khrushchev, a confident man, must have confidence that the problem of livestock shortage is on the way to solution, or he would

[6] MacDuffie, op. cit., p. 85.

never have promised with such public heat that the USSR would surpass the United States in per capita production of butter, meat, and milk by 1962. Another preoccupation is corn, more production of which will help the live-stock situation. Parts of the rich grain areas of the Kuban and North Caucasus are to be turned over to corn. Above all, the Khrushchev government pins its hopes on the Virgin Lands project, which is probably the largest agricultural experiment—or gamble—in the history of the world. Some 87,500,000 acres in southwestern Siberia and northern Kazakhstan have been opened up since 1954, an area larger than Pennsylvania, New York, and Maine put together, and equivalent to not less than one-quarter of the total sown area of the entire United States.

Some 425 new state farms have been created in this huge area, several of them real giants, and 350,000 workers from all parts of the country have been settled here. The intention is to make this the grain bowl of the nation, instead of the Rostov area and the Ukraine. But few trees exist in this enormous steppe, and rainfall is scant; the surface soil is quite good, what we call "dark chestnut," but the subsoil is salty. Sunflowers (a very important crop in Russia, because it is a prime source of vegetable oil), potatoes, corn for silage, and other crops will be planted as well as wheat, but spring wheat predominates overwhelmingly. The pessimists say that the Virgin Lands project is vulnerable to a fantastic degree, and that the whole region may well become a dust bowl instead of a grain bowl, with resultant disaster, if the rains fail in successive seasons, but yields so far have been quite good. One factor not without interest is that the Virgin Lands development was made necessary to an extent by the comparative failure of the collective system in other parts of Russia. Another is that this is the first big development plan to be worked out in the Soviet Union for decades without the use of forced labor.[7] It may be questioned, however, if all the "volunteers" who are on the spot were really volunteers.

The USSR as a whole had its greatest crop in history in 1956. The 1957 harvest fell below expectation, largely on account of bad weather, but even so was as good as any other recent year except the prodigious banner year 1956. The 1956 harvest was 47 per cent above average, but large amounts of the crop were lost because of inadequate storage facilities, bungling, and shortage in transportation.

[7] *New Statesman*, August 18, 1956.

Gist of Industrial Reorganization

Khrushchev, who is a man to be taken with extreme seriousness as we should know by now, announced on March 30, 1957, a plan for the decentralization of Soviet industrial management. His statement, eighteen thousand words long, was the most important public announcement made by any member of the Presidium since the Twentieth Congress (February, 1956), and is one of the most important ever made by a Soviet leader at any time. It followed a tangled period, already alluded to in these pages, of disagreement and controversy on national planning and economy. The Khrushchev "theses" (as his economic proposals came to be called) were adopted by the Supreme Soviet in May, and put into effect at once.[8]

What Khrushchev did was give Soviet economy its biggest shakeup since the First Five-Year Plan. Before this, almost all Russian industry had been run from Moscow. The situation was roughly comparable to that which would obtain in the United States if every American industry, from Du Pont or General Electric to a repair shop employing six people in a Chicago suburb, operated directly under the absolute authority of a cabinet minister in Washington. The stage had been reached in the Soviet Union where, if a factory superintendent needed a new pair of scissors, he practically had to ask Moscow for it. Duplication, red tape, bureaucratic waste, abuse of power, slipshodness, mismanagement, delay, plain silliness, were grave characteristics of the Russian economic picture. Bitter jealousies existed between different administrations. Omsk refused to send some badly needed gypsum to Bashkiria because Bashkiria refused to send some badly needed alabaster to Omsk. "A plant manager in the Ukraine had to ask Moscow's permission before ordering a new piece of machinery from across the street. . . . Soviet bureaucrats in Moscow would send equipment they controlled from one end of the country to the other rather than allow local managers to get supplies from nearby plants run by rival ministries."[9]

[8] The Soviet press went through some fancy antics over this. Of course the Supreme Soviet is a rubber stamp; it had no choice but to approve what Khrushchev had suggested. But Khrushchev had taken unusually wide steps to disseminate knowledge of his proposals, and ensure "popular" support. For instance, no fewer than 514,000 meetings took place all over the USSR between March and May, to discuss the plan; forty million people attended these meetings, and more than two million spoke. Some details in the government's project were modified as a result. This, however, does not excuse such a headline as some that appeared, like "THE SOVIET PUBLIC DRAFTS A NEW LAW."

[9] Malcolm Muir in Newsweek, July 15, 1957.

Khrushchev himself, in his "theses," gave some crazy examples of how things had gone wrong. One factory manager spent 200,000 rubles on a fence separating his plant from a neighboring plant because they were attached to different ministries. One prize story had to do with material for prefabricated housing. At one and the same time, authorities in Krasnoyarsk, in eastern Siberia, were sending huge amounts of prefabricated sheets to Kirov, in Central Russia, while Kirov was sending exactly similar material to Krasnoyarsk. Khrushchev said that this reminded him of Ostrovsky's comedy *The Forest*, in which two characters ask each other where the other is going. One says, "From Kerch to Vologda"; the other says, "From Vologda to Kerch," but in fact neither is going anywhere. Khrushchev concludes: "The same in our case. Administrative chaos!"

Gist of the reorganization scheme, which in theory went into operation on July 1, was abolition of no fewer than twenty-seven of the former industrial ministries, several of which were colossi. In their place, about one hundred regional economic councils were set up all over the country; these, once the confusion attending transfer is done away with, will have very substantial autonomy in their districts. Of the new units sixty-eight are in the RSFSR, and there are eleven in the Ukraine. The frontiers of each correspond with provincial frontiers, and also follow natural economic lines of demarcation. In Moscow, only six of the former industrial ministries survived, all closely associated with national defense—aviation, shipbuilding, electronics, chemicals, medium machine building, and transport construction. Four of these surviving six were subsequently abolished in December, leaving only transport construction and medium machine building, which is believed to be the Soviet apparatus for dealing with military applications of nuclear energy, to be handled in the old centralized manner. New organizations replaced the abolished ministries, under the supervision of Dmitri F. Ustinov, former Minister of Defense Industry. He became a deputy premier, and is now Khrushchev's right-hand man to supervise these important fields.[10]

All in all, the carnage in Moscow was unbelievable. More than twenty huge ministries had to be dismantled, and, in sum, four hundred government bureaus and about half a million civil servants were involved. Not all the civil servants were fired, or had to move to Novosibirsk or Tomsk. The best at the top were probably reassigned to posts in Moscow with the *Gosplan*, State Planning Commission. But thousands had the shock of

---

[10] Not to be confused with Vladimir I. Ustinov, who in the same week became First Secretary of the Moscow City Party Committee, succeeding Madame Furtseva.

their lives. One dry announcement was to the effect that few of the 2,050 employees of the former Iron and Steel Ministry in Moscow had "expressed a desire to go to Chelyabinsk," where steel plays a major role in the new regional council. Khrushchev himself told Joseph Alsop of the New York *Herald Tribune*, in an interview in which he outlined leading details of the reorganization scheme, that "many tens of thousands of engineers and technicians will be released from office work," the inference being that it would do them a lot of good to get out into the open air and work with their hands. One estimate is that Khrushchev has, since Stalin's death, fired or transferred no fewer than 900,000 civil servants, and some 40,000 new appointments have been made to "responsible executive posts." Ruthlessly the dead wood is being chopped away. One curious item, as several connoisseurs of the Soviet economy have pointed out, is that the scheme, although it is known universally as one for decentralizing industrial management, has in truth had the opposite effect; it *re*centralizes it. Moscow still holds all the strings. But Moscow operates through one main agency, the State Planning Commission, instead of multitudinous different competing ministries. Then the chain of command goes down as before through the republics to the new regional councils to the individual mine, shop, or factory. The *top* direction is more centralized than before, but "local initiative, on the plant level, is encouraged." This may have profound consequences for the future, and not merely in economic realms. For instance the new managerial class, with substantial local authority, is almost bound in time to exert a loosening political influence throughout the country.

The basic reason for this whole unprecedented operation was, of course, desire to get more life into the economy, more strength through flexibility and elasticity. A subsidiary consideration was, to a degree, military. Khrushchev concedes this frankly. On November 19 he received Henry Shapiro, of the United Press, for one of the most illuminating interviews he has ever given, in the course of which the following colloquy took place:

H. SHAPIRO: Are military bases losing their importance, with the development of rocket weapons?
N. S. KHRUSHCHEV: Unquestionably. At one time bombers could be stopped by antiaircraft fire, artillery, or antiaircraft rockets, but there is no stopping the ballistic missile.

You will say: But will not the Soviet Union suffer too? Of course we too will suffer great losses. But look at our space and look at Germany, France and Britain. One does not have to be a strategist or a military man to see the difference.
H. SHAPIRO: America also has vast expanses.

N. S. KHRUSHCHEV: Not quite so vast; and it should be kept in mind that American cities—New York, Chicago, San Francisco and others—have a very high concentration of industry. Our industry is more widely dispersed. Moreover, the reorganization of industrial management that we have carried out also ensures more autonomous management of industry. This also improves our strategic position.

H. SHAPIRO: But that is not the main purpose of the reorganization.

N. S. KHRUSHCHEV: No, it is not the main purpose, but a collateral, although very important one.[11]

This interview, like others which Khrushchev has given lately, deserves scrupulously close reading. In it Khrushchev emerges as a person with an extraordinary arc of vision, realism, and quick-witted intelligence. Obviously no one who did not possess these qualities, as well as courage and strength of will, could possibly have put through the reorganization scheme, together with much else. There are still people in the United States and the western democracies who think that Khrushchev is a boorish clown, besotted and tipsy most of the time. It is true that he talks windy nonsense on occasion, but they could not be more wrong.

*

What counts most about Soviet industrialization, like education, is *pace* of development. The USSR is, as is well known, already the second most powerful country in the world from the criterion of total volume of industrial output, as well as quantity of basic industrial goods produced—steel, iron, coal, oil, machine tools, as well as hydroelectric power. Moreover it has reached this position in a comparatively short span of time, in spite of setbacks suffered during the war and other obstacles only too familiar—crudeness in equipment, inefficiency, and administrative "chaos." What it may be like ten years from now, if the decentralization scheme works and production becomes more streamlined, efficiently managed, and abundant, is frightening to think about.

One obvious element of strength is concentration on industries with a military potential. Service industries, in the American sense, hardly exist. The consumer comes last in this country, not first as in ours. Mr. Dulles mentioned recently that the USSR produces only about 100,000 passenger automobiles per year, and seemed to feel that this indicated weakness, not strength, in the Soviet economy. Actually it may well indicate the opposite—

[11] *Pravda* and *Izvestia*, translated by *Current Digest of the Soviet Press*, December 25, 1957.

strength, not weakness. The time could, indeed, be near when the United States, in order to keep up with the USSR in industrial power and military preparation, might have to sacrifice some of its well-known impulses toward fanciness and pleasure, consumption for the sake of consumption, and luxuries. Also, *in time*, the Soviet Union certainly intends to do more for its people in the way of consumer goods, even luxuries, than it does now. As a matter of fact some of its contemporary production is quite respectable. The USSR produced 804,000,000 pairs of hosiery in 1956, 179,000 vacuum cleaners, 3,100,000 bicycles, 22,600,000 clocks and watches, and 1,200,000 cameras.[12]

But to get back to pace. Statistics are available by the shovelful. I will try to spare the reader most. Besides most Soviet statistics are slippery. They tend to deal in terms of percentages rather than hard totals. Even so, some of the percentages have to be respected. Since the inauguration of the First Five-Year Plan (1928) the gross industrial output of the Soviet Union has increased twenty times; of cement, to take one specific item, not less than thirty-four times. Some hard totals should be respected too. Pig iron production was 4.2 million tons in 1913, 15 million in 1940, 33 million in 1955, and 37 million in 1957. The corresponding figures for coal are 29.1 million, 166 million, 391 million, and no less than 462 million; for petroleum, 9.2 million, 31 million, 71 million, and 98 million. Steel rose from 4.2 million in 1913 to 18.3 million in 1940 to 45 million in 1955, and then jumped a cool 4 million in a single year to reach 49 million in 1956. Today it is 51 million. On any terms, these are staggering figures.

Of course failures exist in the Soviet economy as well. These are as a rule frankly stated, and are the cause of much self-castigation. The building material industry is lagging badly, and the housing program fell short of its 1957 goal by 30 per cent. Many roads, where they exist at all, are appalling pools of mud for much of the year, and railroad transportation creaks at the joints. Troubles are incessant in getting fuel up to Moscow. Other cities are starved for fuel. There were serious deficiencies in glass, some machine tools, and farm machinery in 1956. Ore resources are immense, but dwindling sharply at some sites. "Capital investments fell six percent below the target set for 1956, but they were still 17 percent over 1955."[13] Production of pig iron, coal, and electric power increased, but by lower percentages than in preceding years. Automobile prices went up; so did the price of vodka at the end of 1957. Grumbles have been loud, and may get louder.

---

[12] Most textile goods are shoddy, but this condition too may improve in time.
[13] William J. Jorden in the *New York Times*, January 3, 1957.

It is possible, although certainly not probable, that the entire economy of the Soviet Union may break down and collapse someday; nobody can make prophecies for eternity. But two things should be kept firmly in mind. First, the general rise has been persistent and steady. The USSR accounted for only 1.7 per cent of total world industrial production in 1917; in 1955, slightly more than 19 per cent. Industrial production *doubled* between 1951 and 1956. Second, the nature of the Soviet system is such that its economy can presumably be made to bend before it breaks.

Labor, White Collars, and Once More the Consumer

About fifty million men and women have jobs in Soviet industry; the number of industrial workers has shot up to this figure from around thirteen million thirty years ago, a very large and quick gain. Many workers are, however, not skilled, and many are employed wastefully. The average productivity per man in Soviet industry is, like that of the Soviet farmer, far less than that of a comparable American worker. There are more railway workers to the mile in the USSR than any country in the world, even by Soviet figures. Workers not only lack skill; they lack interest in their jobs. The reason why new buildings in Russia crumble so quickly is not merely faultiness of material, but careless, sloppy workmanship. One device typical of the Soviet Union is that, to improve morale in this direction, the rule has been established in some areas that laborers working on a housing project have first priority for rooms in it.

Soviet trade unions have 47,000,000 members. The supreme trade union boss is V. V. Grishin. There are forty-six unions in all, under the All-Union Central Council of Trade Unions, organized on an industrial basis like the CIO. They are, however, not remotely like American unions. They are, in fact, almost the opposite. They do not exist, as do American and British unions, primarily for the benefit of the worker, to get higher wages; their function is not to fight for higher pay at all but to attend to general social services and encourage production. No such thing as collective bargaining with the employer (i.e., the state) is known, and strikes are forbidden, as they were under the Czars. The right to strike is not recognized in the Soviet Union, and there has been no legal strike for forty years or more.

Some ameliorations have, however, recently come to the Soviet worker, and more are promised, including new machinery for settling "individual" labor disputes. (1) The first minimum wage law in Russian history went into effect on January 1, 1957. The wage differs depending on the location and type of industry; 300-350 rubles a month is the average. The wages of more than eight million workers, or roughly one-sixth of the total labor force, went *up* to this minimum when the new law became operative, a sufficient commentary on low Soviet living standards. (2) The forty-eight-hour week was cut to forty-six hours, with two hours off on Saturday. That this reform was taken with extreme seriousness as an important measure of relief to the population tells much. Soviet workers work hard. Saturday is now a blessed day. The government hopes to introduce a forty-one hour week by 1960, seven hours a day for five days, with six on Saturday. (3) A new, substantial, and advanced pension scheme is in effect. Pensions begin for men at sixty, after twenty-five years of service, and for women at fifty-five; the amounts range from 100 to 55 per cent of salary, with three hundred rubles as the minimum. For workers in Arctic regions or those with dangerous occupations, benefits are greater, and about seventeen million citizens are involved in all.

Also—an arresting development—workers now have the right to change jobs without permission; they can thumb a nose at a boss and quit, a privilege that did not exist before. However, two weeks' notice must be given. Nor does this regulation apply to young men and women out of the *tekhnikums,* who, on graduation, are as we know obliged to spend three years at some assigned work in their specialty. After three years they are free to fend for themselves. The regulation permitting ordinary workers to quit employment at will has not been in effect long, but is already having marked social consequences. People are getting mobility; they wander all over the country. I met a schoolteacher from Leningrad who is now running a restaurant in Sochi, and a surveyor born in Vladivostok who is now a librarian in Kiev. The labor turnover has been so great that the government is, in fact, now seeking to modify it. As an example health insurance does not become effective till a worker has been at a post for six months, and vacations are tied to tenure.

Working conditions in plants and factories vary. Some older establishments are, by American standards, deplorable, with bad lighting and ventilation, meager sanitary arrangements, and inadequate safety precautions; some newer are first class. Scale of pay depends not so much on what work a person does, but on the type of industry; if a particular industry is important to the state at a given moment, its help is better paid. A good deal is done to encourage incentive and productivity by way of bonuses, differential awards, and the like,[14] and, of course, it is drummed into workers

[14] Managers are also eligible to substantial bonuses.

all the time that the basis of all success is "material" and that the main "spiritual" value to life consists in "the ability to work well." Not all pay heed. One minor point is that never once in Russia in 1956 did I hear the word "Stakhanovism," which was a shibboleth in the 1930's.[15]

Almost all Soviet industrial plants have facilities for sport and recreation, and big factories invariably possess a House of Culture, which has, among other things, libraries, community halls, a theater, and the like. Here dances are held, games played, and entertainment encouraged. Some of these culture halls are dreary with the almost phosphorescent dreary ugliness of the plants themselves; some, on the contrary, almost manage to achieve a festive look, largely because they are always crowded, animated, and full of young women.

Finally, unemployment does not exist in the Soviet Union;[16] on the contrary, shortage of labor is acute.

*

A white-collar employee of an American corporation visiting a Soviet institution of comparable rank will be in for some surprises. For one thing the offices of the establishment will be secondary to the plant, instead of vice versa which is usually the case in the United States. Also the visitor will note that a considerable number of executive officers in a Russian industrial organization, even engineers, are women. On a superficial level other points may be mentioned. First, there is little of the personal byplay and banter that accompany much American business endeavor and office routine; no coffee break, for example. Bosses are aloof. Second, lunch takes place in a cafeteria on the premises, maintained by the establishment; no corner drugstore, bar, or hotdog stand. Third, nobody has to catch the 5:25; commuting, if any, is by bus. Another point is that jobs are different in function. No Soviet plant has a public relations department or advertising department, office for employer-employee relationships, or even a sales manager and staff. Salesmanship, the first of all occupations in America, does not exist in our sense at all.

*

[15] It meant efficiency and speed-up devices, developed in theory by the worker himself, to increase output.

[16] Except peripherally. Some young people of well-to-do families refuse to work. This annoys the authorities exceedingly, and a new law recently went into effect whereby loafers and "parasites" can be sent off into exile in a different community, not necessarily by decision of a court but by a vote of the community involved.

A last word on the consumer. "It is not bad if in improving the theory of Marxism one throws in also a piece of bacon and a piece of butter." This line is from Khrushchev, and is characteristic. But pressure from the people for more and better consumer goods, as well as food, grows more apparent all the time. On a certain level, the most impressive of all contemporary Soviet statistics is that the waiting list for the Pobeda, the 20,000 ruble ($5,000) small automobile, numbers at the moment one *hundred thousand* citizens in Moscow alone.

Not only do people yearn for motor scooters, silk thread, casseroles, and umbrellas, but for prettier things, articles more gay. They want colored automobiles, not merely automobiles. One exasperated recent letter to *Izvestia* asked why paper napkins and tablecloths cannot be produced with a softer texture and better design. On the other hand, dutiful citizens recognize (or are taught to recognize) that it is easier for a factory manager to continue to produce the usual run of paralyzingly dull, uniform, and standardized products because this helps him to fulfill his "gross output plan."

We do not need to repeat why consumer goods are scant. It is not merely because heavy industrial production takes priority, but because the Soviet economic system *as a whole* is less efficient than ours. Not enough consumer goods exist to go around partly at least because of waste, carelessness, and mismanagement. The problem for the government is vexing, on the rise, and perhaps insoluble. Khrushchev wants above all to broaden the basis of his support, to bring people more closely into the family of government so to speak, but the only substantially effective way to do this is to increase vastly the amount of consumer goods available, which at the present moment cannot be done.

How Socialist Is It?

Not very, if by "socialism" you mean equality of reward.

The chief socialist characteristics in the Soviet system are (a) ownership by the state of all land, without exception, although land is leased to the collective farms; (b) ownership by the state of all means of production; (c) no accumulation of private wealth through conventional business processes, by buying cheap and selling dear; (d) no exploitation of labor for private profit; (e) no stock market or mechanisms for private financial manipulation; (f) national planning and nationally integrated effort, on the fixed, zealously held theory that the country as a whole "belongs" to the people.

Qualifications should, however, be made about several of these points. For instance, peasants sell a great deal of produce on the free market, and make a profit thereby. A woman can knit woolen goods at home, and sell on the free market (of course she can only buy the wool from the state at a price set by the state). Speculators do buy cheap and sell dear, but this is illegal, and dealings on the black market are severely punished. Servants exist, but these are not "exploited." Basically, nobody is permitted to employ labor in the USSR except the state. Also, needless to say, the Russian *state* is probably the biggest and most merciless exploiter of labor that the world has ever seen.

The Soviet authorities take the line that socialism, as a prelude to Communism, already exists, and hundreds of millions of words are printed every year paying tribute to socialist aims and accomplishments. But, as is only too obvious, the Soviet regime is much more state capitalist than socialist.

Some nonsocialist factors are the following, if we define socialism by conventional western terms:[17] (1) The banking system, operated through the State Bank, works for the most part through orthodox capitalist procedures. The government does, however, control credit, dealings in foreign exchange, et cetera. There is no private money market. (2) People can earn salaries or fees up to almost any limit, and disparity in income is a pronounced feature of Soviet society. In theory, anybody can accumulate any amount of capital. There is, however, no means of investing capital except in savings banks operated by the state or state bonds, nor is anybody allowed to accumulate capital by exploitation of basic resources, like oil, or industrial ownership. (3) Wealth may be assigned or passed on to children or others, and the inheritance tax is light, about 10 per cent.[18] (4) The system has most certainly not produced a classless society.

Ownership of private property is an involved subject. A Soviet citizen may own a house, a piano, clothes, a car, and so forth, but not (to choose one item) an airplane, and certainly not a mine, a forest, or a factory. Most socialists, in Russia or out, have no objection to the personal ownership of property, provided that this does not include any means of production. Marx had no objection to the accumulation of private property, and the right of contemporary citizens to possess private property is specifically safeguarded in the Soviet constitution.

Thousands of Soviet citizens own their own homes; I saw a notice in a Russian paper a few days ago offering 2,400 cottages for sale. The usual process for acquiring a house goes like this, and is not unmixed, to understate the case, with capitalist procedures. First the worker must prove that he has

[17] Soviet definition of "socialism" and how it differs from "Communism" is abstruse, but is hardly something to go into here.
[18] There are thirty-five probate offices in Moscow.

been a good worker, and has fulfilled his "plan." He will need recommendation from his trade union or factory manager. He then goes to a bank, where he may borrow up to fifteen to twenty thousand rubles for fifteen years, at 3 or even 2 per cent interest; he pays off the debt in small installments, usually through deductions from his wages. Next, he goes to a local building agency and, if lucky, receives an allocation for land, materials, and labor. Next, he builds his house on the plot assigned, pays the construction company, and moves in. Subsequently he may sell, rent, or bequeath this property. He does not, however, own the land, which belongs to the state in perpetuity and absolutely.

The Soviet government gives distinct encouragement to private housing. One reason is that the public housing program has been so inadequate. In some cases the home builder pays no interest at all on his loan for the first few years. Workers in some communities build houses with their own hands, and not less than one-third of all the housing being built in the Soviet Union today is in the "private" sector.

Overtaking the United States

So many imponderables enter into this question that discussion is difficult. The USSR might (conceivably) blow up. The USA might (conceivably) break down. One element to keep in mind in attempting to sketch the relative economic strength of the two powers is the extreme stress on industrialization in the USSR, which gives the entire Soviet economy a top-heaviness, a lack of balance. Another is that Soviet economy is working at full capacity, straining at the seams. The Russians often criticize the United States for not employing its plant capacity to the utmost, and say that Americans notoriously fail to utilize their resources to the fullest extent, but this is an American strength, not a weakness. American industry has, in theory at least, much more potential for sudden expansion in an emergency than has the Soviet Union. For instance, many USSR factories are already working in two or even three daily shifts.

An admirable (but possibly too optimistic) analysis of this question, whether or not the Soviet Union will overtake the United States in industrial power in the discernible future, was written by Harry Schwartz in the *New York Times*, July 14, 1957. Mr. Schwartz makes several cogent points. First, the high rate of Soviet output must be looked at in perspective; it seems so high nowadays partly because it was so low for many years, and some percentage increases are declining. Second, the Kremlin will, as time

goes on, probably have to accede more and more to further consumer de
mands, particularly in housing. (On the other hand, the Khrushchev regime
is loud in its assertions that the housing shortage will be "conquered" by
about 1970.) Third, labor shortage. Fourth, a large part of the Soviet industrial effort is being shifted from European Russia to Siberia, which
entails massive effort and expense. Fifth, grave difficulties in agriculture.
Also—still to follow Mr. Schwartz—factors not strictly economic may well
come into play, for instance further disaffection in the satellites (which have
been costly enough already), internal forces making for possible unrest in
the Soviet Union itself, and the fact that Russian competition will probably
have the effect of stimulating the western world to greater endeavor. After
all, nobody has a right to assume that the United States is going to stand
still with its hands in its pockets for the next decade.

What really counts is, once again, pace. The United States is today substantially ahead of the USSR in every principal field of production. Gross
national output of the Soviet Union is, as of the moment, only about 42
per cent of that of the United States. But—and it is a very large but—other
important factors have to be considered. The subject is full of statistical
snares, but most experts concede that the present *rate* of Soviet industrial
expansion is at least twice that of the United States, perhaps more. Soviet
output has been increasing in recent years by 10 to 11 per cent a year, a
fantastic figure; it fell last year, but is still in the neighborhood of 7 per cent;
the corresponding figure for the United States is around 3 per cent. The
lesson of these figures is not merely that the Soviet economy is expanding
much faster than is ours, but that, if this present situation continues, it will
be inevitably bound to catch up.[19] Soviet production of steel has gone up
more than 100 per cent in a little over ten years; American production in
the same period, 32 per cent. Soviet production of coal has gone up 60
per cent as against 30 for America; of electricity 80 per cent as against 29
per cent. Several European experts think that the Soviet Union may well
surpass the United States in steel production, the key to everything, by
1970. Another compelling factor is that the present rate of Russian industrial expansion is more than three times that of western Europe. These
are items that need to be seriously digested. We are in a race, and no
mistake about it.

[19] Also, it means among other things that the USSR will presently have substantially more capital goods available for export to its allies and to underdeveloped
neutral countries than it has now; and even today Soviet economic aid to nations
abroad, as well as export of technicians, has reached imposing dimensions. Cf. A. H.
Raskin in the *New York Times*, January 20, 1957.

The USSR does not conceal its extravagant ambitions. The primary goal, to surpass the United States and become the world's first industrial power, is spelled out for all to see. Apparently Khrushchev thinks that two Seven-Year Plans will do the job, the revised current plan and one to follow, and put the USSR neck and neck with the United States on most categories of basic industrial goods by 1972

Some Russian Jokes

A friend says to a friend, "I have just written a book."
"What about?"
"Boy meets girl."
"Ah, a story!"
"They fall in love."
"A romance!"
"They get married and find an apartment."
"Ah, a fable!"

One joke about the USSR and Poland is that in Moscow nobody talks freely except Khrushchev, whereas in Warsaw everybody talks freely except Gomulka.

Khrushchev and Bulganin go to the airport to meet a visiting dignitary. Khrushchev sees that his shoelace has become undone, and stoops to tie it; as he does so, his trousers split. Bulganin hustles him into the waiting room, where an attendant at once comes forward and presents him with a new pair. "Excellent!" Khrushchev exclaims, "But how did you know I needed them?" The attendant replies, "We just heard about it on the BBC!"

A vagrant lies in the gutter, dressed in filthy rags, starving, and almost comatose. Comment of an observer: "Somebody has reached socialism."

CHAPTER XVIII

The Soviet Armed Forces

> What man dare, I dare.
> Approach thou like the rugged Russian bear,
> The arm'd rhinoceros, or the Hyrcan tiger;
> Take any shape but that, and my firm nerves
> Shall never tremble.
>
> —MACBETH, III, iv

> The Russian soldier is perhaps the most faithful
> modern parallel to the Spartan. He would let the
> wolf tear at his vitals without uttering a groan.
>
> —LORD CURZON IN 1889

> I'll put a girdle round about the earth
> In forty minutes.
>
> —A MIDSUMMER NIGHT'S DREAM, II, i

THE USSR has the largest force of men under arms in the world. Hard statistics are almost impossible to obtain—the Russians are more secretive about affairs in this realm than almost any other—but their total military establishment probably numbers at least 4,100,000 men. The corresponding figure for the United States is 2,800,000. The Soviet Army consists of 175 to 200 divisions; probably not more than half of these are activated or ready for immediate service, and Soviet divisions are smaller numerically than American, but even so, the figure is substantial. Moreover—omitting any consideration of China—satellite forces in Europe probably number almost a million men. It is true that, since the Polish and Hungarian explosions, all these are not considered by the Russians to be reliable; nevertheless, something like fifty to sixty-five satellite divisions could probably be put in the field. How many divisions has NATO got? Perhaps sixteen or seventeen.

Nor should we forget that the British are steadily cutting their power in Europe down, and the French are embroiled up to the umbilicus in Algeria.

In general, Soviet military characteristics reflect the nation. The best divisions are very good indeed; the worst are terrible. Some equipment is superb, and may be superior to ours; some is primitive, badly maintained, and obsolete. In the past few years the Russians have made a serious effort to make their army more homogeneous, and reduce the gap between good and bad divisions; since about 1952, equipment has tended to improve. In some elements—for instance motorized transport—the Soviet Union is a very long way behind the United States. Nevertheless we may well pay heed to such statements as the following, from the United States Army *Information Digest*, "The Soviet Army is the only major force in the world today that has a completely new post-war arsenal of weapons in being, capable of fighting either a nuclear or non-nuclear war, big or small, in any kind of climate or terrain."[1]

Any attempt to estimate the proportion of the Soviet budget applied to arms leads to a morass of conflicting and unreliable figures. Khrushchev, reporting to the Twentieth Congress, had a few things to say about military budgets in the western world, without revealing much about his own. He stated:

> In the United States, *per capita* arms expenditure was $3.50 in the 1913-14 fiscal year, $7 in 1929-30, and $250 in 1954-55—a more than seventy fold increase. In Britain, *per capita* arms expenditure increased from £1 14s. in 1913-14 to £2 10s. in 1929-30, and £29 6s. in 1954-55.

In 1956, the Soviet Union spent 97,800 million rubles (about $24 billion at par) for defense out of a total budget of 560 billion rubles, or roughly 17.5 per cent. This works out to about $122 per capita. The 1957 estimates are lower, down by 1,100 million rubles from 1956, and are 16 per cent of the total budget.[2] United States defense expenditure is roughly $38 billion for the present year, not counting foreign aid, or well over 50 per cent of the total American budget. But comparisons like these are full of thorns and pitfalls, because no one knows exactly what is—or what is not—included in Soviet "military" expenditure, and, as always, it is next to impossible to quote rubles in terms of consistent dollar values.

Why should the Soviet military establishment, so much bigger than ours in several dimensions, cost so much less? Why does the United States have to spend almost half again as much more per year on arms?

[1] Jack Raymond in the *New York Times*, July 7, 1957.
[2] In Czarist days military expenditure was about a quarter of the budget.

There are several answers. American military hardware costs more, and industrial wages are higher in the United States. All equipment is more expensive. An American GI gets $85.50 per month, whereas a Soviet private gets $6.00 to $8.00. Moreover American GI's have better food, live in more comfortable quarters, and are given various luxuries. A Soviet soldier— to pick just one item—lives mostly on black bread and soup, and perhaps gets white bread three or four times a year. His life is pared down to the bone, without pampering.

The Soviet government announced in May, 1956, that it intended to reduce its armed forces by 1,200,000 men within a year, with 63 divisions to be dismantled.[3] It is not known whether this order has been fully carried out as yet. For several reasons the Kremlin finds sharp reduction in its armed services, particularly ground forces, advantageous at this particular time. First, it strengthens the Russian hand in disarmament negotiations. Second, it will tend to relieve manpower shortages in industry and agriculture.

As to strategy, the basic Russian concept is still to think in terms of the ground forces—the lowly infantryman—as the vital and paramount factor. It is perfectly well known that attack on Russia, if it comes, will probably come in the first instance from the air; even so, the land of Russia will, sooner or later in the event of war, have to be conquered and occupied by the invader, or so at least Russian strategical thinkers assume. And, to defend the land, the foot soldier cannot be replaced. Even the navy is thought of as a kind of flank for the army. Of course the infantry will be supported by artillery, tanks, and airpower. But, in the main, the Russians hope to rely on the giant, immutable factor of their geography, plus men and tanks fighting on the ground. Subsidiary elements in their strategy: (1) to keep firm control of their seas, in particular the Baltic, at all costs; (2) to maintain the satellites as a *glacis* or wedge of terrain separating Russia proper from a possible invader. The satellites provide two precious elements, space and time.

Russian strategy is, in general, keyed more to defense than attack. A telling indication of this is that the Soviet Union has *no* aircraft carriers, and apparently has no intention of building any. Aircraft carriers are, of course, primarily offensive weapons. Nuclear research and the development of nuclear arms are emphatic in the Soviet Union, but the Kremlin is by no means committed to an exclusive nuclear strategy, even in these post-Sputnik days. Marshal Zhukov, when he was still Minister of Defense, answering a

---

[3] Also 375 warships and other units in the navy were to be given up.

series of questions posed not long ago by Hanson W. Baldwin of the *New York Times*, said that nuclear weapons were not "decisive" in Soviet military planning.[4] The Russians are not (at the moment of writing at least— times may change) even remotely interested in unleashing a nuclear blitz attack on the western world; first, this does not fit in with their ideology; second, fear of retaliation is too great. The Russians think of A-bombs, thermonuclear devices, and ballistic missiles as strictly a checkmate proposition.

We proceed to details:

Army. Properly this is now called the "Soviet Army," not the "Red Army." The appellation "Red" was dropped after World War II, when national symbols replaced those connoting the old revolutionary fervor. Conscripts go in at nineteen, and serve for a minimum of two years. Probably the total enlistment in ground forces is about 2,300,000; of these something less than two-thirds are conscripts, the rest being long-term professionals. One reason why the army is so big is distance, plus difficulties in internal transportation. Before World War II there were, in fact, two quite distinct Soviet armies, one for European Russia, and one for the Far East which, under the command of the renowned Marshal Bluecher, was for a long time almost autonomous.

Mr. Baldwin writes in the *New York Times*: "The order of battle of the active Soviet Army numbers about 175 to 200 divisions. Sixty to 100 of these may be at, or near, full strength; some are at reduced strength; probably at least one-third exist only in cadre form. About 100 to 110 . . . are rifle or infantry divisions; forty-five are so-called mechanized divisions, with many tanks; about 20 are armored. There are still at least five horsed cavalry divisions." Soviet divisions, even though smaller than ours numerically, are believed to have nearly equivalent fire power. Some twenty-two divisions are stationed in East Germany and three other European satellites —Poland, Hungary, and Rumania.

Soviet tanks are good; so are their bazookas, mortars, rocket launchers and medium artillery. Their personnel carriers and the like are inferior to ours, but their jeep, known as a Gaz,[5] is adequate. The Russians go in for simplicity in small arms, stressing sturdiness and avoiding complicated gadgets. Their T-54, the standard medium tank, is faster than the equivalent American tank, and is more maneuverable; it has broader tracks, with less ground pressure per square inch, and carries a 100 mm. gun as against our 90. The American tank weighs more, uses more fuel, and has a higher silhouette. On the other

[4] August 7, 1956.
[5] Standing for Gorky Automobile Plant (*Zavod*).

hand the American M-48 has better armor and a better gun sight, and probably our gun fires with greater initial velocity.

During the great purges in the late 1930's, the Red Army lost *one-half* of all its officers, a staggering percentage. This was, of course, one reason why, during the initial stages of the German attack in 1941, the Russians did badly. Later, as all of us have good reason to know, they did not do badly. Discipline has always been strict. General Eisenhower has an eloquent passage in his *Crusade in Europe*, describing a conversation with Marshal Zhukov in Moscow after the war. He asked Zhukov how Soviet troops cleared mine fields. Zhukov replied that the customary procedure was to send in swarms of infantrymen, regardless of casualties; when the mines had blown up everybody, more or less, the field was adjudged to be clear, and more troops went in. General Eisenhower mentioned wryly what would happen to any American commander who ever indulged in the same technique.

The following is the oath taken by Soviet Army soldiers, and it is taken very seriously:

> I, a citizen of the Union of Soviet Socialist Republics, entering the ranks of the Soviet Army, do take this oath and do solemnly swear to be an honest, brave, disciplined, vigilant fighter, to guard military and state secrets strictly, and to obey all military regulations and the orders of my officers and those in authority over me.
>
> I shall always be ready to defend my country—the Union of Soviet Socialist Republics—at the bidding of the Workers' and Peasants' Government and as a fighter of the Soviet Army I swear to defend it courageously, ably, worthily and honorably, not hesitating to sacrifice my blood and even my life to achieve complete victory over the enemy.
>
> If I wilfully break this solemn oath, then may the stern judgment of the Soviet Law and the universal hatred and scorn of the working people strike me.[6]

Most senior officers are Communist party members; most men in the rank and file are not, but the percentage of party membership is increasing, and in any case the army is a *Communist* army. The party runs the army, not vice versa, particularly since the fall of Zhukov in 1957, even though the role of the "political commissars" attached to army units is much less significant than in former days. During World War II, these officials, who were often not military men at all, could countermand orders of professional officers. Reports were rife, during the Soviet attack on Hungary, of serious disaffection among Russian troops, mass desertions, and the like. In actual fact nothing of the sort took place; there was no movement at all

[6] *If You Were Born in Russia*, by Arthur Goodfriend, p. 75, published by Farrar, Straus and Cudahy.

across the lines, and only five or six individual defections occurred in all. On the other hand, Soviet troops which had been stationed in Hungary for a long time, particularly in outlying districts, liked the Hungarians and did not relish the job of putting them down by force of arms.

One powerful military figure in the USSR is Marshal Ivan S. Konev, Commander of the Army Ground Forces, a first Deputy Minister of Defense, and the officer in charge of military liaison with the satellites, under the Warsaw Pact. Konev, the son of a peasant, was head of the special military tribunal that sentenced Beria to death, and before that, during the war, commanded the southern front below Moscow. Foreign military attachés view his talents with sober respect. He is bald as a croquet ball, and looks something like Khrushchev. It was Konev who took the lead in attacking Marshal Zhukov, his old comrade, when Zhukov was dismissed. Other officers of high rank and influence are Marshal Alexander M. Vasilevsky, who made a great name for himself in World War II, and Marshal Kirill S. Moskalenko, who commands the Moscow military district, and who is Ukrainian. The chief of the general staff is Marshal Vasily D. Sokolovsky, who was chief of staff to Zhukov during the war; the most important of the district commanders, sixteen in all, is probably Marshal Semyon K. Timoshenko, another Ukrainian, who made a vivid record in the war and is now commander-in-chief in Belorussia; he guards the Soviet western frontier. All these officers, are, incidentally, members of the Central Committee of the party.

Marshal Konstantin K. Rokossovsky, of Polish origin, sometimes called the most "brilliant" of contemporary Soviet officers, was Minister of Defense in Poland and a member of the Polish Politburo, put there by Stalin to keep the Poles in order; he was thrown out by Wladyslaw Gomulka in the Polish explosion in 1956, and Moscow had to take him back. He serves now as a Deputy Minister of Defense, and is in command in the Caucasus, on the Turkish frontier. Still another man of consequence is a deputy minister of defense, Marshal Ivan Kh. Bagramyan. One more officer of marked distinction and interest is General of the Army Alexei I. Antonov, a former acting chief of staff. He was Stalin's favorite military expert; Mr. Truman, when he met Russian leaders at the Potsdam conference, was much impressed by his abilities.

Air Force. Something like eighteen to twenty thousand military planes and one million men or more comprise the Soviet Air Force. The Russians are strongest in jet fighters, like the MiG 17,[7] and in newly developed delta-wing craft for the tactical support of ground troops. The main accent is on

[7] Of which a brother of Anastas Mikoyan is the coinventor. The "Mi" in the name stands for Mikoyan.

defense, but long-range bombers are not neglected. Those that most impress foreign observers are four: (1) The four-jet ship which, in American and NATO nomenclature, is called the Bison. It was designed by Andrei N. Tupolev, the best-known of Soviet aeronautical engineers, and is supposed to have a speed of 560 miles an hour, a range of three to four thousand miles, and a bomb load up to ten tons. It corresponds to our B-52, and is probably lighter and has a higher ceiling, but is not so fast and has less range. Still, Mr. Tupolev builds good airplanes, and the Bison is not to be ignored. (2) The twin-jet medium bomber called by us the Badger. It was designed by the illustrious Sergei V. Ilyushin, who won a 150,000-ruble Stalin Prize in 1952 for his work on this and other planes. The Badger has roughly the same speed as the Bison, but its bomb load and range are smaller; it corresponds roughly to the American B-47. A new and better variant of the Badger, with four jet engines, is believed to be in production now. (3) A four-engine turboprop heavy bomber called the Bear, designed by Ilyushin, not particularly fast but of great range and weight-carrying capacity. The United States has no exact counterpart to this massive ship. (4) A twin-engine light jet bomber, a development of the Il-28 called by us the Blowlamp, which the Russians say is supersonic, i.e., it flies faster than the speed of sound. The United States has no supersonic bombers that are operational, but in the summer of 1957 a new craft known as the B-58 Hustler was demonstrated publicly for the first time, and promises to fill this gap soon.

As always, Soviet stresses and accents are unpredictable. One curious point is that the Russians have paid comparatively little attention to aerial refueling, although the Bison can be fitted out as a tanker. This could mean either that they do not think at all in terms of direct aerial attack on the United States, or, on the contrary, that they have other weapons up their long sleeves, like the ICBM. One item about which they have been altogether consistent for many years is the development of parachutist and airborne troops. Attack by parachutists is a Russian invention, and the Soviet Union today has more glider troops and parachutists than all the armies of the rest of the world combined.

The Soviet Air Force has six distinct branches or commands: (1) The Army Air Force, by far the largest and most important. Like the U. S. Tactical Air Command, it is devoted to the support of ground troops. (2) The Air Defense Force, including missiles, aircraft, and antiaircraft artillery. (3) The Naval Air Forces. (4) Civil aviation. (5) The Long Range Air Force, known as ADD, and the equivalent of the Strategic Air Command in the United States. (6) Transport and parachutists. At least one ADD base is believed to be on the Chukchi Peninsula, next door to Alaska, and there are other important installations in Kamchatka.

Nobody knows exactly who runs the Soviet Air Force. The chain of command in the army is clearly marked, but not in military aviation. The Minister of Defense, who at the moment is Marshal Rodion Malinovsky, is in charge of all Soviet military matters—army, navy, air—and is of course the top of the top, but some mystery surrounds the exact function of some of his deputies. Most Soviet officers of supreme rank wear two hats; there is no such thing as a civilian minister, and the highest officers may serve as deputy ministers as well as active commanders in the field, and are often transposed from one job to the other. The ranking air officer of the Soviet Union is an accomplished commander, Air Marshal K. A. Vershinin. His chief of staff is, or was, Air Marshal Sergei I. Rudenko, a Ukrainian. Another officer of consequence, believed to be the commander of the Long Range Air Force, is Air Marshal Vladimir A. Sudets.

The Navy. Here the chief emphasis is on submarines. The Russians have no new battleships, no new heavy cruisers, and no aircraft carriers; what they do have is by far the largest submarine fleet in the world. Probably 350 to 450 submarines have been actually launched, with 600 as the goal; of these 100 to 200 are of long range. The United States has, by contrast, a total of only 105 submarines in commission. Several of these are, however, propelled by atomic power whereas the Soviet Union has no atomic submarines. Submarines are predominantly a defensive weapon; but this does not mean that they cannot be used offensively. The word U-boat is well known. Moreover submarines can be equipped nowadays for the propulsion of ballistic missiles. In fact the Russians have recently taken to boasting that their submarines could not only block American ports, but, sitting out in the open sea, could bomb and destroy targets like New York or inland cities by the use of H-bomb missiles.

Submarine crews need intensive training, and long shakedown cruises in ocean water have been deemed essential. It puzzled observers for a long time that, in spite of their number and the need for training, Soviet submarines were practically never tracked in non-Russian waters. Apparently they seldom left their Baltic or Black Sea sanctuaries, or ventured far from Petropavlosk, near the tip of Kamchatka, the only Soviet naval base directly fronting on the high seas. Then, in June, 1957, three Soviet submarines were seen traversing the English Channel. These, it became known later, had been sold to Egypt, and were en route there. When Russian naval officers are asked why they give so much precedence to submarines the answer is that two-thirds of the Soviet frontiers are water, and that distances are such that each area—Black Sea, Baltic, and so on—needs its own units. Another reason is, of course, that the Russians want to be able to cut off both Atlantic and Pacific shipping in the event of general war. One little-known fact is that most Russian submarines are constructed inland, not at ports, and are shipped to Leningrad or Sevastopol where the parts are assembled, almost as if they were automobiles. How *good* Russian submarines are is unknown.

The navy, submarines aside, does not get much priority in the Soviet defense system; even so, it is the second navy in the world, having surpassed the British. Khrushchev, it seems, has little faith in conventional seapower. When he and Bulganin traveled to England they went on a cruiser, and Khrushchev said that this was all that cruisers were good for—they were sitting ducks, or taxis. During the 1956 air show in Moscow, visiting dignitaries like General Twining were entertained at the House of the Soviet Army, a kind of officer's club; its gardens contain a large pond, and Khrushchev, Bulganin, and company amused themselves by taking their distinguished guests for rowboat rides. Khrushchev pointed to the rowboat, and smiled, "Our navy!" The Soviet Union does, however, keep in commission several Sverdlovsk-class light cruisers, which displace 17,000 tons and carry 5.9 inch guns, and the destroyer fleet is strong. Altogether the personnel of the Soviet Navy probably number 800,000 men.

Ballistic Missiles and the Sputniks. Developments in missiles have come with such disconcerting speed recently, and the whole subject is so unpredictable, reverberatingly confused, and mercurial even on a day-to-day basis, that anything except the briefest comment would be out of place here; this book is, after all, not a newspaper, or even an almanac. On August 26, 1957, the Soviet government announced successful tests of the ICBM, or intercontinental ballistic missile, often called the "ultimate weapon" because it is capable of crossing a continent or an ocean and because no conclusive means of defense against it or intercepting it are known. The democratic world was stirred—and should have been profoundly shocked. The Soviet communiqué did not fail to allude pointedly to certain suggestive items. "The rocket flew at a very high, unprecedented altitude. Covering a huge distance in a brief time the rocket landed in the target area. The results obtained show that it is possible to direct rockets *into any part of the world.*" (Italics mine.) Perhaps the ICBM cannot strike a target with complete accuracy. "Target area" is not a very precise term, although Khrushchev said later that the missile had hit "the bull's eye." In any case it does not matter much if a missile equipped with a hydrogen warhead lands, let us say, in the Bronx instead of Brooklyn. The destruction caused will cover substantial areas in any case.

Subsequently the Russians announced officially that this missile travels at a speed of 13,000-15,000 miles an hour (which means that it could reach New York from Moscow in a matter of minutes), and reaches an altitude of 620 miles before beginning its descent. No details have been given of the type of fuel it uses, aside from the fact that this is "new," or how the Soviet scientists have solved the "re-entry problem"—that is, how the missile is enabled to penetrate successfully the earth's oxygen-laden atmosphere on its descent, and thus hit the target intact instead of burning up.

Then, on October 4, came the successful launching of the first Soviet earth satellite, or artificial moon. Once again the world was stirred—and doubly shocked. The Sputnik has major importance in all sorts of fields, including its propaganda value and usefulness in pure scientific research, but perhaps the most vital and significant thing about it is its launching mechanism, which is of a weight and thrust far beyond anything in possession of the free world at the moment; it staggered scientists everywhere that such a mechanism could have been developed by anybody. Many had doubted—before the Sputnik—that the ICBM *had* been successfully launched; now they could doubt no longer. In fact Khrushchev announced presently that the launching mechanisms of the ICBM and Sputnik were the same, and that the rockets differed only in the character of their heads. Sputnik carried a radio transmitter, but the ICBM carried a bomb.

On November 3 came launching of the second Sputnik, complete with dog. More Sputniks will probably follow soon. The trepidation Americans felt about these developments should not have blinded us to the fact that the incredible Russians had successfully pulled off a magnificent—solid as well as brilliant—scientific achievement. With Laika in Sputnik II, the space age really began. In military fields these developments continue to have coldly staggering implications. For one thing—forgetting about Brooklyn and the Bronx—the Soviet missiles, it became only too obvious, made NATO and American bases everywhere in Europe vulnerable in the extreme. In his interview with Henry Shapiro of the United Press early in November, Khrushchev said that he was convinced that the United States did not have an intercontinental missile because "if she had she would have launched her own Sputnik." (Khrushchev was right.) Then he reiterated that the United States could be reached by Soviet rockets fired from submarines and otherwise, and playfully challenged the United States to a missile shooting match (peaceful) so that we could see Russian prowess for ourselves. A few weeks later Khrushchev received William Randolph Hearst, Jr., and his team for another remarkable interview. He told Bob Considine, not playful this time, that although he would not go in for threats Russia had won the arms race, and could at will strike American cities and bases "off the face of the earth." Maybe this was an empty boast. Maybe not.

By the time these lines are in print the situation may have radically changed, but there is no doubt that, as of the autumn of 1957, the United States was caught badly lagging in the missile race. In the field of the ICBM we have two missiles, the Atlas and the Titan, but it may be a long time before they are operational. The Atlas failed in two launching tests, but was successful in a third in a less than full-length flight; the Titan has never left the ground.[8] But the Soviet ICBM may become operational within a year, or even sooner. Even more embarrassing is the fact, now generally accepted, that the United States is also far behind the USSR in intermediate-range ballistic missiles, the IRBM's. These have a range of from eight to fifteen hundred miles, as against five thousand miles or more for the ICBM. The Russians have been testing their intermediate missile, known as the T-2, since the middle of 1955, and for the past year and a half have been firing five or six a month. The T-2 is supposed to be in active production now. The United States has three different IRBM's in the fifteen-hundred-mile range, the Army's Jupiter, the Air Force's Thor, and the Navy's Polaris. They are believed to have about half the power of the T-2. As of the moment, Jupiter and Thor have been tested successfully, but not Polaris. None is as yet anywhere near being operational. In fact, disconcerting as the fact may be, the United States still has no operational ballistic missile with a range greater than 200-300 miles.

The Bomb. Of all Soviet military and strategical assets, possession of the H-bomb is obviously biggest. So long as the Russians did not have atomic weapons, they were not a serious military problem. They were, in effect, at our mercy. When, however, the Soviet Union broke the American monopoly on atomic bombs in 1949, and in particular when its first hydrogen bomb was successfully exploded in 1953, the balance of power in the world was irremediably changed. The Russians can, any time they want to, destroy the earth, as can we. The Soviet stockpile of A-bombs and H-bombs, probably a thousand or more, is nowhere as big as ours. But neither the size of stockpile nor rate of production has much relevance nowadays. Nor is the Russian

[8] *New York Times,* October 27, 1957.

atomic armory anywhere near as potent, varied, and advanced as ours. As of last summer, the Russians are known to have detonated eighteen atomic or nuclear explosions, many fewer than we. Even so, the Soviet atomic accomplishment should be treated with respect.

In May, 1957, Khrushchev told Polish journalists that the Russians had a bomb so big that they did not dare test it; he said that it would "melt the Arctic ice cap and send oceans spilling all over the world." This, no doubt, was an example of the kind of pictorial exaggeration Khrushchev often indulges in. It is unknown whether or not this was the weapon with the hydrogen-bomb warhead that was successfully tested in October, 1957, and which made a very large explosion. This test followed by a day or two launching of the first Sputnik, but had no connection with it. The bomb was dropped from an airplane at a great height.

*

Several important Soviet deficiencies or weaknesses in military or semi military matters are obvious—inadequate transportation, fuel shortages, clumsiness in much equipment, et cetera. In basic industrial strength, the paramount determinant in a protracted war, the United States is overwhelmingly superior. We produce more steel, more petroleum, more and better machines. The American economy is infinitely stronger than the Russian, more flexible and productive, if only because it is free. The Soviet Air Force has effective planes, but it cannot touch ours. The Soviet Navy has not a fraction of the striking power of the American Navy, despite the number of Russian submarines. The Soviet Army private may be tough, but so is the American GI.

For a long time it was thought that the principal Soviet handicap was its vulnerability to American air attack. It is much easier for the United States to attack Russia by air than vice versa, by conventional means. Using long-range bombers, we have been in a position to envisage assault on key targets in the Soviet Union almost with impunity; we could attack with ease from American bases scattered throughout the world, as well as from carriers in the Mediterranean: from England, North Africa, the Middle East, and Okinawa. But the Russians (we thought) did not have the capacity of hitting us in return substantially, because of the distances involved. They could bomb targets in western Europe and Japan, but not in critical areas of the United States itself. In other words, Moscow appeared to be automatically vulnerable, acutely so, and could be destroyed in a flash; New York and Washington could not. But Soviet development of the ICBM has seriously altered this strategical picture. As things stand today we could be easily hit by intercontinental missiles without warning, at least in theory. We do not know now how vulnerable we may be, although the long-range bombers of the Strategic Air Command are still a prime and powerful deterrent to any aggression or threat thereof.

In any case, some folk in Washington do not like the feel of things. One cannot ignore the testimony of General Curtis E. LeMay, former chief of the Strategic Air Command, who said (May, 1956) that it was his "guess" that the Soviet Union could destroy the United States by a complete surprise attack by 1959. Early in 1957, a Senate subcommittee headed by Senator Stuart Symington reported that the Soviet Union has more combat aircraft than the United States, and was rapidly closing the "qualitative gap" in American production. In May, 1957, a meteorological specialist attached to the Federal Civil Defense Administration told Congress that, in the 1960's, a Russian attack on the United States, using 250 thermonuclear bombs on primary targets, could theoretically kill 82,000,000 people. Moreover these estimates and predictions were made in pre-Sputnik days. They would be even less agreeable today.

A Word about Civil Aviation

All civil aviation within the Soviet Union is, of course, a state monopoly; Aeroflot has no competition, except on flights outside the country, and is run by the Ministry of Defense.

Flying in Russia is apt to be pretty rough. This is an understatement. It is extremely rough. It is also fun, and comparatively safe. Most travelers know by this time that Soviet planes do not (as a general rule) have seat belts. The Russians don't believe in them. Only seldom is a signal given when a plane is about to land, and no one pays attention to whether you smoke or not taking off or landing, although "NO SMOKING" signs exist on some planes. There are no emergency exits on planes on domestic runs. Sometimes a plane will have *one* seat with a seat belt, presumably for somebody sick or for some old-fashioned crank who demands one. And a thing that mystified and bewildered me more than anything in the entire Soviet Union was that seats in some airplanes have *half* a seat belt. The buckle end is there but not the strap that fits into it. Don't ask me what it is good for.

Soviet planes on international routes are newer, cleaner, and better equipped than those used on domestic flights. As always, the Russians like to put on their best face when they are seen abroad. When we flew out of Russia we took Aeroflot as far as Riga because the weather was so bad that the Scandinavian line would not fly. This ship was bright with shiny paint; the cabin had a carpet; the stewardess not only wore a cap and a uniform but she served bits of candy; and we had blankets. You do not get such luxuries on internal runs, and the planes are old and look frightfully beaten up. But the tires, I observed, are usually new-seeming, with sharp treads. The planes have no ground heating system and the door is always, for some reason, kept open during waits at an airport; such waits may be hours long, and if your metal shell of plane has been sitting on the snow, the cabin can be cold— very cold indeed. But, as a rule, some sort of gadget is turned on that provides heat when the plane, after departure, levels off. Planes are not pressurized (except the jets), and long flights are fatiguing. The baggage allowance is only ten kilograms per person (twenty-two pounds), but, so far as I could tell, baggage was never weighed. My wife and I between us had thirty-nine kilos, and never had to pay any overweight at all. I never saw a baggage check in Russia.

In his book *A Russian Journal* published some years ago, John Steinbeck mentioned that Soviet stewardesses seem to have no relation whatever to the passengers; this is still true. Only seldom does a stewardess wear a uniform, and usually she sits alone, in the third seat from the front, during the entire flight, immobile and inert, although friendly. Apparently she has no function except to inform the pilot if something in the cabin goes awry. Only rarely are refreshments served aloft. The planes stop every two or three hours, and you go out for a hurried lunch or dinner at the airport. Sometimes on a long flight you can have six or seven dinners in a row, all approximately the same. The planes seldom taxi all the way up to the apron, and you may have to tramp as long as a quarter of a mile through the frozen snow.

The airports, particularly in remote places in Siberia and Central Asia, are really something. Usually they consist of a line of small wooden buildings, one of which is the restaurant. Sometimes an open washbowl is to be found in the waiting room, and in small airports an incongruous object sits on the table next to the telephone—a flat iron. Presumably this is for passengers who want to press their clothes after a night aloft, but I never saw one used. Incidentally departures of planes are not, as a rule, announced; there are no loudspeakers, bells, or other signals for this purpose, but usually an elderly woman attendant, swaddled in a padded cloak and wearing cloth boots, is assigned to each group of passengers, with the responsibility of getting them aboard in time.

Russian pilots, according to tradition, always fly at treetop or chimney level, but in our case this didn't happen. Usually we flew at about four thousand feet. Every Soviet airliner has conspicuously set up in the cabin a small instrument panel which includes an air speed indicator and an altimeter, so that the passengers—it is good fun—always know how fast they are traveling and how high. Planes are usually crowded. A familiar legend is to the effect that Soviet citizens are immobile, perpetually confined to one community, but this was certainly not true according to our experience. We met people from all over the country on various flights, and movement through the country is incessant. One characteristic of Soviet flight is its astounding informality. If the pilot is feeling friendly, he will hold the plane until everybody has had his supper at whatever airport he has come into. If the stewardess fails to show up, or happens to be left behind, one of the passengers may be asked to substitute for her. On one long flight we took—all the way from Tiflis to Moscow—the door separating crew from passengers kept banging. No one could make it stick shut. The copilot made a halfhearted effort to do so, without luck. So it simply banged open and shut, with an infernal racket, for the whole length of the flight—more than seven hours.

I have said that flying in Russia is apt to be pretty casual. One day, en route from Leningrad to Kiev, we stopped at Minsk, very late because of fierce headwinds. Our interpreter kept warily watching the plane crew as we gulped our soup. Soviet pilots do not like to be late. Suddenly she tapped me on the shoulder and, without finishing lunch, we boarded our craft. In a second, so it seemed, we were taxiing down the snow. I looked out and saw that half a dozen of our fellow passengers, not adequately warned, now stood on the strip wildly beckoning to us and even chasing us along the runway. The pilot brought the plane to a halt at the end of the runway, and within two or three minutes up drove an open truck with our missing passengers. But no one had thought to bring a ladder. No matter. The pilot and copilot simply marched down the length of the cabin, opened the door, and, grasping the passengers by the wrists, hauled them bodily in one by one. After what could not have been a delay of more than a minute, we took off again. A far cry from Idlewild!

In the 1930's a British resident of Moscow made a remark that has passed into legend. "If Russia didn't cover such a large part of the earth's surface and if there weren't so many Russians, this country would be one long laugh."

*

Practically all flight is by contact. If the weather is really bad, Soviet planes do not fly. The pilot before departure telephones the next airport to see what the ceiling is. Soviet pilots, who are extraordinarily skilled, take absolutely no chances, although they are used to conditions that would appall an observer in the United States, and fly in much worse weather than our regulations would ever permit. Standard operating procedure in western Europe is for a plane to carry enough fuel for its destination, plus 6 per cent for deviation, plus one to two hours' holding time over the target, plus enough to get to the nearest alternate field. The Russians think that such extreme precautions are childish. They carry exactly one hour's extra gasoline on a day flight, one and a half hours for a night flight. Senior pilots get 3,500 rubles ($875) a month salary, plus bonuses and special allowances if they fly in the Arctic regions or the southern deserts. There are a good many women pilots, but we never happened to fly with one.

Flying may be rough, but Russian pilots are magnificent and accidents are extremely rare. These are, however, not reported unless a foreigner is involved; local aviation crashes are not considered news, and never appear in the Soviet press. One reason why the Soviet safety record is so high is, the Russians say, absence of competition. Planes do not have to outdo rivals and do not unnecessarily extend themselves.

Aeroflot is the largest airline in the world from the point of view of length of domestic routes, and runs neck and neck with Pan American World Airways in total route mileage. It serves twenty-four cities outside the USSR, most of them capitals of adjacent countries, and 121 within. The standard carrier is the Ilyushin, which exists in two models, and is a powerful, squat thirty-passenger machine. In some respects it resembles our Convair. Aeroflot has nine hundred of these. Also Russian-built DC-3's are still flown on short runs; they are called Li-2's, and some, believe it or not, are surviving American planes delivered under Lend-Lease during the War.

New four-motor turbojets and other models are being tested, including one sleek, ponderous ship designed by Tupolev that is supposed to be the largest and fastest passenger aircraft in the world; it is (the Russians say) capable of carrying 160 passengers from Moscow to London in a little over three hours.[9] Also the world's biggest helicopter, the Mi-6, is in tentative operation, carrying 80 passengers or a payload of 26,000 pounds, as well as

[9] American aviation designers say that we could easily build such planes, but that they would be unprofitable to operate. The Russians of course pay no attention to profit motive or similar "bourgeois" considerations.

several new-type very small planes. The Soviet government does its utmost to encourage domestic aviation in a variety of aspects, and advertisements urging people to fly may be widely seen, but fares are high. The flight from Leningrad to Moscow costs two hundred rubles or fifty dollars; a comparable flight in the United States would be substantially less.[10]

The Soviet Union is the only country in the world, as of the moment, flying full jets on regular passenger runs. The Russian jet-liner, known as the TU-104, carries fifty to seventy passengers, and provides services at astounding speeds, although its nonstop range is limited. Flying time from Moscow to Khabarovsk near the Pacific, a distance of more than six thousand kilometers, is only eight hours and thirty minutes. Moscow-Peking, almost ten thousand kilometers, is flown with only two main intermediary stops, Omsk and Irkutsk. The Soviet delegation to the UN used a TU-104 to fly to New York in 1957. Flying on these jets, it is now possible to get from Paris, via Prague, all the way to Peking in less than a day—in nineteen hours and forty-five minutes, to be precise. So far Russian jets are serving only one city in Europe, Prague. The jet service to Tashkent, in Central Asia, connects with flights to Afghanistan, Pakistan, and India.

[10] All services were, until recently, scheduled on Moscow time, which caused confusion since there are no fewer than eleven time zones in the Soviet Union; now local times are used.

CHAPTER XIX

What Has Russia Got?

> *A specter is haunting Europe—the specter of Communism.*
> —THE COMMUNIST MANIFESTO (1848)

THIS brief chapter is in the nature of a recapitulation. Then we shall take a trip.

The factor that counts most, when we attempt to answer the question what the Russians have got, is challenge. What, in other words, have the United States and the free world to fear? Have we reason to fear, not merely Soviet aggressiveness and indiscriminate nuisanceful troublemaking, but Soviet *success?* Several items may be listed in this general connection, some obvious, some not. Everybody knows that the USSR is the second industrial and second (perhaps first) military power in the world. The era when folk in the West thought complacently and patronizingly that the Soviet Union could not so much as produce an alarm clock that would work is no more. The Sputnik was an alarm clock with a heady ring, if nothing else. Anyway—

Item. Geography, a factor so manifest that it scarcely needs mention again. Not only is the Soviet Union big, but it is situated with vivid capacity for strategic force. It contains the heartland of the Eurasian land mass and, as was said in these pages long ago, it dominates not merely one continent but two. And it is flanked by a buffer screen of satellites on the west, and by the immensity of its partner, China, on the east.

Item. Raw materials. In this regard the USSR is next to the United States incomparably the greatest repository in the world. It is short on some strategic materials, like natural rubber and industrial diamonds, but it is long on a great deal else. The Soviet Union is supposed to have 21 per cent of the world's known coal resources, 20 per cent of iron ore, 33 per cent of forest, hydroelectric reserves almost beyond computation, and the largest

395

black soil area in the world, 247,000,000 acres.[1] It is first in the world in production of manganese, platinum, peat, and several rare strategic minerals; second in coal and iron; and, very important, third in petroleum. Also it has the second largest gold reserve in the world, if a gold reserve can be considered to be a "raw" material. The industrial constellations at Magnitogorsk and elsewhere in Siberia, utilizing vast deposits of zinc, tin, and nickel, are well known. New discoveries in the realm of mineral wealth come frequently. The iron-ore deposits near Kustanai, on the Turgai lowland in Kazakhstan, are supposed by new calculations to amount to twenty *billion* tons, by far the largest such deposit in the world. Another immense newly discovered deposit is in European Russia in the vicinity of Kursk, known as the Kursk "Magnetic Anomaly."

Item. Population. This, we know, is a bit over 200,000,000 now, considering Russia alone; with Communist partners and satellites, including China, it is more than 900,000,000 or almost one-third the total population of the world. *One-third of all mankind lives under Communism.* Moreover the Soviet Union has no demographic problem. It is true that the population increases at the rate of three million a year, and Soviet statisticians like to dwell proudly on such details as that between 1951 and 1955, for example, the population increased by 16,300,000, more than the total population of Scandinavia; but Russia has plenty of room. The death rate has, Kremlin figures say, been cut 75 per cent since the Revolution, and life expectancy has increased from thirty-two years in 1917 to sixty-four today.[2] In any case the Soviet Union could probably support easily a population three or four times its present size.

Item. The regime is in its forty-first year. This means that nobody at present has much knowledge of the past, of pre-Revolutionary Russia, except people over sixty. Hence, indoctrination becomes easier and more effective year by year.

Item. Vitality. Positiveness of Approach. Durability. Toughness.

Item. But toughness alone does not make a people strong. The Russians are tough, but beyond this, in spite of their poverty, they have a peculiar kind of spirit, an *élan.* I do not mean merely that avowed Communists have

---

[1] *Life,* March 29, 1943.

[2] *USSR,* August, 1956. Life expectancy figures are from the speech by M. A. Suslov celebrating the thirty-ninth anniversary of the Revolution. It should be pointed out again that the Soviet birth rate fell sharply during and immediately after World War II, because of casualties and dislocation of much of the population. A labor shortage much more acute than the one that obtains today is forecast for 1960-65, when the children born in 1941-46 reach working age.

faith in their goal, are fantastically disciplined, and share the grim comforts that may come to people of utterly fixed dogma. It is something on top of this, and it is difficult to determine whether it is an expression of Russian or Communist characteristics—probably a combination of both. People are taught (and a great many really believe it) that Russia, the country, is *their* country—they own it. And this gives them a special euphoria, an emotional superiority, quite aside from normal patriotism and the pride that arises naturally from their new position as one of the two supreme powers in the world. Finally, people gain spirit because the believers believe devoutly that the whole world will, sooner or later, become collectivist, and be *one* world run on Soviet lines; that irresistible social and economic forces make Soviet victory inevitable; that, in short, history is on their side.

One factor promoting this *élan* is that vast numbers of Russians now in responsible positions were sons and daughters of illiterate peasants, and have come up from nothing, as has been pointed out in these pages before. But they do not, as young people in America might, think of themselves as "self-made"; they think of themselves as *state-made*. Of course the vision of Russia as a unique motherland is not a Soviet invention, and is by no means new. Literature from Pushkin on talks of the "special destiny" of the Russian people. The fact remains that the contemporary ideology of the system, no matter how it has been distorted and watered down, is what helps to give the regime its positive force, as well as its totalitarian uniformity. This is still the world's first "wholly rational and scientific state." Socialism (as interpreted by the Kremlin) is still the ideal—and not only for Russia, but for the world. The regime still seeks to appeal to underpossessed people everywhere on the basis of socialism, and this is an important factor in its power.

Item. The Soviet Union insists that it stands for *peace*. We shall explore this issue in a chapter below. In any case it is vital to point out that the incessant Soviet stress on peace (even if this seems spurious to our eyes) as well as socialism produces an undeniable effect on small nations, even among American allies in western Europe. Not many countries want to be blasted off the face of the earth because Mr. Dulles is having a quarrel with the Kremlin. Peace and disarmament are magic words to many, and the Soviet government knows full well how to exploit them to the limit.

Item. Planning. No list of Soviet assets, even the most cursory, can omit this. The concept that the entire energies of a nation should be focused to and controlled by a systematized master plan is not merely a source of internal strength, but is a formidable article of ideological export. It is the chief contribution that the USSR has made to social science since the Revolution and is one of the most piercingly seminal concepts ever invented. There is scarcely a country in Asia or Africa, as well as Eastern Europe, without its Three, Five, Six, or Ten-Year Plan.

Item. There are weak and highly vulnerable areas in the Soviet economy, particularly in fuel and power production, agriculture, and transportation, but in general industrial progress has been marked, as is well known. Take one detail only—that since 1926 no fewer than 560 new cities and 1,000 lesser "urban communities" have been created. A feudal society has become (or is becoming) technical and urban, with the concomitant growth of a managerial class—also of headaches without end.

Item. The case might almost be made that poverty, particularly among the peasants, is an advantage to the Soviet regime as well as a handicap. The incessant struggle to make ends meet, on the land and in the factories, all but extinguishes interest in anything else. By keeping its people poor, the government also keeps them submissive. (This is not to say that plenty of discontent does not exist.)

Item. The totalitarian one-party system, plus the threat of terror, excludes any possibility of political opposition. We do not need to labor the point that the Soviet Union is a dictatorship, an utterly merciless one at that. The government is in a position to rule without any regard whatever to popular controls, although public opinion is not ignored. The regime gains cardinal strength by reason of its exploitation of dogma. Anybody dissident is an outcast, a heretic.

Item. Moreover the government of the USSR is an *executive* government par excellence. The cabinet does not have to argue with a congress, and nothing faintly like our Supreme Court exists, with a power to invalidate legislation. Elections are a farce. Laws are issued by decree, and the constitution can be amended at any time by simple executive decision. The executive, making its own decisions, also writes its own ticket. If, today, it decides to lend Afghanistan or Indonesia $100,000,000, all it has to do is do so. Nothing need be justified or explained. All this means, in turn, that important political decisions, particularly in foreign policy, can as a rule be taken more swiftly than is possible under any western government. Also policy can be shifted quickly, and tactics are much more supple and elastic. (It also means that authority can be extraordinarily capricious. No Soviet functionary can ever be sure of holding his job more than from hour to hour.)

Item. The Soviet government is also an extremely realistic government. To cite one minor example—the Communist theory is that monarchy is an anachronism, and royal dynasties a surviving relic of outworn imperialist techniques. But this did not keep the Kremlin from giving a calculatedly enthusiastic reception to Riza Pahlevi, the Shah of Iran, when he visited Moscow in 1956, and to the King of Afghanistan the next year. *The Kremlin knows what it wants.* A good many democracies do not, except loosely. Moreover the totalitarian system imposed on the people helps the Kremlin *get* what it wants. One must never forget or minimize the effectiveness of Soviet unity of purpose. Everything is focused to achieve the single end in view. Such a phenomenon as the competition in the United States between army, navy, and air force in development of ballistic missiles, in spite of the fact that these three services are supposed to be unified, would be inconceivable in the Soviet Union. Also Soviet leadership (no matter who is at the top) is a composite phenomenon. It was stated recently[3] that Mr. Dulles, in conceiving the Eisenhower Doctrine for the Middle East, formulated it "without consultation either with the policy planning staff of the State Department or the National Security Council." An analogous procedure would be utterly unthinkable in the Kremlin.

Item. The Soviet government, which under Khrushchev likes to gamble, is gambling nowadays on the supposition that the United States is not likely to go to war unless it is directly attacked. The fact that we did not intervene in Hungary was, to the Kremlin mind, an apt illustration of this. In several fields, this strengthens the Soviet hand, and gives it leeway in propaganda, political blackmail, and diplomatic infiltration and sabotage. American predisposition toward peace is a major Soviet asset.

Item. Skill in propaganda. The step-by-step methods by which the Russians took advantage of the Suez fiasco are a classic example of their almost diabolical alertness. And the fact that the Soviet government will lie on any occasion, utter the most brazen and black-faced lies without a tremor, plays to its hand. Also money is no object. For instance the USSR is spending $55,000,000 on its exhibit, which will have marked propaganda value, at the 1958 Brussels fair; the United States $11,800,000.

Item. Surely we do not need to mention again the Soviet stress on education and particularly science and scientific research. The library of one *factory* in Moscow (the ex-Stalin automobile works) contains 150,000 books. There were in Moscow in 1921 exactly eight chemical laboratories; today, more than six hundred. I asked one Russian friend what the country *did* with so many physicists, for example. "Ah!" he replied, "we calculate that, say, in April, 1960, we will need 11,762 physicists, with advanced degrees, in certain branches of industry. So we work out today what schools they will go to,

[3] Dana Adams Schmidt in the *New York Times*, October 14, 1957.

what special technical or theoretical subjects they will specialize in. They come out like oil in one of your pipe lines. If we have made a miscalculation, we simply tighten up the pipe and cut off some of the oil. Or we can expand our production of physicists at any time."

Item. Willingness to spend money. Nobody worries about the debt-ceiling in *this* country! The money comes out of the hides of the people, although taxes are extremely low. In one provincial city I asked the chief educational authority how much money he got from Moscow for research projects. Answer: "What we want." The Moscow Higher Technical School has a budget of 100,000,000 rubles ($25,000,000), as much as many American universities.

Item. An effort is made (of course within the circumference of the system) to make government and politics an extremely respected profession, which, to understate the point, is not always the case in the western democracies. Men of rank, in no matter what field—radiologists or irrigation engineers or poets of distinction—become deputies to the Supreme Soviet, and regard such elevation as a signal honor, which (by Russian standards) it indeed is. A distinguished academician will almost always have some other governmental function. A famous ophthalmologist, Professor V. P. Filatov, was a deputy to the Supreme Soviet, and so is the writer Ilya Ehrenburg. The Ukrainian dramatist Alexander Korneichuk is a member of the Central Committee of the Party. And so on almost without end. Everybody of consequence is brought into the functioning of the system and made to play a role.

Item. Another characteristic is what has been well described as the "mobilization potential." This is a regime almost neurotically keyed up, on the *qui vive*, taut, and ready for instant action or change of course. It gives the note of always being in crisis. Of course such keyed-upness may produce deleterious results—instability, slipshodness, extravagant waste of effort, and emotional fatigue. Russia, despite its latent vitality, often appears to be a very *tired* country.

Item. The Russians grasp better than we do some basic realities about Asia, and, as is only too obvious, are in hot, careful pursuit of the neutralist world of Asia and the Middle East. One factor favoring them is that they are partly Asian themselves and have little, if any, color prejudice. They *like* Asians, and get along with them well. Another point is that Moscow may seem to be a pretty miserable place to a sophisticated visitor from, say, London; but to a peasant from China who has never seen Europe before, it may look like paradise. Asians are sometimes repelled by the extravagances of American or western European standards of living. They know that the sparkling luxuries of New York are beyond their present grasp. But Moscow, with its "middleness," is something they can hope to reach, something attainable. One should also point out in this general connection that the struggle for power going on in the world, with unlimited stakes, is for the *whole* world, and that not less than two-thirds of the population of the world is black, brown, or colored. Moreover many Asians, Africans, and Middle Easterners have come to dislike actively American policy, particularly its attempt to create blocs, and no longer trust American leadership.

Item. Our stupidities, mistakes, inertia, overconfidence, lack of imagination, and lack of will and faith.

And What It Hasn't Got

Freedom. Therefore the whole Soviet structure is built on quicksand—so at least devotees of liberty must hope. Much depends on the use the United States puts its free institutions to, in particular in demonstrating to the uncommitted or captive world that what we stand for is right. It is strictly up to the free world to prove that our system is not merely stronger, but the best.

CHAPTER XX

Leningrad and Kiev

We do not cry
For it is truly said:
Our tears are frozen dry,
We have no tears to shed.
—LENINGRAD POET, DURING THE NAZI SIEGE

THE first thing I noticed in Leningrad was that when the train pulled in at 8:45 A.M. it was still pitch-dark. This was in December and the city lies on the 60th degree of latitude; we are far to the north now, level with the lower tip of Greenland. In midsummer Leningrad has eighteen to nineteen hours of sunlight. The second thing I noticed was a building being torn down on the Nevsky Prospekt, one of the most gracious streets in the world in former days, but gaunt and dilapidated now. Workmen were using torches, and bits of molten metal cascaded like fireworks on passers-by below. They had no protection. Nobody paid the slightest attention. Ah, Russia, Russia! The third thing I noticed was a gang of house painters in a corridor in the hotel, sternly wielding brushes from steep ladders—all women.

Our suite was enormous, of five rooms, and was exceptionally embellished. In one salon stood no fewer than twelve Empire chairs upholstered with brilliant orange silk, and the tea service was of solid silver. Some objects were tagged with numbers, as in a museum. A carved cut-glass bowl as big as a bushel basket dominated one large Victorian table, with a heavy fringed cloth, and a glass cabinet held a profusion of porcelain fish, dolls, and puppies—even a morose-looking albatross. There was no commode with any shelves, no place to hang up pajamas, and no wastebasket, in all five rooms. I asked why this opulent hostelry (it got a star from Baedeker in 1914) happened to be called the Astoria. Our guide seemed uncertain: "I think it was named for a rich man in New York."

We came up from Moscow on the night train, the celebrated Red Arrow

Express, the best train in Russia. Equipment on this is from Hitler's train, which the Russians got in reparations after the war. It looked like any European international train with sleek, shiny, blue sleeping cars, and was drawn by one of the largest locomotives I have ever seen. Cars on this line bear the symbol "OK." This, I thought, was a curious place to see American slang, until it dawned on me that "OK" stands for "Oktyabr," the Russian spelling of October. This is the October line, once called the Nicholas line. It goes from Moscow to Leningrad, three hundred miles, without a single curve, bend, jog, or jiggle. Czar Nicholas I wanted it that way, and the flatness of the terrain made it easy to build it so. The Red Arrow covers the distance in eight and three-quarters hours. As is usual in Russia, there is no warning at all when the train starts—no whistles or bells, no cries of "All Aboard." The train leaves and arrives on the dot. We were told that the radio would be playing in our compartment, very low, and that it would be impossible to turn it off because there was no switch except one controlling the whole car. Half true, half untrue. The radio was on, sure enough. Soft music was playing, and it was not unpleasant. After a while our interpreter showed us how to turn it off by pushing a button near the table lamp.

LENINGRAD, the second city of the Soviet Union and the eleventh largest city in the world, has about 2,800,000 people. But there has been no census since 1939, and I asked our guide how he could be sure of this figure; he replied that it was "probably" correct, because it came from the Mayor. Actually it is the official 1956 estimate. Leningrad began life on an island and lies astride more than one hundred different islands today; it is almost as much a water city as Stockholm or Venice, and its multitudinous canals are traversed by no fewer than four hundred bridges. Leningrad has a lot of smog, like Los Angeles, and, unlike Los Angeles, is well known for its fur auctions. It is the most important seaport in the Soviet Union, lying on Kronstadt Bay in the Gulf of Finland; a dredged channel sixteen miles long leads to deep water, and the harbor is one of the largest in the world. Citizens are impressed by the fact that Leningrad receives no fewer than two hundred ships of foreign registry, mostly Scandinavian, every year. The biggest seaport in the Soviet Union—and it receives only two hundred non-Russian ships! No wonder Russians are preoccupied with their isolation.

Leningrad is a principal Soviet gate to the Arctic. Here the first (and only) atomic icebreaker in the world is being assembled, and here is the world's only nonmagnetic survey vessel, the *Zarya*, built of wood, bronze, and non-magnetic metals. The *Zarya's* research work is superintended by the Leningrad Division of the Institute for Research on Terrestrial Magnetism, the Ionosphere, and the Dissemination of Radio Waves—a nice Soviet name.[1] Russia is keenly interested in the Arctic as we know. Fourteen floating weather stations have been set up on Polar floes, to gather and transmit meteorological information; several of these are unmanned. Radio hams are urged to listen in to "North Pole Four."

For a city so important Leningrad does not seem to have much air traffic. I looked at the bulletin board at the airport, and only about forty flights, both incoming and outgoing, were listed that day. La Guardia in New York has as many as a thousand.

Two things chiefly distinguish Leningrad, its surpassing beauty (even if it is miserably run down nowadays) and its past. The skeleton is still imperial, even if much of the skin is missing. The Germans besieged Leningrad for nine hundred days during World War II, but never took it, although they came within seven kilometers of its center. Six hundred thousand Leningraders died, and many buildings still bear niches made by shell fire. And a third characteristic should be noted—culture. Leningrad has (Soviet statistics are, as usual, a mouthful) forty-seven museums, fifty-two colleges, and seventeen hundred libraries. The Academy of Sciences was seated here until it moved to Moscow in 1924. Tchaikovsky, Pushkin, Mendeleev, and Repin are all closely associated with Leningrad. One night we went to the Opera, and the Intourist girl exclaimed breathlessly, "Ah, you are going to hear the new Italian tenor!"[2] A few days before I had been reading *Oblomov*, the heartbreakingly sweet-sour Goncharov novel, and was much struck by a passage mentioning the arrival in Petersburg of—guess what?—a new Italian tenor. This was in the 1850's. Russian themes repeat themselves.

Leningrad differs sharply from Moscow in any number of respects. Moscow is Chicago; Leningrad is Boston. Leningrad has less push than Moscow, and is more down at the heel, but is much more relaxed. A map of the city—wonder of wonders!—is freely available, and I never once saw a picture or statue of Stalin. Moscow is a burly city; Leningrad still smells of lavender. Manners—good manners—still persist here, and people are better dressed; some women even look chic. The main point to make is, perhaps, that Leningrad is basically a *western* city like Paris or Vienna. Moscow, although the capital, is much more provincial. Lord Curzon, when he visited Petersburg

[1] Moscow *News*, April 5, 1957.
[2] The tenor did not do very well, and we left *Traviata* after the first act. People were still crowded in the lobby hoping by some miracle to get in. We gave our tickets to a lady and her husband who were profoundly shocked by our walking out. "What!" the lady expostulated. "Didn't the Italian tenor sing well?"

in 1889, called it a "plagiarism," with "its amusements borrowed from Paris and its pretentiousness from Berlin," in contrast to Moscow, "an Asiatic original."[3]

Leningraders are apt to look down on Muscovites, and the cities are lively rivals, almost as if they belonged to the bourgeois world and were Minneapolis and St. Paul. Leningrad thinks that its new subway is better than Moscow's, but its citizens are civilized enough to make little jokes about it, such as that "the Muscovites come here to see our subway, and we go to Moscow to see theirs." Leningraders are terrifically proud of their ballet, and charge that Moscow "kidnaps" their leading stars. And everybody seems pleased if you say that you like Leningrad better than Moscow, and burst out that it is a "shame" and a "scandal" for a visitor to give long weeks to Moscow and stay in Leningrad only a few days.

Leningrad is also an extremely important industrial city. Here are the S. M. Kirov Plant (steel, locomotives),[4] the biggest porcelain factory in the Soviet Union, the V. I. Lenin Neva Plant (machine building), the Red Triumph Rubber Foundry (the largest rubber plant in Europe), and above all Elektrosila. This last, which experiments with and manufactures heavier electrical equipment than any factory in the world, employs 10,000 workers, and has a technical staff of 2,500 engineers and 1,200 researchers. Such a ratio of technical staff to workers, unknown to the West, is common enough in the Soviet Union. I have heard engineers say that Elektrosila ranks without question with General Electric or Westinghouse in technical know-how. Many factories in the Soviet Union are not well run, but Elektrosila is an exception. And it can undertake work—particularly in the field of exceptionally heavy electrical machinery—beyond anything yet attempted by us, if only because the cost does not matter. One project is a test bay for alternators with the unprecedented capacity of 300,000 kw. Closely associated with Elektrosila and the electrical industry in general is the Institute of Energetics. This, with twelve thousand students and a teaching staff of eight hundred, trains designers and other technical workers. The course takes five years. Most Soviet industries have similar institutes attached, and the scale is vast.

Glimpses Forward and Back

First this great city was a trading post on the junction of the Neva and Okhta, built by the Swedes and called Nienshants. Peter the Great decided

---

[3] But also Curzon described it as "this majestic emanation from Peter's genius."
[4] Known in older days as the Putilov Works.

to create a capital on the marshes here, largely because the location gave him a pivot near the Baltic. Peter did not name it for himself, but for St. Peter.[5] The name was changed to Petrograd in 1914, when the First World War broke out, to get rid of its German taste, and then, for obvious reasons, to Leningrad in 1924.

The city was the capital of Russia for some two hundred years, and its history traverses a sharp, vivid arc. Here the inner heart of Czarist Russia beat; here Peter, Catherine, Alexander, brilliantly personified absolutism. (But they were no more absolutist than Lenin.) Behind the glowing Czarist façade, with its accouterments so floriferously imperial, Petersburg was also the heart of revolutionary conspiracy, agitation, and outbreak. Peter's "window" let in much as time went on. The Decembrist mutiny of 1825 occurred in St. Petersburg; so did the 1905 uprising, and so did both the February and October revolutions of 1917.

Let me be guidebookish for a paragraph or two. After all, no contemporary guide to Leningrad exists in English. One confronts an *embarras de richesse*. The Winter Palace, built under the order of the Empress Elizabeth (1741-62) and hung with baroque statues like gargoyles, is painted a very peculiar and characteristic shade of green—almost the green of a crushed avocado, but more bluish. The great S. M. Kirov Theater, once the Mariinsky, wears this same green, but in a slightly paler shade.[6] The colors of Leningrad are, indeed, fascinating. Near the Winter Palace is the Admiralty building which, under its slim spire, is lemon yellow—not the egg-yolk yellow of the Moscow Kremlin, but a sharper, cleaner yellow. One look at the half-mile-long Admiralty tells the visitor about one preoccupation, at least, of pre-Soviet Russia—outlet to warm seas. Russia was hardly a naval power at all, but the Admiralty was the grandest, the most imposing, of all government buildings of that era. Near by is the old War Office, intersected by a triumphal arch. Our guide said dryly, "It was built to commemorate the Russian victory over Napoleon. I am told that there is a similar arch in Paris to commemorate Napoleon's victory over Russia."

Two architects partly of Italian origin give Leningrad much of its spectacular quality. One, Bartolomeo Rastrelli, was born in Paris, but moved to Russia in 1716; he built the Winter Palace, as well as parts of Peterhof and Tsarskoye Selo, palaces outside the city. The other, who came later, was Carlo Ivanovich Rossi, the son of an Italian ballerina who lived in Peters-

---

[5] *Duranty Reports Russia*, p. 231.

[6] Much in Leningrad has been renamed for Sergei M. Kirov, the Leningrad party boss who was murdered in 1934.

burg. Rossi built the Senate, the ballet school, the library, and the surpassingly beautiful Alexandrinsky Theater, now called the Pushkin. A street is named for him—Street of the Architect Rossi—and indeed all the buildings on it are his, grouped together with exquisite homogeneity. Moscow does not like to acknowledge foreign or semiforeign contributions to its art or history, but Leningrad does not mind a bit.

In this central area of Leningrad, which is comparable in a degree to the Place de la Concorde in Paris, stand two interesting statues. One, in the Square of the Decembrists, is the celebrated equestrian statue of Peter the Great known as the Bronze Horseman. It was created by two French sculptors, and has given its name to a well-known Soviet ballet. Peter, in this statue, charges off into space like a meteor, or the Sputnik. The second is a much more placid representation of Nicholas I, also on horseback, between the somber, iron-colored City Hall and St. Isaac's Cathedral. A little story hangs on this. The City Hall was originally the Mariinsky Palace, built by Nicholas for his queen, Marie. Marie, however, refused to live in this gloomy structure, not because it was gloomy but because her windows faced the rear end of her husband's horse. It had been set up in this direction because the *front* had to face St. Isaac's.

On the crook of the Neva, about a mile away, is the Smolny Institute, which was originally a school for daughters of the nobility. This was used by the Bolsheviks as their first headquarters in 1917 (Lenin's room was on the third floor, No. 95), and is now the headquarters of the local Communist party. Next door is the Smolny Convent, an enchanting blue building of purest eighteenth-century baroque, by Rastrelli. Not far away is the Tavrida Palace, built for Prince Potemkin by Catherine the Great, as a reward for his conquest of the Crimea, during which the famous "Potemkin villages" were fabricated; it serves as a party school today. The Duma held its meetings here, and here in 1918 the constituent assembly, dissolved by the Soviets, had its first and only session. The story is—to go back a bit—that Potemkin, after receiving this sumptuous palace from his monarch-mistress in 1782, sold it for 200,000 rubles. Then Catherine is supposed to have repurchased it and given it to him all over again. Such were imperial moods.

It was amusing to discover, in Leningrad, that youthful Communists have a tidy interest in Czarist gossip. Their attitude is much like that of English people, say, talking about Henry the Eighth with a mixture of affection, curiosity, and intellectual disdain.

One could go on almost indefinitely. The grim Fortress of St. Peter and Paul, on an island in the slate-colored Neva, was the Bastille of Czarist

Russia, just as Lubyanka prison in Moscow was a Soviet Bastille. Churches are all over the place, like St. Nicholas's, shining in turquoise and gold, and the Church of the Resurrection, behind a crazy rococo fence grilled like an iron porcupine. Then we saw the Yusupov Palace, where Rasputin was murdered, and Peter the Great's Summer Palace, which I thought was the prettiest building in all Leningrad, surrounded by sere gardens. In winter, the statues here are concealed by wooden cabins, like outhouses, to keep them from being split by frost. And there are modern sights by the dozen—Lenin's taut high-bodied armored car; the warship *Aurora*, still holding its commanding position in the Neva; and the Finland Railway Station. This is a shabby little two-story ocher building, used only for suburban traffic nowadays, where Lenin arrived to take charge of the Revolution in April, 1917. Outside Leningrad is Peterhof, the Russian equivalent of Schönbrunn or Versailles, built by Peter in 1709 and tinkered with by subsequent monarchs till 1917. Perhaps oddly, the Communists never bothered to change its name until 1944.[7] Also in the environs is Tsarskoye Selo (Czar's Village), another and even more magnificent Russian Versailles. It was badly damaged by the Germans in World War II.

*

And more sights:

Kazan Cathedral. This, modeled on St. Peter's in Rome and built between 1801 and 1811, has the best dome in Russia, and holds the tomb of General Kutuzov. A statue of another great Russian soldier, Barclay de Tolly (who was half Scot) stands outside. Kazan Cathedral was desanctified in 1929, and turned over to the Academy of Sciences; it is now the Museum of the History of Religion. One horrifying set of exhibits shows replicas of torture chambers during the Spanish Inquisition, complete with life-size effigies of prisoners being burned and torn to pieces on the rack. One provocative instrument is a metal snout, which prevented a prisoner from eating; another is a chair studded with iron tacks.

The Natural History Museum. This, the largest museum of its kind in Europe, was founded by Peter the Great. One of its most picturesque displays is of a mammoth, believed to be the only intact (or nearly intact) mammoth in any museum in the world. A hunter found him in Siberia, near the Kolyma River, in 1901, with his head projecting from some newly melted snow; he had been there for anything from six thousand to twelve thousand years. The

---

[7] Then it became Petrodvorets. Tsarskoye Selo is now officially Pushkin, but few people call it so. Pushkin went to school here.

hunter cut off one of the tusks and sold it to an itinerant merchant for a sack of tobacco; this aroused local curiosity, and the Emir of Yakutsk was informed; eventually an expedition from the Academy of Sciences arrived on the spot, hoisted the mammoth (which weighed five tons) out of the ice, chopped him apart, and then put him together again in Leningrad. This museum also has the skeleton of the largest prehistoric elephant in the world, which was found near the Aral Sea in 1940.

The Pavlov Institute. Dr. Ivan Petrovich Pavlov died in 1936. The mark he left is still broad and deep. Pavlov, as everybody knows, worked out the mechanism whereby dogs, as an example, salivate or have other physical reactions in response to such stimuli as the ringing of bells, or mild electric shocks. Even erections can be induced by means of this sort. Pavlov won a Nobel Prize as far back as 1904, and most of his work was done under the Czars; he became nevertheless a Soviet demigod. The reason is not far to seek. Not only dogs are taught to have conditioned reflexes in the USSR. In fact the conditioned reflex principle underlies much in Soviet educational and propaganda techniques, and is a powerful arm of the regime. Pavlov himself retained his independence of mind to the end and was steadily critical of the Communist system, but the authorities knew his value full well and carefully let him alone.

We visited one of the twenty-eight laboratories that compose the Institute, and met the Director, Academician Konstantin M. Bykov. A Leningrader of the old school, he kissed my wife's hand; such gestures are not common in the Soviet Union. The particular laboratory we saw is devoted to the pathology of the nervous system; the atmosphere was that of any good research laboratory, but the equipment looked primitive. On one wall is a portrait of Pavlov; opposite it is a large photograph of his first dog, named Boy, who lived twenty years "and never had a neurosis." One experiment going on today has practical consequences. Hens have been conditioned to lay more than one egg a day, by submitting them to stimuli from light. Also interesting studies are proceeding on senility.

Finally, the *Hermitage.* This, the Leningrad sight above all sights, is a museum ranking with the Louvre or Vatican. It has twenty-five Rembrandts, fifty-one Picassos, Rubenses by the score, two out of the fourteen Leonardo da Vincis in the world, and the most satisfying Titian I have ever seen. There are six different buildings, twenty-five kilometers of corridors, and four hundred rooms in use out of fifteen hundred. The Hermitage has, interestingly enough, no elevators. Cumbersome wooden ramps and slides cover marble staircases, and crates full of pictures are laboriously hauled up and down by muscle power. Once again we see the familiar Soviet characteristic of paying no attention to things that are considered to be nonessential.

Most visitors to the Hermitage, if they get permission, go to the Treasury first. Here is an unparalleled collection of ancient gold objects and ornaments, dating from Helleno-Scythian times; some are as beautiful as the golden objects from the tomb of King Tutankhamen in Egypt—gold laurel leaves, gold buckles and crowns, solid gold leaf stitched to fabrics, brooches made of tiny golden lions. Then, among the fifty-four cabinets packed solid with gold or jeweled ornaments, are objects more modern—some personal jewelry of the Czars. A sixty-piece golden toilet set belonged to Anna, the Empress who ruled from 1730 to 1740; she hated to wash, and used unguents instead. As glittering as anything I ever saw is a blanket given by the Sultan of Turkey to Nicholas I about 1830; it contains eighty-nine diamonds, most of which are bigger than dimes. Next to it is a sword caked in diamonds, like a huge banana set in sparkling sugar.

And now pictures. Upstairs in the attic, through the courtesy of the Hermitage Director, Professor Artamanov, we saw some French Impressionist paintings of the old Morozov-Shchukin collection, which are not yet permanently hung. Altogether more than four thousand pictures are stacked in this attic. Their frames have been removed, and they are tacked against large grooved scaffolds, twenty feet by ten, which slide into a kind of enormous recessed file. The pictures are stuck on these sliding boards like gigantic postage stamps. Such a resplendent display, concentrated in so small a space, exists nowhere else on earth. We saw in profusion Cézannes, Monets, Manets, Gauguins, and a few Van Goghs. On one board there were no fewer than twenty-one Matisses. Imagine seeing twenty-one Matisses unframed, stuck at random on what is in effect a single canvas! On the other side of this panel were fourteen Derains, and then came what are probably the two greatest Matisses in the world, the huge twin murals from the Shchukin house depicting dancers and musicians. Of the Picassos, the most extraordinary is the celebrated Child Harlequin in White with Blue Buttons.

Incident in a Bookshop

A boy heard me talk English in a bookshop, and glided close. Was I American? How did I happen to be in Leningrad? Member of a delegation, i.e., a Communist? I was an object of as much curiosity as if I had been a Fiji savage in a top hat. The boy was nineteen, and was studying to be a philosopher. I asked him what he knew of contemporary American or English philosophy or literature. He said that he "rushed" to the library every week to read the *New York Times*. (American newspapers do not exist on newsstands in Russia, but a few are available to special students in some libraries.)

"How do you find our journalism compared to yours?" I asked. He gave me a quick odd look and said, "One is the more tendentious." I did not need to ask which. But he became guarded, and added, as if to cover himself, "Of course I agree with the tendentiousness!" I did not ask him why, in that case, he "rushed" to see an American newspaper every week. I asked him what he thought of events in Hungary. "A sad history," he replied. "With us there are two minds about it. But—"

Somebody came up, and the boy fled at once.

More about the Dark Pearl of Cities

What Leningrad is proudest of is its theater, literature, and music. At least a hundred magazines and periodicals are published here, and there are no fewer than eighteen main state theaters. Of these the chief are the Kirov (the Opera) and the Pushkin, formerly the Alexandrinsky. Both date from the middle nineteenth century, and the Alexandrinsky, which corresponds to the Art Theater in Moscow, is particularly proud of its noble tradition; for half a century, it was the foremost theater in all Russia.

Fare was varied. We had a choice when we arrived of *Don Quixote* (ballet), J. M. Barrie's *What Every Woman Knows*, *The Fountain of Bakhchisarai* from the Pushkin poem, a play made out of Dostoevsky's *Insulted and Injured*, Rimski-Korsakov's *Sadko* at the Opera, and two modern Soviet plays. Later came *Dangerous Corner*, by J. B. Priestley, and of all things, an adaptation of *Dial M for Murder*, which was bitterly attacked by local critics.

Tickets at the Kirov range from 3.6 to 22.30 rubles. In the buffet (no hats or coats, no smoking) the cheapest chocolate bar was 7.80 rubles, with sandwiches ranging from sausage at 1.35 rubles to caviar at 3.8 rubles. Members of the orchestra (except half a dozen women) wear white tie, and in contrast to the formality of this, the audience swarms with sailors, children, and Chinese. During the intermissions, others in the audience form a grand circle in the upper hall, and march slowly, almost solemnly, four or six abreast. Women do their hair with some attention to western style, and there were even a few evening dresses. I heard people speak French—with a tinny Russian accent. Always in Russia survivors of the *ancien régime*, the few who still survive, can be detected at once; aristocracy leaves adhesive traces. There is something in the very walk of these people which makes them conspicuous and recognizable. They have obvious good breeding and a proud, if muted, electricity in the eye.

The Ballet Russe had its birth in Leningrad more than two hundred years ago, and the oldest and most distinguished ballet school in the country still operates here. This was the home of Geltzer, Pavlova and Nijinsky. The leading ballerinas today are Natasha Dudinskaya, no longer young but probably no older than Ulanova, who came originally from Leningrad, and Ninel Kurgapkina, youthful and rising fast; another, one of the most promising, is Alla Shelest. Forebodingly Leningraders told us, "She is too good—Moscow will take her from us soon." (When I asked who were the leading Leningrad writers, the answer was, "Moscow has snatched them all.")

Above all, Leningrad loves music. Anton Rubenstein founded the Conservatory here in 1862, and its classically beautiful concert hall, with twenty-four dazzling white marble pillars and giant chandeliers, is the only room I ever saw in the USSR that didn't need a paint job. It reminded me of the old Musik-Vereinsaal in Vienna, but is whiter, bigger and more brilliant. We heard here, by good luck, a most extraordinary concert—a stunning performance of Shostakovich's Eighth Symphony which, incidentally, is officially frowned upon for its "subversive" ideological content. The conductor was Yevgeni Mravinsky, the most distinguished and best known in the country, and a musician of intense, controlled authority and fire. Shostakovich was in the audience and he, Mravinsky, and the *Konzertmeister* embraced after the performance, as the enraptured audience cried and cheered.

*

Leningrad, like most Soviet cities, has plenty of complaints. One recently voiced in the newspapers had to do with "intolerable delays" in modernizing a department store on Nevsky Prospekt, which was to have opened in 1955.[8] It failed to do so, however, through the "fault of the Russian Republic Ministry of Trade's Chief Department Store Administration." Other protests have to do with students. Recently *Komsomolskaya Pravda* wrote, "In the past academic year 134 Leningrad students failed to pass the state examinations. . . . The state had taught these students 5 or 6 years, spending hundreds of thousands of rubles on them, and the end result was that state

[8] Incidentally the name Nevsky Prospekt was changed for a time to "Street of 25th of October." Then the unpredictable Bolsheviks changed it back to Nevsky Prospekt.

funds were thrown to the winds. The number of failures is particularly high in the Institute of Precision Mechanics and Optics, and among . . . clinical pharmaceutical students."[9]

One student wrote the following little verse:

> But now I know not where to go
> Nor where my guide or road can be.
> My voice is shy, confiding, low:
> People, lead me, who cannot see!

Komsomolskaya Pravda indignantly took this young man to task: "What produced such a strange, decadent sentiment in a Young Communist League student? How is it that the little hand written magazine *Yeres* (Heresy), comprised of wild verse ineptly patterned after the worst examples of decadent literature, could appear?" A western observer might well say that the appearance of such a poem, in a magazine called *Heresy*, is a hopeful sign.

White Russia

White Russia—correctly Belorussia—is one of the fifteen Union republics, and has always been a "frontier" land, if only because it has no marked frontiers. Since history began, it has been pressed upon by Poland, the former Baltic States, Russia proper, and the Ukraine. The area is 56,000 square miles, about the size of Iowa, with a population around eight million. The *Belorussian Soviet Socialist Republic* is one of the "senior" republics, and, like the Ukraine, is a member of the United Nations. The people are a cross between Great Russians, Ukrainians, and Poles. Before the Revolution, 55 per cent of arable land in the country belonged to the gentry, which was mostly of Polish origin; today there are 5,207 collective farms, embracing almost the entire agricultural population. In the southern quarter of Belorussia are the Pripet Marshes, which until recently formed a district as inaccessible as any in Europe. Now more than three million acres of marshland have been drained. Peat is a major source of fuel.

Germany, when it was forced to withdraw from White Russia toward the close of World War II, wrought inexpressible havoc. The Nazis destroyed ten thousand industrial enterprises, wrecked 90 per cent of the power facilities of the country, and tore up four thousand miles of railway track. Three-quarters of all housing in the country was destroyed. Very nearly every Jew in Minsk, the capital, a preponderantly Jewish city, who had survived up to

[9] *Current Digest of the Soviet Press,* February 13, 1957.

that time went to the gas chambers. Many White Russians certainly did not like the Nazis; but many others did not like the Soviet Union either. Tens of thousands of non-Jewish White Russians, seeking to escape the rigors of the Soviet regime, crossed the border and went over to the German enemy.

Reconstruction of Belorussia began soon after it was freed in 1944. Minsk, utterly destroyed, had to be rebuilt from scratch. Rehabilitation is now more or less complete, and, the Russians say, Belorussian industry now turns out as much product in one week as during the whole year 1913. The Minsk Automobile and Tractor Works today employs more workers than the total of all factories in Minsk province in 1913.[10] Industrialization has, significantly enough, been prompted to a degree by considerations of defense. An industrial city like Stalingrad, the Russians learned in World War II, will be easier to defend than one not industrialized. The accent on education is, as always, also acute. In 1913 (the Russians say) Belorussia did not have a single institute of higher learning, and 85 per cent of the population was illiterate. Today there are no fewer than twenty-nine Belorussian colleges. Before the Revolution, scarcely any Belorussians used the local language. It has been revived with a rush, and today magazines, newspapers, books, exist plentifully in Belorussian.

MINSK is "open" now. Not until recently were foreign visitors allowed in. The symbol of the city is an aurochs, and the population is 412,000. Minsk has a new TV tower, and five thousand sets; its biggest industrial undertaking is the tractor factory.[11] The chief political personages in Minsk are the Prime Minister, Nikolai Ye. Avkhimovich, and the foreign minister, Kuzma V. Kiselev, who frequently represents Belorussia at the UN. He is a cheerful character.

Sovetskaya Belorussiya, the chief local paper, protested recently at "lack of discipline among students" in Minsk. Criticisms voiced by Belorussian deputies at the last meeting of the USSR Supreme Soviet indicate that, despite advances, much still remains to be done in education—also housing. One complaint was that 6,700 of the 11,000 schools in the republic were obliged to operate on two shifts; many primary schools have three shifts, and 1,928 rural schools are housed in rented peasants' huts. "The republic has an acute shortage of cultural and educational institutions. Thirty-five districts do not

---

[10] Most of these statistical details are from USSR, November, 1956.

[11] Two well-known American citizens were, it happens, born in or near Minsk— David Sarnoff, the omniscient seer of Radio Corporation of America, and Max Lerner, author and political columnist.

have any . . . premises for cultural centers." Also complaints were registered about fuel shortages, something very important in the present state of Soviet economy. One deputy, S. O. Pritytsky, stated that a clothing mill at Molodechno (cost 48 million rubles) has been under construction for three years, but the completion was nowhere near, and that this town, a provincial capital, does not have a theater, a modern hospital, a library, or even a water supply and sewage system.[12]

Episode Aloft

We flew from Minsk to Kiev through impenetrable snow and icy mist. The airstrip at Minsk was marked off with small Christmas trees stuck any which way in long lines in the snow like gay, crooked little sentinels. So much in Russia is improvised; so much has a peculiar charming note of amateurism.

A gray-haired man in his early fifties, wearing a cap, sat across from me, and politely asked to see my glasses. He inspected their thick lenses with curiosity, and then took a chamois skin from his pocket. This he cut in half carefully, and gave me half. "Very good for cleaning glasses." This good man was a Leningrad factory inspector. As almost all Russians do, he began to talk about books, and asked me if I had ever heard of Pushkin, Tolstoy, and Yesenin. I replied that I had once known Yesenin's wife, Isadora Duncan, and then picked up a book from my wife's lap and handed it across the aisle, without further explanation. It was the *Collected Poems of Pushkin* in the Modern Library. So we were friends.

Up shot a dark boyish figure from the seat forward. He was a garage mechanic, returning to his home in Kiev. We were joined then by a smiling small shy red-haired man, who was a piano tuner. The stewardess, who spoke French, joined our group. Conversation then became mixed, voluble, and explosive. What was I doing in Russia? I tried to explain. What kind of writer was I? Journalist. They all took a dim view of journalists. How much money did I earn a year? They were stupefied. How much did it cost to visit Russia? I said thirty dollars a day. Silence. The factory inspector from Leningrad murmured quietly, "Soon, under Communism, there will be no need for anybody to have any money at all."

"Have you American money?" asked the garage mechanic. I took out a ten-dollar bill, and he held it up to the light, fingering it slowly and carefully feeling it. Then he asked if I had a hundred-dollar bill. No. He wanted to know what ten dollars would buy in the United States. I replied, giving a

[12] *Current Digest of the Soviet Press*, March 27, 1957.

long and varied list of food and other goods; this was greeted with incredulity, together with the slight touch of contempt that Russians almost always show when they hear about superior American living standards. More questions flowed. "What is the favorite American drink?" I tried, vainly, to explain what Coca-Cola was. "What is whisky made of?" "How much does an American drink a day?" The mechanic, roaring with laughter, said that the normal Ukrainian ration was at least half a liter of vodka with every meal. "Makes us strong!" What was my impression of the Soviet Union? I said, "Mixed!" and added that everybody I met seemed strong and friendly. Nods of approval. Who is the best American violinist? Who is the best American "sportsman"? Then books again. The factory inspector had read Theodore Dreiser's *The Financier* and knew about Mark Twain and Edgar Allan Poe, but had never heard of Hawthorne, Melville, or William Faulkner.

I asked what nationalities they belonged to. The Leningrad man was Russian, and the garage mechanic Ukrainian. The piano tuner with his fringe of red hair, who did not have on a collar or tie, retreated into embarrassed silence; the mechanic answered for him in an uproarious voice, "No nationality, he is Jewish!" The shy piano tuner blushed. I asked how much money each made. Leningrader three thousand rubles a month; piano tuner one thousand; garage mechanic eight hundred. The mechanic added passionately that his wife, a salesgirl in a shoe shop, earned twelve hundred, that their rent was only fifty rubles a month, and that they were perfectly comfortable and well-off. The stewardess, chiming in, said that she earned thirteen hundred. This, she apologized, was a great deal—far too much for a young girl! But she got high pay because she knew French and a little English.

I asked what, if any, were the differences between the Ukrainian and Russian languages.

"*Nyet!*" shouted the mechanic. *Nyet* means "no" or "nothing" in Russian.

"All right," said I. "What's the Ukrainian for *nyet?*"

Something quite different! We went through six or seven words until we found two—*maslo* (butter) and *pivo* (beer) that were the same in both languages.

"Any good restaurants in Kiev?" I asked our friends. "Plenty!" This we found was not quite the case. "Any pretty girls in Kiev?" "Any number!" This too, alas, proved to be an exaggeration.

That evening, dining at the Intourist hotel in Kiev, whom should we find at the next table but our garage mechanic, very drunk, and his wife, who *was* pretty. She had never met an American before. She had a characteristically

Russian temperament—shy as a mouse, but direct and warm. Our mechanic loved her madly. We joined forces, and had a brilliant, majestic debauch. Russians certainly do like to drink. The mechanic insisted on giving us not only drinks but food—including huge pieces of a sticky sweet cake which he tried to stuff physically into our mouths—and must have spent a week's salary, maybe more. After trying vainly to pay my proper share and after topping things off with champagne, which is not a good chaser for vodka, red wine and beer, I gave our host my fountain pen. Instantly, with flashing pride, he tore off his wrist watch, and tried to make me take it in return. He asked if my wife and I had children. I showed him a picture of our boy. He grabbed the shiny Kodachrome print and smothered it with kisses.

The Great World of the Ukraine

"Ukraine" means borderland, and in the old days it was called "Little Russia." Actually it is not little, but quite big, the sixth country in Europe in population. Officially its name is *Ukrainska Radyanska Sotsialistichna Roopubliku*, and it covers 232,664 square miles, about the size of France, with roughly 40,000,000 people. The Dnieper, the third largest river in Europe (after the Volga and Danube), bends through it in a lopsided circle, and it has in all 60,000 miles of rivers. The Ukraine contains one-fifth of the total cultivated area of the entire Soviet Union; it has 15,200 collective farms, and 1,397 machine tractor stations. One out of every five men in the Soviet Army is Ukrainian. The Ukraine has its own flag, in red and blue, and is a member of the United Nations. Fifteen years ago if you asked what the Ukraine meant to the Soviet Union the answer would have been that it was the essential fuel, metallurgical, and grain base of the country. But now Kazakhstan is surpassing it as a bread basket, and its tremendous constellation of industry is being matched by newer industrial developments in the Urals and central Siberia. Even so its importance to Soviet economy is very great; it gives the USSR 75 per cent of its sugar, 60 per cent of its iron ore, 48 per cent of pig iron, 30 per cent of steel, and 32 per cent of coal. Industrial production will by 1960 reach a level twenty-seven times that of 1913, if the calculations of the Sixth Five-Year Plan are fulfilled.[18]

Ukrainian history goes way back; this was the first eastern Slav state, and is the cradle of Russia. It was taken in turn by the Tatars, the fiercely

[18] Among oddities produced by the Ukraine are a rubber plant known as koksagyz, and the tarpan, a variety of wild horse. Another curiosity is silk culture; a particular variety of silkworm has been developed to feed on birch leaves. Also Ukrainians are very proud of their cut flowers, like carnations.

marauding Lithuanians, and the Poles. Kiev was the first Christian city in Russia. Through centuries the Ukrainians have suffered much. Jump to modern times. *Half* the total housing in the Ukraine was destroyed by the Germans in World War II, and fifteen hundred miles of tunnels and shafts were wrecked in the Donets mines alone. There was suffering in another dimension, too. In the Stalin purges in 1936-38 all nine members of the Ukrainian Politburo were shot or disappeared, all twelve members of the cabinet, and forty-five out of fifty-seven members of the Central Committee of the Ukrainian Communist Party.[14]

But these are unquenchable, indomitable people. They have a lively Polish substratum, and a pronounced tradition of revolutionary romanticism. Sometimes they are called "Dnieper-Italians" because they are such volatile, emotional, singing folk. Gogol was a Ukrainian and so was the painter Repin; Dostoevsky was part Ukrainian. The works of Tschaikovsky and Moussorgsky are packed with Ukrainian melodies. Also the Ukrainians, by and large, have a smart—almost glib—sophistication, plus intellectual detachment. We set out for a concert one night, and one of our Ukrainian friends said, laughing, "I am Ukrainian enough to dislike Ukrainian music." I do not think one would ever hear such a remark from a citizen of Moscow about Russian music.

Ukrainians love good food and drink, and have a hearty zest for life. Their special variety of borsch is famous, and chicken à la Kiev is known in good kitchens almost everywhere in Europe—breast of chicken formed into a pouch and filled with melted butter. The Ukraine has a superb beer, called Gigulovsky, and its special vodka, Gorilka, is very good. The caviar in Kiev was superior to any we found elsewhere in Russia; moreover, it was served nicely, even daintily, with slices of lemon on little bowls of ice. Nowhere else in the USSR did I ever see ice on the table.

Industrial development is, by Russian standards, prodigious; so is intellectual development. More than one hundred million books were distributed in the Ukraine last year, and some of the ablest writers in the Soviet Union are Ukrainian, like Alexander Korneichuk, the leading dramatist. His wife, Wanda Wasilewska, also a well-known (and very inflammatory) writer, is a Pole. The country is full of literary magazines, and has newspapers perhaps not quite so stiflingly dull as most others in the USSR; readers are not totally dependent upon *Pravda* and *Izvestia*. The Ukraine has seven universities, 150 colleges and institutes, its own Academy of Sciences, and 34,000 schools. In

[14] Hugh Seton Watson, *From Lenin to Malenkov*, p. 170.

1917 roughly three-quarters of the population was illiterate; today illiteracy is unknown.

Ukrainian is, I have already indicated, a quite different language from Russian. Our Moscow interpreter could not understand Ukrainian. We had to have a second interpreter if the person we saw chose to speak Ukrainian instead of Russian, as several did. Before the Revolution, the Czarist authorities largely suppressed the Ukrainian language in newspapers, theaters, and schools. In 1913 not a single elementary school in the Ukraine gave instruction in the native language. Nowadays all children are taught in Ukrainian, but it is compulsory to learn Russian too. Of approximately 1,050 newspapers now published in the Ukraine, more than nine hundred appear in Ukrainian. Before World War I the Ukraine had seven theaters, all Russian; today there are seventy-four, of which sixty play in Ukrainian. On the other hand, so far as things that count are concerned—government, politics, industry, agriculture—the Ukraine is as thoroughly Russianized today as it was under the Czars.

Does Ukrainian nationalism exist? Of course. There must be millions of Ukrainians who would like to have a country of their own, to be independent, but this does not mean that they are not loyal citizens now.

*

The Ukraine extends all the way from the Carpathians in central Europe to the Crimea, and is full of important cities. Twenty-three have a population of more than 100,000; forty-three have more than 50,000.[15] KHARKOV, with a population of 877,000, is the second biggest city, and was the capital until 1934, when Kiev replaced it. Kharkov is a vital communications center, and has what some people think is the best university in the Soviet Union, as well as a big tractor plant. STALINO (population 625,000) is the chief city of the Donets coal basin (Donbas), "the Ruhr of Russia." Here is a cluster of other formidable industrial towns, like VOROSHILOVGRAD, which makes Diesel locomotives, and ZAPOROZHYE, important for pig iron and aluminum. Along the Dnieper are gigantic dams and hydroelectric installations, including Dneprogres, formerly called Dneprostroi, which produces twice as much electricity as all of pre-1917 Russia, and which was built by an American, Hugh Cooper. The booming city of DNEPROPETROVSK, population 576,000, is a center of steel production and metal working industries. At KRIVOI ROG, about eighty miles away, an ambitious new steel center is being

[15] Shabad, op. cit., p. 440.

built. Then one must mention NIKOLAYEV, on the junction of the Dnieper and the Southern Bug, where Trotsky went to school, and which is well known for shipbuilding; KERCH in the Crimea which has iron ore; KRAMATORSK, a machine tool center; and KHERSON, on the Black Sea, a textile focus, and in the old days the seat of much British capital. Nor should one forget the steel mills at ZHDANOV on the Sea of Azov, the manganese deposits near NIKOPOL, and the "Salt City" of SLAVYANSK.[16]

In the western Ukraine, near the Polish border, is the ancient and splendid city of Lvov, "the City of Lions." This, more familiarly known as Lemberg, was Polish until the end of World War II, and the Poles, even if they don't say so, still think of it not only as being Polish, but as a precious incubator of Polish history and culture second only to Cracow. They would like to have it back. Before the war, Lvov had a quality almost like that of Bruges or even Siena. Recently it was opened to tourist traffic. Further west is UZHGOROD, the capital of what is now called Transcarpathia; a more familiar name for this area stretched on the rack of the Carpathians is Ruthenia. The population is an intricate mixture of various Slav stocks. The Russians took it because it gives them a common frontier not merely with Czechoslovakia (to which it once belonged) but with Hungary. There was no ethnic justification. It is the extreme western projection of the Soviet Union into Europe.

*

The Chairman of the Council of Ministers of the Ukraine is Nikifor T. Kalchenko, and the Foreign Minister is L. F. Palamarchuk; both are sons of peasants. Mr. Palamarchuk has never made as much of an impression at the UN as his well-known predecessor, Dmitri Z. Manuilsky, who was a boss of the old Comintern. A more interesting character is the deputy chairman of the Ukrainian Supreme Soviet, Sidor Artemovich Kovpak, a remarkable guerrilla chieftain with a romantic history, and a writer of distinction as well. He raised the countryside against the Germans in World War II, and before they withdrew had more than a whole division of guerrillas under his command, behind the German lines. Kovpak received the Order of Lenin on his seventieth birthday early in 1957, and is a national hero.

[16] If these names are not confusing enough, it is easy to make them more so. Stalino was once known as Yuzovka, and Dnepropetrovsk as Yekaterinoslav. Yuzovka was named for a Welsh engineer, Hughes, who founded it.

Kiev, a Pleasant City

But what really matters in the Ukraine is KIEV. This ancient city is built on flowering hills overlooking the Dnieper, and bulges with pretty parks and gardens; hence one of its nicknames, the "Green City." The atmosphere is totally different from that of Moscow, and the visitor feels here little of the coldness, the spoiled arrogance of Leningrad. Kiev exudes sophistication, stability, and charm. During summer the city is half-deserted, and thousands of citizens play on the sandy Dnieper beaches. But Kiev has important industry, including the Gorky Tool Plant, although most of its industry has been moved into Siberia. Housing development is lively, but not lively enough; there are nine hundred miles of new streets, some of which are so new that they have not yet been named. The Mayor, O. I. Davidov, a mechanical engineer by profession, is one of the ablest administrators in the country.

Kiev has about 1,200,000 people, and is the third biggest Soviet city. The population is 15 per cent Jewish. The 1939 population was around 800,000, but the Germans killed more than 150,000 men, women, and children during their occupation, and another 50,000 fled. So, in reality, Kiev has jumped from roughly 600,000 people at the end of the war to double this figure. No wonder the municipal services have been strained. Near the middle of town is a ravine known as Baby Yar; here lie the remains of no fewer than 140,000 Kievan citizens, mostly Jews, murdered in cold blood by the invading Nazis. When the Germans were forced out, they systematically blew up most of the center of the city, leaving it a ruin.

Kiev is the oldest city in the USSR; it goes back to A.D. 862, and is sometimes called the "Jerusalem of Russia." Here is some of the holiest of holy Russian ground. It was founded by three legendary brothers, members of an old princely family, by name Khoriv, Satchek, and Kiy; from "Kiy" comes the name "Kiev." It became in time the capital of the Kievan Rus, and, for several centuries, was the most important city in eastern Europe. Then the Tatars came, and Russia, so to speak, moved north. Kiev has always been a crossroads, ideologically and otherwise. During the 1918-20 civil war it changed hands no fewer than *thirty* times.

Three things in three totally different fields interested me. (1) A poster advertising a movie showed a gangster with *a drawn revolver*. Such a poster would, in Stalin's day, have been unthinkable anywhere in the USSR. Anything depicting violence against constituted authority was not, to put it mildly, countenanced. (2) In the Kiev hotel, which is comfortable, bread is toasted on one side only. This is supposed to make it taste better, and does. (3) Outside Kiev are the only clover-leaf highway intersections I saw in Russia. It is, as always, paradoxical that the Russians advance so swiftly in some divisions of technology, and are so laggard in others. It is now possible to travel by car from Kiev to Kharkov, but the trip (only about two hundred miles) will take eight to ten hours. Between Kiev and Odessa the road is not even open, which is as if there were no road between Kansas City and St. Louis.

Conversation in Kiev can be quite outspoken. One morning we passed some dilapidated shanties, and our guide said, "These are the slums for people who say we have no slums." I asked another young man if he went to church. Reply: "Of course not. I am a pagan like my grandfathers in the ninth century." The intelligentsia is, of course, thoroughly indoctrinated. I asked a youngster if he thought of himself as being more Ukrainian than Russian, or vice versa. Reply: "I think of myself as a Ukrainian who believes in socialism for all of the Soviet Union, including the Ukraine." I asked him if he hated Germany. "We never hated Germany as such—only the Nazis and fascists." Sight-seeing one day we passed under a lacy bridge—a kind of lover's leap. Our guide said that before 1917 young people, unhappily in love, often committed suicide here, but that since the Revolution in 1917 people do not kill themselves for romantic reasons.

One movie running in Kiev while we were there was *Miss Mend*, which is a satire about young people in the United States; another was a deliciously witty and engaging travelogue on London, narrated by the Director of the Puppet Theater in Moscow, Serge Obraztsov. Kiev is more receptive to things external than most Soviet cities. Calling on one official, we saw an eight-volume set of Abraham Lincoln behind his desk.

Kiev University, named for the Ukrainian poet patriot Taras Shevchenko, is one of the foremost in the Union.[17] It is a bright red structure, and behind this lies a story. Students made a demonstration here a hundred years ago, which the authorities could not quell. So they painted the University red, with the words, "If our students won't blush with shame, at least the building will." The University of Kiev was founded in 1834, and has 705 teachers and 6,200 students. The Rector is a specialist in machine building, and

---

[17] The local Opera is also named for Shevchenko. He was a serf, born in 1814; he showed talent as a writer and painter, and a group of artists and writers bought him from his owner for three thousand rubles, and gave him an education. He spent twelve years in Siberia as a political exile, and then returned to Kiev, where he died. He is the first of Ukrainian national heroes, largely because his poems and paintings attacked serfdom.

the general emphasis is, of course, on science. Most students are Ukrainian, but there are some Czechs, Poles, North Koreans, and Chinese—also one Canadian.

History is close to the visitor in Kiev. One important street, Vladimirskaya, is named for St. Vladimir, who introduced Christianity to Russia in A.D. 988. As a matter of fact, this worthy's name was not Vladimir at all, but Basil. He was a prince of Kiev who, as Byzantine influence grew, decided to renounce paganism. But he did not know which faith to choose—Islam, Judaism, or Christianity. Except for an accident, he might have made Kiev officially Jewish, and all Russia might be Jewish today. For a time, as he sought to make up his mind, Basil veered toward Islam, but then discovered that the Moslem creed prohibited alcohol—intolerable thought! Eventually he decided in favor of Christianity, renamed himself Vladimir, and became the first saint of the Russian Orthodox Church. This Basil-Vladimir did not, however, even after adopting Christianity and baptizing thousands of his subjects in the icy waters of the Dnieper, surrender some of his pagan habits; for instance he kept a harem of eight hundred wives in the village of Vasilkov, fifteen miles from the capital. Its ruins may still be seen today.

One pleasant sight in Kiev is the National Museum, which contains a charming Velásquez—a coral-pink Infanta. Another is the luminous pale blue palace built by the Czarina Elizabeth, daughter of Peter the Great. Elizabeth led a very fancy life. At one time she owned fifteen thousand dresses, and behaved accordingly. In her mature years, she left St. Petersburg for Kiev, to live in retirement and repentance. However, she resumed her frolics, though she was over sixty, and had a celebrated love affair with a choirboy. Her palace is now a reception hall for the Ukrainian parliament next door. Sic transit gloria.

But the outstanding spectacles of Kiev are the churches. This is Rome. One is St. Vladimir's, still an "active" church and crowded with worshipers. Another, St. Andrew's, with five blue and white spiky domes, was built by the architect who contributed so much to Leningrad—Rastrelli. The legend is that long before Kiev was founded, St. Andrew stood on this site with its splendid view of the Dnieper, and proclaimed that this should be the location of a great city. A church here, he said, would be so gloriously situated that it would need no bells to give notice of its location. Hence, to this day, St. Andrew's has no bells. Then we must mention St. Sophia, built in 1037, pure white with a soaring blue bell tower. The first library in Russia was established in this church, and it contains some fascinating mosaics, as beautiful as those in Ravenna. Also the tomb of Yaroslav, one of the earliest and greatest of Kievan princes, is here; the marble coffin, on an iron floor, weighs six tons. Not many people recall that this ancient Ukrainian potentate had position enough, in the eleventh century A.D., to marry off one of his daughters to Harold, King of Norway, another to Andreas I, King of Hungary, and a third to Henry I, King of France.

Not far away, near the river, is the picturesque tomb of the brothers Askold and Deer, princes of Kiev. In 1182 a group of Viking merchants came to Kiev; Askold and Deer received them courteously, and were then treacherously murdered. The leader of the Vikings, Prince Oleg, presumably out of contrition, subsequently announced that Kiev would become the mother of all Russian cities. Another well-known tomb is that of Kochubei and Iskra, colonels in the service of Peter the Great. They were betrayed by a Cossack chief named Mazepa, during the war against Charles XII of Sweden, and, by error, were executed. Pushkin and Byron both wrote poems about this episode.

The supreme sight of Kiev is the Pechersk Monastery, sometimes called the Lavra. The oldest church in this ancient compound dates from A.D. 1051, and the campanile, which rises three hundred feet, was the tallest structure in the city until the new TV tower was built. The Nazis, when they evacuated Kiev, did their best to destroy the Lavra, out of sheer wantonness. It had no military significance. Mines blew up most of the site, including some of the loveliest monuments in Europe, like the St. Assumption Cathedral built in the eleventh century. The Lavra, next to Zagorsk near Moscow, is commonly regarded as the "holiest" institution in all Russia. The cellars contain some extraordinary mummies.

CHAPTER XXI

Across the Black Sea to the Caucasus

*Scratch a Russian and you get a Tatar; scratch a
Tatar and you get—a Tatar.*

—OLD PROVERB

THE headwaiter in Odessa, the "Gem of the Black Sea," wore a dinner
jacket, something rare in the Soviet Union, and looked impeccable—except
that he had on a green striped shirt. When we walked into the Intourist
restaurant, eyes followed us as if they were attached to strings operated by a
puppeteer—eyes starving, ravenous, for the sight of something different,
something fresh. Odessa is the dingiest, most dog-eared city I saw in the
USSR; it looks as if mold were growing all over it. Toward the edge of the
city, along the Black Sea beaches, are rows of scrofulous old buildings,
tottering on their foundations behind ruined shabby gates. Once these were
the houses of the rich; today they are sanitaria for the proletariat.

ODESSA (population about 600,000) has a distinguished past. Its opera
is—or was—the most famous in Russia after that of Moscow, and the city
has always been well known as a music center. Tchaikovsky conducted the
first performance of the *Queen of Spades* here, and two of the most notable
contemporary Soviet virtuosi, David Oistrakh and Emil Gilels, are Odessan.
The opera is decorated in red, gilt, white; it has crimson armchairs, and the
high vaulted ceiling is covered by frescoes representing scenes from Shakespeare. Also Odessa was a considerable literary center, and next to Leningrad
was probably the foremost "writer's city" in the country in older days.
Odessa had a reputation for political liberalism under the Czars. Partly
this was because it was close to Turkey; the Czars wanted it to be loyal at all
costs, and so gave its people special privileges. Also Odessa was the scene
of one of the most infamous pogroms in Russian history; thousands of Jews
were massacred here in 1905.

425

Odessa, the fourth city of the Ukraine and its most important port, dates from 1794. It is one of the four "hero cities" in the USSR; during World War II it withstood siege by the Germans for sixty-nine days before it fell. Today the population is largely Ukrainian, with strong Russian and Jewish communities (probably, despite the Nazis, the town is still 20 per cent Jewish) and with some Greeks, Spaniards, and Italians left over from older days. Odessa is a big tourist center; about 200,000 Soviet citizens visit it every year, putting up at its sixty sanitaria and forty rest homes; also a good many non-Russian visitors come in. French and Italian cruise ships call here every summer. The name "Odessa" comes from Ulysses. The Greeks built an outpost called Odissus in the fourth century A.D., about thirty miles from the present site; centuries later, the Turks established a post near by called Yeni Dunia, or New World. Catherine the Great, when she set up the town as a fortress to prevent further incursions by Turkey, chose the name Odessa.

This is headquarters not merely for Soviet maritime operations in the Black Sea, but for whaling and other expeditions into the Antarctic. Leningrad and Murmansk are Russia's gateways to the Arctic, and Odessa similarly serves the Antarctic. Work on Antarctic affairs is closely pressed.

I have never seen anything more forlorn and decrepit than the streetcar tracks leading to the suburbs—limp, twisted pipes of metal that look made of putty; it is a miracle that anything can run on them. Most of the cars are (as in all Soviet provincial towns) operated by women. The former Vorontsov Palace, named for a well-known nineteenth-century governor, is now the House of Pioneers. The old stock exchange is now a concert hall. Most street signs exist only in Ukrainian—not in both Ukrainian and Russian, as is the case in Kharkov and Kiev. Pushkin lived here briefly, and there are the inevitable Pushkin streets and monuments. Also Odessa is the site of the ophthalmological institute founded by the renowned Dr. Filatov, a pioneer in the technique of corneal transplants, who died last year.

The Duke of Richelieu emigrated to Odessa from France in 1789, and later Alexander I made him governor general; a statue stands to his memory on the waterfront today. It is an odd monument indeed, because it was hit by a shell from a British warship in 1854, during the Crimean War, and there the shell still is, stuck like an iron mango in the body of the statue. Near by is a broad flight of steps leading from the quays to the city proper. They will be remembered by anybody who saw Sergei Eisenstein's old film *Cruiser Potemkin*.

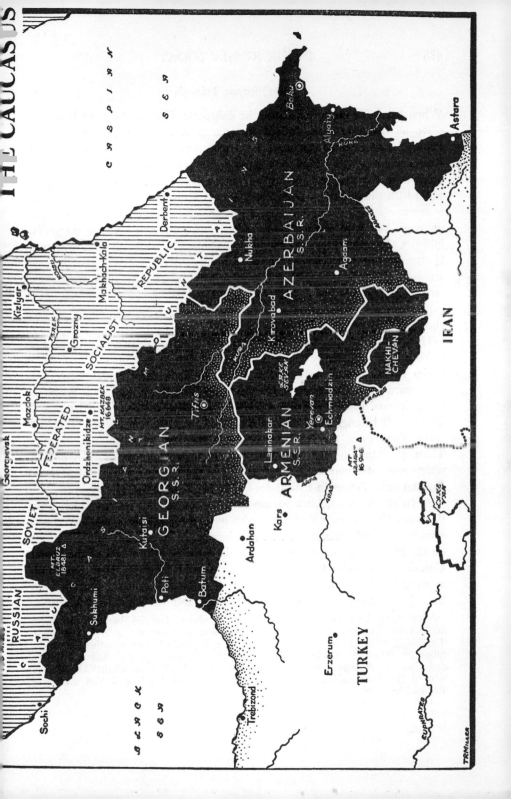

The Crimean Triangle

When Mark Twain visited Russia he called the Crimea the most beautiful place he had ever seen. Indeed its scenery is entrancing. The Crimean Peninsula, as anybody can see from a map, hangs down from the body of Russia like a pendant held by a slender chain; the Perekop Isthmus which holds it to the mainland is only five miles wide. To one side is a body of water with the odd name Putrid Sea. The "Green Peninsula" of the Crimea is at once a crossroads of history, a garden, and a complex anthropological museum. We have reached a subtropical area now, and here are magnolia, hibiscus, bougainvillaea, eucalyptus, camphor, in a flamboyant Rivieran landscape. But the Crimea can be cold in winter. The sky the day we arrived was the color of an ugly bruise on a thumbnail. At Yalta, the mountains were powdered with fresh snow, and, without turning your head, you could see roses in the foreground and pines glazed with an icy frosting just above.

History leaves mixed-up traces here. The original inhabitants of the Crimea were apparently Celts, who named the area Tauris. The Greeks began to colonize it early, and Greek settlements have existed since the fifth century B.C. Caesar made the Crimea a Roman province and, centuries later, it was ruled by other Italians, including Pisans, Venetians, and Genoese. It belonged to Genoa, strange as this may seem, for two hundred years. Then came the incursion of the Tatars in the thirteenth century. These predatory Moslem invaders set up their khanate at Bakhchisarai, which was later conquered by the Turks: the peninsula did not become Russian until Potemkin took it for Catherine II in 1783.

A tragic episode relates to modern Greeks in this area. About forty thousand Greeks, including many who were actually Greek nationals, were rounded up and evacuated from their homes in the Crimea and elsewhere on the Black Sea, and were summarily deported to other parts of the Soviet Union, in particular Central Asia, after World War II. They were not, as were the Crimean Tatars,[1] accused of disloyalty or collaboration with the Nazis; Stalin simply wanted to uproot and destroy this community

[1] See "The Lost Peoples" in Chapter IX above. Russian barbarity in these matters was bad enough; German barbarity was also something to reckon with. The Nazis invading the Crimea executed 79,276 people in two months. One order called for "the summary killing of all Jews, gypsies, insane people, Asiatic inferiors, and Communist party functionaries and officials." Rudolf Lowenthal, "The Extinction of the Krimchaks in World War II," *American Slavic and East European Review*, April, 1951.

as part of his program to liquidate all "foreign" blocs within Russia. The operation was a climax to the "anticosmopolitan" campaign. Nobody knows how many of these unfortunate Greeks survive today, and the Greek government, despite stern effort, has never been able to get in touch with them. These Greeks, it should be emphasized, were not vagabonds or refugees, but represented a solid, enlightened, commercial class that had lived in the Black Sea region for generations, if not centuries. Nor were they guilty of any crime. But Stalin thought that they were too close to foreign bourgeois influences, and so they were wiped out.

Crimea belongs these days to the Ukraine, although its population is probably not more than 20 per cent Ukrainian. Before the liquidation of the Crimean Tatars its status was that of an autonomous republic; then it was joined to the RSFSR, and in 1954 was transferred to the Ukraine, with which it has close economic ties, as a gesture to the Ukrainians and to honor the three-hundredth anniversary of the union of the Ukraine and Russia.[2] It is not yet known how, or where, the rehabilitated Crimean Tatars will be absorbed, but the work of transplanting them has begun.

The principal Crimean sights are the old Khanate Palace at Bakhchisarai, and the "hero city" of SEVASTOPOL, which withstood siege by the Nazis for 250 days. This is the chief Russian naval base on the Black Sea. Oddly enough the spot—to go back to another war—where the Light Brigade charged at Balaklava, near Sevastopol, is not marked, and tourists will have a hard time finding it.

We drove from SIMFEROPOL, the capital, which was known as Al-Mechet under the Turks, along precipitous corniced roads and through seaside villages, to Yalta on the sea. In 115 kilometers we never saw a gas station except for one at Alushta, a town built by Byzantines in the sixth century. This was, however, the most heavily traveled road we encountered in the entire Soviet Union; it groaned with trucks. No railroad serves the villages along the shore. There are no billboards, but at regular intervals stand small framed posters. These identify whatever collective farm happens to be near by, or describe local achievements—what power schemes are in the works, what the coal industry is doing, and statistics of grain production or viti-culture. Plaster statues stand at sharp turns in the climbing road; these statues are very primitive indeed, depicting a boy with a fish or a girl holding a basketball aloft. Statistics, culture, sport! You can't get away from them anywhere in the Soviet Union.

[2] *New York Times*, May 5, 1957.

The Pretty Town of Yalta

YALTA, like spas in France, lives on health. The population of this little town is only 34,000, but something like 300,000 people visit it every year, some of them tourists, but most sick or tired people coming for a cure. Yalta has thirty-nine sanitaria, and twice as many rest homes; the difference is mainly that a physician's approval is necessary for entrance into a sanitarium, and medical care is given; the rest homes are for people on holiday. Vacation is called "rest" in the Soviet Union.

One of the newer sanitaria, the Ukraina, is devoted mainly to heart and neurological cases. Dr. Boris A. Sokolov, a youthful neurologist from the University of Kharkov, took us around. Originally this sanitarium, a showplace, only received patients who belonged to the trade union of the Ministry of Lumber and Paper. Now the system has been changed, and all the sanitaria, under the direct supervision of the Ministry of Health in Kiev, take in people without regard to their particular trade-union affiliation. Patients must, of course, be passed upon by their local doctor, who then recommends them for admittance, and their trade union, whatever it happens to be, pays for part of the cure. The fee for the normal stay—twenty-four days—is 1,400 rubles, or $350 at par. Rooms in this establishment are double, with a private bath between each. Guests get five meals a day, including tea and a cup of yoghurt at 10 P.M. I looked at the dinner menu. There was a choice of three hors d'oeuvres, five soups, and seven meats—something luxurious and unusual for the USSR. Everything was clean, and the place looked comfortable, if plain. One patient we talked to was a coal miner with arteriosclerosis; another was a bookkeeper from Kiev, suffering from upset nerves.

Arriving in Yalta, we put up at a hotel also called the Ukraina. There is a certain monotony to names in the Soviet Union. The uniformity of Russian hotels, which is oppressive throughout most of the Union, is relaxed here. The state china was different, and the ash trays were, a merciful relief, flat. But we saw guests in "state pajamas"—coarse garments in black, green, and white stripes—which are identical everywhere from Smolensk to Vladivostok, and which are sometimes impolitely called "concentration camp pajamas." People lounge in them in the corridors and lobbies, as if they were suits, without robes. A Soviet hotel can be very cozy, but the pajamas themselves are hideous. Choice of movies the night we arrived: Bread, Love and Dreams, with Gina Lollobrigida; one Finnish importation and one Viennese; a wide-screen Soviet film, *Leningrad Nights;* and a documentary showing, of all things, life in New York, Chicago, and Los Angeles. Our guide asked us if wide-screen movies existed in the United States. When I said we must have ten thousand theaters equipped to project these, he looked hurt.[3]

Mr. Roosevelt, when he arrived in Yalta for a conference quite well known, stayed at the Livadia Palace, a graceful structure which once belonged to the Czars, and which was the favorite residence of Nicholas II. It is a rest home nowadays, holding seven hundred workers. Dining tables are crowded together throughout the whole building, even in the room Roosevelt used as an office. Mr. Churchill and the British delegation stayed at the Vorontsov Palace in a near-by village called Alupka. This edifice, now a museum, was built in the early nineteenth century by an English architect, Edward Blore, and looks like an Elizabethan Gothic castle combined with a Moorish palace. Large marble lions, with enticing coy smiles, guard the front steps; then come busts of Demosthenes, Socrates, Aesculapius, and Euripides, the only representations of classic Greek art I saw in Russia. We asked where Stalin had resided during the Yalta conference. Consternation. Soviet citizens never like to admit defeat, but our guides did not know, and agitated researches were at once pursued. No result. Security considerations have been ingrained here to such a degree that even today, twelve years afterward, it is still unknown where Stalin stayed.[4]

The house where Chekhov lived for some years is in Yalta, and its lower floor is a museum. His widow, a veteran actress named Olga Knipper, still lived on the upper floor at the time of our visit, aged eighty-six; she died a few months later. Also living here but secluded from the tourists who swarm in is one of Chekhov's sisters, M. P. Chekova, aged ninety-three. The house, in distinct contrast to that of Tolstoy in Moscow, has an intimate air, reflecting Chekhov's own sensitiveness and modesty. One of his most profoundly moving stories, "The Lady and the Dog," is laid in Yalta, but whether or not he wrote it here I do not know. The walls are brightly whitewashed, and windows with tall double curtains look through a screen of cypress to terraces and the sea—very Mediterranean. But everything else

---

[3] Prices in the shops: tennis balls, 4.65 rubles (Yalta has the only tennis court I saw in the USSR); an alarm clock, 110 rubles; ornaments for Christmas trees, colored balls and the like, 3.70 rubles each; a large lithograph of Voroshilov, 120 rubles; a man's necktie, 4 rubles 10. Once more, divide by four to get dollar values at par.

[4] We found out later in Moscow that he put up at Simeiz, a village near by, in a palace once owned by the Yusupovs; I hope our earnest and hard-working Yalta guides read this footnote.

is quintessentially Russian—a white tile stove, narrow iron bed, souvenirs of the première of *The Cherry Orchard*, a pile of yellowing visitors cards underneath a samovar, old-order Russian bric-a-brac, and faded sepia photographs of Rachmaninoff, Chaliapin, the youthful Gorky, and other friends. There are no books in the house—a phenomenon somewhat puzzling. Also puzzling is the fact that Chekhov, the gentlest of men, kept a revolver in his medicine chest.

Black Sea Cruise

Looking down from the Nikitski Botanical Garden, with its crumbling statuary and shabbily proliferating growth, we saw at dusk an apparition on the waterfront, a floating jewel, a blur of phosphorescent light. It was a ship. It was none other than the *Pobeda* (*Victory*), which rides the Black Sea like an amphibious centaur. We rushed to the dock, and found that it was sailing that night for Sukhumi, our own destination. But we were booked to go to Sukhumi by automobile and plane. We decided forthwith to travel by the *Pobeda* instead. The response to this was very Russian. Intourist meets all challenges!—even a change in plans so radical. The local Intourist office was closing for the day, but we opened it. We needed rubles, but the girl who had the key to the cashbox had gone to the movies. We found her. She had no idea of the rate of exchange for Finnish marks, the foreign money we carried, and took our word for what the rate in Moscow was. A comparison for all this would be for two Russians in New York to decide at the last moment to cancel their flight tickets across the Atlantic, and take the *Queen Mary* instead, a scant hour before its departure—then dig out a Guaranty Trust Company cashier from Radio City Music Hall, and get him to change money in a hotel room at a rate taken on nothing but faith.

There followed the pleasantest two or three days we had in the Soviet Union. The *Pobeda*, originally a German liner called the *Magdalena*, ran before the war from Hamburg to South America; briefly then she served as a British hospital ship. The Russians got her, together with several other German merchant vessels, by way of reparations after World War II, just as the French got the *Europa*, which they renamed the *Liberté*. The *Pobeda*, a staunch and pretty ship, displaces fifteen thousand tons, and cruises at fifteen knots. In summer, she takes Soviet tourists abroad, visiting Naples, Le Havre, Antwerp, Stockholm, and other European ports. The inclusive fare is 4,200 rubles ($1,050) first class, 3,000 rubles ($750) second class, for a twenty-six-day cruise. Each Soviet tourist is given a handout of $47 in American cash, for purchasing souvenirs; how this exact sum is arrived at I do not know. If anybody still thinks that Russia has produced a classless society, he should travel on the *Pobeda*. There are not merely three classes but four, and every cabin conspicuously bears its category on the door—Third, Second, First, and (believe it or not) "Deluxe First."

We had a bathroom done in blue-green tile, the only modern bathroom I saw in the USSR, and the toilet paper was nonstate. A crisis came when Zoya, our assiduous blond interpreter, found that she was sharing a small cabin with a man. The purser thought that she was being unnecessarily fussy, but moved her to another cabin. The boat, like all conveyances in Russia, takes off without warning; no shouts, no bells. The *Pobeda* has little deck space, and no deck chairs. No drinks are served in the bar, but only in the dining room; we saw one really sensational drunk, who rolled halfway down a stairway. The library, the site of the former smoking room, reminded me of Russian airports—dingy, improvised, shut in, but with a friendly *je m'en fiche* atmosphere.

The best things to eat were the soups, and, as always, bread. All over this part of the Union, bread is not black, as in the north, but has a consistency and color like American protein bread. One evening a ship's officer came up to us, shook my hand with a mighty grip, beamed all over, and announced that Russia had just won the Olympic Games. Such pride! We met on this boat a shipbuilder, Mr. Z. His first questions were: (1) were we rich; (2) what was my profession; (3) what did we think of the Soviet Union. He had read Fenimore Cooper and, inevitably, Howard Fast. He patriotically rebuked us for not having stayed longer in Leningrad, his native city, asked why the United States insisted on inflicting on foreign visitors the indignity of fingerprinting, and was horrified to hear that Washington, D.C., does not have a national theater. And, like all Russians, he talked of peace. "Of course there cannot be a war. We lost twelve million dead. There is nobody in this country who did not lose somebody. It takes one minute to destroy, and then a whole generation to rebuild." There was a note of anger and positive fear in his voice. Russians are literally terrified at the thought of war.

The pace of the *Pobeda* is leisurely, with long stops at successive ports of call. We put in at NOVOROSSIISK, where a fierce wind nailed us to the pier for hour after hour. We went ashore, and, plodding through thick wet snow, sticky like marshmallows, reached the end of the dock area, where we signaled a bus, hoping to be taken into the town. The driver looked at us as if we were apparitions from another planet. Up drove a small car, and the youth driving it, with devil-may-care insouciance, offered us a lift—in fact, took us for an hour's sight-seeing tour, through a driving snowstorm. Balls of snow came at us, as if shot from guns. This young man had just had an afternoon of sport in the countryside, shooting rabbits. Some people do have fun in the Soviet Union. Novorossiisk is a grain and cement center, which under the Czars was capital of the "Government of the Black Sea." French financial interests were strong here in those days. When the invading Germans left Novorossiisk in 1943, not a building was left undestroyed; today not an iota of damage remains. But what struck me most was that, so far as we could tell, there was not a single café in the whole city, not a place to sit down, chat with our guide, who had a characteristically Russian volubility, and have a drink. We saw nothing but the lean walls of factories and tenements, blotched with snow. I felt like a mouse nibbling at an icebox.

*

The eastern shore of the Black Sea, the Pontus Euxinus of the ancients, is even more extravagantly pretty than Yalta. A little train plodded along the coast, keeping pace with our ship; the smoke from its locomotive took on and maintained the shape of a white cypress. Toward nightfall lights begin to blink but they are weak and strung far apart; each gives an individual blob of illumination, like a necklace of widely separated pearls. Sochi, the site of the Greek Nisis, is the most "fashionable" health resort in the Soviet Union. Here are the massive sanitaria once belonging to the Ministry of Agriculture, the Ministry of the Coal Industry, and the Ministry of Metallurgy, as well as lesser ones for workers in leather, textiles, and food processing. Along one road we saw a high, solid wooden fence, half a mile long and without an aperture; even the beach is screened off. In this enclosure are villas reserved for leading members of the Presidium; here too Stalin often stayed. In the parks—the standard "Park of Culture and Rest" and others—large nude statues rise, some of plaster, some painted the color of tinfoil, symbolizing various aspects of recreation or sport. I should say "almost" nude. Always we must reckon with Soviet puritanism. The statues have neat little plaster G-strings.

The main Sochi squares are hung with posters, like signs in a convention hall, which announce that by the end of the current Five-Year Plan the country will produce 593 million metric tons of coal, 135 million metric tons of oil, and 40 million cubic meters of gas. Another sets up marks for expected increases in production:

MEAT—200%
MILK—195%
EGGS—254%

Another:

HOSPITAL BEDS—28%
PLACES IN NURSERIES—44%
KINDERGARTENS—45%

Even on a holiday in Sochi, you never get away from the regime and its barrage of blistering statistics.

Another town further down the coast, SUKHUMI, is the capital of Abkhazia, and has fifty thousand people. It is a resort like Sochi, but is less chic. This is where Trotsky, ill with a mysterious fever, sulked after Lenin's death. Tobacco, grapes, and tea are local products; we bought here the only oranges we saw in the USSR, price 15 rubles ($3.75 at par) for four.[5] Sukhumi has one astonishingly good restaurant. Food is weighed and charged for according to weight, exactly as in a shop. The waiter takes your order; then the man at the counter, unshaved and in a sweater, slices off slabs of meat or bread, weighs them, and you pay. In the hotel we came across several demonstrations of the local character. I mislaid our key; the chambermaid found it after much commotion, and, handing it to me, knelt and kissed it gratefully as she passed it over. Such dramatic people! When we checked out, a porter with shaven skull who might have been a hundred years old tottered after us to give us something precious that we had no doubt lost, or unaccountably left behind. It was a crumpled bit of Kleenex.

The monkey nursery of the Medical-Biology Station of the Academy of Medicine of the USSR, founded in 1927, is in Sukhumi. This is a well-known research establishment, which studies and experiments on monkeys in relation to human disease. Breeding is in charge of what is, aptly enough, called the production department, and six generations of animals have been born here. The laboratory has four main departments—oncology, biology, radiobiology, and neuropathology—and one of the directors, Dr. Georgi Ivanovich Kondakov, took us around. Artificial reproduction of malignant tumors in apes is a special object of study, and in another series of experiments monkeys are deliberately turned into neurotics. The neurosis

[5] But in summer oranges are plentiful.

is produced by submitting the beast to mild electric shocks, in the Pavlov manner. Dr. Richard E. Shope of the Rockefeller Institute for Medical Research visited this establishment not long ago, and I quote a brief passage from a subsequent report: "Another method used was to separate a male and a female who had lived together for a long time . . . and place the female in a nearby cage with a new male. The old male gets violently disturbed by what he sees in the other cage and, after some three months, develops a severe neurosis, and may even develop gastric erosions, coronary disease, etc."

Monkeys are kept outdoors uncaged, and flip from walls to trees on a protected terrace. To see them being fed tangerines is an odd sight. Most human beings in the Soviet Union do not get tangerines.

Abkhazia (population around 330,000) is a curiosity, an autonomous republic affiliated to Georgia. Turkish influence is marked in this area, particularly in architecture. The Abkhazians have their own language, which is totally different from either Russian or Georgian; it derives from Latin, but uses a modified Russian script. Children here may go to Abkhazian, Georgian, or Armenian schools, but all are obliged to learn Russian as well as their own language. Street signs in Sukhumi are in three different languages— Russian, Georgian, and Abkhazian.

Nikolai Arastovich Geria, aged forty-six, is Abkhazian Minister of Education, and a familiar Soviet type. He is also an impressive human being— dedicated, confident, competent, and tough. Officials like this rise out of the humblest beginnings. But, as I have pointed out in a chapter above, they never say that they are "self-made," as Americans might; they say that they are made by socialism and the Soviet regime. Mr. Geria's mother and father were both illiterate peasants, poorest of the poor, and he was one of many men we met with this same background. How proud they are of their evolution!

Geria, after the Revolution, got free primary and secondary schooling in Sukhumi, and then made his way to the University of Leningrad. He received a degree in history, and returned to Sukhumi to teach. Meantime he had become a member of the Communist party, and rose in the local administration. He became deputy minister for education ten years ago, and has been full minister since 1954. He wore an old blue neckband shirt when we saw him, without collar or tie.

Before 1917, Mr. Geria told us, Abkhazia had exactly one secondary school, so inferior that it did not even have the right to give a diploma. Now ninety-four secondary schools are functioning, the degrees of all of which are good for college entrance. There were 48 primary schools before the

Revolution; now 424. There are three teachers' colleges, and everything possible is being done, Mr. Geria said, to promote the national culture and literature, including publication of books in Abkhazian. Of the primary schools, 170 teach in Abkhazian, 90 in Georgian, 80-90 in Armenian, and 70 in Russian. This more or less follows the population ratio. Several interesting communities live in or near Sukhumi. One is descended from Negro slaves who were brought in here from Africa by Georgian princes several hundred years ago. Another is a group of Estonians. These derive from the mass deportations after the war, when thousands of Balts, particularly Latvians and Estonians, were bodily transplanted from their homes and dumped without mercy elsewhere throughout the country. The theory was that the Estonians would be "happy" in Sukhumi, because they are a seafaring people and have the Black Sea now (instead of the Baltic) as their front yard. The Estonian side of the story may be quite different. But—not to condone the crime of uprooting them—Sukhumi is probably a pleasanter place to live than the primitive wastes of Kazakhstan.

Abkhazia has several ministries of its own—education, roads, industry, justice, construction—which are autonomous. For the rest, administration comes from Tiflis, the capital of Georgia, or Moscow. The Ministry of Foreign Affairs in Moscow is represented here. I asked why. The answer was equivocal: "Why should we have any foreign office at all, since our only interest is in peace?"

The Caucasus Frontier

The Caucasus, an abundantly vigorous and exciting region, lies between the Black Sea and the Caspian, on the magnificent mountain-*cum*-valley shelf where Europe and Asia meet. It differs as much from the rest of the Soviet Union as Mexico, let us say, differs from Saskatchewan. About nine million people live in the Caucasus in three different Union republics, Georgia, Armenia, and Azerbaijan. Their "independence" is, of course, a fiction. In the last analysis, no matter how strong the accent is on local identity, the Caucasus is as much ruled by Moscow as Janos Kadar or Siberia.

I have visited the Caucasus twice and have always marveled, as any visitor must marvel, at the concentration it provides of natural wonders. Here is Mount Ararat, with Little Ararat perched beside it like a tent; here are no fewer than nine mountains higher than Mont Blanc, including Elbruz, the highest peak in Europe. Here are cities bustling with industry like Baku, and tribes of primitive mountain folk who have scarcely reached the perimeter of civilization; here are modern roads and railways, pipe lines, oil refineries, machine tool factories, built on the silt of centuries. The valley of the Rion is the original home of the pheasant. The Caucasus is the richest region in the USSR—largely on account of petroleum. It is rich in folklore, too. Noah and Jason left their legendary traces here, and Prometheus was chained to the sharp lofty peak (16,540 feet) known today as Kazbek.

Above all this area is a colorful patchwork of customs, races, creeds, and languages. One authority writes, "Nowhere else in the world is there so great a variety of races and peoples, or such diversity of speech and custom in so small an area as here."[6] As an example, seventeen different languages are spoken in one small district, and altogether the region holds fifty or sixty different "nationalities." When I first visited Erivan, known in Armenian as Yerevan, the capital of Armenia, in 1928, I saw street signs not merely in five different languages, but in five different *alphabets*—Russian, Armenian, Georgian, Arabic, and Latin. Once, and it was a pleasant small adventure, I rode on horseback up into the hills to visit the unknown Khevsuri country; here live people who are believed to be descendants of refugees from the Crusades, and who still possess authentic crusader's armor. The Caucasus is a crossroads as well as a mountain fastness, and it has echoed for centuries to the tramp of conquerors—Khazars, Arabs, Turko-Mongols, Persians, Byzantine Greeks and Seljuk Turks. "During the 1500 years that Tiflis was the capital of the Georgian kingdom, it was seized by the enemy and either razed or burned 29 times."

This was the last region in the Soviet Union pacified after the Revolution. Georgia in particular, with its superb national tradition, held on to a Menshevik regime bitterly hostile to Moscow for a considerable period, and the civil war in the Caucasus as a whole went on till 1921.

*

Armenia, about as big as Belgium, with 1,600,000 people, has a geography of peculiar fascination. Parts of it look like the roof of the world. A great lake, Sevan, lies more than a mile and a quarter high, and is bigger than all the lakes in Switzerland put together. Somehow one associates Armenians with seaports, trade, and low-lying crowded bazaars, but their country of origin is lofty, empty, and has immense horizons. Most Armenians are of peasant stock, and, if only because they have been persecuted so unmercifully, are

[6] This and the following quotation are from the old Intourist *Guide*.

intensely chauvinistic. For a long time Armenia was part of Georgia, but Georgians and Armenians are altogether different people, and even today do not like each other much. Armenia, in contrast to aristocratic Georgia, with its profusion of landowning nobles, was a country of small, humble, and tenaciously worked individual farms. Today 99.7 per cent of the peasants are in collectives. Armenia has, incidentally, one of the oldest Christian churches in the world, with headquarters at the ancient capital Echmiadzin.

A good many Armenians came back from residence abroad, after their diaspora, and re-established themselves in their homeland in the period between the wars. Many of these, thoroughly disillusioned, would now like to get out. They can't. One of the conspicuous social patterns in Armenia is rivalry between the old stock, predating the Revolution, and the newcomers.

The capital is YEREVAN, an interesting animated city (population 385,-000); another important town, on the Turkish border, is LENINAKAN, once known as Alexandropol. Yerevan sits directly under Mount Ararat (16,916 feet). Industry is being built up, and mineral resources—particularly copper—exploited. Armenia, like everything in the Soviet Union, seeks to stress applied science too, and Yerevan has a solar electric station, for production (if it works) of energy from the sun.

Some straws in the Armenian winds, similar to others we have encountered in the Soviet Union, are these. Komsomolskaya Pravda printed recently an article complaining about "laziness" among students at Yereven State University. There is "no genuine liking for labor among students," and "snobbish attitudes toward manual labor are tolerated by the Young Communist League." It is no secret "that some [Armenian] graduates of higher educational institutions have an absolutely false conception of life; they see it as a bed of roses." The city has thirteen thousand university students, but not a single one "volunteered" for work in Central Asia, when "patriots" from all over the Union were urged to go to work on the Virgin Lands.

Reporting to the Supreme Soviet in February, 1957, Deputy S. Kh. Matmishyan asserted that the Ministry of Machine Building in Moscow had "failed to settle the problem of full utilization of the productive capacity" of several Armenian factories. "The small hydro-turbine plant and compressor plant are capable of doubling output without new construction, if given small amounts of additional equipment." Again: "Only one of Armenia's eight shoe factories operates in two shifts. With normal provision of raw material, this factory could increase output by approximately 800,000 pairs of shoes a year." "Matters are even worse with respect to . . . the

Leninakan Bicycle Plant." Also: "Within the Armenian Republic the railroad sector from Alaverdi to Leninakan has been electrified. But this sector is so short that the electric locomotives are utilized entirely inefficiently for brief runs, and consequently the 37 million-ruble capital investment in electrification yields little return." Finally it is noted that Moscow authorized construction of a pilot plant for processing materials for a special kind of optical glass back in 1949. "However, eight years later, nothing has been done." Bureaucracy![7]

*

Azerbaijan, on the Caspian, differs totally from Armenia. Most of it is arid steppe or semidesert, and it is predominantly Moslem; three-fifths of the people are of Turkish stock.[8] Also, because of its oil resources centering on Baku, it is much richer. Part of its frontier is with Iran. Azerbaijan covers 33,089 square miles, about the size of Portugal, and has about 3,400,000 people, fewer than Chicago. It has cotton as well as oil, and is in fact a very big cotton-producing area. Oil and cotton are, oddly enough, connected here by a material called gumbrin; this, a by-product from the oil refineries, is used as a fertilizer on the cotton fields. One unusual crop is guayule, the Mexican rubber plant. Azerbaijan, which was almost totally illiterate before World War I, is proud of its literary activities now. The State Publishing House issued 350 titles in Azerbaijanese in 1956, with a circulation of more than five million volumes. The works of Lenin have been republished 218 times, to a total of 2,204,000 copies. This is, of course, part of the familiar Soviet pattern. So is the fact that the local Academy of Sciences has twenty-five different research institutions, and works in a variety of specialized technical fields. So is the disclosure recently that a pipe rolling plant was ordered by Moscow to start operations although its "production cycle," after four years of work, was not ready, and its blooming and billeting mills were not even assembled. There are times when the Soviet Union seems to be populated by children gone slightly mad.

BAKU, a European city on the edge of Asia, looks like a port in Texas. Oil derricks rise from the sea. Untrained workers stream into it from the

[7] *Current Digest of the Soviet Press,* January 30, 1557, and March 27, 1957,
[8] Recently a new postage stamp was issued in honor of one of its citizens, Makhmud Eivazov. He is the oldest citizen of the Azerbaijan Republic, and probably the oldest man in the world; he has been a sheep farmer for more than a hundred years, still works on a collective farm in his mountain village, has twenty-three children, and is 148 years old.

barren hinterland, and as a result it is a somewhat turbulent city. A recent decree of the Presidium of the Azerbaijan Republic Supreme Soviet states that "the manufacture, possession, sale, and carrying of daggers, hunting knives, and similar cold steel weapons without proper authorization will henceforth be punished by five years in jail." Baku has 901,000 people, and is the fourth biggest city in the USSR. Petroleum development here is not a new phenomenon; Baedeker in 1914 mentions that the "naphtha springs" of Baku supply the whole of Russia with petroleum. The Nobel interests had a big financial stake here under the Czars.

The leading political personality in Azerbaijan in contemporary times was Mikhail Bagirov, a former prime minister, who was also for a brief time an alternate member of the Presidium of the Central Committee of the CPSU. He was a Beria man and was executed in 1956.

Georgia, the Jewel in the Crown

This republic has strong picturesque identity. First, the name. The country is called Gruziya in Russian, Sakartvelo in Georgian, and Vrasian in Armenian. It was named for St. George, who, although he never actually visited Georgia, holds a place in Georgian folklore almost like that of St. Patrick in Ireland. Georgian history goes back at least two thousand years, and the people were Christianized—by St. Nina, a Cappadocian girl—in A.D. 324. One of its last native kings was named, romantically enough, Hercules, and it was not incorporated into Russia until 1801. For more than a hundred years the Czars did their best to abolish Georgian nationalism and Russianize the country, but never with complete success.

Georgia has roughly four million people, and the population is two-thirds Georgian. Armenians form a 10 per cent minority. The area (29,498 square miles) is about that of South Carolina. The country, as a "sovereign" republic within the Union, has its own proud flag, red with a blue stripe on top. Two small items give some indication of Georgian background. Until the 1917 Revolution, every seventh citizen was a "nobleman," and Georgian princes made gallant sport all over the world. Second, the traditional Georgian drinking cup, which may be found in even the poorest house, is conch-shaped. Georgians are famously hospitable people, and once such a cup is filled with an appropriate libation, it cannot be put down until the entire draught is consumed.

The language, as different from Russian as Arabic is from English, is extraordinarily complex; there are thirty-three letters in the alphabet, and nouns inflect to seven cases. The names of most Georgians end with "shvili" or "adze"; both mean "son of." There were no schools of higher learning before the Revolution, and illiteracy probably reached 85 per cent; today there are nineteen colleges in the country, and literacy is near 100 per cent, except among surviving very old people. Most Georgians are bilingual, but many do not speak Russian well. School children are obliged to study both languages, but a Georgian child in a Russian school begins with the Russian language in his second year, whereas the study of Georgian, in the case of a Russian child, does not start until considerably later. In other words, Russian comes first. But before the Revolution, *all* instruction had to be in Russian, and *all* organizations worked exclusively in the Russian language. Today, at least in the realm of culture, the main emphasis is on Georgian. For instance 70 per cent of all plays produced at the National Theater are in the Georgian language. I was astonished, walking past this theater, to see that posters advertising its performances not only appeared in Georgian, but that no translation into Russian was provided.

Georgians are, of course, Orientals. They have hair black as midnight and lustrous dark large eyes; most do not resemble Russians from the north at all. I asked several if they considered themselves to be "European" or "Asian." The usual reply was that, as loyal Soviet citizens, they were European, but in other respects still Asian. One evidence of Orientalism is the position of women. Even today, women remain for the most part secluded. Only seldom did we see a Georgian woman in a restaurant, and sleeping cars on the Georgian trains are strictly segregated—the only place in the Soviet Union where this is true. You won't find a pretty girl in the upper berth in Georgia.

A substantial industrial effort has been made here. Georgia's second town, KUTAISI, has a well-known motor works, and the steel plant at RUSTAVI is a show-place. Automation is making progress. And all manner of smaller industrial activities are developing—food processing, textiles, furniture. Manganese deposits are important and, at the other end of the industrial spectrum, Georgia has the best-known champagne factory in the Soviet Union. It produced nine *million* bottles of champagne last year, several of which— on the occasion of our visit—we drank. One of the few light touches I encountered in the USSR was provided by this establishment—a large rococo statue in the courtyard, with a cherub holding a magnum of champagne aloft, between figures of Lenin and Stalin. The factory is new, clean, and well operated. The champagne runs from *Brut*, devoid of sugar, through various shades of dry to sweet; the dry wines are equal to anything produced in France, I thought. But perhaps I gained this impression after a lot of tasting. One curiosity: the Russians dismiss any talk of vintages, and consider classification of wines by year to be an archaic and bourgeois procedure. They assert that, by proper mixing, any year can be made as good as any other. Crazy, wonderful people!

The Georgian cabinet has about twenty ministers, of whom all are Georgian except one, an Armenian. There are no Russians. The chairman of the Presidium of the Supreme Soviet is a youngish man, Miron D. Chubinidze; he rose, like most of his colleagues, from illiterate peasant stock. The chairman of the Council of Ministers, prime minister, is Givi D. Dzhavakhishvili, an engineer by profession. I asked Georgians about their special position in the Union. Typical answer: "The tragedy of Georgia is that it has always been alone—for two thousand years surrounded by enemies. But with the victory of the great October Socialist Revolution, we have acquired brothers. Georgia has lived for centuries, but Soviet Georgia for only thirty-five years. In the Union is our happiness." I asked about relations with the sister republics. The answer, all over the USSR, is always the same, "Backgrounds of the individual fifteen republics may be different. We think of the Armenians, for example, as our cousins. It is inconceivable that bad relations could exist among the republics, because all are united by the fraternal bond of Moscow."

The statements above are, of course, rubbish. Moscow does not extend fraternity; it *rules*. And, as a matter of fact, Georgia has the most independent spirit of any of the Union republics, and is the one which, if by some miracle it ever got the chance, would probably be the first to secede. Political sentiment is still closely tied up with national pride, and people here, no matter what pious double-talk or "double-think" they engage in, are *Georgian* patriots. Stalin was a Georgian, and so was Beria. Under them, Georgia was highly favored. It got big appropriations.[9] When Stalin died Georgians certainly must have felt something of the relief that came to people everywhere in the Soviet Union; nevertheless, Stalin was Georgia's own, and, to a certain extent, he is missed. The only overt political disturbance in the USSR in many years occurred in Tiflis in March, 1956, on the third anniversary of Stalin's death. Stalin was not mentioned in the press—not a word—and citizens resented this; the next day students demonstrated all over the town, carrying Stalin portraits. This was, it is important to point out, not so much an anti-Soviet as an anti-*Russian* demonstration. The authorities were quick to act. Several university people were punished for having

[9] An odd point is however that Stalin only visited Georgia once in his twenty-nine years of power.

permitted "outbursts of nationalistic speculation," but no punishments were severe. Then a mass meeting was held, in which leaders pointed out to the students that Stalin indubitably did have good qualities, but that the "cult of personality" was wrong. Then Moscow sent hundreds of agitators through Georgia explaining this point further. One observer made a wry joke about all this. "The Georgians don't really like Stalin, but say that they like him only in order to annoy the Russians."

We ourselves had a vivid little experience in this field. One day in Tiflis we met with eleven distinguished members of the Georgia Writers Union. No fewer than three Stalin Prize winners were present, among them Georgi Leonidze, who has won a Stalin Prize three times. Others were the translator of Shakespeare into Georgian, a deputy to the Supreme Soviet in Moscow, the leading Georgian poet, the best-known author of Georgian children's books, a specialist in linguistics who was a member of the Georgian Academy of Sciences, and the editor of an important newspaper. The walls rang with good talk. We were jovial and hearty. After a while I asked a question about Stalin—whether, since de-Stalinization, writers felt freer. Dead embarrassed silence followed. I explained that in Moscow, when I asked a similar question at the Moscow Writers Union, the reply had been vigorously affirmative. Then, guardedly, warily, the Georgians conceded that things had lightened up for them too, and so de-Stalinization was welcomed. I put in the remark, "Even though Stalin was a Georgian?" The grave answer came, "In spite of the fact that Stalin was a Georgian!" Then these good men ceremoniously gave us a copy of a handsome anthology of Georgian verse, in English, and all inscribed it. We said good-by, went out to do some sight-seeing, and did not return to our hotel till nightfall. There, on the lookout for us, was one of our writer friends. He had been waiting for hours in the freezing lobby, and he had with him *another* copy of the anthology; he insisted on taking back the one we had received that morning, and giving us this instead. My wife pointed out that the first copy was uniquely precious to us, since all eleven writers had autographed it. The new copy was autographed too, by the same eleven!

Upstairs, alone, we looked curiously at the new copy wondering what could be the reason for this mysterious and dramatic switch. We found out that several sentences in the foreword had been clumsily scraped out with a razor, and, from the context, it was clear that the erased passages must have been glorifications of Stalin. Obviously, our friends did not want us to know that they had *ever* been Stalinists. They did not care to be on record with *anything* contrary to current trends. This episode, minor as it is, has relevance. These writers, let me repeat, were not children, but were creative people, elite as well as sophisticated. They must have known that we would see the evidences of mutilation and guess what this meant. And think of the trouble they had taken to round up eleven men and get eleven new signatures, after our meeting had broken up that morning.

Tiflis, Now Called Tbilisi

"Tiflis means hot water and ten minutes after I arrived I was in it." So wrote a youthful journalist many years ago. He was referring to the fact that Tiflis had, at that time, a grandiose bathing establishment. Tiflis does not, however, quite mean "hot water"; the correct translation is "hot springs." The word is a Russian distortion of the old Georgian name for the capital, TBILISI, which has now been restored to use. The population is 635,000, of which 80 per cent is Georgian. The city is strikingly divided between old and new, with handsome modern structures on one side of the Kura River, and Turkish-style wooden buildings, creaking hovels, set against a bluff on the other. The river cuts through the town jaggedly like a defile.

The hotel was really something. For two days running the temperature in our room was forty-five degrees, and it was freezingly cold outside. We were moved at last to another, warmer room. I will attempt to describe it. It had mottled purplish walls of rough plaster; heavy red velvet curtains, hung with derelict lace, across the leaky windows; patched white slip covers over massive furniture; light switches jutting out of cracked glass discs; and the inevitable big bad oil paintings, hung out from the walls on twine. The bathroom had a brown tile floor, cracked and buckled, and, over a wash-basin that didn't work, a broken mirror was suspended by grocery string. The door did not close or lock. Next to the blotched tub was a mat of wooden slats. The wire waste basket would hold nothing, and the electric wiring was exposed. Our Georgian interpreter asked us one evening what the best hotel in New York was like. He was perfectly serious when he said, "Does it differ in any way from this?"

The Intourist office had Chinese, East German, Armenian, and, of all things, Albanian newspapers. As always, unity with the satellites is emphasized. This was the first, and only, time in my life I have ever seen an Albanian newspaper. And there were the usual copies of *Taras Bulba* (Gogol) and *War and Peace*. In the restaurant, which has a wild, ornately convivial atmosphere, men wore pullovers back to front, without ties. A tall and exceptionally good-looking Georgian drifted in, wearing a scarlet cardigan with a blue scarf twisted around his neck. He looked like a king-fisher out among gray sparrows. Some good things to eat may be found in Tiflis restaurants, and the *vinogradny sok,* grape juice, is the best in the Union. The wine is full of bounce. One renowned Georgian *plat* is turkey in cream with a sauce made of crushed walnuts, and another is *shihirtma,* an exemplary sweet-sour chicken soup.

Tiflis has an astounding main street, named nowadays for the classic Georgian poet, Rustaveli.[10] Everything is here—the Supreme Soviet, the House of Pioneers (formerly the Palace of the Viceroy), the Opera, the National Theater (once known as the Theater of the Georgian Noblesse), the Marx-Lenin University, the two leading hotels, the post office, and the National Museum, which is painted in Leningrad green. Several buildings are made of a bright yellow—almost orange—sandstone, which comes from a village quarry near by called Volivisi. Churches built in the fifth century used this stone; so did a bridge built in 1951; Georgia has continuity. At one end of Rustaveli is the best statue of Lenin in the Soviet Union. It is by an artist named Topuridze, and depicts Lenin clutching his cap with his left hand, while the right hand is stretched out in a commanding gesture, with fingers extended and separated like a starfish. Bookshops are, as always, crowded. People stood in line for cheap prints. We tried to buy a book on ancient Georgian architecture (sold out), and the Georgian translation of Shakespeare (sold out). The chief local newspaper, *Zarya Vostoka* (*Dawn of the East*), is well known. Along the streets, women in Kurdish costume are to be seen, with red silk pleated skirts. But the Georgians look down on the Kurds, and the picturesqueness of their national dress is not admired—indeed it is considered to be an anachronism. The streets are filthier than any I have ever seen, except in certain areas of New York.

Tiflis, in the familiar pattern, is crowded with pedagogical, biological, veterinarian, agricultural, and other scientific institutes. Its Institute of Marxism-Leninism, distinct from the Marx-Lenin University, is working on a history of the Georgian Revolution. The National University, founded in 1918, has six thousand students, and the Rector, a professor of mathematics named Victor Kupradze, is supposed to be one of the most enlightened men in the Soviet Union. All teaching is in Georgian, but the faculty of philology has a Russian division. Tiflis has tolerable parks, and its athletic stadium, opened in 1956, seats 45,000 people. A pugnacious little funicular climbs one of the hills surrounding the town, and two TV towers have been built. Programs are, however, described as being "experimental" still. One amuse-

[10] In Czarist times it was called Golovinsky Prospekt.

ment park has a special children's room, as is common all over the Soviet Union, where parents can, so to speak, check and park their youngsters.

The National Museum (Director, Professor Amiranashvili), well organized and well run like almost all Soviet museums, contains some of the most ancient and beautiful icons in the world. One fragile silver masterpiece, magnificently jeweled, goes back to A.D. 886, and several are even older. The museum still buys from private collections, and treasures still crop up. One of the biggest icons in the world (tenth century) is here. Its central square measures five feet by three, and is heavily studded with glowing jewels; the wings are slightly smaller. Parts of this gigantic work of art were broken off and lost in earlier days, and both the Metropolitan Museum in New York and the Hermitage in Leningrad have fragments of its soaring halo. This museum also has good examples of the national work in enamel, which is *the* thing here, and a collection of old princely relics.

The most famous sights of Tiflis are the old churches. One is the Cioni (Zion), built in the fifth century; it was destroyed by invading Turks and Persians no fewer than seven times, but always rose again, and is still an active church. It is, in fact, the headquarters of the present-day Georgian Patriarchate, and we attended a service there. Across the Kura River is Metekhi, traces of which go back to the sixth century. This structure, which was used as a prison under the Czars, has a ten-sided conical tower, with a point like a blunt, fat pencil.

About twenty miles outside Tiflis, on the Georgian Military Road that leads northward into Russia, is MTSKHETA—try to pronounce it. This was the capital of the country until the fifth century, and the Georgian Patriarch lived here until the 1300's. The vestments of Christ are supposed to have been found here, brought from Golgotha by a merchant. Its church, built in the eleventh century and called Sveti Tskhoveli, Tree of Life, was made originally out of wood from a near-by cedar grove, which—for some reason —symbolized Christian impulses of the day. Later it was reconstructed in stone and, by special orders from the king and patriarch, who wanted a taller church, it gained a cupola. Before this all Georgian churches had been basilicas. This too is still an active church. Three Georgian kings are buried here, including Gorgaslan (Wolf's Head), who died in A.D. 501, and the last king of independent Georgia, whose reign ended exactly thirteen hundred years later.

Georgia today has a lively cultural life, and the Georgian theater is popular. Two favorite items in its repertory are *Oedipus Rex* and *Othello*, and a modern Yugoslav comedy, *Doctor of Philosophy*, was playing while we were there. The Opera, a structure named for a Georgian composer who died in the 1920's, Paliashvili, has orange plush armchairs, and compares favorably to the Bolshoi in Moscow. We saw a stunning performance here of a Paliashvili work called *Daïssi* (*Twilight*); it was like a combination of Wagner and Berlioz, and depicted thunderous events in the life of an early Georgian king.

Literary life is, of course, abundant. There is plenty of tradition. Mayakovsky was born in Georgia, and Gorky had his first book published here. Georgians like to write about their past (in particular folklore) but cannot, in these dour days, neglect modern themes. The State Publishing House issues about five hundred titles a year; translation of foreign works is not done from a Russian text, as heretofore, but directly from the original. Poe, Byron, Scott, Shelley—the Georgians are a poetic people—are high favorites, together with Dickens, Mark Twain, O. Henry, and—you guessed it—Howard Fast. Among Russian authors the leaders seem to be Turgenev, Gorky, Sholokhov, and a poet, Mikhail Lukonin.

Life is not all poetry in Tiflis, but proceeds at homely levels. I quote the following, if only to show what average preoccupations are. It appeared in *Izvestia*, April 7, 1957.

> There can be no question but that railroad stations are supposed to serve passengers. Unfortunately, letters indicate that there still exists a bureaucratic system that is incompatible with the norms of civilized service to citizens. This is how passengers are greeted at the Tbilisi station:
> "On a cold night a comrade and I got off the train at the Tbilisi station," writes reader N. A. Krayevsky. "We were both unwell and had come to Tbilisi for operations at one of the hospitals there. We both had certificates of illness, travel orders, and other documents given to us by physicians. We hadn't the money to go to a hotel, so we decided to stay in the station until morning. But . . . at the Tbilisi station all passengers, no matter when their trains arrive, are ordered out of the station by the railroad official on duty and by the militia."

Comrade Krayevsky and his companion had a hard time. Officials would not look at their documents, and they were chased out into the streets. They collapsed outside, but managed to get to a dispensary, where they received treatment.

Izvestia comments: "Comrade Krayevsky's indignation is understandable. The Tbilisi station officials take a heartless attitude toward passengers! . . . The Ministry of Transportation is not inclined to change these 'regulations' (if you will pardon the expression) concerning service to the passengers, but they must be changed!"[11]

What a people!

This Is Sparta

One morning in Tiflis it was cold, cold, cold. A chill rain, that would become snow at any moment, froze the bones. It was very early—about 6 A.M.—and still quite dark. We were driving to the airport, shivering, and suddenly near a factory or a school, I do not know which, we saw a line of about two hundred young men running swiftly through the icy gloom, and doing complicated, vigorous calisthenics as they ran. This was their routine drill before showing up at their desks or machines. And, in the freezing cold, they were *naked to the waist*.

This is Sparta, I thought.

And indeed, a few moments later I knew that it *was* Sparta, because I saw some helots—old women with clumsy brushes, sweeping dirt and refuse off the cold, grim streets.

[11] *Current Digest of the Soviet Press,* May 15, 1957.

CHAPTER XXII

Antique Worlds of Central Asia

In all other parts of the world light descends upon earth. From holy Samarkand and Bukhara, it ascends.

—OLD PROVERB

The conquest of Central Asia is a conquest of Orientals by Orientals.

—LORD CURZON IN 1889

SAMARKAND, the old capital of the Emperor Tamurlane and the anchor of the ancient silk road across Asia into China, is a perfumed name. It has delicate, aromatic associations for most of us, as if it were a magic city, or something remembered in a dream. People have called Samarkand "a combined Delphi and Athens," a "green jewel on a withered hand," and "the glory and wonder of the Asiatic continent." For centuries it was undefiled by western eyes, and was one of the most remote as well as legendary cities in the world. The story, which was difficult to verify on the spot, is that only two European visitors ever reached it in the four hundred years from 1450 to 1850. Nowadays, getting to Samarkand is a routine matter. It is only about seven and a half hours from Moscow by a direct daily flight, and is conspicuous on Intourist itineraries.

Indeed, if it were not for its majestic and romantic ruins, SAMARKAND today would be nothing more than another Soviet provincial town, that happens to be in Central Asia. It lies, nicely situated, at an altitude of two thousand feet, on an oasis in the Zeravshan Valley, and is surrounded by rotund mountains shining with snow. The snow shines in the winter, anyway. In summer, the temperature in Samarkand can reach 120 degrees Fahrenheit. The population is 170,000, with four main communities which do not mix much—Uzbeks, Russians, Armenians, and Jews. The Uzbeks

450

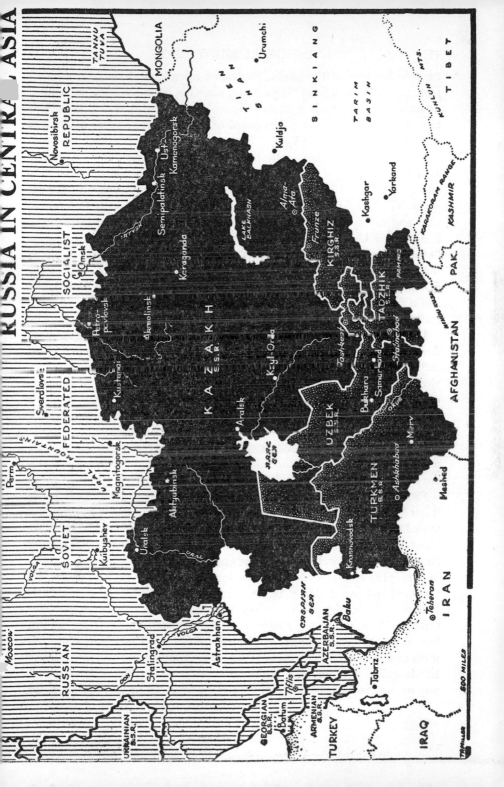

form 60 per cent of the whole. The name Samarkand derives from Uzbek roots meaning "fruit" and "sugar," and there are seven thousand students at its university. The town is often afflicted by earthquakes, and it is unlikely that any of its citizens have ever heard of James Elroy Flecker's poem, *The Golden Journey to Samarkand*.

Streets are broad, abundantly lined with pleasant trees, and paved with asphalt; the atmosphere is not "Oriental" or pungent at all, but is western and businesslike. There must be a *medina* (native quarter), but we did not see it. The Uzbeks look like Moroccans, except that they wear Russian fur caps and tall Russian boots, if they can afford them. Street signs are in Russian and Uzbek, and the airport even has a neat little sign in English, "EXIT TO LANDING." Some little girls wear bright dangling earrings and have their brows marked with kohl; a few Moslem women still wear veils. The first person I looked at carefully sat next to us in the hotel restaurant. He had a completely shaven skull and a solid mouthful of gold teeth, and was scraping flies off his cropped head with a table knife.

If the restaurant is crowded, people ask to sit down at your table, or sit down without being asked, in the familiar Russian manner. A splendid old lady in a white beret, who ran the restaurant and looked like the last survivor of some eccentric British aristocratic family, or the Madwoman of Chaillot, was, however, alert to keep such advances at the minimum. We had, that first evening, delicious food—a *solyanka* (meat soup), delicate little meat patties made of veal and onion, a superlative *shashlik*, and choke cherries and pomegranates for dessert. There were two movies at our disposal later—a Mexican picture about Wetbacks, and a Russian film made out of an old Italian story, Goldoni's *Mistress of the Inn*.

Samarkand was the ancient Maracanda. No one knows how old it is, but it has been mentioned in chronicles since the fourth century B.C., when the walled city had a diameter of ten and a half kilometers. Here Alexander the Great murdered his comrade Clitus, and married the handsome princess Roxana ("for political reasons," our guide interjected). The Arabs took it in A.D. 712, and Scheherazade, no less, is supposed to have spent her thousand and one nights in this magical vicinity. The Samarkandians were known as Sarts, the old name for Uzbeks. Imperial heyday came later. Genghis Khan, the most formidable of Mongol destroyers, set up his rule here in the thirteenth century, and he was followed by Tamurlane, who made it his capital in 1369. Later came conquest by Chinese and Russians. Czarist Russia spilled over into the Turkistan wastes, and the Trans-Caspian Railway reached Samarkand in 1888. Very few people, taking this railway today, realize that it was built more than seventy years ago under the Czars. Samarkand was made capital of Uzbekistan by the Bolsheviks, but the capital was moved to near-by Tashkent, a larger and more important town, in 1930, partly for convenience and partly to discourage Moslem "nationalism."

The following are the signal sights of Samarkand. We were lucky in our escort, Professor Ivan I. Umyakov, professor of antiquities at the University of Samarkand. A venerable Leningrader, Professor Umyakov studied for the Foreign Office in the last days of the Czars, and was trained by the foremost Russian orientalist of the time, V. V. Barthold. Umyakov kept on with his studies after the Revolution, came out to Central Asia, and has taught in Tashkent and Samarkand for more than forty years. Probably he is the paramount living authority on the area, and his career is an interesting example of continuity in a turbulent and changing time.

The Observatory. This was built by the Emperor Mirza Ulug-Beg, grandson of Tamurlane, who lived from 1409 to 1449, and was an astronomer by avocation; in fact he was known as "Prince of Astronomers." Sloping stone tracks leading into a deep, dark orifice like a well, on a hilly site on the outskirts of the town, show where his telescope was posted. Ulug-Beg's mathematical calculations have been translated into English, and are indication that, even in Central Asia in medieval times, men had inquisitive scientific minds and did fruitful work.

The Registan. This, with its adjacent buildings, was the central square of Tamur's city in the fifteenth century. Facing it is the rectangular façade of a mosque, with a tall bluntly pointed arch; adjoining are three *madrasahs* (schools) with double rows of pointed Moorish cloisters. The most notable is the Shir-dar. The blue tipped minarets, on each side of the central structure, are still standing, but one is aslant, and is wired to scaffolding to keep it from toppling; restoration work is in progress. The impression as a whole is that of a broken-down Alhambra.

Lord Curzon, when he visited Samarkand in 1888, called the Registan the "noblest public square in the world," even outranking St. Mark's in Venice. Its buildings are roughly of the same period of the Taj Mahal in India, and of the same type, but deteriorated. All over the place are broken, glowing bits of tile; they keep falling off the monuments in small bits, and you can stuff your pockets with them, if so inclined.[1] Here, for centuries, the Moslems of Central Asia had their heart and focus; here students were trained, pilgrims greeted, and Islam perpetuated.

[1] The 1914 Baedeker placidly says, "The abstraction of colored tiles and other relics is promptly and severely punished by officials."

Nearby I noticed a large statue of Stalin, painted silver. Of these, Russian art factories must have turned out tens of thousands, and it is not surprising that Samarkand still has one. Then the loudspeaker began to shout—news of Hungary and Suez—and a jet noisily split the sky above us. Indeed, the centuries coalesce in this part of Asia.

The *Debi-Hanum*, which Tamurlane built for one of his wives, a Chinese girl. Here the mosque and *madrasah* are almost totally in ruins. The mosque was built (1399-1404) to commemorate one of Tamur's spider-like military expeditions. A large arch remains, and behind this half a dome and one pure perfect cylinder of a minaret. In all these monuments, what is most notable is the surviving tile, which is radiant; the dominating colors are green and blue. Birds nest in the broken columns of Debi-Hanum today, and the site is so far gone that, despite all effort, it is impossible to restore it.

The *Shah-i-Zind*. This means "Living Czar," and is a street—or rather stairway—of resplendent ancient monuments. Small mosques and tombs sit along a narrow, steep passageway, and some of the graves date from the eighth century. Most members of Tamur's family are buried here. Two bulbous turquoise domes are patchily covered with a crisp frizzle of weeds, which grow in cracks in the plaster, and look like hair on a bald green skull. The tile of the Shah-i-Zind is white, coral, chrome yellow, a blue the color of cornflowers, and a deeper blue, like sea water seen at sunset.[2]

Above all, the *Gur Emir*, or tomb of Tamurlane himself. Across a small rough courtyard stands this soaring edifice, with its double series of pointed arches on either side of an arched doorway shaped like a hollow phallus; surmounting it is an enormous beet-shaped dome, covered with green-blue fluted tile, in spiral convolutions. The walls inside are made of solid onyx (like parts of the Moscow subway today) and other precious materials. Tamur's sarcophagus is black, constructed out of a rare stone known as nephrite; other tombs, including that of his religious instructor, are white. Tamur's block of nephrite is said to be the largest single piece of this material ever known; the inscription on it reads, "Were I alive today, mankind would tremble." Tile on the Gur Emir is mainly in four colors of blue—a gray powdery pastel shade, turquoise, a brilliant ultramarine, and dark blue-green. The dark blues came in during the fourteenth century, and were introduced by Tamurlane. *White* tile was, incidentally, not used after Tamur's accession, for reasons unknown.

Tamurlane's grave was opened not long ago and his bones brought to

[2] Baedeker reports the presence here of a copy of the Koran six feet wide but, if it survives, we did not see it.

Tashkent, where they could be better kept. This Mongol potentate, who liked wide horizons, must have been a small man physically; probably he died of tuberculosis. He was lame, and his right hand was withered. Russian scientists, by using evidence from the bones, do their best to construct replicas of the actual faces of historical figures like these; Tamurlane was not handsome. He was a canny monarch. Once, on a trip, he sent back emissaries with false news of his death, in order to see how his sons would respond. On his death at seventy in 1405, he ruled the earth from Mongolia to the Danube, almost the same area covered by Communist states today.

*

Between Samarkand and Bukhara, the plane makes one stop. Distances are short, and I am prepared to swear that the identical radio program, carried by loudspeakers, saw us off at Samarkand, greeted us at our intermediate stop, and welcomed us at Bukhara. This was the nearest thing to the radio in George Orwell's 1984 that I came across in the Soviet Union. Also the taxi which met us at the Bukhara airport, with a line of checkers around the body, was obviously the same type we had used in a different city two hours before. Uniformity conquers all.

Although the plane follows a valley fertile in summer, we scarcely saw a road or a house. One decrepit village was laid out in the shape of a gourd. Some of the dry water courses looked as if they had been drawn by a thick brush with pale blue whitewash, against the tiger-colored earth. Then came outcroppings of savage, brilliant red rock, as red as fire engines. And then, of all things, arose a violet lake, on the edges of which lay lines of white foam, not snow as I first thought, but salt. Close to Bukhara signs of irrigation appear. Villages on the brown-purple land looked like heaps of pebbles, but surrounding them were small green irrigated areas, some of them oblong, some in the shape of jelly beans.

Samarkand to Bukhara and Tashkent

BUKHARA, sometimes called Bokhara, is smaller than Samarkand, more primitive, and more homogeneous; it is not split between old and new, and a great many people still live more or less as they lived hundreds of years ago. The city walls, dimly crenelated, are so broken down that the towers look like stalagmites, and the black cobbles in the streets are the stoniest, spiniest, and sharpest I have ever seen anywhere—like pointed lumps of coal. Bukhara is famous for its maroon, square-shaped rugs. These, however, were not made in the town; Bukhara happened to be the market where most of them were sold.[3] On a road leading into the city I saw men trampling on what seemed to be white crushed stone—cotton. A road is flat, and as good a place to handle cotton as any.

Bukhara, so remote and off the conventional track, is not served by Intourist. One thing may be said about this city with the utmost confidence— here live seventy thousand people who have never seen a flush toilet. An estimable English lady, visiting it recently, gave it as her opinion that "to go to the bathroom in Bukhara you need stout boots." Here, too, we enter what might be called the real gold tooth territory. An astounding number of people have all, or most, of their teeth solid gold. I asked a pretty girl at a hotel if she were an Uzbek, and her indignant reply was, "Do I look like an Uzbek?" I do not know what she was, probably Russian or Tatar, but her mouth fairly yawned with its weight of gold.

Mostly the population is Uzbek and Tadzhik, but a strong Jewish community still survives. Tamurlane brought the Jews in from Mesopotamia.

History has known Bukhara for at least two thousand years. Alexander the Great stopped here, and Bukhara was the scene of his well-known wrestling match with a lion. Other conquerors came, one after another; for a time, around A.D. 1000, Bukhara was the most celebrated place of learning in all Asia. Students and pilgrims journeyed to it from afar, until Genghis Khan burned it to the ground and slaughtered most of its Arab inhabitants (1220). Marco Polo is supposed to have said of it, *"Quant il orent passé cel desert, si vindrent a une cité qui est appelée Bocara, moult noble et grant."* Under the Russians, after the middle of the nineteenth century, Bukhara had a semiautonomous status, and was ruled, at least titularly, by its emir. Slavery existed—on the open market—until about 1870. People tell highly unpleasant stories about the last emir, who was dismissed from his throne and exiled in 1920, when the Bolshevist regime took over after a period of civil war. He tossed people into pits where they were slowly devoured by vermin, and maintained a harem of some four hundred girls and boys.

The site Bokhariots are proudest of is the Manari-Kazyan, or Tower of Death, a tall minaret adjoining a tatterdemalion mosque. This was built in 1127, and for centuries was the town scaffold. That is, condemned criminals were executed by being tossed to death from its top, if they were not

[3] "Bokhara" rugs are manufactured mostly in Ashkhabad, Kerki, and Chardzhou in Turkmenistan.

assigned to the vermin pits. A tuft of what seems to be green hair surmounts the Tower of Death today—a stork's nest. The old fortress, with its ocher dried mud walls, has interest. A museum has been set up here, which contains relics of Bukharan history. One chart shows the governmental "chain of command" under the Czars. The czar is at the top, needless to say; citizens are at the bottom, and at the very bottom is a drawing of a man being hanged. In this museum I saw a knout. I had never seen one before. It is an evil object, with a wooden stock; the rope is made of leather bound with wire, and is as thick as a man's wrist at one end, tapering to a tip an inch in diameter. A sleepy sight is the emir's palace, flanked by a stagnant pool. This edifice, with its pale gray lattices, has also been converted into a museum. Cheek by jowl with old Chinese porcelain and cloth embroidered with gold we saw contemporary posters, some of which depicted Red Chinese aircraft gleefully knocking off American Sabre jets in Korea.

Bukhara's School of Divinity, nine hundred years old, still functions. We talked with the Rector, who, sleepy eyed and richly bearded, resembled Moslem dignitaries in northern Nigeria or Morocco. He has been in charge of this establishment for more than thirty years, and has one hundred students, who take a nine-year course. Graduates go out all over Central Asia as *mullahs*, or priests. I asked what percentage of the population of Bukhara still attended religious services. The Rector, after a pause, evaded this question and said that many people "prayed at home." I asked if his congregation included any members of the Communist party. No. "But maybe they pray at home, too." Then the Rector asked us how many practicing Moslems lived in—the United States.

*

TASHKENT, the capital of Uzbekistan, is an altogether different article. This is a modern industrial city. It is a vital link in the Soviet air route into India, and is a metropolis not merely for Uzbekistan, but for all five of the Central Asian republics. Tashkent—the name means "city of stone" —is the seventh biggest city in the Soviet Union, and has 778,000 people. When the Russians occupied Central Asia, their procedure was the same as that adopted by the great French colonizer, Marshal Lyautey, in Morocco decades later, namely to build new quarters for the Europeans without wrecking the existing native cities. So, like Rabat, Tashkent has a modern and an old city side by side. The old native ruler of Tashkent, from whom the Czars took over in 1865, was known as the "Half-King." According to

Soviet statistics, the population of Tashkent today is 65 per cent Uzbek, 11 per cent Russian. (Tadzhiks, Kazakhs, Tatars, and Armenians make up the rest.) A more detached estimate is that Russians, coming in in greater number year by year, now comprise at least 50 per cent of the population. Tashkent has, among other things, what is said to be the largest cotton mill in the world.[4] Juxtapositions are quite sharp here; men tend the most modern machinery while their wives, if Moslem, may still be seen wearing absolutely opaque black veils made of horsehair. The night we arrived *Trovatore* was playing at the Opera—what a thing to find in the middle of Central Asia! The Opera itself, a large building occupying a whole square, was built actually during World War II, as if to indicate that Tashkenters (or their Russian bosses) had confidence about the outcome.

Nature can be generous in the Tashkent gardens. We ate strawberries that looked like pieces of marzipan—one could not believe that they were real—big as plums, pale pink in color, and deeply pitted. Yellow-red apples are shaped like pears, and grapes have the form of cashew nuts, or small blunt boomerangs. We visited the son of the venerable Mufti of Tashkent. He gave us some roses that must have been six inches wide. Our chambermaid, when we returned with them to the hotel, at once embraced them passionately as if they were like no flowers ever seen before. As always with Russians (except the poker-faced politicians), the transition from emotion to gesture is instantaneous, and the gesture is as a rule extravagant.

One night we went to the circus, and saw, in what was otherwise a disappointing performance, the foremost of Russian clowns, Durov. Later a man, strolling with his wife, followed me down the dark street. He caught up, took me lightly by the shoulder, and peered into my face. "Tourist!" he exclaimed. Then his hand shot out like a piston, he shook mine, and said no more. But with that one word he expressed more than amply his envy of the outside world and fervid secret alliance with it.

The most startling thing in Tashkent, as well as in several other Central Asian towns, is the astonishing number of amputees. Within moments of arrival, along the streets and in the markets, we saw cripples hobbling. Some begged; some sold pencils and shoestrings. One man had both legs and an arm gone. There were hundreds of others less drastically crippled. At first I thought that these unfortunates might have been shipped down there because the climate is salubrious. I should have known better. A few years ago the authorities decided to clean up Moscow, Leningrad, and other metropolitan Russian cities of their more obvious disfiguring elements—confirmed alco-

[4] Except possibly one at Barnaul (in Siberia), also in the USSR.

holics, incorrigible delinquents, and the like. Of people who deface society, amputees are, of course, the most conspicuous. So tens of thousands of them were simply picked up, corralled, and shipped out to remote places in Central Asia, and here they stay. Unless able to work, they are not given wooden legs. In order to keep them from starving, the local administration gives them things to sell.

*

The mayor of Tashkent, Minavar Tursunov, is a forty-two-year-old Tash-kenter. With him, when we talked, was his associate Rasul G. Gulamov, secretary of the Communist party of the city, also forty-two and a Tashkenter. We sat with them for several uninterrupted hours. (The telephone did, it is true, ring twice, but our hosts did not answer it.) Soviet officials believe in concentration. Mr. Gulamov, although he was only in his thirties at the time, preceded Mr. Tursunov as mayor. Once every two years the city council is elected—by secret, direct ballot, we were told. Of course there is only one ticket. Then an executive committee of nine is named, and the nine choose the mayor from out of their own number.

These young men talked as officials in Cincinnati or Leeds might have talked. They were hard-headed, alert, and proud of their municipal ac-complishments. Their biggest problems are housing and utilities. I told them that, in most large American cities, mayors stood or fell on the efficiency of their police, and that crime, graft, gambling, and transportation were important items. Mr. Tursunov raised his eyebrows. Crime and graft do not exist in Uzbekistan except on a petty level, and such things as automobile traffic, parking, and so on, present no problems to Tashkent as yet.

Housing is an extremely serious and in fact agonizing issue, as it is every-where in the Union. "Before the Revolution, nobody had a plan!" exclaimed Mr. Gulamov. The idea that anything could ever have existed without plan-ning was, to these young men, utterly unbelievable. "People could put up houses where they wished!" Now, residential building in Tashkent is care-fully controlled, but there isn't nearly enough of it. Last year 42,000 square meters of new living space was built, enough for about 4,600 people, and, as in Kiev, "satellite" housing developments were set up in the suburbs, with private building permitted. This year, the state hopes to provide 74,000 more square meters of housing, with 45,000 to be built privately. "We are a rich state. We can afford this. Also the Union government helps us. Moscow gave Tashkent an 800 million ruble grant this year."

Tashkent had no running water before the Revolution, and little electricity. Only one street, Karl Marx Street (formerly Cathedral Avenue), had electric lighting at night. Nowadays a modern sewage system functions, but the amount of water available is limited.

Tashkent's most urgent problem, when the Bolshevik regime took over, was the liquidation of illiteracy. This has been successfully accomplished. Forty years ago exactly one Uzbek in Tashkent held a college degree; he was the son of a merchant, who became a lawyer. There were no schools of higher learning at all. Today education is compulsory for everybody, and illiteracy has disappeared, except among a few surviving old people. In addition to its University, Tashkent has 17 colleges or institutes and 153 schools; there are 125,000 students. Of these, between 65 and 70 per cent are said to be Uzbek. But not all the rest are Russian. Schools exist for all the recognized national minorities. But a Kazakh boy going to a Kazakh school in Tashkent has to work hard; instruction is in his own language, but both Russian and Uzbek are compulsory as well. So three languages have to be absorbed. Children in Russian and Uzbek schools are also obliged to learn still another language if they reach the upper grades—English, German, or Hindi. We are close to India here.

Nasrulla Akhundi, a poet and the secretary of the State Publishing House of the Uzbek SSR, gave us a glimpse of things literary. Five hundred titles were published in Uzbek last year, with a total distribution of nine *million* copies; this is the more remarkable in that almost all Uzbeks speak and read Russian, in which many of the same books are available. Recently Mr. Akhundi completed translations of Pushkin and the Ukrainian poet, Shevchenko. The most popular classic authors are Tolstoy, Chekhov, and Turgenev, translations of which did not even exist in Uzbek before the Revolution; among moderns, Sholokhov and Fadeyev are being translated now. I asked about western literature. *Othello* and *King Lear* appear on the Uzbek stage in Uzbek. *The Gadfly*, by Mrs. Voynich, has been translated, and so has Howard Fast's *Freedom Road*. As usual, polite incredulity greeted my remark that Mr. Fast is not particularly well known in the United States. It was interesting that Mr. Akhundi had never heard of John Steinbeck, and that the names Evelyn Waugh and Graham Greene meant little. But he knew about Jack London. All Russians do. Any American who tells any Russian that Jack London is *not* a supremely great writer will have heavy going.

Uzbek is of course a totally different language from Russian, but it is written in Russian script nowadays, and printed in the Russian alphabet with an additional character or two. The old alphabet was Arabic. Uzbek literature goes back to a poet of the fifteenth century, Alishir Navoi. Many observers think that, far from having stimulated the Uzbeks to a literary renaissance, the Soviet system has set them back. They are allowed to use their own language, yes, but not their own alphabet, which means, in a sense, that the true basis of culture is cut off. It is as if the British, say, taking over Hong Kong, had forced the Chinese to write in English characters. On the other hand standardization of the alphabet all over Central Asia, first into Latin and then Cyrillic, assisted greatly in the fight against illiteracy and helped speed up industrialization.[5]

There are ten large functioning mosques in Tashkent, and several smaller, to serve the Mohammedan population. We happened to visit the Barracan, a religious school, on a Friday, the Moslem Sabbath, and the adjacent mosque was crowded. The Grand Mufti, who is ninety-six, is titular leader of the Moslem community not merely in Uzbekistan, but in all Central Asia.[6] There are about twenty million Moslems in the area as a whole. Soviet policy is, in theory, to respect Islamic institutions. Religious practices are not (again in theory) interfered with. In plain fact, the Moslem church exists only on sufferance, and has been separated from all its vital roots. Obviously, a Soviet public school does not stress Islam, to put it mildly. I asked the Mufti's son if any members of his congregation ever went to Mecca. Yes. A limited number of pilgrimages—say twenty or thirty—are permitted every year; an applicant addresses himself to the Moslem authorities first, and his name then goes to the government for approval. I asked about the position of women, who, in most Moslem lands, lead severely circumscribed lives. Here women have equal rights with men, and all Mohammedan girls are obliged to go to school. Polygamy is, of course, illegal by terms of Soviet law, but it is not actually forbidden; polygamous marriages are, however, rare.

Professor T. D. Dzhurayev, formerly a deputy minister of education for Uzbekistan, is the representative in Tashkent of VOKS, the Society for Cultural Relations. His father, illiterate, was a worker in a textile factory, "who dyed thread all his life." (Soviet officials are always astonished to hear that, in the United States, thousands of prominent citizens have fathers who were workers.) He graduated from Tashkent University after World War I,

[5] Another point, supporting the argument that Russianization has stunted rather than encouraged the Uzbek revival, is that the Uzbeks, like peoples in the Caucasus, find their best literary flowering in epic and lyric verse, also folk songs, and it is impossible to do much with these forms under socialist realism. Free expression is of course unknown.

[6] He died while this book was in press.

became a specialist in the history of the Communist party, and has been a party member since 1943. Before the Revolution, Professor Dzhurayev told us, Uzbekistan was "nothing." Heavy industry scarcely existed, and the population was 98 per cent illiterate. Nowadays not less than 65 per cent of the local budget goes to education. Forty years ago Uzbekistan had 145 doctors; today, more than ten thousand. What about relations with the neighboring republics? "Very close!"—particularly with Kazakhstan, which bounds half of the Uzbekistan perimeter. The two neighbors recently set up a joint enterprise for the irrigation of a desolate area known as the Hungry or Golodnaya Steppe. Basically relations between the republics consist of "exchange of experience, plus friendly competition." This was talk exactly like what we heard in the Ukraine and Georgia. I asked about local nationalism, and the good Professor was bewildered. He sought to explain that Uzbekistan *was* a nation, and had, like the other republics, the "right" to secede from the Union at any time. I did not ask what would happen if any Uzbek political leader tried to put the right of secession into effect.

*

These three cities—Samarkand, Bukhara, Tashkent—are all in *Uzbekistan*. This republic, though not the biggest in Central Asia, is the richest and most advanced. The population is about 8,500,000. An oddly shaped entity, it covers an area almost exactly the size of California; 50 per cent is desert, and a large region to the northwest, the Kara-Kalpak ASSR, is so much a wasteland that, even today, it is mostly terra incognita. Uzbekistan has about two-thirds of the railway mileage of Central Asia, 80 per cent of the cotton area, and a pronounced industrial development. Oil has been found in the Fergana Valley, and hydroelectric developments are ambitious. There are steel mills (at Begovat) a copper refinery at Almalyk, and coal deposits near Tashkent. The people have a characteristic national costume; men wear an embroidered skull cap which they seldom take off, even when at meals.

Central Asia in General

Central Asia is such a large entity that generalizations are difficult; in fact, there is no such thing as "Central Asia" from a strict political or geographical point of view. In older days the whole vast area was called "Turkistan" loosely, and its distinguishing marks were remoteness, aridity, and inaccessibility. Today it consists of five republics—Uzbekistan, Kazakhstan, Turkmenistan, Kirghizia, and Tadzhikistan. The region stretches all the way from the Urals and Caspian to the borders of China and Mongolia, from the vicinity of Stalingrad to the frontiers of Afghanistan. It faces the Pamirs and the Hindu Kush, which merge into the Himalayas and form "the Roof of the World." Most of it is an unending flat plain, and most of its rivers drain into inland seas, like the Aral Sea, the fourth largest lake in the world. Two of these rivers we know from the history books: the Syr Darya, which was the ancient Jaxartes, and the Amu Darya, or Oxus.

This is the impregnable inner core of the Eurasian continent. The first Aryans, our forefathers, probably rose out of this ancient heartland. You would not believe it to look at the people today. Of course, Turks, Arabs, Persians, Baluchis, Tatars, Chinese, all left their traces here, and invaders have been known from Macedonians to Cossacks. Also Central Asia was the starting point for the great migrations into Europe led by Genghis Khan and Tamurlane. The Tatars and Mongols who sacked Moscow and established the Golden Horde on the Volga came from here; so did the Huns, who reached the Danube.

One historical determinant was aridity. The Kara Kum Desert in Turkmenistan is, as an example, as sterile and bony as the Sahara, and is known as "the Grave of Caravans." The Intourist Guide says that "progressive desiccation," which reduced the cattle ranges and left cities to die of thirst out in the desert, forced the Mongols westward. I came across this passage in Bertrand Russell's classic Freedom Versus Organization, page 200. Mr. Russell is arguing, in his discussion of Karl Marx, that the processes of dialectical materialism cannot explain everything in history:

> History can be viewed in many ways, and many general formulae can be invented which cover enough of the ground to seem adequate if the facts are carefully selected. I suggest, without undue solemnity, the following alternative theory of the causation of the Industrial Revolution:
> Industrialism is due to modern science, modern science is due to Galileo, Galileo is due to Copernicus, Copernicus is due to the Renaissance, the Renaissance is due to the fall of Constantinople, the fall of Constantinople is due to the migration of the Turks, the migration of the Turks is due to the desiccation of Central Asia. Therefore, the fundamental study in searching for historical causes is hydrography.

Czarist forces, in the reign of Alexander II, moved in on Central Asia in the 1860's. The movement was roughly analogous to the development of the American West at approximately the same time. The Russians dealt with various Asian princelings as we dealt with Sitting Bull. The British believed at that time that Russia had aggressive designs on India, which prompted their advance; most modern historians are inclined to discount this view. The Russians slopped over into Central Asia because it was adjacent, empty, and of value. They filled a vacuum, without specific ulterior design. In any case, Samarkand was captured in 1868, Fergana in 1876, and Merv in 1884. The chief weapon of penetration, after military conquest, was the Trans-Caspian Railroad, mentioned above. The engineer first asked to create this spiny little railroad was none other than Ferdinand de Lesseps, the builder of Suez. Until the railway, to get to Central Asia was an almost unimaginably difficult and dangerous adventure. Even under the Czars, the region was sealed off. The chief building erected in each occupied town was the Military Club. The Czarist administration functioned in part through the agency of the two emirates, at Bukhara and Khiva, and was an example of what later came to be called, in other parts of the world, "Indirect Rule." In some directions the Czarist government did much good, and its activities resembled to a degree those of the first British colonists in East Africa. The local administrators starved education, but they built communications. They sought to end tribal warfare, established law, abolished various barbarities, and, to a degree, improved public health. In one field they differed radically from the British. They had no color bar. Social discriminations existed, of course, and practically nothing was done to lift the general cultural level of the aboriginal population, but there was no discrimination *solely* on grounds of color or race. This sensible attitude survives in Bolshevist techniques today.

What Central Asia means to the Soviet regime can be expressed mostly by one word—Frontier. The whole area, now being developed at a perfervid pace, is an inordinately rich repository of natural and potential wealth—in cotton, grain, oil, minerals without number, and hydroelectric power. Vast irrigation works have been put forward, and populations shifted. Agriculture has been collectivized, and transportation improved.[7] The chief Soviet accomplishment is supposed to be industrial. As compared to 1913, the gross output of Kazakh industry has increased thirty-three times; Kirghiz industry thirty-seven times; Tadzhik industry twenty-four times.[8] Central Asia as a

[7] A major item in penetration has been the Turksib Railway, built in 1930, which links Tashkent with Novosibirsk and the industrial cities of Siberia. The man mainly responsible for building it was an American, Bill Shatov, who had been an IWW organizer.

[8] According to Khrushchev's Report to the Twentieth Congress, p. 68.

whole, an untapped wilderness forty years ago, produced last year 300 per cent more electric power than the entire Middle East. The desert blooms, not with roses, but with factories.

The Russians, as always, announce their plans and achievements with a certain neat dash. The following is the complete text of a recent decree of the Presidium of the Uzbek Republic Supreme Soviet:

> ON FORMATION OF THE CITY OF YANGI-YER IN THE GOLODNAYA STEPPE. The petition of the Tashkent Province Soviet Executive Committee is to be granted and a city under province jurisdiction is to be formed in the center of the Golodnaya Steppe (on the territory between the railroad station of Ursatyevskaya and Spur No. 58).
> The newly formed city is to be named Yangi-Yer. SH. RASHIDOV, CHAIRMAN OF THE PRESIDIUM. D. ILKHAMOVA, SECRETARY OF THE PRESIDIUM.[9]

In several other fields Central Asia has interesting importance. Mainly this is because much of it is still extraordinarily remote, difficult of access, and seldom visited. Back in 1931, the Red Army made its first experiments with mass parachute drops in Central Asia. Here, today, most Soviet work in ballistic and guided missiles, A-bombs, and thermonuclear devices is believed to go on. Semipalatinsk, in northeast Kazakhstan, is supposed to be a testing center roughly equivalent to Las Vegas, Nevada. Another important focus is Leninabad, in Tadzhikistan, and, according to some reports, missile development is concentrated in closed areas of Turkmenistan, near the Caspian. The Sputniks are believed to have been launched here, and also the first Soviet intercontinental ballistic missile.

If there is any political "situation" in Central Asia, it lies far below the surface. In this field a curious Soviet circumlocution comes into play—people are judged to have both "reserved" and "day-to-day" characteristics. A Kazakh or Uzbek is encouraged to have pride in his racial origin, culture, and folkways, but this is all "reserved." As far as his political behavior is concerned, he is Russian. He can go to his own theaters, read his own newspapers, and attend the local mosques, but as a Soviet citizen he belongs to Moscow. I heard one Russian say, somewhat fancifully, that this system closely resembles that which obtained in the United States during the period of mass immigration late in the nineteenth century. A Pole, let us say, or an Irishman, arriving in New York was permitted, without limit, to retain any of his national characteristics that pleased him. He could speak his own language, associate with his own fellows, join his own clubs, and identify him-

[9] *Current Digest of the Soviet Press*, May 22, 1957.

self strongly with his ethnic group. But he had to become an American *citizen*, if he wanted to enjoy the full benefit of American nationality, and his children were obliged to learn English in a public school.

In general the Soviet idea is to make each individual nationality closer to *Russia* than to any of the other republics.[10] Intermarriage between Russians and the native population does not, an incidental point, occur often, although we saw blond Kazakhs in Alma-Ata. In course of time, obviously, the local communities will inevitably lose some of their national characteristics, and in fact their nationalism is already being steadily watered down. For instance, Kazakhs nowadays comprise only about 30 per cent of the population of Kazakhstan, and more and more Russians are streaming in. To recapitulate: there are no doubt plenty of Central Asians who dislike Russians and the Soviet system, although their pace of development would have been much slower without Soviet rule. But no overt signs exist of discontent, and relations between Russians and their subpeoples are harmonious on the whole. This is not a dissatisfied area at all on *national* grounds. Soviet-controlled education, year by year, does its calculated work, and the administration has brought substantial economic progress and substantial economic benefits to many.

On paper, Central Asians participate to a fairly wide extent in pan-Union affairs. Some 147 Central Asians are deputies to the Supreme Soviet of the USSR, and of the total membership (133) of the Central Committee of the Communist Party, thirteen come from Central Asia. William O. Douglas, Associate Justice of the United States Supreme Court, visited this area in 1955 and wrote an article for *Look*, "Soviet Colonialism—Product of Terror." This, along with Mr. Douglas's subsequent book, *Russian Journey*, was bitterly resented in the Soviet Union, but, I found, people who criticized it had as a rule not seen the actual text, but only comments on it by Soviet propagandists. One point Mr. Douglas makes is that all *political* leadership, no matter how it is window-dressed, is Russian. And the KGB is extremely watchful in these regions. Four justices of the Supreme Court of the Soviet Union, representing the four republics which Mr. Douglas saw, took the unprecedented step of writing a reply to his charges, which *Look* published (May 29, 1956). These justices deny that, as Mr. Douglas said, special courts exist for the trial of the favored Russians, that minority sentiments are "ruthlessly stifled," and that the leading posts in industry are held by Russians. To this last charge, the Central Asian justices say that the director

[10] *Russia and Her Colonies*, by Walter Kolarz, p. 260.

of the Leninabad silk mills is a native Tadzhik, that the head of the Kazakh Petroleum Corporation is a Kazakh, that the chief engineer of the Uzbek Coal Trust is an Uzbek, *und so weiter.* But, on balance, most Americans who visit Central Asia will agree that Mr. Douglas was a pretty good reporter.

*

Finally, the detainees. All over Central Asia these luckless transplants are to be found—colonies of "lost peoples." We have mentioned them earlier in this book, first the communities of Poles, Balts, and Ukrainians who were moved bodily from their homes during collectivization and the purges, and, second, citizens of the abolished "nations"—Volga Germans, Crimean Tatars, Kalmuks, and the various Caucasian groups who were literally wiped off the map. These latter have all been rehabilitated but the process of getting them back to their homelands is slow and complex, and countless thousands of unfortunate detainees still live in Central Asia. Some, like the amputees mentioned above, are virtual beggars; some managed to create new lives in Kazakhstan or Kirghizia, and are not so badly off. The Soviet nationality policy in regard to the Uzbeks and Kazakhs is something Russians boast about, but—until very recently—the Central Asian detainees were never mentioned. The ban on visiting them was utter. It was not even acknowledged that the detainees existed. They had been formally "abolished" —victims of a Soviet "nationality policy" of quite a different kind.

"The Russian Texas"

Kazakhstan is perfectly enormous. With 1,062,242 square miles, it is by far the biggest of the Central Asian republics, and, next to the RSFSR, is the biggest republic in the Union, covering 11.9 per cent of its whole area. *Kazakhstan* is bigger than all of western Europe, one-third the size of the entire United States, and four times bigger than the state of Texas, if anything can be four times the size of Texas. About half of Kazakhstan is desert, and in its whole expanse only 8,500,000 people live. This is one of the most underpopulated areas of its size and consequence in the world, and, obviously, as industrialization proceeds, may easily become a useful reservoir for draining off Russia's surplus population.

It took us nineteen hours in a nonpressurized two-motor plane to fly from Moscow to Alma-Ata, the lonely Kazakh capital. This route is a milk-run line, with a number of local stops. It was as if one should cross Texas on a line Houston–Dallas–San Antonio–Amarillo–El Paso. For hour after hour, we saw nothing but flat fields of snow. At airports, the snow reminded me of the Italian cheese known as *ricotta*—moist and cohesive; if you cut off a slab, it would hold together. Near the towns, the shriek of locomotive whistles sounded, as they sound in the lonely parts of Rhodesia or the American West. We stopped at Uralsk across the Russian border from Kuibyshev; at the great air junction Aktyubinsk, where waitresses in crisp white aprons served us; at Kustanai in the north, which we reached after crossing a prong of Siberia; at another big junction, Akmolinsk, where we changed planes (Russian fellow passengers had to spend the night here, but we were given another plane and went on); at Karaganda at 3:00 A.M., where we saw the lights of big office buildings flashing as they might flash in an American city late at night; at Balkhash, on a lake incredibly isolated; and finally Alma-Ata.

Kazakhs differ substantially from Uzbeks, and are, by and large, less advanced. They are round-faced, and look oriental; the long-faced Uzbeks resemble Arabs. Kazakhs speak a language partly Mongol in origin, whereas Uzbek resembles Persian. The alphabet, like Uzbek, has been Russified, with the original Arabic lettering abolished in favor of Cyrillic. Kazakhs are, in general, more assimilated, or perhaps one should say more submerged, than the other Central Asian peoples; hence they seem colorless. Few citizens wear national dress. The case might be made that Kazakhstan, except in its southeastern quarters, does not properly belong to Central Asia at all. Czarist penetration did not begin until about 1890, long after the rest of Central Asia was conquered and occupied. Originally, when the Soviet Union was formed, Kazakhstan had in fact the status of an autonomous republic within the RSFSR; it did not become "independent" until 1936, many years after Uzbekistan became a "country" on its own.

Several Kazakh cities have interest. SEMIPALATINSK, on the Irtysh River, is a center for meat packing (as well as possibly for hydrogen bombs); Dostoevsky served in the Czarist army here. Pavlodar, near the Siberian border, has the biggest harvester combine factory in the Soviet Union. There are lead mills at Chimkent, where we stopped on one flight, and textile mills at Aralsk on the Aral Sea. KARAGANDA, with a population near 350,000, is one of the biggest coal mining centers in the USSR, and is a boom town thriving with new industry. It is also famous—or infamous— for another reason; at Karaganda was the largest and most dreaded slave labor camp in the USSR, next to Vorkuta in the Arctic. Most of the area is still strictly closed, and passengers flying through Karaganda are not allowed to leave the airport. UST-KAMENOGORSK, to which Malenkov was shipped off in 1957, has about 100,000 people; here is a two-million kw electric station and one of the largest lead and zinc plants in the country.

The principal importance of Kazakhstan is, of course, its mineral wealth. A chemist in Alma-Ata told me that every element in the periodic table is to be found here. Kazakhstan is the first producer of copper, lead, and zinc in the Soviet Union, the third in coal, and the third in oil. It is one of the largest producers in the world of molybdenum, and has considerable wealth in other strategic minerals. Animal and vegetable wealth are conspicuous as well. The republic produced last year no fewer than sixteen million tons of grain, largely by reason of the new Virgin Lands development, and it is the biggest cattle and sheep producer in the Union. From 1924 to 1939, 19 billion rubles ($4,750,000,000) were invested in Kazakhstan industry and agriculture, according to Soviet statisticians. For the current Five-Year Plan alone, 29 billion rubles ($7,250,000,000) have been appropriated. A boom area indeed!

Kazakhs are predominantly Moslem, and I asked one young Communist official about religious matters. Reply: "Do not forget that the Soviet Union is the fourth Moslem power in the world. We do not intend to lose this position. Therefore it would be very foolish of us to deny freedom of religion to our Moslem population." I asked him about political matters, and if any substantial number of Kazakhs would like to be free of Soviet rule. Up to this point this official had not admitted to any knowledge of English, but my question surprised him so much that he answered in English without thinking, "Absolutely not!" He smiled. "Go to the market and ask." But it would have done no good to ask.

*

ALMA-ATA, the capital, lies at the extreme southeastern edge of Kazakhstan, only about a hundred miles from China. It is more than 2,800 miles distant from the other end of the Kazakh Republic. Few countries have capitals so far off center; it is as if the capital of France were Saint Jean de Luz.[11] Alma-Ata, called Verny in Czarist times, was a garrison town without much historical interest, but its location is spectacular—against a backdrop

[11] Actually Alma-Ata only became the capital of Kazakhstan in 1928. Before that the capital was at a town called Kzyl-Orda, in the remote interior, but this was too primitive for modern administration. Orenburg, now known as Chkalov, in the RSFSR, was the capital before Kzyl-Orda.

formed by the tremendous Tien-Shan range of mountains. It is the center of an apple-growing region, and the name means "Father of Apples." ("Verny," incidentally, means "loyal." Alma-Ata is so far away that, in Czarist days, officers were sent here only if their loyalty was thought to be absolute.)

The population is around 330,000, two-thirds of which is Russian. There are many amputees and detainees. Under the Czars Alma-Ata was a favorite place to send political exiles, if only because it is so distant, and the Bolsheviks followed suit; this is where Trotsky was sent when Stalin banished him. During the liquidation of the kulaks, a good many Ukrainians were dumped in the Alma-Ata region; later came Volga Germans and the Greeks. During the Stalin purges some Yugoslav Communists resident in Russia disappeared. It is known that they were shipped to Alma-Ata, but even though they are (or were) Yugoslav citizens, they have never been heard of since.

Alma-Ata wants to be Saint Moritz. At any rate the town is building what is called an "Olympic" skating rink, on the slopes of the majestic hills near by. To reach it, one must traverse a road that would be bad for the middle of Ethiopia, or England in the time of Stonehenge.

In the town, a dreary town, some of the militiamen are women. In the bazaar, an egg cost 1.40 rubles, mangy ducks were stamped with blue ink to show that they had passed sanitary inspection, and I saw a man pull a mule's hoof out of a truckload of cabbages and try to sell it. But guess what was playing at the Opera that night—*Faust!* We went to a Kazakh concert. The conductor had on white tie (but with a turned-down soft collar) and tails. Among the performers, in the national costume, were girls with sleek long black braids of hair, in blue hats, white puffed-out dresses and billowing white skirts, and tall men in embroidered skull caps and pink velvet pantaloons, who sang and played stringed instruments that had a plangent, tinny sound. Between the acts a young man with black slanting eyes came up to us and said, in English, "What language were you speaking?" I replied, "English." He said, "Good-by!" and fled. (This was, I suppose, about the hundredth time that something of the sort happened to us in Russia.)

In the hotel, a dreary hotel, the headwaiter told us that he had lived for many years in China, and had been boss of the second-best restaurant in Shanghai. I asked him why he had returned. His groan was gloomily expressive. "Was my home."

Portrait of a Kazakh dignitary. Short, Mongoloid in feature, with dark discerning eyes, about forty-five. He came from a poor peasant family; his father and brothers worked for kulaks. At eleven, he set out to earn a living, herding cattle. His home town, in the Kustanai region, was remote and underdeveloped, and he did not get to a school until he was fourteen. He went to Moscow University, became a biologist, returned to Kazakhstan, and at the local university taught the biochemistry of plants for eighteen years. He became a member of the Communist party, and is today a deputy to the Kazakhstan Supreme Soviet and a member of its Academy of Sciences. He was the *first* man of his tribe, the Avgukshek, ever to learn to read and write.

This worthy citizen, Professor Temirbai B. Darkanbayev,[12] is none other than Rector of Alma-Ata University. His life story resembles closely thousands of other life stories in the Soviet Union, as we should know by now. This is a prototype of the "new" Soviet man. He wanted to emphasize to us that the state had supported him during all the years of his education from the age of fourteen through twenty-four. When I mentioned that hundreds of thousands of successful Americans had also gone to schools supported by public funds for a decade or longer, he blinked. Professor Darkanbayev was, as is natural, very proud of his institution, which was founded in 1934. He receives regularly technical and scientific journals from the United States, and he and his colleagues were well informed about American developments in their fields. He said, "Alas, American scientists are not so well informed about us." He thought, like almost all Soviet citizens, that responsibility for the Iron Curtain was entirely American. Alma-Ata University has six thousand students, of whom 44 per cent are Kazakhs.[18] In some faculties the instruction is in Kazakh, but all students are obliged to know Russian as well. The largest department, is, inevitably, physics and mathematics. Professor Darkanbayev told us that before the war Kazakhstan did not possess a single institution of higher learning. There was not a single scientist in the entire area, and not a single native doctor. Now nearly all Kazakhs can read and write, hear their own music, and go to their own theaters, in the familiar Soviet pattern.

Kazakhstan has its own Ministry of Foreign Affairs, although its foreign affairs are nil. The minister, Tulegen T. Tazhibayev, was a member of the Soviet delegation to the UN in 1956. We talked with a somewhat stiff but very alert young man, Murolla Sagendekov, one of his deputies. His life story—he is only thirty-one—bears lessons. He was born in Guryev, an oil town on the Caspian, and came from the poorest peasantry—up from noth-

---

[12] Most Kazakh names end in "ayev."
[18] Altogether thirty-four different nationalities are represented from all over the USSR.

ing. But he got primary education, went into the Red Army when he was sixteen, and after the war managed to make his way to the Institute of International Relations in Moscow, where he studied for five years. He joined the Communist party, and spent two years traveling all over Kazakhstan as an agitator-propagandist, representing *Agitprop*. I asked him if Kazakhstan hoped, in time, to have diplomatic relations with other nations, and to be represented at the UN. "Of course." I asked him if, some time at the UN in the future, it was conceivable that Kazakhstan might ever vote against the USSR. "Certainly. We are a sovereign state. But disagreement with Russia would be unlikely." He even *believed* that Kazakhstan was a "sovereign" state. I asked what Kazakh foreign policy was. "Our only wish is that peace can be saved. Those of us who were at the front know what war means."

Our Last Three Republics

Kirghizia, a mountainous area south of Kazakhstan, has a long common frontier with China. On the west, Uzbekistan jabs into it. The area is 76,718 square miles, about the size of South Dakota, and the population 1,900,000. The Kirghiz are a distinct people, allied to Mongols, but with their national characteristics largely blunted; the mountaineers are called "Black Kirghiz." Here are some of the highest, most massive mountains in the world, and Kirghizia has the tallest peak in the Soviet Union, Mount Stalin, 24,406 feet. Near by is another almost as high, known as Pobeda (Victory) Peak.

The capital, FRUNZE, formerly Pishpek, is a somewhat turbulent little city, with perhaps 190,000 inhabitants. It is proud of the fact that it was allowed to set up its own Academy of Sciences two years ago.[14] Frunze, even more than Alma-Ata, is a home for castoffs. Amputees are here in great number; every other person seems to be a cripple. And in a valley above Frunze, successive villages almost resemble (perhaps this metaphor is not apt) pavilions at a world's fair; there are Chechen, Ingush, Crimean, and Volga German villages, one after another.

Not everything goes smoothly in Kirghizia, particularly in agriculture. Here, in the pattern only too familiar, are excerpts from a speech by Alexander I. Makhno, a Kirghiz deputy to the Supreme Soviet of the USSR:

> Machine and tractor stations experience an acute need of spare parts and repair supplies. . . . Sometimes stations have to send over to the province center or even the republic center for a three-ruble part. . . .

[14] *Moscow News*, April 10, 1957.

The working parts of ploughs and seed drills wear out fast. The planning agencies overlook these characteristics of our republic. The
quotas of allocated plough shares, moldboards, and discs for ploughs
and of moving parts for tractors are utterly insufficient. . . .[15]

Further to the south, in the Pamirs, is *Tadzhikistan*. Most of its frontier
is with Afghanistan, and nothing separates it from Pakistan but a narrow
corridor. It is much less industrialized than Kazakhstan, and hence there
are not so many workers from outside; the population is still fairly homogeneous, and is probably still 75 per cent Tadzhik. The Tadzhiks, quite distinct
from Kazakhs and the Kirghiz next door, are a mountain people of Persian
origin, who speak a language akin to Persian. They were pushed up into
their mountain strongholds by Mongolian invaders. An American president
once visited this remote area, and shot here a specimen of the *Ovis poli*, or
great mountain sheep, one of the rarest of the world's large mammals. His
name was Theodore Roosevelt.

Tadzhikistan covers about 55,000 square miles, roughly the area of Florida,
and has 1,800,000 people. The capital is STALINABAD, once known as
Dyushambe. Another town, LENINABAD, is the former Khodzhent; long before
that it was called Alexandria, Alexander the Great set up a city here, and
named it for himself. Tadzhikistan, like all the other republics, has its complaints. "Local industry has a fish-catching brigade, but few fish are caught.
Geologists have found several deposits of coal in the Pamirs, but these
are not exploited, because the necessary equipment is lacking. Meantime
we haul in salt and coal from great distances. . . . There are dozens of large,
rapid rivers in the Pamirs. Yet, in 1956, we have not built a single collective
farm power plant. . . . Large quantities of canned vegetables and fruit are
brought into the Pamirs every year, though the province could meet all its
needs for these canned goods itself." These items are all from a recent
letter to *Pravda* and refer to conditions in the Gorno-Badakhshan Autonomous Province, part of Tadzhikistan.[16]

Tadzhikistan is, of course, hot after culture; also tourists. The Tadzhik
Academy of Sciences has a language and literature institute, and has
recently issued a new edition of the works of Omar Khayyam, who is considered to be a Tadzhik author. As to tourists, a Tadzhik Society for Cultural Ties with Foreign Countries was established a year ago, and is looking
for customers. The scenery is stupendous, and adventure may still be found
on this roof of the world. About forty foreign delegations from twenty

[15] *Current Digest of the Soviet Press*, March 27, 1957.
[16] *Ibid.*, November 28, 1956.

different countries—including Britain, France, Norway, Mexico, and Brazil—
have visited Tadzhikistan recently, although it is one of the most isolated
and inaccessible regions on earth. An elaborate Tadzhik "festival of the
arts" was held in Moscow in April, 1957.

Turkmenistan (area 187,000 square miles, almost twice the size of West
Germany; population 1,400,000) is the least known of all the Union
republics, and the one most closed off. The capital is ASHKHABAD, and the
country is 85 per cent desert. The southernmost point in the Soviet Union
is here, approximately on the same latitude as Algiers. The people are
mostly Moslems of Turkic stock; many are nomads.

The main local problem is irrigation; people are delighted to point out
that Lenin himself announced this way back in 1918. Here are the black
sands of Kara Kum, one of the bleakest deserts in the world, and the ruins
of towns like Nissa, the capital of ancient Parthia. Ashkhabad, a sizable
industrial city, was once known as Poltoratsk. It was in large part destroyed by
an earthquake in the late 1940's, and has not yet been altogether rebuilt.
KRASNOVODSK is an important port on the Caspian. But the most interesting
town in Turkmenistan is probably Merv, known as MARY, which was
built by Nestorian Christians in the sixth century, and is where Genghis
Khan is reputed (A.D. 1219) to have slain a *million* people. Merv, on a
famous oasis, was the embittered focus of Anglo-Russian tension a hundred
years ago, when the Russians were thought to be advancing toward India;
British wits of the day, deploring the possibility of armed conflict, warned
citizens against "Mervousness."

In this whole area, only twenty-five women could read and write in 1925.
Educational advance has been considerable. Nowadays what counts most
about the Turkmenian Republic is mineral development. Here, under the
thick brittle blanket of rock and desert, incalculably rich deposits of oil,
potassium salts, sulfur, gypsum, and radioactive elements are believed to lie,
and geological exploration, if bungled and dilatory on occasion, is being
carried out with verve.

*

So now we return to Moscow. It is time. We flew over the wastes of
Kyzyl-Kum, another formidable desert, and the crinkled edge of the Aral
Sea. Between Samarkand and Aktyubinsk we made only one stop, at a place
I could not find on most maps, Dzhusaly. Perhaps secret work on ballistic
missiles goes on here. Anyway a big sign in English stood at the airport gates
—EXIT FORBIDDEN FOR UNACCOMPANIED PASSENGERS.

CHAPTER XXIII

The Russians Gamble for the World

I like the Russian people, but I abhor the Russian system of government and I cannot trust the word of those at the head.
—THEODORE ROOSEVELT in 1905

The strictest loyalty to Communist ideas must be combined with the ability to make necessary compromises, to scheme, to sign agreements, to zigzag, to retreat — anything to hasten the coming to power of Communism.
—LENIN

AND now, nearing the conclusion of this long book, we must face the knottiest, most abrasive questions of all. Does the Soviet Union want war? Certainly not. The Russians know full well that a nuclear war, even if it did not actually destroy them, would set them back untold years. The key to almost everything in Soviet foreign policy is that the Russians want peace, but they do not think of the concept of "peace" as we do and they want peace *on their own terms*. (So, of course, do we; the difference is that we are open to reasonable compromise, which they are not.) Their definition of coexistence is altogether different from ours; they mean by peace and coexistence *absence of a shooting war*. Moreover, their major long-range political aim is still what it once was—to win the world without a war—and they stand to gain by anything that lets them free to pursue their own devices abroad without interference. The Russians want peace, but they are still gambling for the world.

This conception is utterly basic to Soviet policy, and goes back many years. The Kremlin wants to be let alone if only in order to consolidate its regime. The publicist Karl Radek explained this as well as anybody twenty-odd years ago, before he was purged, and the doctrine has never changed:

475

The object of the Soviet Government is to save the soil of the first proletarian state from the criminal folly of a new war. To this end the Soviet Union has struggled with the greatest determination and insistency. . . . The defense of peace and the neutrality of the Soviet Union . . . is the central problem of Soviet foreign policy. The Soviet Union follows the policy of peace because peace is the best condition for building up a socialist society.[1]

Not only does the Soviet Union not want war; it no longer takes the official line that war is inevitable. Khrushchev is the best person to quote in this connection. His vision is that a vast "Zone of Peace" has emerged in the world in recent years including first, the Soviet Union and its associated powers, and second, the bloc of neutralist "peace-loving" states emerging now in Africa and Asia. "This zone embraces vast areas inhabited by nearly 1,500 million people—that is the majority of the population of our planet." He proceeds: "The achievement of collective security in Europe, the achievement of collective security in Asia, disarmament, these are the three cardinal problems the solution of which can lay the foundation for firm and lasting peace." Then:

There is of course a Marxist-Leninist precept that wars are inevitable as long as imperialism exists. This precept was evolved at a time when (i) imperialism was an all embracing world system, and (ii) the social and political forces which did not want war were weak, poorly organized, and hence unable to compel the imperialists to renounce war . . . . In that period this precept was absolutely correct. At the present time, however, the situation has changed radically. Now there is a world camp of socialism which has become a mighty force. In this camp the peace forces have not only the moral but also the material means to prevent aggression.[2]

The Russians, he concludes, must display vigilance, but war is not "fatalistically inevitable."

The Soviet Union, in the event of atomic war, would almost certainly lose its precious new industrialization, since industrial cities would be the first to be bombed. Industrialization is the chief reward the Kremlin has given its people for the Spartan sacrifices that have been demanded; for this reason as well as others the Russians will, it may be assumed, be wary of risking war. But, of course, there are acute and pressing dangers. A witty Briton in Moscow once said, "Soviet foreign policy is a policy of extreme realism based on total unreality." The realism is based on the fact that the

[1] "The Bases of Soviet Foreign Policy," *Foreign Affairs*, January, 1934.
[2] From the Report (not the speech) to the Twentieth Congress, February, 1956.

Russians know what they want. The unreality is based on their peculiar disingenuousness, naïveté, capacity for self-deception, and profound lack of knowledge of what the rest of the world is like. They are, let us say once more, an excessively provincial people. Soviet bad manners are not likely—if we keep our heads—to make a war, but Soviet ignorances could. There is always the possibility that they will overreach themselves in a diplomatic maneuver, and miscalculate western reactions. The chief danger of war is in the realm of blunder. On the other hand the Kremlin knows (just as the United States knows) that a point *could* be reached in an international altercation that *could* make war inevitable, and therefore it is unlikely that the Soviet Union, under present circumstances, will go too far. Dancing on the brink, whether by Mr. Dulles or anybody else, is ticklish business.[3]

Meantime, Soviet foreign policy has three permanent, overriding principles. First, perpetuation of the regime. Second, the closest wariness and vigilance to forestall, dissipate, or counteract any consolidation of force against the regime and its satellites, and to attack by all indirect means such consolidations that already exist, like NATO. Third, as to the rest of the world, pick up pieces where they fall.

Beneath this superstructure, in the realm of tactics, any number of factors may be mentioned. "Timing, flexibility, deception" are, in the words of an American official document, obvious characteristics of Soviet foreign policy. Since the United States is the most powerful opponent, the major objective is always to nullify American superiorities, if possible. The Soviet Union would like to keep nuclear weapons out of Europe, and to abolish nuclear tests. It wants disarmament, but strictly on its own terms. It wants a foothold in the Middle East, at the same time that it asks for international agreement to preclude the use of force in the Middle East. It would be willing, however, to stop any shipments of arms there, if the other powers would do likewise. It doesn't want Norway and Denmark to be sites for missiles, and has told these countries—also Turkey, Iran, and Japan—in no uncertain terms that if missile attacks were ever launched from them against the Soviet Union, retaliation in kind would be "energetic." Also Khrushchev has offered to withdraw Soviet troops from eastern Europe, if the United States gets out of Germany and the NATO area. The bargain would be a good one for the Kremlin, if only because Russian troops, having withdrawn from Europe, could get back there much more quickly in the event of

---

[3] There are, however, observers who wonder if "Bolshevik irrationality cannot go to the lengths of self-destruction." Cf. Geroid Tanquary Robinson in *Continuity and Change in Russian and Soviet Thought*, p. 377.

an outbreak than could American troops from across the Atlantic.

In a word, Soviet foreign policy is to do anything possible to weaken the United States, meantime stirring up ferment wherever possible. It is also American policy to do anything possible to weaken the Soviet Union. The United States believes in exerting pressure against Russia through "containment," and it steadily propagandizes for liberation of the satellites.

Soviet policy goes by zigzags, although the end is always the same. In the old days, this zigzagging was most conspicuous geographically; an almost "rhythmic" alternation took place between attention to Europe and to the Far East. Zigzagging occurs today in toughness of thrust; the alternations are between aggressiveness and relative placidity.

Techniques, targets, may vary, but the USSR never ceases trying to play for advantages, no matter how minute. Nowadays, the chief target area is certainly the Middle East, into which it has already effectively penetrated. But more remote areas in Asia are not neglected, particularly Afghanistan, Burma, Ceylon, and Indonesia. As to Europe, anything that tends to separate the United States from Great Britain or France or that weakens West Germany is greedily welcomed. In regard to techniques, there are several. The Czechoslovakian armament deal with Egypt was an obvious case in point, and so, even more significantly, is the recent arms build-up in Syria. The hundred-million-dollar credit to Afghanistan was followed by a similar grant to Indonesia. The Russians, just as we do, go in for "economic" aid to their associates, and spend a lot.[4] Khrushchev has stated that long-term credits amounting to 21,000,000,000 rubles ($5,250,000,000 at par) have been granted to the satellites, and very large sums are being spent steadily on economic aid projects in other parts of the world, particularly Egypt. Czechoslovakia is outfitting Egypt with a rubber processing plant, a shoe factory, and a ceramics factory; seven bridges and an electric power plant are to go to Egypt from Hungary; an enamelware factory is to be provided by Poland; and the East Germans are to build a shipyard in Alexandria. Aid is not merely financial. For instance a nuclear laboratory is to be established in Cairo, under Soviet auspices, and a program has been set up for training Egyptian scientists.[5]

Soviet economic aid goes not merely to satellites and close friends, but to almost anybody who will accept it. In August, 1957, Russia offered Iran an

---

[4] Soviet use of arms shipments and economic aid as political weapons is a comparatively new development. Stalin was extremely hesitant about giving arms to any non-Communist states, and did not believe much in economic aid.

[5] Dana Adams Schmidt in the *New York Times*, July 23, 1956.

"unlimited credit" at 2 per cent interest for heavy industrial development, and a month later announced an agreement whereby it will build a glass factory in Istanbul, Turkey. (Iran, be it noted, is a member of the Baghdad Pact, and Turkey belongs to NATO as well. The Kremlin is delighted to cross fences when it can.) Burma is receiving from the Soviet Union a steel plant, a theater, a hospital, and a technological institute in exchange for 400,000 tons of rice. The Russians are helping to finance building of a major steel factory in India, and are assisting in oil development in the Punjab. Yemen is getting arms, and the Sudan is giving the USSR cotton in exchange for technical help, including a geological survey. Russia has offered to assist Nepal in its five-year agricultural and industrial development plan, and is busy in several realms in Indonesia.

Another word about the Middle East. There are half a dozen reasons for Russian interest in this agitated region. One is the very fact that it is agitated, and a good pool to fish in. Another is that the Kremlin has always considered the Middle East to be a kind of vent, which keeps the USSR from being completely encircled; it wants to nullify the Eisenhower Doctrine, and keep this vent thoroughly open. Again, Soviet pressure here weakens the American position, not merely in the Middle East itself, but all over the Afro-Asian-Arab world. This is where the old colonial order has most conspicuously broken down, and where the western allies are most divided, fumbling, and vulnerable. Still again, it is advantageous to have a military position in the eastern Mediterranean. Further if the Russians want to stage an external diversion to conceal troubles at home, the Middle East is an ideal spot, with any amount of explosive tinder conveniently on hand. Finally, it is good for Soviet prestige elsewhere in Asia and the Arab world to assist Moslem states. Above all, the Middle East means *power*. Soviet maneuvers in the Middle East are, incidentally, seldom operated through party channels. All is done strictly in the old-fashioned way, by direct contact with governments or politicians. Communism, as such, plays no role.

The worst Soviet headache in foreign policy has to do with the European satellites. The lesson of Hungary is that Russia will not give up any European satellite without a fight. But two auxiliary considerations embarrassing to the Kremlin should be mentioned, particularly in reference to Poland. The first is that the Russians know full well that, if for instance they were forced to make an armed intervention in Poland on the Hungarian model, the country would burst into savage nationalist flame. The second is that Gomulka and his fellows know this too, and even if they are being well behaved and quiescent at the moment, they are in a better position than ever before to twist the Kremlin's tail, in moderation. An important factor operating against the possibility of war is Soviet fear that the satellites are "unsafe," and cannot be trusted. On the other hand, Gomulka *is* a Communist, and it may be that he needs Moscow as much as Moscow needs him.

The Communist Empire

This consists of the following units in Europe:

Country	Area (sq. miles)	Population
Albania	11,100	1,394,310
Bulgaria	42,796	7,350,000
Czechoslovakia	49,354	13,089,000
German Democratic Republic (East Germany)	41,380	16,500,000
Hungary	35,905	9,808,000
Poland	120,442	27,089,142
Rumania	91,654	17,489,794
Yugoslavia	98,700	17,557,000

Yugoslavia is not a satellite, but is Communist. It was flung out of the Kremlin orbit in 1948. Since Stalin's death, Khrushchev and Tito have, so to speak, kissed and made up three different times, but Yugoslavia pursues its own policy. Nor can Poland be considered to be a true satellite any longer, in the sense that it takes orders from Moscow, although as a *Communist* country it is closer to the Kremlin than is Yugoslavia.

And in Asia:

Country	Area (sq. miles)	Population
China (Chinese People's Republic)[6]	3,911,209	582,603,417
North Korea (Korean People's Democratic Republic)	49,114	10,750,000
North Vietnam (Democratic Republic of Vietnam)	62,808	13,000,000
Outer Mongolia (Mongolian People's Republic)	614,350	920,000

The total population of Communist states in the world, including the USSR, is thus more than 900,000,000, spread over a very wide area indeed—from Berlin and the Adriatic all the way to the Pacific, and including most of southeastern Europe, the great Eurasian plain, and parts of southeast Asia.

Nor is this all. There are, as everybody knows, Communists of varying tints

[6] Including Tibet.

and shades in practically every country in the world; some are underground, some above. The largest Communist party in the world outside the Communist bloc is in Italy. The Italian Communists polled a total popular vote of 9,500,000 in 1953, or 35.6 per cent of the electorate, and the Italian parliament (590 members) has 143 Communists, not counting some 200 fellow travelers and left-wing socialists who usually vote Communist. France has more than four million Communists, a quarter of the electorate; there are about 150 Communist members in a chamber numbering 628. Then, quite without regard to the official parties, one must keep in mind surreptitious Communists, agents, spies, and underground workers in a variety of other countries, including Great Britain and the United States.

As to Asia, pertinacious Communist influence exists almost everywhere. In the last Indonesian elections (September 1955) the Communists received six million votes, or 17 per cent of the total. There are powerful Communist factors at work in Indonesia, right to the top of the state. Communists control one state in India, are a strong and growing force in Laos, and are capable of making mischief in Japan and even Okinawa. And wo must mention again countries in the Middle East like Egypt, Syria, and, in a somewhat different category, Yemen. Egypt and Syria are allies of the Kremlin, if not puppets. One point of marked interest and importance, which is often neglected by Americans, is that a country may become friendly to Moscow not merely by reason of Communist subversion or blandishment, but because it *likes* aspects of Communism and Russian policy, admires socialism and national planning, and has reached a point in social evolution where the Soviet system appears to offer more than ours. Almost all undeveloped Asian (and African) nationalisms are left wing, and would be left wing and perhaps anti-American even if the Kremlin did not exist. People want education, technological advance, economic amelioration, and, above all, neutrality. American policy, for instance in supporting the Baghdad Pact, is bitterly resented in several countries at least, and it is we, not the Russians, who are accused of being the troublemakers.

The European Satellites

The European satellites still follow to an extent their pre-Soviet characteristics; Communism has not by any means stamped out the old, ingrown national patterns. An Albanian may be a Communist, but he remains an Albanian just the same, and is a totally different article from a Bulgar or a Czech. Poland is still romantic and volatile; Czechoslovakia is still business-

INSIDE RUSSIA TODAY

like, stolid, and obedient. The Bulgars have a strong tradition of being pro-Russian, and this still plays a large role in their affairs. Yugoslavs and Bulgars have been at odds for generations, and still are. East Germans are, it is quite obvious, different from Rumanians. Moscow takes the general line that all the satellites are partners, but insists on as much subservience as it can get. So, even though national characteristics survive, a massive *Gleichschaltung* has stricken the entire area.

There are, however, important stirrings. Omitting Yugoslavia, Poland is the most revisionist and independent-minded of the Communist countries. Khrushchev, when he went to Warsaw in a vain attempt to forestall Gomulka's coup in October, 1956, said, "We could have squashed Poland like a bedbug, but did not do so." He could not do so now, except at the gravest risk of civil and perhaps international war. The Poles have achieved an astounding amount of liberalization, particularly in such realms as agriculture and a loosening of intellectual yokes. On the other hand Gomulka is a firm and dedicated Communist, and wants good relations with the Kremlin. A little *bon mot* is apposite. The story is that in Poland you can criticize the Polish government until the cows go home, but not the USSR. In Yugoslavia you can criticize the USSR all you want, but not the Tito government.

After Poland, the most revisionist state is, curiously enough, probably Hungary. Janos Kadar, the prime minister, was a Titoist, who was imprisoned and put to torture by the old-line Hungarian Stalinists, and he wants Hungarian Communism to be as "national" as possible. East Germany probably comes next from the criterion of relative independence from Moscow. This is because it is technically advanced enough to be able to resist, to an extent, Russian efforts to pull it into the Soviet economic orbit. Next, Rumania. The states most thoroughly inert or subjugated are Czechoslovakia, Bulgaria and Albania. The Czechs, who have a lucrative industry and who are much more prosperous than any other satellite, are still led by outright Stalinists, as is East Germany. There has been no shakeup in the hierarchy here. On the other hand, the *worst* Czechoslovakian Stalinists, like Rudolf Slansky, the former party secretary, were liquidated by "moderate" Czechoslovakian Stalinists some years ago, and hence present no problem. Albania and Bulgaria are docile for different reasons. The Albanians hate the Yugoslavs, and Marshal Tito has never bothered to conceal his contempt for Enver Hoxha, the Albanian puppet ruler; therefore Albania, out of fear of Yugoslavia, tends to keep close to Moscow. The situation in Bulgaria is more complex. But even in Bulgaria, beaten into conformity as it has been, and for years as flat as a cabbage patch overrun by a bulldozer, impulses toward liberalization are felt nowadays. In particular the Bulgars (also the Albanians) would like more contact with the United States.[7]

To sum up, the satellites are pursuing different evolutions under the Moscow cloak, and, although it would be a gross exaggeration to say that any is on the point of breaking loose, a lively fermentation, almost a tumult, is evident almost everywhere. The consequent dilemma for the Kremlin is perplexing. It is, in a word, "how to run the system without Stalin." It is altogether impossible to put eastern Europe back under direct control of Moscow, under outright Kremlin discipline. The Italian Communist leader, Palmiro Togliatti, said after Khrushchev's speech to the Twentieth Congress, "The Soviet model is not and cannot be obligatory any longer."[8] Walter Lippmann wrote recently, "The communist world, what with the growing strength of China and the increasing nationalism of the European satellites, can no longer be held together, as in Stalin's day, by imperial fiat from Moscow." The dilemma is, as a matter of fact, analogous to one which also marks Soviet domestic affairs, though not to such a dramatic degree. Put in its bluntest terms, it is that the Russian oligarchs cannot afford to tighten up too much, but at the same time cannot afford to let go. If they continue to rule exclusively by arbitrary force, they lose all contact with the people. But if they liberalize too copiously, then they risk further disaffection, and possible eventual revolt.

The Kremlin needs the satellites—needs them badly—for a variety of reasons. Prestige is one; so is military security; so is desire to extend the Soviet system. On the other hand, the satellites cost Russia plenty. The Hungarian episode set the economy of the entire region back terrifically; one estimate is that physical damage alone amounted to a billion dollars. For a long period the Russians were in a position to fleece the satellites, and duly fleeced them; now this position has changed, and the satellites are demanding more economic freedom and fairer financial treatment from Moscow. Whereas, three years ago, the USSR probably drew in five billion dollars a year from the satellites, today it is putting out a billion.[9] Then one must consider political factors, such as the possible effects on the Soviet Union internally of alterations and developments of mood in the satellite

[7] See an illuminating series of articles from the satellites by Harrison E. Salisbury, published late in the summer of 1957 in the *New York Times*.
[8] *New Statesman*, June 23, 1956.
[9] According to the London *Times* (May 14, 1957), the Soviet government was compelled to sell gold heavily in western European markets early in 1957, in order to ease the strain of satellite economic demands.

structure. What is the ordinary Russian going to think when he learns that the Poles have won substantial economic as well as civil liberties? "Family" quarrels within the Soviet orbit may turn out to be a much more dangerous threat to Soviet power than western "imperialism" or "encirclement" ever was. The Russians may discover in time, like the British, that to maintain an empire can be an extremely expensive business.

Speaking of empire, the fact is relevant that the western "imperialists" have freed from colonial bondage about 600,000,000 people since 1945, which happens to be almost the same number that Communism has taken over. India is free; Pakistan is free; Burma, Malaya, and Ceylon are free; so are Tunisia, Morocco, Israel, Libya, the Philippines, and Indonesia; so is Ghana, so is the Sudan, and so will be Nigeria soon. But Bulgaria, which was once a sturdy upright little nation, has gone down the drain, even if it wriggles, and so has Czechoslovakia with its magnificent democratic tradition under the elder Masaryk, to say nothing of other satellites still in a state of slavery, petrifaction, or forced feeding.

Russia and China

China, holding almost a quarter of all mankind, is important enough to the Communist world already; if, as projected, it becomes a great industrial power its importance will be vastly augmented; the Chinese say that they will have by 1975 a steel industry equivalent to that of all western Europe. Does Russia run China? Certainly not! Does China run Russia? By no means! One observer in Moscow told me, "The worst place in the world to find out about Sino-Russian relations is Moscow." By this he did not mean to indicate surreptitious hostility, but that Peking played its own hand carefully, and did not expose it more than was necessary. Russia and China—particularly in their joint position vis-à-vis other Communist areas—are somewhat like two partners in a business united by a common aim but with different points of view, and with unruly junior executives to keep in order. Or, to change the metaphor, Russia and China resemble to a degree a husband and wife who get along pretty well, bound by the same essential interests, but who have sharp disagreements on how to spend money and bring up the children.

Russia cannot "run" China for several reasons. One is that China is too big; certainly it would be very difficult indeed for the Kremlin to exert pressure on China by force, if this should ever be necessary. Second, China has the prestige that goes with seniority, and cannot possibly be brushed off as a parvenu or puppet. The great Chinese Revolution which overthrew the

Manchu dynasty in 1911 predates the Russian Revolution by several years;[10] also Mao Tse-tung has a seniority in the international Communist movement that no Russian leader can match. Moreover, the Chinese Communists conquered China without intervention by the Red Army, and in fact without Russian help at all. Stalin for a time backed Chiang Kai-shek. Another point is that, during the period of Soviet assistance to the Chinese in the 1930's, the Russians gave advice to the Chinese Communists that came near to wrecking them. The Russians, operating by the book, neglected local Chinese considerations and stuck to the orthodox Marxist line that the revolution must be made by the proletariat in the cities; Mao, in contrast, chose to get out into the countryside, and build up his movement on the peasantry. China has been somewhat wary of Soviet counsel ever since. In any case, the Russians cannot possibly pretend to have done much to assist the Communist conquest of China. Even today, Peking's attitude to Moscow has elements of superiority, and is somewhat patronizing.

Mikoyan led a Russian Communist party delegation to Peking to attend the Eighth Congress of the Chinese Communist party, but, interestingly enough, the visit has never been returned. Multitudinous exchanges of missions have taken place on lower levels, for instance in reference to everything from agriculture to drama; the fact remains that no official Chinese *party* delegation has ever visited Moscow. During 1956, when a great deal of the most urgent and controversial business was on the boards, the Chinese for long months did not even have an ambassador in Moscow.[11] Before this, during the later Stalin period, the Chinese were not at all happy about some things that went on in the Kremlin. They deplored the rupture with Tito. When Mao visited Moscow late in 1949 bargaining of the most stringent sort took place, particularly in regard to Russian economic demands on China. "Had it not been for the hardening of United States policy toward Red China [at that time], the Peiping Government might well have decided to break openly with Moscow as Marshal Tito did in 1948."[12]

The Russians, on their side, are nowadays very solicitous of Chinese sensibilities, even tender. Khrushchev said in the summer of 1957, "China follows a Marxist path in her own Chinese way, but that is no cause for quarrel. China is a large, original country. She does not copy anything. Differing ways to socialism are only tributaries to the main stream." After the Hungarian

[10] Of course the 1911 revolution in China was not a Communist revolution.

[11] This however does not necessarily mean much; perhaps relations between Moscow and Peking were handled by direct contact. In any case a Chinese chargé d'affaires was on hand.

[12] Sydney Gruson in the *New York Times*, June 4, 1956.

crisis, the Chinese prime minister, Chou En-lai, visited Moscow, Warsaw and Budapest, in the capacity of a broker or middleman trying to ease the situation. He did not take an anti-Russian line; quite the contrary. He told the Hungarians to behave themselves, warned Gomulka severely against the dangers of counterrevolution, and had tart words for Tito. All this being true, it is revealing that Moscow should have found Chou's intermediation so convenient. The Russians needed Chinese authority and prestige in order to restore their position and authority in eastern Europe, and were grateful. Chou's own attitude toward the Kremlin seemed to be a bland "Don't be worried, comrades; leave everything to me."

On February 17, 1957 came the celebrated "Hundred Flowers" speech by Mao Tse-tung, who is head of both the Chinese Communist party and the Chinese state, and who thus holds a position in China technically superior to that of any Russian leader in Russia. This speech, seventeen thousand words long, was not made public until June; it has a seminal importance to Communist affairs similar to that of Khrushchev's speech to the Twentieth Congress, and has in fact been called a more "radical" repudiation of Stalinism than the Khrushchev speech.[18] It reverberated, with piercing undertones, throughout the whole of the Communist world. Mao reversed not merely Stalinist policy but contemporary Kremlin policy by stating that "contradictions" can exist in a Communist society between the ruling classes and the people. In Marxist jargon, the term "contradictions" means "disagreement." "Disagreement," in turn, can easily be transmuted into "struggle." Before this, it had been basic Communist doctrine that the "contradictions" that exist in bourgeois states, and which are supposed to cause their eventual collapse, do not and cannot appear under Marxism, where in theory there is "perfect unity between the ruler and ruled." Moreover Mao went on to say that Communist leaders would be "in danger politically" if mistaken policies led to the "just dissatisfaction of the masses." He recommended "democratic freedoms" for citizens so long as these are kept within bounds, and uttered the phrase, "In every field let one hundred flowers blossom, and one hundred schools of thought contend." Strong stuff! It was, at least, too strong for Khrushchev. When, it will be remembered, Khrushchev talked on TV to the United States and Daniel Schorr asked him whether or not contradictions of the type Mao had in mind existed in the Soviet Union, he replied, "We believe that we have no contradictions of that nature." Subsequently this sentence was cut out of the Khrushchev text when it was distributed within Russia, and even eliminated from the film shown in Soviet movie houses.

[18] Isaac Deutscher in the *New Statesman*, June 29, 1957.

On the other hand, it is only fair to add, the Kremlin rulers some months later gave wide public circulation to Mao's speech, in which the passage about "contradictions" in China is included. In fact *Pravda* gave three of its six pages to the speech, without comment or interpretation. What is one to make of this? First, the Chinese are, like the Russians, trying to fill the "doctrinal vacuum" left by Stalin, and are therefore obliged to experiment with changes in ideology. Second, Khrushchev must have thought in the first instance that Mao was going too far for Soviet audiences, and then reconsidered. Third, both the Chinese and Russian publics have it on the authority of their own bosses that the expression of dissent does not contravene Marxism. This however does not mean that much dissent is apt to be permitted.[14]

Mao was remarkably candid about Hungary. He said that the Communist party in Hungary "simply disappeared in a matter of a few days, and the whole state threatened to disintegrate." One reason for the enunciation of the "contradictions" theory was, no doubt, to give opportunity for the expression of disagreement, and thus to keep revolts like that in Hungary from reoccurring. He was also remarkably candid about China, saying that the Chinese Communists had liquidated no fewer than 800,000 opponents of the regime between 1949 and 1954, when the terror was stopped and "persuasion and education" substituted instead. This tidbit was, incidentally, censored from the text of the Mao speech released to the *Chinese* people.

Sino-Russian co-operation in China today is expressed mostly in economic fields—industrialization projects, hydroelectric developments like one proposed for the River Amur, railway administration, and the establishment of joint scientific councils. Russian engineers are all over the place in China, and multitudes of Chinese are studying in Russia. Even so there is a tendency on both sides not to allow contact to be too close. For instance the Russians do not particularly want their people to learn that, in China, strikes are legal, whereas in the Soviet Union they are not. Jealousies and rivalries in a variety of areas may come in time—even direct conflict of national interests. But at the moment no signs of serious differences between Russia and China are discernible.

One curious point is that, some folk in Moscow say, the Kremlin hopes that the United States will *not* recognize Red China in the future. The Soviet Union wants to keep China all to itself, and, if the Chinese Communist regime gained American recognition and entered the UN, Moscow's

[14] In China Mao backtracked significantly from the "hundred flowers" position within a few months, and blossoms that emerged had their heads whacked off.

influence on Peking might be diffused. Also the Russians want to learn more from the Chinese. I heard a Russian lady say, "The Chinese are subtler than we are, more dexterous and more experienced. Our policy is too blunt—we don't know how to get around things. Hungary would never have happened if we had had Chinese advice."

Comintern to Cominform to What?

The Russians are gambling for the world, but world revolution as an avowed, overt policy is out of the window. The period in which all Communist parties all over the world were bound in a tight interlocked structure devoted to concerted and all-embracing internationalist revolutionary conspiracy is no more. This is probably the most striking of all manifestations of the de-Stalinization process.

The Kremlin will of course do anything possible to make its system stronger anywhere and to reduce the power and prestige of the free world. Infiltration, arms shipments, political blackmail, economic aid, propaganda, espionage, are the familiar weapons, and have not been superseded. But the approach is different, and the accent is no longer pronouncedly conspiratorial. The Russians are determined to hold on to the existing Communist states but not prepared to risk much—in the nuclear period—to get more. Khrushchev is convinced that Sovietism is the irresistible wave of the future, that in time Moscow will certainly inherit the earth, and that Communist governments will take power everywhere, if only because, as time goes on, the "superiority" of socialism to capitalism will be made overwhelmingly manifest, and people everywhere will flock voluntarily to the "socialist" camp. The Kremlin thinks, in other words, that the game is in the bag already. World revolution incited by Moscow is no longer an element in policy because it is no longer considered to be necessary. Moreover the whole stress of Soviet policy since the middle 1940's has been toward *national* development.

It might even be said that the present Kremlin leadership would view with active distaste—even fear—the prospect of Communist revolution in certain countries. Suppose, let us say, Denmark should go Communist. Denmark is a member of NATO, and Greenland is part of the Danish realm; on Greenland are located several important American bases and installations. Presumably the United States could not possibly tolerate the establishment of a Communist government in Denmark with power over Greenland, and presumably would go to almost any length to inhibit such a development.

Certainly, to Russian eyes, Denmark is not worth an atomic war. Moscow is more important to Moscow than Greenland or Copenhagen.

Another factor, for which several elements are responsible, is that the international Communist movement is not by any means what it once was. Probably there are at least twenty million Communists in non-Communist countries in the world today, but almost all have been infected to some degree by the virus of "national" Communism. Tito's defection, the emergence of Communist China as an independent force, the Khrushchev speech, above all the events in Hungary, have all diluted Kremlin authority for the time being, and have led to "polycentrist" tendencies. The rigid discipline of former days can no longer be readily imposed, and fragments of the Communist world run themselves. Togliatti in Italy has one kind of relationship to Moscow; Thorez in France has quite another. The American Communist party is split into three feeble wings, and the Kremlin and *Daily Worker* spit confused fire at each other day after day.

All this is rudimentary. Nevertheless it has had important effects on levels high as well as low. Toward "international" Communism, the United States still maintains the most resolute hostility. But toward "national" Communism the attitude is somewhat different. The United States is giving substantial aid to both Tito and Gomulka. President Eisenhower said at a press conference on August 21, 1957, "Tito is in a far different position with respect to the free world than are Communist countries that are directly controlled by Communism. In other words it is international Communism that spells the greatest danger to the United States, not that we approve of Communism anywhere, but international Communism and subordination to the views of Moscow are one thing. Independent Communism is something else."

Of course the "national" movements may revert to Moscow in time, and the Kremlin may return to an active revolutionary policy at some future date convenient to its aims. United States policy is to try to wean Tito away from the Kremlin and thus keep an aperture in the Iron Curtain permanently open, but it may not work out this way. These are unstable times, and in the Communist orbit one violent and unexpected switch follows another. Tito and Gomulka met in Belgrade in September, 1957, and announced that they were not "national Communists" at all.

President Eisenhower was asked if he thought that the Soviet penetration of Syria was, in effect, part of a Communist conspiracy, a deliberate effort to take the country over, at the press conference quoted above. His answer was, "Well, I think this: I think that is the ultimate aim, but, of course, an ultimate aim of that kind is kept very definitely under cover, because one of the things, when you go on, you appeal to the spirit of nationalism. I am talking now about the Soviet. They appeal to the spirit of nationalism in the country, telling them that through this method, you are independent, you run your own affairs, but when they get a hold of the thing, they find out too late that they are being run from somewhere else."[15]

Go back a bit. To appreciate how remarkable Khrushchev's position is today it is necessary to see the picture in perspective. The Bolsheviks were, in theory, "stateless" at the beginning in 1917, and Lenin seized power in Russia not exclusively in the name of Russia, but as an international socialist. It is interesting, however, that Lenin himself realized that world revolution was going to be a headache; he called it the "greatest difficulty" of the Russian Revolution, as well as its greatest historical "problem." The Third International or Comintern, the official vehicle for world revolution, was founded in 1919. Presently struggles between Stalin and Trotsky paralyzed it, and it met only twice after 1934. Then Stalin killed it in 1943—partly because it had become ineffective, partly as a token of friendship to the Allies in World War II. Not only was it killed but, in the familiar Soviet manner, its memory was blotted out. For instance a town called Comintern (in Russian Komintern) had its name changed to Novoshakhtinsk. But Communist parties all over the world remained active. Then in 1947 came the establishment of the Communist Information Bureau, or Cominform. This was not an international agency, as was the Comintern in theory, but an agency of the Soviet government, largely devoted to the satellites. The split with Tito made it useless, and it was formally abolished in 1956. It only met once after 1949.

Khrushchev harps on the present position in almost every speech. He says that it is "ridiculous to think that revolutions are made to order," and denies any plan to interfere "in the internal affairs of countries where capitalism still exists." New "forms of transition to socialism" will appear, so that revolutions will not be necessary. In June, 1957 Khrushchev received a Japanese journalist, Tomoo Hirooka, editor-in-chief of the *Asahi Shimbun,* Japan's most important independent newspaper, for an interview to which I have already alluded. Khrushchev said to Mr. Hirooka:

> It is not we who influence the activity of the Japanese communists, but the teaching of Marxism-Leninism. I personally do not know the secretaries of the Japanese communist parties. I have never met them, but we have our ideas in common. We believe that Marxism-Leninism

[15] *New York Times,* August 22, 1957.

is right. . . . Marx showed that capitalism is inevitably succeeded by another system, communism, just as capitalism replaced feudalism in its time. Such is the inexorable law of social development. . . .

Listen further:

You are a newspaper editor and the editor of a bourgeois newspaper and you believe that the capitalist system is a good one. You are free to stand by your opinions. What you think is your own affair. . . . I believe that communism will triumph in Japan. I am convinced of this because I am a communist. But when will this victory be? This depends on the Japanese people. I believe in them and in their power. The Japanese are a stubborn people and they will gain victory. You would like the bourgeois system to exist forever. And I should like communism to prevail.

Khrushchev repeats that he sympathizes with the Japanese Communists, but nevertheless will not allow himself to intervene with Japanese affairs. "Intervention in the internal affairs of other countries always brings nothing but harm. Each fruit ripens in its time and according to conditions. This also applies to revolution. The Japanese people themselves must decide what system they are going to have." Then Mr. Hirooka puts in politely, "The most important thing is not to foist one's ideology upon another. Communism, if it comes, must be brought by the people voluntarily." Khrushchev concludes, "We are for that. I agree with you. This is exactly how it should be."[16]

No Soviet leader has ever talked in quite these accents before.

Some Soviet Blunders

No one, not even fellow travelers in backward Asian areas, should be permitted to think that the Kremlin is omniscient, invincible, or even always right. We have talked much in this book of Communist successes. But there have also been Communist failures, errors and gross stupidities. One, caused by overconfidence and a total misreading of the American mind, was the blockade of Berlin, which produced the Air Lift in retaliation. Also a miscalculation by Stalin led indirectly to the foundation of NATO—a result he certainly did not foresee or intend. We are all apt to forget nowadays that the Soviet Union was invited to be a participant in the Marshall Plan; it refused. Had the Russians allowed their satellites to accept Marshall Plan aid, and entered the project themselves, it is quite possible that the North Atlantic Treaty Organization would never have been established. Another

[16] *Current Digest of the Soviet Press*, August 7, 1957.

curious Soviet blunder, on the technical level, came at the outbreak of the Korean War. The Russians boycotted the session of the UN Security Council which voted to put the United Nations into the field to resist North Korean aggression. They would certainly have vetoed this decision. There would have been no difference to the result, but they could have made plenty of nuisance and delay.

Will the Russians Conquer the World in Thirty Years?

Perhaps. It is possible. It depends on how stupid we are. But it is altogether unlikely that this will happen *unless* the Western Powers commit some gigantic and egregious folly, like plunging into war, or suffer prolonged and prostrating economic collapse. Russia may however, with luck, and unless the democratic world shows a great deal more discipline, unity, and grasp of new realities than it has recently been showing, make very strong advances. One factor to keep in mind is that no country has ever succumbed to Communism except after exhausting warfare, with the constituted government broken down and intolerably corrupt (e.g. China), or as a result of outright occupation by the Red Army (*e.g.* the European satellites), with the exception of Czechoslovakia.

CHAPTER XXIV

Peace, Coexistence, and the United States

Russia is always defeated, but never beaten.
—CZARIST PROVERB

FOLLOWING is an exchange of notes between Walter Bedell Smith, the American Ambassador, and Mr. Molotov, the Soviet Foreign Minister, during the beginning of the Cold War in 1947. Mr. Smith wrote:

During the year and a half that I have resided in the Soviet Union I have been obliged with the deepest regret to witness in the Soviet press an increasing flood of half truths, distortions of truth and utter falsehoods about my country and my government. I have tried to overlook this incendiary press campaign, feeling that to take issue with a myriad false or incorrect statements would simply be adding fuel to the flame of hatred toward my country which the Soviet press has apparently undertaken to kindle in the hearts of the Soviet people.

However, an occasion has now arisen when I must break this self-imposed rule. An article by one Boris Gorbatov just published in *Literary Gazette* No. 39 is so wantonly libelous in its personal attack on the President of the United States that I cannot permit it to pass without the strongest protest. It has thoroughly shocked me. . . .

I must assure you in the most solemn terms that every fair-minded American citizen, regardless of his political opinions, will be deeply affronted by this article and will feel that he in some way shares the personal insult thus gratuitously offered to President Truman.

I cannot recall that Dr. Goebbels, of unsavory memory, at the height of our common struggle against Nazi Germany ever stooped to greater ridicule and vituperation against the head of an enemy country than has Mr. Gorbatov against the chief executive of a friendly and allied state. In this connection, I would never have believed that a Soviet writer would permit himself, or be permitted, to draw an analogy between the President of the United States and our recent common enemy, Hitler. Mr. Gorbatov goes so far as to imply criticism of Pres-

493

ident Truman for associating with the President of Brazil, our faithful and devoted ally in the recent war, to whom is unwarrantably imputed some prior association with the Axis powers. Any unprejudiced observer, familiar with the course of history since 1939, would agree that such criticism comes with extraordinarily bad grace from a Soviet writer.

I cannot believe that Mr. Gorbatov's article represents the opinion of the Soviet Government, and I therefore request that it be officially disavowed and if, contrary to my belief, it has the approval of the Soviet Government, I would appreciate a statement to that effect.

This was Molotov's reply:

Acknowledging the receipt of your letter of September 25, I must state that I do not consider it possible to enter into a discussion with you of the article of the writer B. Gorbatov in the *Literary Gazette*. . . . and cannot accept the protest you have made in that connection.

However, inasmuch as in your letter you decided to undertake a general evaluation of the Soviet press and from it is obtained a completely perverted picture of the situation, I must state my disagreement with your point of view on the Soviet press.

Despite your allegation, the Soviet press more than the press of any other country whatsoever, especially aims to elucidate as broadly as possible the actual situation and true facts of the life of other countries, attaching special significance to the strengthening of friendly relations between peoples. . . . Any move or approach . . . toward the strengthening of normal relations between countries and toward the support of universal peace invariably encounters warm support in the Soviet press, and this is so generally known that it needs no reaffirmation whatsoever. It is by no means possible to say [this] regarding the . . . American press which is so widely encouraged by the most reactionary circles in the U.S.A. and which not only from day to day inserts lying and slanderous articles regarding the U.S.S.R. and its statesmen, but also inflames hostility between peoples, and which does not meet with any serious support whatsoever in the U.S.A., which is of course, Mr. Ambassador, well known to you regarding which there are not two different opinions in international democratic circles.[1]

One can only be relieved that today things are not quite so bad as this.

Policy Toward the US, and Vice Versa

Russia, I have stated in the preceding chapter, does not want a war if only because peace serves its national interests better. Today's Russians are not reckless, bloodthirsty marauders or territorial expansionists like Hitler. Nor does the United States want war. But is coexistence with the Soviet Union

[1] *The Strategy and Tactics of World Communism*, House Document No. 619, 80th Congress, 2nd Session. Report of Subcommittee No. 5.

possible, and on what terms? Both the United States and the Soviet Union, while each denies that it has any aggressive characteristics, continually seek to undermine or destroy the relative power of the other, which makes for dangerous and cumulative tensions. Meantime, we have to coexist, since the alternative is nuclear war. It is better (under most circumstances) to be alive than dead. But how is coexistence possible?

Can the United States, Great Britain, or any country of the free world coexist with a dictatorship? Perhaps—democracies have certainly coexisted with dictatorships before. We coexisted with Czarist Russia.[2] In fact the United States coexists with several dictatorships at this moment, like Spain, and even has cordial relations with them. Can the United States coexist with a country that tells lies blatantly and wantonly as an instrument of national policy? Perhaps—there are plenty of liars in the chancellories of the world, and even some at home. But can we coexist with a country that does not disguise its hope for eventual Communization of the world, that uses its own fraudulent conception of "peace" as a mask for persistent and incorrigible nibbling at the foundations of peace? Can we coexist with a country without civil liberties or free access to information, a country with no right of protest for citizens and one impossible to reach? Can we, above all, coexist with people rooted and steeped in a faith, a political documentation, an accent on life, diametrically opposed to ours, as well as fiercely competitive? Difficult! But we have to try.

Soviet bad manners, superficial as such a consideration would seem to be, play a substantial role in all this. Americans, like most other inhabitants of the earth's surface, hate to be deceived, pushed around, and mocked. Moreover, more than most peoples on the earth's surface, Americans like to be liked, and take it badly when they are not. And, although the Russians are a friendly people and individual Americans are almost always treated with courtesy, and it would be difficult to engender a popular or genuine anti-American movement in the USSR, there is no doubt that the Soviet government simply does not *like* America, if only because we are as strange and alien to them as they to us.

In a book some years ago I gave several reasons for Soviet bad manners.[3] One is that a lot of Russians don't know any better. Another is that they think that braggadocio will impress their own satellites. Another is that, to

---

[2] The Czars gave us trouble on occasion. Not often is it remembered that the Monroe Doctrine was promulgated partly because Alexander I, the creator of the Holy Alliance, prodded Spain into threats of intervention in the Western Hemisphere, and made mild trouble for the United States elsewhere.

[3] *Behind the Curtain*, p. 341.

keep the world in turmoil so that they can pick up plums that drop, bad manners are often necessary. Still another is that they are uneasy in sophisticated society, make blunders out of inferiority and sensitiveness, and brag and bluster not because they are strong, but because they lack confidence. Khrushchev, while he was in London, made some bitterly anti-British remarks in private. A neutral statesman remonstrated, saying that such wild talk only served to defeat Khrushchev's own ends. Khrushchev replied frankly that he knew this to be right, but couldn't stop himself. He said, "We Russians have lived in a state of siege for a generation and are apt to be afraid and say and do the wrong things."

In fact, although one unmistakable Soviet hallmark is an overriding optimism, based on faith and discipline, fear plays a very definite role in Russian policy—fear of the possibility of dissent at home, fear of further trouble in the satellites, fear for continuity in their leadership, fear that the whole gigantic apparatus of the "first socialist state" will break down, through inherent defects or a process of profound economic failure, and, most important, fear of direct military attack. The United States, let us remember, has been invaded only once in its entire history, during the War of 1812, and then with little damage. But look at Russia and its exposed and vulnerable western frontier! Russia has been invaded from the west fourteen different times in 150 years, and one city, Minsk, has been under foreign occupation 101 times since its foundation.[4] True, the Russians always managed to get rid of the invaders. This, however, took time, lives, and effort, and the Soviet Union doesn't want to have to go through the painful and laborious process ever again. To sum up this point: the Russians keep up the Cold War partly because they fear that we will make it hot.

General Lauris Norstad, the Supreme Allied Commander in Europe, said in June, 1957 that the West now had the capability of destroying "absolutely" the USSR's capacity to make war in "a matter of hours." This statement was made before the USSR fired its first long-range missile and before the Sputniks, and these events may have changed the strategic position considerably. Even so, items like this do not improve Soviet feeling toward the United States. Khrushchev's reply was, "Such unreasonable hotheads [as Norstad] exist, and we must not forget about them. We do not want to be like the lamb who is defenseless against the wolf. . . . We must have teeth . . . so the wolves may lose their skins and maybe even more—their heads."

Meantime, both because their philosophy teaches them to believe it explicitly and because it is seductive propaganda to the less enlightened

[4] John Fischer, *Why They Behave Like Russians*, p. 9.

regions of the world, the Russians say that the reason we, the United States, keep up the Cold War is not merely for political advantage, but for economic gain. Talking to Joseph Alsop of the New York *Herald Tribune*,[5] Khrushchev said, "We believe . . . that the United States is carrying on the material and psychological preparations for a third world war. Perhaps the purpose is to start a European war and to have the peoples of Europe fight each other—something that happened for a period last time, when the United States *made a lot of money.*" (Italics mine.) On another occasion he said that the capitalists do not liquidate the Cold War because it is so "profitable."

The Russians know, profits or not, that what won both World War I and World War II was the weight of the American *industrial* as well as military potential. This is not the only reason for their fixation on industrialization, but it plays a role. They know that what makes the United States strong—stronger than they are—is industry. Therefore they must attempt to overtake the United States in industrial power. Meantime, they seek to give themselves comfort by saying that the United States is "weak," "imperialistic," and "corrupt."

No matter what muscles and sinews the Soviet Union has, as well as new weapons, if war broke out between the United States and Russia tomorrow the United States would probably win, and perhaps win quickly. But this does not mean necessarily that Russia would be *conquered.* It would not be an easy country to occupy, garrison and administer, even after an atomic blitz, and a good many fingers, or even cities, might be burned on our side of the water even before the period of occupation began. Nobody but an idiot can want a war, which means that we ought to eschew idiotic policies.

Examine Russian attitudes further, in the light of American behavior. Suppose, flying over the United States at regular intervals, appeared a series of large balloons carrying photographic and other apparatus for mapping the American terrain, and dropping propaganda material by parachute. We would not like it a bit. There would be a screech of outrage loud enough to rock the Grand Canyon, or silence Niagara. Yet the United States not long ago peppered the Russian air with such balloons.[6] Or suppose Russian military bases should be built up and manned in, let us say, Haiti, Newfoundland,

[5] February 20, 1957.
[6] The Soviet answer was quite characteristic. The Kremlin made a formal protest, put captured balloons on display in Moscow, and, as if to give warning that these objects could not be laughed off or disavowed by the Americans, blandly offered to send them back to the United States, so that public exhibits could be made of them in New York and Washington!

and Hawaii, with massive bombers poised for instant action and aimed at the industrial cities of America. Moreover, suppose that an international pro-Russian military force, trained to a razor's edge and equipped with nuclear weapons, held firm positions across Canada, and constantly held conspicuous maneuvers. We would not like it a bit. We might even find ourselves touchy, exasperated, and afraid.

Bases and NATO are the chief Soviet grievances. Why, the Russians ask, does the United States "encircle" the Soviet Union with bases, from Okinawa to Morocco, from England to the eastern Mediterranean, if not in preparation for attack?[7] It is difficult, if not impossible, to explain the *raison d'être* of our bases without going back to events now largely forgotten. Nobody on the Soviet side has ever been informed that the United States, hoping in good faith for a peaceful world, cut its military establishment to the bone after World War II, and was to a large degree disarmed. Then it discovered that the Soviet Union, while giving lip service to peace, was in fact launching a flagrant policy of political expansion. The Kremlin imposed satellite governments on the peoples of eastern Europe in direct violation of agreements made at Yalta, and, as a matter of sheer common sense, the United States set about defending its position. Russia started the Cold War, not the United States.

Subsequently the free world was subjected to a series of extremely unpleasant shocks and blows, from the coup in Czechoslovakia to the invasion of South Korea. Moreover, it might be pointed out that, until Russia got the atomic bomb in 1949, the United States could have obliterated the Soviet Union overnight, without fear of retaliation, but refrained from doing so. (During this same period, before NATO, it is also true that the Russians could probably have taken western Europe in a walk, but likewise refrained from doing so.)

Also the Russians accuse the United States of hypocrisy little short of monstrous. Americans call themselves "democratic" and "peace-loving" but perpetually launch imperialist adventures, like the recent arms-lift into Jordan. But this was a tit-for-tat riposte to the loading up of Soviet arms in Syria. The Russians ask if, for instance, the United States would possibly permit a Communist revolution to succeed in, let us say, Cuba or Bolivia.

---

[7] Khrushchev in his conversation with the Japanese editor already mentioned said, "If the Americans were to return to you the island of Okinawa, I would approach our government with a proposal to turn the islands of Habomai and Shikotan over to Japan." Russian occupation of these islands has obstructed negotiations for a Russo-Japanese peace treaty. Then: "It is my opinion that you do not press the USA sufficiently to make it return the island of Okinawa."

If, they proceed, the United States would without doubt put down such a business by force of arms or less direct means (as was done in Guatemala), they, the Russians, had an equivalent right to put down an uprising in Hungary which would have installed an anti-Communist regime in Budapest.

As to the situation today, the Russians assert not merely that they believe in and want coexistence, but that it is a feasible proposition, on their terms. As a matter of fact coexistence, which does not necessarily mean co-operation, serves their aims well. They are spectacularly clever operators, and they have a fixed long-range view. They accept and promote the concept of coexistence not merely to avoid or preclude a worsening of relations that might lead to war, but because it gives them convenient room, as well as time, to move around in. One must never forget: *Russian long-range policy is offensive*, even if it forswears direct offensive means.

To prove that coexistence is a correct policy even within orthodox Marxist tenets, Khrushchev goes back to Lenin. Actually, Lenin can be quoted for or against it. His view followed tactical considerations at the time he spoke. Khrushchev, however, insists that, at present, coexistence is not tactical in Soviet foreign policy, but "fundamental." Of course! It removes the danger of war (except by accident) and gives Soviet plans leeway to mature. There is no alternative to coexistence except "the most destructive war in history." Let coexistence be competitive, and let the best man win.

The Soviet line on coexistence poses, it is unnecessary to add, problems of the gravest and most penetrating nature for the United States. It would be unpleasant to have a war, and doubly unpleasant to lose one. But it is also possible to lose a peace.

The best hope for the future is in the realm of cultural and intellectual exchange. Anything in the field of legitimate policy that tells Russia what America is like is to the good. Instead of doing our best to keep Russians out of the country, we should do our utmost to entice them in; the United States is still the best single advertisement for the United States. No doubt, if Soviet tourists should arrive in any number, spies and *agents provocateurs* would be among them; never mind; in time they will be caught. American cultural and scientific missions—also tourists—should, conversely, be urged to go to Russia in great numbers. Anything that lets air in serves our purpose. And we should try to take advantage of the new fermentations going on in the USSR and in particular of the *genuine* desire for peace held indisputably by the rank and file of the Soviet people. Our policy should not be to frighten Russia, or needlessly irritate it. Show the people of the Soviet Union what a supermarket is, let them see clover-leaf highways and housing projects and new machines better than theirs; open their windows, open their eyes and minds. Anything that breaks down Russian provincialism, isolation, blindness, ignorance is useful to American policy. Of course, as coexistence proceeds, the Russians will tend to be more, rather than less, on guard against western penetration and influences, which makes for difficulty. They will feel that they must strengthen their "ideological defenses," as relations with the West improve. No coexistence in the realm *of ideas* is going to be tolerated. All in all the Soviet door is not going to be easy to pry open; the difficulties are gritty and exhausting. But we have little to lose by trying.

Above all, we should try to break down the implanted Russian conviction that the United States is an enemy. The Kremlin almost always seeks to present America as the country par excellence of ruthless capitalist exploitation. The United States is an enemy because it is run by money. Most Russians have utterly no conception of American aims and accomplishments in such fields as social welfare. Nor have they even the remotest comprehension of what democratic governments in Europe, like those in Great Britain or Scandinavia, are doing for their citizens. If you tell a Russian that, almost everywhere in the world, the aim of decent governments is the same, namely the betterment of the people as a whole, it will be quite an eye-opener, even if he does not believe it. Russians have no realization whatever of the spectacular American record in education, labor legislation, social security, participation by the public in "capitalistic" enterprises, equalization of income, housing and pension schemes, health insurance, rent control, old age insurance, child welfare work, federal aid to farmers, regulation of utilities, highway and reclamation work, and scores of similar items. This is why the distribution of publications like *Amerika* in the Soviet Union is so important. (It is also the reason why the Russians, exasperating as always, do their best to keep the circulation of *Amerika* limited, and hedge it in with all manner of restrictions.)

Meantime, a long period of stalemate is before us. It could last forever. Maybe it will. The Russians cannot attack us, for fear that their country and their precious revolution and regime will be destroyed. We cannot attack Russia, without the grave risk that western Europe will be overrun, and the United States itself attacked. The United States should be strong—that goes without saying; it should also be patient, not so touchy as it is, less committed to the all-out Cold War approach, less dogmatic in our assumption that Communism is bound in time to disappear, more aware of the enlivening changes that are without doubt going on in the Soviet Union, more sensitive and sympathetic to liberalizing developments in the satellites, less heavy-handed in the Middle East, more realistic about China, and, above all, not afraid. The Russians are tough, yes, but so can we be tough. But peace or even "nonfriendly coexistence" should rest on understanding and lack of fear as well as on strength and toughness. Above everything, there should be more information and knowledge—of each giant about the other.

Glimpse Concluded

Several chapters in this book carry their own conclusions and I have several times made tentative generalizations on trends.[8] So little remains to be said in final summary. The following factors might be mentioned or reiterated, aside from such obvious items as technological advance, education, and the Sputniks:

First, Khrushchev's Russia is radically different from what preceded it, although basic and essential characteristics of the system remain the same. Momentous and pointed changes have come since the death of Stalin. This served to fling doors violently open, and no one knows what may emerge. Already the rigor mortis characteristic of the previous era has been replaced by something much more dynamic, more fluid and experimental. Russia is, in truth, in full process of evolution, of a very fluctuating sort, which is one reason why forthcoming events are so unpredictable. The pace of events today is inordinately fast.

Second, the regime is, so far as any man can tell, stable, although there may be serious rivalries and dissensions within it. But there are no indications whatever of counterrevolution. Pious wishful thinkers in the State Department and elsewhere seemingly base their policy on the hope that, some bright day, the Soviet Union will conveniently crumble and collapse. This hope is shared by very few, if any, serious observers on the spot in Moscow. One should remember that the Soviet Union has been ruled by one regime for forty years; few, if any, modern dictatorships have lasted so long. It has survived the deaths of both Lenin and Stalin, and is the only totalitarian system to reach a third generation (perhaps "generation" is not quite the correct word) of dictators.

But, *third*, no dictatorship is likely to be eternal, if only because history is based on people. Few dictatorships die a natural death. The death or overthrow of Khrushchev might release unknown disrupting forces. A war might

[8] A reader who happens to pick up this book at this point is cordially invited to glance at Chapter IV above, also Chapter XIX.

conceivably let in enough free air to destroy the Soviet Union. Yet it was born in one war, and survived another. In the *very* long run, the Soviet Union may disintegrate or even collapse if it does not root itself more firmly in the will and desires of the people, for at least two reasons: (1) Even in the most merciless police state, a point may be reached where the cost (in energy, blood, or money) of keeping people permanently suppressed is greater than the return derived; (2) People are, after all, the raw material from which government arises, and sooner or later pressure from them is bound to exert a certain force. The present rulers of the USSR realize this full well, and are far more conscious than Stalin ever was of the necessity not merely to placate the people, but to pull them further into the body of the state.

Fourth, dissent certainly exists in the Soviet Union, and strong fermentations are at work. There is discontent in any jail, but this does not mean that a jailbreak is imminent.

Fifth, what has gone on since Stalin's death cannot be fully understood without grasping that one aim of the regime is to institutionalize itself, that is, re-establish the *party* as the "primary center of power." The yawning vacuum left by Stalin, whose rule was utterly personal as well as all-embracing, had to be filled somehow. First came the experiment with collective leadership. Now Khrushchev is the top totem on the pole, but this does not mean that the principle, at least, of collective leadership has been given up. Khrushchev got rid of Malenkov and company by a skillful manipulation of the Central Committee, and by assembling votes; the procedure would have been very different in Stalin's day. The fact that Molotov, Malenkov, and Kaganovich were not put up for public trial or shot was an exceptionally significant event. If they had been shot, it would have been Stalinism all over again. That they were not shot, or even severely punished, does not prove that the Soviet Union has got around to the western idea of tolerating opposition, but it does demonstrate a profoundly new and important trend. Similarly Zhukov was ousted without being punished at all.

Sixth, it would be nonsensical to call Khrushchev "liberal" in the true sense, but his government is the most temperate the Soviet Union has had since the Revolution. We do not need to repeat countless items in de-Stalinization already mentioned in this book. The most important for the ordinary citizen is the reduction in accent on arbitrary police power and the end of overt terror. There may, of course, be a reversion to terror at almost any time.

Seventh, the main characteristic of the Soviet government, distinguishing it from all other governments in the world, even other dictatorships, is the extreme emphasis on *secrecy*. We should also mention again conformity and uniformity, which secrecy abets, and the stress on *executive* decision. Secrecy is important for another reason; it keeps Soviet adversaries from knowing fully what is going on, and hence makes it difficult to establish effective counter policies.

Eighth, characteristics of the party are changing, and a society based on the party hierarchy is being supplanted by one based in part at least on the new technical elite, the so-called managers. Despite lip service, few citizens pay much attention to the party *as such* any more. I have already mentioned that probably not ten thousand Soviet citizens would give their lives for Karl Marx. What counts is nationalism and the *regime*, which is interlocked with the party but which is quite a different thing. Moreover in the future more power is bound to come to the technical and professional men, many of whom have very little interest in traditional Communist or party principles, if only because they will demand it. This in turn may gradually cause a transformation in the entire structure of government and society. It is possible that the rising technical class may outgrow Communism altogether.

Ninth, we must mention again Soviet relations with the satellites. Is the Soviet empire cracking up? To a certain extent, it has already cracked up. It may be counted on as axiomatic that the Moscow regime will do everything in its power to prevent further defection, and will not give up eastern Europe without a fight, even if it was Khrushchev himself who pulled the cork out of the satellite bottle. But the paradox already alluded to in these pages remains, and is the most grinding problem in external relations that the Kremlin has—how to maintain the substance of Soviet control without making this so conspicuous that resentment on the part of the subject nations will increase, and become unmanageable. Meantime Hungary was a very damaging blow indeed to the Kremlin. All over the world Communists left the party, or were bitterly troubled and disillusioned, and the uncommitted and neutralist nations, which the Russians want to woo and court above all, were profoundly shocked, not merely because of Soviet brutality but because the Russians suppressed a *popular* movement by reactionary means.[9]

Tenth, the Soviet Union certainly wants peace, and considers nuclear war with the United States "unthinkable." But, as explained in passages above, it wants peace on its own terms. (As do we.)

[9] The Yugoslav Communist Milovan Djilas said, and went to jail in Yugoslavia for saying it, "The wound which the Hungarian Revolution inflicted on Communism can never be healed."

Now, *eleventh,* to revert to domestic affairs, the chief Soviet weaknesses in the physical sphere are in agriculture, finance, and housing. Also bureaucratic slipshodness, overlapping, and plain dumb bungling and hidebound rigidities have made the industrial program lag somewhat. The principal aim of the Khrushchev project for decentralizing industry is to increase efficiency. Meantime, the basic wealth of the Soviet regime still comes mostly out of the hide of the peasant, the caste system inflicts painful pressure on the population, and consumer goods are scant. Most citizens live out their lives against a background inexpressibly burdensome, crude, and dreary.

Twelfth, let me put in a final word about culture. The Soviet record in education, particularly scientific education, is striking, and "culture" is talked about without end. But it is a very peculiar kind of culture. The Russians are blind as adders to anything in the realm of culture (except science) that does not suit their own particular ends. Take a list of men who have contributed indispensably to the enlightenment of contemporary mankind, who are household names abroad, or lesser figures whose function it has been to contribute art or enjoyment—the average Soviet citizen will never even have heard of them. Freud, Jung, Croce, Proust, Conrad, Joyce, Yeats, Henry Adams, Thomas Mann, Henry James, Bertrand Russell, Schweitzer, Frank Lloyd Wright, T. S. Eliot, Eugene O'Neill, and countless others who are among the essential creators of our modern intellectual or artistic world are absolutely unknown or are condemned in the Soviet Union. Soviet citizens today, despite their proud emphasis on "culture," simply are not world citizens. On most points they are as uncivilized and unschooled as Bantus in Bechuanaland.

Finally, we must take note for the last time of Russian mixed-upness, turbulence, contradictoriness, and love of mystification. The Soviet Union is a kind of monstrous, seething beehive, out of which almost anything can come—hope, bitterness, faith, ardor, idealism, cynicism, despair. The Russians are both bleak and grandiose; both primitive and ambitious. No people fumble so much as the Russians do; no people are so advanced in one corner of a field, so backward in the next; no people are both so technically proficient and so clumsy; no people are more capable of being, almost at the same time, both exalted and cast down. There are times when the entire country seems to be populated by mad children, or hobgoblins at some obscene circus in a wilderness.

People often say that the Russians are a magnificently human and attractive people under a callous, mendacious, and detestable government. I have said so myself. I like Russians. But, unimportant as the statement is, I for one would willingly die if by so doing I could prevent the export of the Soviet system to, let us say, a country like Denmark. But such statements do not get us very far. It does little good to call names. The gap between Soviet government and Russian people becomes steadily smaller, less pronounced, as the years go by, and we must attempt to deal with Soviet matters as they *are*, not as we would like them to be. The Russians, like the weather, are here to stay—moreover here to stay as extremely serious competitors. Perhaps the two most important things to say are (a) they are strong, not weak; (b) they do not want war. Whether we like it or not it is our duty as a people presumably more secure and adult, as well as free, to try to understand not merely their vagaries but the essentials of their position—to know the full nature of our adversaries, comprehend frankly their massive power, and, if possible, live side by side with them peaceably even if difficulties largely of Russian making appear to be insuperable. This is strictly to American self-interest.

Appendix on Personalities[1]

Aristov, Averky Borisovich. Full member of the Presidium of the Central Committee of the Communist Party, USSR. He corresponds more or less to Suslov as a party specialist, but his activities are more on the domestic side. He has been one of the party secretaries, with interruptions, for a good many years, and deals largely with administrative and personnel matters. Like Kuusinen, he became a full member of the Presidium when Stalin enlarged it in October, 1952; then he was dropped when Stalin died in March, 1953, and came back in June, 1957. The main thing characterizing Aristov is that he represents Siberia, and is symbolic of Khrushchev's attempt to modify the old system of complete concentration of power in Moscow, with Muscovites running everything. Khrushchev, in contrast, has as we know tried to pull in people from everywhere—his own people, of course. Aristov was born in 1903 and spent most of his career in various Siberian posts. When he wears a cap he looks like a good old New York City taxi driver. He has been party secretary at Krasnoyarsk, Chelyabinsk, Sverdlovsk in the Urals, and in particular Khabarovsk near the Pacific. For years he was known as "boss of Siberia."

In 1955 he became chairman of the Foreign Affairs Commission of the Supreme Soviet of the RSFSR, an odd post considering that, so far as is known, he has never been outside Russia except for one brief trip to North Korea.

Belyayev, Nikolai Ilich. Full member of the Presidium. Like Aristov, he has spent much of his career in Siberia, and was party chief for a long period in the Altai region, north of Kazakhstan. Little is known of his origins and he did not reach any position of rank until the 1940's; his specialty, aside from Siberian administration, has been agriculture, particularly grain products. Under Khrushchev, he is deputy chairman of the party bureau dealing with the RSFSR. Late in 1957 he became party boss in Kazakhstan. He has white hair and is a somewhat colorless personality. In November, 1955, he led a Soviet delegation to Bulgaria, on the invitation of the Bulgarian National Assembly. One should always keep in mind the intensity with which the Soviet government seeks to preserve the illusion, to its people, that Russia, China, and the European satellites are true sisters— great islands of "socialism" which must stick together at all costs, and defend themselves against the depredations of the wicked external world. Soviet propagandists love to have it both ways. For years, they boasted that Russia was the only socialist state; now they boast with equal fervor that it is one of many.

Sample of Belyayev's talk:

[1] Also see Chapters VI and VII above.

507

The imperialists are trying to weaken and disunite the camp of socialism, to undermine it. This has been demonstrated by the events in Hungary. The counter-revolutionary uprising in that country was carefully prepared and directed by the imperialist powers. However, the schemes of the imperialists have failed. Events in Hungary have not only failed to produce a victory for the counter-revolution, but have actually made the camp of socialism still more united.

The announcement of the new Eisenhower-Dulles doctrine on the Near and Middle East means that the most powerful imperialist power, the United States, is now coming forward to take the place of the old colonial powers with the object of seizing the positions lost by them and preserving the income and super profits of the oil and other monopolies. . . . Many millions of dollars are being allocated to sugar the pill of this new slavery, this new form of colonial domination of the peoples of the Near and Middle-East.[2]

Once more the sour, wearisome party line!

Benediktov, I. A. Former USSR Minister of State Farms, now Minister of Agriculture for the RSFSR. One of the ablest men in Russia, Benediktov served for a time as ambassador to India. Frequently the Soviet Union picks men with no experience of foreign affairs (as does the United States, for different reasons) and gives them ambassadorial posts abroad, partly because of the shortage of competent men, partly to round out their experience.

Bobrovnikov, N. I. Mayor of Moscow. He took over this post from Mikhail Yasnov, who became for a time chairman of the Council of Ministers of the RSFSR. The mayoralty of Moscow is often an important steppingstone to higher posts. Bobrovnikov, something unusual among Russians, is a very large man physically, and has a lively personality.

Brezhnev, Leonid I. Full member of the Presidium, and one of the most powerful men in Russia. For some years he was boss of Kazakhstan, the largest Soviet republic after the RSFSR. He was, in fact, so closely identified with Kazakh affairs that he was little known in Moscow (except to people at the very top) until 1956. Brezhnev comes from Moldavia near the Rumanian frontier, but is of Russian origin; he was party secretary in Moldavia for some years. His eyebrows are as dark and thick as those of John L. Lewis. Brezhnev has always been primarily a party man, and, except for one brief period in the Defense Ministry, has never held a governmental post. He became an alternate member of the Presidium in February, 1956, when Khrushchev was beginning to reach out for men identified with the Union republics, and a full member in June, 1957. He is reputed to be tough and able. Anybody who ran the immensity of Kazakhstan would have to be. Kazakhstan is landlocked, and it may therefore seem surprising that Brezhnev's other specialty has been, of all things, the Soviet Navy. But the Soviet government always seeks to make its coming men as versatile as possible.

In a recent speech, delivered when he presented the Order of Lenin to Omsk province, Brezhnev mentioned that the 35,500,000 hectares of virgin land now

[2] *Current Digest of the Soviet Press*, February 27, 1957.

being sown to grain in Siberia and northern Kazakhstan constitute a larger area than the total grain-producing regions of nine European countries, including France, Italy, and West Germany. He is full of the usual lip service to socialism:

> If the Soviet Union was able to achieve such successes in a short period of time, it means that our socialist system has every advantage over the capitalist system. This is why we have every reason to say to the gentlemen-bourgeois critics: "Is it not time for you to stop your sinister hollering about our socialist regime? Is it not time for you to look more soberly at the historical facts and consider which system is more progressive, the capitalist or the socialist one?"
>
> Of course, it is difficult for them to understand this, but all honest people on earth can see that history itself long ago passed sentence on the capitalist system, which is rotten to the core.[3]

Ignatov, Nikolai G. Full member of the Presidium, who has been a party secretary in Leningrad, Voronezh, Krasnodar, and Gorky. He has specialized in organizational questions, is a firm Khrushchev supporter, and has been called the principal trouble-shooter in the party. He is a heavy-set, heavy-minded man. Under Stalin he was a candidate member of the Presidium for a brief interval.

Kalnberzin, Yan E. Alternate member of the Presidium since June, 1957. Little is known about him except that he is a Lett, and was party secretary in Riga for some years.

Kirilenko, Andrei P. Alternate member of the Presidium and industrial specialist. He is a veteran organizer who has been party secretary in Sverdlovsk and, before that, in Dnepropetrovsk in the Ukraine. He is Ukrainian.

Kirichenko, Alexei Illarionovich. Full member of the Presidium, boss of the Ukraine, one of Khrushchev's closest associates, and a man of considerable interest both actual and potential. He was born in the Ukraine in 1908, in a village near Poltava. His father was a private in the Czarist Army, and he had little education; he went to work for a living at eleven, and became a railroad worker and mechanic. Then, in the pattern we have seen several times, his latent abilities were recognized by those above him, and he was pulled out of the mass and given special opportunity for education—first in manual training at the Kherson Motor and Tractor Repair School, then as a senior mechanic on several state farms, and finally at an agricultural engineering institute. His two specialties have always been agriculture and transport.

For some years Kirichenko ran Odessa, and rose to be party chief for the whole Ukraine in 1953, in succession to Khrushchev under whom he had served for eleven years; people say that he is the first chief of the Ukrainian party organization in many years who "does not speak Ukrainian with a Russian accent." He has been a deputy to the Soviet of the Union for a long time, and is a member of the Presidium of the Supreme Soviet of the USSR. Kirichenko is a large, heavy, blunt-mannered man with few social or other graces. Although predominantly occupied with Ukrainian affairs, he has, in the stereotyped way, done his duty abroad on several occasions.

[3] *Ibid.*, February 27, 1957.

He led the Russian delegation to the Second Congress of the Rumanian Workers Party in Bucharest, and, along with Suslov, represented the USSR at the last Communist party congress in France. His speeches, except those that deal with strictly Ukrainian matters, sound like those of any other Soviet leader; all could have been mass-produced like sausages or nuts and bolts, and perhaps they are. Sometimes, aside from the usual defiant quality, Kirichenko gives forth a note of wistfulness, almost as if he were a man who had been blackballed from a club. But as a rule he follows the standard pattern:

> During the years of the Soviet regime . . . a mighty Ukraine Socialist power emerged. . . . Cultural work in the Ukraine bears witness to the undeniable fact that precisely under socialism every possibility is created both for an un- precedented growth of the culture of whole nations and for an all-around de- velopment of the creative ability of each individual member of society. . . . [Representatives of] world reaction are bending all their efforts to slander the idea of friendship among peoples and to denigrate the principles of proletarian internationalism. They stop at nothing in their slander.[4]

Korotchenko, Demyan Sergeyevich. Another Ukrainian, and an alternate mem- ber of the Presidium. Briefly under Stalin he was a full member. He was a party secretary in the Ukraine from 1939 to 1947, and the chairman of the Council of Ministers of the Ukrainian SSR for some years after 1947. He is close to Khrushchev. He is about sixty-seven, began life as a manual laborer, and has consider- able prestige as an Old Bolshevik.

Kosygin, Alexei Nikolayevich. Deputy Chairman of the Council of Ministers of the USSR, and an important member of the "technical aristocracy." He was born in 1905, and first became a member of the Council of Ministers when he was only forty-one; when he entered the Presidium under Stalin, he was its youngest man. His career has been full of ups and downs. He was dropped from the Presidium in 1953, and has flitted in and out of various offices; nobody in the Soviet Union is ever sure of a job for long. Kosygin rose from the humblest begin- nings. He was for some years a manual laborer, and then a foreman in a textile plant. He became mayor of Leningrad in 1938, and in quick succession held three important cabinet posts under Stalin—Textiles, Light Industry, and Finance. He was a protégé of Zhdanov's, but somehow managed to survive the purges attending the "Leningrad Case," although his immediate superiors were shot. By this time (1948- 49) he had already served a term as premier of the RSFSR, a post requiring con- siderable organizational capacity, and had become deeply involved in planning. He was a leading executive in the *Gosplan,* and from this perch entered the Presidium again. He is believed to be very close to Khrushchev, and is often talked of as Bul- ganin's successor as prime minister. Kosygin visited Great Britain in 1955—his first trip abroad. All in all, a man to watch.

Kovrigina, Maria D. This lady is Minister of Health. She is a doctor of medicine, and is the only woman in the Soviet Union to have full cabinet rank. (Madame

---

[4] *Ibid.,* May 15, 1957.

Furtseva outranks her in the party hierarchy, but is not a member of the cabinet.) Recently Dr. Kovrigina, an earnest character, visited the United States.

Kozlov, Frol Romanovich. A newcomer, who since June, 1957, has been a full member of the Presidium. Koslov went to work in a textile factory at the age of fifteen, became a leader in the Komsomol organization, and was given advanced education at the Leningrad Polytechnic Institute. He earned a living in a metallurgical factory, and concurrently rose in the party apparatus; he has been party chief in Leningrad since November, 1953, and thus inherits a position once held by such eminent figures as Zinoviev, Kirov, and the celebrated Zhdanov. In 1956 he visited Rumania. He likes to call political opponents "Talmudists." He worked for a time as a subordinate to Malenkov in the Central Committee, and for a time held an important government as well as party post—he was Minister of State Farms, although his career has never had anything to do with agriculture. Then Khrushchev pulled him out of agriculture and assigned him to party work. Lately he became Premier of the RSFSR.

Kuzmin, Iosif Iosifovich. A big white hope, who is the new planning "czar." As with Kosygin, his main line of development has been through the government, not the party. Kuzmin is an engineer by profession, and is not only head of the State Planning Committee but is First Deputy Chairman of the USSR Council of Ministers. He is, it is believed, the only man in Soviet history ever to become a First Deputy Prime Minister without being a member of the party Presidium. How Khrushchev first became struck with him is unknown.

Kuzmin was born in 1910, went to school in Leningrad, and worked there as a machinist. Once more, we have the spectacle of a man rising from the very bottom to the very top. He got a job in an armaments plant in Moscow, became secretary of the factory's party bureau, was picked out as a potential leader by his superiors, and, in the familiar fashion, was given special education and opportunities. He went into agricultural machine building, worked on the old Commissariat of Grain Procurement, became a trade-union executive, and got a foothold in the Gosplan.

Despite all this, Kuzmin was so inconspicuous on the national level that he was not even a delegate to the Twentieth Party Congress in 1956. This Congress, however, gave him a post on the Central Auditing Commission, an important body, and, a little later, he became a member of a special committee of the Supreme Soviet (although he was not a deputy) with the job of "reviewing amendments to the Soviet constitution and other legislation pertaining to the reorganization of industry." Then Khrushchev suddenly picked him out to become chairman of the Gosplan in 1957, one of the key posts in the country. His right-hand man on this is Kosygin. Obviously Kuzmin is a prime example of the new type of Soviet administrator-technician. Associated with him are six chief planners, all of whom are men to watch, not merely because they are the active superintendents of the whole Soviet industrial structure under the decentralization scheme, but because of their possible future importance as technical men who are not exclusively party stalwarts. Their names are perhaps worth mention—Mikhail V. Khrunichev, Vasili P. Zotov, Nikolai I. Strokin (who are all deputy chairmen of the Gosplan), Alexander F. Zasyadko, Yefim S. Novoselov, and Grigori S. Khlamov. All have rank as ministers, and are able men.

Latsis, Vilis. President of the Soviet of Nationalities, one of the two houses of the Supreme Soviet or "parliament" of the USSR. Latsis is a Lett, born near Riga in 1904, the son of a worker, and a writer by profession. While teaching himself to write, he earned a living as a fisherman, lumberjack, stevedore, and ship's fireman, until his first novel, *Son of a Fisherman*, made him a success. He dropped writing for politics in 1940, and became Minister of Home Affairs and then prime minister of Latvia when the USSR annexed the Baltic States. He went back to writing in 1945, and has published several novels, the best known of which is *The Storm*, and has had several plays on the boards. Probably he is the only professional author in the world to be head of a parliament.

Lobanov, Pavel Pavlovich. President of the Soviet of the Union, the second of the two Soviet houses of parliament, whose job corresponds roughly to that of Speaker of the House of Representatives in Washington. Lobanov is an interesting character. An agronomist by profession, he succeeded the celebrated T. D. Lysenko as president of the All-Union Academy of Agricultural Sciences, when Lysenko was de-Stalinized. Born in 1902, Lobanov joined the party in 1927, received advanced training in agricultural economics, and has held all manner of jobs, mostly in the realm of agriculture and genetics. He was Commissar (minister) for Grain and Livestock State Farms as far back as 1938, and also ran animal husbandry. In 1956 he led a Soviet agricultural mission to Ireland. As a deputy to the Supreme Soviet, he represents a constituency in Siberia, and holds the interesting post of Chairman of the Council for the Application of Atomic Energy to Agriculture. Of course men like Latsis and Lobanov are figureheads so far as exerting power in their own jobs is concerned.

Mazurov, Kirill T. Party Secretary of the Belorussian SSR and an alternate member of the Presidium since 1957. He is the first Belorussian to reach Presidium level.

Mukhitdinov, Nuritdin Akramovich. An Uzbek, he is the first representative of one of the "exterior nationalities" to reach the Presidium. Khrushchev brought him in from Tashkent, and made him a candidate member in February, 1956. He became a full member late in 1957, taking Zhukov's place. His specialty is agriculture, particularly cotton, and he is supposed to be one of the most competent administrators in the country. Mukhitdinov was born in 1917 in an obscure Uzbek village, the son of peasants. He joined the Communist party in 1942, and at once rose steeply, becoming party secretary in a town near Samarkand by 1947. Cotton was in a bad way then, and Mukhitdinov aroused national attention by criticizing severely the local authorities. He became chairman of the Uzbek Council of Ministers, i.e., prime minister, in 1951, when he was only thirty-four, and also served as party chairman. Local squabbles forced him out for a period, whereupon he was brought back to power by Khrushchev himself. Subsequently he moved on to Moscow. In 1956 he represented the Soviet Union at the Eighth Congress of the Chinese Communist party in Peking, and is steadily being given more authority. He is a deputy to the Soviet of Nationalities in the USSR, representing the Namangan electoral district, as well as to the Supreme Soviet of the Uzbek SSR; he is a member of the Budget Commission of the Supreme Soviet of the USSR, and holds other honorary posts.

Mzhavanadze, Vasily P., alternate member of the Presidium and party secretary for Georgia. He is the first Georgian to reach national eminence since Beria.

Ponomarev, B. N. Strictly a specialist in party affairs, particularly in regard to relationships with Communist parties abroad. He is a watchdog on the satellites, and usually accompanies Khrushchev on his trips to eastern Europe.

Pospelov, Pyotr Nikolayevich. A candidate member of the Presidium, who is the party theoretician par excellence. Pospelov ranks as an Old Bolshevik, and is an academician and a professor of historical sciences; the most doctrinaire of intellectuals, he looks like a bespectacled ascetic, and has held all manner of important posts. He was editor of *Pravda* for nine years, has been chairman of the Central Committee of the party, no less, and served for a long period as director of the Marx-Lenin Institute.

In these and other capacities, Pospelov had the ticklish job of revising Leninist scripture from time to time, to fit meandering shifts in the party line. He was a member of the editorial board of *Bolshevik*, the theoretical organ of the Central Committee of the party, for no fewer than twenty-three years; this periodical, now known as *Kommunist*, was intermittently purged, and Pospelov, a sinuous character, was the only one of its editors to hold his position from first to last, without interruption. Also he has been head of the chair of party history at the Higher Party School and the Academy of Social Sciences, attached to the Central Committee. He has published about eighty historical works, served for long in the All-Union Society for the Dissemination of Political and Scientific Knowledge, won a Stalin Prize for his share in a history of the Civil War, wrote a standard two-volume work analyzing party theory, and is a member of the editorial board of the Great Soviet Encyclopedia. Four times Pospelov has been chosen to make the address given in Moscow every year to commemorate Lenin's birth. The one in 1951 has been called the "hate America" speech. Pospelov took the line that the United States was the "inspiring agent" of European military intervention against the Soviet Union in 1918-20, and, pulling out an old chestnut, said that American "imperialism" was the principal agency which fostered and reared—Adolf Hitler!

Pospelov was born in 1898 in a town called Konako, now in Kalinin province. He went to school at Tver, began revolutionary activity in his youth, and rose to be secretary of the Tver organization of textile trade unions in 1917. He did "responsible party work" during the October Revolution and the civil war, and then resumed his studies at the Institute of Red Professorship in Moscow. Pospelov has always paid close attention to German and Polish matters, and on several recent occasions has been a member of missions to Warsaw and Berlin. Also, in the interests of the faith, he has visited Bulgaria and Albania. A terrifying man.

Ryzhov, Nikita. Former Minister of Light Industry, now Ambassador to Turkey. His parents were both mill workers, and he himself started work at a loom at the age of seventeen.

Suslov, Mikhail Andreyevich. Full member of the Presidium since 1955. A tall stringy man who wears pince-nez like Molotov, Suslov gives a mixed impression;

he has a sensitive poetic face, but his voice is harsh and his manner sanctimonious, even forbidding. To a degree, he resembles an old-style American missionary trying, in some barbaric place, to convert the stubborn heathen, but is even more of a zealot. Suslov is seldom seen publicly, and has been called the most unpopular man in the Soviet Union.

His special province is international party relations, and he is often described as being an unreconstructed and vigorous Stalinist still, capable of making mischief. Like Shepilov, whom he closely resembles in career, he has always been predominantly a propaganda specialist. He has never held a governmental post. For a time he and Khrushchev were the only members of the party secretariat who were also full members of the Presidium, and Suslov is the senior member of the party secretariat, having served on it since 1947. A good deal of his work has been with the satellites.

Suslov, the son of a peasant, was born in 1902. He came up in the conventional way through the Komsomols, and joined the party in 1921. He went to a special workers' school in Moscow, studied at the Moscow Institute of International Economy, and did postgraduate work at the Communist Academy. There followed organizational and propaganda work in various parts of Russia, and he was charged, in 1944, with the ugly job of "restoring the Soviet regime" in Lithuania. Then, in 1947, he became director of *Agitprop*, and, like Shepilov and Pospelov, was also editor of *Pravda* for a time.

Volin, Anatoli. President of the Supreme Court of the USSR, that is Chief Justice. His prestige as a jurist is high. He is the son of a fisherman who, even as do American boys, studied law at night.

Yelyutin, V. V. All-Union Minister for Higher Education. He is a metallurgist by profession, in his middle fifties. An American publicist who called on him recently described him as "good-looking and vital, energetic and self-confident."

Bibliography

ANTONOV, S. *Poddubki Songs*. Foreign Languages Publishing House, Moscow, 1953.
ARMSTRONG, HAMILTON FISH, editor. *The Foreign Affairs Reader*. Harper & Brothers, New York, 1947.

BAEDEKER, KARL. *Russia, with Teheran, Port Arthur, and Peking*. Leipzig, 1914.
BAILEY, THOMAS A. *America Faces Russia*. Cornell University Press, Ithaca, New York, 1950.
BARGHOORN, FREDERICK, C. *The Soviet Image of the United States*. Harcourt, Brace and Company, New York, 1950.
BARGHOORN, FREDERICK C. *Soviet Russian Nationalism*. Oxford University Press, New York, 1956.
BAUER, RAYMOND A.; INKELES, ALEX; KLUCKHOHN, CLYDE. *How the Soviet System Works*. Harvard University Press, Cambridge, 1956.
BECK, F. and GODIN, W. *Russian Purge and the Extraction of Confession*. The Viking Press, New York, 1951.
BECKER, CARL. *Modern History*. Silver Burdett Company, New York, 1931.
BERLIN, ISAIAH. *Karl Marx*. Oxford University Press, London, 1948.
BEVAN, ANEURIN; STRACHEY, E. J.; STRAUSS, GEORGE. *What We Saw in Russia*. Hogarth Press, London, 1931.
BOORMAN, HOWARD L.; ECKSTEIN, ALEXANDER; MOSELY, PHILIP E.; SCHWARTZ, BENJAMIN. *Moscow-Peking Axis*. Harper & Brothers, New York, 1957.
BULLITT, WILLIAM C. *The Bullitt Mission to Russia*. B. W. Huebsch, New York, 1919.
BULLITT, WILLIAM C. *The Great Globe Itself*. Charles Scribner's Sons, New York, 1946.
BURNS, EMILE, editor. *A Handbook of Marxism*. Victor Gollancz Limited, London, 1935.

CARR, E. H. *The Bolshevik Revolution*, Vols. I-IV. Macmillan and Company Limited, London, 1954.
CARR, E. H. *The Romantic Exiles*. Penguin Books, Harmondsworth, 1933.
CARROLL, WALLACE. *We're in This with Russia*. Houghton Mifflin Company, Boston, 1942.
CARTIER-BRESSON, HENRI. *The People of Moscow*. Thames and Hudson, London, 1955.
CHAMBERLIN, WILLIAM HENRY. *The Russian Enigma*. Charles Scribner's Sons, New York, 1943.

515

CHAMBERLIN, WILLIAM HENRY. *Russia's Iron Age*. Little, Brown, and Company, Boston, 1934.

CHARQUES, R. D. *A Short History of Russia*. E. P. Dutton and Company, Inc., New York, 1956.

CHURCHILL, WINSTON S. *The Aftermath*. Charles Scribner's Sons, New York, 1929.

COATES, W. P. and ZELDA. *Soviets in Central Asia*. Lawrence and Wishart Limited, London, 1951.

CONNOLLY, CYRIL. *The Missing Diplomats*. The Queen Anne Press, London, 1952.

COUNTS, GEORGE S. *The Challenge of Soviet Education*. McGraw-Hill Book Company, Inc., New York, 1957.

CRANKSHAW, EDWARD. *Cracks in the Kremlin Wall*. The Viking Press, New York, 1951.

CRANKSHAW, EDWARD. *Russia and the Russians*. The Viking Press, New York, 1948.

CRANKSHAW, EDWARD. *Russia Without Stalin*. Michael Joseph, London, 1956.

CRONYN, GEORGE W. *A Primer on Communism*. E. P. Dutton and Company, Inc., New York, 1957.

CROSSMAN, RICHARD, M.P., editor. *The God That Failed*. Harper & Brothers, New York.

CURZON, HON. GEORGE N., M.P. *Russia in Central Asia*. Longmans, Green and Company, London, 1889.

DALLIN, DAVID J. *The Changing World of Soviet Russia*. Yale University Press, New Haven, 1956.

DEAN, VERA MICHELES. *The United States and Russia*. Harvard University Press, Cambridge, Massachusetts, 1947.

DEUTSCHER, ISAAC. *Stalin*. Oxford University Press, New York, 1949.

DEWEY, JOHN; BEALS, CARLETON; RUEHLE, OTTO; STOLBERG, BENJAMIN; LAFOLLETTE, SUZANNE. *The Case of Leon Trotsky*. Harper & Brothers, New York, 1937.

DOUGLAS, WILLIAM O. *Russian Journey*. Doubleday and Company, Garden City, New York, 1956.

DRIBERG, TOM. *Guy Burgess—A Portrait with Background*. Weidenfeld and Nicolson, London, 1956.

DUDINTSEV, VLADIMIR. *Not by Bread Alone*. E. P. Dutton and Company, New York, 1957.

DURANTY, WALTER. *Duranty Reports Russia*. The Viking Press, New York, 1934.

DURANTY, WALTER. *The Kremlin and the People*. Reynal and Hitchcock, Inc., New York, 1941.

DURANTY, WALTER. *Stalin & Co*. William Sloane Associates, Inc., New York, 1949.

DURANTY, WALTER. *USSR*. J. B. Lippincott Company, Philadelphia, 1944.

EBON, MARTIN. *Malenkov*. Weidenfeld and Nicolson, London, 1953.

EHRENBURG, ILYA. *The Thaw*. Harvill, London, 1955.

ETHRIDGE, WILLIE SNOW. *Nila* (as told to Willie Snow Ethridge by Nila Magidoff). Simon and Schuster, New York, 1956.

FADEYEV, A. *The Rout*. Foreign Languages Publishing House, Moscow.

FAINSOD, MERLE. *How Russia Is Ruled*. Harvard University Press, Cambridge, 1953.

FARSON, NEGLEY. *A Mirror for Narcissus.* Doubleday and Company, Garden City, New York, 1957.

FISCHER, JOHN. *Why They Behave Like Russians.* Harper & Brothers, New York, 1947.

FISCHER, LOUIS. *Russia Revisited.* Doubleday and Company, Garden City, New York, 1957.

FISCHER, MARKOOSHA. *My Life in Russia.* Harper & Brothers, New York, 1944.

GOODFRIEND, ARTHUR. *If You Were Born in Russia.* Farrar, Straus and Company, New York, 1950.

GORDEY, MICHEL. *Visa to Moscow.* Alfred A. Knopf, New York, 1952.

GRANIN, D. *Those Who Seek.* Foreign Languages Publishing House, Moscow.

HAMILTON, G. H. *The Art and Architecture of Russia.* Penguin Books, Baltimore, 1954.

HAZARD, JOHN N. *The Soviet System of Government.* University of Chicago Press, Chicago, 1957.

HIGGINS, MARGUERITE. *Red Plush and Black Bread.* Doubleday and Company, Garden City, New York, 1955.

History of the Civil War in the U.S.S.R. Co op Publishing Society of Foreign Workers in the U.S.S.R., Moscow.

History of the Communist Party of the Soviet Union. Foreign Languages Publishing House, Moscow, 1939.

HUGHES, LANGSTON. *I Wonder As I Wander.* Rinehart and Company, Inc., New York, 1956.

HUNT, R. N. CAREW. *Marxism Past and Present.* Geoffrey Bles, London, 1954.

ILIN, M. *New Russia's Primer.* Houghton Mifflin Company, Boston, 1931.

KAZAKEVICH, E. *Heart of a Friend.* Foreign Languages Publishing House, Moscow.

KELLY, MARIE NOËLE. *Mirror to Russia.* Country Life Limited, London, 1952.

KENNAN, GEORGE F. *Russia Leaves the War.* Princeton University Press, Princeton, 1956.

KETCHUM, RICHARD M., editor. *What Is Communism?* E. P. Dutton and Company, Inc., New York, 1955.

KIRK, LYDIA. *Postmarked Moscow.* Charles Scribner's Sons, New York, 1954.

KOESTLER, ARTHUR. *Arrow in the Blue.* The Macmillan Company, New York, 1952.

KOESTLER, ARTHUR. *The Invisible Writing.* The Beacon Press, Boston, 1954.

KOESTLER, ARTHUR. *The Yogi and the Commissar.* The Macmillan Company, New York, 1946.

KOLARZ, WALTER. *Russia and Her Colonies.* Frederick A. Praeger, New York, 1952.

KOSMODEMYANSKAYA, L. *The Story of Zoya and Shura.* Foreign Languages Publishing House, Moscow, 1953.

KRAVCHENKO, VICTOR. *I Chose Freedom.* Charles Scribner's Sons, New York, 1946.

KRIVITSKY, W. G. *In Stalin's Secret Service.* Harper & Brothers, New York, 1939.

KVESELAVA, M., editor. *Anthology of Georgian Poetry.* State Publishing House, Tbilisi, 1948.

KULSKI, W. W. *The Soviet Regime*. Syracuse University Press, Syracuse, 1956.

LASKI, HAROLD J. *Communism*. Williams and Norgate Limited, London, 1927.
LAUTERBACH, RICHARD E. *These Are the Russians*. Harper & Brothers, New York, 1944.
LAUTERBACH, RICHARD E. *Through Russia's Back Door*. Harper & Brothers, New York, 1946.
LEE, IVY. *USSR—A World Enigma*. Ernest Benn Limited, London, 1927.
LENIN, V. I. *Selected Works*, Vols. I-XII. Co-operative Publishing Society of Foreign Workers in the U.S.S.R., Moscow-Leningrad, 1934.
LIDDELL HART, B. H., editor. *The Red Army*. Harcourt, Brace and Company, New York, 1956.
LITTLEPAGE, JOHN D. and BESS, DEMAREE. *In Search of Soviet Gold*. Harcourt, Brace and Company, New York, 1937.
LOCKHART, R. H. BRUCE. *Memoirs of a British Agent*. Putnam, London, 1932.
LVOV, ANOKHIN B. *Galina Ulanova*. Foreign Languages Publishing House, Moscow, 1956.

MACDUFFIE, MARSHALL. *The Red Carpet*. W. W. Norton and Company, Inc., New York, 1955.
MAKEEV, NICHOLAS and O'HARA, VALENTINE. *Russia*. Ernest Benn Limited, London, 1925.
MARTIN, JOHN STUART. *A Picture History of Russia*. Crown Publishers, Inc., New York, 1956.
MARX, KARL. *Capital*. The Modern Library, New York, 1932.
MARX, KARL and ENGELS, FRIEDRICH. *The Russian Menace to Europe*. The Free Press, Glencoe, Ill., 1952.
MASARYK, THOMAS G. *The Spirit of Russia*. The Macmillan Company, New York, 1919.
MAYNARD, SIR JOHN. *Russia in Flux*. The Macmillan Company, New York, 1948.
MEAD, MARGARET. *Soviet Attitudes Toward Authority*. Tavistock Publications Limited, London, 1955.
MENON, K. P. S. *Delhi-Chungking*. Oxford University Press, London, 1947.
MILLER, JACOB. *Soviet Russia*. Hutchinson's University Library, London, 1955.
MIRSKY, D. S. *A History of Russian Literature*. Alfred A. Knopf, New York, 1955.
MOORE, BARRINGTON, JR. *Soviet Politics—The Dilemma of Power*. Harvard University Press, Cambridge, 1956.
Moscow. Foreign Languages Publishing House, Moscow, 1955.

OSBORN, R. *Freud and Marx*. Victor Gollancz Limited, London, 1937.

PANOVA, VERA. *Looking Ahead*. Foreign Languages Publishing House, Moscow.
PARES, SIR BERNARD. *A History of Russia*. Jonathan Cape, London, 1926.
PARKES, HENRY BAMFORD. *Marxism, an Autopsy*. Houghton Mifflin Company, Boston, 1939.

PETROV, VLADIMIR and EVDOKIA. *Empire of Fear.* Frederick A. Praeger, New York, 1956.
PETROV, VLADIMIR. *Soviet Gold.* Farrar, Straus and Company, New York, 1949.
Pocket Guide to the Soviet Union. Issued by Intourist Vneshtorgisdat, Moscow and Leningrad, 1932.
POLEVOY, B. *A Story about a Real Man.* Foreign Languages Publishing House, Moscow, 1952.

REED, JOHN. *Ten Days That Shook the World.* The Modern Library, New York, 1935.
Report of the Royal Commission on Espionage. Sydney, Australia, 1955.
RICE, TAMARA TALBOT. *Russian Art.* Pelican Books, West Drayton, Middlesex, 1949.
ROBERTS, HENRY L. *Russia and America.* Harper & Brothers, New York, 1956.
ROMANOVA, E., editor. *This Is America. Stories.* Foreign Languages Publishing House, Moscow, 1951.
RUSSELL, BERTRAND. *Freedom versus Organization.* W. W. Norton and Company, Inc., New York, 1934.

SALISBURY, HARRISON E. *American in Russia.* Harper & Brothers, New York, 1955.
SCHUMAN, FREDERICK L. *Russia Since 1917.* Alfred A. Knopf, New York, 1957.
SCHWARTZ, HARRY *Russia's Soviet Economy.* Prentice-Hall, Inc., New York, 1954.
SETHE, PAUL. *A Short History of Russia.* Gateway Editions, Inc., Chicago, 1956.
SETON-WATSON, HUGH. *From Lenin to Malenkov.* Frederick A. Praeger, New York, 1953.
SHABAD, THEODORE. *Geography of the USSR.* Columbia University Press, New York, 1951.
SHUB, BORIS and QUINT, BERNARD. *Since Stalin.* Swen Publications Company, Inc., New York, 1951
SHUB, DAVID. *Lenin.* Doubleday and Company, New York, 1948.
SIMMONS, ERNEST J., editor. *Continuity and Change in Russian and Soviet Thought.* Harvard University Press, Cambridge, Mass., 1955.
SKOSYREV, P. *Soviet Turkmenistan.* Foreign Languages Publishing House, Moscow, 1956.
SMITH, WALTER BEDELL. *My Three Years in Moscow.* J. P. Lippincott Company, Philadelphia, 1950.
SNOW, EDGAR. *Pattern of Soviet Power.* Random House, New York, 1945.
SOBKO, VADIM. *Guarantee of Peace.* Foreign Languages Publishing House, Moscow, 1951.
SPRIGGE, C. J. S. *Karl Marx.* Duckworth, London, 1938.
STALIN, JOSEPH. *Leninism,* Vols. I and II. Co-operative Publishing Society of Foreign Workers in the U.S.S.R., Moscow, Leningrad, 1934.
STANISLAVSKY, KONSTANTIN. *My Life in Art.* Meridian Books, New York, 1956.
STEINBECK, JOHN. *A Russian Journal.* The Viking Press, New York, 1948.
STEVENS, LESLIE C. *Life in Russia.* Longmans, Green and Company, London, 1954.
STIPP, JOHN L., editor. *Soviet Russia Today.* Harper & Brothers, New York, 1956.
SULZBERGER, C. L. *The Big Thaw.* Harper & Brothers, New York, 1956.

THOMPSON, DOROTHY. *The New Russia.* Henry Holt and Company, New York, 1928.
TREVIRANUS, G. R. *Revolutions in Russia.* Harper & Brothers, New York, 1944.
TROTSKY, LEON. *The History of the Russian Revolution.* The University of Michigan Press, Ann Arbor, 1955.
TROTSKY, LEON. *The Living Thoughts of Karl Marx.* David McKay Company, Philadelphia, 1939.
TROTSKY, LEON. *My Life.* Charles Scribner's Sons, New York, 1930.
TROTSKY, LEON. *The Revolution Betrayed.* Doubleday, Doran and Company, Garden City, New York, 1937.

VON ECKARDT, HANS. *Ivan the Terrible.* Alfred A. Knopf, New York, 1949.
VON RAUCH, GEORG. *A History of Soviet Russia.* Frederick A. Praeger, New York, 1957.
VOYCE, ARTHUR. *The Moscow Kremlin.* University of California Press, Berkeley and Los Angeles, 1954.

WELLS, H. G. *Russia in the Shadows.* Hodder and Stoughton Limited, London.
WHITE, W. L. *Report on the Russians.* Harcourt, Brace and Company, New York, 1945.
WILLIAMS, ALBERT RHYS. *The Soviets.* Harcourt, Brace and Company, 1937.
WILSON, EDMUND. *Red, Black, Blonde and Olive.* Oxford University Press, New York, 1956.
WILSON, EDMUND. *To the Finland Station.* Doubleday and Company, Garden City, New York, 1955.
WILSON, MITCHELL. *Live with Lightning.* Little, Brown and Company, Boston, 1949.
WINTER, NEVIN O. *The Russian Empire of To-day and Yesterday.* L. C. Page and Company, Boston, 1913.
WOLFE, BERTRAM D. *Khrushchev and Stalin's Ghost.* Frederick A. Praeger, New York, 1957.
WOLFE, BERTRAM D. *Three Who Made a Revolution.* Beacon Press, Boston, 1948.
WOOD, JUNIUS B. *Incredible Siberia.* Lincoln MacVeagh, The Dial Press, New York, 1928.

YOUNG, GORDON. *Stalin's Heirs.* Derek Verschoyle, London, 1953.

ZINNER, PAUL E., editor. *National Communism and Popular Revolt in Eastern Europe.* Columbia University Press, New York, 1956.

Among standard works of reference I used the *World Almanac,* the *Information Please Almanac,* the *Statesman's Year-Book, The Home Book of Quotations,* edited by Burton Stevenson, *Political Handbook of the World* (published by the Council on Foreign Relations), W. L. Langer's *Encyclopaedia of World History,* and the *Encyclopaedia Britannica.*

Notes, Names, and Sources

First I want to thank several members of the staff of *Collier's Magazine*, now defunct, who first suggested this Russian assignment and made it possible for me to take the trip—Paul C. Smith, Ken McArdle, and Theodore H. White. Mr. White provided much stout and discerning counsel. Similarly my cordial thanks are due to Gardner Cowles, Dan Mich, and William Attwood of *Look*, which valiantly took over the *Collier's* commitment, and printed a fourteen-thousand-word article on Russia (April 2, 1957) soon after my return. Two chapters of the present book have appeared in condensed form in *Harper's Magazine*, and I would like to express my appreciation to John Fischer, Editor-in-Chief of *Harper's* and members of his staff. Also I want to thank Hobart Lewis of *Reader's Digest*, which gave hospitality to another article. Finally in this general realm I must, as always, render abundant thanks to my publisher, Cass Canfield, chairman of the executive committee of Harper & Brothers, whose steady patience, encouragement, and editorial acumen helped me without end. Some authors are lucky in their publishers.

Theodore Shabad, author of *Geography of the USSR* and a member of the staff of the *New York Times*, read with care and discrimination my entire manuscript, and put me right on innumerable details not merely about Russian geography, but Russian nomenclature, orthography, and political and historical matters. But, if any errors remain, they are my fault, not Mr. Shabad's. My best thanks to him. The whole manuscript was also read, to my substantial benefit, by my friend Alexander Lindey, attorney-at-law.

I have dozens of times in the course of this long book cited or quoted from the *Current Digest of the Soviet Press*, published weekly in New York by the Joint Committee on Slavic Studies. I would like to express grateful acknowledgment to its editor, Leo Gruliow, for permission to use material from his admirable magazine.

A good many friends and acquaintances in New York and Washington gave us the benefit of their knowledge, wisdom, and discernment about Soviet affairs before we set out for Moscow: some did so again on our return. In particular I want to thank the following, whom I list at random: Professor Roman Jacobson of Harvard University, distinguished authority on Slavonic languages; Dr. Richard E. Shope of the Rockefeller Institute for Medical Research, who made available to me a memorandum of great interest; Dean Acheson, former Secretary of State; Joseph Barnes, publisher, author, and former correspondent in Moscow of the New York *Herald Tribune*; Hamilton Fish Armstrong, editor of *Foreign Affairs*; Dr. Philip E. Mosely, former director of the Russian Institute of Columbia University and subsequently Director of Studies at the Council on Foreign Relations, New York; Marshall Mac-

Duffie, author and attorney, whom I have several times cited in these pages; Alfred H. Barr, Jr., Director of Collections of the Museum of Modern Art, New York, who was my indispensable guide on matters having to do with art; Mr. and Mrs. Faubion Bowers; my good friend Alexander Liberman, Art Director of the Condé Nast Publications, and Mrs. Liberman; Miss Helen Stevenson (before she became Mrs. Robert Meyner) and Miss Colette Schwartzenbach; George F. Kennan, former American Ambassador to the Soviet Union; Hanson W. Baldwin, Harrison E. Salisbury, Harry Schwartz, and Clifton Daniel of the *New York Times*; Morris Ernst, New York attorney, author, and stimulator-at-large; several members of the State Department; and above all William Benton, former Assistant Secretary of State and Senator from Connecticut, who is publisher of the *Encyclopaedia Britannica*. Mr. Benton took exhaustive notes during his recent trip to the Soviet Union, and drew up memoranda of unique interest and value, all of which he generously made available to me.

In London we had the benefit of good talks with the Rt. Hon. Hugh Gaitskell, M.P., leader of the Labour Party and former Chancellor of the Exchequer; David Astor, Lajos Lederer, and other friends on the *Observer*; Sir Isaiah Berlin, who told us much in brief compass; Barbara Ward Jackson; Kingsley Martin and R. H. S. Crossman, M.P., of the *New Statesman*; Her Excellency Madame Vidaya Lakshmi Pandit, the Indian Ambassador; Edward Crankshaw, one of the best-informed of contemporary observers of the Soviet scene; Iverach MacDonald, foreign editor of the *Times*; my old friend and colleague Louis Fischer; and various members of the British Foreign Office, who, I imagine, will prefer not to be named. In particular I want to thank Hamish Hamilton, my London publisher, and Baroness Moura Budberg, with whom my friendship, always to be cherished, goes back many years.

As to people in Moscow and elsewhere in the Soviet Union, I prefer not to give any names of Russians other than those already mentioned in the text. Among visitors we profited from the conversation of J. B. Scott, of Crompton Parkinson, Ltd., London; Samuel Rosen, M.D., the well-known New York ear specialist; J. S. Seidman of Seidman and Seidman, certified public accountants; Dan Weiner, who was doing a series of photographs for *Fortune Magazine*; and Miss Shelley Rohde of the London *Daily Express*. Then I must mention that David Douglas Duncan, one of the most brilliant and distinguished of American photographers, was our day-by-day colleague and companion in Moscow; we were fortunate to have the pleasure and profit of his company. Amiable hours spent in the Hotel National and elsewhere are not to be forgotten.

Finally I must mention with appropriate as well as profound thanks my wife, Jane Perry Gunther. All I need say is that without her neither trip nor book would have been possible.

*

Without being too hard-and-fast or pedantic about it I have tried to include footnotes in the text identifying all quotations or citations of importance. If I have neglected any acknowledgment of sources, I am sorry. Following are additional attributions, notes, and names.

NOTES, NAMES, AND SOURCES

523

Foreword

The Milton quotation appears in G. H. Hamilton's *The Art and Architecture of Russia*. I found the Churchill quotation in Schuman, cited in the bibliography, p. 352, a book from which I have learned much; it is particularly useful in the field of Soviet foreign relations. My statement that the Soviet Union graduates four times more doctors of medicine than does the United States comes from a good American authority, but has been disputed. Mark George Field says in a recent issue of *Look* that the correct ratio is 2.35 to one. Statistics about champagne are from the *Current Digest of the Soviet Press*, hereafter to be called *C.D.*, March 5, 1957. Incidentally Russia produced 203 billion cigarettes last year, about half of American production. The claim that the USSR has more university students than all of western Europe was made by M. A. Suslov in his speech commemorating the thirty-ninth anniversary of the Revolution, November 7, 1956, quoted in *C.D.* Details about the H-bomb and industrial use of the atom may be found in *Fortune*, February, 1957. Four valuable articles appeared in this issue, "The Condition of Communism" by Emmet Hughes, "The Crisis of Soviet Capitalism" by Gilbert Burck and Sanford S. Parker, "Russia: the Power and the People," and "How Good Is Soviet Science?," together with other material including some magnificent photographs by Dan Weiner. Several details about the Sputnik are from William J. Jorden in the *New York Times*, October 5, 1957, and November 24, 1957.

Chapter I

The quotation from Anne O'Hare McCormick is from *Harper's Magazine*, May, 1946. The observation that it takes the sun eleven hours to cross the USSR is from an editorial in *Life*, March 29, 1943. Wolfe, *Three Who Made a Revolution*, p. 12, mentions that European Russia is bigger than all the rest of Europe. The item about Edmonton is from the *World Geo-Graphic Atlas*. Stevens, cited in the bibliography, (p. 372) mentions that Asia begins at the Volga, as do several other writers. Figures about navigability of rivers are from Hanson W. Baldwin in the *New York Times*, March 26, 1956. I mentioned in news stories written for the Chicago *Daily News* as far back as 1928 that everything decorative has disappeared from the Soviet Union and that life is stripped to the very bone—also that there are seldom interruptions during an interview. Details of tourist traffic are from an early issue of *USSR*. The number of pianos produced in the Soviet last year is from *C.D.*, March 6, 1957. Gordey, p. 28, mentions that three traffic violations are the lifetime quota. Mr. Justice Douglas (*Russian Journey*, p. 8) has sensible things to say about interpreters. Louis Fischer in *Russia Revisited*, p. 115, says that the real reason for the Soviet Union's inveterate hatred of the West is fear of the "contagion of freedom." Also see Deutscher, cited in the text. Several writers mention the Soviet tendency to ambivalent thinking. I want to thank the amiable and efficient Gabriel Reiner of the Cosmos Travel Bureau in New York City for help in getting us our visas and arranging transportation.

Chapter II

It never occurred to me that Moscow could be as far east as Jerusalem until I saw this in Winter's *The Russian Empire of To-day and Yesterday*, p. 369. This is an old book still of substantial value, in which I have taken many soundings. Moscow was called "an inland Constantinople" by Lord Curzon back in the 1880's. The quotation about the Kremlin is from Lauterbach, *These Are the Russians*, p. 26. For a quick résumé of the history of Moscow see *Time*, September 15, 1947; the Pushkin quotation is from this. Figures on book publishing and other details are from the guidebook *Moscow*, a guide inadequate in the extreme but the only contemporary one available. Statistics on telegrams and wine come from *Sovetskaya Rossiya*, January 3, 1957, quoted in *C.D.* For scientific matters see *USSR*, Nos. 1 and 5, and *Fortune*, February, 1957. Maynard mentions the analogy between the exposed bodies of Lenin and Stalin and those of early Christian saints. The best description I have read of the jewels and works of art in the Kremlin Museum is in Kelly, and Stevens, as always, is an observant, sensitive, and penetrating guide. Morris Ernst, the New York attorney, suggested several details in this chapter, as did William Attwood, National Affairs Editor of *Look*. *Moscow*, p. 140, talks about tree planting and takes a different view from mine. Alec Horsley in *Russian Journey*, a useful small pamphlet describing a visit to Russia by a British religious delegation in 1954, has some illuminating passages. Literary associations of sites in Moscow are from *Moscow*. For housing see William J. Jorden in the *New York Times*, September 11, 1956. Gordey, *op. cit.*, mentions that you are not allowed to throw cigarette stubs on the street. The item that the battle of Kharkov cost more lives than American casualties in the war against Japan is from Edgar Snow, *Stalin Must Have Peace*.

Chapter III

For more on Glavlit, see Bedell Smith, p. 293. MacDuffie mentions that it is impossible to lose anything in the USSR. B. J. Cutler surveys the Barzov case in the New York *Herald Tribune*, May 16, 1957. American correspondents are subjected to intermittent running attack by the Moscow press; a conspicuously virulent example of this appears in *Komsomolskaya Pravda*, December 21, 1956, translated by *C.D.*, January 30, 1957. The photograph of a Negro and a white girl in enthusiastic embrace appeared in *Soviet Woman*, August, 1956. Items about per capita alcohol consumption are from *C.D.*, April 10, 1956. I want to thank warmly all the American and British resident correspondents in Moscow, who shared their wisdom with us most generously; never in any city have I met a more distinguished and alert as well as friendly group. It is invidious to mention some and not others, since all were without exception helpful, but I cannot refrain from acknowledging specifically our debt to Henry Shapiro (United Press), Irving Levine (NBC), Daniel Schorr (CBS), Edmund Stevens (*Look*), and Welles Hangen (formerly the *New York Times*). Members of the diplomatic corps were also exceptionally hospitable, and we had talks, one or several, with the American,

British, Canadian, Indian, French, Dutch, Swedish, Sudanese, Egyptian, Turkish, Afghan, Italian, Austrian, Norwegian, Yugoslav, and Bulgarian ambassadors, as well as the Belgian, Polish, Israeli and Greek chargés d'affaires. Above all I want to thank cordially Charles E. Bohlen, the American Ambassador, and the well-informed members of his staff.

Chapter IV

President Eisenhower's statement quoted at the head of chapter was made at a press conference and was printed in the *New York Times*, January 24, 1957. An admirable account of Moscow attitudes today is "Russia Revisited—Moscow Dialogues, 1956" by Philip Mosely, *Foreign Affairs*, October, 1956. The item about Harlow H. Curtice's brother is from *Time*, October 8, 1956. Khrushchev's statement that Americans have "freedom to die" is from his interview with a Japanese journalist, several times mentioned in the text and published in *C.D.*, August 7, 1957. Ignazio Silone in *The God That Failed* (p. 99) accounts for Russian willingness to make sacrifices by the suggestive theory that such sacrifices are personal contributions to "the price of collective redemption." Details about Soviet broadcasts are from General Alfred M. Gruenther, former Supreme Commander of NATO, *New York Herald Tribune*, April 10, 1957. That propaganda broadcasts even reach Eskimos is from "Soviet Monopoly of Northern Canadian Air," London *Times*, August 10, 1957. The quotations from the religious group in Ruthenia are from *C.D.*, as is the remark by the writer Zaslavsky.

Chapter V

By far the best guide to party and governmental structure is Fainsod. Harrison Salisbury discussed possible threats to the Khrushchev leadership a few weeks before the June, 1957 coup, a remarkable example of journalistic prescience, in the *New York Times*, May 12, 1957. The Khrushchev-Voroshilov interchange is from the *New York Times*, November 19, 1956. The anecdote about Voroshilov and Lenin's works comes from William Benton, publisher of the *Encyclopaedia Britannica* and former Senator from Connecticut.

Chapter VI

Both Marguerite Higgins' "The People's Mr. Khrushchev," New York *Herald Tribune*, August 19, 1957, and Stewart Alsop's "Khrushchev Gets Tough," New York *Herald Tribune*, September 22, 1957, mention that Khrushchev's chief quality is that he "genuinely believes in the Marxist doctrine." *Time*, July 22, 1957, mentions that Stalin ruled through a private secretariat, not merely the police. Crankshaw (*Russia and the Russians*, p. 132) makes the same point. Khrushchev's remarks about having worked at capitalist enterprises are from *C.D.*, January 9, 1957. For Khrushchev's role in the Ukraine purges and much other discerning elucidation see Isaac Deutscher, London *Times*, July 11, 1957. Marshal MacDuffie, the perspicacious New York attorney who has seen Khrushchev more often than any nonofficial American and who misses nothing, once asked Khrushchev what exact color his eyes were. He did not get a satisfactory reply. Mrs. Eleanor Roosevelt, characterizing Khrushchev after her interview with him late in 1957, believes that his outstanding characteristic is that he is a peasant. Maynard, p. 20, mentions beards. I did not know that Lenin was clean-shaven when he arrived in Russia in 1917 until I came across this item in Schuman, p. 91. My friend Daniel Schorr was the journalist who had the colloquy with Marshal Bulganin about extension of his stay in Moscow. Mr. Schorr stayed. For Malenkov, Yezhov and the Leningrad affair see Harry Schwartz in the New York Times, October 12, 1952 and July 7, 1957. The Malenkov quotation about responsibility is from Time, April 16, 1956; also see "Stalin's Sinister First Lieutenant" by Edgar Snow, Saturday Evening Post, May 17, 1952. The quotation from Shepilov is from the Sixth Review of USIA operations, January 1–June 30, 1956. Some details about Zhukov's career are from a personality sketch in the New York Times, July 5, 1957. Lauterbach, These Are the Russians, has much interesting material on Zhukov. The Eisenhower quotation about Zhukov is from the New York Times, February 2, 1957. Sources for Marshal Malinovsky are the New York Times, October 27, 1957, and the New York Herald Tribune, October 27 and October 29, 1957.

Chapter VII

For much biographical material here and in the "Appendix on Personalities" I am indebted to a confidential official source. Also several piquant details come from the table talk of a particularly discerning member of the diplomatic corps in Moscow. The Russians often call their old leaders "demigods"; see the article in the Encyclopaedia Britannica on Peter I. For Mikoyan in Baku see Duranty (Stalin & Co. pp. 163-5); this also has interesting material on Shvernik, Voroshilov, and Kosygin. Duranty, out of fashion in his later years, was one of the grandest reporters on things Russian who ever lived; his contribution to the understanding of the Soviet Union in its formative years was inestimable. He could be irreverent, but he was a superb realist. Details about Matskevich and Yelyutin are from William Benton, who had long talks with both. USSR (September, 1956) is my source for Latsis. For terror and forced labor any amount of documentation is available. See particularly William Henry Chamberlin's "The Evolution of Soviet Terrorism," Foreign Affairs, October, 1934, and "The Truth About Soviet Russia's Fourteen Million Slaves" by Max Eastman, Reader's Digest, April, 1947. For the traitor Malinovsky see Shub, p. 112. That a Ministry of State Security was established as early as 1811 is from Charques, p. 154. Winter (p. 438) mentions that there was a double police system under the Czars. I have paraphrased several sentences in this chapter from my Inside Europe.

Chapter VIII

Basic sources for historical matters are Pares, Maynard, Winter (for the perspective of former days), and Charques, whose book is the best brief history of Russia I have read. Several picturesque details about early history are on the authority of Winter. I have also drawn on Langer, Martin, and the Encyclopaedia Britannica. The quotation from Marx is from his essay on India, which may be found in Burns, A Handbook of Marxism, p. 194. A penetrating description of the influence of Byzantium on Russian affairs is "Russia's Byzantine Heritage," by A. J. Toynbee, an article in Horizon. "Great gatherer of the Russian land" comes from Voyce,

p. 15. The phrase "Wild East of Europe" is from H. G. Wells. Herzen invented the term "baptized property" (Becker, p. 466). The item about 300,000 serfs is from Charques, p. 140, who also (p. 157) mentions analogies between Alexander I and Stalin. The episode about six thousand strokes of the rod is from Bertrand Russell's *Freedom versus Organization*, p. 37. Kelly, p. 173, quotes the Marquis de Custine about Nicholas I's extravagances. For Marx, Berlin is indispensable as well as brilliant, and Sprigge very useful; also see Wilson's *To the Finland Station*, one of the best studies of early socialism ever written. My analysis of Marxist theory closely follows Becker. For Marx on the French, Germans, and Jews, see Parkes, pp. 263-4. Wilson is particularly interesting (p. 397) on Marx and the Jews; also the fact that Marx was never personally interested in economic gain. Schuman (p. 19) quotes Marx as saying he was glad that he was "not a Marxist" when dogmatic excesses by his disciples disappointed him; also Schuman notes that Marx might well be horrified by what is going on in the Soviet Union today, a point of view reached independently by me. Shub discusses the evolution whereby early revolutionary thought became socialist (pp. 12-19). Max Lerner once wrote of Lenin in the *New Republic* (August 30, 1939), "There is probably nothing in the history of political thought that equals in dramatic power Lenin's achievement in linking in his own life the analysis and enactment of revolution." For the origin of the name "Lenin" see Bertram Wolfe, *op cit.*, an interesting footnote on p. 153. For some of Lenin's personality traits see *USSR*, No. 1. The Gorky quotations are from Wilson, pp. 383 and 451. That 7,300 editions of Lenin's works have been published to date is from *C.D.*, May 29, 1957. The phrase "greatest event in history since the reformation" is from Harold Laski, *Communism*, p. 45. That four-fifths of Red Army officers were former Czarist officers is from Liddell Hart, p. 27. The quotations at the end of the section on Lenin are from Maynard, p. xii, and from Vice Admiral Leslie C. Stevens, "The Russian People," *Atlantic Monthly*, May, 1952, an extraordinarily illuminating and useful article, as is his "The Russian Doctrine," which appeared in the same magazine the month following. The interviewer to whom Stalin spoke about human will was the late Walter Duranty.

Chapter IX

Some of my geographical material comes from Shabad, the standard text. For literary associations I have used Mirsky. The Great Northern Sea Route is described in the Moscow *News*, December 5, 1956. For the Arctic in general see Bruce Hopper, "The Soviet Conquest of the Far North," *Foreign Affairs*, April, 1936. Complaints in Komi are from *USSR*, No. 11. Protests made by the Bashkir deputy are from *C.D.*, June 26, 1957. The item that Zhdanov was party boss in Gorky for twelve years before spending the same time in the equivalent job in Leningrad is from Duranty, *op. cit.*, p. 149. The London *Times* (July 12, 1957) mentions the British expert who built the arms factory at Tula for Peter the Great. The item about wrist watches is from *C.D.*, January 30, 1957. For several details about Siberia in the old days I am indebted to that splendid old reporter-bulldog, the late Junius B. Wood of the Chicago *Daily News*. *USSR* (No. 7) mentions town "warmings" in Siberia. Movement of workers to Siberia is analyzed by Harry Schwartz, *New York Times*, April 8, 1956. Lauterbach, *Through Russia's Back Door*, p. 59, is authority for the statement that the journey across Siberia took a year until the Trans-Siberian was built. Opening of the new

Yakutsk University is described in *C.D.*, November 14, 1956. Statistics *in re* Sverdslovsk's industrial production are from *C.D.*, June 19, 1957. Estimates of the Kuzbas coal reserves are from Max Frankel, *New York Times*, July 23, 1957. For Novosibirsk see Douglas, *op. cit.*, and Welles Hangen in the *New York Times*, August 23, 1956. Shabad describes the two islands in the Bering Strait where American and Russian territory comes closest to meeting. A pamphlet by Nikolai Mikhailov called *Sixteen Soviet Republics*, published by the *Soviet News*, contains much statistical information but should be used with caution. For Moldavia see *C.D.*, March 27, 1957. Most of my information about the Lost Peoples comes from a private but highly authoritative memorandum. Also see Kolarz, the best published source.

Chapter X

Vera Micheles Dean, "Russia, Menace or Promise," a pamphlet published by the Foreign Policy Association (July-August, 1946) has useful background on governmental matters. Jack Raymond vividly describes a meeting of the Supreme Soviet in the *New York Times*, July 15, 1956. For dictatorship "over" the proletariat see Parkes, p. 14. A recent speech by Allen W. Dulles, Director of the Central Intelligence Agency (*New York Times*, September 21, 1957) mentions that the "international ideological fervor of the international revolutionary communist movement" is dwindling. Details about *Agitprop* are from *C.D.*, February 13, 1956; also see "The Soviet Man," *Reporter*, August 16, 1949. The Guillaume quotation is from Liddell Hart (p. 238). Trotsky's phrase "Dictatorship of the Secretariat" comes from Duranty, p. 91. Bertrand Russell, *op cit.*, has the best analysis of Marxist errors I have ever seen, and Schuman makes the point that Marx would have been much shocked by the contemporary welfare state. Communism as an expression of "the will of history itself" is from Koestler, *The God That Failed*, p. 65. Lenin's remarks about ethical and moral considerations are quoted in Shub. The quotation from *Bolshevik* is from Kulski, p. 15. Wolfe is authority for the statement that the Russian state was the largest landowner and employer of labor in the country. For recent evaluations of Russian history by various historians see Dwight MacDonald in *Politics*, Spring, 1948. The quarterly *Foreign Affairs* has published innumerable articles on Russia since its foundation, many of them of marked interest and value; four particularly notable are "The Sources of Soviet Conduct," by X (George F. Kennan), July, 1947; "Stalin on Revolution," by Historicus, January, 1949; "Generalissimo Stalin and the Art of Government," by O. Utis, January, 1952; and, one of the most luminous studies on a Russian theme ever written, "The Silence in Russian Culture," by Isaiah Berlin, October, 1957.

Chapter XI

I have used the Khrushchev text as it appeared in a pamphlet published by the *New Leader*, "The Crimes of the Stalin Era." For the Dennis article see B. J. Cutler in the New York *Herald Tribune*, July 27, 1956. Whittaker Chambers in "The End of a Dark Age" (*Life*, April 30, 1956) brilliantly expresses the view that the Khrushchev speech strengthens international Communism, not the reverse, by making it "radioactive" again and thus reopening "an unparalleled struggle for men's minds." Khrushchev's remarks about Stalin as a great Marxist are from the *New York Times*, January 2, 1957; other words from him on the subject are, "The imperialists call us Stalinists. Well, when it comes to fighting imperialism we are all Stalinists." References by Khrushchev to God are from *C.D.*, August 21, 1957. That twenty-eight different anti-American plays appeared in Moscow in the immediate postwar period is from Stipp, p. 213, quoting Gordey. The items about Gandhi are from the *New Statesman*, March 9, 1957. Exceptionally valuable correspondence about Russia appears intermittently in the *New Statesman*. For fascinating details about rehabilitation see "More Re-writing of History," by Alexander Dallin, in a special issue of the *New Republic* (June 11, 1956) devoted to the Soviet Union. Schuman has copious details about de-Stalinization. For Stalin on linguistics, see Kulski, p. 83.

Chapter XII

I found the Lenin quotation about Hungary in a recent *New Statesman*. *Pravda's* reply to the letter of British Labour Party leaders is from *C.D.* A recent article in *Encounter* has much revealing information on student resentments following the Hungarian affair. Khrushchev's remarks about Hungary and paprika are from the *New York Times*, April 16, 1957. My account of the Khrushchev coup in June follows closely the *New Statesman*, July 20, 1957; also see Harry Schwartz and Harrison Salisbury in the *New York Times*, July 7 and July 14, 1957, as well as dispatches from Warsaw by Sydney Gruson. The Dulles speech cited above mentions why Khrushchev had good reason to fear Malenkov. Much in this and the preceding chapter comes from the conversation of British friends in Moscow and elsewhere.

Chapter XIII

The Herriot quotation is from *The Red Army*. "The Soviet School Child" (*Ladies' Home Journal*, February, 1956), by Dorothy Thompson, was so far as I know the first article ever printed in an American popular magazine analyzing the challenge of the new Soviet educational system; it is an extremely penetrating as well as prescient piece of work. The *New Statesman* (September 15, 1956) mentions the fatigue caused to students by excessive work, and steps taken by the authorities to counteract this. A report recently issued by the United States government, *Education in the USSR*, contains much valuable statistical matter about Soviet education; I have drawn on it, as published in the *New York Times* (November 11, 1957), for several details. But most of my information on education was gathered by word of mouth. MacDuffie, *op. cit.*, makes the point that Moscow University is a higher building than any except seven in the United States. *Fortune*, February, 1956, says that "the best Soviet minds are attracted into science because freedom is such a scarce commodity elsewhere in Soviet life," and mentions how disconcerting it is to find science flourishing so successfully in a police state (p. 118). An article on Soviet science in the London *Observer* (August 18, 1957) has figures on the earnings of scientists and intellectuals. A letter to the writer from Stuart Chase mentions the importance of the scientific method as a liberalizing influence on Communism. Background about the Academy of Sciences may be found in "Science in the USSR," by J. D. Bernal, *New World Review*. Details about the atom plant at Obninsk are from *First in the World*, Soviet News Booklet No. 2, published in London, 1956. In typical Soviet fashion this document describes the plant thoroughly but does not reveal where it is. Harry Schwartz discusses the Soviet atom smasher in the *New York Times*, October 6, 1957, and mentions that Soviet scientific advance is only made possible by depressing the living standard of the people. Also see William J. Jorden in the *New York Times*, April 12, 1957. For abstracting see the *New York Times* dispatch cited in the text, as well as *C.D.*, April 10, 1957, and several articles in the New York *Herald Tribune*. The quotation from Dr. Oppenheimer is from *Fortune*, February, 1956. For the physicist Kurchatov, see the *New Statesman*, May 5, 1956. The statement that the Russians have had no failures in launching satellites was carried in a dispatch to the *New York Times*, November 16, 1957. Serge Fliegers of International News Service was the correspondent with whom Zverev, the Soviet Finance Minister, discussed the cost of the Sputnik project.

Chapter XIV

The Yesenin poem appears in Maynard, p. 1. André Gide (*The God That Failed*, p. 190) defines formalism. Harrison E. Salisbury has an acute analysis of Soviet literary ferment and of the Dudintsev novel in the *New York Times*, January 13 and 14, 1957. Lauterbach (p. 115) mentions Stalin's reaction to Simonov's poetry. Some details about Stalin Prizes are from a Soviet pamphlet *The USSR—One Hundred Questions Answered*. The criticism of *Yellow Metal* is from *C.D.*, June 12, 1957. The Marshak poem is from his *Verses for Children*, published in the *Soviet Literature for Young People* series, Moscow. The item about Tikhanov is from *C.D.*, January 9, 1957; those about Conan Doyle, Dumas, and the reindeer book are from the same, September 18, 1957. A recent article in *USSR* (No. 11) has a laudatory article, "Plays from Dostoevsky's Works." The reference to Clifford Odets is from *C.D.*, February 13, 1957. For Longfellow see a letter by Albert Parry in the *New York Times*, August 29, 1957, also *USSR*. For the Encyclopedia in general see William Benton in the *New York Times*, "The Party Line from A to Z," January 22, 1956. *C.D.*, November 6, 1957, has the *Pravda* headline about the Sputnik. Several details about journalism are from William Benton. See in particular his "The Voice of the Kremlin," *Britannica Book of the Year*, 1956.

Chapter XV

The Mayakovsky poem is from "The Two Deaths of Alexander Fadeyev," by George Paloczi-Horvath, London *Sunday Times*, April 28, 1957. An engaging introduction to the Russian theater is "Curtain Time in Moscow," by Kenneth Tynan, *Harper's Magazine*, March, 1956. *The Muses are Heard*, by Truman Capote, has some wonderful glimpses of show business and other characteristics of Soviet life, truer than truth. Current trends in Soviet painting are described in the London *Times*, August 15, 1957, "A Glimpse of Art and Artists in Soviet Russia." Also see Ralph Parker, "Art and Soviet Life," *New World Review*, April, 1957, a discerning article. Details about the Mikhalkov play on Shostakovich appear in Gordey, p. 142. Isaac

Stern's report on his experiences in Russia may be found in the *Reporter*, August 9, 1956. The number of movie theaters in the USSR is from the *Statesman's Year-Book*; it seems to me somewhat large. For some details about TV I am indebted to my friend Irving R. Levine, Moscow correspondent of NBC. The Sputnik joke at the circus is from the *New York Times*, that about twenty years is from *Look*, reported by Earl Wilson.

Chapter XVI

The Nechayev-Bakunin quotation is from Shub, p. 15. For divorce see the *New Statesman*, October 27, 1956, and the *New York Times*, July 7, 1956. If my memory is correct it was Henry Wales of the Chicago *Tribune* who coined the phrase "Just marriage is grounds for divorce in Russia." The item about swearing is from *C.D.*, July 10, 1957, as is that about whistling to girls in the United States. "We Saw How Russians Live," by Bruce and Beatrice Gould, together with "Report on Russian Youth," by Robert Griscom, *Ladies' Home Journal*, February, 1957, has interesting material on social patterns. The speech by the Patriarch Alexei appeared in *C.D.*, February 13, 1957. Also see *C.D.* (September 4, 1957) for religious weddings in the Ukraine. Charques (p. 49) is authority for the statement that the Zagorsk monastery was the largest landowner in Russia. D. J. Cutler discusses Christmas in the New York *Herald Tribune*, December 26, 1956. *C.D.* carried the items about Buddhists and Jews in Dukhara. For the situation of Jews in general see, among much else, a brief news note in the *New Statesman*, February 2, 1957; articles by Dr. Morris N. Kertzer, secretary of the New York Board of Rabbis, in the *New York Times*, July, 1956; "Soviet Jews Fear Outcome of Purge," by Judd L. Teller, New York *Herald Tribune*, July 16, 1957; "The Plight of the Jews in Russia," by Rabbi Joseph Miller, *Look*, November 27, 1956; and several articles in the *New York Times* by Cyrus L. Sulzberger. Crimes and their punishment are from various issues of *C. D.* So is my list of protests and complaints. As to sport see William Benton, "Soviet Use of Sports as Part of Cold War," New York *Herald Tribune*, March 8, 1956. The *Encyclopaedia Britannica* ("Russia," p. 699) mentions the former Soviet antipathy to sports records. George F. Kennan in his celebrated article "The Sources of Soviet Conduct," *Foreign Affairs*, July, 1947, signed "X," mentions that "Soviet power bears within itself the seeds of its own decay." See Louis Fischer, *Reader's Digest*, January, 1954, for mention of the fact that multitudinous Russian prisoners of war sought to stay in Germany after World War II. An expert analysis of Soviet inertness is *Soviet Opposition to Stalin*, by George Fischer, included in Stipp, p. 166. As to boredom, I wrote in *Inside Europe* more than twenty years ago that the Soviet Union has become "the dullest country on earth, charted, organized, planned out to the last detail—cut, dried, and bound." A good survey of student opinion, "What Russian Students Think," by Merle Fainsod, appeared in the *Atlantic Monthly*, February, 1957.

Chapter XVII

Writers about Soviet economic affairs are bound to be in debt to Harry Schwartz, author of *Russia's Soviet Economy*. Budget figures are from USSR, No. 15; figures on trade from *Time*, September 16, 1957. For repudiation of state loans, see *Life*, April 29, 1957. For the background of planning, I have drawn on my old *Inside Europe*. Walter Duranty (*Duranty Reports Russia*, p. 362) said some cogent things about planning back in 1929, for instance, "From a strictly dispassionate standpoint, the Bolshevik Five Year Plan is a superb political invention. It gives esoteric stimulus to a people whose roots are deep in mysticism, and yet corresponds to the severely practical surface of outward Marxism." Also Maynard, *op. cit.*, points out how the planning concept evolved naturally from the Marxist theory that "the curve of history can be plotted out." For agriculture in general I have made use of a U.S. government memorandum. The item about Omsk and Bashkiria is from *C.D.*, July 10, 1957; that about the fence between rival factories appeared in the *New York Times*, May 7, 1957, and that about Chelyabinsk in the same, July 1. That 900,000 civil servants have been ousted is from the *Economist*, May 11, 1957, and that 40,000 new executives have been appointed is from the *New Statesman*, May 25, 1957. Joseph Alsop points out in the New York *Herald Tribune* (February 15, 1957) that service industries hardly exist in the USSR. *C.D.*, July 17, 1957, mentions paper napkins and pocket umbrellas. The item about the waiting list for the Pobeda is from William J. Jorden in the *New York Times*. In the summer of 1957 a series of articles by Mr. Jorden, "The People of Russia," provided fascinating details about conditions of work and wages in various Soviet occupations. Two views of Russian factories are "Russia's Weaknesses," by G. Warren Nutter, *U.S. News and World Report*, March 1, 1957, and "A First Hand Report on Russian Industry," by Dr. Weldon H. Brandt, *Mill and Factory*, July 1956. The joke about finding an apartment appeared in the *Saturday Review*, September 8, 1956.

Chapter XVIII

I owe much in this chapter to the conversation of Hanson W. Baldwin, also to his written work, for instance "The Soviet's Armed Forces," a series published in the *New York Times* in March, 1956, and subsequent articles in August, 1956, and July, 1957. Details of recent Soviet military budgets are in David Dallin, *The Changing World of Soviet Russia*, p. 340. Liddell Hart, *op. cit.*, p. 414, is my authority for rates of pay and the diet of Soviet privates. Some details about Soviet aviation are from *Life*, July 9, 1956. Khrushchev's remarks about the "big" bomb appeared in the *New York Times*, May 31, 1957. Authority for several details about missiles is the *New York Times*, October 6, 1957. The interview with Khrushchev by Henry Shapiro appeared in the *New York Times*, November 15, 1957; that by Bob Considine in the New York *Journal American*, November 24-25, 1957. Details about Soviet civil aviation are from the *World Almanac*, 1957, p. 442, and various aircraft manuals. That airline schedules are now based on local instead of Moscow time is from *C.D.*, March 27, 1957.

Chapter XIX

The item about iron ore reserves is from *C.D.*, June 26, 1957. Details of new towns and urban communities are from *USSR*, No. 4. See Stipp, p. 79, for Russia's old-time concept of a "special destiny." The phrase "wholly rational and scientific state" is from Leslie C. Stevens, "The Russian People," *Atlantic Monthly*, May, 1952, cited above. The Harvard Report mentioned in the text points out the "instant mobilizability" of the Soviet Union, and describes it as a society "existing in a state of perpetual emergency." Receptions in Moscow to visiting royalty and their significance are mentioned by B. J. Cutler in the New York *Herald Tribune*, July 12, 1956. Harry Schwartz, "The Real Threat of Moscow's Missile," *New York Times*, September 15, 1957, describes cogently the ability of Soviet leaders to concentrate all their energy and resources to a single end.

Chapter XX

Basic geographical matters are on the authority of Shabad. Some of my Leningrad and Ukraine statistics, which may be suspect, are from *USSR*, No. 6. The Curzon quotations are from *Russia in Central Asia*, p. 28. For prerevolutionary items I have drawn partly on Winter, as always an invaluable source. The item about Pavlov and hens is from a report by a recent United States medical mission to the USSR. The complaint about the Leningrad department store is from *C.D.*, January 16, 1957. The old Intourist *Guide* is still the best available authority for details on many Soviet cities. Horsley, *op. cit.*, p. 26, mentions how valuable industrialization may be in connection with defense. That one out of every five men in the Red Army is Ukrainian is from John Fischer, p. 23. The Intourist *Guide* mentions the use of Ukrainian themes by such Russian composers as Tchaikovsky. Details about Ukrainian newspapers, theaters, etc. are from a memorandum by William Benton. That the Czarina Elizabeth had fifteen thousand dresses is from Charques, p. 123.

Chapter XXI

Baedeker, the Intourist *Guide*, and Winter are prime sources for early material. MacDuffie, p. 233, mentions that restaurants sell food by weight. Details about industry in Azerbaijan are from *C.D.*, March 20, 1957, as is the item about carrying of daggers in Baku, April 3, 1957, and the figure about Lenin's books. Charles W. Thayer, "I Found Russia Changed," *Saturday Evening Post*, March 31, 1956, mentions that Georgian women do not share compartments with men on trains.

Chapter XXII

The quoted descriptions of Samarkand are from Curzon, p. 211, and *Duranty Reports Russia*, p. 372. Douglas and MacDuffie both assert that only two Europeans reached Samarkand in four hundred years. Martin, p. 242, is the source for the inscription on Tamurlane's tomb. The Marco Polo quotation is from Curzon, p. 151. For all nationality questions the best authority is Kolarz. He points out (p. 255) that by conquering Central Asia Russia has become an Asiatic power without losing her separate status as a European power. Chester Bowles, "Report from Russia," New York *Post*, March 10, 1957, mentions the analogy between American expansion in the West and Russian expansion in Central Asia. Maynard is among historians who minimize the seriousness of the Russian threat to India in the late nineteenth century. Coates (p. 117) is the source for the item about Verny and loyalty. Details on Tadzikistan are from *C.D.*, February 13, 1957, and May 15, 1957. The item about "Mervousness" is from Curzon, p. 13.

Chapter XXIII

The quotation from Theodore Roosevelt is from Bailey, p. 185. Another apposite Roosevelt quotation from the same source (p. 198) is, "Russia is so contemptible, so treacherous and shifty and so incompetent that I am utterly unable to say whether or not it will make peace." This was said in reference to the Russo-Japanese War in 1905. Present attitudes in the satellites are well summarized in the *New York Times*, July 21, 1957. Also see "New Era in Eastern Europe" by Jack Raymond, a pamphlet published by the Foreign Policy Association in its Headline Series. Details about what the satellites cost the Soviet Union are from C. L. Sulzberger in the *New York Times*, May 6, 1957, Marguerite Higgins in the New York *Herald Tribune*, May 20, 1957, and *Fortune*, February, 1957, p. 107. The passage by Walter Lippmann is from the New York *Herald Tribune*, July 16, 1957. Harrison Salisbury (*New York Times*, January 27, 1957) states well the central dilemma of Kremlin policy vis-à-vis the satellites and in a bulletin issued by the Foreign Policy Association outlines basic Soviet policy toward the United States. The London *Times*, March 6, 1957, suggests that nationalist developments in the satellites will, in the end, be more dangerous to the USSR than western "imperialism." The line from Khrushchev about China is from *C.D.*, December 26, 1956. Sources for Mao's "One Hundred Flowers" speech are the *New York Times*, June 20, 1957, the Manchester *Guardian*, June 13 and 20, 1957, and the *Economist*, May 11, 1957. For the background of Sino-Russian relations see Louis Fischer, "China and Russia—Allies or Rivals," *Reader's Digest*, July, 1954. For Chou's trip to Europe after the Hungarian affair see Joseph Alsop, New York *Herald Tribune*, January 18, 1957. Edward Crankshaw (*Cracks in the Kremlin Wall*, p. 123) points out that the early Bolsheviks were stateless. See also A. J. P. Taylor (*Observer*, June 30, 1957). Crankshaw (p. 176) says that the Russian rejection of Marshall Plan aid was the real starting point of the Cold War. Schuman, *op. cit.*, p. 360, describes fully Molotov's rejection of this offer and also explains interestingly why the Soviets boycotted the UN session on Korea in June, 1950.

Chapter XXIV

John Plamenatz, quoted in Stipp, p. 257, points out that the Russians may be "pedantic, rude, and wearisome" but are not "mad." I owe several pungent details in this and the preceding chapter to the conversation of British and Indian friends. The lines from Khrushchev about General Norstad are from *C.D.* A suggestive survey of problems in American foreign policy is "Is Our Reappraisal Agonizing Enough?" by Barbara Ward Jackson, *New York Times*, July 22, 1956. Also see the Kennan article cited in the text, "Overdue Changes in Our Foreign Policy," *Harper's Magazine*, August, 1956. One should also take note of Mr. Kennan's words in "A Fresh Look at Russia," Foreign Policy Association, June 15, 1957. Mr. Kennan says that it is a "gross and dangerous oversimplification" to assume that Soviet policy is based primarily on aggressive military considerations. Also: "I deplore the frequent insistence on ignoring all gradations in the Kremlin's relations to fellow travelers and other groups in third countries friendly to Soviet policy, to portray all these people as merely the blind stooges of Moscow and to impute their acts and words exclusively to Moscow dictation. Such relationships have existed and still do to some extent; but there is also such a thing as normal Russian influence, and there are people who support Soviet policy for reasons of their own without accepting any bond of discipline to Moscow." A recent issue of the *New Statesman* mentions efforts toward "institutionalizing" the Soviet regime. Eric Sevareid in "A Change in the Air" (*Reporter*, June 13, 1957) discusses tellingly some differences between the Stalin and Khrushchev regimes. Walter Lippmann in the New York *Herald Tribune* (July 9, 1957) has cogent things to say about the Khrushchev *coup d'état* of June, 1957. My concluding remarks about Hungary are paraphrased from a private memorandum.

Index

537

THE UNION OF SOVIET
SOCIALIST REPUBLICS

ARCTIC

NORWEGIAN
SEA

SPITZBERGEN

FRANZ JOSEF
LAND

BARENTS
SEA

UNITED
KINGDOM

ESTONIAN
S.S.R.

NORWAY

NOVAYA
ZEMLYA

LATVIAN
S.S.R.

SWEDEN

DENMARK

Murmansk

KARA
SEA

(WEST)
GERMANY
(EAST)

FINLAND

LAKE
ONDOGA

Tallinn

Archangel

RUSSIAN

Vorkuta

LITHUANIAN
S.S.R.

Riga

Leningrad

KARELIA

SOVIET
S

BELORUSSIAN
S.S.R.

POLAND

Vilnius

Minsk

RU
SOCI

HUNG.

Moscow

Gorky

Perm

EUROPE
ASIA

URAL MOUNTAINS

Kiev

Kazan

Sverdlovsk

Tobolsk

RUMANIA

Kishinev

Kharkov

Saratov

Kuibyshev

Chelyabinsk

Odessa

Magnitogorsk

Omsk

Novosi

BULGARIA

Sevastopol

BLACK
SEA

Rostov
on-Don

Stalingrad

Uralsk

Astrakhan

Karaganda

Semipal

MOLDAVIAN
S.S.R.

TURKEY

Batum

Tiflis

CASPIAN
SEA

ARAL
SEA

LAKE
BALKHASH

UKRAINIAN
S.S.R.

Yerevan

GEORGIAN
S.S.R.

SYRIA

Baku

Alma-Ata

Frunze

ARMENIAN
S.S.R.

IRAQ

Tashkent

AZERBAIJAN
S.S.R.

Ashkhabad

Bukhara

Samarkand

Stalinabad

Merv

IRAN

AFGHAN.

PAK.

KASHMIR

SAUDI ARABIA

TURKMEN
S.S.R.

UZBEK
S.S.R.

TADZHIK
S.S.R.

KIRGHIZ
S.S.R.